VOLUME II: THE WAY OF THE SEEDED EARTH

PART 3

MYTHOLOGIES OF THE PRIMITIVE PLANTERS: THE MIDDLE AND SOUTHERN AMERICAS

JOSEPH CAMPBELL

HISTORICAL ATLAS OF WORLD MYTHOLOGY

VOLUME II

THE WAY OF THE SEEDED EARTH

PART 3

MYTHOLOGIES OF THE PRIMITIVE PLANTERS: THE MIDDLE AND SOUTHERN AMERICAS

PERENNIAL LIBRARY
HARPER & ROW, PUBLISHERS NEW YORK

GRAND RAPIDS, PHILADELPHIA, ST. LOUIS, SAN FRANCISCO
LONDON, SINGAPORE, SYDNEY, TOKYO

THE WAY OF THE SEEDED EARTH. MYTHOLOGIES OF THE PRIMITIVE PLANTERS: THE MIDDLE AND SOUTHERN AMERICAS. Copyright © 1989 by The Joseph Campbell Trust. All rights reserved. Printed in the Netherlands. No part of this book may be used or reproduced in any manner whatsoever without written permission except in the case of brief quotations embodied in critical articles and reviews. For information address Harper & Row, Publishers, Inc., 10 East 53rd Street, New York, NY 10022.

Library of Congress Cataloging-in-Publication Data
Campbell, Joseph, 1904–1987.
Historical atlas of world mythology/Joseph Campbell. p.   cm.   Bibliography: p.   Includes index.
Contents: v.2. The way of the seeded earth. pt.3. Mythologies of the primitive planters : the Middle and southern Americas.
ISBN 0-06-055159-3 : $.—ISBN 0-06-096352-2   : $
1. Mythology. I. Title.
BL311.C26   1989
291.1'3—dc20   89-8387

89 90 91 92 93 10 9 8 7 6 5 4 3 2 1
89 90 91 92 93 10 9 8 7 6 5 4 3 2 1   (pbk.)

BOMC offers recordings and compact discs, cassettes and records. For information and catalog write to BOMR, Camp Hill, PA 17012.

TABLE OF CONTENTS

AGRICULTURAL

DEVELOPMENTS
IN THE
MESOAMERICAN MATRIX

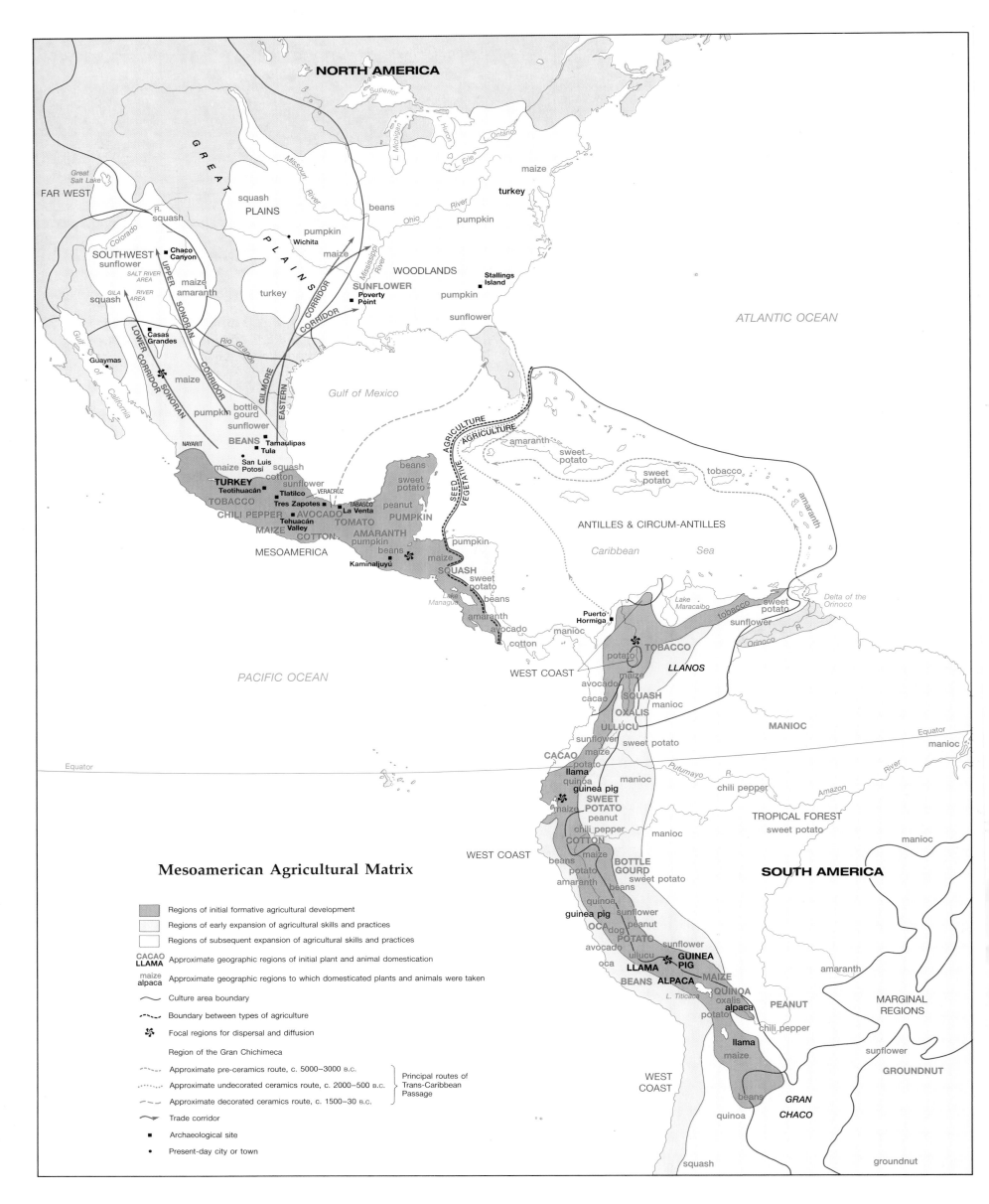

NORTH AMERICA

Great Salt Lake

FAR WEST

Superior

maize

turkey

G R E A T

squash
PLAINS

beans

L. Michigan

Huron

Ontario

Erie

pumpkin

Missouri River

Ohio River

maize

R.
squash

Colorado

pumpkin
Wichita

SOUTHWEST
sunflower

■ Chaco
Canyon

SALT RIVER AREA

maize
amaranth

WOODLANDS

turkey

WOODLANDS

SUNFLOWER

Stallings
Island

GILA RIVER AREA

squash

P L A I N S

UPPER SONORAN CORRIDOR

maize

Poverty
Point ●

pumpkin

ATLANTIC OCEAN

Gulf of California

● Guaymas

■ Casas
Grandes

LOWER CORRIDOR SONORAN

maize

GILMORE CORRIDOR

EASTERN CORRIDOR

Rio Grande

Gulf of Mexico

sunflower

pumpkin
bottle
gourd
sunflower

BEANS ■ Tamaulipas
■ Tula

NAYARIT

maize
squash
cotton
sunflower

■ San Luis
Potosí

TURKEY
Teotihuacán ■

TOBACCO

Tlatilco ■

■ Tres Zapotes

VERACRUZ

CHILI PEPPER

■ La Venta

AVOCADO
Tehuacán
Valley

TABASCO
TABASCO

MAIZE

TOMATO

beans

sweet
potato

AGRICULTURE
AGRICULTURE

amaranth

sweet
potato

sweet
potato

tobacco

AMARANTH

COTTON

pumpkin

MESOAMERICA

beans

Kaminaljuyú ●

PUMPKIN

peanut

SEED VEGETATIVE

pumpkin

maize

SQUASH

ANTILLES & CIRCUM-ANTILLES

Caribbean   Sea

amaranth

sweet
potato

beans

Lake Managua

PACIFIC OCEAN

amaranth

avocado

cotton

manioc

Puerto
Hormiga ■

Lake Maracaibo

tobacco

sweet
potato

sunflower

Delta of the Orinoco

amaranth

potato

TOBACCO

Orinoco R.

WEST COAST

maize

LLANOS

avocado

cacao

SQUASH

manioc

OXALIS

MANIOC

ULLÚCU

Equator

sunflower

maize

sweet potato

CACAO

potato

Equator

llama

quinoa

guinea pig

manioc

Putumayo R.

chili pepper

Amazon River

TROPICAL FOREST

sweet
potato

manioc

SWEET
POTATO

peanut

chili pepper

manioc

COTTON

maize

SOUTH AMERICA

WEST COAST

beans
potato
amaranth

BOTTLE
GOURD

sweet
potato

beans

quinoa

guinea pig

sunflower
peanut

OCA
dog

POTATO

avocado

ulluco

sunflower

oca

LLAMA

guinea pig

GUINEA
PIG

MAIZE

amaranth

manioc

BEANS

ALPACA

QUINOA

PEANUT

MARGINAL
REGIONS

oxalis
potato

alpaca

chili pepper

llama

sunflower

maize

GROUNDNUT

L. Titicaca

WEST
COAST

beans

*GRAN
CHACO*

quinoa

squash

groundnut

Mesoamerican Agricultural Matrix

Regions of initial formative agricultural development

Regions of early expansion of agricultural skills and practices

Regions of subsequent expansion of agricultural skills and practices

CACAO
LLAMA   Approximate geographic regions of initial plant and animal domestication

maize
alpaca   Approximate geographic regions to which domesticated plants and animals were taken

Culture area boundary

Boundary between types of agriculture

Focal regions for dispersal and diffusion

Region of the Gran Chichimeca

Approximate pre-ceramics route, c. 5000–3000 B.C.

Approximate undecorated ceramics route, c. 2000–500 B.C.

Approximate decorated ceramics route, c. 1500–30 B.C.

Principal routes of Trans-Caribbean Passage

Trade corridor

■   Archaeological site

●   Present-day city or town

THE TIDE OF HISTORY

Draw a line from San Francisco to Wichita; drop two verticals to the Tropic of Cancer: enclosed is an area that the Aztecs knew as Gran Chichimeca (Great Land of the Chichimec), the meaning of Chichimec being, Son of the Dog. It has been suggested that this may be a depreciatory term, about equivalent to the Greek βαρβαρία "land of the barbarians" (land of those strange to Greek manners, foreign, not speaking Greek). However, the Huichol Indians of the Sierra Madre Occidental, in Nayarit (just south of the Tropic of Cancer), speak of themselves as lineal descendants of "the Dog" and survivors of the Great Flood, from which only one man and one woman escaped.[1] Of all the peoples of that still largely undeveloped mountain area which lies directly along an ancient trade route from south to north, the Huichol have held most tenaciously to their pre-Columbian heritage. The name Chichimeca, therefore, may carry positive mythological, rather than (or, at least, as well as) negative sociological, implications.

Evidences are every day increasing of a substantial trade carried on over centuries between the peoples of Chichimeca and the civilizations of Mexico. Excavations conducted since the early 1970s at Casas Grandes in Chihuahua, for example, have unearthed there a large trading outpost established specifically for the conduct of this Chichimecan trade, which was in full career from c. A.D. 1050 to 1350, the very period known to the archaeology of the Southwest as Developmental Pueblo (see pages 274–276). Charles C. Di Peso reports that his own findings at this station have included "warehouses holding literally millions of shells…perforated and strung to make necklaces," brought apparently from a site near present-day Guayamas, in Sonora. "Another type of shell," he continues, "…was a large univalve, which could be used as a trumpet…to make the deep, resonant sound associated with the horned or plumed serpent—the god Quetzalcoatl."[2]

The commodity that the Casas Grandes merchants required from the north, evi-

339. A mythological theme outstanding throughout the range of the early planting cultures is of death as the generator of life. Excavated from a grave site at Tlatilco (see pp. 255–257), a mask of baked clay showing life and death as one. The principal and most characteristic early planting culture rendition of this paradoxical theme is in the mythological scenario of a divine being, slain and buried, from whose remains the food plants grow.

Across the Pacific, in Cambodia, seventh century A.D., an equivalent image fashioned in stone was of a Hindu mythic savior known as Hari-Hara, who in one person united Vishnu the Preserver (the left side) and Shiva the Destroyer (the right). Still further westward along the tropical belt, we find the East African Basungwe, once from the neighborhood of Zimbabwe, with a legend of the Lord of Life and Death as a royal presence in the Underworld, his right side alive and comely, the left rotting, crawling with maggots.

In Haitian voodoo lore (originating in Nigeria) the possessing-god Ghede, Lord of Cemeteries and Death, is equally Lord of Sexuality and a patron of children. Souls of the dead enter the Underworld by the passage that he guards, and the deities of life emerge by the same road from the same depth. As Death, he is a glutton; as Life, his dance is of copulation. He is wise with the knowledge of both worlds; and when he appears (by possessing — or "mounting" — someone at an invoking ceremony), he wears a pair of dark glasses, from which he knocks out the right lens: for with his right eye he watches those present, lest anyone steal his food, while with his left (protected from the sun's glare) he surveys the universe.[1] Of especial interest is the testimony of Ghede; for when this god mounts his carriers (or "horses"), they are bereft of any sense of self, behave and speak compulsively, and, recovered, know nothing of what they did or said. Their bifocal (life/death) behavior and knowledge are, thus, not of themselves individually, but compelled from an inner transpersonal "vision center" of which their intellects know nothing.

dently, was turquoise, an indispensable component of much of Middle American religious art. And in exchange for this, their second trade staple was birds acquired from the South: parrots, scarlet macaws, and green macaws. "The natural habitat of these birds," Di Peso notes, "does not extend north beyond Veracruz. Yet their remains were found in abundance at Casas Grandes, some 800 miles north, and in sizeable numbers in Arizona and New Mexico."[3] In fact, at Casas Grandes the remains of breeding pens have been found: "adobe boxes open at the top, which in use were covered over with fabric matting. The hutches were equipped with roosting holes. Eggshell remains and remains of skeletons of birds as young as two weeks were also found at the site, leaving little doubt that it was a breeding center."[4]

Copper bells, or crotals, of the kind known to the Hohokam culture were another item of the commerce. "Strictly speaking," states Di Peso, "a bell has a clapper; a crotal has a loose object inside an enclosed space. The copper crotals were made by the 'lost wax' method. …Copper work is found first in South America," he points out, "later in Mexico, and still later in the U.S. Southwest. Looking at the dates of copper artifacts, one can almost see knowledge of copper metallurgy working its way up the west coast of Mexico to Casas Grandes."[5]

The elaborate irrigation systems found both at Casas Grandes and in the Hohokam Gila and Salt River areas (see Map 29) add to the impression of direct connection. Di Peso is even of the opinion that the Hohokam may have been immigrants from Mesoamerica into the Southwest. As he writes: "The Hohokam's knowledge of irrigation, and their expertise in working shell, stone, and bone mark them as aliens in the Chichimecan sea. Their settlements are set apart from the villages of the indigenous Qotam. And the Hohokam built such Mesoamerican-style structures as ball courts and truncated mounds. There were religious similarities as well. For example, the Hohokam appear to have included in their pantheon the Mesoamerican war god of the black shining mirror, known as Tezcatlipoca."[6]

Map 26.

253

This enterprise, however, was late in the long history of the passage of Mesoamerican influences into regions north of the Rio Grande. Not only was it late, but it was organized and deliberate—an enterprise, as Di Peso suggests, like that of the Hudson Bay Company in the seventeenth and eighteenth centuries, as an outpost in northeastern North America of the interests of Great Britain. Among the Aztec there was a hereditary guild of armed merchants known as *pochteca*, who traveled into distant lands seeking luxury goods for the royal house. The lands of the hostile tribes they would take by force, or if unable to do so, they would provoke incidents that would lead to the intervention of the Aztec army. It has been suggested that both the Toltecs and the pre-Toltec builders of the Early Classic metropolis of Teotihuacán (c. A.D. 100 to 600) must also have known such

340. From the fifteenth-century Mextec *Codex Borgia* 55, Aztec *pochteca*, symbolic illustrations allegorical of eternally wandering stars: (**a**) the Wanderer of the North, and (**b**) the Wanderer of the South. Members of an influential and respected guild of international travelers — combining the qualities and functions of merchants, army officers, and cultural propagandists — they bear the traveling-pack (*thamamalli*) supported by the broad head-strap (*mecapalli*); a quetzal bird is perched upon one of the packs.

aggressive merchant colonists and explorers. One cannot but think of Queen Elizabeth's princely pirates, Sir Walter Raleigh and Sir Francis Drake. In any case, the extent of the commerce and commercial empires of Teotihuacán and Toltec Tula (c. A.D. 900 to 1200) throughout the first millennium A.D. is only now coming into view. We see the signs of influence from Chaco Canyon (New Mexico) to Kaminaljuyu (Guatemala) and Yucatán.

Very much earlier influences out of Mexico into and across the Chichimecan north have been traced along the corridors represented in Map 26. They begin with the very beginnings of plant domestication in

Middle America, and continue with increasing effect, through millennia, to the period of the Aztec empire.

The first signs already appear during what is known to American archaeology as the *Period of Incipient Agriculture (c. 6500 to 1500 B.C.)*, when in Middle America the transition was made from Paleolithic hunting and foraging to a settled Neolithic style of village life and farming (see pages 254–256).

The *Mesoamerican Formative Period (c. 1500 B.C. to A.D. 100)* is characterized by two distinct yet intermeshing developments. The first is of the native farming villages now everywhere appearing—in the high-

341. La Venta Monument 19, a sculptured stone tablet c. 800 B.C. Olmec, Tabasco, Mexico.

The prominence of the serpent in the mythologies of agriculturally based societies — whether of the primal, tribal class (such as are dealt with in this volume) or of the later, historical orders (the biblical, for example) — is a mystery of profound psychological and sociological import. Repeatedly shedding its skin to be born again, the serpent — like the moon that sheds its shadow in rebirth — typifies life-energy and consciousness locked within temporal space, delivering and suffering births and deaths.

Fluent in movement as the waters flowing over and fertilizing the earth, yet with their fiery forked tongues flashing tirelessly as lightning from a storm-laden sky, serpents appear to incarnate the elementary mystery of life, wherein apparent opposites are conjoined. In the grandiose symbolic theatre of Nature's spectacles, however, where a striking contrast can be seen between the serpents' bondage to the earth and the release of birds to untrammeled flight, an irreducible may be inferred as between earthly and heavenly powers. (Compare I.1:**68**.) In Genesis 3:14–15, for example, the serpent is cursed by a sky god and set at enmity to "the woman," with whose mystery, in most agriculturally based traditions, it is identified and thus revered. The aim of Indian yoga, in contrast, is to bring the female "serpent power" (*kundalini*) — which is to say, the will in nature as known to temporal consciousness — to knowledge of itself as identical with unconditioned being. Such a realization is what is connoted iconographically by any conjunction of lunar and solar symbols, of which the serpent and sunbird are everywhere primal examples.

Quetzalcoatl, the Aztec "Feathered Serpent," who as Evening Star dies with the sun but then as Morning Star is resurrected as herald of the light, is the best-known Mesoamerican symbol of this life-fostering realization of eternity as incarnate in the forms of time. In the unexpectedly early appearance of this archetype in Monument 19, a crested rattlesnake supports on its prodigious coils a priestly figure wearing a jaguar mask and holding in his extended right hand a little bag or basket (probably a container of powdered copal, used in Mexico to this day as incense), while the left hand, awkwardly turned palm out at the wrist, is in a position that everywhere in the Orient would be interpreted as the "boon-bestowing hand posture" (*varada-mudra*) of a divinity (see II.1:**49**). That the Olmec artist even overstrained his art to render this gesture in profile suggests that already in earliest Mesoamerica, long before its appearance in the East, the gesture must have had some such meaning.

lands, in the lowlands, in the temperate northerly zones, and in the rain forests of the south—each essentially self-sufficient, yet exchanging goods (and no doubt ideas as well) over wide ranges. The second, altogether distinct development, is to be seen in the sudden appearance and flowering in tropical Tabasco and Veracruz, of a constellation of symbolically structured ceremonial centers governed by a priestly elite and of the order not at all of a Neolithic village culture but of a hieratic, literate civilization: the Olmec (see pages 260–267). Its dates (c. 1200 to 200 B.C.) parallel those of the Formative folk villages of the era, but its rise, flowering, and decline are not of the same order of life as theirs. Moreover, the mythologies and ritual styles of the subsequent Middle American Classic and Postclassic Periods, from A.D. 100 to 1519, cannot be understood as developments simply out of the folk base. They are continuations, with new inspirations and applications, of the impulse of the Olmec. The major cult, for example, of the Feathered Serpent (Kukulcán of the Maya, Quetzalcoatl of the Toltec and the Aztec) is already announced in Olmec art from c. 800 B.C. (see Figure 341).

The art of the Early Formative villages, however, was typically of ceramic figurines, not at all monumental, but with a lifelike charm, vitality, and humor. Olmec influences can be identified, here and there, but in the main the statement is of a healthy and joyous popular culture. Our

342. Dual-faced "Pretty Lady" figurine of terracota, from Tlatilco, Valley of Mexico, Middle Preclassic Period, c. 1200 to 700 B.C.

first clues to the dominant mythological archetypes structuring the works and days of these earliest of America's planting communities come to light in these clay figurines, the most numerous and best preserved of which are from the site of Tlatilco, in the great clay pit of a brickyard twenty minutes by automobile from the heart of Mexico City.

Here in the early 1940s, a bonanza find was uncovered of prehistoric graves filled with ceramic figurines of an elegant local style (Figure 344). As elsewhere in Early Formative Middle America, the most typical image is the standing female nude. There is no point in pretending—like so many exact scholars of these matters—that we do not know who she is. What we do not know exactly are the uses to which her images were applied and by what names she was invoked in her various manifestations and functions. But that she is the great goddess-mother of us all and in the context of a planting culture's inevitable order of interests was associated with the earth, we can surely know. A comparable series of ceramic female figurines from sites of a comparable culture stage (some 5000 years earlier, c. 6000 B.C.) is perfectly understood from both Asia Minor and southeastern Europe. At Tlatilco her double-headed forms are interesting and may refer (as they do in Old Europe and the Ancient Near East) to the dual domination of the goddess in the worlds of the living and the dead (as Demeter and Persephone, Inanna and Ereshkigal). Support is given to this probability by the findings at Tlatilco of forms that are half skeleton and half alive (Figure 339). The statement here is obviously of life and death as one—life out of death and death out of life—a dominant theme throughout the dominion of the planting cultures, underlying the frenzy of human sacrifice along their whole range, from Mexico, through Polynesia and South Asia, to Equatorial Africa. No evidence has yet turned up, as far as I know, of human sacrifice in the villages, but in the Olmec ceremonial centers it was apparently the central occasion, as it became and remained, certainly, throughout the Classic and Postclassic stages of Mesoamerican civilization.

343. Uncovered, 1942, at Tlatilco, a site near the center of Mexico City, were burials in which the corpses had been interred with caches of pottery and ceramic figurines (dated c. 1200–700 B.C.), the products of a prosperous early-agricultural community, whose ancestors had occupied the site from as early as 1500 or even 1700 B.C.[2] They cultivated maize, squash, and chili peppers; hunted deer, rabbits and waterfowl with javelins propelled by spear throwers; caught fish and shrimp in the lakes; and fattened for food a breed of small dog. Their remains betray connections with other early communities far removed, "some," according to Miguel Covarrubias, who supervised the excavating, "extending as far north as the Ohio Valley, as far south as Honduras, and all the way to the Peruvian north coast."[3]

344. About the Tlatilco artifacts Covarrubias has written: "Their art was simple and unassuming, but gay and sensitive, free of religious themes. This is evident in the effigy vessels, in the clay figurines, some as large as a baby, finely modeled and highly polished, which must have required considerable skill in the potter's art, and particularly in the small, solid figurines, even if, to judge by their uniformity and large numbers, they were made by mass-production methods.

"Hundreds of complete figurines and thousands of fragments have come out of the earth at Tlatilco in a most varied range of styles; most of them are of women with small breasts, short arms, slim waists, and large, bulbous legs; some are standing, some seated, others carrying babies on their hips or caressing a small dog held in their arms. The figures of women are invariably naked, and it seems that feminine coquetry was limited to painting the face and body and wearing elaborate headdresses, of which there is an unlimited variety. Occasionally they wear abbreviated garments, such as turbans and short skirts, which seem to have been made of grass in some cases, of cloth in others, worn low at the hips. Figurines of exceptionally fat women wearing such skirts are shown in dance poses, and it is possible that these skirts were worn for dancing. The feminine figures generally show the hair shaved off in patches or worn bobbed in the back, with a long lock on each side reaching down to the waist in front. Another lock of hair was worn over the forehead, held in place by a band or garland decorated with leaves or tassels and placed at a jaunty angle like a modern lady's hat. The hair is usually painted red, suggesting that they dyed their hair, perhaps bleaching it with lime as among the Melanesians or tinting it with red achiote (*bixa orellano*) seeds, as is still done by the Colorado Indians…

"They also made representations of men, considerably rarer than those of the women, wearing loincloths

(and sometimes leggings and skirts), as well as vests, garters, turbans, and helmets. A pair of figurines found in a Tlatilco burial perhaps represent shamans: each is accompanied by a dwarf, and each of the shamans wears a small mask. Ballplayers have also been found, with the characteristic belt, helmet, and knee pads, the right hand bound with a rope, perhaps to hit the ball [a striking example of these stalwart fellows is pictured in the lower right corner]. Apparently they used beds or sofas rather like ours, and from Tlatilco came an amusing group in painted clay, showing a chief or warrior comfortably reclining in bed, with a woman coyly seated at his feet. Both men and women painted their bodies in characteristic patterns with red, black, yellow, or white paint, supposedly by means of clay seals and roller stamps, decorating their thighs with geometric designs, concentric circles, and patches filled with cross-hatching. They also painted their faces with symmetric patterns over the mouth and cheeks and across the eyes. A peculiar fashion was to decorate one side of the body, leaving the other unpainted.

"The Tlatilcans were apparently little concerned with religious symbolism, though the figurines must have served a ceremonial purpose; the motifs on their pottery and clay stamps were purely decorative, and little in their art could be called representations of deities. However, a rather unusual and fascinating concept is found in certain feminine figurines with two heads or, stranger still, two sets of features on a single head: two noses, two mouths, and three eyes, reminiscent of certain paintings of Picasso, perhaps connected with the idea of twins. There are also figurines of jaguar-like beings or persons wearing jaguar masks; old crouched men, probably representations of the fire god; and strange masks of clay, one of which (**339**) shows a face of which half is contorted with a hanging tongue and the other half is a human skull, perhaps representing the idea of life and death; there are also half-human, half-jaguar faces that have a strange counterpart in the probably contemporary Chavín culture of Peru."[4]

345. Mushroom stone with jaguar-based stipe, from Kaminaljuyu, Guatemala. 346. Ceramic from Colima, Mexico, of celebrants encircling a mushroom (likely *Pslocybe mexicana*) as if it were the *axis mundi*. 347. Mushroom stone from Guatemala.

A stone image from an important site on the Guatemalan Pacific Coast, Kaminaljuyu, near Guatemala City (see Figure 345), provides a clue to the possible existence already in the *Late Formative Period (c. 300 B.C. to A.D. 100)* of another constant Mesoamerican interest—namely, in the inward, visionary transformation of consciousness produced by hallucinogens. A number of these so-called mushroom stones have been recovered from sites in highland Guatemala, and although their function is a matter of speculation, their relevance to a still-surviving Mesoamerican cult in which hallucinogenic mushrooms play a central role is not unlikely.[7] In the north, the dominant hallucinogen is mescaline, as rendered in peyote, though other plants are also used, often with more dangerous effects—for example, jimson weed (*Datura stramonium*), which the Huichol personify as the wicked enemy, Kieri, of the peyote champion, Kauyumari (see Figure 348).

The Formative Period ended with the Olmec civilization dissolving into the beginnings of the Mayan in the south and, in the north, in the Valley of Mexico, with the abrupt appearance at Teotihuacán of what has been termed the first fully urban culture in the New World. An elaborate hieroglyphic script, an extremely complex calendar, an architecture of great pyramid temples, and a social order symbolically structured marked the rise during the *Classic Period (c. A.D 100 to 900)* of the great Aztec civilization.

348. *The Power of the Tree of the Wind (Kieri)* by Hakatemi, beeswax and yarn on plywood, c. 23.5″ × 23.5″. The Huichol believe Kieri — their personification of jimson weed (*Datura stramonium*) — to be a wicked and dangerous sorcerer to whom offerings must be made to ward off evil.

It was during the *Early Classic Period (c. A.D. 100 to 600)* of the flowering of Teotihuacán that there were established in northern Mexico, at about the latitude of the Tropic of Cancer, two trading outposts for commerce with the Gran Chichimeca. One we have already noticed (see II.2:124) at the root of the two eastern corridors of Map 26, in southwestern Tamaulipas and San Luis Potosí, at the edge of the desert habitat of the hallucinogenic cactus, peyote. The other was at the base of the two Sonoran corridors, in what is now the state of Dur-

ango.[8] The passages of goods, techniques, and ideas to the north before the establishment of these early trading outposts had been fortuitous and piecemeal. The bottle gourd, as we have seen (II.2:124) reached Tennessee and Kentucky before 2500 B.C., apparently by way of the early eastern Mexican corridor, yet the same gourd arrived in the Chichimecan southwest only c. 300 B.C., by way of the corridor of the Upper Sonoran Complex. In c. 2000 B.C. pottery appeared in Georgia, Florida, and Alabama, but had to wait until 200 B.C. to appear (by trade) at the Koster site (I.2:210) together with maize, which by c. 300 B.C. had already appeared in the Southwest (without pottery), and by around 200 B.C. was known to the Cochise desert tribes of Utah and Colorado. Beans came next to that area, and by A.D. 500 the maize-beans-squash symbiotic complex was established throughout the region. By that time, cotton and turkeys had been acquired by the Anasazi Basket Makers, and the more intentional, commercial, introduction of Mexican products and ideas had begun.[9]

When, at last, pottery arrived in the Southwest, between c. A.D. 1 and 500, it appeared in as many as four different forms, all anticipated by ceramics to the south. From c. A.D. 500 to 700, another kind appeared, resembling in detail the Chupicuaro pottery of the Mexican west coast, and by that time the Hohokam with their Mexican ball courts had arrived.[10]

Comparably, in the East, but more

remotely and with a greater contribution of local forms and adaptations than ensued in the Southwest—also, with contributions by way of the Caribbean seaway—the great complexes of Adena (c. 800 B.C. to A.D. 800) and Hopewell (c. 200 B.C. to A.D. 500) were not miscellaneous assemblages of fortuitous odds and ends, but total and consistent structures (see I.2:212–214). The bent knees of the figurine of the Adena stone pipe (I.2:**346**) suggest an Olmec form; its earspools, a Mexican. Pipe-smoking, however, was an Eastern Woodland invention, unknown to Mexico until brought there as a return gift, by way of the Gilmore Corridor in reverse. Tobacco, on the other hand, does not appear on the scene until c. A.D. 1000, at two Missouri River drainage sites: Mitchell, South Dakota, and Brewster, Iowa. The origins of this weed, however—which has been called "The Red Man's Revenge"—are unknown.[11]

Finally, with the culminating *Postclassic Period (A.D. 900 to 1519)* of the expansive Toltec and Aztec military empires, we see the rise and flowering of the Mississippian Civilization in the East, c. A.D. 700 to 1700 (see I.2:210–218), and in New Mexico the phenomenon of Chaco Canyon, c. A.D. 1050 to 1350 (see pages 274–279). It is interesting to compare the numerous absolutely straight roads of that development (see Map 31) with the highways of the South American Incas (see Map 42), c. A.D. 1200 to 1532, their great coastal road of 2520 miles, from Tumbes in the north of Peru to Talca in central Chile, and the Andean Road of 3150 miles, from Quito in Ecuador again to Talca.[12] Whatever the explanation may be, one has the sense, in contemplating the incredible ruins of the civilizations of America that are gradually coming to light, of a majesty and spiritual force yet to be fully recognized and appropriately interpreted. For, as Spengler has written of the manner of its extinction: "This is the only example of a Culture ended by violent death. It was not starved, suppressed, or thwarted, but murdered in the full glory of its unfolding, destroyed like a sunflower whose head is struck off by one passing. All these states—including a world power and more than one federation—with an extent and resources far superior to those of the Greek and Roman states of Hannibal's day; with a comprehensive policy, a carefully ordered financial system, and a highly developed legislation; with administrative ideas and economic traditions such as the ministers of Charles V could never have imagined; with a wealth of literature in several languages, an intellectually brilliant and polite society in great cities to which the West could not show one single parallel—all this was not broken down in some desperate war, but washed out by a handful of bandits in a few years, and so entirely that the relics of the population retained not even a memory of it all. Of the giant city of Tenochtitlán not a stone remains above ground. The cluster of great Mayan cities in the virgin forests of Yucatán succumbed swiftly to the attack of vegetation, and we do not know the old name of any of them. Of their literature three books survive, but no one can read them.

"The most appalling feature of the tragedy was that it was not in the least a necessity of the Western Culture that it should happen. It was a private affair of adventurers, and at the time no one in Germany, France, or England had any idea of what was taking place....A few handguns and cannon opened the tragedy and brought it to conclusion."[13]

349. Cortés and his army marching on Mexico City, a color copy of an original painting by Father Pichardo from *Histoire Mexicaine depuis 1221 jusqu'à 1594*, a seventeenth-century manuscript.

THE OLMEC ENIGMA

"Coming suddenly to light within a few decades from the depths of time, a civilization totally unknown to us has emerged, with its compelling evidence and its mysteries, with its style and its gods, forcing us to recognize it as being the earliest of all those that man has built on the American continent, and perhaps as the 'mother civilization' of the New World."[14]

Thus the distinguished French Americanist, Jacques Soustelle, describes the recent archaeological discovery and reconstruction of a civilization that appeared abruptly, c. 1200 B.C., in a region of tropical rain forest, sluggish rivers and extensive swamps, along the southern shore of the Gulf of Campeche, in Tabasco and Veracruz.

"The Olmecs were the first," Soustelle declares, "to construct vast ceremonial centers, to sculpt bas-reliefs and statues in the round, to group together horizontal monoliths or 'altars' and stelae, to carve hard stone. They invented symbols that remained in use until the Spanish Conquest, more than two thousand years after them, and probably a system of writing and a highly perfected calendar as well. Their civilizations flourished from Veracruz to Michoacán, from Guerrero to Costa Rica."[15]

The first notice of the remains of such a civilization, lost to history, resting hidden in an apparently pristine wilderness, had been chanced upon at Tres Zapotes, in 1862, by a laborer clearing jungle for an hacienda. What looked to him like the bottom of a prodigious pot buried upside down proved to be, when the earth was dug from around it, the top of a colossal carved stone head (Figure 350a). Archaeological excavations in the region were not undertaken, however, until the late 1930s, when one astonishing monumental complex after another came to light.

The most imposing of these was at La Venta, situated on a parcel of elevated land,

350. Discovered in 1862 and first excavated in 1864, the Colossal Head (*in situ,* above) known as Tres Zapotes Monument A was in 1868 the first Olmec monolith to receive wide attention, when a drawing of it was published (by José Maria Melgar y Serrano in *Semanario Ilustrado*). Forgotten for a time, this marvel was re-excavated in 1938 by Matthew Stirling (whose expedition gathers around it, above). At least a dozen similar gigantic sculptures of heads have to date been identified from several different sites in the Olmec heartland (see **Map 27**).

Fashioned from basalt, Monument 1 (left) from San Lorenzo is 9 feet 4 inches tall and dates c. 1200–900 B.C. The stone, according to Michael D. Coe, is from Cerro de Cintepec, "70 kilometers northwest of San Lorenzo and a great deal further by the circuitous water route by which the monuments must have reached their final destination."[5] The pitting is of the period and intentional. Why? Many monuments at this site and at La Venta were deliberately mutilated. Coe has suggested a popular revolt c. 900 B.C., after which, in his words, "an entire Olmec state fell into disarray....San Lorenzo," he observes further, "is subsequently abandoned," but La Venta goes on to even greater brilliance, and so does Tres Zapotes."[6]

A second suggestion has been of ritual destruction to deprive the monument of its mana after the death of the personage portrayed.[7] A third might be of the vandalism of some rival cult, like that wrought by the zeal of the early Christians upon such great sanctuaries of antiquity as Eleusis, Delphi, and Epidaurus.

The Olmec World

- ☐ Olmec heartland
- ■ Olmec monument
- ▲ Other Olmec sites
- ☐ Olmecoid monument
- △ Other Olmecoid sites
- + Mountain top
- — Present-day International boundary

Map 27. The unannounced and unexplained appearance in the swamplands of Veracruz and Tabasco of the Olmecs' masterful sculptural tradition—from huge basalt heads to tiny jade figurines—is a phenomenon unmatched in the history of civilizations.

352. Although the Colossal Heads evidence subtle yet significant stylistic variations, their distinctly similar physical features and headgear suggest to some that they were raised to honor dead (perhaps Negroid) chieftains.[8] At right is Monument 2 from San Lorenzo.

351. Since most of these huge basalt heads were in ancient times relocated and subsequently suffered over the years additional displacements, discussions about the significance (if any) of their original placements and geographic orientations remain at best a speculative exercise; but that these magnificent creations demonstrate an extraordinary mastery of the art of carving stone (carving, moreover, without the use of metal tools) is incontrovertible. Above is an eroded specimen, originally from La Venta and now in a museum; at right, another example, this one from Tres Zapotes, seems to be emerging from the ground.

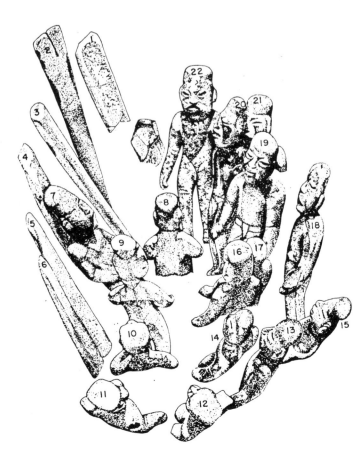

353. Throughout Mesoamerica it was customary to bury offerings in a systematic relationship to either the buildings or a courtyard or a center line that bisected the site (see **Map 28**). This custom made it possible for so-buried offerings later to be easily located, examined, and, if circumstances dictated, removed. The famous figurine offering (above) from La Venta, for example, was so precisely marked that years after its burial beneath several floors of clay (variously colored clay floors, in fact, a feature that seems to have been unique to the La Venta site) "the Olmecs themselves were able to open a pit of exactly the right size on the precise site in order to inspect these figurines."[9]

Three interpretations of the arrangement of this mysterious scene have been proposed by the excavators. The first possibility is that the figurines of jade and serpentine be viewed as facing the one made of a conglomerate of granite sand. Dark buff in color, this exceptional piece contrasts strongly with the greens and grays of the rest. Its present gritty appearance may have been caused, the excavators suggest, by chemical action of the soil. There is evidence, in fact, that another figurine originally stood beside this one, backed against celt number 3, where two pieces of badly decomposed schistose material were recovered, which, when cleaned, appeared to be fragments of a figurine's arms.[10]

The second suggested view of the arrangement of figurines envisions the five characters numbered 8, 9, 10, 11, and 22 as being central to the composition and dominating it. Number 7, accordingly, may represent a captive or other important presence, but the main figure of interest, by this interpretation, is number 22, who appears to be confronting the oncoming file. "It is worth noting," the authors remark, "that this figurine was the most spectacular in appearance of all this group, being made of bright green jade with numerous black inclusions which gives a very striking appearance. The features of this figurine were also most haughty and commanding."[11]

The third suggested interpretation of the organization of this mysterious offering has to do with an apparent arrangement of figurines in pairs: 8–9, 10–11, 12–14, 13–15, 16–17, 18–19, and 20–21. The figures numbered 7 and 22, then, stand alone, and again, number 22 appears to be the real center of the action.[12]

The figurines range in height from 6⁵⁄₁₆″ to 7⁵⁄₁₆″. Many of them had traces of bright red cinnabar paint on their feet and their legs. Some appear as if they may have been painted all over.[13] The tall heads may reflect the practice of intentional cranial deformation by tightly binding the head during infancy. The slightly bent-knee or slouching stance of the figurines is a trait characteristic of carved images throughout Oceania and in equatorial Africa. The absence of genitalia may represent an extension to earliest Mesoamerica of the shamanic practice of ritualistic sex-change or transvestism (see I.2:173–175 and **Map 38**).

354. Carved jade mask discovered at La Venta, Olmec Preclassic, dated c. 800–200 B.C.

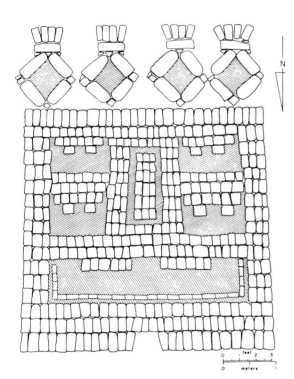

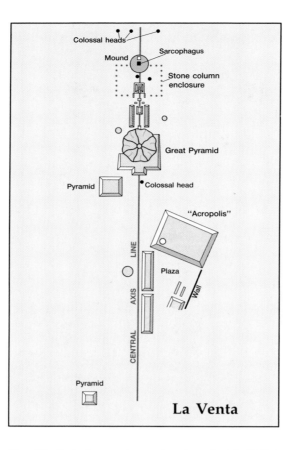

Map 28. Note the precise and systematic orientation of the major buildings along a hypothetical center line that bisects the site.

355. Unearthed at La Venta were three nearly-identical mosaics (below and at right), each of which seems to represent a stylized jaguar face (see the schematized drawing at left). Excavation evidence indicates that immediately after these intricate constructions were initially completed, they were "buried," that is, covered over with a layer of clay. Given what has been learned about similar Olmec practices in other contexts, it seems reasonable to conclude that the creators of these jaguar mosaics clearly intended them to be, not part of a practical floor, but rather an elaborate ritual offering.

about two square miles in area, in the midst of a swamp some ten miles up the Tonalá river, which flows between Tabasco and Veracruz. The dominant feature at this site is a roughly conical pyramid of built-up clay, 103 feet high, fronting a long rectangular plaza oriented eight degrees west of true north (Map 28). Along the line of this orientation, as well as at other undoubtedly symbolical positions within what is clearly a ceremonial compound, there have been uncovered no fewer than nineteen deeply buried "massive offerings" (as they are now called), of which the most extraordinary is a cluster of standing, beautifully finished, eunuchoid figurines (Figure 353), two of jade and thirteen of serpentine, arranged in a semicircle facing a sixteenth, of a reddish-brown or buff conglomerate stone, standing with its back to an array of six tall slabs of polished jade.[16]

Is the company listening to an address? Or is the sixteenth about to be sacrificed?

The basis for a possible answer may be implied in three more of the discovered "offerings," which are, namely, three separately buried, yet almost identical, rectangular mosaic panels (Figure 355), each measuring approximately 15½ feet by 20¾ feet, and each composed of close to five hundred small, polished blocks of serpentine arranged to suggest a jaguar mask.[17]

a

b

356. Some intimation of the ceremonial secrets of La Venta can be gleaned by a close examination of the mysterious iconography of Altar No. 5 (height: 5'1"): (**a**) South side, featuring glyphs of helmeted figures holding jaguar-masked boys; (**b**) front view, of a cross-legged figure with a boy supine in his lap; and (**c**) details from the North side.

357. Olmec jade figurine of standing man holding (presenting as an offering?) a "were-jaguar" child, c. 8⅝" high, Southern Mexico, c. 1000–500 B.C.

Throughout the ranges of both Middle and South American religious art the figure of the jaguar, in the form especially of the ornamental jaguar mask, appears and reappears like an obsession. The were-jaguar, furthermore, is a prominent figure in Middle and South American folk mythologies. And in every one of the recently excavated Olmec ceremonial centers unmistakable indications have been found of offerings to a jaguar god. A clue to the mythology of this god is suggested by two greatly (and apparently deliberately) damaged images of stone from two neighboring sites, Rio Chiquito and Potrero Nuevo, some fifty miles southwestward of La Venta. As interpreted by their discoverer, Matthew W. Stirling, these appear to represent a woman lying on her back with a jaguar in intercourse on top of her;[18] and since many of the most characteristic Olmec figures and figurines portray a distinctive type of were-jaguar boy, it has been suggested that these ambiguous little fellows may have been regarded as representing the progeny of that miraculous conception.

A hauntingly suggestive monument of uncertain meaning at La Venta is the carved monolith known as Altar No. 5 (Figure 356), which, in fact, may not be an altar, but a throne. From a deep hollow on its anterior face a mitred personage emerges, bearing on his arms a child, as though in offering. The northern face of the same block shows another such dignitary, clasping a child that seems to be struggling to break free. And on the opposite, southern face are two more elaborately ornamented functionaries, each with a child in his arms. A jade figurine (Figure 357) now in the Brooklyn Museum suggests that at some moment in whatever

ceremonial these images represent, both the celebrant and the presented jaguar-boy were naked. Figures 359a–d, are of celts, hachas or "votive axes" on which anthropomorphic representations of the jaguar-god himself appear, while in Figure 358, which is of a jaguar-child, zoomorphic and anthropomorphic features are indistinguishably conjoined.

Was the ritual represented in these finds of an actual child sacrifice? Or was it, as Ignacio Bernal suggests, a ceremony with "a dynastic meaning, showing the importance of the child as heir to the throne?"[19] Michael D. Coe suggests that "the feline element in Olmec art" anticipates the mythology of the Aztec jaguar-god Tezcatlipoca, pointing out: "1) that the main point of Mesoamerican theogony [myths of the origin and genealogy of the gods] was to confirm royal power, and 2) that the entire origin myth, like the Memphite Theogony of the Egyptians, was recited at the accession of a new king so that he, chosen by Tezcatlipoca himself, might know who he was and that his people might know him."[20]

In the folk-beliefs and mythologies of both Middle and South America the jaguar has inherent shamanic associations; in fact, as Peter Furst has defined the case: "shamans and jaguars are not merely equivalent, but each is at the same time the other."[21] At a critical moment in the history of the Olmec sites, as registered and even illustrated in their magnificent monuments, a dominating shamanic elite evidently assumed charge of a cultural and related spiritual transformation that amounted, as Jacques Soustelle has described it, to a "prodigious mutation that took the Olmecs from tiny hamlets to cities, from culture to civilization; and we use the word 'mutation,'" he adds, "deliberately, for there is no evidence of a 'formative' evolution, a gradual maturation over several centuries. This indeed constitutes," he concludes, "the very heart of the Olmec mystery. The sudden passage to a superior level thanks to individuals of genius? Innovations suddenly brought in from the outside?—but if so, by whom and from where?"[22]

The critical date of the Olmec event is c. 1200 B.C., which nicely matches that of the Late Shang dynastic capital at An-yang (Honan), c. 1384–1025 B.C.; also, that of the legendary fall of Troy to the Achaeans (destruction by fire of Troy, c. thirteenth century B.C.), as well as the entry into northwest India of the Vedic-Aryans. Evidence of an earlier occupation of a number of the Olmec jungle sites from possibly c. 1500 B.C. has suggested to some that a local formative development may have anteceded the abrupt appearance in the area of both great and small stone monuments in a sculptural style fully achieved.[23] No signs, however, have yet been found of formative beginnings of any kind. Moreover, great styles in art do not evolve, they appear, as manifestations of intelligible insights, after which, as in the course of time the originating impulse fades, there is a devolution to secondary interests, applications, and effects. Likewise, in the history of any mythologically structured

358. Tantalizing insights into Olmec mythology are suggested by this three-inch-high jade figurine (pierced for use as a pendant) of a polymorphous "were-jaguar" boy, in the throes of transformation.

359. Ceremonial celts with incised anthropomorphic representations of the "jaguar-god" abound in Olmec Mesoamerica: (**a**) specimen probably from Oaxaca, c. 7¹³⁄₁₆″ tall; (**b**) the jadite Kunz celt, first described in 1889, 10³⁄₁₆″ high; (**c**) "votive ax" from the region of Veracruz, 11″ in height; and (**d**) hacha from La Venta Tomb E.

civilization (and there is none known that was not originally so structured), as the initiating metaphysical insight fades and the connotations of the metaphoric customs are forgotten, practical political and economic purposes take over, the integrative principal no longer holds, and the civilization goes to pieces.

At the Olmec sites, from c. 600 B.C. onward, there are signs, increasingly evident, of a decline of this kind, until by c. 100 B.C. the civilization was extinct and its heritage of symbolic forms had been passed on to the Maya. Bernal has termed this season of devolution, Olmec III. His Olmec I is of the period from c. 1500 B.C. to the epochal "mutation" or "quantum leap," as it has also been called, of c. 1200 B.C., after which, during Olmec II, for a period of six centuries, there flourished in the torrid swamp and river lands of a Mesoamerican jungle the first monumental civilization of the New World.

One of the most remarkable aspects of the Olmec phenomenon is the very wide diffusion of the evidences of its influence. On the west coast, in the highlands of the Sierra Madre del Sur, in both Oaxaca and Guerrero, these evidences are such as to suggest an Olmec colonial presence exerting a formative influence on the local agricultural populations from as early as c. 1000 B.C.[24]

At Tlatilco, for example, among the figu-

a

b

c

d

rines of a local style were other objects of a distinctly Olmec cast (Figure 361), "establishing," as Miguel Covarrubias, who had supervised the dig, declared, "the contemporaneity and relationship of these two puzzling cultures."[25] The period of the burials from which the objects were retrieved was c. 1200 to 900 B.C.,[26] exactly that of the sites in Guerrero and Oaxaca. Also, as Soustelle has shown, at a succession of sites southward, along the coastal way from below Tonalá in Chiapas to the Peninsula de Nicoya of northwestern Costa Rica, monuments have been identified of distinctly Olmec craftsmanship and origin: at Pijijiapan, Ojo de Agua, El Sitio, San Gerónimo, Abaj Takalik, Piedra Parada and, in El Savador, Las Victorias.[27] "In the southernmost border region of Mesoamerica, in Costa Rica," Soustelle suggests, "the jade deposits of the Nicoya Peninsula perhaps served as a pole of attraction drawing to this region Olmec traders or explorers—half traders and half warriors—traveling down the Pacific coast from Tonalá and Pijijiapan by way of Las Victorias."[28]

"If we observe on a map the areas occupied by the Olmec world," Ignacio Bernal has remarked, "we see that they cover most of Mesoamerica...."[29] And yet, the Olmec cannot be said to have been the masters of an empire. The explanation generally proposed and accepted for the broad reach of their influence is of trade, undertaken in the first instance to establish and maintain a

360. Concave mirror of polished hematite, pierced to be worn as a pectoral, from La Venta.

This remarkable mirror is one of eight that have been recovered. According to a technical report published by the excavators: "The polish of the specimens is excellent and probably represents the limit of perfection that the material will allow....The radius of curvature becomes progressively greater as the edge is approached. The effect is almost identical with the modern practice of parabolizing optical reflectors. This outer flattening improves the performance of a reflector that focuses radiant energy."[14]

The focal length is so long, however, that it is impossible to concentrate enough heat to ignite a fire.[15] Instead, "an even more fantastic use could have been as a 'camera obscura.' These mirrors can throw a picture of the landscape on a surface placed near the principal focus. All that is required is some shading of the screen on which the picture is to be projected."[16] Some sort of magical or symbolic use may have been made of such reflections. Whatever the case, as the excavators unequivocally remark, these mirrors "stand out as the most unique pieces of precision stoneworking of the La Venta culture."[17]

flow of jade, magnetite, ilemite, and the other luxury goods required for the fabrication of the status symbols of an elaborately ornamented theocratic aristocracy: decorated cotton mantels, earrings, lip-plugs, pectorals, and the like.[30] Protection of the trade routes required the establishment of guardian "gateway communities" at critical points along the way, while in stations of major concern, colonial factoring communities would have come into being.

For there was already in America at the time of the Spanish Conquest a well-traveled system of highways that with hardly a break extended from Chaco Canyon, New Mexico (see pages 276–277; Map 31), to Santiago in Chile (see pages 369, 375–376; Map 42); and, as it now appears, the beginnings of the type of interregional trade and traffic represented by these foot-worn thoroughfares must be ascribed to the earliest centuries of La Venta, when basalt and other materials not to be found in the surrounding swamps were already being turned into symbolic monuments on that astonishing little island of but two square miles.

Nor was all the traffic by land: see Map 26.[31] In the course of a discussion on the dating, form, and function of the pyramid at La Venta, Gordon Willey called attention to the fact that at Poverty Point, Louisiana (about 250 miles up the Mississippi River), there stands "the earliest pyramid in the eastern United States....It is enormous,"

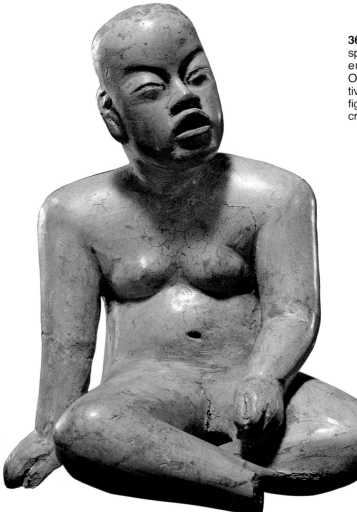

361. That a significant Olmec influence was widespread in Mesoamerica is demonstrated by the proliferation at various non-Olmec sites of so-called Olmecoid figurines (that is, figurines that are suggestive of those made by the Olmec), such as: (**a**) seated figure of white slip, 6½" high, from Tlapacoya; and (**b**) cross-legged figure from Tlatilco.

he declared, "and its radiocarbon dates are just about the same as those from La Venta."[32] And from a much later period (not determined), at a site on the savannahs around Lake Okeechobee, Florida, there has been retrieved a silver jaguar mask (Figure 363) which also points to Veracruz.[33] As envisaged by Soustelle:

"It is still too early to try to understand exactly what the Olmecs were doing when they left their normal habitat and ventured forth into regions so distant and so different from their own. They were seeking, as we have said, raw materials such as jade and serpentine, and perhaps certain varieties of obsidian as well: artifacts made of extremely rare green obsidian, scarcely ever found outside of the region of Pachuca (state of Hidalgo), in the northeast of Mexico, were discovered at Ayotla and at San Lorenzo. If, as we may suppose, Olmec travelers or colonists engaged in trade—like the Aztec *pochteca* many centuries later—they must have brought from their place of origin objects or goods that would pique the interest of the peoples who dwelt on the central plateau: the feathers of tropical birds, rubber, cocoa, carved jade pieces perhaps. These Olmec traders may thus have initiated a certain current of exchanges between *Tierra Caliente* and *Tierra Fría*—the Hot Lands and the Cold Lands—that, practically speaking, has continued uninterruptedly ever since and that serves to explain in particular how it happens that precious feathers, balls of rubber, tropical plants such as cacao trees, and jade pieces are shown in the fresco paintings on the walls of the palaces and sanctuaries of Teotihuacán."[34]

"Certain portions of this immense zone of diffusion of Olmec civilization were probably administered by individuals (priests? government functionaries? military personnel?) who had come from the 'metropolitan area,' representing, for example, the leaders of La Venta. Other regions might well have been peopled by Olmecs but allowed to administer themselves. Still others doubtless preserved the basic features of their traditional culture, their language, and their gods, but assimilated, more or less profoundly, certain traits of the more sophisticated civilization that had reached them.

"Although we know so little about Olmec religion, it is legitimate to presume that it played a large part in the dynamic expansionist thrust of these people. In world history, proselytism is always a powerful factor in cultural diffusion. Perhaps Olmec 'missionaries' journeyed along the long routes of Mesoamerica in order to spread the cult of the jaguar god....

"More cultural and religious than military, more commercial than administrative, the spreading over a wide area of a civilization rather than a power, what we call the 'Olmec empire' was chronologically the first, in this part of the world, of those great human edifices, of those groupings of peo-

362. The lower fragment of Tres Zapotes Stela C was discovered by Matthew Stirling in January 1939. Depicted on one side is a "weeping-jaguar" (arguably Cocijo, the Zapotec rain god), and on the other, signs that are of numbers, the notation being the same as that used later by the Maya: each bar is a 5; each dot is a 1. The lowest element is a day-sign corresponding to the Mayan "6 Etz' nab" (something very like "Thursday [Thor's day] the 6th"). The upper numbers represent this weekday's position in the month, the year, a cycle of twenty years, and (beyond that, see below) a megacycle of twenty such greater cycles of ever-cycling time. Hence, the designation, "Long Count" that has been given to this type of Mesoamerican calendar.

When restored with the addition of a second fragment (the upper, discovered about 1972), the inscribed date on Stela C now reads: 7 Baktuns, 16 Katuns, 6 Tuns, 16 Uinals, 18 Kins. Considering that, in the Long Count, 1 Baktun = 20 Katuns and 1 Katun = 20 Tuns and 1 Tun = 20 Uinals and 1 Uinal = 18 Kins and 1 Kin = 1 day, the signs on Stela C accordingly add up to 1,125,698 days from the base date of the Long Count calendar. Now, if the base date of the Mayan Long Count was, as some suppose, October 4, 3373 B.C., then the date here inscribed would, according to that reckoning, be November 4, 291 B.C. If, however, the base date of the calendar was, as others believe, August 13, 3113 B.C., then the date recorded on Stela C would be September 2, 31 B.C.[18] Both dates are for the Olmec, however, very late. Soustelle has therefore suggested that the Long Count of the Olmec may have been based on an earlier date than the Long Count of the Maya.[19] The question has not been resolved.

ples, that successively bore the imprint of Teotihuacán, of the Maya cities, of Tula, of Tenochtitlán. For the first time, a dynamic outpouring of thought and action, of art and of commerce, a religion, and a style transcended the narrow limits of a village. This was the decisive step, the threshold approached but not crossed by other Indians such as the Pueblos: the transition, or rather mutation, that two thousand years after the first faltering steps in the domain of agriculture, transformed the life of the Mexican peasant by inventing the city, the crucible of new ideas."[35]

363. From the Fort Center site, Lake Okeechobee, Florida, comes this silver mask (or tablet), depicting either a jaguar face or a "spider motif."[20]

AGRICULTURAL RITES

AND MYTHS OF
MIDDLE AMERICA

The Desert Cultures

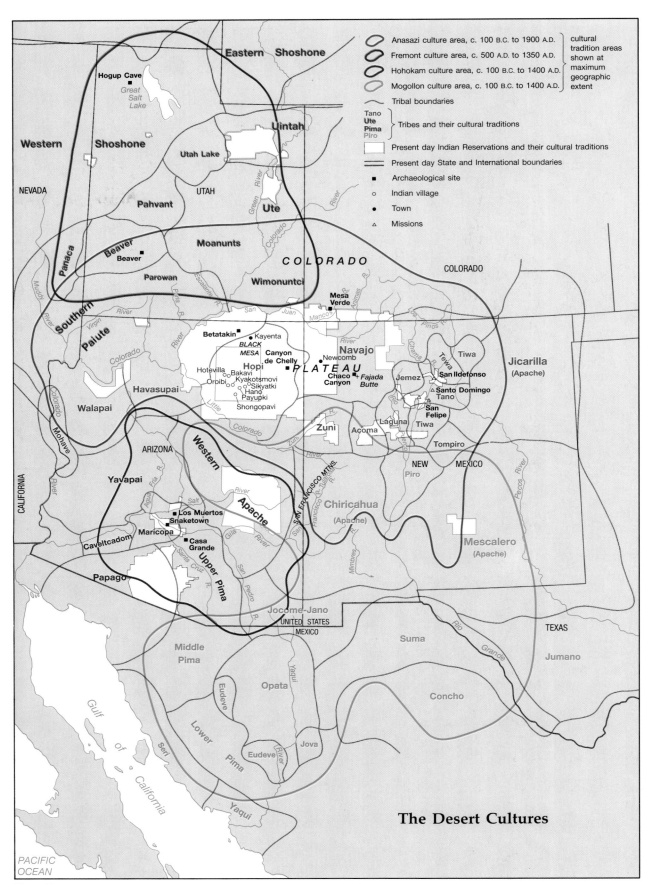

The Desert Cultures

Map 29.

From as early as 8000 or 7000 B.C., the whole area from Oregon to northern Mexico and from the Pacific Coast to the eastern foot-hills of the Rocky Mountains was occupied by a scattering of so-called Desert Culture tribes subsisting, not by big-game hunting, but by plant gathering; and whereas, over the rest of the continent, the prime signs of the time were Clovis, Sandia, and Folsom points (see I.1:35–36), the distinguishing stone artifacts in this region were milling stones for the grinding of wild seeds. The atlatl, or spear-thrower, also appears, however, and, as the animal remains suggest, small-game hunting must have contributed to the economy. Caves and rock shelters were inhabited, and by about 4000 B.C. the domesticated dog had arrived—like the atlatl, from Asia. Among the characteristic manufactures were baskets, nets, the crude milling stones, simple bone tools, and small stone projectile points, stemmed or notched.

By c. 300 B.C. in Arizona and western New Mexico the people of a specific local desert culture known as the Cochise had begun practicing a form of agriculture based on maize, beans, and squash which had been developed in Mexico between 6500 and 1500 B.C.[1] and was to become in time the characteristic agricultural form of North America. As described by Carl Sauer, this cultivated triad formed a "symbiotic complex," without an equal anywhere. As he describes it: "The corn plants grow tall and have first claim on sunlight and moisture. The beans climb up the corn stalks for their share of light; their roots support colonies of nitrogen-fixing bacteria. The squashes or pumpkins grow mainly prone on the ground and complete the ground cover. In lands of short growing season, all three may be planted together at the same time, the corn then being of early maturing kinds. In lands of long season, the corn was planted first, the other two later in the hills of the corn. With few exceptions all three were grown together. By long cultivation varieties of all were selected, able to grow to the farthest climatic limits of Indian agriculture."[2]

A second new appearance in the Cochise area at that time was the pit-house dwelling: huts of poles, bush, and clay, built over pits of from ten to forty inches in depth, entered by way of a stepped tunnel. There is no known evidence of any such building style either in Mexico or in the eastern United States. One suggestion is that it may be a reflection in the New World of a Late Paleolithic (Gravettian) mammoth hunters' house-form of c. 25,000 years ago.[3] Be that as it may, its sudden appearance in the American Southwest, c. 300 B.C., was in the Cochise Mogollon area (southwestern New Mexico and southeastern Arizona), after which it spread through the rest of the culture.

Farther west, in the more arid parts of what is now central and southern Arizona (largely along the Salt and Gila rivers), a remarkable local development out of the general base arose that is known to archaeology as the Hohokam culture. Its most striking feature was a network of irrigation canals, of which the first element, three miles long, was already functioning, watered from the Gila River, in the first centuries A.D. By the fourteenth century there were over 150 miles of such canals in the Salt River valley alone. Ball courts, resembling those of the Mayan ceremonial centers in Guatemala, appeared here between A.D. 500 and 900, and the art of casting copper bells in wax molds, between A.D. 900 and 1100, after which date the villages of pit-houses, which had occasionally been walled for defense, gave place to large, multiple-storied communal buildings. Early in the fifteenth century, for reasons unknown, this extensive organization of interdependent settlements broke down, and the Hohokam culture disintegrated. The modern Papago and Pima, both of which tribes are of a Uto-Aztecan language stock, are believed to be its descendants.

The Pima, who have remained in their traditional locales—the valleys of the Gila and Salt rivers—still practice a form of agriculture made possible only by controlled irrigation. They have returned, however, to the one-room dwelling, and during years of drought (which are frequent) are reduced to the ancient desert resource of small-game hunting and seed collection (largely of jackrabbits and mesquite beans). The Papago, who appropriately call themselves the Bean People (also, Desert People, in contrast to the Pima as the River People), are even more dependent on primitive desert-foraging than their relatives. Dwelling as they do in the arid hills of southernmost Arizona and northernmost Sonoma, they are thrown back upon what is known as flash-flood farming. Immediately following the first rains, they plant what seeds they have in the alluvial fans at the mouths of washes.

And yet, the elegant little fragment of myth that was confided to Natalie Curtis,

364. Reconstruction, based on posthole patterns and fallen timbers from various structures, of a typical pit-house of the Late Pithouse period.

365. The Pima pithouse tradition continued into the twentieth century: *Ceremonial Ki-Pima*, 1907 photograph by Edward S. Curtis (1868–1952).

around 1904, by the old Pima chief Hovering Hawk may well have been a particle of ancient Hohokam mythology from the great periods of the ceremonial ball courts, c. A.D. 500 to 1400. "I will sing an old, old song," he told her, "a song sung by the Creator at the beginning of the world.... The story tells of the beginning of all things, and there are many songs in the story. To tell it rightly and to sing all the songs would take all night and longer. So I will only tell you, shortly, just a part of it, and sing you the one song.... White people say that our dances and our songs are not good. We are glad that you say it is no harm for us to sing.... It is well that you have come to do this thing for us, but we have not much money to offer you in return. The white people living up above us on the river have taken all the water, so that our fields are dry. We are poor."[4]

A history closely parallel to that of the rise, culmination, and abrupt dissolution of the Hohokam village complex between c. 300 B.C. and c. A.D. 1400 unfolded in the Mogollon culture area as well—there where the pit-house dwellings had first appeared. That was a culture notable especially for the beauty and variety of its potteries. Already in its earliest appearance, Mogollon pottery (the first in the Southwest) was graceful and expertly made. The Mogollon villages were at first of circular pit-house dwellings, which by A.D. 700 had become rectangular. From c. A.D. 1, however, there were in many of the villages very much larger structures which served apparently as ceremonial chambers, and these were of various forms: circular, bean or kidney shaped, square with rounded corners, **D** shaped. Generally regarded as ancestral to the Pueblo Kiva, twenty-three or more have been identified in the area, and seven have been excavated and described.[5] Stress-bearing walls of masonry were introduced to the Mogollon

a

c

b

366. Throughout the North American Southwest, an extraordinarily diverse profusion of prehistoric paintings adorn isolated rock outcroppings, desolate caves, and seemingly inaccessible canyon bluffs. Although increasingly endangered by the passage of time, the ravishment of the elements, the maliciousness of vandals, and the encroachment of civilization, these iconographic treasures nonetheless still provide invaluable intimations of ancient ways. Herewith, a selective sampling: (**a**) 1930 photograph of anthropomorphic figures in Classic Vernal style, from Dry Fork Valley, Utah; (**b**) from Barrier Canyon, these pre-Fremont pictographs are suggestive of aboriginal Australian ancestral figuration (see I.2:**246**); (**c**) an eight-foot-long, horned and plumed, Mogollon serpent, decorated with stepped motifs that possibly represent clouds, from the Diablo Dam site in Texas; and (**d**) a colored transcript of a composition that Campbell Grant, author and illustrator of a comprehensive study of Chumash rock painting, considers to be "the most elaborate and colorful pictograph in Chumash territory." Grant continues, "It shows considerable overpainting to the right, where cruder work is overlaid with beautifully executed designs. This painting originally covered most of the cave walls, but the wind has eroded all but these paintings on the roof."[21] The Chumash, a great Indian nation that in pre-Colonial times occupied a substantial territory along the coastline in southern California, by 1839 had virtually ceased to exist.

d

culture zone c. A.D. 900, and during the classical, so-called Mimbres period, c. A.D. 1050 to 1200—which was graced by an especially striking pottery (see Figures 367–368)—pit-house dwellings gave place to apartment buildings of from forty to fifty rooms, one to three stories high, constructed around a plaza. But then again, as in the Hohokam zone (and again for reasons unknown), these substantial settlements were abandoned, and all trace (in this case) of the population has disappeared.

367. Hohokam red-on-buff pottery, Sacron phase (c. A.D. 900–1100):

(a) Gila shoulder olla with plaited and spiraling decorations, c. 13″ × 18⅓″, Casa Grande, Arizona.

(b) Shallow plate with crane, c. 1½″ deep × 9″ diameter, Middle Gila River Valley, Arizona.

368. Classic Mimbres (c. A.D. 1000–1150) Black-on-white hemispheric vessels, Mimbres River Valley, New Mexico. All have had a hole punched in them (that is, been "killed") before being placed over the face of a corpse; depicted are **(a)** anthropomorphic reptile figure, c. 3¾″ × 8¾″; **(b)** opposing pronghorn antelope, c. 4⅞″ × 11⅛″; **(c)** anthropomorphic bird with fish, c. 4″ × 9″; and **(d)** male figures with a feline in a "cornfield," c. 3½″ × 10″. Barbara L. Moulard provides a context: "Mimbres constitutes both a regional branch as well as a chronological period of Mogollon development…concentrated along the upper Gila, San Francisco, and Mimbres River valleys. Classic Mimbres Black-on-white pottery was adumbrated in…the final phase of the late Pit House Period [c. A.D. 750–1000, when] the Mimbres region experienced direct contact with the highly developed Hohokam [who] appear to have been most accessible early in their development to influences from Mesoamerica. Mexican traits continued to diffuse into the Hohokam region and the culture grew in power until c. A.D. 900–1100. The development of Mogollon pottery painting prior to the Classic Mimbres Period closely resembles that of the Hohokam from A.D. 700 to 1100. During the eleventh century, Hohokam influence gradually withdrew from the Mimbres region. At the beginning of the eleventh century, the Mimbres area underwent major social and organizational changes reflected in the move from pit house dwellings to surface cobblestone masonry pueblos."[22]

The Kiva

The third and only enduring flowering out of the early Cochise ground was that known as the Anasazi, of which the Pueblo are the inheritors. The geographical center of this development lay northward of the Hohokam-Mogollon zones, in that still magnificently beautiful area (studded today with national parks and monuments) where the four states of Utah, Colorado, Arizona, and New Mexico come together. The name Anasazi is from a Navaho noun meaning Ancient Ones, and indeed the history of this region, as it now appears, tells of the force of a single, ancestral, *cultural* continuity, which took into its fold and shaped to its own archetypes peoples of a number of distinct racial and linguistic stocks. The Navaho, Apache, Athabascan, and various Pueblo communities, for example, are of at least four separate stocks: Uto-Aztecan, Penutian, Tewa, and Keresan.

Yet all share, as though it were their own, the origin myth of an emergence from the womb of the earth (usually by an ascent through three subterranean stages), the legend of a tribal wandering before settling in their present station, and an adventure cycle of the heroic deeds of young, twin, monster slayers, whose miraculous lives are rehearsals of a series of standard mythological motifs: virgin birth, father quest, perilous journey (to the Sun) with magical aid (from Spider Woman, from the daughter of the Sun, and from various spirit messengers), paternity tests and recognition followed by initiation to self-knowledge, return to the earth with augmented powers (lightning arrows, arcane knowledge, and so on), and a series of culture deeds of Herculean type that clear the land of threatening presences. There are, furthermore, a number of other standard elements associated with these narrative motifs: colors of the four directions, one central and four cardinal mountains, sunwise circumambulation, and the ritual use of sandpaintings and of prayer sticks—all of which, by the way, were also features, until 1959, of the Tantric Buddhist ritual arts of the monasteries of Tibet.

The primitive Cochise inhabitants of the Anasazi area were a people known as Basket Makers, dwelling in caves or in shelters of poles and adobe, cultivating maize and pumpkins, and fashioning, as their name suggests, excellent baskets. Then around A.D. 500, turkeys, bean crops, and cotton were added to their holdings, and pottery (sun dried) was introduced; along with these, from the Mogollon area, came pit-houses, both as domiciles and as ceremon-

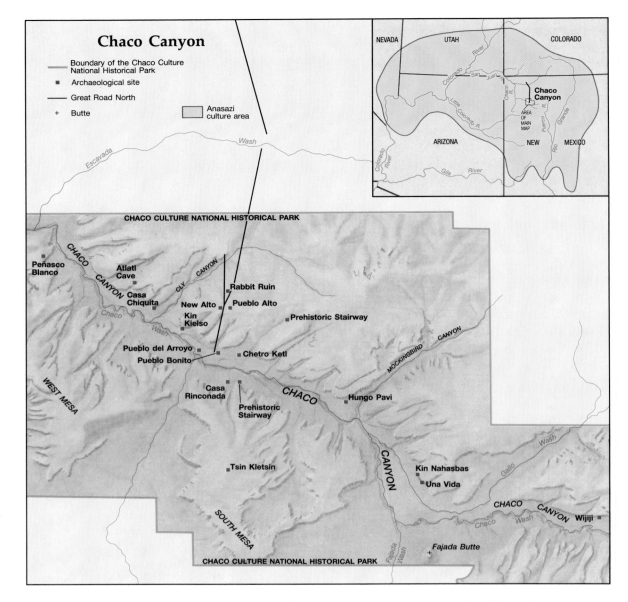

Map 30. With its impressive pueblo ruins, its network of arrow-straight roadways, and its rich ceramic tradition, Chaco Canyon offers ample evidences of what has become known as the Chaco phenomenon, a major cultural influence in the prehistoric North American Southwest.

ial chambers. At Juniper Cove, at the foot of the Black Mesa, six miles south of Kayenta, there has been excavated a large structure of the ceremonial kind, situated about one hundred feet from a late Basket Maker pit-house village. It was thirty-six feet in diameter, with a continuous bench encircling the interior, an entrance with descending steps, four large posts near the corners, which had supported a flat roof, and a central fire pit on a raised platform; the date was c. A.D. 650 to 700.[6] Through the following three and a half centuries (the period known as *Developmental Pueblo,* also as *Pueblo I and II:* c. A.D. 700 to 1050), the interiors of these Anasazi "great kivas" became standardized in arrangement and greatly enlarged. There is an example in Cahone Canyon, near Ackman, Colorado, of a date c. A.D. 855 to 872, showing a diameter of no less than eighty-one feet.[7] And among the great system of ruins at the site known as Pueblo Bonito in Chaco Canyon (New Mexico), there is a prime example from this period, known as Kiva Q (see Figures 369–370), the floor plan of which[8] presents a readily read statement of the standard main features (all mythologically symbolic) of an early Pueblo kiva.

The only exceptional element in this kiva is the entrance from the south, instead of the north; the other elements are standard for the Developmental Pueblo period. The columns are not only structural, but also (undoubtedly) symbolic of the mythic mountains of the four quarters below ground, which support the plane of this earth. For the kiva is itself the underworld, and those initiates within it, seated on the encircling bench or in action performing ritual tasks, are in imagination identical with the world-supporting and world-generating cosmic and ancestral powers that are personified and made visible in their ceremonials. Within the kiva they have stepped back, as it were, behind the veil of time of the beginning, as well as down below the floor of sunlit space, and their flickering light now is of the "old god," fire, the sun's terrestrial counterpart, a beloved and major god throughout Middle America.

The presence of the sipapu in the floors of these first kivas of the Anasazi pueblo culture gives tangible evidence of an emergence myth already central to the ritual lore of that otherwise undocumented period of exclusively oral transmission. The symbolized Place of Emergence, furthermore, is today interpreted—as we have learned (see I.2:241–243)—as the womb of a living mother earth, who is the mother, not only of mankind, but also of the beasts and birds. The sipapu in the kiva, therefore, is an altar symbolic of the female power, as the other altar, the raised firebox, must have been of the male as engendering fire: the "old god" *huehueteotl,* as the Aztecs termed this prime giver to mankind, not only of the fire of life, but also of the hearth-fires of civilization. Thus through archaeology it appears that the reverence in these sanctuaries was of the two great mysteries of the boons of life and culture: the *yin* and the *yang* (to use the Chinese terms), the dark and the light, moist and dry, female and male. The informing mythological tradition was specifically of an emergence myth of all life arising from a female earth. And already, there was a governing society or priesthood of initiates (not individual shamans) charged with the maintenance and celebration of relevant rites.

369. Photograph of Kiva Q looking south. The arrows indicate the depth of probable rebuilding of the outer wall. Specialists doubt that the antechamber is of prehistoric construction.

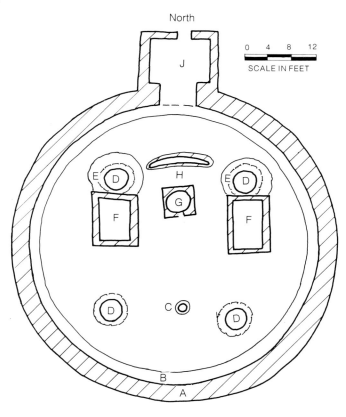

North

SCALE IN FEET
0   4   8   12

370. Plan of Pueblo Bonito's great Kiva Q (Pueblo Bonito II): Its interior diameter averages forty-four feet. Its floor is nine feet below the plaza level and six feet four inches below the level of the entrance chamber (**J**), descent from which must have been by a ladder. The chamber is encircled by a permanent stone bench (**B**) against the wall (**A**). Four columns (**D**) once supported a flat roof. Two vaults (**F**) — for the storage, possibly, of ritual gear — abut the southern columns, and between them is a raised rectangular masonry firebox (**G**), with a rectangular draft opening to the north. The dimensions of the vaults are six feet eight inches (north to south) by four feet eight inches (east to west). The original height of the firebox may have been about two feet. A floor slot (**H**), which when uncovered was found to be filled with shale up to the floor level, has been interpreted as being a base for some kind of fire screen. And approximately mid-way between the two northern columns is what is known as a *sipapu* (**C**), a hole symbolic of the Place of Emergence. Circular in form the *sipapu* is fourteen inches in diameter and nine inches deep, features well-made masonry walls, and is floored with a stone slab through the center of which there is a circular hole (compare the hole in the center of a Huichol *tepari*: Figures **417** and **418**). The *sipapu* is directly in line, on the north-south axis, with the firebox and the fire screen.[23] Although Kiva Q is larger than the other kivas at Pueblo Bonito, its interior arrangement can be seen as prototypical of the architectural features of most other kivas.

Cycles of the Sun and Moon

Pueblo Bonito, five stories high with some 832 rooms and kivas, was but one of a number of Developmental Pueblo and *Classic Pueblo* (*Pueblo III*, c. A.D. 1050 to 1300) settlements centered in a vast ceremonial and commercial complex around Chaco Canyon, New Mexico. A related ruin some fifty miles northwestward, on a milelong mesa near Newcomb, New Mexico, nearly covers the mesa top with at least 1200 rooms.

In those centuries the entire canyon floor was laced by numerous roads, many as wide as thirty feet, running perfectly straight for miles out to the north, south, east, and west, with stairways cut into rock walls to ascend and descend obstructing mesas and with causeways across the low spots. Trodden only by sandaled or bare human feet — since there were neither beasts of burden nor wheeled vehicles in pre-Columbian North and Middle America — they supported what must have been a lively traffic of porters bearing produce from the surrounding farms, household goods, and luxury articles for the wealthy, as well as the tens of thousands of timbers from forests twenty to thirty miles distant to serve as beams for the building and repair of the numerous multiroom dwellings. There is evidence, also, of an import and export traffic, with itinerant merchants arriving from and departing for the great capitals to the south: Pre-Toltec Teotihuacán (c. 100 B.C. to A.D. 650), Toltec Tula (Tollan) (c. A.D. 750 to 1168), Aztec Tenochtitlán (c. A.D. 1150 to 1521).

Regulation of the public affairs of a civilization of this magnitude, dependent on agriculture for its life in a marginal agricultural zone, demanded as a first necessity a binding of the whole to the seasonal tasks of the local agricultural year, and this in turn required the maintenance of a seasonal watch on the heavens. The binding of the community was then to be achieved by way of a year-round calendar of festivals articulated by this watch. And as in every other known early agricultural society, so here in the North American Southwest, the sense of an essential spiritual accord between the social and celestial orders, with the well-being of the community understood as a function of this accord, contributed to the flowering of a mythology of personified cosmic powers functioning simultaneously in the heavens and on earth. Conformance with their celestially announced order yielded health, wealth, and progeny, whereas the slightest deviation broke the connection.

The annual passages of the sun northward and southward, back and forth, as marked by the movement along the horizon of its points of rising and setting, were

the first and most obvious signs to be watched. To this day in the Hopi village of Walpi, Arizona, for example, the festivals preceding the winter solstice (about December 21, when the sun turns to its southward course and days begin to grow longer) are determined by sunset-horizon observations; those before the summer solstice (about June 21, when the northward turn is made and the nights begin to grow longer) by sunrise horizon. Sunset observations are conducted from the rooftop of the Bear Clan's matriarchal house, which is in the center of the main house group of the pueblo; those at sunrise, from the tip of the First Mesa. As the critical day approaches, observations of the controlling celestial body (sun or moon, depending on the festival) are made each day by the chief of the particular kiva in charge of the occasion, and on the relevant evening (when the sun has reached a specific position or the moon has entered a specific phase), this watcher calls for a smoke talk. There the leading members of the society settle upon a proper date, and at sunrise of the following day this date is announced by a crier chief. Preliminary exercises of prayer, meditation, and fasting from salt and meat are undertaken in the kivas while the altars, prayer sticks, and other elements of the ceremony are being prepared, and the public ceremonials then commence either four or eight days after the announcement and continue for either five or nine days (four or eight sleeps). On the final day there is a culminating performance, usually featuring a dance by the sponsoring kiva or kivas.[9]

A remarkable invention, unique (as far as is known) in the history of astronomical observation, has been lately recognized in the apparently casual arrangement of the three stone slabs shown in Figure 374.[10] Their site is a narrow ledge about thirty feet below the summit of an isolated sandstone butte some 475 feet high, Fajada Butte (Figure 373), which stands guard, as it were, at the southern gate of Chaco Canyon. On June 29, 1977, a week after summer solstice, a young artist in search of petroglyphs, Anna Sofaer, of Washington, D.C., having made her way up to this rocky shelf by way of a narrow chimney inhabited by

372. A sense of timelessness surrounds Walpi (seen here in an Edward S. Curtis photograph), where the Hopi of today still maintain their ancient tradition of harmonizing their daily lives with the cosmos through a ceremonial cycle set in accord with observations of sunrise-sunset horizons.

371. Pueblo Bonito, largest of Chaco Canyon's eight prehistoric towns (pueblos), is **D**-shaped, covers three acres, and contains between 650 and 800 rooms — as well as five large kivas and thirty-three smaller ones — all stacked around a large central plaza, dominated by a great kiva and bisected by a row of rooms. Across its straight-walled front, entrance to the plaza is blocked by a single-story row of rooms forming a continuous wall that rises to perhaps five stories, in the rear, where the ancient town curves into the shadow of the mesa cliff. Large logs from the highland areas (forty-seven miles away) were carried to Pueblo Bonito for use as timbers in its roofing. Ring-dated logs indicate that the construction was begun c. A.D. 919 and was completed by c. A.D. 1085.[24]

Map 31. Enhanced aerial photography of Chaco Canyon and environs has established the existence of a network of straight roadways, many thirty feet wide, interconnecting towns within the canyon and linking it to various outliers up to sixty-five miles away. When cliffs were encountered, the road was not rerouted; instead, stairs or footholds were carved. Since the Chacoans had no wheels and, further, the roads neither accommodate draft animals nor facilitate foot travel, it is surmised that they had some symbolic or ceremonial significance.[25]

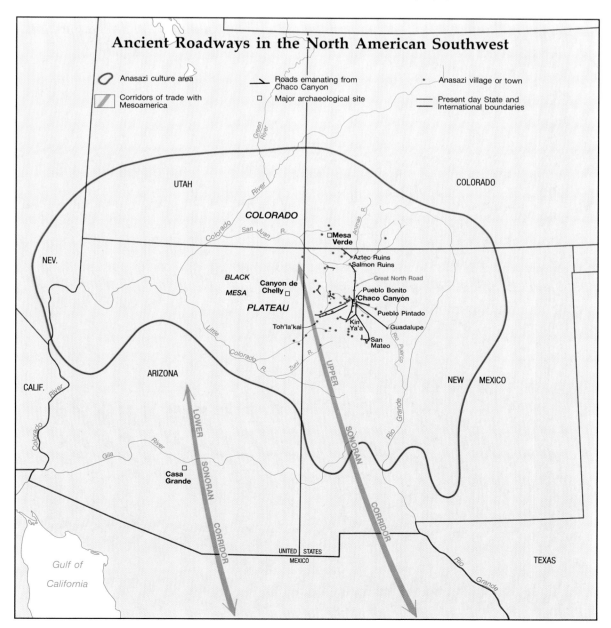

Ancient Roadways in the North American Southwest

rattlesnakes on the west side of the butte, worked her way around to the southeast face and, having arrived at this arrangement of slabs, looked behind them. It was about eleven in the morning. And what she saw was a daggerlike, vertical shaft of sunlight moving slowly, as though alive, down through the center of a spiral petroglyph. In about twelve minutes the dart of light had passed completely down the spiral and disappeared.

Ms. Sofaer and her colleagues have since assiduously studied the construction, both by day and by night, for the summer and winter solstices, for the spring and fall equinoxes, and by moonlight.[11] They have found that the construction is both a solar and a lunar calendar. On the rock face behind the vertical slabs are engraved two spirals, a larger of nine and a half turns and a smaller, to the left, of two and a quarter. Toward noon on the day of the summer solstice, a dagger of living light passes through the center of the larger spiral while, in a related effect, a small spot of light, hardly noticeable, shines for but two minutes somewhat to the left of the lesser spiral.

Through the following months of July, August, and September, these two beams move steadily, day by day, to the right,

373. On isolated Fajada Butte, at the southern edge of Chaco Canyon, Anna Sofaer in 1977 discovered a unique Anasazi solar-lunar calendar.

until on the day of the fall equinox, September 21, the leftward beam, now much longer than at first, cuts through the center of the lesser spiral. Thereafter, the rightward movement continues, and this second beam ever lengthens. By noon on December 21, the day of the winter solstice, the two darts, now of equal length, perfectly frame the larger spiral, after which the movement, day by day, is from right to left. At noon on March 21, the day of the spring equinox, the positions of the light beams are exactly as they had been September 21, and by the summer solstice the cycle is completed.

As for the moon, the research teams studying these petroglyphs have established that the patterns formed by moonlight shining between the slabs are as clear as those of the day, and when the moon's declination is anywhere between the solar extremes of plus 23.5° and minus 23.5°, the patterns formed are the same as those of the sun. However, in the course of a cycle of nineteen years, the moon's declination, for a part of that time, goes beyond these solar limits. This periodic extreme was not reached again until 1987, when photographs taken on November 8 (the night when the moon attained the most northerly extreme of its nineteen-year excursion) confirmed predictions by Sofaer and others that the rising moon, shining on the verti-

cal slabs, casts a shadow which is tangent to the left edge of the spiral.[12] It has been noticed that the count of the lines of nine and a half turns crossing any diameter is 9 + 10 = 19, and we know that once every nineteen years there is a full moon on winter solstice eve.

The dating suggested for this extraordinary observatory is c. A.D. 950 to 1150, the period of the greatest population density and architectural development of the canyon.[13] Ms. Sofaer and her colleagues have recently undertaken studies of the roadways and architecture of Chaco Canyon that suggest that Chacoan involvement with cosmology also influenced the construction of their Great North Road,[14] which heads from the ceremonial buildings of Chaco Canyon directly north for a distance of some thirty-five miles to Kutz Canyon, an abyss of eroded badlands. The road seems to have been built primarily as an expression of the Pueblo belief in the north as their place of origin, where they emerged from the worlds below and where the spirits of the dead return. Chacoan cosmological involvement is also evidenced in the orientations of individual pueblos, as well as in interpueblo alignments.[15] Moreover, the large Chaco pueblos form a complex regional pattern that displays the Chacoans' sense of harmony between their society and the cosmic order.[16]

374. The Anasazi calendar utilizes three large rock slabs (**a**) to baffle and focus both the sunlight and the moonlight (**b**), so that significant celestial intervals are marked by a sliver of illumination (**c**) that falls upon and traverses one or another of the spiral petroglyphs on the adjacent cliff face.

375. A seasonal calendar showing the position of the light dagger on the petroglyphs at each equinox and at the summer and winter solstices.

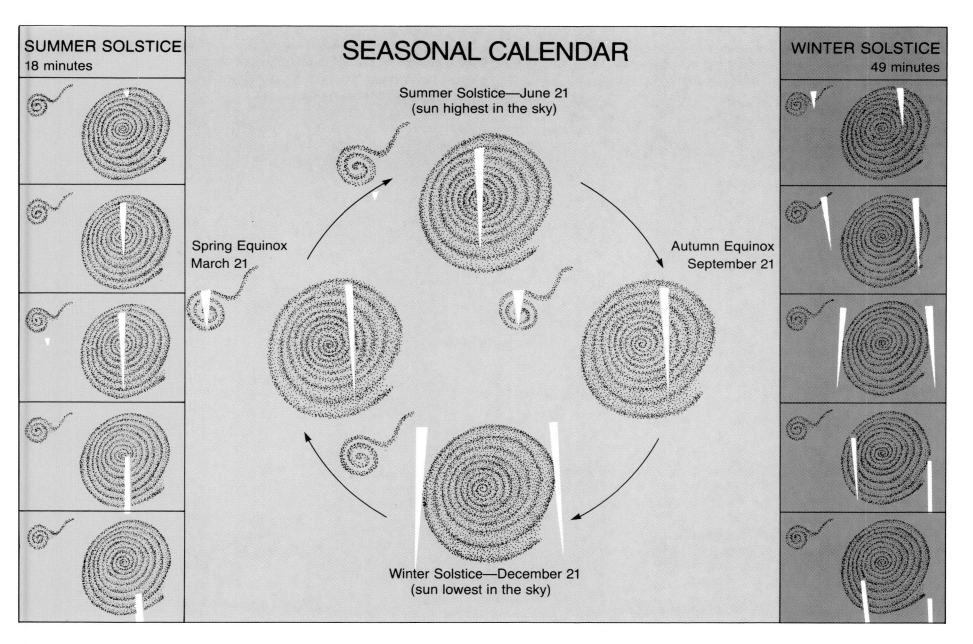

SUMMER SOLSTICE
18 minutes

SEASONAL CALENDAR

WINTER SOLSTICE
49 minutes

Summer Solstice—June 21
(sun highest in the sky)

Spring Equinox
March 21

Autumn Equinox
September 21

Winter Solstice—December 21
(sun lowest in the sky)

The Spirits of Life

The sense of a play of transcendent energies into the round of the seasons and their labors comes to expression with especial clarity in the annual cycle of solar and lunar festivals of the Hopi. Remote on their desert mesas, these have been, of all the Pueblo inheritors of the Anasazi, the least affected by Europeans. Many of the Rio Grande ceremonies (at Santo Domingo, San Ysidro, San Ildefonso, San Felipe, and Santa Ana, for example) were early converted into Christian festivals, their dates determined, consequently, not by signs in the heavens, but by the calendar—for it has already been 400 years since, in 1540, the Spanish entered the Southwest and in 1598 made it their own. In 1629 their priests established a Hopi mission at Awatovi, but the Pueblo Revolt of 1680 ended that adventure and, although Spanish authority was reimposed in 1694, the Awatovi mission was not resumed. Drought, smallpox, and Navaho raids have wrought their devastations; U.S. Indian agents arrived about 1870, and in 1897 a government boarding school was opened, to break traditional patterns and assimilate Indian children into the white community, with trade goods replacing native arts and the Christian myth, native thinking. Yet even today, without fail, every year at the time of the winter solstice, the first kachinas appear from their invisible homes. Others follow in increasing number, until by February all are present in the kivas, generating life anew. And at the turn, then, of the summer solstice, with harvest time drawing near, the kachinas, having served, are bidden farewell in a ceremony of departure, and dismissed to their homes for another year.[17]

The breakup of the Classic Anasazi civilization, of which the Pueblos today are the inheritors, followed two decades of drought at the end of the thirteenth century, 1276 to 1299, just when the Navaho and Apache were moving in. There followed a period known as *Regressive Pueblo* (*Pueblo IV*, c. A.D. 1300 to 1700), which saw a scattering of Anasazi populations southward and eastward. The great Classic centers were abandoned, and new pueblos arose in central New Mexico, along the Rio Grande, and in western New Mexico and Arizona. The languages now spoken are of four unrelated stocks: Uto-Aztecan, Tewa, Zuni, and Keresan. The eastern are patrilineal, the western, generally matrilineal.[18] Clearly, the peoples today are not of one strain. Yet all participate in what appears to have been the fundamental Anasazi heritage of an emergence mythology associated with kiva priesthoods and a ritual art of prayer sticks and altars, sand paintings, wall paintings, symbolically masked per-

376. First Mesa, with Walpi in the foreground.

377. About the Hopi annual ceremonial cycle (events and times of which may vary at First, Second, and Third Mesas), Barton Wright, a noted authority on the Hopi, comments: "The rich tapestry of Hopi ceremonial life is interwoven by the belief that nature and God are one and that the universe is totally reliable if properly approached. Every object possesses a spirit or animus of its own which can be coerced to intercede for the Hopi in his dual world of the natural and the supernatural. This balanced cosmos is envisioned as the natural world, where objects have mass and solidity, and a preternatural world of spirit beings, substanceless shapes of evanescent mist, the physical world's mirror image. The important forces of this universe are given living form in beings who will, through the performance of ceremonies and rituals by the Hopi people, be obligated to assist them."[26]

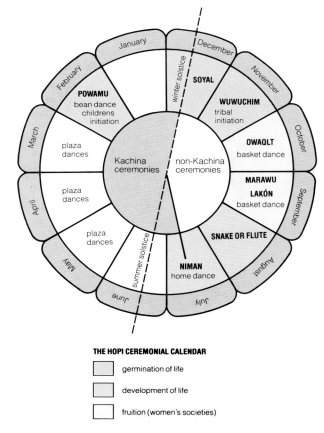

THE HOPI CEREMONIAL CALENDAR

- germination of life
- development of life
- fruition (women's societies)

formers, and a calendar governed by cycles of the sun and moon, as well as a distinctive body of folktale motifs, story plots, and popular mythic characters.

The opening festival of the Hopi ceremonial year is called Wúwuchim (from *wu*, "to germinate," and *chim*, "to manifest").[19] Its season, known as the Initiates' Moon, is the lunar month just prior to that of the winter solstice, and its first major ceremonial is the making of the New Fire in the secrecy of the Two Horn Society's kiva. "Life began with fire. Thus we begin," a Two Horn chief explained to the author Frank Waters,[20] whose *Book of the Hopi* is a compendium of information from thirty-two Hopi elders. "The Two Horn Society's symbol of two horns," states Waters, "designates knowledge of, and remembered experiences in, the three previous worlds as well as in this present Fourth World. Their six directions altar represents the First World at the time of Creation, with colored sands spread to the four primary directions: yellow for the West, blue for the South, red for the East, and white for the North. An ear of dark mixed corn is laid for the Above, and an ear of sweet corn for the Below. The wooden backdrop of the altar is

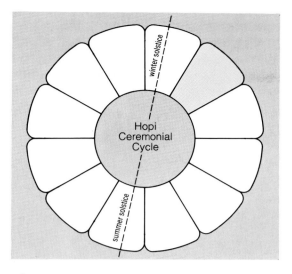

WÚWUCHIM (Tribal Initiation)

During Wúwuchim, a most sacred ceremony that begins (and ends) the annual ritual round, young men are initiated into tribal societies responsible for the performance of the ceremonial cycle, thus insuring the survival, not only of the Hopi's village life, but also of their religious traditions.

379. Enroute from Sichomovi to Walpi, Two-Horned Society members in traditional garb carry flat trays of cornmeal. Photograph by Joseph Mora.

380. Inside the One Horn Kiva at Oraibi, *plaques* (baskets) filled with cornmeal in which *páhos* (prayer sticks) have been planted. Photograph by H. R. Voth, purportedly the only person ever permitted to photograph inside the kivas.

378. Two-Horned Society "priests" in their kiva at Oraibi, photo by H. R. Voth, a Mennonite clergyman who lived with the Hopi, 1893–1902, and amassed a vast pictorial record of ceremonies.

painted with the corresponding colors of the successive four worlds, and there are symbols of the primary elements: fire, earth, water, air represented by eagle down."[21]

It may surprise the reader to recognize here the same four elements known to the Greeks. They are represented, also, on the Aztec Calendar Stone which was dedicated in 1479, over a decade before the landing of Columbus.

Within the Two Horn kiva the First Fire is struck from flint, caught by native cotton, and kept burning with coal from the nearby desert outcrops, while prayers are addressed to Mácaw, the god of death, but also of the fire of life, which bursts from his domain in volcanic eruptions. The flame is then carried to the other kivas responsible for this festival: the Wuchim, the One Horn, and the Flute.[22]

Of especial interest here is the society of the One Horns. In contrast to the Two Horns, whose knowledge is of the previous worlds as well as of this fourth, the authority of the One Horn kiva is of this earth alone. On its altar the symbolic forms are the figure of a woman holding a child and a six-foot lance with a sharp flint point. The Twin War Gods are its patrons. The elder sits at the northern pole and the younger at the southern of the world axis, keeping the earth properly rotating. They give warning of anything going wrong by sending along the axis vibrations to which the One Horn members are attuned. And on their altar is a little bell of baked clay symbolic of this attunement.

The second major Wúwuchim ceremonial, celebrated on the fifteenth night of the moon and known as the Night of the Washing of the Hair, is of the initiation of young men. It is so profoundly meaningful and holy that for its celebration the pueblo is magically sealed off from the world for that night by a member of the One Horn Society, who, when evening falls, emerges from his kiva in full ceremonial attire and symbolically closes all four roads of access to the mesa by drawing four lines with sacred cornmeal across each. No one dares to cross these. Beasts and birds that do are found dead, they say, the next morning. In the village every door is closed, every window is hung with blankets, the streets are empty, and all is quiet and dark.

The kiva in which the youths are assembled is called the One Way Trail. It is the underworld, from which they are to emerge like the First People. In its floor is the sipapu of emergence from the two lower underworlds, and the ladder upward through the opening in the roof is the One Way Trail. There is a fire in the fire pit, by the dim light of which the young men are watching a priest who is recounting to them the history of mankind's rise through successive worlds. With fire, life began in the first. A tabu was broken; that world was destroyed and mankind mounted to the second, where again a tabu was broken and a perilous ascent made to this third world of the kiva, where the initiates are now assembled.

His narrative concluded, the priest partly covers the fire pit with a flat rock, so that there is only a faint red glow, when down the ladder, dimly appearing as though from the sipapu, members of the other kivas arrive, ceremonially robed and with large white four-pointed stars over their faces. They gather and stand around the dim fire pit, sounding a low hum and a strange blowing of breath. Both the pitch and the volume slowly rise as, down the ladder, a silent, white-robed, lone figure descends with an immense star over its face. "I am the Beginning and the End," this apparition declares, then ascends as quietly as it came.

The visitants now become agitated and noisy. The flat rock is shoved completely over the fire pit and the kiva is absolutely dark. A yell sounds and the company, in wild confusion, throwing off its stars and robes, rushes naked for the ladder, to escape before this world, too, is destroyed. The rungs extend to each side beyond the ladder poles, so that two or three can climb at a time, the terrified initiates among them, contending for the exit. On emerging, each is drenched with a bucket of water and greeted by the village chief, called Father of the People. The Crier Chief is there as well, and a member of the Coyote clan, called Guardian of the People, whose function it is to "close the doors." And when all have come out, the Father calls down into the dark hole of the empty kiva, ordering anyone there remaining to come up.

Wet and naked as newborn babes, the initiates are gathered to a nearby home, where their hair is washed in nine successive bowls of yucca suds, which represent (as Frank Waters was told) the seven stages of the Road of Life (three worlds already passed, this the fourth, and three to come) plus the realm of Sótuknang (the god governor of the universe, creator of all ceremony) and that of Taiowa (the Creator, whose light blazes in the sun).[23]

The final event of Wúwuchim is a public dance by the associated kivas, whose members appear in the village in two long parallel lines. Between them is the drummer, and on the outside the asperger with his bowl of water and eagle feather who sprinkles each dancer. It is noticed that the four leading Two Horns are maintaining a rhythm out of accord with the rest. With their knowledge of previous worlds, they are keeping time to an unheard rhythm, unbroken by time and space. The dance threads through the village four times, and on the fifth appearance all but the four leading Two Horns are naked save for breechcloths—in anticipation of a Bath Ceremony now administered by the women, who all come running to pour buckets of cold water (and not all of it clean, by any means)[24] over everyone but the Two Horns, taunting the dancers and being taunted in turn, with all terminating in a roughhouse around the kivas.

Finally, out of their kivas come the One Horn members, striding without voice to the brittle clatter of the small clay bells in their hands. They circumambulate the pueblo countersunwise, signifying an earthly, in contrast to the heavenly, sunwise round. The sun is now setting. A few minutes later the Two Horns make the same circuit, and so the festival ends.[25]

381. Four priests (Tawȧkwaptiwa in the lead), carrying cornmeal in *plaques*, prepare to follow Mastop Kachina to the Flute Spring, where the Soyál Chief will present him with a special *pàho* before he departs to the west. This simple sequence of events begins Soyál, a ceremony of world renewal celebrated during winter solstice.

Soyál, the winter solstice festival, is announced already the next day by the appearance on the desert, coming from the east, of a kachina in turquoise helmet and white robe, staggering like a child learning to walk. This is Soyál Kachina, the first kachina of the year, signifying life reborn and to be followed next day by a terrifying figure, Mastop Kachina, whose black attire and mask, showing white stars on each cheek, tell of the interstellar distances from which he has arrived. He is the unmitigated power of male energy. (Compare his Mandan counterpart, described by Catlin, I.2:228.) Entering the village, he grabs a married woman from the crowd and simulates copulation, then descends into the Soyál kiva and, after bestowing there his blessings for the coming year, departs westward to his shrine at the bottom of the cliffs.[26]

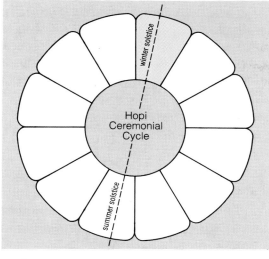

SOYÁL

384. During Soyál, seed corn (carried here by Kachina Mana) is sanctified to increase its yield, the village is ritually cleansed of all misfortune, and the sun is turned back from its southern course so that it might come again to the Hopi.[27]

The term *kachina*, as understood today, has four references, the last three of which are inflections of the first: (1) a personified charge of the energy of life, (2) a ceremonial costume and mask representing such a personification, (3) a ceremonial celebrant wearing such a costume and mask, and (4) a doll representing the personification, fashioned originally for the instruction of children, now also as an *objêt-d'art*, for pleasure, or for sale to tourists, museums, or collectors.

The holy season, which in the West is a celebration of the birth of the world savior, is on the Hopi mesas welcomed chiefly within the kivas with symbolic rites, "establishing," as they say, "life anew for all the world."[27] Its season is of the full moon around the moment "when the sun is turned back," which is a conjunction (as we have seen, page 279) that occurs once

382. Barton Wright's painting of Soyál Kachina, the first kachina to appear each year.

383. Mastop Kachina, the second to appear, c. 6⅛" tall, made of pine, paint, and owl feathers.

every nineteen years. There are no spectacular public dances. Prayers are addressed to the sun, who is the deity of this festival, and prayer sticks placed before an altar six miles to the east. Formerly, every four years, a virgin (usually of the Soyál chief's family) was sacrificed at this season. Today, the Hawk Maiden, ceremonially attired, simply sits for a time in the Soyál kiva, watching rituals for the germination of crops. After sixteen days of such rites, the festival is concluded with a four-day rabbit hunt, followed by a feast and a ceremony of blessing.[28]

Through the following two lunar months kachinas arrive in increasing number, both to empower the seeds now being planted and to instruct and discipline children in the knowledge of the laws of their own nature. Kachinas do not visit the Rio Grande pueblos, where there is sufficient water for crops. The only other favored

pueblo is Zuni, but the Hopi say that since these spirits emerged from the underworld with themselves, those that the people of Zuni know must have been originally of the Hopi. They all live, it is said, to the west, on the San Francisco Peaks, and their appearances at Oraibi, Walpi, and the other Hopi-mesa villages are to ensure the timely occurrences of the rains which in those parts are the *sine qua non* of life.

a

385. Joseph Mora's paintings of some of the kachinas appearing during Powamu, when children of proper age are initiated into the mysteries of the kachinas, whose cooperation the Hopi seek during the coming growing season: (**a**) Wupamo, who is a guard; (**b**) Owangazrozro, an ogre clown, among whose functions is that of inter-kiva messenger; (**c**) Tumas (Crow Mother), who leads both the Powamu procession and the children's initiation; (**d**) Powamu, who performs the dance during which the kachina dancers are shown to be men; and (**e**) Avachhoya, the distinctively costumed Speckled Corn Kachina.

b

e

d

c

284

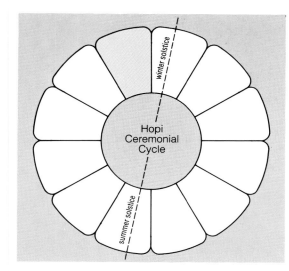

PAMURTI

386. Performed during Pamurti (Jan. to early Feb.) are so-called social dances; many, such as this Buffalo Dance, have religious overtones.

387. An 1893 assembly of kachinas of Powamu.

At the start of the festival of Powamu, during the lunar month (mid-January to February) of the full presence in the pueblos of the kachinas of that year, beans are planted in the kivas at the first appearance of the new crescent moon. They are diligently watered, ritually smoked over, and sprinkled with sacred meal, so that by the eighth day the first sprouts have appeared. In the kivas, meanwhile, and in public, there has been ceremonial dancing: as many as two hundred kachinas together appearing on some of these occasions, praying, singing, and dancing, both to help the corn, beans, and other crops to grow, and to confirm the Hopi themselves in their faith in the power of the life-force represented in these masks to bring health and beauty to their lives.

Children between six and ten are being at this time initiated into their own kachina societies. They are given little gifts by the masked dancers. But there also are brief but painful whipping rites to which they are subjected, while for those who are disobedient, there are warnings of monstrous Scare Kachinas, for whom they had better watch out.

By the time this festival is approaching its end, the bean sprouts in the kivas have grown and been cut. Tied into small bun-

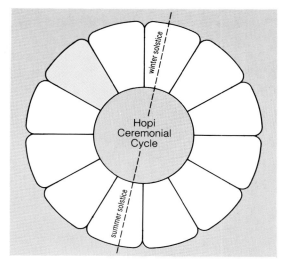

POWAMU (Bean Dance)

dles, they are carried by kachinas to all the homes in the pueblo, together with presents for the children: kachina dolls and plaques tied with bean sprouts for the girls, and for the boys, moccasins and painted bows and rattles. A final, grandiose procession in the village plaza of all the kachinas and initiates brings the whole occasion to a climax with singing, dancing, and various kachina appearances. Then a Kachina Father cries out for all the mothers to cover the eyes of their uninitiated children, one of the kachinas yanks off his mask, and they all disappear into the kivas. So the festival ends. The bean plants, which have been blessed, are carried to various shrines and then home, for a concluding feast.[29]

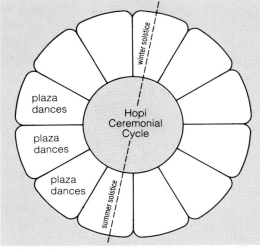

PLAZA DANCES

In the spring and early summer the Hopi hold performances of the Plaza Dances: Line Dances, in which all kachinas are the same (as in **388**, below, where Ota line dancers are accompanied by the White-Faced Kachina Girl [Alo Mana] and a side dancer), and Mixed Dances that involve a variety of kachinas, all differently masked and costumed. Now, regardless of outward appearances or what they might otherwise represent, all kachinas are believed to be rain-bringing supernaturals and, although each offers its own special blessing, their dances now bring to the mesa the moistures of the underworld. Prominent during the Plaza Dances are Hopi clowns, both the "Mudheads" (Koyemsi Kachinas, see **389**) and the striped Hano Clowns (Koshari Kachinas, **390**).[28]

389

390

388

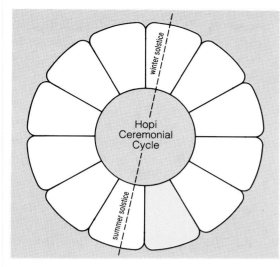

NIMAN (Home Dance)

The ceremony of departure at the time of the summer solstice, when the crops have matured and the kachinas' work is done, is called Niman Kachina (Home Dance) and assigned to the lunar month Niman-muya (Home-going Moon). Earlier in the spring, a number of eagles' nests will have been identified in the sides of nearby cliffs and marked with prayer sticks, inviting the great birds to come willingly to the villages to be sacrificed after this ceremony. The hunters, then, either lower themselves on ropes or climb by perilous ledges to remove from the nests the birds too young to fly (in former years, sometimes as many, they say, as twenty-five), which then are brought with great honor to the village and tied by the feet to eagle platforms on the rooftops.

A second preliminary to the celebration of this season is the pilgrimage by three selected men for the gathering of spruce.

They carry special male and female prayer sticks some forty miles northeastward to Black Mesa and into a long, desolate canyon, where there is a cave at the top of a rocky, spruce-and-pine-covered ridge, and within the cave, a sacred pool that is known as Kisiwu (Spring in the Shadows). The cave is approached with ritualized precautions. The prayer sticks are planted, prayers are recited, and next morning, to a selected spruce tree the leader prays: "O Spruce Tree, we have come for your leaves, to be used for our clothes, so come with us!" They bless the tree, leave a prayer stick before it, and without touching it, turn to other trees and gather from them their branches, for the spruce tree is thought to have a special magnetic power that draws to it the rainclouds. As John Lansa of the Badger Clan, Oraibi, who had performed the pilgrimage twelve times, explained to Frank Waters: "It is the spirits of the spruce, the clouds, and the rain who give this life to us, you understand. So we offer our prayers again to the male and female branches, and we invite all the spirits to our village to take part in the ceremony."[30]

At dawn on the morning of the Home-going Dance, two fresh spruce trees, a male and a female, are standing in the otherwise empty plaza. From a nearby housetop a tethered eagle screams, and the kachinas enter in single file, led by the Powamu Chief, who is unmasked, wearing an embroidered kilt and a single eagle feather. The Kachina Father and his assistant follow, with some thirty Hemis Kachinas (Faraway Kachinas, a reference to the distant

realm from which these presences have come and to which they are now to return) and eight or more Kachina-manas (Kachina Mothers) behind. Their bodies are black and their masks are yellow on the left side and blue on the right, with blue cloud-terrace crowns rising high above, tufted with heads of wild wheat and eagle feathers. Deer-hoof and turtle-shell rattles adorn their right legs, straps of bells their left. Spruce branches hang from their belts; spruce twigs are stuck in their arm bands; in the left hand each carries a feather and a twig of spruce, in the right a rattle; and there is a ruff of spruce around the throat. In contrast, the face masks of the Kachina Mothers are orange. Each wears the classic squash-blossom hair whorls of the Hopi unmarried maiden, a black manta, a red and white blanket, and white deerskin boots. Each carries, besides a pumpkin shell, a notched stick and the scapula bone of a sheep or deer, with which to accompany the music.

"After entering the plaza, they stand silently," states Waters, "the *kachinas* in a long line, the *kachina-manas* behind them. The Powamu Chief sprinkles each with cornmeal from a sack worn on his breast. The Kachina Father encourages them with talk. Then suddenly the leader of the *kachinas*, standing in the middle of the line, shakes his rattle. The powerful legs lift and stamp; the low, strong voices break into song—a day-long dance and song, beautiful and compelling, but with infinite variations in which are found its deepest meanings."[31]

391. In preparation for Niman, early in the spring, the Hopi clans go to special eagle-hunting grounds (each has its own), where, with proper ceremony, they remove from nests fledglings that they bring with great honor back to the village, where they are tied by their feet to rooftop platforms. There the eaglets remain and flourish, until the Niman ends, and they are with ceremonial reverence "sent home."

392. At first light, into the plaza file the Hemis Kachinas, spruce-adorned and bearing children's gifts (here, cattails), and the Home Dance begins.

The line is along the north side of the plaza. Dancing, it moves westward, curves southward, and breaks before a circle is formed, "just as the pure pattern of life was broken," Waters states, "and the First World destroyed." The line moves to the west side and again curves and breaks, signifying the dissolution of the Second World. All move, then, to the south side, and again the pattern breaks, in the way of the World before this. But there is no fourth position taken, because in this Fourth World we do not yet know whether its circle is to be broken or formed.[32]

The cosmological pattern of three with a fourth implied and open is suggested, also, by the day's program of three appearances of the dancers, at sunrise, mid-morning, and late afternoon until sunset. Armloads of significant gifts are again distributed to the children. At the closing dance the year's brides attend, attired in their wedding robes. And when it ends, the Kachina Father delivers a word of farewell:

"It is now time for you to go home. Take with you our humble prayer, not only for our people and people everywhere, but for all the animal kingdom, the birds and insects, and the growing things that make our world a green carpet. Take our message to the four corners of the world, that all life may receive renewal by having moisture. I am happy that I have done my small part in caring for you this day. May you go on your way with happy hearts and grateful thoughts."

The leader of the kachinas shakes his rattle to show that the message is accepted and will be delivered. The spectators step forward to pluck twigs of spruce from the kachinas to carry home, and separate to let them file from the plaza and away. The two spruce trees are carried from the plaza. At the same time, as Waters tells, "the great proud birds waiting on their platforms are 'sent home' with the kachinas. No blood is shed during their sacrifice. The clan leaders ascend to the housetop platforms, wrap a blanket around the head of each and as gently as possible snuff out its life."[33]

It is supposed that the kachinas in their distant world experience winter and spring during our summer and fall, so that on returning home they will again be engaged in ceremonials. Here on earth, meanwhile, it is important to bring a final burst of rain, so that the flooded washes will deposit fresh soil for new crops. And in this function the famous Hopi Snake-Antelope Ceremony alternates from year to year with a Flute Ceremony, during the lunar month known as the Big Feast Moon (Nashanmuya) of late August.

393. In this 1901 photograph taken at the Hopi village of Shungopovi, Hemis Kachinas dance the farewell ceremony that "sends the spirits back to their various homes and encourages them to continue to send their benefits to the Hopi although they will not return again till December."[29] As the sun sets, they file silently westward, out of the plaza. No one follows. When the kachinas arrive at Kachinki (Kachina House), their cliff-edge shrine, there is a disrobing and unmasking ceremony. Then, members once again of the human community, they return to the village. The next day, the Powamu Chief leads the final *tangave* (religious plan act), the closing of the kivas.

394. Simultaneously, clan leaders reverently enfold the eagles in blankets and "send them home."

Inside the house, when the eagle's body is cold, its feathers are gathered for ceremonial use, and

the body is ritually "buried, head to the west, with cornmeal, *piki*, tobacco, and prayer feathers."[30]

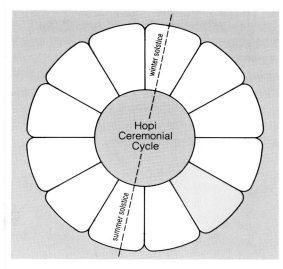

ANTELOPE-SNAKE / FLUTE DANCES

Hopi Ceremonial Cycle

winter solstice

summer solstice

Preparations for the Snake Dance commence in the kivas of the Antelope and Snake societies with the usual preparation of prayer sticks, fasting, and setting up of altars. The Snake Society's altar carries the images of two Snake Maidens. That of the Antelope Society—set up on a sand painting of the four directional colors with at each corner a small cone of sand (called a cloud mountain) into which a hawk feather is stuck—represents the world as formed by earth, air, water, plant life, and mankind. These preparations require eleven days, after which the Snake members set out on their four-day task of searching the desert for rattlesnakes, sidewinders, gopher snakes, bull snakes, and the rest, coming back with some fifty or sixty.

Meanwhile, in the Antelope kiva there has been ritually consummated a symbolic *hieros gamos* ("sacred marriage"). A young virgin already initiated into the women's Snake Society—her forehead, chin, and throat painted white, the rest of her face painted black; her hair loose, with a small eagle-down feather attached to it; and wearing the customary woman's black manta and a red and white cape, to which there have been added a Snake Dancer's kirtle and a necklace of turquoise and shell—is conducted by the Snake chief into the Antelope Society's kiva, where, in the role of Snake Maiden, she is the living counterpart of the two Snake Maiden images on the altar of the Snake kiva. In her hands she carries an earthen jar containing prayer sticks, corn, melon, squash, and bean vines. And she is greeted in the kiva by the Antelope chief and the Antelope Youth, a young man in whose hands are an Antelope fetish and a snake. His hair, too, is loose, with a small downy feather tied in front. And his chin, too, is painted white. He is wearing a white ceremonial kirtle, and his body is ash grey, but with white zigzag lines drawn on the torso, arms, and legs.

The Snake Maiden is seated on the south side of the Antelope kiva's symbolic altar, and the Antelope Youth on the north. Between the altar and the fire pit is an earthen bowl full of yucca suds, and before the altar, a woven plaque full of many kinds of seed. The maiden and the youth are conducted by their chiefs to the bowl, and there a full wedding ceremony is performed, after which the Snake chief washes the maiden's hair in the yucca suds, and the Antelope chief the youth's. The two chiefs exchange places and the Snake Maiden's hair is washed by the Antelope chief, the Antelope Youth's by the Snake chief, following which exchange, the wet locks of the couple are braided together and the two conducted to the northern bench, where the maiden is seated on the plaque of seeds that the Antelope chief has just placed there. It is midnight. Through the ladder-opening in the

395. Late in the afternoon on the final day of the Snake-Antelope Ceremony, as Antelope Dancers (painted ash-gray) await beside the cottonwood kisi filled with snakes, the Snake Dancers enter the plaza and begin their climactic circling dance.

kiva roof the bright stars of Orion's Belt can be seen. A chanting begins, which drones on until the same stars are at the western horizon. Trying not to fall asleep, the Antelope Youth and Snake Maiden remain seated together until the chanting stops, when they are blessed, separated, and taken by their guardians to their separate homes.

The ritual obviously is of the mystery of the two that are spiritually one though physically two, as symbolized in the mythological image of the androgyne. This is an image known, not only to most planting-culture mythologies, but also to every mystical tradition of the world (see I.2:142, Map 33). In the context of a planting society's interests, the function of a ritual reestablishing this image is to reactivate, through what James G. Frazer called "imitative sympathetic magic,"[34] the energies of what is conceived to be the creative ground of all temporal conditions. In the context of a mystical tradition where the same image is proposed as a theme for contemplation, its function is to release the mind from the bondage of the body by uniting it with an image transcendent of temporal conditions. Obviously, the two functions are related. And by analogy, of course, the biological act of a male and female in the union out of which a new life is born gives evidence beyond question of the life-producing power of this mystery.

Now, for a planting culture, which is necessarily committed—in contrast to its hunting-and-gathering neighbors—rather to generating life than to killing and collecting, this mystery of the two that are one and the one that makes two and the one-plus-one that makes three, is of unrelent-

ing importance. Moreover, since there is everywhere a tendency for the practical, magical aspect and the inward, mystical aspect to run together, we find—as among the Hopi, for example—disciplines of fasting and spiritual exaltation (in the kivas) integrally associated with the conduct of the public ceremonials. In fact, according to native belief, it is the set of the mind of the performers, no less than the patterns of their rites, that determines the results.

A second matter of essential concern is the precise coordination of the natural and

396. Each dancer carrying a snake (in his teeth, its body symbolically aligned with his own) is guided around the dance ground by a partner (a so-called hugger), who all the while strokes the snake with his eagle-feather snake whip.

ritual orders, and this involves not only attention to the intermeshing of the lunar, solar, and various stellar cycles, but also associated interpretations of the flora and fauna of the neighborhood. In the case, for example, of this Hopi marriage in the Antelope kiva of the Snake Maiden to the Antelope Youth, the snake, as Waters points out, which dwells deep in the earth out of which mankind originated, is equated with the lowest of man's psychological centers, that associated with the generative organs, whereas the antelope is associated with the highest center in man; for "its horn," as he tells, "is located at the top or crown of the head, the *kópavi*, which in man is the place of coming in and going out of life, the 'open door' through which he spiritually communicates with his Creator."[35] Also: "Running Antelopes make the sound of thunder whose vibration stimulates the clouds to come out of their shrines."[36] The clouds come out of their shrines to send rain; the Serpent Maiden, out of her kiva, to incubate the seeds of life! And in both instances it is the antelope that functions as the summoner, the awakener, of the life-bearer. The antelope here is male and associated with the head and consciousness; the serpent is female and associated with the generative energy of life. The ritual of her

397. When every snake has been danced, they are placed in a circle of cornmeal, and the Dancers quickly gather up handfuls to take back to the desert, where they are released to carry a message of renewal to the four corners of the earth.

marriage is an appeal, as it were, to the energies of life to come out, as she has come, from their unawakened virginal retreat.

The serpent is associated also, it appears, with the moon, which sheds its shadow to be born again, as the serpent its skin, to be born again. And the antelope, then, as of the head and consciousness, is symbolically an agent of the sun. The marriage, accordingly, is of the solar and lunar energies, which, though apparently two are in fact one, as in the Navaho version of the legend of the twin heroes, where, although the elder was begotten of the Sun and the younger of the Moon, Where the Two Came to Their Father was the house of the Sun.

Waters has noticed what is indeed a remarkable likeness of this Hopi system of symbols to that of India's Kundalini Yoga (see pages 378–379),[37] where the energy of life—all life—is symbolized as female, a female serpent coiled upon itself in a spiral of three-and-a-half turns and lying asleep, not only deep within the earth, but also, in the same way, deep within the lowest energy center of the body. The aim of the yoga is to wake this Serpent Maiden, coiled in upon herself, and bring her up the spine to full consciousness, both of herself and of the spiritual nature of all things. She is awakened by the sound of the energy of the light of consciousness (the sound of the syllable "om"), which is brought to her first

on the rhythm of the breath, but fully heard only when she has uncoiled and ascended to the center of the heart, whose animal symbol (remarkably) is the antelope—swift as the wind and thus, the vehicle of the wind, the breath (Sanskrit, *prāna*; Latin, *spiritus*), the spirit. The Serpent Maiden, Kundalini, has thus left three worlds to rise to this spiritual center: the first, of her home base; the second, at the level of the genitals (sex); the third at the level of the navel (will to power, aggression), and this the fourth world, where, as the Wúwuchim initiates within the kiva heard, there is the "sounding of a low hum and a strange blowing of breath," the sound of the syllable "om." Awakened, the Serpent Maiden will now pass on along the One Way Trail of this fourth world, through three more, to the crown of the head, the seventh ($3\frac{1}{2}+3\frac{1}{2}=7$), as the initiates at the Washing of the Hair learned of three worlds already passed, this fourth, and three to come.

The high moment of the Snake Dance arrives on the sixteenth day of the festival, when the performers, one by one, step up to the kisi (the evergreen shelter housing the tangle of gathered snakes) and, stooping low, straighten up with a snake between the teeth, caught and held just back of its head. With the dancer's left hand the upper part of the snake's body is held level with the heart, and with the right hand the lower length of the reptile, level with the waist. The illustration of the idea of the Kundalini could hardly be improved: the serpent energy to be uncoiled from its place of rest in the lower pelvic centers (position of the right hand and lower length of the serpent), by virtue of an awakening at the center of the heart (left hand and upper body of the serpent), leading to the knowledge of a higher order of life and consciousness in the centers of the head, the inner eye and the opening at the crown (position of the serpent's head by the head of the dancer). Also relevant to this reading of the Hopi rite is the Hindu idea of two secondary nerves running alongside and crossing to right and left of the central

spinal trail up which the Kundalini is to rise. One is known as *iḍa* and carries lunar energy; the other, as *pingala* and carries solar energy. Before the Kundalini can be waked and brought up the central way of the *suṣumna*, the energies of these two have to be brought together and recognized as of one transcendent source, as in the mystic marriage in the Antelope kiva of the Serpent Maiden and Antelope Youth before, in the dance, the serpents are lifted and carried in the dancers' mouths.

Next day the snakes are returned to their desert, to carry back to their hidden homes the good tidings of the ceremonially confirmed accord of the Hopi with the natural order.

On alternate years, the ceremonial celebrated in this place is, in its public phase, a simple enactment of the Emergence. Known as the Flute Ceremony and conducted by the Blue Flute and Gray Flute societies (*iḍa* and *pingala?*), the members gather at Flute Springs at noon on the sixteenth day of the moon and come in a winding procession up the mesa into the village. Leading all the way are two small girls who, at intervals, toss little rings upon cornmeal lines drawn on the ground. In the plaza the people sing to the music of the flute and then simply disperse.[38]

Finally, there follow the three terminating festivals of the whole ceremonial round—Lakón, Márawu, and Owaqlt—performed by the women's societies.

398. Watercolor of a Snake Priest—not a kachina; rather, member of a Hopi warrior society—by Joseph Mora, who, living with the Hopi from 1904 to 1906, labored to document accurately (in authentically detailed paintings and in several series of sequential photographs) the rich tapestry of ceremonial life that he feared would soon disappear.

399. The Flute chief carries *paho* and cornmeal to the Flute Spring during the Flute Ceremony. Frank Water notes: "No Hopi ritual is as simple and mystifying to the casual visitor as that portion of the Flute ceremony he is allowed to witness. It is simply a procession winding up the mesa and into the village, headed by two small girls who periodically toss little rings upon cornmeal lines painted on the ground. In the plaza the people sing to the music of a flute, then silently disperse. That is all. Yet this simple ceremony embodies in song and symbolism the whole pattern of man's Emergence to the present world."[31]

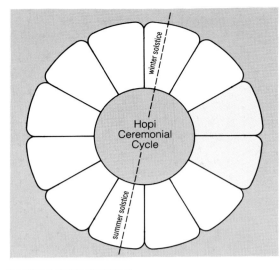

WOMEN'S SOCIETY DANCES

400. During the afternoon public ceremony, the Lakón Manas, carrying baskets, form a great circle. Chanting, they raise them—first to one breast, then to the other—then lower them to their groins.

Lakón, of which the meaning of the name has been lost, is celebrated in two sessions. The first is at corn-planting time in late May and early June, when four women and the Lakón chief (a man) enter the kiva for eight days of prayer, fasting, and singing, while the chief makes and consecrates prayer feathers. The second session, also of eight days, begins on the day in late September when the sun is seen to rise over a point between Oraibi and Hoteville, known as Where Two Rocks Lean on One Another. For four days the members pray, sing, and eat no salt or meat. On the seventh night, when the Lakón chief, who is watching the sky, sees the Pleiades rise, he enters the kiva, where the women are singing. From their altar they take up lightning sticks, cloud sticks, prayer feathers, and corn (leaving only the sand painting on the floor), elevate these four times ceremonially, and after replacing them, file from the kiva. The Pleiades are now at the western horizon, and daybreak is near. The women, each holding in one hand cornmeal and in the other hand three prayer feathers, follow a trail along the mesa top, pausing for prayer at certain shrines, then proceed down the rocky face of the cliff to a huge volcanic boulder whose top is covered with small brown nodules surrounded by curious whorls, which are taken to represent the embryo within the fetal membranes of the womb. The maiden members rub their hands over these whorls, offerings are left at a shrine below the boulder, and the company files up the cliff to prepare for the public ceremony.

Four maidens are chosen to represent the cardinal directions. With their feet and faces powdered yellow and wearing cloud headdresses of eagle feathers and the feathers of tropical birds, each receives four ears of corn appropriately colored: yellow for the Maiden of the West, blue for the Maiden of the South, red for the Maiden of the East, and white for the Maiden of the North. The others of the kiva have formed a circle in the plaza, and when the four appear a cloud design is drawn with corn-

401. A Joseph Mora watercolor of a Lakón Mana.

meal on the ground before them. In its center is placed a small ring of cornhusks, at which each in turn tosses her ears of corn. This they do four times, after which they are led into and around the singing circle and stationed at their cardinal points. The Maiden of the West rolls the cornhusk ring toward the east and quickly throws her corn at it. The remaining three follow in sequence, and then joining the other women in song, they fling plaques and baskets over the singers' heads—west, south, east, and north—as gifts to the crowd.[39]

Márawu—the word means Leg Decoration—follows in September and October. The first four days are spent in the kiva by the four leaders, two of which are men, fashioning prayer sticks, fasting, and praying. On the fifth day, the other members come in, and on the seventh a ritual is performed before the altar of specially blessed sand supporting eagle feathers alternating with a number of wooden figures and painted slabs (representing Márawu women and their guardian spirits, as well as clouds, rain, and corn of the four directions). Corn of the colors of the four directions is laid upon the altar, and in the center is a bowl of water that has been blessed. The ritual is of songs recapitulating the story of world creation: first the earth, then the vegetation, animals, and man, at the end of each of which stages the world is blessed. Dawn now is showing through the ladder opening, at which time the Village Chief and Crier Chief come down into the kiva and announce: "I want all of you to come out of this kiva. We must all come to the light." Holding hands in a long chain they climb, unable to touch the ladder except with their feet and so with difficulty and slowly, to simulate the difficulties of mankind's emergence to the Fourth World. They go to the east to greet the sun and then return to prepare in the kiva for their public appearance.

All wash their hair and dress in the usual black manta and red and white ceremonial cape, except three young virgins selected to be the Márawu Maidens. One is to be the Caller, to sing more loudly than the others, directing the changes of the songs. She wears eagle feathers in her hair, and each cheek is painted with a brown stripe down from the eye. In her left hand she carries a long rod with two eagle feathers on the top and a long streamer of horsehair, dyed red; and on her right wrist, a fox pelt that hangs to her ankles. Each of the other two selected maidens wears part of a decorated wedding dress that falls below the hips and

a kirtle that reaches to the knees. Two circles, like garters, are drawn, one high on the thigh, the other just above the knee, from which four vertical stripes, front, back, and sides, are marked down the legs. (From this, the name of the ceremony.) On their heads are fastened four upright blue sticks joined at the top with eagle feathers. Down feathers are bunched at the back of the head, and each cheek is painted, like the Caller's cheeks, with a brown stripe from the eye.

The woman leader then conducts the company out of the kiva to the plaza, where they form a circle with an opening to the east. The three Márawu Maidens follow, each carrying a small hoop or ring made of cattails, which they toss onto lines of cornmeal drawn on the ground before them by one of the two male leaders. Having tossed the rings, they throw at them their feathered sticks. This they do four times. On arriving in the circle, they are given bowls of water and of sweet cornmeal, of which each kneads two rolls of dough. One goes to the west and then to the south, throwing a roll each time over the circle of singing women to the men outside, who try to catch it. The second maid

goes tossing to the east and then the north; the older women, meanwhile, dancing and singing, throw gifts of food to the spectators. And at intervals throughout the day this pretty little game is repeated.

Owaqlt, meaning Melons on the Vine, is the last and least important of the women's ceremonies. It may be given any time between Márawu and Wúwuchim and is referred to, commonly, as the Basket Dance. Its altar, kiva rituals, and public dance repeat, essentially, the forms of Márawu, except that its maidens wear a horn on the right side of the head and a squash blossom whorl on the left, and throw to the bystanders, not food to eat, but baskets.[40]

And so, it is with the bountiful, playful joy and generosity of the women's ceremonials that the annual cycle is carried on from harvest time to Wúwuchim. The mood and flavor throughout is erotic, of maidenhood and motherhood, their charm and readiness to bear, yield, and provide for the future. And with that the cycle rolls to another round.

402. Singing, the Lakón Manas shield their faces with the beautifully woven food baskets that have given to the Lakón Ceremony the name by which it is popularly known: the Basket Dance.

293

NORTHWEST MEXICO: THE HUICHOL

The Land and Fruit of Eternal Life

Dwelling in the highlands of Nayarit, just below the Gran Chichimeca, exactly at the entrance to the Lower Sonoran corridor (Map 26), where in pre-Conquest times there were settlements from the coast to the Sierra,[41] the Huichols are the inheritors of a substantial Mesoamerican tradition. The whole rich area was almost completely destroyed, as Carl Sauer and D. D. Brand report of its archaeological remains, "because it was overrun in 1530 and 1531 by about as hard a gang of killers as Spain let loose anywhere in the New World and because in those days there was no stay upon the killing propensities of conquerors."[42] Their introduced diseases did the rest, so that, as Betty Bell reports of Nayarit, Jalisco, and Colima: "Within a few years of the Spanish conquest the Indian population had declined sharply.... Moreover, many Indians abandoned their settlements and fled into the mountains of northern and eastern Jalisco, and into the Sierra de Nayarit. These areas remained unsubjugated for many years after the conquest."[43] Such is the area in which the Huichols now dwell.

They are of the Uto-Aztecan linguistic stock, related in speech to the Hopi, Toltecs, and Aztecs, and thus of the Gran Chichimeca in origin. Their legendary place of emergence, *Wirikuta,* is the desert between the Rio Grande and San Luis Potosí, where grows the plant of eternal life, *hikuri,* the desert-cactus peyote. Annually, pilgrimages are undertaken by small parties under the leadership of a shaman (*mara'akame*) to harvest this fruit of the knowledge of immortal being. It is a journey of some three-hundred miles each way, along a route punctuated by holy sites, a passage to be accomplished during the dry season between the harvest festivals of October and rain ceremonies of February. In December 1966, two anthropologists, Peter Furst and Barbara Myerhoff, joined such a party under the conduct of Ramón Medina Silva, who besides being a *mara'akame,* was an artist (creating yarn paintings) and

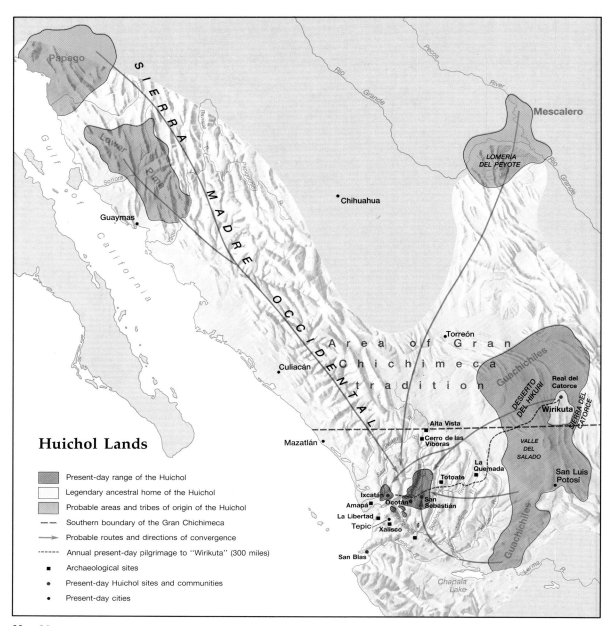

Huichol Lands

- Present-day range of the Huichol
- Legendary ancestral home of the Huichol
- Probable areas and tribes of origin of the Huichol
- – – Southern boundary of the Gran Chichimeca
- → Probable routes and directions of convergence
- ------ Annual present-day pilgrimage to "Wirikuta" (300 miles)
- ■ Archaeological sites
- ● Present-day Huichol sites and communities
- ● Present-day cities

Map 32.

a musician (playing the fiddle). The preferred manner of travel would have been to walk; but with all the photographic and recording gear a compromise was granted, namely, transportation by camper to the edge of Wirikuta. Each member of the party had an established place in the vehicle, and the decorated antlers symbolic of *Kauyumari*—the Sacred Deer Person, who is identical with the hallucinogenic cactus plant itself—were attached in front to the foremost part of the camper.

The party gathered at Ramón's little rancho and there engaged for three days in last-minute preparations. "Every *peyotero* works for weeks," states Furst, "to prepare his or her own prayer objects, ceremonial

arrows, and decorated votive gourds, or even a miniature version of the large folk-art yarn paintings."[44] While the others sewed, strung beads, adorned hats, and so on, Ramón occupied himself preparing Kauyumari's antlers, wrapping them with colored yarn, and attaching ceremonial arrows along with eagle and hawk feathers hanging freely to blow in the wind; every now and then he put his hands to his mouth to make the call, or whistle, of the deer.[45]

To return to Wirikuta, all had to become gods, and on concluding his preparations, Ramón revealed the names he had dreamed for them. He would himself be Grandfather Fire, who in the beginning raised the heavens by placing four great trees in the corners of the world. His paternal uncle, Carlos, who had already gone on pilgrimage eight times, would be Our Father Sun, and another relative, Sebastián, who in his youth had failed in his aspiration to become a shaman and now was afraid of becoming a sorcerer, would be Deer Snarer, patron of the deer hunt. Francisco, whose age was variously given as between 70 and 110, would be Our Great-Grandfather; Lupe, Ramón's wife, Our Mother Maize; Victoria, her niece, Our Mother of the Children; and Pablo, married to Carlos's daughter, Elder Brother Deer Tail. In a sense, this hunting god, Deer Tail, and the Sacred Deer Person, Kauyumari, are aspects of a single power: that represented as at once the hunter and the hunted in the dancing Animal Master of the Paleolithic cave, Les Trois Frères.[46] Barbara Myerhoff, finally, was identified with the deity Eyebrow of the Peyote (a fuzz in the center of each peyote which senses the ritual condition of the seeker), and Peter Furst, as driver of the camper, became the Arrow That Guard Us.

In conclusion, a sort of Last Supper was served of water and tortillas, before, during, and after which everyone prayed, offering water and bits of tortilla to the quarters and to Grandfather Fire; following this event a number of restrictions were in effect—among others, abstentions from salt, washing, full meals, sexual intercourse, and ample sleep.

403. Ramón Medina Silva (c. 1926–71), Huichol *mara'akame*, artist, and, according to Peter T. Furst, a "superb reciter and singer of the sacred myths and songs,"[32] here plays the "bow drum."

404. *Nearika for the Deified Sun,* by Ramón Medina Silva, 1966; yarn and beeswax ("yarn painting") on plywood (24½″ × 23¼″) representation of a god disk (see **418**) of Tayaupa (the Sun God), who, in Peter T. Furst's explication, is surrounded (clockwise from top) by: a double-headed eagle, the manifestation of the sky goddess Our Mother Young Eagle Girl; a sacred deer, representing Elder Brother, the stag that appears to the peyote pilgrims (*peyoteros*) and transforms, in death, into the sacred peyote cactus; a maize plant representing the young maize goddess; one of the terrestrial water goddesses (identified by a bottle gourd containing sacred water) who reside in the water holes

405. *Tatewari, Our Grandfather Fire,* yarn painting by Ramón Medina Silva.

that the *peyoteros* visit on their way to Wirikuta, the peyote's desert home in north-central Mexico; a branched cactus; a rain serpent with white-candle offering; the wild figwood box in which the old earth-mother goddess, Great-Grandmother Nakawe, saved one man, a black female dog, and seeds of beans, squash, and (above all) the five sacred colors of maize (see **419**) from the flood that drowned the world and the previous races of human beings (when the land dried out, the dog transformed into a woman who became the mother of the Huichols and other humankind); and a blue deer, the manifestation of the Huichol culture hero, Kauyumari.

The first act of the pilgrimage was to gather food for Grandfather Fire, who would be kept alive during the journey by four companions remaining behind. Ramón prayed over the wood, holding each piece aloft to the quarters, while all chanted and the mood became very solemn. From his house Ramón then brought out a stone disk—about two feet across and two inches deep—meant to cover the sacred opening that goes down to the center of the earth, from which Grandfather Fire was born. Scooping a hollow in the ashes and covering it with this stone, he recited prayers to the fire for success and then covered all with wood arranged to point east-west and north-south, after which everyone, in single file, made a ceremonial circuit around the flame.[47]

406. In a ceremony that for the Huichol is as ancient as time itself, the *peyoteros* contemplate Tatewari on the edge of Wirikuta.

Conversing with his apprentice Prem Das (see p. 302), Huichol *mara'akame* (Don Jose Matsuwa) (see **413**) spoke of Tatewari's power: "Anyone who really listens to great-grandfather fire will learn how alive he is, how alive the whole earth is, and the sun. These are our great-, great-, great-grandparents, and they can teach us and help us so much. But as our ancestors, who are living and seen as everything around us, they need one thing: our love. The ceremonies are hard. It's a sacrifice—to stay awake all night, sing from your heart for hours, dance with all your life upon the earth, to fast and pray for everyone. But look at me. I am an old man and I do it, and every time I do it I exhaust myself, yet Tatewari always restores me with *kupuri* [life force]."[33]

The next event was a ceremony of the restitution of innocence. Around the fire, each in turn arose, acknowledged the four directions, and in formalized speech named the names of all those with whom he had ever had illicit sexual relations. For each name Ramón tied a knot in a cord drawn from his quiver, and at the end of each revelation brushed the candidate down with his plumes and then shook them into the fire. Then the pilgrim shook and brushed himself, his clothing, and his gear into the fire, which he then circled back to his place. The knotted string was elevated, prayed over, and cast into the flames: and from this moment to the end of the course, the pilgrims knew each other as the Ancient Ones.

Ramón then placed one end of his deer-skin-strung bow in his mouth and, holding the other between his toes, with a ceremonial arrow beat on the string a rhythm which told Grandfather Fire that all was well and in readiness. From his quiver he took a cactus-fiber cord that he passed twice around the circle, first in front of, then behind, the pilgrims, after which he scorched it in the fire and returned it to his quiver. At last, he blew a horn and took up his violin, and the company danced and sang through the night. Anyone harboring resentment after this ceremony risked terrifying, even maddening, peyote visions in Wirikuta.[48]

The camper with its cargo of gods en route to the land of the knowledge of eternal life punctuated the adventure with stops at which Ramón recounted the related legends: tiny water holes, small caves, tree stumps, little clumps of rock, heaps of pebbles (compare pages I.2:135–137). On approaching a place called in Spanish La Puerta (but in Huichol, The Vagina), he required the curtains to be drawn, so that those on pilgrimage the first time (the *primeros*) should not see until properly instructed; and a short way beyond this portal he required the camper to stop. All descended and knelt in a semicircle, and with prayers for all and for each, he blindfolded the *primeros*. Here, in the Mythological Age, the First Pilgrims

wept: some of those now present did so, too. The company returned to the camper and drove on.

Proceeding, bumping over sunbaked cactus reaches, onward deeper into the natal zones of their lives, pausing here and there for little ceremonies, here and there to pass the night, at last the assembly arrived at the place called Where Our Mothers Dwell: a little cluster of water holes, from which a sacred water flowed that was to be drunk and sprinkled over each. In the First Peyote Hunt the female members met and joined the males at these springs, where even now they abide in the form of snakes.

Among those "Mothers" here to be brought to mind was old Nakawé, The One Who Came First, who, after the flood, remade the world. She is an old old woman with very long hair, who, leaning on her staff, walks alone in the Sierras. With her staff, she recreated the animals and plants and, while the earth was still soft, sent the

Macaw to scoop up mountains with its beak. In her canoe she had saved a single man, Watákame, and a little black she-dog, with which the man subsequently dwelt.

One day, on returning from clearing the fields, Watákame found his hut set in order. Next day, this happened again. To learn the secret, after next setting out he circled back to hide and to watch. Then he saw the little dog remove her animal skin and become a lovely young woman, who set to work about the house. The man stole the animal skin and burned it [as in the Eskimo version of the same old tale, see I.2:184], and the woman became his wife. Together they repopulated the earth, and the Huichol, as their descendants, know themselves as Sons of the Dog [see page 253].

At this very holy shrine, Where Our Mothers Dwell, Ramón removed the blindfolds from the *primeros'* eyes and, as they looked about in wonder, recounted legends of the Ancient Ones, pointing to places where they had stopped and rested

go to Wirikuta. Because the old man, the tiny baby, they are the same."[50]

Driving north through San Luis Potosí, the company at last arrived at Real de Catorce, a former colonial mining town on the border of Wirikuta, which, as Myerhoff describes it, is "a flat stretch at the base of two sacred mountains...a featureless brush desert of creosote and cactus." The interior, where the cactus grows, can be reached only on foot, "for there are no roads or even paths into the center of the region."[51]

Here they would leave the camper. All got out and went to look for deer tracks, for, according to the legend, the first peyote appeared, in the beginning, in the tracks of the first deer. When they returned, a brush fire was built; and after an interlude of praying, talking, and singing, Ramón drew from his quiver the scorched cactus-fiber cord for the ceremony of "knotting in." It was passed twice around the circle, first in front, then in back, of the *peyoteros,* while Ramón twanged his bowstring. Then he summoned each to his side, to kneel holding one end of the string, while he prayed and tied a knot in it. Carlos tied the knot for Ramón; then Furst and Myerhoff were knotted in. No one was to sleep that night. Remaining awake, all were to hold right thoughts, to be of one mind, and to ask Grandfather Fire and Our Father Sun for the strength they would be needing the next day in Wirikuta, whence they all had been born.

407. *The Shaman and the Sorcerer,* yarn painting by Eligio Carrillos Vicente, Huichol shaman of Nayarit, Mexico; yarn and beeswax on plywood, 23½" square.

The two paths, of the healing shaman (*mara'akame,* upper left) and the bewitching sorcerer (*tiyukewaya,* center right): Kauyumari, Elder Brother Deer Spirit, is perceived by the apprentice after eating peyote (below center) and peering into the passageway (*nierica*) that leads to the Realm of the Gods (*Tajeima*). Also perceived through this passageway is the cause of illness (central figure of the panel), whose destructive power can be seen rising from its head. The opposite, healing power of the life force (*kupuri,* upper left), descends to support the healing shaman, beneath whose winged spirit is the prayer bowl offered in the sacred land, Wirikuta, to beg for healing powers strong as corn seeds — strong enough to cure illnesses of all kinds.

The two starlike lights above the deer to the left represent the wisdom bestowed by Kauyumari on the apprentice who has chosen to use his knowledge rather to help people than to harm them. This is a decision made by every apprentice when the powers are first revealed to him. Some decide to use their powers for healing, and these then become shamans. Others decide to use them to shift events to their own advantage, offering their special talents for hire or using them to inflict harm. These become sorcerers, like the figure (upper right) with poisons pouring from its mouth and destructive powers rising from its head (emanations visible only to the healing shaman).[34]

on the First Peyote Hunt and had eaten, sung, or talked with the animals. The mood of the company here changed to banter, and a language of "reversals" came into play. Ramón told Myerhoff that her hair was now cactus fiber; himself, the Pope; his wife, Lupe, an ugly boy; Victoria, a *gringa;* and Francisco, a *nunutsi* ("little child"). The camper was now a burro that would stop if it ran out of tequila; the miserable ruts that passed for roads were a paved highway. Someone sneezed, and the laughter was uproarious; for according to one of the conventional reversals, the nose had become the penis.[49]

"When the world ends," Myerhoff was told, "it will be as when the names of things are changed during the peyote hunt. All will be different, the opposite of what it is now....There will be no more difference. No more man and woman. No child and no adult. All will change places. Even the *mara'akame* will no longer be separate. That is why there is always a *nunutsi* when we

his arrows into the peyote blood (which only he could see) and with this substance anointed the forehead, cheeks, eyes, and breasts of each god present.

One can understand why the Spaniards thought they saw in many of the Mexican rites satanic parodies of their own sacraments. Here is the deity incarnate actually sacrificed on a cross (of arrows), so that his flesh and blood should become his worshipers' spiritual food to eternal life.

With his knife Ramón next dug the peyote carefully from the ground, leaving some of the root, "so that the deer might grow again from his bones"; then slicing from the center outward, he placed a segment of the plant in each pilgrim's mouth, after touching it to the recipient's forehead, cheeks, and eyes.

The hole was then covered with gifts, and the company, still whispering, fanned, stalking out over the desert. After several hours, they returned, their baskets heavy with cactus. "Now," Ramón said, "we must leave as quickly as possible. It is dangerous to remain longer." And they left at a run, as though in peril, arriving at their camper to find the Old God, their fire, still aglow. The next day was spent searching for more peyote, then sorting, admiring, and packing the harvest; and that night, for the first time on the trip, much peyote was eaten, with laughter at first, but then a falling into silence, each alone, as Myerhoff tells, "engrossed in his private view of beauty and light."[52]

The final ceremony occurred only after the camper had rolled back into the yard of Ramón's rancho. The fire had been kept burning by the four who had remained and were now silently standing with lighted candles in their hands. All circled the fire, thanks were chanted to the gods, the bas-

Leaving their fire burning by the camper, at dawn they crossed the railroad tracks to a little stand of stunted trees that marked the perimeter of the sacred land, where they made again a fire, to which each brought a stick. Then the company fanned out, searching for tracks. Their manner was of stalking, stooping, whispering, and moving through the brush on tiptoe. Ramón, discovering signs of the passing of earlier Huichol searching parties, bade his company move on, and in single file they walked for three hours, until he gave the sign for all to fan out. After a time, he again gave a sign. He had seen the deer.

All gathered behind him as he drew his arrow and readied the bow. All prayed as he stalked carefully to within a few feet, aimed, and shot into the base of the plant an arrow aligned east-west, then quickly another, north-south. The peyote-deer was secured. Ramón, approaching, placed beside it, to the west, the horns of Kauyumari; he then cleaned the ground around the flat-topped plant, which was about two inches in diameter, and beckoned all to sit around it. With his plumes sweeping downward, he combed back into the plant the multicolored rays of energy (*kupuri*)— to most eyes invisible—which had spurted upward when the deer was struck. The company then presented their offerings: decorated gourds of sacred water, ceremonial arrows, yarn paintings, antlers, beads, miniature deer snares, and lighted candles. Then naming in a long chant the gods they represented, they knelt in a circle and wept, while Ramón dipped the tips of

According to Barbara G. Myerhoff's recounting of her experience, having at last arrived at Wirikuta, the party of *peyoteros* "begins to search for the peyote [**408**], which is tracked by following its deer tracks. When the tracks are sighted, the *mara'akame* stalks the peyote-deer, and cautiously, silently drawing near, slays it with bow and arrow. Blood gushes upward from it in the form of an arc of rays....The *peyoteros* weep with joy at having attained their goal and with grief at having slain their brother; his 'bones,' the roots of the peyote plant, will be cut away and saved, to be buried in the brush so that he may be reborn. The peyote is removed from the earth, and the resultant cavity surrounded with offerings [**409**]."[35]

Brother Deer and Mother Maize

410. On the peyote pilgrimage in Wirikuta, Ramón, chanting, uses a blessed arrow to show the *peyoteros* a location with sacred significance.

There were two related ceremonies to follow the Peyote Hunt. The first, the Cleansing of the Spines, took place in the Sierra several weeks after the party had returned and involved, among other rituals, the clearing of small fields for planting of maize: one for Grandfather Fire, another for Our Father Sun, and so on, for all the deities represented on the trip. The second would then be a Deer Hunt, in which the deer was to be caught in a snare and neither bow and arrow nor gun might be used.[54]

"I will come up," said Ramón, "there beside him, there where the snare is. He is in the snare, he looks up at me, saying as he does so, 'Ah this is the death of me!' There he lies down, he stretches out before me of his own will. I speak to him. I ask that he understand. He calls to me, 'I am taking leave of my life, my life is darkening.' That is how it is. Here where my brother, the deer, roams, I have succeeded once again. I am able to place him on my shoulders. I have [his] blood to place on my

ceremonial objects. Once more we have our life.

"And when I bring him back those others will say, 'Here you are with Our Brother. Now the earth will be able to bring forth once more, now it finally will.' I will say, 'That is what I am saying to him as I carry him here on my shoulders.' I will place him gently down on the ground. The women pick him up, they lay him gently down on their capes so that he will be well honored. They give him to eat, they give him to drink. They feed him the sacred grasses which he likes. He is in his place. I skin him. I extract his heart. I cut it through the center. I cut it into pieces. I take his blood, I paint it on Tatewari [Grandfather Fire]. I paint it on his house. I anoint the earth with it. I anoint the *útsa*, the arrows, all the ceremonial objects. That is how we obtain our life."[55]

The echo here of Väinämöinen's hunting of the bear in the *Kalevala* (see I.2:150–151) is too evident to be missed. As Myerhoff has remarked: "In the deer hunt, and the manner of his death, one detects evidence of the recency of the Huichols' past as hunters and their incomplete transition to agriculture. The concept that the animal is man's brother who sacrifices himself to the hunter willingly at the request of the

411. Cross-stitched embroidery, collected (1976–77) by Susan Eger in San Andres, depicting a deer in a field of peyote flowers. "For the Huichols," Myerhoff explains, "peyote as a sacred symbol is inseparable from deer and maize....The deer is associated with the Huichols' idealized historical past as nomadic hunters;

the maize stands for the life of the present...; and peyote evokes the timeless, private, purposeless, aesthetic dimension of the spiritual life, mediating between former and present realities and providing a sense of being one people, despite dramatic changes in their recent history, society, and culture."[36]

kets were set down, and peyote was distributed to be eaten. Then Ramón removed from the coals the stone disk he had put there, and each male of the company dropped into the uncovered hole a small package of wild tobacco wrapped in maize husk and yarn; after this the stone was replaced and wood once more moved to cover it. Dipping some dried flowers into his gourd of sacred water, Ramón now touched with them the crown of the head, cheeks, and lips of each present, then took from his quiver the string of knots that represented their unity and passed it twice around, once before and once behind; then he summoned each to come and grasp the string to the right of the knot that represented himself while he slowly untied it from the other end. The string was then passed over the fire for the last time and returned to the basket of the *mara'akame*. A small bowl of salt was brought out, and Ramón, calling each before him, placed a pinch of salt in his mouth—which broke the fast, and with that the mystery play was ended.[53]

Guardian of the Species, the fact that the deer does not die, for 'his bones are given to Tatewari, and in this manner, Tatewari, with his power, revives the deer and a new one is born'—these are ubiquitous features of hunting ideologies."[56]

Another sign of the incomplete transition is the character of the *mara'akame*, who is regarded by the Huichols and treated also in the anthropological literature as a shaman—yet a shaman of very different kind from the ecstatics of Siberia. In the estimation of two investigators: "More than two-thirds of Huichol males over the age of eighteen are either fully initiated, or well on their way to becoming *mara'akame*."[57] In fact, already in early childhood both the boys and the girls are introduced through the annual ceremonials to the structuring mythological symbols of Huichol culture, so that by the age of ten they can begin their training and by twenty become fully initiated *mara'akame*.

Two factors have contributed to the production of this spiritually supportive situation: one, the unbroken vitality of the native ceremonial heritage, and the other, the inward illuminations of peyote. "Through their observance of and participation in the ceremonies," state the observers, Susan Eger and Peter Collings, "children come to understand the sacredness of peyote and learn to esteem it at a very young age. Most children, although given peyote to taste and to play with when they become curious about it, do not actually consume it in doses large enough to produce visions until at least eight years of age. But…by the time they actually do partake of peyote, they are sufficiently clued in not only to experience prototypical, expected visions, but to interpret them with some degree of accuracy and to remember their significance."[58]

"Thus," they suggest, "Huichol culture in an abstract way can be thought of as a kind of school for high priests, since its entire belief system and way of life is directed toward providing motivation for becoming a *mara'akame*, instilling the self-discipline required, providing memory training, and making the individual worthy of this exalted profession….The knowledge does not simply come down from the elders; rather, each person must learn it anew through the use of the tools of the Huichol religion, the most important of which is peyote."[59]

Actually to press on to the attainment of the status of a recognized *mara'akame*, however, requires, first, the arrival at an explicit decision to do so, and then, unflagging labor. More generally, the ideal for the individual is the achievement of completion, "completing oneself," this being identical with what is understood as "being Huichol."[60] And this cannot be realized simply by participation in general ceremonies and attention to secular duties. There is an inward life to be developed as well, by way

412. Huichol child, his cheek adorned with a sun-spiral of ground yellow root.

of the visions of peyote and translation of the beauty of those visions into works of art. Many have observed that most Huichols are excellent artists, and for the women this is the usual way to completion. Quoting Eger and Collings again:

"The religious path of the Huichol woman offers more than standing in her husband's shadow. If she desires, as a great many women do, she can set out to excel at various crafts, to become an expert at embroidery work, weaving and beadwork—a master artist. This is believed to be the destiny of every 'good woman,' as she will learn to bring the powers of the supernatural into her artwork and life. …'Good women' are not at all hard to find among the Huichols….They excel in the arts, because they produce art not only for the sake of art and economics, but for the sake of preserving their collective cultural knowledge, thereby completing their destinies as Huichol women….The most dedicated do not sell any of their work from the time they begin until they have attained completion—a period of from five to ten years."[61]

The decision to become a *mara'akame* involves, in contrast, an absolute and exclusive dedication. As described by a Huichol of about twenty-four:

"You must not think of anything but becoming a *mara'akame*, nothing else. and if you do this, then god will see you, look at you, hear you, and he knows all. He will test you to see if you can bear so many years dedicating yourself only to this, give you tests to see if you pass. He will tell you that every year you go to the peyote desert, from the time you leave to the time you return you may not eat salt, for five years you must do this.

"When you go to the peyote desert, thinking only of becoming a *mara'akame*, you will eat the peyote and speak to the deer, and say, 'I come here to learn how to be a *mara'akame*, I think only of this. I don't know anything, but what do you know?'...Speak to the peyote with your heart, with your thoughts. And the peyote sees your heart and then you can eat as much as you want, with total confidence you eat it, without fear you eat five, ten, fifteen, twenty, it doesn't matter. And you sit there thinking, what will I see, how will it be? But in a little while you lose all your thoughts, and then in a little while you

413. Entranced, shaman Don José Matsuwa, leading a ceremony, sings "the old songs."

begin to see and hear beautiful things, moving, beautiful things, *nearika*, and you don't move, you just sit there watching, as though at the movies. And if you have luck, you will hear things, and receive things that are invisible to others, but that god has given you to pursue your path."[62]

A second strain of endeavor essential to the apprentice is the accumulation of power objects through which to communicate with the Ancient Ones and inhabiting spirits of the Huichol world. This requires,

301

as Eger and Collings point out, "years and years of traveling about the Huichol homeland, and a good deal of luck to locate the numerous power objects in the mountainous and precipitous terrain"—this being one of the main reasons, they note, why women rarely become shamans: "it is just too difficult a task for a woman with children."[63]

Alliances with animals are important in this training. Different animals have different powers. And as for the actual potency, finally, of the gathered power objects—crystals, snake tails, feather wands, cactus spines, and so on—all stored together in the *mara'akame*'s power basket (*takwatsi*), there is an anecdote told of old don José Matsuwa, a *mara'akame* on into his nineties, by Prem Das, a young American, who, after a season of studies in India, apprenticed himself to this master. They were driving back, one night, from Wirikuta to their rancho in the Sierra Madre, when, in Prem Das's words:

"Only a few miles outside San Luis Potosí I had to pull over to check my right front wheel, which was emitting a strange, whining sound. Lupe, the only one still awake, asked why I had stopped. I checked the wheel and told her that it was oozing grease; most likely a seal had broken, and the bearings were beginning to grind. She decided to wake up don José and inform him. She spoke to him in Huichol; finally he mumbled a reply, yawned, and asked to be let out of the car. I got out with him to show him the damaged wheel. Nodding his head, still half asleep, he asked for his *takwatsi*; Lupe handed it to him through the window. When I saw him take out a prayer plume and in all seriousness begin to 'feather off' or psychically 'dust off' the tire, rim, and then the whole car, I could barely keep from bursting out laughing.

"'It's O.K. now, let's go,' he said, getting back into the car. I stood there bewildered, wondering how I could drive the car in this condition over two hundred miles of rough roads, over steep, dangerous mountain passes, and at night.

"I thought I would at least give it a try for a few miles. I got in, turned to look at don José, only to see he had gone back to sleep, then started up. After driving about ten miles at 30 m.p.h., I pulled over again to doublecheck the wheel. It had quit making the whining sound, but I felt sure it was still leaking grease. A quick look assured me it was not, and as I got back in, don José said, 'What's wrong? Come on, let's go. Your car is fine. Now start passing those trucks again.'

"We drove all night and arrived in Tepic early next afternoon. After buying some candles, chocolate, and cigarettes, we headed out on an old, bumpy dirt road for some twenty-five miles, where it ended in a Mexican rancho community. I could not believe it. The car had made the whole trip with no problem."[64]

When and where the ancestors of the present-day Huichol passed from hunting to agriculture is unknown. Nor do we know when peyote became the sacrament of their spiritually inspired lives: not simply a hallucinogen for shamans, but the ultimate teacher and highest concern of the culture. The inspired mythologization of the landscape of the peyote hunt—all the way from the point known as La Puerta, past the freshwater springs called Where Our Mothers Dwell, on and on, beyond

414. *The Shaman's Dream*, 32″ × 48″, yarn painting; lower right, speech glyphs (dotted lines) link a dreaming shaman to a votive bowl (prayer) and to visions of the source of all life and every living thing, Great Grandmother Nakawe's fertile growth.

415. *Three Sacred Peyotes*, 24″ × 24″, yarn painting by Ramón Median Silva. A vision of three peyote cacti, rendered in x-ray style (to show both what appears above ground and the root stock below), emitting their fluorescent rays of power.

Real de Catorce, into the desert—suggests a long and intimate experience of the region. But experience of what kind? The associations are not simply historical, suggesting actual or imagined ancestral events or migrations, but in the profoundest sense mythological, representing accurately the universally known stages of an inward, *psychological* journey: a turning from the world and plane of common daylight consciousness, to pass through zones of increasing interest and danger, to reach, ultimately, in a desert beyond the bounds of reason—where pairs of opposites are reversed, time and eternity come together, each is all and all are one—the treasure of an actual experience of a blissful ground of unity, in which all temporal stress and strivings are at rest. The pattern is exactly that of the visionary journey which I have designated the "Monomyth" in *The Hero with a Thousand Faces*,[65] even to the last detail of the imperiled flight from the blessed land when the trophy of the quest has been obtained.

We have already referred (page 258) to a large trading outpost in the Sierra de Tamaulipas, at the edge of the peyote desert, dating from the Early Classic (c. A.D. 100 to 600). Were the Huichol at that time a desert tribe delivering peyote to the merchants of that frontier station?

They are agriculturalists today, in the western Sierra Madre, cultivating in their rugged highland retreat maize, beans, squash, and cucumbers, while dwelling in established ranchos—farmsteads ranging in size from the single patio of one family to clusters of related compounds. Moreover, the archaeology of the area reveals, as we have learned (page 258), all the signs of a significant commerce for centuries—south to north and north to south—by way of the two Sonoran corridors (see Map 26), passing directly over the present Huichol domain. What role, if any, did the ancestors of these people ever play in that trade?

Many have remarked the likeness of the Huichols' sacred architecture and religious paraphernalia to the ritual gear and kivas of the Pueblos. As Furst points out, the circular Huichol temple, which is known as a *tuki* or *tukipa* ("house for all"), is strikingly like the "great kivas" of the early Southwest. "The circular *tukipas*," he writes, "like the circular Great Kivas of Chaco Canyon with which they share many features, are really the former domestic architecture writ large—since the *tukipa* is the house of the gods (or the deified ancestors), who would not feel at home in unfamiliar surroundings....As the mythology tells us," he continues, "the prototype of the circular *tuki* is the primordial council house of the gods, which Tatewari instructed the people to build after the transformation by fire of one of their number into the sun [an Aztec theme] and the sun's subsequent birth from the earth."[66] As Furst continues the myth:

416. *How We Contemplate Hikuri in Wirikuta,* yarn painting by Guadalupe, widow of Ramón Medina Silva. Of this interval in the *peyoteros'* ritual, as she experienced it, Barbara Myerhoff observes:

"On the evening following the ritual slaying and token consumption of the first peyote, the pilgrims seat themselves before the fire surrounded by their companions and eat several rounds of their best peyote. This generally quiet affair is the first release they have had from the earlier intense camaraderie and demanding conformity to ritual. Each one is now alone in his or her inner world, for it is not the custom, as the Huichols say, to talk of one's visions."

When later she discussed her observations with Ramón, he explained: "One eats peyote and sees many things, remembers many things. One remembers everything which one has seen and heard. But one must not talk about it. You keep it in your heart. Only one's self knows it. It is a perfect thing. A personal thing, a very private thing. It is like a secret because others have not heard the same thing, others have not seen the same thing. That is why it is not a good thing to tell it to others." Meyerhoff concludes, "All that is said is that ordinary people see beautiful lights, lovely vivid shooting colors, little animals, and peculiar creatures. These visions have no purpose, no message: they are themselves."[37]

Because the young sun had traveled far and faced many obstacles in his journey from west to east through the underworld, he was weak and, instead of rising to his proper height, fell back upon the earth, bringing the sky down with him. Tatewari raised the heavens by placing four giant trees in the four corners of the world—one to support the sky in the west, another in the east, a third in the south, and a fourth in the north. That done, he ordered the people to carve a large stone disk and make a shaman's chair exactly like his own, so that the Sun God might travel from east to west across the sky without tiring and again threatening the earth with a cosmic conflagration.

That done, Tatewari instructed the people to build the first *tukipa,* so that the gods might hold council in their proper house. He walked in a circle to mark off the walls and ordered four trees to be cut and set in the four corners as supports for the roof. In the center of the *tukipa* he dug a hole on which he placed a tepari [a "god disk"] with an opening in the middle, and next to it the people, under his direction, constructed a rectangular hearth, beneath which he made a place for himself [compare the Great Kiva plan of Figure 369].

When the gods assembled in council, the people carved for each his own *tepari,* which was also his *nearika,* his likeness. The "Little Old One," Greatgrandmother Nakawe, the old earth goddess who is sometimes conceived as both male and female, likewise was given her *tepari,* her seat of stone. And because the trees of the sacred directions were also gods, Tatewari gave them each a *tepari.*[67]

417. Above left, a disk of the Sun in the wall of a *shiriki,* the oratory or god house found on most Huichol *ranchos* and in front of *tukis,* larger circular district temples; above right, a sacred disk *(tepari),* 12″ in diameter, incised and painted (two deer, three fish) for placement in a *shiriki* wall, where each successive offering of incense and candle sanctifies it more; collected (1934–35) by Robert Mowry Zingg, an early-twentieth-century student of Huichol ethnography.

418. Two *tepari* collected in Tuxpan, in the Sierra Madre Occidental, by Carl Lumholtz, who undertook in the 1890s three expeditions to Mexico and wrote the classic *Symbolism of the Huichol Indians,* in which he observed: "All sacred things are symbols to primitive man, and the Huichols have literally no end of them. Religion to them is a personal matter, not an institution, and therefore their life is religious — from the cradle to the grave wrapped up in symbolism."[38]

Below left, a *tepari* of volcanic stone, 16″ in diameter, with symbolic renderings of such deities and sacred animals as rain goddesses (snakes), Kauyumari (deer), and a peyote flower. Bottom right, a stone *tepari* (same size) with paintings of a double-headed—"all-seeing" — eagle (Our Mother Young Eagle Girl, the sky goddess) and a dove (the maize goddess), as well as an emergency hole, through which deities enter to participate in *tuki* ceremonies.

"In explaining the tradition," states Furst, "Ramón insisted that a fifth tree—'the tree that reaches from the earth to the sky'—had been placed in the center of the first *tukipa.* But that tree could be seen only by the shaman, he said, because it was the hole through the *tepari* in the center of the *tukipa* and the center of the world. Here Ramón spoke the universal language of shamanism, describing the world axis as the cosmic opening through which gods and shamans travel from one plane to another."[68]

Apparently, what we have here is a mythological fusion of at least two distinct traditions, facilitated by a third: one from the south, associated with agriculture, circular council chambers symbolic of the universe, an emergence legend, and a pantheon of ancestral male and female powers whose dwelling in the beginning was beneath the earth; another, from the north, associated with the hunt, shamanic individuals, a mythology of animal masters, and visionary journeys between planes of phenomenal and noumenal realities; and then a third, originating in the north-central Mexican peyote-desert itself, whereby the personal shamanic vision became translated into a communal event. The identification of peyote, not only with the deer, but also with maize (though less

emphatically), testifies to its service to both traditions, as well as to their amalgamation. The deer as the Animal Master of the hunters and maize as the Corn Mother of the planters are equivalent symbols of the mystery of the life-sustaining energy of that singular ground—transcendent of reason, yet identical in all—to which the mind is opened through the radiance and the beauty of peyote.

The hole, the "cosmic opening," in the center of the *tepari* is symbolic of this breakthrough into eternity. At Pueblo Bonito II, in Chaco Canyon, such a disk was discovered in Kiva Q at the bottom of the *sipapu* (see page 275). And during Ramón's consecration of the hearth of Grandfather Fire (see page 295), he placed such a *tepari* over a hollow among the coals and ashes. In the wall of every Huichol "god house" (*tuki*, or *tukipa*), there is such a "god disk" beneath the roof, as a kind of gable stone, "so that Father Sun may see in."[69] If a myth or mythic symbol be defined as a *metaphor transparent to transcendence*,[70] then every detail of the Huichol landscape, every ornamental motif of their culture and every ceremonial occasion of their lives is such an opening.

The Huichol legend of the origin of maize, like that of the Ojibwa (see I.2:207), represents the cultivated plant, not simply as the gift, but as the very body of a divinity. There the legend was of a divine youth; here, closer to the tropical source, it is of a maiden. Ramón called his version of the legend "The Story of Our Roots." "It is the story," he said, "of the maize we adore, that which we hold sacred, because it is our nourishment, it is our life. That is why we must know it well."[71]

419. *The Five Sacred Colors of Maize*, yarn painting, c. 23¾" square, by Guadalupe, after one by Ramón. For the Huichol, these sacred colors (yellow, white, speckled, red, and blue, the most sacred), are personified as young maize goddesses, each manifesting as a bundle of corn and together coalescing into Our Mother Kukuruku, the maize deity that appears as a wild dove.

The Story of Our Roots

A long time ago there was a woman who lived in a small rancho alone with her son, Growing Boy. They were very hungry, had nothing to eat, no maize, no squash. The boy, alone one day in the woods, heard the notes of a dove above him in the trees. Starving, he took aim. But it was Our Mother Dove Girl, the Mother of Maize. She warned him not to shoot, but to follow her to her house, where there would be maize. Growing Boy followed. In her house she gave him a gourd bowl of sour maize porridge and then a bowl of five small tortillas. As he ate, the bowls were replenished, and he found he could not finish it all. Our Mother Dove Girl had read his thoughts, and he realized with embarrassment that she knew he had been afraid there would not be enough to fill him up. When he thanked her she offered to give him some maize to take home to his mother. Then five maize girls came forward, one for each of the five colors. Very pretty little girls, all in their fine clothes! "Who will go with this boy?" she said to them. They sat there embarrassed, silent. Nobody? "But," said the Mother of Maize, "he should not be left to go hungry."

All continued to sit, silent, and Dove Girl, the Mother, scolded, until at last Purple Maize Girl came forward, very beautiful, with rosy cheeks, well-painted cheeks, with ear ornaments, bracelets, sandals—really beautiful. Our Mother Dove Girl, the Mother of Maize, told Growing Boy that he was to build the girl a house with a shelf in the center, a ceremonial shelf, on which Purple Maize Girl should be placed, as though on an altar. He agreed and arrived at home with the girl, whom he presented to his mother. She became angry, saying, "Oh, you have brought back a woman, another mouth to feed. You were to bring back maize." He explained that she *was* maize, and told how she was to be treated. And so, the house and shelf were constructed, and the maize girl remained. Growing Boy went out into the fields to plant, and then things began arriving, piling up in the house, all the colors of maize. "Ah!" he said to the girl, "Someone is giving us lots of maize." "You have found your life," she told him. "You are going to start to work now, seeing the way things are." That girl: she had all the virtues of maize.

The boy went out into the fields to plant, having told his mother not to make Purple Maize Girl work, not to let her grind, for she was delicate. She should remain where she was, on her shelf. But as the mother was grinding, she began to have bad thoughts about the girl. Working so hard, she felt sorry for herself, while the girl sat up there, a lazy person, beautifully dressed, while she was working. The poor girl became ashamed and came down to help the mother grind. She ground on the metate—that girl who was Purple Maize. As she ground, all that came out was blood—pure blood. That cornmeal was blood. Because the girl herself was maize. She was grinding herself, and every time she pulled back, what appeared was pure blood.

Growing Boy came running back, and when he saw what was happening, rebuked his mother. She denied any blame, but weeping, he said to her: "Ah! You let it slip from our grasp. That is what you have done. It all has come to nothing." He tried to stop the bleeding, the bleeding of Purple Maize girl, putting cornmeal where the blood was, where the poor arms had been. Then, during the night, she departed forever. "Here I cannot stay," she said to herself. "It is dangerous here. There are too many things I cannot control. I thought I might stay, but I see now, it is best to return to my mother. I am unhappy here: ill at ease."

Poor Growing Boy! In the morning he found her gone. He followed her trail to where he had received her and asked Our Mother Dove Girl to return her. But, although his heart was pure, he was refused. "No," the Mother of Maize replied to him, "she did not work out with you."

That is what Our Mother of Maize told Growing Boy. And that is why some of us have maize, others not. Those people did not properly care for it. They did not adore it. And just that was why the spirit preferred to leave their place, returning to its Mother, where there was no danger. Only the shell was left, a rotten shell.

That is why, among us, this is such a sacred story. It is very sad, very hard, this story. Maize is our nourishment. We have to work for it. We must gain it from the earth. We must treat it well, as a sacred thing, so that it may not leave us.[72]

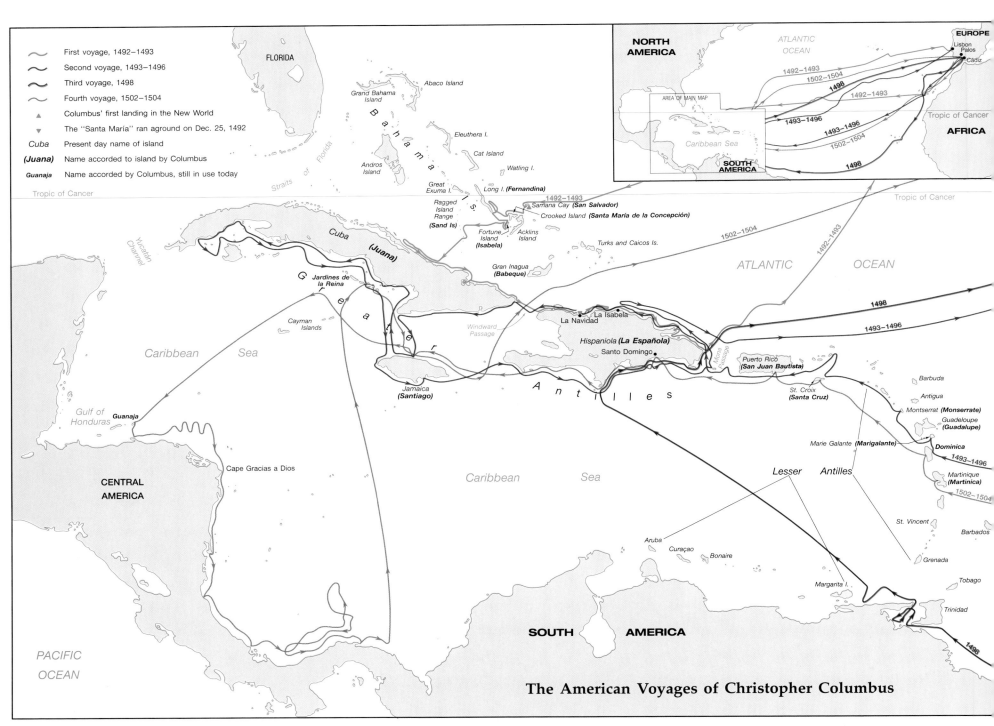

The American Voyages of Christopher Columbus

Map 33.

The location of Columbus's first landing in the New World — fancifully depicted, left, in a fifteenth-century woodcut (**420**) — had always been a vexed question that, if unresolved, would have rendered approximate any such cartographic recapitulation of his American voyages as that presented here (**Map 33**). Various authorities, interpreting over the years in various ways the same data — namely, the Admiral's own log, the text of which is known only from a paraphrased transcription made by priest-historian Bartolomé de las Casas for his celebrated *Historia de las Indias* (see II.2:227–228) — have pronounced that historic site to be no fewer than nine different islands.

Now, without certain knowledge of which island is the one Columbus named San Salvador, it becomes impossible, of course, to chart his subsequent route or to ascertain with any confidence the identities of those islands that he later visited, naming them, in turn: Santa María de la Concepción, Ferdandina, Isabele, and so on (as pictured in the quaint 1493 woodcut [**421**] at right).

It was therefore an event of no small consequence when recently Joseph Judge reported in *National Geographic* that, after five years of painstaking interdisciplinary research, he was at last able to write with reasoned assurance: "Christopher Columbus first came to the New World at reef-girt, low, and leafy Samana Cay, a small outrider to the sea lying in haunting isolation in the far eastern Bahamas, at latitude 23°05′ north, longitude 73°45′ west."[39]

A NEW WORLD DISCOVERED AND DIVIDED

From the *Journal of the First Voyage of Christopher Columbus, Friday, October 12, 1492:*

Two hours after midnight, at a distance of two leagues, land appeared. They shortened all sail, remaining with the mainsail, which is the great sail without bonnets, and lay to, waiting for day, a Friday, on which they reached a small island of the Lucayos [Bahamas], which is called in the language of the Indians 'Guanahani' [now Samana Cay]. Immediately, they saw naked people, and the admiral [Columbus] went ashore in the armed boat, and Martin Alonso Pinzón and Vincente Yañez, his brother, who was captain of the Niña. The admiral brought out the royal standard, and the captains went with two banners of the green cross, which the admiral flew on all the ships as a flag, with an F [Ferdinand] and a Y [Ysabella], and over each letter their crown, one being on one side of the cross and the other on the other. When they had landed, they saw trees very green and much water and fruit of various kinds. The admiral called the two captains and the others who had landed, and Rodrigo de Escobedo, secretary of the whole fleet, and Rodrigo Sanchez de Segovia, and said that they should bear witness and testimony how he,

before them all, took possession, as in fact he took, of the said island for the king and queen, his sovereigns, making the declarations which are required, as is contained more at length in the testimonies which were then made in writing. Soon many people of the island gathered there. This which follows are the actual words of the admiral, in his book of his first voyage and discovery of these Indies.

"I," he says, "in order that they might feel great amity towards us, because I knew that they were a people to be delivered and to be converted to our holy faith rather by love than by force, gave to some among them some red caps and some glass beads, which they hung round their necks, and many other things of little value. At this they were greatly pleased and became so entirely our friends that it was a wonder to see. Afterwards they came swimming to the ships' boats, where we were, and brought us parrots and cotton thread in balls, and spears and many other things, and we exchanged for them other things, such as small glass beads and hawks' bells, which we gave to them. In fact, they took all and gave all, such as they had, with good will, but it seemed to me that they were a people very deficient in everything. They all go naked as their mothers bore

them, and the women also, although I saw only one very young girl. And all those whom I did see were youths, so that I did not see one who was over thirty years of age; they were all very well built, with very handsome bodies and very good faces. Their hair is coarse and short, almost like the hairs of a horse's tail; they wear their hair down over their eyebrows, except for a few strands behind, which they wear long and never cut. Some of them are painted black, and they are the color of the people of the Canaries, neither black nor white, and some of them are painted white and some red and some in any color that they find. Some of them paint their faces, some their whole bodies, some only the eyes, and some only the nose. They do not bear arms or know them, for I showed to them swords and they took them by the blade and cut themselves through ignorance. They have no iron. Their spears are certain reeds, without iron, and some of these have a fish tooth at the end, while others are pointed in various ways. They are all generally fairly tall, good looking and well proportioned. I saw some who bore marks of wounds on their bodies, and I made signs to them to ask how this came about, and they indicated to me that people had come from other islands, which are near, and wished to capture them, and they had defended themselves. And I believed and still believe that they came here from the mainland to take them for slaves. They should be good servants and of quick intelligence, since I see that they very soon say all that is said to them, and I believe that they would easily be made Christians, for it appeared to me that they had no creed. I, Our Lord willing, will carry away from here, at the time of my departure, six to your highnesses, that they may learn to talk. I saw no beast of any kind in this island, except parrots."[73]

And so it began, and so it continued, up and down the American coasts, in the various names of the various Christian kings and queens of Spain, Portugal, France, and England (always in the name of God, with intention to Christianize, regardless of any claims of natives to the regions they inhabited), until by October 12, 1892, four hundred years after that divinely witnessed landing, the native order of culture and life in the Western Hemisphere was extinct. There has never been anything like it in the history of the planet. Like a plague the virus of Christian love went across the continents, leaving in its wake museums where there had formerly been populations.

422. In a rare woodcut from 1493, King Ferdinand bestows his blessing on Christopher Columbus and crew, who, upon reaching Mundus Novus (the "New World"), encountered a native populace, now believed to be the Lucayan.

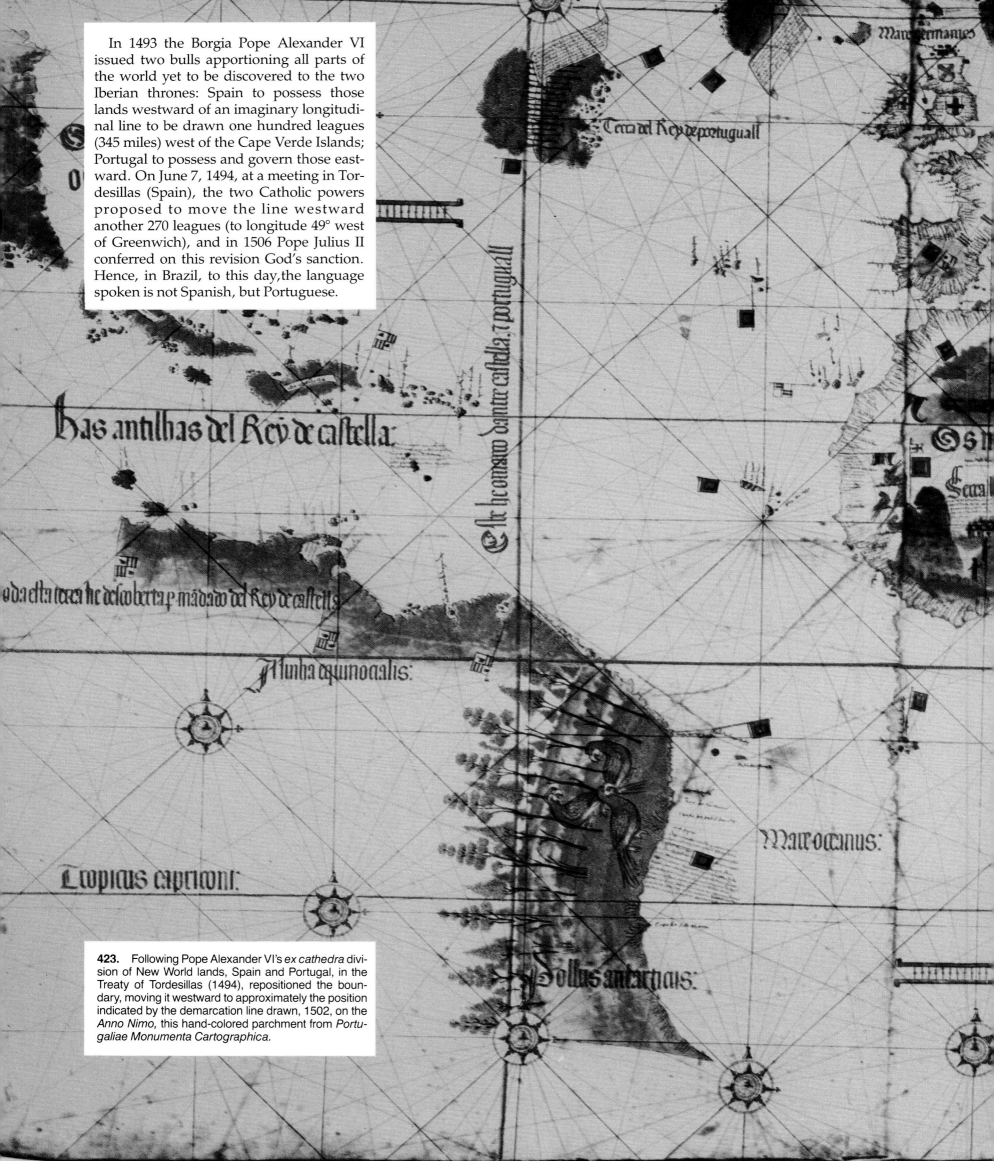

Circulus articus:

Maremanies

Terra del Rey de portugall

In 1493 the Borgia Pope Alexander VI issued two bulls apportioning all parts of the world yet to be discovered to the two Iberian thrones: Spain to possess those lands westward of an imaginary longitudinal line to be drawn one hundred leagues (345 miles) west of the Cape Verde Islands; Portugal to possess and govern those eastward. On June 7, 1494, at a meeting in Tordesillas (Spain), the two Catholic powers proposed to move the line westward another 270 leagues (to longitude 49° west of Greenwich), and in 1506 Pope Julius II conferred on this revision God's sanction. Hence, in Brazil, to this day, the language spoken is not Spanish, but Portuguese.

Las antilhas del Rey de castella.

El termino entre castella. 7 portugall

Tropicus capricorni.

Polus antarticus:

Mare occeanus:

423. Following Pope Alexander VI's *ex cathedra* division of New World lands, Spain and Portugal, in the Treaty of Tordesillas (1494), repositioned the boundary, moving it westward to approximately the position indicated by the demarcation line drawn, 1502, on the *Anno Nimo,* this hand-colored parchment from *Portugaliae Monumenta Cartographica.*

Inter Cetera

Alexander, bishop, the servant of the servants of God: To our most dear beloved son in Christ, King Ferdinand, And to our dear beloved daughter in Christ, Elizabeth Queen of Castile, Legion, Aragon, Sicily and Granada, most noble Princes, Greeting and Apostolic Benediction.

AMONG OTHER WORKS acceptable to the divine majesty and according to our heart's desire, this certainly is the chief, that the Catholic faith and Christian religion, especially in this our time may in all places be exalted, amplified, and enlarged, whereby the health of souls may be procured, and the barbarous nations subdued and brought to the faith.... For which, as we think you worthy, so ought we of our own free will favorably grant all things whereby you may daily with more fervent minds to the honor of God and to the enlarging of the Christian empire, prosecute your devout and laudable purpose most acceptable to the immortal God. We are credibly informed that whereas of late you were determined to seek and find certain islands and firm lands far remote and unknown (and not heretofore found by any other) to the intent to bring the inhabitants of the same to honor our redeemer and to profess the Catholic faith…you have, not without great labor, perils and charges, appointed our well-beloved son Christopher Colonus (a man surely well commended as most worthy and able for so great a matter) well furnished with men and ships and other necessities, to seek (by the sea where hitherto no man has sailed) such firm lands and islands, far remote and hitherto unknown, Who (by God's help) making diligent search in the Ocean, has found certain remote islands and firm lands which were not heretofore found by any other. In which (as is said) many nations dwell, living peaceably and going naked, not accustomed to eat flesh. And as far as your messengers can conjecture, the nations inhabiting the aforesaid lands and islands believe that there is one God Creator in heaven: and seem apt to be brought to the embracing of the Catholic faith and to be imbued with good manners: by reason whereof, we may hope that if they be well instructed, they may easily be induced to receive the name of our savior Jesus Christ. We are further advised that the aforenamed Christopher has now built and erected a fortress with good munition in one of the aforesaid principal islands in which he has placed a garrison of certain of the Christian men that went thither with him: as well to the intent to defend the same, as also to search other islands and firm lands far remote and as yet unknown. We also understand that in these lands and islands lately found, is great plenty of gold and spices, with diverse and many other precious things of sundry kinds and qualities. Therefore all things diligently considered (especially the amplifying and enlarging of the Catholic faith, as behooves Catholic princes following the examples of your noble progenitors of famous memory) you are determined by the favor of Almighty God to subdue and bring to the Catholic faith the inhabitants of the aforesaid lands and islands.

We, greatly commending this your godly and laudable purpose in Our Lord, and desirous to have the same brought to a due end and the name of Our Savior to be known in those parts, do exhort you in Our Lord and by the receiving of your holy baptism, whereby you are bound to Apostolical obedience, and earnestly require you by the bowels of mercy of Our Lord Jesus Christ, that when you intend for the zeal of the Catholic faith to prosecute the said expedition to reduce the people of the aforesaid lands and islands to the Christian religion, you shall spare no labors at any time, or be deterred by any perils, conceiving firm hope and confidence that the Omnipotent God will give good success to your godly attempts. And that being authorized by the privilege of the Apostolical grace, you may the more freely and boldly take upon yourself the enterprise of so great a matter, we of our own motion, and not either at your request or at the instant petition of any other person, but of our own mere liberality and certain science, and by the fulness of Apostolical power, do give, grant, and assign to you, your heirs and successors, all the firm lands and islands found or to be found, discovered or to be discovered toward the West and South, drawing a line from the pole Arctic to the pole Antarctic (that is to say) from the North to the South: Containing in this donation whatsoever firm lands or islands are found or to be found toward India, or toward any other part whatsoever it be, being distant from, or without the aforesaid line drawn a hundred leagues toward the West and South from any of the islands which are commonly called De los Azores and Capo Verde.

All the islands, therefore, and firm lands, found and to be found, discovered and to be discovered from the said line toward the West and South, such as have not actually been heretofore possessed by any other Christian king or prince until the day of the nativity of Our Lord Jesus Christ last past, from which begins this present year being the year of our Lord 1493, when so ever any such shall be found by your messengers and captains, We, by the authority of Almighty God granted unto us in Saint Peter, and by the office which we bear on earth in the place of Jesus Christ, do for ever by the tenor of these presents, give, grant, assign, unto you, your heirs, and successors (the kings of Castile and Legion) all those lands and islands, with their dominions, territories, cities, castles, towers, places, and villages, with all the right, and jurisdictions thereunto pertaining: constituting, assigning, and deputing, you, your heirs, and successors the lords thereof, with full and free power, authority, and jurisdiction....

Furthermore, We command you in the virtue of holy obedience (as you have promised, and as We doubt not you will do in mere devotion and princely magnanimity) to send to the said firm lands and islands, honest, virtuous, and learned men, such as fear God, and are able to instruct the inhabitants in the Catholic faith and good manners, applying all their possible diligence to the premises....

It shall therefore be lawful for no man to infringe or rashly to contrary this letter of our commendation, exhortation, request, donation, grant, assignation, constitution, deputation, decree, commandment, prohibition, and determination. And if any shall presume to attempt the same, he ought to know that he shall thereby incur the indignation of Almighty God and his holy Apostles Peter and Paul.

Given in Rome at Saint Peters: In the year of the incarnation of Our Lord 1493. The fourth day of the nones of Mary, the first year of our Pontificate.[74]

THE ANTILLES

In 1515, Bartolomé de Las Casas, the first Catholic priest ordained in the New World, returned to Spain to protest before the emperor the enslavement and inhuman abuse of natives by *conquistadores* zealous only for gold and enrichment. His *Historia de las Indias*[75] and *Brevísima relación de la Destrucción de las Indias*[76] are lurid documents of the holocaust; and in 1517, in desperation, he proposed the importation of African slaves, who would be better able than the Indians to endure and survive the forced labors. So it is that today the Caribbean population is not red but black, with little remaining of either evidence or knowledge of the earlier population.

Columbus's reported recognition of two distinct peoples in the isles of his discovery is the earliest recorded anthropological observation in the New World. Those of his first meeting were the comparatively gentle Arawakan Taino; the others, the invaders, were the Caribs, after whom the Caribbean has its name, and from whose

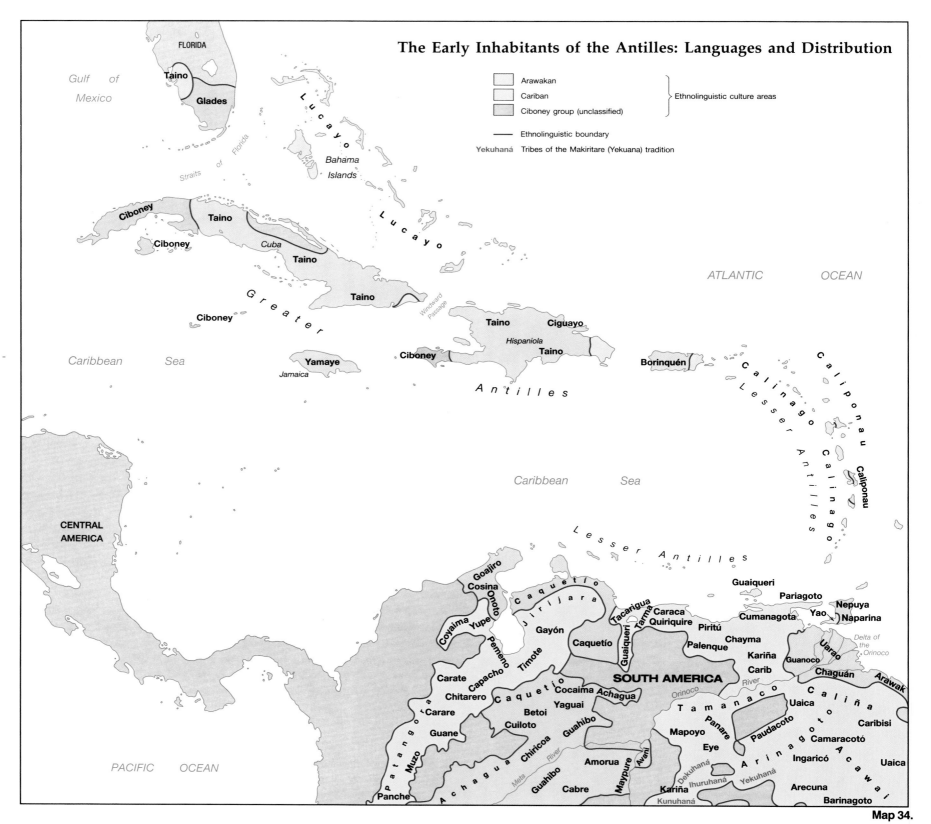

The Early Inhabitants of the Antilles: Languages and Distribution

Arawakan
Cariban
Ciboney group (unclassified) } Ethnolinguistic culture areas

—— Ethnolinguistic boundary

Yekuhaná Tribes of the Makiritare (Yekuana) tradition

Map 34.

custom of eating their enemies the word "cannibal" comes. An early account of the character of these Caribs can be found in *Historia de los reyes católicos, Don Fernando y Doña Isobel,* a work based on the words and letters of Columbus and composed c. 1510 by Andrés Bernáldes, an acquaintance of the great Admiral of the Ocean Sea and the parish pastor of a town, Los Palacios, near Seville:

"There are there, at the entrance of the Indies, certain islands, which the Indians of the islands already mentioned call Caribs, which are inhabited by certain people whom they regard as very ferocious, and of whom they are much afraid, because they eat human flesh. They have many canoes with which they go about all the neighboring islands and steal whatever they can, and take and carry away captive such men and women as they can, and kill them and eat them, a matter for great wonder and amazement. They are more ill formed than the others only in the fact that they have this evil custom; they are a very powerful race and have many arms, for they use arrows and bows of cane, and they set a sharp flint in the arrow head, or fish bones, in place of iron, which they do not possess. They wear their hair long like women, and are dreaded as ferocious by the people of the islands already mentioned, and this is because the other people are very cowardly and very domesticated and without malice, and not because the Caribs are strong or because our men have to take more account of them than of the others. And in the islands of the Caribs, and in the other islands mentioned, there is gold beyond measure, and an infinite amount of cotton; there are especially spices, such as pepper, which burns more and has four times as much strength as that which we use in Spain, and is regarded by all the people of these islands as very useful and very medicinal. There are bushes of flax, aloe, gum-mastic and rhubarb, and many other things, as it seemed to the said Columbus. There are no four-footed beasts, or any animals such as there are with us to be seen in such of the islands as were discovered, except some small curs, and in the fields some very large mice, which they call hutias and which they eat and which are very savoury; and they eat them as rabbits are eaten here and they regard them as of the same value. There are many birds, all different from those here, and especially many parrots."[77]

424. Seated figure of wood with inlays of conch shell, from Jamaica, c. 26¾" high. Atop the figure's head is a bowl, part of a platform extending from its back, that apparently once held a powder used for ceremonial purposes. Visible from the rear are skeletized ribs.

The Taino

a

b

c

425. Differing in subject depicted, in medium, and in quality of execution, a diverse array of carved, tri-cornered, enigmatic zemis have been recovered from sites scattered throughout the Antilles. Here arranged are several specimens from Puerto Rico: (**a**) dated c. A.D. 1000–1500, c. 7½" long, a head of gray stone dominated by an elongated nose; (**b**) 4" long, a fish-mouthed personage with flexed legs; (**c**) a gaping figure of white marble, 3" in length, evidencing a distinctive headdress and perforated earlobes; and, from Santo Domingo, (**d**) a conical head of stone, 7" high. While acknowledging that some others consider these strange Antillean artifacts and their like to be merely "decorative mortars," the noted scholar of Mesoamerica Frederick J. Dockstader nonetheless concludes: "From whatever side we approach the subject, we come back to the conclusion that they were idols, or zemis. If they were not actually worshipped, they assumed forms which were duplications of idols that were worshipped."[40]

d

The native Americans first confronted by Columbus and his landing party were the Taino, a tribe whose language was a dialect of the largest and most widely spread linguistic stock of South Ameica, the Arawakan, which at that time was spoken by resident tribes from Florida to Paraguay and from the Andes to the Atlantic (see Map 43). And since some fifty Arawakan languages survive in South America as spoken tongues to this day (in Colombia, Venezuela, Guyana, French Guiana, Surinam, Bolivia, and Peru), it has been possible for the distinguished linguist and historian, José Juan Arrom, of the Cuban Academy of Arts and Letters, to reconstruct by a controlled comparative method, from certain documents of the period—most notably, the Catalonian friar Ramón Pané's *Relación acerca de las antigüedades de los indios*[78] (completed c. 1498)—an abstract of the mythological foundation of the ritual life of the Taino at the moment of the Conquest.

The Taino were extinct 100 years (three generations) after that first landing of Columbus. Pané, however, who arrived on the second voyage (1493–94), was directed by Columbus himself to live with the natives, to learn their language, and to make note of their beliefs. His manuscript has disappeared, but three redactions have come down to us: an abstract in Latin by Pedro Martir de Anglería, quotations by Las Casas in his *Apologética historia de las Indias*,[79] and a full translation into Italian by Alfonso de Ulloa, printed in Venice in 1571. Through all this, of course, as Arrom remarks, "the Taino words have suffered considerable alteration…not infrequently the same term appears in differing forms in the versions of Ulloa, Anglería, and Las Casas."[80] By means, however, of a scrupulous translation of Ulloa back into Spanish, with attention not only to Las Casas and Anglería, but also to the known Arawakan counterparts of the *distorted* Taino terms, Arrom has succeeded in restoring the mythic vision of the primary race of the American Aegean.

"They believe," states Pané, "in a Great Lord who dwells in the sky and is immortal, whom no one can see and who has a mother but no beginning, and they call him *Yócahu Bagua Maórocoti*."[81] *Yócahu* is a proper noun composed of *yoca* (meaning "yuca") and *hu*, an intensifying suffix. Yuca—not to be confused with Yucca—is a flowering plant, *Manihot esculanta* (known also as cassava, manioc, and mandicot),

426. Also from Santo Domingo, this ingenious prehispanic nose-pipe, 3⅜" high and 2⅛" wide, was clearly intended for ritual use, realistically depicting Maquetaurie Guayaba (*guayaba*, "guava"), the mythic figure described by Pané as being the Lord of Coaybay, the Land of the Dead.

that is cultivated throughout the American tropics for its tuberous roots (see page 342), from which a bread-flour and an alcoholic beverage are prepared and, today, in North America, tapioca and a laundry starch. *Bagua* was the word for "ocean." *Maórocoti* is composed of the privative prefix *ma-* plus the noun *órocoti*, "grandfather." Hence, *Yócahu Bagua Maórocoti* yields the meaning "spirit, without male ancestor, of the yuca and the sea." Another title recorded by Pané is *Yucahuguamá*, composed of *yucahu*, "spirit of the yuca," plus *guamá* or *wamá*, "lord."[82]

Dance festival of the Haitian Taino in honor of their image of the Mother of God, after an eighteenth-century engraving in Picart's *The Religious Ceremonies and Customs of the Several Nations of the Known World* (London, 1731–37).

The image of the goddess here shown (Figure **428**, at right) is an invention not of the native American, but of the European, imagination, even to the trident in the idol's right hand. Its counterparts exist only in sixteenth- and seventeenth-century woodcuts and engravings of imagined scenes of occultism, diabolism, and sorcery (see Figure **427**, above), the obvious present implication being that since the gods of the heathens are devils (2 Kings 5:15: "There is no god in all the earth but in Israel"), the religious festivals of the New World were invocations of Satanic forces, comparable to the rites of the Witches' Sabbath.

The five, instead of three, heads of the idol must have been inspired by the friar Ramón Pané's mistaken five names of the Taino goddess: Atabey, Yermao, Guacar, Apito, and Zuimaco (see p. 314). The two seated idols to the left are Gothic devils, even to the trident in the raised left hand of the one to our right. The form of the temple itself is an invention of the artist. And the drums are of a British fife-and-drum corps: Taino drums were not properly drums but hollow-log gongs (see the example illustrated in the upper right corner of Figure **435a**). Yet through all these distortions, the engraving reflects two eyewitness accounts of an actual Haitian Taino festival in honor of the Mother of God, one by the Spaniard Francisco López de Gómara,[41] and the other by the Italian Girolamo Benzoni[42] (herein translated, in part, on page 318).

"Their stone zemis [images]," states Pané, "are of various shapes. There are...[among others] those with three points, which they believe give rise to the yuca."[83] Arrom sees this as an evident reference to the numerous three-pointed stone images (see Figures 425a–d) that have been known to scholarship—though uninterpreted—for some time.[84] These are almost certainly representations of Yuca-huguamá and, as Arrom suggests, "were used in agricultural rites...whereby they were buried in the *conucos* [garden plots], so that their magic might fertilize the sewn ground and so, increase the harvest."[85] As he points out, "it was a fundamental idea of the peoples of America, with respect to their agricultural gods, that the plants bequeathed by those gods to mankind were manifestations of the very bodies of the gods themselves, perennially renewed in their immortal substance."[86] The idea of a "great spirit," a "high god" (in Andrew Lang's and Father Schmidt's sense, see I.2:139), as a personificaton of the living ground of all being, is likewise a shared theme of all of the major Amerindian mythologies. (Compare Letacost-Lesa on Tirawa, I.1:8; the Winnebago tale of the visionary who desired to see Ma-o-na, I.2:204–205; and the words of Chief Seattle, I.2:251.)

The second divinity recognized by Pané was the mother of that supreme being who had a mother but no beginning. "They called her by five names," he wrote: "Atabey, Yermao, Guacar, Apito and Zuimaco."[87] Las Casas, however, rejected this list with the observation that "since Pané was by birth a Catalán, he did not speak quite well our Castilian tongue."[88] Yermao, he observed, was a misconstruction of the Castilian noun hermano, meaning "brother," and Guacar was the name, therefore, not of Atabey, but of her brother. Las Casas simply ignored both Apito and Zuimaco, which leaves but two of Pané's five names to be interpreted: Atabey, or Attabeira (Anglería's version of the same) and Guacar.

Atabey and Attabeira were apparently derived from the noun itaba ("lake," or "lagoon") plus era ("water"), itabo being a term still in use in the Antilles in the sense of a "pool or reservoir of fresh pure water…with springs rising from the bottom." Atté, the vocative form of an Arawak word for "mother," is another element which, Arrom suggests, may have entered into the shaping of this water-goddess's name.[89] For the Water Mother is a well-known figure in a number of South American (Carib as well as Arawak) origin myths, and this Water Mother's brother, typically, is the Moon. Guacar, which is here his name, is composed of the pronominal prefix wa- ("our") and katti, or kairi ("moon," or "month") kairi itself being compounded of the noun ka ("force") and iri ("menstruation").[90] There is a Cariban legend (reviewed on page 330) in which the Moon Brother of the Water Mother is the cause of his sister's menstruation.

"Most of the chieftains [caciques]," Columbus wrote, "have three stones which they and their people hold in great reverence. One, the say, is good for the grain and vegetables that they sow, another to help women bear without pain, and the third to bring water and sun, when these are lacking."[91] Arrom suggests that stones of the first kind must have been the three-pointed zemis symbolic of Yócahu (Figures 425a–d, 429). Stones of the second kind would have been little images of the Water Mother herself, as patroness of childbirth. The stones of the kind to bring rain and sun were undoubtedly images of the mythological twins Boinayel and Márohu, as represented in the zemi of Figure 430.

"And they say," Pané reported, "that the Sun and Moon rise from a cave in the country of a cacique named Mautiatihuel, and that the cave is called Iguanaboina, and they hold it in high regard. And they say it is all painted, not with any figures, but with foliages and the like. And there are said to be in that cave two small zemis of stone, about half the length of an arm; and they appear to perspire. Which zemis, they greatly revered. And when there was no rain, they would enter that cave to visit them, whereafter it would rain. And those zemis were

429. This head of polished stone, c. 8³⁄₁₆" high and 5¼" deep, from Puerto Rico, is almost certainly yet another representation of the master of Coaybay, the Antillian realm of the dead (see **426**). When viewed from the side, this zemi exhibits a radically inclined forehead, suggesting that its creators were practitioners of artificial cranial deformation.

430. Stone amulet, c. 2" tall, of two conjoined anthropomorphic figures with incised teeth, hands, and toes; Taino, c. A.D. 1000–1500.

named, one, Boinayel, and the other Márohu."[92]

The name Mautialtihuel, however, means Son of the Dawn, or Lord of the Region of the Break of Day. "It would therefore," as Arrom remarks, "not have been the country of any actual, historical cacique, but of some mythical being corresponding to the god whom the Aztecs call Tlahuizcalpantecuhtli, 'Lord of the House of Dawn.'. . . The reported cave in the country of that cacique, consequently, could not have been anywhere on the island of Española, but the cosmic opening through which the sun rises to illuminate the earth, and into which it descends and disappears, when from it the moon rises."[93] Iguanaboina, according to Arrom, would not have been that cave, since the two stone zemis, Boinayel and Márohu, belonged to a very different story from that of the rising and setting of the spheres of the day and night. Iguana is the lizard iguana, whose serrated dorsal crest suggests the solar rays of a beautiful day, while boina is a word related to boíuna (mboi, "serpent"; una, "dark"), the dark serpent that in many American mythologies connotes rain-laden clouds. The name of the first twin, Boinayel, therefore, means Son (-el) of the Dark Cloud-Serpent (boina), while that of the second, Márohu, is a compound of ma- ("without"), aro ("clouds"), and the intensifying suffix -hu. In short, the mythological twins of the Cave of the Radiant Iguana and Dark Serpent were the Lord of Good Weather and his twin, the Lord of the Rain.[94]

The detail of the sweating stone zemis is readily explained, Arrom suggests, since they were kept in a cave whose temperature would have been a great deal lower than that of the humid tropical air outside, and the entrance of a group of worshipers would have brought in enough of the moist warmth to cause a condensation, such as can appear on a glass of cold water. In any case the long eyes and axial nose of each of the twins were designed, as Arrom perceived, to channel the drops of such a condensation; so that the twins of this zemi would have seemed not only to be sweating, but also to be crying.[95] And Frazer, in The Golden Bough, has shown that a shedding of tears has at times been employed as a magical means to bring rain.[96]

Mythologies of the Hero Twins are prominent throughout the world, but emphatically in the Americas, where the two appear under many guises; in cosmogonic myths as the Sun and Moon or, as in the Navaho legend Where the Two Came to Their Father (see I.2:244–248), as the twins sons of the celestial lights. In that Navaho tale, the two, when fully empowered, become four, representing the four quarters of the earth and sky. In the following Taino legend, the Exploits of the Four Twins of One Birth, recorded by Pané c. 1494, the mythological twins are four throughout.

The Exploits of the Four Twins of One Birth

There was a man called Yaya, whose name we do not know. He had a son called Yaya-el, who wanted to kill him, and so, was exiled. For four months he was exiled, after which his father slew him, packed the bones in a mortuary urn, and hung the urn from the roof, where for some time it remained.

Then Yaya one day said to his wife, "I would like to see our son, Yaya-el." She was pleased. So, taking down the urn, he turned it upside down to have a look at the bones, but what fell out were fishes, large and small. And seeing that the bones had turned into fish, the couple ate them.

Evidently, as thus recorded by Pané, what had been related to him as a folktale was actually the deformed fragment of a cosmogonic myth. For the syllable *ia* means "life energy," the informing *élan vital* that distinguishes animals, plants, and man from inert matter. *Ia-ia* is the superlative, suggesting that originally the man Yaya must have been a god personifying the energy of life, the source of which is beyond knowledge. Hence, his true name is unknown. And the suffix *-el* means "son," so that Yaya-el is simply "Yaya's Son."[97]

The mythological theme of a god's or king's son sacrificed either by or to his father could not have been unfamiliar to the padres, who, in their own ritual of the mass, daily celebrated something of the kind as the highest mystery of their faith. The association of the sacrificed Son with a fish meal must also have been familiar, both from the Gospel episode of the miracle of the loaves and fishes,[98] and from the fish meal of Friday (Good Friday), not to mention the early Christian symbolization of Christ himself as a fish, Greek *ichthys*, through an acrostic reading of the letters of this Greek noun as initials of the five words, Iēsous CHristos, THeou Yios, Sōtēr, "Jesus Christ, Son of God, Savior."

The bizarre Taino myth continues:

When one day Yaya had left his house to go to inspect his gardens, the four sons arrived of a woman who had died in giving birth to them. Itaba Cahubaba, she was called, The Blood-bathed Old [Earth] Mother.[99] She had been cut open and the four taken out. The first was called Deminán Caracaracol; the other three were nameless. And when Yaya had departed from his house, these four entered to get the mortuary urn. Only Deminán dared to take it down, but all were gorging themselves on the fishes it contained when Yaya was heard returning. In haste to hang the urn up, they hung it badly. The urn fell, broke, and out poured so much water that it flooded the earth. Many fish came too. The origin of the sea was from that urn. And the brothers, terrified, fled.

They came to Bayamanaco's door and perceived that the old man had been cultivating cassava. "Bayamanaco," they said, "is our grandfather." And determining to learn from him the art of preparing food from that plant, Deminán decided to go in.

For cassava (manioc, yuca), when improperly prepared, is painfully and deadly poisonous. The proper preparation requires the use of fire to volatilize the toxic prussic acid. The implication, therefore, of Deminán's confrontation with his grandfather was that he had come to ask for the release to mankind of two essential secrets: (1) the art of preparing cassava and (2) the means of producing fire.

But who, then, was this grandfather Bayamanaco? The name of the Aztec firegod, Huehueteotl, means The Old God. Bayamanaco was evidently his Taino counterpart,[100] even as Tatewari, Grandfather Fire, is today his counterpart among the Huichol (see page 295).

Now when Deminán entered Bayamanaco's house and presented his request, the old man put a finger to his nose and blew at him a charge that struck his back between the shoulders. It was full of the powdered tobacco that he had been using that day as snuff, and when Deminán returned to his brothers, his back was in great pain. He told them what had happened. They looked and saw that a tumor had appeared. It was swelling to such a size that Deminán was on the point of death. The brothers were unable to open it, until they gave it a blow with a stone axe, and out came a living female tortoise. So in that place the four built their home and reared the tortoise.[101]

Pané's account concludes at this point with the baffled words: "Of this tale I could learn no more; and of little help, what has here been writ." Anglería in his Latin version states that what was born from the tumor was the woman through whom the four brothers engendered the human race. Figure 432 demonstrates, however, that the creature was indeed a tortoise. Moreover, there is an Amazonian Cariban tribe, the Waiwai, dwelling at the juncture of the Esequibo and Mapuera (1°N, 59°W), whose creation myth opens with a female tortoise.[102]

"The brothers," Arrom suggests, "having ended their cosmic escapades, settled down at last in a definite place, built a durable house, and set themselves to the task of engendering mankind.... They had acquired fire, cassava, and tobacco, and had passed from the primitive stages of a wandering foraging band to the position of a settled agricultural community with a situated population, liberated living conditions, and customs relatively advanced. They had passed, as Lévi-Strauss would say, 'from the raw to the cooked,' from the natural to the civilized state. As the four children of Mother Earth and as personifications of the winds of the quarters, they were now to become the patriarchs and civilizers of mankind—the ancestral founders of the Taino culture."[103]

431. From Santo Domingo, melancholic crouched figure of black stone, c. 12⅞" × 2⅞", one of the many "crying idols" that have been found.

432. Ceramic effigy figurine—arguably Deminan Caracaracol, the named first son of Itaba Cahubaba, the Blood-bathed Old (Earth) Mother—with a tortoise growing on his back (see text), c. 15⅞" tall. Found, 1916, on an altar in a cavern in Santo Domingo by Theodoor de Booy, this thin-walled statue has been called by Frederick J. Dockstader "a tour de force in the ceramic arts."[43]

The Arawak

Writing of the native cultures of Map 34, Julian H. Steward, general editor of the six-volume *Handbook of South American Indians*,[104] remarks on the shattered condition of the evidences remaining in these first areas entered by the Europeans as well as on the reduced condition of the surviving natives. "A comparison of data from the modern tribes with those from the early chroniclers and from archaeology," he writes, "shows that all but the very backward and isolated tribes have suffered drastic changes. Gone are the intensive horticulture, the dense population, the large villages, the class-structured society, the mounds, temples, idols and priests, the warfare, cannibalism and human trophies, the elaborate death rites, and even the technological and esthetic refinements evidenced in the early metallurgy, weaving, ceramics, and stone sculpture. The modern tribes who retain a predominantly aboriginal culture have come to resemble the Tropical Forest tribes [of Map 37] rather than their own ancestors. They carry on small-scale slash-and-burn farming, and many of them now hunt and fish more than they till the soil. They live in small villages, weave simple cloth, and make only plain pots. Their society is unstratified, their religious cults are scarcely remembered, and the principal survival of former days is the shaman."[105]

With respect specifically to the Antilles (Map 34), he names three distinct waves of occupation that had populated the islands before the landing of Columbus. The first was of a primitive hunting-and-gathering people, the Ciboney, from the north, evidently Florida. The second was of the Arawak, a people from South America of an advanced Formative Culture stage typical of the Circum-Caribbean cultures (Map 35). The third was of the Carib, who were also from South America, but from the interior, the tropical forest (Map 37). Though relatively recent arrivals, these last had already occupied the Lesser Antilles (Grenada, Martinique, Guadeloupe, and the rest), but had been stopped at Puerto Rico. The Ciboney had been reduced to parts of Cuba and the southwest peninsula of Haiti. The Arawak were in possession of the rest of the Greater Antilles and the Bahamas.[106]

Of the Ciboney, next to nothing is known but that they occupied at one time the greater part of Cuba and a large part of Haiti. Very primitive hunters and gatherers, living in caves and temporary shelters, they subsisted primarily on sea foods,[107] and their disappearance has been complete. Not even of their language do we have a clue.

433. *Arawak Village*, c. 1850 painting by George Catlin, oil on cardboard, 19⅜" × 24⅞."

Of the Antillean Arawak, the Taino, however, sufficient evidence remains to demonstrate that Columbus in his judgment of the poverty of the culture was deceived. The culture level, as just remarked, was of an advanced Formative grade, supported by intensive farming. Moreover, it was of a kind with—though less developed than—the mainland civilizations of Mexico and Peru. Steward describes these tribes as follows:

"The Circum-Caribbean tribes differed from the civilized peoples of the Andes and Mexico in the elaboration of the basic sociopolitical and religious patterns. Among the latter, social classes were more complicated, more fixed by heredity, and more strongly and endogamous. In the Circum-Caribbean area status was somewhat mobile and, though hereditary rank was not absent, status often could be obtained by warfare. The civilized peoples had achieved political states, with rulers of dominions and even empires, and their warfare was directed toward conquest and tribute. The Circum-Caribbean tribes had

434. *Four Arawak Indians*, oil on cardboard by George Catlin, 18⅜" × 24⅜", c. 1850.

One of the few extant historical accounts of the pre-hispanic inhabitants of the Antilles is that provided by Gonzalo Fernández de Oviedo y Valdés in his *Historia general y natural de las Indias islas y tierra firme del mar oceano*, first published in 1535 and reissued in 1851. Redrawn from this original source are the various artifacts shown below (**435**): (1) Christopher Columbus's coat of arms; (2) the Southern Cross, used by the conquistadors for navigation; (3–6) various types of Taino drums; (7) the tube used by Taino for sniffing *cohoba* snuff; (8) a Taino hammock, as set up when they are traveling; (9) the circular house (*caney*) used by Taino commoners; (10) the rectangular house (*bohio*) used by Taino chiefs; (11) the genital covering worn by Taino men before the arrival of the Spanish; and (12) the kind of stone ax used by the Taino to hollow out canoes. At right (**436**) is a facsimile reproduction of a page of the original publication.

only incipient states, and warfare furthered personal ambition rather than political ends. Its purpose was cannibalism, display of human trophies, capture of female slaves, and, in some cases, taking of sacrificial victims. In religion, Mexico and the Andes had succeeded in separating shamanism from temple worship, and they had a special class of priests dedicated to community worship in temples. The Circum-Caribbean peoples also had temples, but their shamans performed not only as priests but also as medicine men. [Compare the Huichol *mara'akame*.]

"In their material arts the civilized peoples of Mexico and Peru excelled mainly in the elaboration of the processes which they shared with the Circum-Caribbean tribes. The greater variety of crops and better

Sexto.   **Fo. lrj.**

llaman Canoas. Las quales son ð vna pieça o vn solo

¶ blando plinio en las cosas de la india oriental dize lib. vj. cap. veynte y tres / que Moðusa alboaða esta en vna region lla mada concionada: desde la ql region se lleua la pimienta al puerto llama ðo Becoreton nauezillas ðe vn leño. Estas tales nauecipareo yo que deuen ser como las que aca vsan los Indios: que son desta manera. ¶ En esta Ysla Española y en las o tras partes todas destas indias que hasta el presente se saben / en todas las costas de la mar y en los rios que los christianos han vi sto hasta agora / ay vna manera de varcas / que los indios llaman Canoa / con que e llos nauegan por los rios grãdes, z assi mis mo por estas mares de aca. delas quales v san para sus guerras y saltos: y para sus con trataciones de vna Ysla a otra / o para sus pesquerias y lo que les conuiene. E assi mes mo los christianos que por aca biuimos no poðemos seruir nos delas credaðes que es tan en las costas dela mar y delos rios gran des sin estas Canoas. Caða Canoa es de vna sola pieça o solo vn arbol. El qual los indios vazian con golpes de hachas de pie ðras enastaðas / como aqui se vee la figura dellas y con estas cortã o muelen el palo aoca ðolo: y van quemando lo que esta golpeaðo

y cortaðo poco a poco: z matanðo el fuego toman a cortar y golpear como primero / y continuanðo lo assi hazen vna barca / quasi de talle de Artesa o ðornajo: pero honda z luenga y estrecha: tan grande y gruessa co mo lo sufre la longituð z latituð ðel arbol de que la hazen: y por debaro es llana / y no le ðeran quilla como a nuestras varcas y na uios. Estas he visto de porte de quarenta y cinquenta hombres: y tan anchas que po ðria estar de traues vna pipa holgaðamen te: entre los indios caribes flecheros. Por que estos las vsan tan grandes o mayores como he dicho z llaman las los caribes Pi raguas: y nauegan con velas de algodon, y al remo assi mismo con sus Nahes (que assi llaman alos remos.) Y van algunas vezes bogando de pies y a vezes sentados: z quã do quieren de rodillas. Son estos Nahes como palas luengas: y las cabeças como v na muleta de vn coro: segun aqui estã pinta ðos los nahes o remos: y canoa. Ay algũas ð stas canoas tã peqñas q no cabé sino dos

methods of cultivation made their farming more productive. Their pottery was better made and esthetically far superior, especially in painted decoration; their weaving involved many special techniques; and their handling of stones, whether in construction or in sculpture, outranked that of the Circum-Caribbean peoples. The Andes also had metallurgy, which became part of the Circum-Caribbean culture, and domesticated animals, which did not. The Circum-Caribbean cultures are distinguished from the civilized peoples not only by their lack of the latter's elaborations but also by their possession of certain material items probably derived from the Tropical Forest....

"That the Andean and Mexican civilizations differ from the Circum-Caribbean culture more in elaboration than in essential form or content means that they grew out of something generally similar to it and that each acquired its own emphasis. It must be postulated, therefore, that a Formative Period culture once existed from Mexico to the Andes, and perhaps farther."[108]

Among the known features testifying to a common ground are large villages of up to 3000 persons, carefully planned and enclosing ball courts. That such a game should have been developed independently among the Maya of Guatemala, Taino of Puerto Rico, and Hohokam of Arizona, is hardly likely, even though the rules of the game did differ from region to region (as do those of British rugby and American football or, indeed, of American football as played in 1912 and in 1981). The Puerto Rican version of the game is described by Irving Rouse as follows from contemporary Spanish accounts: "As many as 20 persons participated on a side. They used a rubberlike ball made from the gum of a tree. The players had to keep it in the air without crossing a line, knocking it out of the court, or touching it with their hands and feet. Each time one of the sides failed to do this, its opponents scored a point. The spectators sat around the court on slabs of stone, the chiefs on their carved wooden stools.

"Both men and women played this ball game, but never together (except that the young men of the village occasionally opposed the young women). Often village played village, using the large courts outside the villages. The chiefs sometimes offered prizes.

"The ball games and other contests were accompanied by dancing, which also took place upon ceremonial occasions, such as the marriage or death of a chief, before and after victory in battle, and during the autumnal festival in honor of the chief's zemis. The more solemn dances were organized by the chiefs, who sent messengers to inform the people; the more jocular ones, however, took place without authority; sometimes the men and women danced

437. *Five Carib Indians*, painting done by George Catlin c. 1850, oil on cardboard, 18⅜″ × 24⅜″.

together; sometimes they had separate dances....

"Three kinds of musical instruments were used to accompany the songs and dances: drums, rattles, and a kind of castanet. The drums were actually gongs hollowed out of logs. Like modern matracas, the rattles consisted of gourds filled with stones; those of shamans had split handles. For castanets the Taino used little plates of metal attached to the fingers. Only the chiefs and principal men were accustomed to play these instruments, but the ordinary people wore strings of small shells on their arms and legs when dancing, to give a rattling sound."[109]

Birth, marriage, death, going to war, curing the sick, initiation and puberty rites all seem to have had their ceremonies (called by the Spaniards *areitos*) in which song and dance played a part. "The Spaniards lived for some time in Hispaniola," states Anglería, "without suspecting that the islanders worshiped anything but the stars, or had any kind or religion...but after mingling with them for some time...many began to notice among them divers ceremonies and rites."[110] Apparently the most important of these—or at least the most conspicuous—was a festival in honor of the Mother of God celebrated by the Haitians and described by two observers, an Italian, Girolamo Benzoni,[111] who traveled in the New World from 1541 to 1556, and a Spaniard, Francisco López de Gómara, of whose account the following is a translation:[112]

"When the cacique celebrated the festival in honor of the principal idol, all the people attended the function. They decorated the idol very elaborately; the priests arranged themselves as a choir about the king, and the cacique sat at the entrance of the temple with a drum at his side. The men came painted black, red, blue, and other colors or covered with branches and garlands of flowers, or feathers and shells, wearing shell bracelets and little shells on their arms and rattles on their feet. The women also came with similar rattles, but naked if they were maids, and not painted; if married, wearing only breechcloths. They approached dancing and singing to the sound of the shells, and as they approached the cacique he saluted them with a drum.

"Having entered the temple, putting a small stick into their throat, they vomited in order to show the idol that they had nothing evil in their stomach. They seated themselves like tailors and prayed with a low voice. Then there approached many women bearing baskets and cakes on their heads and many roses, flowers, and fragrant herbs. These formed a circle as they prayed and began to chant something like an old ballad in praise of the god. All rose to respond at the close of the ballad. They changed their tone and sang another song in praise of the cacique, after which they offered the bread to the idol, kneeling. The priests took the gift, blessed, and divided it; and so the feast ended. But the recipients of the bread preserved it all the year and held that house unfortunate that was without it."[113]

As Hartley Burr Alexander has remarked of the pitiful scraps of information that have come to us from the Caribbean: "As in the case of myths, so in the case of rites, it is chiefly those of [the Arawak of] Haiti which are described for us; but there is little reason to doubt that these are typical of all the Greater Antilles."[114]

The Carib

The whole interest of the Caribs of the Lesser Antilles was in war—specifically, war in conquest of the Arawak. "The youths," states Irving Rouse, "were taught to value courage and endurance and were periodically rubbed with the fat of slaughtered Arawak to make them brave. When they had reached the age of becoming warriors they' were tested in these qualities. The youth having been seated on a stool in the center of the carbet [the men's house], his father crushed a bird over his head, scarified his body, and rubbed the cuts with pepper sauce. Then the boy ate the heart of the bird, to give himself courage, and his father beat him. He had to endure the entire ceremony without flinching. When it was over he lay in a hammock and fasted for three days. Then he demonstrated his skill in wielding a club and was accepted into the company of the warriors, being given a new name. His father gave a feast in celebration.[115]

"Each warrior kept his female captives and her children as slaves, incorporating them in his family. The male captives were tortured, killed, and eaten at a feast celebrating each victory. For five days beforehand each prisoner was kept without food in the house of his captor, bound onto one of his hammocks. Then he was brought into the carbet, where the villagers had assembled. They thrust burning brands into his sides, cut his flesh and rubbed in pepper, and shot his body full of arrows, trying (usually without success) to make him cringe. Then one of the old men of the village dispatched him with a club. The Carib cut up his body, washed the flesh, and roasted it, catching the fat in gourd containers. This fat was kept by the chiefs, who used it to season the food during later feasts. Some of the flesh also was kept until later, but most was eaten then with many signs of enjoyment. The most courageous warriors received the heart, the women arms and legs, and the other men the rest of the body.

"At this time the chiefs recounted the exploits of the warriors, and they took the names of the enemies they had killed. A sponsor was chosen to present the new name, and he received gifts of ornaments in return. At this time, too, the fathers gave their daughters to the successful warriors to be their brides."[116] "The men with the most wives were considered the most prominent…. The wives were treated as servants; they dressed and fed their husbands, cleaned and thatched the houses, tilled the fields, and carried all burdens. Their husbands could abandon them without ceremony, in which case the younger children remained with the mother and the older children were divided according to sex.[117]

"The Carib sometimes killed the old and infirm. They feared the dead and never mentioned their names. When a man died all the relatives examined his body to satisfy themselves that he had not been killed by sorcery. The body was washed, painted, oiled as in life, flexed, and wrapped in a new hammock. It was placed upon a stool in a grave dug in the carbet, near the wall in the case of an ordinary person but in the center if the man were prominent, its eyes were weighted shut, and mats were added to protect it from the soil. The grave was not filled for ten days, during which the relatives brought food and water to the corpse twice a day and lamented over it. A fire was built around the grave to purify it and to prevent the deceased from catching cold. The deceased's possessions were either cast into the fire or placed in the grave; sometimes the house was burned too. In prehistoric times a slave or a dog was killed and put in the grave to care for the dead person. If the deceased were a warrior, the chief delivered a funeral oration, extolling his exploits. There was also a feast over the grave, accompanied by dancing. The close relatives fasted and cut their hair in mourning; some time afterward they held a second feast over the grave. In the case of a chief the Carib sometimes burned the corpse and mixed its ashes into a drink."[118] According to some accounts, all brave Caribs at death entered a paradise where they waged successful war forever against the Arawak, while cowards were enslaved in the future world to Arawak masters.[119]

438. Picart engraving of the manner in which the Carib increase their courage before battle: ceremonially attired chieftains, using long tubes, blow an unidentified powder into the faces of the dancing warriors. Even today, various Amazonian tribes ingest hallucinogenic snuff in a similar way.

Of the myths and legends of the island Caribs no more than fragments are preserved. Their reputation for ferocity was such that the Spaniards made no attempt to occupy and settle the Lesser Antilles. As Rouse remarks, "There was no gold there, and the agricultural potentialities did not compensate for the difficulty of subduing the Carib."[120] In 1623, however, the British and the French moved in. First driving the

Carib from St. Kitts, the British went on to colonize Nevis, St. Lucia, Barbados, Montserrat, and Antigua, while the French settled Guadeloupe, Martinique, Désirade, Marie-Galante, St. Lucia, and Grenada. Meanwhile the Dutch came along for a share of the kill and occupied Montserrat and Antigua. After 1650 missionaries arrived to reside among the quelled Indians. They learned to speak the native language, and what we know of the culture is from their reports.[121]

Besides the lurid accounts of their cannibalism, undoubtedly the most striking of the Carib's reported traits is the custom of the couvade, whereby, at the birth of a child, the father is put to bed to participate in his own way in the birthing. The ritual is based on the idea of a mystical relation between father and child. When reported of the Caribs, it was first received as extraordinary, or even absurd. It is an institution, however, that is found throughout the forest culture and among many peoples of tropical Asia. It has also been reported of the Basques. Diodorus Siculus reports it of the ancient Corsicans;[122] Strabo, among the Thracians, Scythians, and Celts. "The women themselves after giving birth," Strabo tells, "go on with agriculture and also tend their husbands, putting them to bed in their own steads."[123] The nineteenth-century anthropological theorists Edward B. Tylor, Ling Roth, and E. Sidney Hartland, among others, believed the couvade to be in the greatest force among tribes in which matrilineal kinship was in process of transition to patrilineal, the frequency and elaboration of the custom diminishing with the gathering strength and prevalence of paternal kinship.[124] Yet, even where kinship is reckoned through both parents, observances linger which are based upon what E. Sidney Hartland called "mystical sympathy."[125] One offered explanation is that a part of the father's being is, in these societies, supposed to have been separated from him and born in the child, so that both the father and the child require attention. Another view is that under conditions which exalt the privilege of motherhood, as is the case in a matrilineal context, these rites bear witness to the concurrent responsibilities of fatherhood: the father thereby demonstrating his spiritual connection with the child, whose physical connection with the mother admits of no argument. But actually, in most aboriginal societies rites such as those that have been called the couvade are observed by both parents: food taboos, avoidances of contact with others, and abstention from work of all kinds. Recognized as a moment of deep wonder, involving grave dangers—both physical and psychological—the birth of a child is an occasion set apart for both of those responsible.

Among the Carib, as related by Irving Rouse: "Sexual intercourse was forbidden during pregnancy. The birth often took place by a fire. If it caused trouble, the woman drank a juice made from a certain root. Afterward she washed the child in a stream and placed it in a tiny hammock or on a couch of leaves. If the birth had taken place at night, the men of the house bathed themselves so that the child would not catch cold.

"For several days after the birth the mother fasted, eating only dried cassava

439. *Watchdog of the House of the Dead*, c. 3'3" tall, from the Dominican Republic. "Named Opiyelguobirán [*opiye*, 'spirit of those absent'], this idol has four legs, like a dog; is of wood; and at night often leaves its place to run through the forest. They go to find and lead him back, tied up; but he again escapes. And when the Christians came to Española, he fled, they say, to a lagoon, to which they traced him by his tracks. But he has never again been seen; nor is anything more known of him."[44] One might ask (it has been suggested) whether the night forays of this Antillean Cerberus might have been meant to guide the recently deceased on the uncertain journey to Coaybay. Or was it to warn shades at large on nocturnal adventure—with a barking inaudible to the living—to return to their underworld dwellings before the break of day, when by the light of the sun they would be transformed into wandering ghosts?[45]

and drinking warm water. The father, on the other hand, practiced the couvade. Immediately after the birth he complained of pains, went to a separate hut, and lay in a hammock. He remained there for at least forty days after the birth of his first child, and for four or five days after the birth of other children. During this time he went out only at night and avoided meeting anyone for fear that they might tempt him to break his fast, thereby making the mother sick and the child cowardly. At first he took no food. After five days he was permitted to drink corn beer and after ten days to eat manioc bread in increasing quantities. He ate only the insides of the bread, the crusts being hung up in the hut until the end of the forty-day period, when they served as the basis for a feast in the village carbet. Preceding the feast the father was brought into the carbet, was stood on two large flat cakes of cassava, and was scarified by two men chosen by the carbet chief. A mixture of urucú, pepper seeds, and tobacco juice was rubbed into the cuts, and the blood which fell from them was daubed on the face of the child, so that he would have the courage shown by the father in undergoing scarification. The man was then fed the two cassava cakes upon which he stood and also fish, which he had to spit out. He went back to bed for several days and had to abstain from the flesh of animals for a period of six months or a year, lest the child become deformed."[126]

There is little doubt that these people entered the Caribbean from the mouth of the Orinoco, as had (probably) the ancestors of the Taino before them. Whereas the Taino were of a Circum-Caribbean background, however, the Carib (as already remarked) were from the deep rain forest area, very much farther up the river, and so skilled were they in the management of boats that some authorities have called them river nomads. According to Rouse they had vessels of four kinds: pirogues, large canoes, small canoes, and rafts. "Both the pirogues and the canoes," states Rouse, "were dugouts, but the sides of the former were built up with planks, sewn together and pitched with bitumen. The average length of the pirogue was 40 feet (12 m.); some were large enough to carry 50 persons. Each one had a keel, a raised and pointed bow, a series of plank seats, and a flat-topped stern carved with an animal's head (maboya) to frighten the enemy and often decorated with a barbecued human arm. The larger variety of canoe was 20 feet (6 m.) long. It, too, had a series of seats and also thwarts against which the paddlers leaned their backs. Both the stem and the stern were high and pointed; there were holes in the gunwales to which the travelers could attach their belongings. The smaller type of canoe was just large enough for one person; it had a flat stern and served mainly for fishing. The rafts consisted of a series of logs, lashed to two transverse bars.

"The pirogues and canoes seem to have been better finished than the Arawak canoes. Their sides were smoothed, polished, and often painted to represent Indians or maboya spirits. In historic times (and perhaps earlier) the pirogues had three masts and the canoes two, each supporting a sail made from cotton or from palm leaf matting. (Some sources say the pirogues had topsails as well as the usual square mainsails.) The paddles were spade-shaped, like those of the Arawak; that of the steersman was one-third longer than the rest."[127]

Of the myths and legends of these aggressive people only summaries and fragments survive; yet these suffice to make known the burden of the tradition. And by good chance there has been lately brought from the upper reaches of the Orinoco (the region from which the Caribs sprang) the whole length of a cycle of tales that matches and clarifies the mythology of these vestigial fragments.

440. *A Fight with the Peccaries—Carib*, 17³⁄₁₆″ × 24¹⁄₁₆″, an oil-on-cardboard view of early Antillean life, painted by George Catlin, c. 1850.

441. The Yekuana, aptly dubbed "river nomads," still navigate the Orinoco River and its tributaries, exactly as their Carib ancestors once did.

SOUTH AMERICAN

AGRICULTURAL
RITES AND MYTHS

CENTRAL
AMERICA

Caribbean   Sea

Goajiro
Calamari
Caquetío
Caraca
Chayma
Carib
Palenque
Uarau
Tolú
Carate
Bubure
Timote
Guamo
Guamontey
Caliña
Chocó
Patangoro
Achagua
Yaruro
Tamanaco
Camaracotó
Acawi
Caliña
Galibi
Baudo
Chibcha
Guahibo
Sáliva
Mapoyo
Makiritare
Casapare
Macusi
Trio
Pijao
Achagua
Piapoco
Pauxiana
Arawak
Barbacoa
Manapai
Baré
Mauaco
Ararau
Oayana
Oyampi
Colorado
Carijona
Cubeo
Bora
Macú
Waiwai
Moheyana
Apalai
Aruan
Tucujú
Teremembé
Quitu
Cofán
Manabí
Quijo
Jumana
Manáo
Apanto
Arára
Pacajá
Tembé
Gamela
Teremembé
Cañari
Záparo
Yagua
Marawa
Catauishi
Ibanoma
Mura
Yúma
Maué
Maué
Curuaya
Yuruna
Cradahó
Manayé
Guanare
Potyguara
Shapra
Jívaro
Mayna
Cutinana
Uaraicú
Catuquina
Curina
Paumari
Mura
Mundurucú
Cayapó
Crahó
Timbira
Geicó
Cariri
Chachapoya
Mochica
Chimú
Hivito
Canamaré
Ipuriná
Caritiana
Urupa
Parintintin
Tupiocón
Nambicuara
Tapanhuna
Cayapó
Tapirapé
Xavante
Aricobé
Amoipira
Caeté
Casma
Campa
Amahuaca
Araona
Toromona
Caviña
Apiaca
Bakairí
Acroa
Canoeiro
Tupiná
Tupinambá
Rimac
Machiganga
Orari
Acroa
Camacán
Nazca
Quechua
Cana
Movima
Mojo
Paicone
Paresí
Cayapó
Cherente
Chicriabá
Patacho
Cavana
Mosetene
Guarayo
Bororó
Goyá
Nacnanuc
Yuracare
Aymará
Chiquito
Guató
Kaingáng
Otí
Purí
Chicha
Lipe
Zamuco
Moro
Tereno
Opaie
Tupí
Cayapó
Tupinambá
Chiriguano
Mataco
Sanapaná
Tupí
Tamoyo
Atacamans
Humahuaca
Pilagó
Chiripa
Guaraní
Pinaré
Juri
Toba
Mocoví
Guaraní
Caringuá
Carijó
Kaingáng
Abipón
Comechingón
Carijó
Tapé
Minuane
Charrúa
Querandi
Huarpe
Allentiac
Mapuche
Millcayac
Araucanians
Pehuenche
Puelche
Divihet
Chechehet
Puelche
Gennaken
Poya
Tehuelche
Huilliche
Chono
Téuesh
Tsoneca
Ona
Yahgan

*Strait of
Magellan*

ATLANTIC OCEAN

Equator

PACIFIC OCEAN

Tropic of Capricorn

Tarapacá
Copiapó
Picunche

Culture Areas in South America

	Circum-Antilles
	Tropical Forest
	Tropical Aquatic
	The Andes
	Marginal Forest
	Pampas-Patagonia-Pacific Archipelago
⌒	Present-day International boundary
Cubeo	Tribe

Watunna: A Cariban Creation Cycle from the Upper Orinoco

The Rain-Forest tribe in the interior of Venezuela from whom—during a season of fifteen years, from the late 1940s to early 1960s—the French ethnographer Marc de Civrieux collected the material of this cycle are the Makiritare, a people of the same Cariban linguistic stock as the boat-warriors of the fifteenth-century Caribbean. Their first experience of the Spanish took place only in 1759, after which the usual attempt to subdue and missionize was followed by a succession of revolts, withdrawals of the Spanish, and returns. These ugly episodes are reflected in the later portions of the cycle in a way that illustrates—with an ironic turn at the end—the ability of myth to assimilate alien matter. The earlier episodes, however, are of ancient heritage, and the evidence of their counterparts in the reports from the Caribbean testifies to the ability of a living mythology to maintain its fundamental sense and structure even through enormous transformations of the historical environment.

Hartley Burr Alexander has summarized the main themes in the recorded origin myths of the Caribbean Caribs:

1. The sky is eternal.

2. The earth, at first soft, was hardened by the sun's rays.

3. Louguo, the first man, came down from the sky.

4. Other men were born from his body.

5. After his death he ascended to heaven.

6. The First Race of men were nearly exterminated by a deluge, from which the lucky few escaped in a canoe.

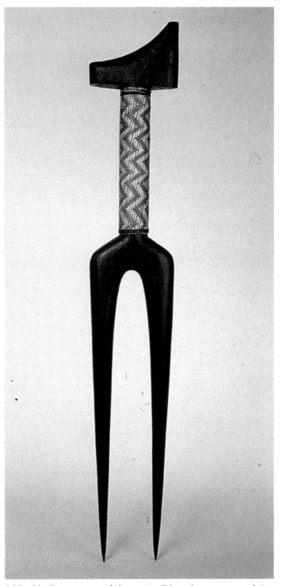

442. Yaribaru, one of three traditional weapons of the Yekuana—"tree" (*ye*), "water" (*ku*), "people" (*ana*): that is, "Canoe People"—of the Upper Orinoco and its tributaries. In Yekuana origin myths, the yaribaru belonged to Vulture.

7. After death the soul of the valiant Carib ascends to heaven.

8. The stars are Carib souls.[1]

In addition, Alexander points out that Maboya, or Mapoia, the Great Snake, was the god who sent the hurricane, and that

there were many other Maboyas—dangerous spirits to be feared (projections by the Caribs, one might say, of the ferocity of their own natures). Good spirits were also recognized, however, so that a rudimentary dualism of beneficent and malignant spirits motivated their universe.

In the following creation cycle of the Cariban Makiritare at the headwaters of the Orinoco (whence the Caribbean Caribs sprang), the dominant character throughout is an unrelenting creature of evil, Odosha, who frustrates at every turn the creative projects of the earthly incarnations of the light of the highest sky. The dualism here is even stronger than in what has been learned of the Cariban myths from the sixteenth century. Indeed, such a dualism of good and evil, with evil everywhere triumphant, is something quite exceptional, even alien, to the spirit of other native American mythologies. It is almost Zoroastrian and may have been influenced by the idea of the Christian devil and his host, who everywhere "wander through the world seeking the ruin of souls."[2] Indeed, I know of only one other aboriginal tradition in which anything comparable can be found, namely, the Melanesian (across the Pacific) of two opposed creator brothers: To-Kabinana, the creator of good things, and To-Karvuvu, who produces the bad or spoiled, but is stupid, not deliberately evil. According to that mythology, however, although the course of creation has involved accidents and misfortunes, there is in the cosmogonic process nothing of intrinsic evil—unlike the Zoroastrian, Christian, and Makiritare mythologies of Angra Mainyu, Satan, and Odosha. Ironically, at the conclusion of the Makiritare myth, the satanic figure, Odosha, is identified as the god of the Spanish priests and musketeers, while their own, native American incarnation of the light of the highest sky, Wanadi, assumes the role of the crucified Redeemer.

The following, then, is an abstract of some of the leading episodes of this long, rich, and now, at last, fully published Cariban recitation of the epic of creation.[3]

443. Women singing *avanso catajo*, the type of Watunna sung (by women only) before planting a new garden. David M. Guss, author of *To Weave and Sing* (a seminal study of Yekuana art, symbol, and narrative), points out that "listening to stories among the Yekuana turned out to be an entirely different proposition than I had originally imagined. There were no neatly framed 'storytelling events' into which the foreign observer could easily slip, no circles of attentive youths breathing in the words of an elder as he regaled them with the deeds of their ancestors. Rather," Guss explains, "Watunna was everywhere, like an invisible sleeve holding the entire culture in place. Derived from the verb *adeu*, 'to tell,' it existed in every evocation of the mythic tradition, no matter how fragmentary or allusive."[46] The only distinction made in the singing of Watunna is between individual (*achiudi*) and collective (*ademi*) singing. *Achiudi Watunna* is sung for widely varied occasions, including: while making a canoe, before using a new child's sling or hammock, over menstruating women, when fasting, or before the first eating of a new food; *ademi Watunna*, on the other hand, is sung only on three occasions: (1) as shown here, before the annual planting of a new garden, (2) when building a new house, and (3) when someone returns home after a long departure.

Cycle of the First Emanation

All was sky and light, and the highest sky, Wanadi—created by the Invisible Sun—gave life and light to the Sky People. Thinking to make people on earth, he sent down his Emanation, Seruhe Sanadi, who shook his rattle, chanted, smoked, and through the power of his quartz crystals created the Old People. When born, however, he had cut his own navel cord and buried the placenta, which rotted, producing Odosha, an evil, hairy creature wishing to master the earth. Odosha saw a man fishing. "If you kill that man," he told the Old People, "you will have fish." They did so and became animals. Then Seruhe Sanadi returned, defeated, to heaven.[4]

Cycle of the Second Emanation

Wanadi sent down Nadeiumadi, a second Emanation, who, when he saw the people who had become animals dying, said: "But now I am here. They will live again. Death is unreal. It is one of Odosha's tricks." Nadeiumadi had brought down with him Huehanna, a beautiful stonelike egg that was full of unborn people. You could hear them inside, laughing, singing, dancing. With his head in hands, sitting, smoking, thinking, he shook his rattle, sang, and dreamed that a woman was born: Kumairiawa, his mother. "You will die," he thought. And she died. But he knew that death was unreal.

Summoning the Orange-winged Parrot to help bury Kumairiawa, he next called the Capuchin Monkey to watch over Huehanna. "You guard the grave," he told the Parrot. "When Kumairiawa comes out, that will be a sign for the unborn to leave Huehanna." Then he left to go hunting, but forgot his medicine bag full of herbs, tobacco, quartz crystals, and Night. (For there was then no night in the world.) The Monkey had been warned not to open that bag.

The earth moved, a hand stuck out, the grave opened, and the Parrot screeched. Nadeiumadi came running, but as he ran everything went dark, for Odosha had spoken to the Monkey. "Open!" the Monkey heard, as though in a dream. "Open, and learn a secret!" He opened and, when Night burst out, fled in terror.

Now, Odosha had sent a hairy dwarf to watch the grave, and when this fellow called, "She's coming out!" Odosha pissed into a gourd, which he gave to the Lizard to fling at Kumairiawa the moment she appeared. The poisonous urine covered her, her flesh roasted, and the bones fell apart, so that when Nadeiumadi arrived in the night, there was nothing he could do. Gathering his mother's remains into a basket, he picked up Huehanna and carried it to Mount Waruma, where he hid it; then he went on to Ahuena, the heavenly lake of eternal life, into which he threw the bones. Kumairiawa there returned to life, and there she is living still. And so the earth was left a second time to Odosha.[5]

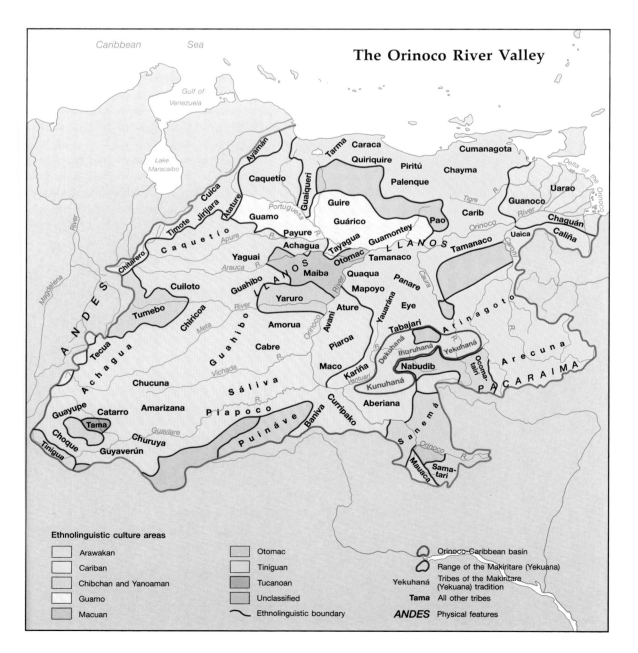

The Orinoco River Valley

Ethnolinguistic culture areas

Arawakan
Cariban
Chibchan and Yanoaman
Guamo
Macuan

Otomac
Tiniguan
Tucanoan
Unclassified
Ethnolinguistic boundary

Orinoco-Caribbean basin
Range of the Makiritare (Yekuana)
Yekuaná — Tribes of the Makiritare (Yekuana) tradition
Tama — All other tribes
ANDES — Physical features

Map 36. The Makiritare (known to scholarship also as Mayonkong, Yekuana, or Dekuana; to themselves, however, as So'to) are a people of Cariban linguistic stock inhabiting a mountainous region of rain forest and riverways on the uppermost Orinoco, in Venezuela. Their legendary place of origin is the area eastward of Mount Paru, whence stream tributaries to the Amazon and to the Orinoco. A single group originally, they split, as they grew, into four: the Dekuhana, Yekuhana, Kunuhana, and Ihuruhana; the last, whose name means "Headwater People," dwelling still in their legendary place of the beginnings.

Now the name So'to means "twenty," which is the number of toes and fingers of the human body. The name therefore signifies "human being," and is thus a term reserved for speakers of the So'to tongue. All speakers of languages unintelligible to the So'to are regarded as animals to be feared. And indeed, the neighboring Kariña, to the east—whose tongue, though also of Cariban stock, is alien to the Makiritare—are greatly feared by them. In their myths the Makiritare portray the Kariña shamans as jaguars out hunting for people to eat. Their own shamans are also envisioned as being jaguars, of course, but at least they are not hungry for Makiritare.

The long and complex origin legend common to all four of the Makiritare subgroups, as recently made known to the world by Marc de Civrieux,[47] is the best reported single cycle of myths yet collected from any quarter of the South American forest. Its recitation is an essential feature of the *Wanwanna* festivals, whereby the young men are initiated and new communal houses and fresh gardens are inaugurated. As observed by David M. Guss—de Civrieux's translator and, for a time, collaborator—its rituals "include dancing, singing, drinking, and a trance-like communion leading to a total collective frenzy."[48] The festival is introduced by the deep mooing sound of long horns (made of a certain bark) approaching along a jungle path. The sound "is identified," states David M. Guss, "with that of the jungle spirits and calls the supernatural beings to the village to participate in the *Wanwanna*."[49] Such horns are known to nearly all of the South American Tropical Forest tribes (see **487**).

Cycle of the Third Emanation

Creation of the Celestial Ceiling

Wanadi blew on his quartz crystals, and there appeard a third Emanation, Attawanadi, who immediately created the visible sky, sun, moon, and stars, whereupon, the people, in their animal bodies, began emerging from caves. They had neither houses, nor hammocks, nor food.[6]

House-making

Attawanadi's first act was to go to the food mistress, Iamankave, and ask for food for the earth. "Fine," she said, and she sent a messenger down with cassava. Odosha, however, while Wanadi was away, disguised himself as Wanadi and, choosing two children, taught them to copulate. The Old People never had done that. Now they started, and got sick and died. The cassava messenger left them, and again there was no food. "What am I going to do now?" thought Wanadi. "These people hear only Odosha. I must make new people."

Going to Wanahidi, a mountain on the Kuntinama, he built for himself the first house. Odosha, however, on seeing this, built right in front of it a house of his own. "I see," thought Wanadi, "I am going to have to work fast." He brought down into his house twelve people, Wanadi's People. They were strong and wise. But Odosha then brought into his own house many people, evil and destructive. Wanadi sat down, elbows on knees, head in hands, dreaming food. But no food came, for Odosha was

dreaming hunger right in front of him. "We can do nothing here," Attawanadi said to the twelve and departed with them to where Wade lived. Wade was the grandfather of all sloths. He was good, the most powerful of the Old People's shamans. He lived in a cave, and whenever he wished to, could appear in his sloth form. "We're fleeing from Odosha," Attawanadi said. "Very well," said Wade, "stay here." So there they stayed, and from there Wanadi would go out to hunt, to fish, and to make houses.[7]

444. Men completing the infrastructure for the roof of an *atta*, a Yekuana roundhouse designed, built, and envisioned as a replica of the cosmos; it will be used as a communal dwelling, housing between forty and one hundred people.

445. A critical part of the process of house-building is the playing of *wana*, the twin flutes that are an integral part of Yekuana ceremonies. The *wana*, although similar to Yurupari sacred flutes (see Figure **487**), are not considered secret.

Felling of the World Tree

One day one of the starving people said, "I know the cassava road. I'll go and bring back food." He was the Kinkajou. Climbing, he reached heaven and came to the house of the Yuca Mistress, Iamankave. There, in a fenced-off garden, grew the great Food Tree, and the Kinkajou, assisted by Iamankave's son, contrived to hide a splinter of its wood beneath his tail. Caught and nearly killed by Iamankave, he nevertheless escaped and returned to the earth, where he drew out the splinter and planted it.

Overnight a great tree grew. However, it had been planted very far from the people. A woman was sent to obtain from it a sprout, which again took root, and again overnight an immense tree grew, so vast that, like a roof, it covered the earth, every branch budding and bearing fruit. Marahuaca was its name. But it was so tall that no one could reach the fruit. Then branches began falling, killing people; and, crying for help, they ran to Attawanadi and surrounded him.

Attawanadi then made a new people, the Birds, to fly and harvest the fruit; but when they did so, much of it fell, and things were no better than before. Then said Semenia, the chief of the Birds: "Let us stop this gathering. Let us fell the tree and plant gardens." (It was thus he who taught us to cultivate.) But the felling of Marahuaca was not easy.

Four toucans began; then more toucans arrived, and woodpeckers. They chopped all day and rested at night, but in the morning Marahuaca was whole again. So then they labored in turns day and night; but the tree, when cut through, did not fall. Squirrel was sent to the top to investigate. The branches, he found, were caught like roots in the sky. It was an upside down tree. Semenia sent him back with an ax, and when Marahuaca fell, the earth shook. The people had taken refuge in caves, and when they came out, it was raining: the first rain. "Now," Semenia said, "we can plant." From the rain the rivers were born and ran like snakes across the earth.[8]

446. Designed, built, and envisioned as a replica of the cosmos, after some four to five months of intermittent labor, the *atta*, with its newly thatched roof in place, is at last completely finished.

447. Home to about one hundred and twenty-five people, the village of Canaracuni, near a tributary of the Upper Caura River, Estado Bolivar, Venezula. Approximately thirty traditional Yekuana settlements are scattered throughout the upper Orinoco; each village is viewed as being an *atta*.[50]

329

Brother Moon

Attawanadi now decided to bring the unborn people forth from Huehanna. He told this to Nuna, the moon, who was a cannibal, hungry for people to eat, and immediately Nuna rose to the highest sky, where the door (which is never opened) to the house of Wanadi (who is never seen) is watched by guardians. "I am Attawanadi," Nuna said to the guardians. "I have come for Huehanna, to bring forth people on earth." Deceived, the guardians reported to Wanadi. "Very well!" said he. "Let him have it." So when Attawanadi himself arrived and asked to be given Huehanna, the guardians said, "We just gave it to you." And he returned, perplexed, to the earth.

Now the moon had a sister, Frimene. "What's that?" she asked, when she saw him with Huehanna. She knew that he had stolen it. "It is full of unborn people," she thought. "I cannot let him eat them. I'll hatch them and be their mother." So when he left the house, she hid the beautiful egg-shaped thing in her vagina. Returning, he looked for it. "Did Wanadi come?" he asked. "Did he come and take Hue-hanna?" But he saw his sister's stomach and knew what she had done.

That night, lying in her hammock, listening happily to the songs and laughter, drums and horns of the unborn people in her stomach, Frimene heard approaching footsteps. Something fell into her hammock, and hands began feeling and searching all over her. She pressed her legs together; the hands tried to separate them, and at dawn the presence had left. "What was that?" she thought. "Was it Odosha? Nuna? Wanadi, looking for his children? Was it a dream?"

Next night she covered her face and body with the black *caruta* oil that our women use for body paint, and when again those steps approached and something fell into her hammock, one of the hands, feeling, forced its way between her thighs, reached into the cave, and touched and tried to grasp Huehanna. She began to bleed (which is why our women bleed when the moon passes), and again, when day dawned, she was alone. Going out, she met her brother in a field. His face and body were stained black. "I've found him out!" she thought, and fled. We can still see those stains on the moon's face.[9]

448

449

450

451

Among the Yekuana, David M. Guss observes, "all economic activities are strictly divided along sexual lines, and even when both sexes participate in a single activity some form of gender differentiation will be employed....But most activities demand no such collaboration, and the daily working lives of tribal members are spent almost exclusively in the company of their own sex."[51] Above, an elderly Yakuana woman (**448**); at right, a young girl cares for a younger sibling (**449**), one of her primary responsibilities; a two-year-old girl (**450**) wearing jewelry having protective qualities; this girl of marriageable age (**451**), adorned with face paint, recently menstruated for the first time.

452

453

454

The principal responsibilities of Yekuana women are the maintenance of the gardens, the growing of food, and the processing of their main staple crop, bitter yuca (*Manihot utilissima*), which is such a labor-intensive activity (see **462–468**) that, as David M. Guss points out, "it is no exaggeration to say that a Yekuana woman, working in necessary collaboration with all other adult females in her extended family, spends a full ninety percent of her working time involved in some aspect of yuca production.... In addition to this lengthy preparation process, the women are also responsible for all domestic maintenance: the drawing of water, the gathering of firewood, the serving of food, and the collection of game left out on the trails by the men who have shot it. When there is no game to collect, the women may supplement the village diet by gathering grubs, ants, or sacred worms called *motto*. Even when uninvolved in the physically demanding daily regime of food preparation, women relax by making the two principal artifacts used in it—yuca graters and carrying baskets."[52] Herewith a sampling of women's activities, clockwise from above left: (**452**) weaving a hammock on a simple loom, an activity little pursued of late, since most hammocks are now obtained by trade with neighboring tribes; (**453**) weaving a *wuwa*, the all-purpose carrying basket (**454**) used to transport firewood, game, fish, and household possessions, as well as to carry yuca from the gardens to the village; (**455**) preparing fermented *iarake* from yuca; and (**456**) weaving a woman's *muaho*, the bead apron that is the most intricate item of a woman's wardrobe.

456

455

The Great Water Mother

When Frimene, running, came to the Orinoco, she splashed into it and turned into an enormous anaconda. "I am the River Mother, Huiio," she said, and, diving to the bottom of the rapids, there built her house. The rainbow that we see where the rapids foam is her feathered headdress.

Presently Attawanadi, searching for Huehanna, came to Nuna's house and asked if anyone there knew where it might be. "My sister hid it in her stomach and ran off," Nuna replied. Turning, Attawanadi dashed into the forest, shouting for everybody to help find her. All night there was hooting and hallooing, until at dawn Huiio lifted her immense serpent form from the water, cried, "Here I am!" and then dove, and the rainbow marked her way as she swam downriver.

Arrows flew and so filled the Water Mother's body that she looked like a porcupine. Over she fell, and Huehanna shot into the air. Falling on a rock in the rapids, it burst, and the unborn people, in the form of fish eggs, flew all about. So were born the fish, crocodiles, anacondas, and other water dwellers. And Huiio, leaving as reminders to us her body covered with arrows and the rainbow, departed to the lake of eternal life, where she lives today in the center of the highest sky.

Then Manuwa, the Jaguar, approached and took a bite of the serpent flesh. That was the first eating of meat. When the others saw the red blood flow, they all pressed in for a mouthful. All the rivers, however, began to rise, and flooded the earth, and the people fled to high cliffs and caves. Then the Great Water went down, and they returned to gorge themselves on the body of the Water Mother.[10]

331

Cycle of the Twin Heros

The Fire Theft

The people had no fire at that time, but the Jaguar's wife, Kawao, the Toad-woman, had fire in her stomach. That was her secret. When alone, she would open her mouth, pull the fire out, cook dinner, then pull it back with her tongue, and when her husband returned, "How do you do it?" he would ask. "By the heat of the sun," she would answer. He was not very bright, and so she had him fooled.

Now the day they killed the Water Mother, Toad-woman found on the shore two fish eggs, which she took home to hatch. The warmth of her fire opened them, and two boys were born:

Shikiemona, the elder, and Iureke. Right away they walked, talked, and were not infants any more, but unruly pests, playing pranks on people, now as boys, now as fish, cockroaches or crickets. "I am your mother," Toad-woman told them, and they knew nothing of their Water Mother's death.

"How do you do it?" they asked, one day, when she had ordered them out of the house, in order to be alone to cook. "By the heat of the sun," she answered. "No," they said, "that wouldn't do it." Angry, she beat them and threw them out, and they went directly to the river, dove, and turning into fish, swam to the bottom of the rapids, where they came to an enormous house. They called. No one answered. They went in. "Nice house," Shikie-

mona said. "I feel I've been here before," Iureke said. They found two hammocks, got in, fell asleep, and in dream saw their mother, Huiio, the Great Serpent. "This is my house, your house. I am your mother," she told them. "Wanadi is your father: not the Toad and the Jaguar. They killed and ate me. I live now in the sky. The Jaguar plans to kill and eat you. You must kill him first." They woke, found a gourd of black *caruta* oil, then slept and dreamed again. "That was my gourd for painting myself," they heard. "If you throw it away, the rivers will rise, and their waters will cover the earth. Those who ate me were many, down to the smallest."

They woke and, returning to the Jaguar's house, asked the Toad-woman for dinner. In order to cook, she ordered them out, but only Shikiemona left. Iureke hid in the roof to spy. "Good," she thought, "they're gone." But in her pan she saw the younger brother's reflection. "What are you doing up there?" she called; "Get out!" "I can't," he answered. "I've lost an eye and can't move. But I won't look. I'll look at the ceiling." He had fixed one eye in the back of his neck, and this watched as she opened her mouth, blew fire under the pan, then shot out her tongue, and took the fire back. "Dinner's ready," she called. Iureke, replacing the eye, came down; Shikiemona entered, and with a large scissors the woman approached the two to kill them. "Boys! Let me cut your hair," she was saying. But they sprang upon her. "Throw it up!" they yelled. "Bring that thing out of your stomach!" She tried, terrified, but choked. They slit her mouth, and out gushed the fire. (That is why toads have wide mouths today and a lump in their throat that goes up and down.) Iureke pounced upon the fire, and cutting up the Toad, they made a stew of her with chili peppers. When they heard the jaguar coming home for his meal, they quickly went out and hid the fire in two trees. Iureke hid half of it in the wishu tree, Shikiemona half in the kumnuatte. When we want fire we remember this. We take wood of the wishu and wood of the kumnuatte and rub the two together. Right away, the fire jumps out. Those two boys, in the beginning, hid it for us in two trees. Because of that, people now eat well.[11]

457. Men making sieves (*manade*), a type of *waja*, the twill-plated flat baskets used as plateware.

458. Below, four examples of "painted" *waja* that feature bichromatic twill plating.

The Eye-juggling Game

Sitting facing each other, the boys were playing their eye game. "Catch!" said one, tossing an eye to his brother. "Catch!" said the other, tossing it back. Jaguar, hunting to kill them, arrived, but on seeing the game, became curious. "What's this?" he asked. "We're airing our eyes," they said. "They were covered with dreams this morning. Now they're clean and dry." "I also dreamed last night," said Jaguar, "and I'd like to see better, too." "Well then, give us your eyes. We'll wash them for you." And he gave them both his eyes.

"Are they ready yet?" he presently asked. "They're really dirty," the boys answered. "They're covered with dreams. Just hang on a little." Laughing, they tossed the eyes back and forth. "Here, catch!" they teased. "No, please!" he cried. "We'll put them out on this rock to dry. They're really beautiful!" the boys told him. Then Wadakane, the Crab, came by. "Give those eyes a turn," the boys called to him. He turned them; they continued to roll; they hit the water: "Plump!" The Jaguar screamed, "They've fallen in!" and striking out a paw to find them, hit the Crab and split his skull. (So crabs now have split skulls.) The boys were just laughing. "Let's go fishing!" they said, and swam away.

The Vulture flew down, expecting a meal. "Here I am!" he said. The Jaguar whined, "I can't see. I've lost my eyes. Who are you?" "I'm Vulture. I'll find you a new pair." Flying off, he returned with two wonderful eyes. They were a bit too large, but he shoved them in. So now jaguars have big beautiful eyes, and are good hunters.[12]

The Great Water

The People were all together, feasting, many of them drunk. "Let's punish them now," Shikiemona said. Iureke agreed, and diving, they swam to their mother's house, recovered the gourd and threw it away. Then the rivers, rising, covered the earth. Only two tall palms were left standing, reaching all the way to heaven. These the boys climbed and, making a platform between them, looked down, day after day, until the flood withdrew to the Caribbean. When they then came down, the palms turned into Mount Moriche, and the brothers looked around. "Everybody's dead," they said, and together ascended to the sky.[13]

459.

The End of the Mythological Age

Wahnatu and Wetashi, Our First Parents

The Old People had departed to the sky, leaving their animal bodies on earth, along with their food plants. "How can I keep these plants from getting lost?" thought Attawanadi. "The animals can't take care of them." He went to Mount Dekuhana, took clay, shaped it and with fire dried it, shook his rattle, lit his cigar, sang, blew smoke, and so made Wahnatu, the first man. "You are a So'to," Wanadi told him. "You will make slash-and-burn gardens." [So'to—True People—is the name by which the Makiritare know themselves.] Then Attawanadi made Wetashi, the first woman, to plant the gardens her man was to prepare. And Attawanadi then made for these two a house.

At Mount Marahuaka, where the great tree had once stood, Wahnatu cleared a garden plot. "The conuco's ready," he told his wife. "Now we'll celebrate. You make the yuca beer; I'll make the bark horn." He climbed the mountain to find bark, made the horn, and then blew it: "Wooo-wooo-wooo." Down came the Bird and Animal Masters, all of them, dancing and singing. "Did you call?" they asked. "We'll help you celebrate." They made a dance stick to beat the earth and summon Food Spirits from below; they cut bamboo and made clarinets and flutes, then played them. "This," they said, "is our voice. Listen and learn the story of how we felled the great tree." They gave him feathers to wear; made dance pendants, hats, and palm-leaf dance skirts; then painted themselves while he watched to learn the patterns. And when they had taught him all, they left, promising to return when his gardens were ready and he blew his horn.

"My, you are beautiful!" exclaimed Wetashi when she saw her husband returning. When everything was ready, he blew the bark horn. "Your beer is ready," said the horn, but all the woman heard was "Woooo-wooo-woooo!" Singing, the Masters arrived, and Wahnatu, listening, repeated their song of the felling of Marahuaca. Wetashi, however, neither heard nor saw the visitors, but only her husband's repetitions of their teachings.[14]

Attawandi, Odosha, and the Soldiers of the Cross

Having fashioned Wahnatu and Wetashi, Attawanadi left to find places to make other people. At Maipures Rapids he made the first Spaniards, but before he could give them a house, Odosha arrived, and he had to leave. Downstream he then made the Puinave tribe and gave them a fine big house. "Wanadi is bad," Odosha told the Spaniards. "He left you with nothing, yet has made a fine house for those new people downstream. Make war on them and take their house." Immediately, they marched, beat and killed the Puinave with clubs, took their house, and went on to get Wanadi. That is how war, injustice, and theft began.

At Angostura [now Ciudad Bolívar] Attawanadi made another white man to replace the Spaniards ruined by Odosha. He made a merchant, wise and rich, with a beautiful house and goods of every kind. "You are a merchant," Attawanadi told him. Forever traveling around,

460

461

462

463

464

465

The Yekuana, like other residents of the Tropical Forest, grow yuca in slash-and-burn gardens and use age-old techniques to process the plant. After a plot of jungle has been clear-cut, the vegetation is left in place to dry out. Later, the plot is burned off (460) and planted with yuca. While the yuca is growing, the garden is regularly tended and carefully weeded (461). When the yuca is ready for harvesting, the women dig up and peel the large tubers (462), fill their *wuwa* baskets, and carry them back to the village (463). In the workhuts shared by each extended family (464), the tubers are grated, and the wet pulp is stuffed into long mesh yuca presses (*tingkui* or *sebucans*) that are carried (465) to an elaborately constructed device known as *tingkui-yedi* ("the *sebucan* teeth"), where they are hung and stretched (466) to squeeze out the prussic acid. When dried, the chalky yuca pulp is forced through *manade* baskets that act as sieves. The resulting flour, spread on hot grills (once made of stone, but now of iron), is transformed into cassava (467), which, if not eaten at once, is dried (468) and stored for future use.[53]

466

467

468

he became Wanadi's friend to the poor. Our grandfathers would go to his village for his wares.

Then at the mouth of the Essequibo, on the shores of the Caribbean Sea, Attawanadi made another white man, Hurunko, the Dutchman, rich, strong, and very wise. But while he was making still another fine house at Caracas, Odosha's Spaniards arrived.

"We're here!" they said. "Whose village is this?" "Mine," said Attawanadi. "No, ours!" they said. "Everything on earth is ours." "I am Wanadi. I made you," Attawanadi said. "You are not Odosha's. Now give up this robbing and killing of people. Go back to your own place. I'll give you everything you need."

They grabbed him, tied him to a pole, took him to a mountain top, and left him there with a guard, who was to watch and to shout when he died; then they went to plunder Caracas. But Attawanadi—by dreaming "I am free!"—got loose and turned the guard into a rooster. "Wanadi's gone!" the rooster crowed. Returning, the soldiers couldn't figure it out.

They searched and found Attawanadi at his home on Kushamakari. They now had gunpowder, mountains of it, but he blew on it, and it turned into a cloud. Though surrounded, by dreaming he turned the soldiers into pigs, cattle, and horses. That is where all those began. A few, however, escaped and caught him by surprise. Then their priests arrived, the padres.

"Who are you?" the padres asked. "Where do you come from? Who is your father?" "I am Wanadi," Attawanadi replied. "My father is Wanadi, and I come from the highest sky." "You lie," they said. "You are Odosha." They began whipping him with vines. "Whose village is this? Whose house? Whose earth?" "All mine," Attawanadi said. "I made it all. I made you!"

So they sent for a post in the form of a cross. A cross: that is what they called it. They nailed him to it with iron spikes, and again set the rooster to watch. At dawn he crowed, "Wanadi's gone!" They arrived and saw the body hanging. "Here he is!" they cried. But the rooster continued to crow, "He's gone! Wanadi's gone!" Three times he crowed. "Shut up!" the soldiers yelled. "He's here! You're a worthless watch."

The body was like a corpse. It was, however, a trick. He had withdrawn his Emanation. The rooster knew that, the padres and the soldiers didn't. "We killed him," they said. "He was Odosha, not Wanadi." And they kept the cross as a reminder. They like to make crosses to show people. "On this post," they say, "he died." They didn't know, and they still don't know. They were tricked. Attawanadi got away.[15]

Wanadi's Farewell

When Wanadi, at the rapids of Kunukunuma, said goodbye to the So'to, he first spoke, then made a feast. They danced, drank, and sang for three days. "I am going," he said, "going back to the sky. Odosha has made himself master of the earth. There is war, sickness, death, every kind of evil. But I shall come back, Odosha will die, and this present earth will no longer exist. The sun, moon, stars, and all are going to fall to the earth, and you will then see the True Sky, as it was in the beginning. Wanadi's light will again be seen, and I shall return as a new Emanation, the new Wanadi of the new earth, myself again, with another body.

"You are all now going to die, as I did in Caracas. But it will not be real, only a trick for Odosha. In my Sky Place your food and houses are awaiting you. It will be only your bodies that die. Your eternal spirit-doubles will depart through the Heaven-door. They will ask its Keeper—the Scissors Master—for allowance to pass, and the good he will let go by. These will climb by many ladders to their houses in the Sky. But the bad will be sliced to bits in the door and, falling back down to earth, will remain forever with Odosha—to die with him when the world ends.

"In my Sky Place there are no wars, only peace, food, and happiness; no sickness or disease; life never ends and there is no night."

Then he turned and spoke separately to the twelve who had been living with him at the place of Wade, the sloth. "I can't take you all to Heaven," he said. "You will remain on earth for now. But I have made for you another house, the New Kushamakari, in which to wait for me. The light from Heaven shines there, Odosha can't get in. I shall come for you when I return."

The twelve went off to hide in Kushamakari at the Duida, there to wait for the end of the world. We can see the mountain, but not their house. There are guards hidden along the way, and a giant bat that lives in a cave. Shamans, yes, they can see the house. They go right up to the door, and speaking through it to its people, tell them all about us and ask for power, health, food, and wisdom.[16]

469. A Yekuana woman, carrying in her arms a child and bearing a *wuwa* filled with yuca grown in the Conuco, returns to her village.

470. Yekuana dancers, wearing skirts made of cokerite palm, sing *Wasai yadi ademi hidi*, the Watunna (taking two to three days to sing) that welcomes back a group of travelers gone from the village for a long period of time.[54]

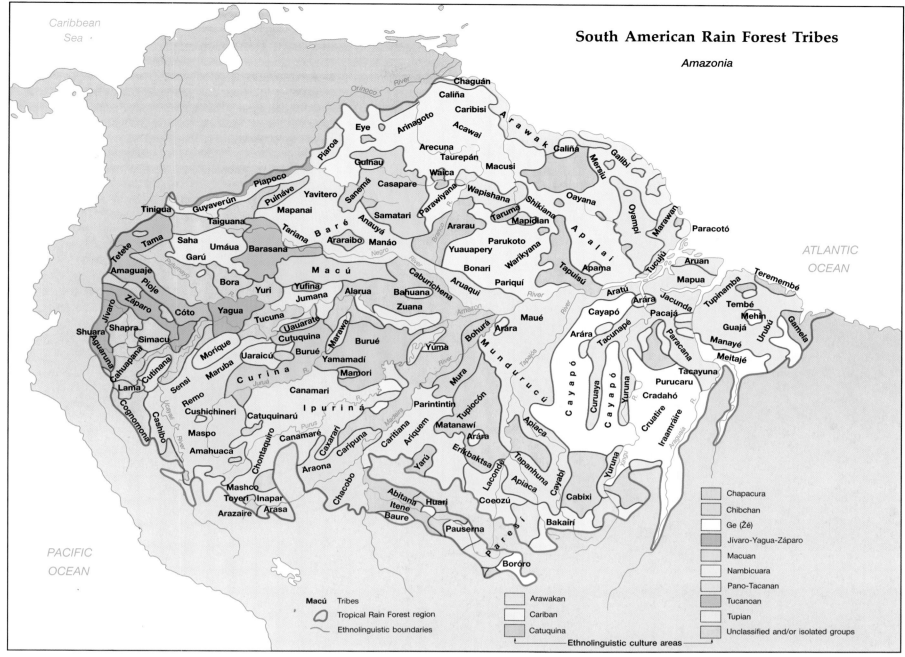

South American Rain Forest Tribes

Amazonia

Caribbean Sea

ATLANTIC OCEAN

PACIFIC OCEAN

Chaguán
Caliña
Caribisi
Acawai
Eye
Arinagoto
Arecuna
Taurepán
Piaroa
Guinau
Macusi
Caliñá
Galibi
Mersiu
Piapoco
Yavitero
Casapare
Parawiyana
Wapishana
Shikiana
Oayana
Oyampi
Marawan
Guyaverún
Puináve
Mapanai
Samatari
Anauyá
Tarumá
Mapidian
Apalai
Tinigua
Taiguana
Tariana
Baré
Ararau
Yuauapery
Parukoto
Warikyana
Tapuisú
Tucujú
Paracotó
Saha
Umáua
Barasaná
Araraibo
Manáo
Manáo
Bonari
Aruaqui
Pariquí
Aruan
Mapua
Tetete
Tama
Garú
Macú
Caburichena
River
Amaguaje
Pioje
Bora
Yuri
Yufina
Jumana
Alarua
Bahuana
Zuana
Amazon
Maué
Aratú
Cayapó
Arará
Jacunda
Tupinamba
Teremembé
Záparo
Cóto
Yagua
Tucuna
Uauaraté
Marawa
Burué
Yúma
Bohurá
Arára
Tacunapé
Pacajá
Paracana
Tembé
Mehin
Guajá
Shuara
Shapra
Simacu
Morique
Cutuquina
Burué
Yamamadí
Mamori
Mura
Munducurú
Arára
Cayapó
Curuaya
Cayapó
Yuruna
Purucaru
Cradahó
Tacayuna
Manayé
Meitajé
Urubú
Gamela
Aguaruna
Cahuapana
Cutinana
Sensi
Remo
Maruba
Uaraicú
Curina
Canamari
Ipuriná
Parintintin
Tupiocón
Apiaça
Cruatire
Iraamáire
Cognomona
Lama
Castibo
Cushichineri
Catuquinarú
Cexararí
Caripuna
Cariñana
Ariquem
Matanawí
Arára
Erikbaktsa
Tapanhuna
Cayabí
Yuruna
Maspo
Amahuaca
Chontaquiro
Canamaré
Araona
Yarú
Laconde
Apiaça
Cabixi
Mashco
Toyeri
Inapar
Arasa
Arazaire
Chacobo
Abitana
Itene
Baure
Huari
Coeozú
Bakairí
Pauserna
Paresí
Boróro

Legend

Macú — Tribes
Tropical Rain Forest region
Ethnolinguistic boundaries

Arawakan
Cariban
Catuquina

Chapacura
Chibchan
Ge (Žé)
Jívaro-Yagua-Záparo
Macuan
Nambicuara
Pano-Tacanan
Tucanoan
Tupian
Unclassified and/or isolated groups

Ethnolinguistic culture areas

Map 37.

471. A sequence of sketches, first reproduced (1557) in *Warhaftige Historia und beschreibung eyner lantschaff der Wilnen / Nacketen / Grimmigen Menschen fresser Leuthen / in der Newenwelt America Gelegen....Da sie Hans Staden von Homberg aus Hessen durch sein eygne erfarung erkant....,* depicting an island settlement (**a**) of Tupinambá, who, engaging in constant intertribal warfare, attack a neighboring palisaded village (**b**) to gather the captives—one such newly-captured prisoner is here pictured (**c**), dancing, surrounded by celebrating women—that they needed for their elaborate ceremonials, during which the hapless victims were clubbed to death and eaten (**d**–**e**) amidst much frenzied drinking, singing, and dancing.

Possessed of religious and social values centered upon such continuous internecine fighting and ritualistic cannibalism, the Tupinambá—the collective name of all Tupian-speaking South American Indians, including those groups of slash-and-burn farmers, river people, and coastal navigators known individually as the Potiguara, Caeté, Tupinikin, Tupinambá, and Guarani—were the sixteenth-century masters of a domain that included the entire Brazilian seacoast, from the mouth of the Amazon River in the north all the way south to Porto Alegre, as well as a substantial portion of the adjacent interior.

472. Employing a hunting technique common to many of the protohistorical peoples inhabiting the various tropical forests ranged throughout the equatorial belt, a Hoti Indian in the Guana Highlands (Venezuela) uses an enormous blowgun and a tiny poisoned dart to fell his treetop prey.

The Desana Creation Myth

The Sun Father's Intention

In the beginning, the Sun Father, Creator of all things—who is not the daily sun that is seen passing overhead, but an eternal yellow light, invisible to physical eyes—produced the universe, not by any act or word, but by mere purpose or intention; and the rays of this "yellow purpose" or "intention" now penetrate and sustain all things, both visible and invisible, in a universe of three levels. The middle level is of this earth and of the color red. Below is a "River of Milk," bathed in a pale green light, the color of coca leaves, while above is a level of two distinct zones: one white, yellow, and orange, of the visible sun and moon; the other blue, of the Milky Way.

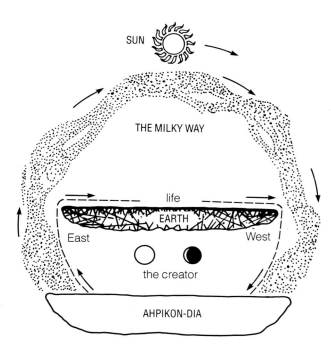

473. Graphic representation of the structure of the Desana cosmos.

This Milky Way is described as an immense and dangerous river, seething with the seeds of life, but also with putrefaction, vomit, and disease. It takes its rise from the River of Milk and arches overhead, flowing from east to west, tossed by the winds of the high heavens. Known as "Wind Current," this high zone is that to which people are carried in vision by hallucinogenic drugs, the most important of which is a powder, sniffed through the nose, prepared from a vine known as *vihó* (from the verb *vihíri*, "to inhale, to absorb"). Vihó Man is its guardian, himself in a state of perpetual trance. His dwelling is the Milky Way. And it is to him that shamans address themselves, to be brought through him, in his meditation, into visionary touch with the other great invisibles. For the Milky Way is the place of meeting and communication between supernatural and earthly beings.[17]

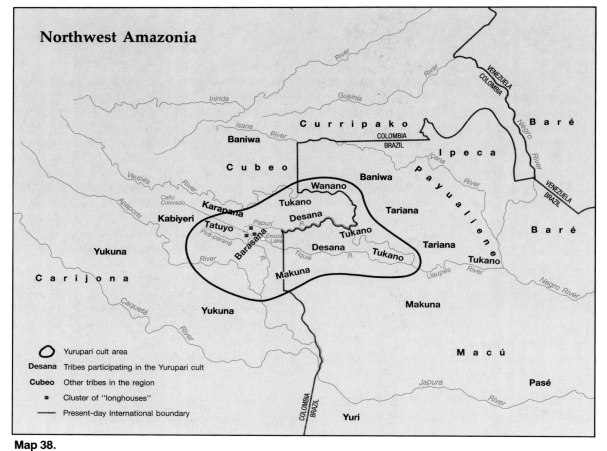

Northwest Amazonia

○ Yurupari cult area
Desana Tribes participating in the Yurupari cult
Cubeo Other tribes in the region
■ Cluster of "longhouses"
— Present-day International boundary

Map 38.

The Maternal Snake Canoe

The coming of mankind to inhabit the middle level of the universe was a paramount feature of the Sun Father's first intention. He produced in the River of Milk an ancestral male of each of the many tribes of the Vaupés region and appointed for them a spiritual guide named "Fermentation Man" or "Flowing Forth [Ejaculating] Man" to conduct them to this earth. They were brought in a live Snake Canoe, named "Fermentation Placenta," painted yellow on the outside with a long black strip along its back and black diamonds along the sides, but inside, red, where the people sat. And whenever they came to rapids (there were many on the long journey), the waters rose and they passed over. At Ipanoré, on the Vaupés River, however, the Snake Canoe struck a rock and the people scattered forth through an opening at the prow.

All human beings are connected in their lives by an invisible umbilical cord that runs back through the rivers to the cosmic womb in the River of Milk, and the Snake Canoe that traced the journey is the sign of that connection.

When the people had dispersed, each went to the place to which Fermentation Man had assigned him, and to each there had been given, also, the token of an assigned manner of life: a bow and arrow to the Desana; fishing gear to the Tukano, Pira-Tapuya, Vaiyára, and Neéroa; a manioc grater to the Kuripáko; and to the primitive Makú, a blowgun and a basket.[18]

The peoples of this northwest Amazonian rain forest are of greatly differing culture stages intermixed: foragers, hunters, fishers, and horticulturalists, with significant influences, also, from the civilizations of the Andes. And the mythologies, accordingly, are composite as well. The Desana, for example, take pride in themselves as hunters; yet fishing and horticulture contribute greatly more than the hunt to their economy; and although the Old Stone Age mythic figure of the Animal Master looms large in their rites and thinking, the structuring energies of their universe are mixed of female and male aspects, with their only culture heroes, two females: (1) a Melusine-like water spirit and ancestress, known as The Daughter of the Aracú fish (an important species of food fish in the riverine economies of the Amazon), and (2) The Daughter of the Sun.

474. This tree lizard (*Plica plica* L.), although rare, is the principal manifestation of *Vaí-mahsë* (*vaí*, "fish"), the Desana "Master of Animals," who, when he thus appears, "tries to bite menstruating or pregnant women or to whip them with his long tail that, like the arm of payé, contains magical splinters and thorns that he can shoot out to cause sickness. For the men, however," Gerardo Reichel-Dolmatoff continues, "his manifestation as a lizard represents no danger but is rather a sign of friendship and protection."[55]

The Daughter of the Sun

The Daughter of the Sun [vaguely, of the Sun Father, as well as of the visible sun] had not reached puberty when her father lay with her at Wainambí Rapids, violating thus, his own first law, against incest. Then the Moon, his twin brother, becoming jealous, tried to seduce her, and the Sun, in revenge, removed from him his feather crown, thus reducing his light. All of which so upset the Moon that for the next three nights he hid his light entirely; and this he continues to do, every month. He is obsessed, furthermore, with sex and at night descends in the form of a man to cohabit with women in their sleep. It is said that he even opens graves to violate and to eat the dead. The stain of the menstrual blood of the Daughter of the Sun remains marked upon his features.

But the Moon also has beneficent powers. Dew, which is called the "saliva of the moon," influences the growth of plants and the gestation of pregnant women. Magical herbs are under his influence, and since many are used in love potions, his fascination with sex is evident even here. His cycle coincides with the cycle of women, whose loss every month of menstrual blood is in memory of the blood lost by the Daughter of the Sun when she lay with her father at Wainambí Rapids.

It is said that she remained with him thereafter as his wife, but thought so much about sex that she became thin, ugly, and lifeless. During her next menstruation, the sex act hurt, and she no longer wanted even to eat. Where she lay dying on a boulder at Wainambí rapids, her imprint can still be seen. But then the Sun, her father, performed for her the invocation to be used when girls attain puberty. Chanting and puffing tobacco, he thus revived her.[19]

475. Standing at the approximate spot where the Pira-piraná river crosses the Equator, this petroglyph illustrates an episode in Tukano mythology.

476.

The Coming of Night

In the beginning there was no night, only the yellow light of the Sun Father's intention. When the people set forth in their Snake Canoe, however, the Sun gave to each something to carry, and to one, a small black purse, tightly closed. The journey being long, this keeper of the purse became curious. He opened it, and out swarmed such a multitude of black ants that their number obscured the Sun Father's light, and that was the First Night. Fermentation Man tried to correct things by giving to each a firefly; but this light was weak and the ants continued to pour forth. The people implored them to go back into their purse, but in vain. Then the Sun Father himself came down with a stick with which to beat the purse, and this compelled them to return—but not all. Those refusing remained in the forest, and from that time there have been ants and anthills.

The First Night is known as the "Night of the Ant," and the man who opened the purse, as "Man of the Night."[20]

Supernaturals

Among the supernaturals put forth in the beginning as intermediaries between the Sun Father and this earth were, first, in the sky, the Beings of Day, in charge of the spiritual development of mankind; next, in the rivers, the Beings of Blood, representing the rules of physical health and the good life; in the Milky Way, Vihó Man, who, is mixed of negatives and positives, being a master of disease and witchcraft, no less than of visionary inspirations; and in the dark region beyond the most distant west, the Night People of sorcery and witchcraft, there established to be the punishers of all who disregard tribal custom. An Owner of Thatch is in charge of palm leaves for the roofing of malocas, and in the wilderness are two Animal Masters: one for the forest beasts, the other for the fish, the first residing in a large maloca within certain forested rocky hills, the other in such a maloca beneath the waters of the rapids. And then finally, there is the Jaguar, whose color is the very yellow of the Sun Father's intention, whose roar is as the voice of the Sun Father, heard in thunder, and whose presence on earth is as the Father's security watch.[21]

The visible sun and moon, meanwhile, rotating in their courses, far above the Milky Way, are brothers (whether twins or not is unclear), representing in our visible world two aspects of the original "yellow intention." "The moon," states Reichel-Dolmatoff, in interpretation of this brother pair, "is called *nyamí abé*, or 'nocturnal sun,' a name that clearly suggests that, basically two aspects of the same thing are involved. The moon is part of the Sun, a negative, evil part."[22]

But there is mention, also, in this mythology of an invisible Moon, of which the visible one is representative; and this can only mean that, although the "yellow purpose" or "intention," of which this world is a reflex, is in its origin transcendent of duality, in its effects and operation in space and time—whether visibly or invisibly—it is dual: not only evil and good, but also dark and light, creative and destructive, female and male (compare II.1:**81**).

341

The First Maloca

The Sun caused the first maloca to be built at the place now called Wainambí, ordering the Beings of Day, the Beings of Blood, and Vihó Man to instruct the people in the art of building homes. Vihó Man, however, brought sorcery and sickness, which hid in the cracks and crannies of the houseposts. He also persuaded the eagles that were sitting in the trees about the big maloca, chewing coca (so that their beaks were flecked with white), to set nets to entrap the people. The Beings of Blood, however, contrived to entrap the eagles themselves, wrapped them in their own nets and threw them into the Milky Way, where they became transformed into the beneficent protectors of malocas that they are today. Moreover, the people at the time were taught protective invocations; also, the art of setting up invisible protective enclosures around their malocas, and invisible nets at their doors.[23]

The Daughter of the Aracú Fish

At that time there were only men. The animals and the fish had wives; so too, the Master of Fish. But none of the company of the Snake Canoe had yet a wife to beget descendants.

The men, one night, were feasting and dancing, when the daughter of one of the wives of the Master of Fish, an aracú fish, saw the yellow light of their fire and, coming out of the river to watch them all, fell in love with the Desana. He gave her honey to eat and she remained with him. One can still see the imprint on the rock of her buttocks where she lay with him. Sons and daughters were then born to them, and these were the first sib of the Desana tribe.

But at that time the invocations to be recited when a woman gives birth were unknown. As a consequence, when the Daughter of Aracú bore her first child, the scorpion and a large black ant, who were watching, licked the blood, and their sting now makes one vomit and feel pain like the pains of childbirth. The stingray ate the placenta, and its sting, too, produces pain. The centipede and a large black spider licked the blood, and they now look like the umbilical cord and vagina. The bat, formerly a bird, became as now, a thing of filth. While the woman herself, who had been afraid to go to the river to bathe because of all the animals that were there, became covered with lice. A bird who noticed her in this condition sang: "This lazy woman! She perhaps doesn't know about invocations." Hearing that, the Daughter of Aracú invented, then and there, the invocations for the ritual bath following childbirth.

Moreover, it was this Daughter of Aracú who planted the first garden. She planted manioc, which she had brought from the underwater malocas of the Aracú; and when these people saw her washing their manioc tubers in the river, they tried to carry them off, but failed. She not only washed the roots, but also invented the long tube through which the manioc has to be squeezed to remove its poison.

Others declare that when the Daughter of the Aracú Fish gave birth to her first child, she took it to the river to bathe, and that the fish, recognizing the babe as one of their kin, came and rubbed themselves against it. The mother then

went to work in her garden, and the infant's father, noticing the congregation of fish at the place of his child's bathing, took his bow and arrow and killed them. When the mother returned and saw all her relatives dead, weeping she carried them back to the water, went into it herself, and never again was seen.[24]

478. A *tipití* (see **464**) is used to extract prussic acid from bitter manioc (*dëhkë*), the staple crop of the Desana, who, Reichel-Dolmatoff notes, distinguish "*boréka dëhkë*—according to myth, it is related to the sib *boréka*; starchy manioc, *bo'o dëhkë*, also having a mythological origin; white manioc (*boréri dëhkë*); yellow manioc (*diári dëhkë*); and one kind called *nopára*, said to have been introduced from the territory of the Karihóna Indians."[56]

The Great Flood

When everything had been created, the world began to be filled with plagues and monsters. No one knows why. Kidnappers and ravishers appeared in the guise of friends along the trails, carried off women and raped them. Others, like large horseflies, brought terror and disease, the hum of their wings being like the sound of a bull-roarer, whose voice is the sound of the radiance of the Sun.

The Sun took note of this situation and, deciding to assume charge, ordered, first, a great flood, and the monsters drowned; then a great drought, and everything caught fire. The armadillo's once fluffy tail was burned off and only one little bird was saved. That was 250 years ago. But in time, life returned, renewed.[25]

477. Derived from yagé-induced hallucinations, the design painted on the front of this maloca, situated on the Pirá-piraná river, depicts the Master of Animals amid a series of abstract symbols.

The First Death

The Sun then sent his Daughter to the earth to teach the people how to live. And what she taught them was, to make pottery, to use baskets, to eat fish and certain wild fruits, and to make fire with fire sticks. The first death in the world was of one of her sons, of which there were two, both apprenticed to become shamans. One was doing very well, but the other, because he was always thinking of women, declined in health and died. His copper earrings had turned, so that their concave parts faced inward, and that was an ominous sign. When he died, the Daughter of the Sun taught the people proper burial rites, after which she departed, returning to the River of Milk, out of which she had appeared. The grave in which the body is buried is the womb to which the corporeal part returns, while the womb to which the part that is spiritual goes is the womb of the River of Milk.[26]

Origin of the Yagé Vine and Coca Plant

When one of the daughters of the Animal Master was pregnant with the pain of childbirth she went to the river shore and lay twisting in anguish. An old Desana woman, wishing to help her, took her hand, but with the writhing, one of her fingers broke off. The old woman kept it in her household, but a young man stole it, buried it, and there grew from it the hallucinogenic yagé vine [*Banisteriopsis caapi*].

A second daughter of the same Animal Master, writhing on the shore in the same condition, was likewise helped by an old woman. Again a finger broke off, which the woman buried, and from this there grew the coca plant.[27]

479. A Tukano woman mixes coarse manioc flour (*pogá*). Other by-products of manioc production are starch (*verá*), tapioca (*bo'óru*), the squeezed-off liquid (*nyohká*), and the leftover scraps (*pulí*).

The Hallucinogenic Voyage

The ceremonial imbibing of an infusion of yagé (Desana, *gahpí*) is known as *gahpí irí-inyári*, from *irí*, "to drink," and *inyári*, "to see." It is experienced as a visionary journey, back along the riverway of the original maternal Snake Canoe to the River of Milk, whence all have come. The participants in the rite, sitting in the center of the maloca, are adult males exclusively, being guided on their visionary way by the voice of a holy man, or Sun priest (*kumú*), who interprets to them the shared vision as it unfolds its revelation. At the rear of the building are the women, who are not allowed to drink yagé, yet play an important part in the ceremony. "Drink, drink!" they sing. "This is why we were born. Drink, drink! For this is our task. By drinking they will come to know the traditions of their fathers. By drinking, they will be brave. We are to help them."

The hallucinogenic liquid is kept in a special pottery vessel (see Figure 481) manufactured by an old woman, who, before firing it, polishes the surface with a very hard and smooth yellowish stone. The vessel is of three parts: a yellow base, red body, and blue top, with the globular red body bearing white and yellow designs, such as adorned the Snake Canoe. As Reichel-Dol-

480. A Tatuyo Indian displays the hollow dancing staffs used during ceremonial gatherings.

matoff was told by Antonio Guzmán, his Desana Indian interpreter and informant:

As mankind arrived in this world in the Snake Canoe, so will it now undertake the journey of the return.[28] One of the men dips from the vessel a small cupful of the liquid and, repeating rapidly, "*Ma, ma, ma!*" [Take, take, take!], carries it to the others, who, while in silence drinking, smoke tobacco to enhance the hallucinations. The kumú, in a loud voice, then declares: "I am the central person, the only one left. Therefore, I am to teach you." And in a hypnotic tone, with great precision, he begins explaining and directing the voyage.[29]

During the first moments, there is talking, a general questioning of the kumú, with him in turn inquiring of each concerning the clarity of his visions. Some may see only lights and, feeling nauseated, withdraw, to the deprecating laughter of the women, who continue with their insistent chant: "Drink, drink, drink!" Those remaining are experiencing a violent current of air, as though of a strong wind bearing them away. That—as the kumú explains—is the Wind Current of the Milky Way, mixed of vomit and disease, together with the seeds of life. They begin descending toward the River of Milk. Walls of fluttering, floating cloth enfold them. Lights appear, growing stronger, which become a moving, luminous mass. When the plunge occurs into the River of Milk, shapes of differing colors, moving, changing in size, come into view. These—the kumú's voice is telling—are the forms of the Beings of Blood, the Beings of Day, Vihó Man, the Daughter of the Aracú Fish and Daughter of the Sun. The sound of the kumú's stick-rattle is heard as the voice of the Sun. The light is seen of the Yellow Intention. A distant music is heard, and the buzz of a hummingbird's wings, as it moves from flower to flower, sucking honey. All the figures of myth and the mysteries of nature appear: the Animal Master in his house within the rocky hills; the Yellow Squirrel, representative of the Sun's generative power, its rodent teeth a magical force that gnaws and penetrates; the Cock-of-the-Rock, who stands watch before the dancing grounds of the forest herds....

For a blessed time—perhaps half an hour—the canoe company, in silent rapture, floating in the River of Milk, participates in the experience of the first things of the universe. The earth plane, viewed from below in this way, is transparent, like a large, extended cobweb with the light of the sun shining through. Its threads are the rules men live by. Toward the sunrise there is a vast lake, into which are pouring all the rivers of the earth, and in the west, where the sun sets, is the dark place of the Night People of sorcery and disease. The River of Milk itself is "Paradise" [*ahpikondiá*]. And as the canoe company rests there, at the Alpha and Omega, the beginning and the goal, they are at peace.

But then the images fade. A music can still be heard in the distance, but the forms, the colors, and the movements are no more. The trance dissolves, and the men are sitting around, conversing and drinking chicha. They have beheld the web of the laws of life, the light of the Sun Father's Intention; the chanting of the women has ceased; they have voyaged far and well.[30]

481. One of the special tripartite pottery vessels in which the Desana keep yagé, the hallucinogenic infusion that induces their visionary revelations.

Sun Priest (Kumú) and Shaman (Payé)

The character of the holy man, or Sun-priest (kumú)—whose role as conductor of this spiritual voyage to Ahpikondiá corresponds precisely to that of the Huichol *mara'akame* on the geographically simulated voyage to Wirikuta (above, pages 294–299)—is of the greatest importance to the spiritually grounded architecture of Desana life. Figure 482 shows the manner of organization of the inhabitants of a Desana communal dwelling. The roof-beam (gumú) is likened both to the Sun-priest (kumú) in the structure of the society and to the Sun Father himself and his light in the structure of the cosmos. For, as Reichel-Dolmatoff learned, "the maloca is the uterus of the sib and as such its structure corresponds to that of the Cosmos."[31] By analogy, the cosmos, then, is the uterus of all things, and as the Sun Father's Yellow Intention is the supporting principle of the cosmos, so is the roof beam, of the house. Its name, *gumú*, is recognized as equivalent to *kumú*. Moreover: "Although it is laid horizontally, it has the meaning of a 'ladder' that penetrates the cosmic levels and forms an axis."[32] Compare the archetype of the pole, or ladder, up which the Siberian shaman ascends (I.2:172).

"According to tradition," states Reichel-Dolmatoff, "the office of the kumú was created by the Sun Father who determined that these men should be called upon to perpetuate moral teachings in the highest ethical sense."[33] The kumú identifies himself with the function of the roof beam, gumú, and through his identification with the role of the Sun and transmission of tradition gives stability to his society. It seems that the office is hereditary, transmitted from father to son. The apprenticeship lasts several years, and in it are emphasized the interpretation of images produced by the drug, yagé, the giving of constructive advice, and the power of conviction in the settling of social conflicts. The kumú's province is of wisdom and meditation.

"Generally speaking," Reichel-Dolmatoff reports, "a kumú does not live in the maloca of his group but occupies an isolated dwelling with his nuclear family. There he receives visits from people who resort to him; he may also take part in certain collective rituals, celebrated in the malocas of the different sibs of the neighborhood. On these occasions the kumú occupies an important and highly respected position. When officiating the kumú puts on a red skirt-like garment of barkcloth decorated with short feathers. On his head he wears a feather crown different from those used in dances; the feathers are short and white, rising horizontally from their ring-shaped base. On his arms he wears several wide bands woven of very fine fibers, adorned with feathers and with

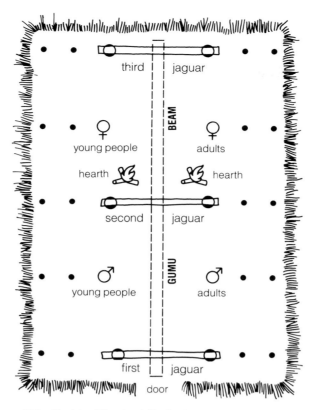

482. Sketch of the ritual distribution of a maloca.

483. This Tukano man proudly wears a necklace of jaguar teeth and a polished quartz cylinder.

interwoven diamond motifs. Hanging from his left elbow he wears a large black palm seed in which he keeps some little red and white feathers as well as a red pigment to paint his face. This adornment is the exclusive privilege of the kumú and publicly represents his authority; a cylinder of quartz hung from his neck complements this costume.

"Although the kumú occasionally intervenes in some rites of the life cycle, his main function consists of pronouncing the *go'a-mëë bayari*, the 'songs of god,' that are sometimes sung on the occasion of large gatherings when gifts of food are distributed between phratries. During these ceremonies, which may last for two or three days, people bring quantities of smoked fish or wild fruits that the kumú receives and keeps in his house.

"After having recited invocations to the Sun, offering him these foods, he distributes them among the participants in the gathering. This ceremonial distribution is called *abé kóa*/sun-gourd bowl, and the food is interpreted as consecrated, coming directly from the divinity. This ceremony generally takes place at the end of the first rainy season, between May and June, and begins at dawn. The kumú faces east to greet the rising sun. Because at this time of the year the fish begin to run, and it is also the time in which the new planting is begun in the fields, the main objective of this ceremony is to ask the Sun for abundance and the fostering of growth.

"On the occasion of these rites the kumú sometimes uses a small altar-like object that consists of a woven box of the leaves of a certain palm. The box is called *go'á-mëë komóro*/god's chest, and in it the kumú keeps his ritual objects. Among these objects there are several anthropomorphic figurines of wood some twenty centimeters in height that represent the Sun, the Daughter of the Sun, and *Emë kóri-mahsë* [the Being of Day]. These figurines are made by the kumú himself or by some youth who is still unmarried and has not yet had sexual relations. It is also said that in the past these figurines were made of stone and were carved with sandstone tools of a white color that were extracted from a lagoon located near a rapids on the Mihpinya, a tributary of the Macú-paraná. For the invocation of the Sun, the kumú places his little figurines on the box and then dances in a circle around them. During this dance he marks the beat with a stomping tube decorated with two black stripes and a series of triangles, representing the designs of the Snake-Canoe.

"On a much higher level than the payé [the shaman, see below], the kumú is a luminous personage who has an interior light, a brilliant flame that shines and unveils the intimate thoughts of all people who speak to him. His power and his wisdom are always compared to an intense light that is invisible but perceptible through its effects. The manifestation of this luminous energy is the 'penetrating glance' that is attributed to the kumú, his capacity of fathoming the psyche of a person and of thus knowing his intimate motivations. From time to time the kumú summons a person who has not lived according to the traditional norms, and on other occasions he is approached spontaneously to discuss some personal problem. The dialogue which then develops has the character of a confession. It is here that a concept called *penyóri* enters. This word is derived from *peri*/to hear, and *nyóri* that designates the effect of the 'penetrating glance.' *Nyóri* is the impact that the words of the kumú make, the sudden insight that then leads to comprehension." As explained by Antonio Guzmán, Reichel-Dolmatoff's interpreter and informant:

"The entire conversation is directed to *Ahpikondiá*. When concentrating (*pepiri*) in this manner, one sees, one is there." And again: "After conversing in this way with the kumú, one goes away relieved."[34]

I have quoted this passage at length for the clarity of its exposition of the role and character of the Desana Sun-priest (*kumú*), as distinguished from the shaman (*payé*). Between the two, according to Guzmán, the relations generally are of mutual respect, since they represent distinct structuring functions in the architecture of Desana life, much as, in the structure of the maloca, the function of the roof beam (*gumú*) is distinct from that of the cross beams, known as "jaguars," which is a term that is applied, also, to the payé.

"The most important part of the structure," states our author in discussion of the maloca, "is formed by the 'three red jaguars,' represented by three pairs of large forked posts and their respective beams, located at the two extremes and in the center of the building. These three 'jaguars,' which are sometimes painted red and adorned with black spots, are interpreted as the guardians and the most important fecundating forces of the dwelling; they 'cover' (*bëári*) the occupants."[35]

The jaguars are grounded, we observe, on the earth, whereas the roof beam (*gumú*), which rests upon them, hangs, as its were, in space. Comparably, the efforts of the shaman, the payé, are dedicated to the earthly, economic concerns of the inhabitants of the maloca, while the Sun-priest, the kumú, is concerned chiefly with their spiritual well-being. And although the latter does, indeed, officiate in the fertility ceremony of food distribution, just described, its form, as Reichel-Dolmatoff points out, "is far removed from the crude sexual symbolism that characterizes other ritual activities, and it is evident that what is involved is a true cult in which the problem of mere earthly existence has been sublimated."[36]

In that author's view, the historic background of the Sun-priest tradition is to be sought in the "sub-Andean priest-temple-idol complex"[37] of the South American Formative Culture Stage; whereas the role, in contrast, of the shaman is of an old, hunting and gathering, Paleolithic tradition, modified and adapted to the circumstances of a settled, village style of existence. According to our author:

"In order to become a payé an individual must have demonstrated since childhood a profound interest in the religious traditions of his culture besides having a good knowledge of myths, genealogies, and invocations. He must know how 'to sit on his bench' and reflect; he must practice sexual abstinence, and he must also be a good drinker of chicha, a good dancer and singer, and he must be able to give sound advice to others. He should not be too fond of women, and he must channel his sexual

484. This remarkable photograph, taken (1928) at an unspecified location in the Brazilian Amazon, records an interval in a Yurupari initiation rite. The identity of the celebrants is no longer known.

energy toward other goals; however, he should be a family man. The most necessary quality is that he have the capacity to achieve well-defined hallucinations when he takes a concoction, and to be able to interpret them. Also, in the learning of myths and traditions what is involved is not so much a good memory but a capacity for interpreting their symbolism, and of 'hearing the echo' of the tales told by tradition.

"It is at about twenty-five years of age that a person begins to show these qualities, and it is then that formal training is begun. The office of the payé is not hereditary but depends on personality type, recognized early in childhood by other members of the group, observed and evaluated in detail, and, from that time on, fostered by the older men."[38]

"In Desana the payé is called *ye'e*, a word that also means jaguar and, in effect, the payé is said to be able to change himself into this feline. The word is derived from *ye'éri*/to cohabit, *ye'éru*/penis, and the payé is thus a phallic instrument that intervenes with its power (*ye'e tulári*) directly in the process of biocosmic procreation. His characteristic attributes are also phallic; in the first place we have the stick-rattle (*ye'egë*), the payé's staff of command and his 'voice.' The payé also possesses the phallic weapon, the ceremonial hoe. The cylinder of quartz that every payé carries is called *abé ye'éru*/penis of the Sun Father, and represents semen. Lightning, besides its luminous aspect, is produced when a payé casts his quartz and is in itself a symbol of fertilization. When lightning strikes nearby, the payé goes to the spot to collect from the ground fragments of quartz because these particles are a very dangerous seminal matter and have to be neutralized. The gourd rattle that the payé uses in his rituals is called *nyahsáru*, a word derived from *nyahsá*/a white ant that stings; allusion is

made to the swiftness with which these insects disperse when their nests are touched, the same swiftness with which the noise of the rattle spreads. The rattle is a prolongation of the payé's arm, and the dry seeds that produce the sound represent the movement of the splinters [or thorns of the *macana* palm that the payé is supposed to carry] locked up in his arm. When he shakes the gourd rattle these splinters are shaken toward the victim. The splinters or thorns are always imagined to be carried in the left forearm because otherwise any blow the payé might strike with his right hand, perhaps during an unimportant quarrel, would be fatal. The left side is always associated with death and the forces of evil.

"In order to establish contact with supernatural beings, the payé uses the hallucinogenic powder of *vihó*....The ability to have visions by means of *vihó* and the power of establishing this contact determine the potential capacity of a payé. A payé ought to view the Milky Way as a road, the hills and pools as malocas, and animals as persons. Those who do not react in this manner to the hallucinogenic drug see only clouds and stones, and 'the birds laugh at them.' In their trance they tear off their loincloths and walk around naked, without shame; they even urinate or defecate in public. But others, the truly experienced payés, control these impulses; they are transported to the Milky Way or to the 'houses' of the hills or the waters, and there they talk and negotiate with the beings occupying these places. Then they return and rejoin their bodies that meanwhile have remained in their hammocks as if asleep."[39]

The Animal Master: His Malocas in the Hills

The principal task of the payé is to visit the abode of the Animal Master (*Vaí-mahsë*), there to negotiate for a certain number of game animals to be killed in exchange for the deaths of an equivalent number of human beings, whose souls would be then reincarnated, not in the usual way, as hummingbirds, but as game animals in replenishment of those the hunters would have killed.[40] The Animal Master is a mercurial figure, described generally as a dwarf with body painted red and covered with the juices of magical plants, by whose strong odor his presence can be known. He appears also in the form of a small lizard that is quite rare and lives in dry clearings at the foot of large rocks. In this aspect he likes to bite menstruating or pregnant women, or to whip them with his long tail, which, like the left arm of a payé, contains splinters and thorns that shoot out and cause sickness. *Vaí-mahsë*, his name, is derived from *vaí*, meaning "fish," but is applied to the Master of Animals as well as to the Master of Fish, who fundamentally are of one being, though in two functions, each dwelling with his charges. As described in Reichel-Dolmatoff's *Amazonian Cosmos:*

"In the rain forests of the Vaupés there exist, here and there, rock formations that stand out like dark islands on the horizon. These isolated hills or ridges often have steep walls and flat, mesa-like plateaus and are full of caverns and dark recesses. These uncanny places are the dwellings of *Vaí-mahsë*, where, surrounded by his animals, he dominates the forest. The rapids of the rivers, where the torrents pass between huge rocks and form deep whirlpools, are the dwelling places of *Vaí-mahsë* as protector of fish. Both places are imagined as large malocas regardless of whether they are in the hills or under the water; there the creatures live and thence they go forth to the forest or to the river.

"These 'houses of the hills' or 'houses of the waters' are sacred and dangerous places. The rapids are, of course, unavoidable passes for the traveler and are navigated in silence, but the hills of the forest are avoided at all times. Besides being the places where the animals live, the houses of the hills also contain illness, and their dark and inhospitable aspect indicates this danger. The cracks, caverns, and tunnels are the entrances to the interior of the hills, to the great malocas of the animals. There, within their dark interior, the gigantic prototypes of each species exist, and thousands of animals are kept—deer, tapirs, peccaries, monkeys, rodents, and many more, in a great community similar to that of human beings."[41]

The Animal Master is not only the guard-ian of the animals of his maloca, but also their procreator, a personification of their sexual life. And yet, at the same time, he is the patron of hunters and a hunter himself. His weapon is a short red wand, highly polished, which he carries with him when he goes into the forest, and when he points this at an animal, it falls down dead. It is said that hunters have seen this occur. He is interested, also, in women, especially those who have not yet reached puberty, for whom he lies in wait. Or he follows women who walk in the forest or on riverbanks alone. He may appear, then, as a fish, a squirrel, or a lizard, and, causing them to fall asleep, cohabit with them, as in a dream. But after a short time, then, they die, and at the place where the act occurred there will be an abundance of animal or aquatic life.[42]

When the shaman, the payé, on his hallucinogenic quest, arrives in the Animal Master's house, either in the hills or in the waters, *Vaí-mahsë* receives him willingly and shows him his animals hanging in bunches from the rafters. The payé indicates those that the hunters have asked him to release, and when the price in souls has been agreed upon, *Vaí-mahsë* shakes the relevant rafters to wake the animals selected, which then go out into the jungle to be killed. "The price," it is said, "is charged 'per shake' and sometimes more are awakened than had been agreed upon and the payé must reopen negotiations."[43]

"But sometimes," Reichel-Dolmatoff found, "the payés go to the hills, not in their hallucinations but in reality, to affirm their requests and to foster the fertility of the animals. On many of the hills the rock walls are covered with pictographs representing various animals and fertility symbols, where generations of payés have drawn, in red, yellow, or black, the forms of game animals. The drawings show deer, tapirs, monkeys, rodents, turtles, and birds, together with phallic and uterine symbols; the stripes and diamonds of *pamurí-gahsiru,* the mythical snake that brought men to earth, are also depicted. Sometimes these rock walls are true palimpsests with a superposition of drawings that, through the centuries, show changing styles. At times the figure of a jaguar dominates the multitude of representations, just as the fertilizing power of this divine beast dominates the jungle."[44]

All of this surely is amazing: 18,000 years and as many miles away from the Temple Caves of the Dordogne and Pyrenees!

485. On the Upper Inirida River, a rock shelter, painted with game animals and abstract symbols, where the Master of Animals dwells. Reichel-Dolmatoff explains: "In the rain forests of the Vaupés there exist, here and there, rock formations that stand out like dark islands on the horizon. These isolated hills or ridges often have steep walls and flat, mesa-like plateaus and are full of caverns and dark recesses. These uncanny places are the dwellings of *Vaí-mahsë (ëhtëngë ví'i,* "hill house"; *Vaí-mahsë ví'i,* "*Vaí-mahsë*'s house"), where, surrounded by his animals, he dominates the forest."[57]

347

The Yurupari Cult

Yurupari is a word of unknown origin that appears in the literature of anthropology as the name of a ceremonial complex widely spread among the forest tribes of the upper Amazon. The dominant feature is an elaborate ritual exercise involving processions of initiated males to the accompaniment of bark trumpets. Females and males not yet initiated are forbidden the sight of these instruments. Distributions of fish, game, and wilderness fruits are associated with the ceremonies, which include as an essential feature the initiation of young men. (Compare the Mandan Okipa, I.2:226–231.) Theodor Koch-Grünberg, whose researches in these regions during the first decade of this century opened them to systematic scholarship, published in 1910 the following version of the Yurupari origin legend, obtained from the Yahúnga—a people of Tucanoan stock inhabiting (in his time) eight malocas at the junction of the Pirá-paraná and Apaporís rivers.

Many many years ago, there came out the great Water House, the dwelling of the Sun, a little boy who sang so beautifully that people flocked from near and far to see and to hear him. His name was Milómaki, the Son (*maki*) of Miló. But when the people who had heard him returned to their homes and ate fish, they all fell dead. Incensed, their relatives seized the boy, who had meanwhile become a youth, and, setting him on a great funeral pyre as an evil wretch who had slain their kin, set it afire.

The youth, however, continued to sing marvelously to the end. As the flames enveloped his body: "Now I die, my son," he sang; "now I am leaving this world!" As the body swelled with the heat, the song continued: "Now my body bursts. Now I am dead!" And indeed, the body exploded, Milómaki died, and the flames consumed him.

But his soul ascended to heaven, and that very day, from the ashes there grew a long green leaf that increased perceptibly as one watched, and, expanding, was by the next day a tall tree: the first paxiuba palm. There had been no such tree before that. Of its wood the people made large flutes that in a marvelous way reproduced the sound of Milómaki's singing. At the time of the ripening of wilderness fruits, men blow such flutes to this day, and dance thereby in honor of Milómaki, the producer of all edible fruits. Little boys and women are forbidden to see those instruments. Any woman who should do so would die. Any boy, would eat earth, become ill, and die, too.[45]

486. For most of the Amazon's riparian inhabitants, fishing (whether with spears, bows and arrows, traps, or, on significant festive occasions, such "fish poisons" as barbasco), although a continual pursuit that provides much of the protein in their daily diet, is considered an activity of a lower status and of less importance than hunting.

a

487. Played most often in association with men's rites and ceremonials, flutes made of twisted bark are pandemic in Amazonia: (**a**) a Yekuana plays the *wana*, twin flutes that, unlike sacred Yurupari flutes — a contemporary Tukano example of which (**b**) is remarkably similar to two Yahúnga models (**c–d**) drawn (c. 1903) by Theodor Koch-Grünberg — are not kept hidden from women and uninitiated males; (**e**) Kamyura versions of the instrument.

"In this myth," remarks Koch-Grünberg, "the tribal hero appears as the culture hero, the generator of vegetable growth, and is of a distinctly solar character. He is the Sun itself. He comes from the east, out of the great 'Water House,' wanders over the earth, and departs in flames to heaven. The burning of a hero to death because of his magical character is a feature common to many of the myths to be found in South America."[46] "Interesting," he adds, "is the reference here to the sea. The sea appears in the legends of many inland tribes, suggesting the probability of migrations, either of the peoples themselves, or of their legends."[47]

The Desana Snake Canoe, we recall, *ascended* the earthly rivers in its passage from the mythological River of Milk. Writing of the "Tropical Forest Tribes," Robert H. Lowie, in his introduction to Volume 3 of the *Handbook of South American Indians*,[48] makes a very strong point of the influence of river travel on the spread of both peoples and culture throughout this heavily forested part of the world. "The very wide distribution of certain traits in the area," he observes, "is correlated with navigation. Thanks to their mobility, the canoeing tribes were able to maintain themselves in the midst of boatless populations, to travel with ease over periodically inundated tracts, and to diffuse their arts and customs over enormous distances.…Accordingly,

earthenware decoration in Santarém [on the lower Amazon] may precisely duplicate details from the Lesser Antilles."[49] And in the same way (I would add), the Yurupari bark trumpets that are being made today in the upper Amazon look very much like those depicted in de Bry's sixteenth-century engraving, *The Queen-Elect is Brought to the King* (See I.2:**387** and II.1:**45**), which was copied from a watercolor by Jacques de Moyne de Morgues, painted in Florida in 1564.

Two thoroughgoing studies of the Yurupari as practiced by the Barasana, a Tucanoan-speaking people on the Pirá-paraná river in the Vaupés area of Colombia — *The Palm and the Pleiades: Initiation and Cosmology in Northwest Amazonia*, by Stephen Hugh-Jones,[50] and *From the Milk River: Spatial and Temporal Processes in Northwest Amazonia*, by Christine Hugh-Jones,[51] his wife — opened the whole complex to view in a fresh light at the very moment of its imminent disappearance.

"In the Pirá-paraná area," writes C. Hugh-Jones, "the influence of the rubber trade was first felt in the latter half of the nineteenth century and the industry reached its height in the first decade of this century. After that it went into a gradual decline until the Second World War brought a sudden increase in demand. By 1970 there were rumours that the market was approaching total collapse and that

government support for the industry was to be withdrawn. White rubber gatherers (*caucheros*) entered the Pirá-paraná from the Vaupés and Apaporis and, in most cases, carried off the able men by force, often killing others and raping women. Many Indians tell how the reprisals against the brutal intruders were also extended to fellow Indians who had directed them to hidden longhouses. The location of longhouses was an indication of white activity, because Indians fled to the headwaters and concealed approaches to their longhouses when times were bad, and then moved back to the larger rivers as white people withdrew.

"Besides reducing the population and disrupting social life in these ways, the rubber trade introduced new diseases on a large scale. It also changed Indian culture and aspirations by creating new needs for white men's merchandise. But the *caucheros* did not purposefully attempt to change Indian culture from within by altering patterns of social and domestic life. Their very lack of interest in Indians as anything beyond a workforce to be ensnared in an eternal credit system meant that those who escaped their recruiting drives continued to live in a traditional way. By the period of our fieldwork, the methods of *caucheros* were less violent, but nevertheless very variable. Many Indians born in the upper Pirá-paraná were permanently living in rubber camps on the Vaupés and beyond, while others in the lower Pirá-paraná worked regularly on the Apaporis for a part of each year.

"The missionaries played a complementary role to the *caucheros*: proclaiming themselves to be against the economic exploitation of Indians, they set out to convert and 'civilise.' The first missionaries to enter the Colombian Vaupés area were Montfortians, who settled along the Papuri following an exploratory voyage in 1914. They destroyed longhouses and burnt ritual goods, and forced the inhabitants to build wattle-and-daub villages, each with its own church. The manner in which they waged their war against sin softened over the years, especially with the replacement of the Montfortians by Colombian Javerians in 1949, but the aims remained basically the same until around 1970 when there came a wave of radical questioning of missionary policy from within. As the methods of persuasion became more gentle, the bond between Indian and missionary strengthened in economic content. The labour required to build airstrips and to feed and maintain mission headquarters and boarding schools was bought with manufactured goods. As these became indispensable, Indians found themselves dependent on mission centers and so the inflationary spiral of demand for manufactured goods began. Such demands are met by working for the missions and this both accelerates the acquisition of mission values, and increases mission power by augmenting capital resources such as airstrips, buildings and so on. In this way, the act of earning manufactured goods strengthens the acculturative force and so creates the desire for more goods.

"Many Pirá-paraná Indians had visited mission centers outside the Pirá-paraná area long before missionaries visited them and all were familiar with the elements of Christianity. The Vaupés marriage system, which requires each man to find a wife from beyond the area occupied by his own linguistic group, creates a network of alliances which facilitates the spread of missionary culture well beyond the limits of missionary activity. However, at the time of my fieldwork, the disparity between longhouse life in the Pirá-paraná and missionary village life in the surrounding areas seemed to have dampened the exchange of women across the divide, so that Pirá-paraná society taken as a whole was relatively endogamous and culturally distinct (in terms of existing culture rather than traditional culture) from the rest of the Vaupés."[52]

The Hugh-Joneses, after an initial survey trip down the length of the Pirá-paraná, made themselves at home in the maloca (situated on the Caño Colorado) of the Meni Masa sib of the Barasana. The Meni Masa is one of a group of five sibs, each with its maloca, separated from its neighbors by two or more hours of travel by trail or canoe. According to S. Hugh-Jones, the Meni Masa rank in the middle of this group of five, those sibs ranked above being referred to as "our elder brothers" and those below as "our younger brothers," each being associated with a specialist ritual role. The Meni Masa are "warriors." Of the two sibs above, the Koamona are "chiefs," the Rasegana, "dancers and chanters," and of the two below, the Daria are "shamans" (*kumua*, see pages 345–346) and the Wabea, "cigar lighters" or servants.[53]

"Barasana society is rigidly divided along lines of sex," Hugh-Jones points out. "Men and women use different doors to their house, spend most of their waking lives apart from each other and are periodically and forcefully reminded of their separateness by the Yurupary rites that form the subject of this book. Working amongst them as a married couple was a distinct advantage. Minimally, it established that, in spite of being a foreign man, I was relatively safe and had not come there to take their women. It meant that we were recognized as being mature enough to be fully incorporated into adult life even though our lack of children was the subject of ribald comments. But most important of all, it meant that we became familiar with Barasana society from the point of view of both sexes. Though we never specifically divided topics of research between us, the nature of the society itself imposed a division on our work. Though my wife was barred from secret male ritual, she was able to talk freely with the men and to discuss topics normally kept secret from women. But for me, the world of women was relatively closed."[54]

The crucial finding of the Hugh-Joneses with respect to the Yurupari complex among the Barasana was that it culminates, not in one ceremonial, but in two: a minor, known as Fruit-House, and a major, known as *He*-House (*He*, pronounced as in *hen* with the *n* omitted). The term *He*, according to Hugh-Jones, "refers in particular to the sacred flutes and trumpets; more widely, it is perhaps best translated as 'ancestral' and refers to the past, to the spirit world and to the world of myth. At its widest range, it implies a whole conception of the cosmos and of the place of human society within it."[55] In other words, *He* means, "mythological."

"The Barasana have an unusually rich and varied corpus of myths which are treated with considerable respect," Hugh-Jones continues, "and which form the basis of shamanic knowledge and power. The myths describe the establishment of an ordered cosmos and the creation of human society within it; the human social order is seen as part of this wider order, as timeless and changeless and beyond the immediate control of human agency—it is, or should be, as it was created in the past."[56]

This, it is safe to say, is an Elementary Idea (see I.1:8, II.1:28, 73) informing *all* aboriginal mythologies. According to this view: to change in any way the form or manner of use of any myth, ritual, or artifact, breaks its connection with the mythological ground through which the energies of eternal life enter the empirical sphere of spatial and temporal processes. The astounding conservatism of aboriginal cultures can be attributed largely to this idea.

"The *He* state," Hugh-Jones goes on to explain, "implies a state of being prior to, and now parallel with, human existence.

488. Koch-Grünberg drawing (c. 1905) of Yurupari rites as celebrated by Tuyúka Indians on the Rio Tiguié. Advancing behind the warning calls of the sacred flutes, the men in file (some, with forehead straps, carrying woven baskets), make their way from the river to the ceremonial maloca.

Originally everything was *He* and the pre-human, man-animal characters of myth are the *He* People from whom human beings developed by a process of transformation. The *He* People and the *He* state, wherein lies the power of creation and order, are thus in the distant past. But it is also an ever-changeless present that encapsulates human society and which exists as another aspect of reality, another world. When *He* is viewed as the past, human society is in danger of becoming increasingly distant and separated from this wider reality and source of life—the effects of this [passage of] time must be overcome. As the present, this other world is seen as separated in space; human society is in danger of becoming out of phase with this other reality and spatial separation must be mediated. The *He* state is known through myth; it is experienced and manipulated through ritual and controlled through spatial and temporal metaphor."[57]

One more paragraph, and this elegant summary of what I would number as one of the fundamental Elementary Ideas of all aboriginal mythic thought and ritual procedure, can be concluded.

"At birth, people leave the *He* state and become human, ontogeny repeating phylogeny; at death, people once again enter the *He* state and become ancestors to be reborn at future births. In life, people enter into involuntary contact with the *He* state through dreaming and illness, through menstruation and childbirth and through the deaths of others. All such contact is uncontrolled and dangerous. [Hence, we may add, the rituals of protection.] It is also possible to enter into voluntary and controlled contact with the *He* state and to experience it directly. The power and position of the shaman lies precisely in his ability to experience and manipulate the *He* state at will; such people are seen as living on two planes of existence simultaneously. Other men can enter into contact with the *He* state through rituals at which the shamans act as mediators. Though all rituals involve such voluntary contact, it is during the rites at which *He* instruments are used that this contact is achieved to its fullest extent. The *He* instruments represent the living dead, the first ancestors of humanity. This regular and controlled contact with the outer world, which gives power to control life and which ensures the continuance of society in a healthy and ordered state, is reserved for adult men. Its complement lies in female fertility and powers of reproduction. Women ensure the reproduction of people; men ensure the reproduction of society."[58]

Where Sacred Things Are Seen

The most important and elaborate of all Barasana rituals is that known as *He wi*, "*He* House," or *He iaria wi*, "House where *He* are seen." It is also, of all the rites, the most dangerous, and very few shamans have the power to conduct it. At one level, it is the rite of initiation of young boys into the men's secret cult of the sacred flutes and trumpets. But since the sight of these is forbidden to women, the ritual also serves to underscore and maintain the tension between the sexes. Barasana marriage is exogamous. All the wives in every patrilocal maloca, consequently, are from other malocas, other sibs. But the instruments represent the ancestors, the descent line, of the local maloca and its sib, who, in the context of the ceremony are adopting into their substance a new generation of young men, so that the social organism grounded in *He* (the mythic past and mystic present) should continue alive into the future.[59]

As Hugh-Jones has observed: "Women ensure the reproduction of people; men ensure the reproduction of society." There are, accordingly, specific women's rites associated with menstruation, birth, and nourishment: moments of great mystery and, consequently, of danger. And the counterparts of these in the domain of the male sex are the dangerous *He* rites for the continuation of the culture. In fact, the ability of women to menstruate and the possession by initiated men of the *He* (the instruments) are seen as complementary and mutually exclusive. There was a time, it is even said, when the women stole the instruments and the men then menstruated. The women then had control. But the men regained the instruments and the women menstruated. Implied is the idea,

as Hugh-Jones has noted, "that the sex that controls the *He* and which does not menstruate will be the one that is politically dominant."[60] But also implied is that the women have the *He* in themselves, and that it is this that causes them to menstruate. The *He*, as we learn from one of the myths, is in their hair.

"It is for this reason," Hugh-Jones points out, "that when the men took back the *He* from the women, their victory over them was double-edged. They regained only one kind of *He* (instruments) which implies political dominance, but they lost another (women's hair) which implies menstruation and the power to create children."[61]

"*He* House," he suggests, "can perhaps be interpreted as a symbolic act in which adult men give birth to the initiates. In order to give birth, men must first be opened up and made to menstruate."[62]

"It is entirely appropriate therefore," he concludes, "that after *He* House, the initiates should be confined in a compartment, as are menstruating women, and referred to by expressions which, in their feminine form, refer to women in this condition."[63]

The three-day ceremonial is preceded by a day of preparations, with increasing separation of the sexes: women in the rear of the house, making manioc beer, the boys to be initiated among them, and the men sitting in front of the house on the plaza. At dusk (which marks the beginning of the first day), the younger men come playing the *He* up from the river, where the instruments have been kept hidden. Immediately on hearing them, the women rush out the rear door to the surrounding scrub, and for the rest of the night the flutes and trumpets are played round and round, outside the maloca. The attendant shamans have meanwhile been chanting and flicking whips to drive away illness. One of them brings smoking beeswax on a potsherd out onto the plaza, where he fans the smoke to the four directions. Others blow their breaths over piles of tobacco snuff that is then blown in large quantities through tubes up

489. A Barasana maloca, in the Rio Pirá-piraná region, that has been converted from an ordinary dwelling to a mythic house by being painted with decorations (modeled after the patterns on the bodies of the ancestral anaconda) that represent visions seen while under the influence of yagé.

the men's noses, causing them to vomit. All communication at this time is being held to a minimum, in whispers.

At the first light of dawn, the *He* are played into the house, where they circumambulate the men's area sunwise. The elders are now sitting in groups at either side of the men's door, the shamans on stools, the others on mats. The women have again rushed out the back door into the bush, to protect their power to menstruate and give birth.

Around 9 A.M., the leading shaman hands around a ceremonial cigar over which he has blown spells, together with a gourd of blown coca. Two more gourds are placed in the middle of the house, one containing red paint, the other snuff. The paint is known as the "blood and flesh of *He*." Any woman touching it would immediately menstruate. The men wipe it over their bodies, especially the temples and navel; for, as they say, "It makes us live." And the snuff, mixed with beeswax, they wipe with a stick over their legs and knees to protect against the stabbing pains of what are known as "water spears" which they would otherwise experience when ritually bathing—all other contact with anything of water being forbidden during the period of the rite.

Protected thus, the company now proceeds to the river in back of the maloca, to bathe. The shamans both lead the procession and follow, flicking their whips aggressively, and the instruments are played as far as to the edge of the clearing around the maloca. At the river they are placed in the water to give them a good sound, and in total silence (to protect against possible attacks by *He* jaguars) the elders bathe while the younger men wash only their face and hands. Back in the maloca, all drink amply of the beer (blown over by the shamans) which the women have prepared for them, and a long chanting session is held.

In the course of the afternoon of this first day, the long flutes known as Old Macaws are decorated with feather ruffs and their engraved designs are filled with manioc starch. Two elders then put on jaguar-tooth belts, elbow ornaments and feather crowns, and dance the decorated flutes up and down the middle of the house, after which the Old Macaws sound continuously, played by relays of elders.

Toward dusk the initiates are brought in. Their hair has been cut by the women, who have also painted them black from head to foot. Having been summoned by the shamans to appear, they are carried in on the shoulders of elders and set down to stand by the men's door in a row, linked by their little fingers. Here they are given kana berries (*Sabicea amazonensis*) to eat, to strengthen them for the rite's ordeal, and eating, each is looked over by an elder.

When the berries have been consumed, the boys are led to a mat before the shaman's enclosure and told to sit in a foetal posture, without moving. The ceremonial cigar and some blown coca are brought to them, after which each is served by the leading shaman a small sip of the hallucinogenic drink, yagé, drawn from a potion freshly prepared by himself at a station outside the maloca. Upon entering the building with it, he had paused at the door, to draw on the ground a figure known as the Yagé Mother [Figure 490], using pounded yagé bark as a paint and throwing the rest of the poundings up onto the maloca roof. Then he had entered

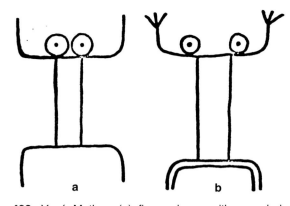

490. Yagé Mother: (**a**) figure drawn with pounded yagé bark on a Barasana longhouse floor during *He wi* ritual (recorded, 1970s, by S. Hugh-Jones); (**b**) petroglyph on a rock in the Vaupés river above Jauareté (recorded, 1900, by E. Stradelli).[58]

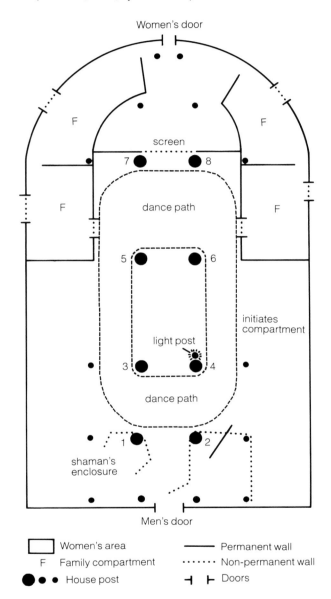

491. Maloca interior, as configured for the *He wi* rites: the temporary walls, special enclosures, and screen that separates the men from the women will remain for the duration of the event (see text).

and all the men had picked up *He* instruments for the moment of the revelation. Solemnly blowing the flutes and trumpets, walking very very slowly with the ends of the long instruments held very close to the ground, the men of the maloca pass before the initiates' eyes, showing to them each instrument, and the boys behold the *He* for the first time.

Following this event, there is a long session of chanting, and apart from the sounds of the chanting voices, the flutes and trumpets, almost total silence reigns in the house. Toward midnight, the conducting shaman carries his pot of yagé to a place between posts five and

six, calling to the company to come drink. One by one, the youngest first, clutching staves and acting out spearing, they advance in inverse order of seniority. Each is given yagé and blown coca, drinks, eats, and returns to his place, and when all have partaken, there follows another parade of the *He*.

When a chanting is heard, soon after midnight, of two voices within the shaman's enclosure, the guardian of the initiates ignites some beeswax taken from a gourd and proceeds twice around the dance path, sunwise, followed by the younger men blowing trumpets, and the initiates blowing short flutes. This procession is the climax of the festival. The women are out at the edge of the forest, listening for falling trees, and should any such sound be heard, it would be understood as an evil omen, presaging the wasting away and death of the participants.

The next events are of violence.

Two elders in full regalia (wearing bark-cloth aprons, belts of carved rose-colored shell, hanks of monkey-fur string on their backs, sacred elbow ornaments, and headdresses of egret and macaw feathers) step outside the building and sound out there the decorated Old Macaw flutes. Those are *He* spirits, fierce spirits, ancestors of the living and very dangerous. "I will kill you," they are saying. They are challenging the initiates to become as fierce as they. And the company, responding, grabs staves and whips, and lines up on either side of the room. The flutes enter, played with ends raised high in the air, and the company, rushing up and down the side aisles, acts out spearing.

Two gourds are next placed between posts one and two; one contains snuff, the other, beeswax mixed with coca. One by one, the members of the company, initiates first, the rest in inverse order of seniority, come up, wipe snuff on their knees, and eat pinches of coca. Then the episode of the challenging pipes and rushing about with staves and whips is played through a second time.

The two elders with the Old Macaw flutes now join the two chanting shamans, then return to playing the flutes, and during their playing blown coca from the beeswax gourd is passed to the older women, behind the screen between posts seven and eight. Receiving it, they eat the coca and apply blown red paint to their bodies. The Old Macaw flute men now are chanting with but one of the two shamans. The other has gone with a bundle of whips to stand before the women's screen.

All present run up the side aisles, acting out spearing, and stand in two groups by the shaman. One by one, starting with the youngest, they go forward and, standing with their legs apart and with their arms held above their heads clutching a staff horizontally in their hands, they are whipped on the leg, thigh, abdomen and chest. Holding their arms out in front of them, these are whipped too. After each person is whipped, he runs back to his place, acting out spearing as he goes. Finally the shaman comes back to the men's end of the house where he too is whipped by another elder.

After all this, more yagé is served and a chanting is commenced before the screen at the female end of the house that continues until dawn; at which time, the leading shaman comes with a pot of blown black paint, and the initiates and younger men begin to paint each other's

Diagram labels (Figure 491):

Women's door

F · · · F
screen
7 · 8
dance path
F · · · F
5 · 6
initiates compartment
light post
3 · 4
dance path
1 · 2
shaman's enclosure
Men's door

Women's area — Permanent wall
F Family compartment — Non-permanent wall
● ● ● House post — Doors

legs and body. Those painting each other establish by this act a ritual brotherlike relationship and will speak of each other henceforth as *yu suori,* "my paint-partner." Formerly, according to report, the initiates were then made to stand in a row, their G-strings were cut, and the *He* instruments blown over their penises, after which they went out naked to greet the morning and to play the short flutes.

The morning of this second day is celebrated with another instrument parade, featuring Old Macaw, another long chanting session, and a general drinking of beer. About noon there is still another parade, during which the two leading shamans play a special type of trumpet (not otherwise seen in this ceremony) called Old Callecebus Monkey. Snuff to prevent illness now is served to everybody, men and women

as well, and finally, just before dark, the flutes and trumpets are again paraded twice around the room in a ceremony called "ending the dance." They are then taken outside and from the flutes the feather ruffs are removed. Mats are laid out near the women's screen and all but a few of the elders go to sleep there. It is thought dangerous for the initiates to sleep at the men's end of the house, where the Sun and the *He* people, having power there and desiring to keep the initiates with them forever, might send dreams of eating fish (a food forbidden at this time) and thus kill them.

The final day is of concluding rites. At dawn, the flutes are played inside the house, the trumpets around the outside. The shamans blow spells over snuff to be applied to the knees and water is drunk in small quantities, to prevent

danger both from the morning dew and from the bathing soon to follow. Then all go to the landing, where the instruments are immersed, the initiates and younger men bathe, and the shamans fill the Old Macaw flutes with water in such a way that it spurts out the sound holes. This is the flutes drinking and vomiting. The initiates drink water from the flutes, and what remains is poured over them to make them fierce. Certain leaves are crushed into water that is drunk to cause vomiting, to clean out the *He* poison and residual yagé, and the initiates then bathe, while two elders play the Old Macaw flutes.

The women have meanwhile prepared a meal and taken all the food and goods in the house out onto the plaza. When the men return, the feather ruffs are put back on the flutes, which are then played by various elders, the last being the two who had been the *He* spirits earlier in the festival. When they have finished and the shaman removes their feather headdresses, he blows spells on their heads and wipes his hands over them lightly, flicking off invisible, harmful substances. He does the same for everyone who wore headdresses during the services; for if this were not done, the men would be in danger of attack from jaguars and of headaches caused by the silverfish that eat feathers.

The meal is eaten on the plaza. The *He* instruments are wrapped in fresh leaves, taken down to the river, and hidden again in the mud under the water. The whole house is swept out thoroughly and fumigated; for it is saturated with *He* poison, which must be removed by shamanism, to protect the women from becoming ill. An enclosure of woven leaves is built just inside the men's door on the left and there the initiates sling their hammocks. The shamans blow spells on the hammock and, once the initiates have been installed there, the screen shutting off the women's quarter of the house is removed. The initiates' compartment is built in such a way that they can go in and out without seeing or being seen by the women at the other end of the house. The women fear the initiates, [Hugh-Jones explains] for if they have any contact with them, *He,* in the form of an anaconda, enters their bodies and they die.

For the initiates the end of this period [of seclusion and restrictions] is signalled by the total disappearance of the black paint applied to their bodies at the start of the rite. The end of the period is marked by the eating of capsicum pepper, blown over by the shamans. On seeing the *He,* the participants become *He* people (*He masa*) and *He* enters their bodies. This gradually leaves the body as the paint fades from the skin. For the elders, the period lasts one month; for the initiates and younger men it lasts two months. Pepper is thus blown twice, once for the elders, once for the initiates. During the period of restrictions, the men are described as *bedira,* a state when people fast and undergo restrictions. The same word also applies to menstruating women.[64]

492. Barasana celebrants, dressed in ceremonial regalia and under the influence of yagé. When the Barasana put on feathers and paint, they enter into mythic time and become ancestral spirits.

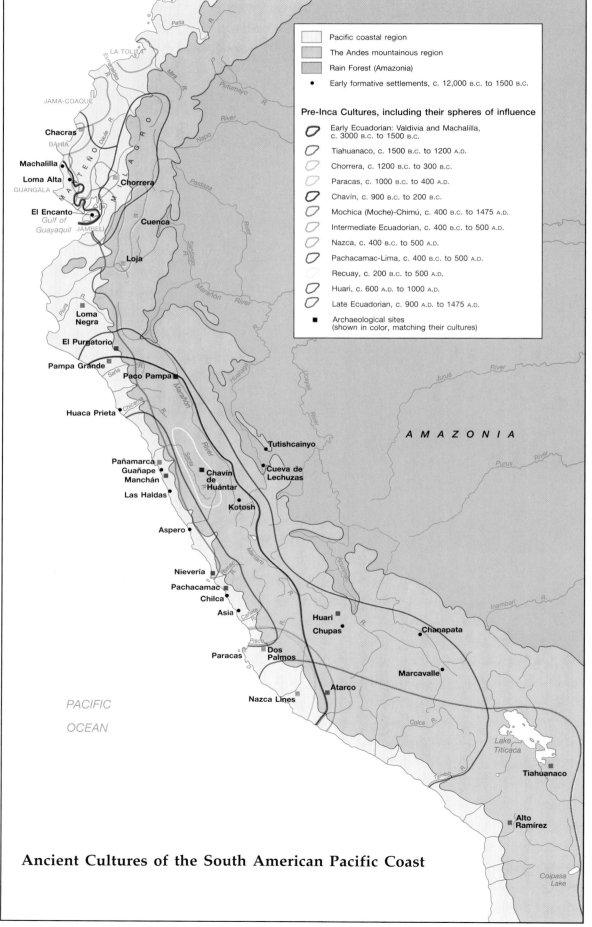

Ancient Cultures of the South American Pacific Coast

Within the map legend:

Pacific coastal region

The Andes mountainous region

Rain Forest (Amazonia)

• Early formative settlements, c. 12,000 B.C. to 1500 B.C.

Pre-Inca Cultures, including their spheres of influence

Early Ecuadorian: Valdivia and Machalilla, c. 3000 B.C. to 1500 B.C.

Tiahuanaco, c. 1500 B.C. to 1200 A.D.

Chorrera, c. 1200 B.C. to 300 B.C.

Paracas, c. 1000 B.C. to 400 A.D.

Chavín, c. 900 B.C. to 200 B.C.

Mochica (Moche)-Chimú, c. 400 B.C. to 1475 A.D.

Intermediate Ecuadorian, c. 400 B.C. to 500 A.D.

Nazca, c. 400 B.C. to 500 A.D.

Pachacamac-Lima, c. 400 B.C. to 500 A.D.

Recuay, c. 200 B.C. to 500 A.D.

Huari, c. 600 A.D. to 1000 A.D.

Late Ecuadorian, c. 900 A.D. to 1475 A.D.

■ Archaeological sites (shown in color, matching their cultures)

Map 39.

Valdivia (Ecuador) and the Old Pacific Culture

In December 1960, a door opened from the local North and South American scene to the much larger, of World History, when Emilio Estrada, a young Ecuadorian businessman who had adopted archaeology as a hobby, excavating at a rich pottery site near the little fishing village of Valdivia, on the Guayas coast of Ecuador, unearthed part of the castellated rim of a shattered ceramic vessel, which he recognized (no doubt with a shock) as similar in both form and decoration to a type of Middle Jomon ware (c. 3000 B.C.) from prehistoric Japan.

Estrada had already published in 1958 a monograph in Spanish classifying some 36,000 potsherds, numerous pottery figurines, and an assortment of artifacts, variously of stone, bone, and shell, uncovered at his site. Three carbon-14 dates had fixed the period of his finds between 2493 and 2093 B.C. Similarities had been noted, furthermore, to known potteries of matching date from two sites to the south, in coastal Peru, Guañape and Ancon, as well as two to the north, Monagrillo and Puerto Hormiga, on the Colombian Caribbean.[65]

Following his recognition of the Jomon connection, Estrada got in touch with Clifford Evans and Betty J. Meggers, at the Smithsonian Institution in Washington, D.C., who had done archaeological fieldwork in Ecuador, Brazil, Guyana, and Venezuela, as well as on Ponape in Micronesia. As she has told of their reaction to what for them was astounding news:

"Having been taught in graduate school that transpacific contacts were irrelevant to explaining the origins of New World traits, we reacted with skepticism. When we examined his sources, however, we found to our surprise that the similarities were closer and more numerous than anything we had been able to find within the Americas. Following the rules traditionally employed by archaeologists for establishing affiliations made it necessary to infer that Jomon and Valdivia were related. This implied a transpacific contact about the beginning of the third millennium B.C."[66] For, as she declares: "If an ocean did not separate Japan and Ecuador, no archaeologist would hesitate to infer the common origin of 5000-year-old potteries from sites in these two countries."[67]

Estrada died in 1961 at the age of 45, three months before the publication of their co-authored announcement of this discovery in *Science*, February 2, 1962.[68] In 1963, Meggers and Evans, on a special visit to Japan, were there able to inspect and to compare the collections of excavated materials from Early and Middle Jomon sites, both on Honshu and on Kyushu, and, after analyzing the evidence, came to the conclusion "that pottery was introduced from western Japan to Ecuador, and that other early occurences in the Americas were derived from the Valdivia complex."[69] In 1965 their final report was published,[70] and from every quarter of the academic community expressions came, and have come flying ever since, of incredulity, indignation, and even insult.

The first question, of course, is of the possibility of a transoceanic voyage at that early date from Kyushu to Ecuador. Meggers and Estrada had modestly suggested "a boatload of Early Middle Jomon fishermen," caught by a storm too far from shore and carried by currents along the great circle route, eastward and then southward to the Guayas coast.[71] But they need not have been so modest. The voyage could have been intentional and of many more craft than one.

The opening, formative years of the Jomon culture of earliest post-Paleolithic Japan date from c. 11,000 B.C. Ocean levels at that time were some fifty feet lower than today, but rising as the last of the glaciers melted. The people of the islands were not of the race of the historic Japanese, but of unrelated stocks as different from each other as the Caucasoid Ainu from Siberia and the Southeast Asian Austronesians from the island world then coming into being with the gradual flooding of Old Melanesia (see I.1:30, and I.1:**Map 8**).

From the very start of this earliest postglacial age, a number of distinct Jomon traditions were already in formation in various parts of the islands, suggesting, as

Chester S. Chard has observed, "the existence of separate ethnic or tribal groupings."[72] What now appears to be the earliest ware is from the Fukui Cave in Kyushu, radiocarbon dated at $12,700 \pm 500$ years ago,[73] which is equivalent to c. 11,200–10,200 B.C., the earliest date for pottery (as far as I have learned) in any part of the world. The origins of the art are unknown. The people of the time were of a hunting-fishing-gathering stage. Evidence of deepwater fishing at the Natsushima site, near the mouth of Tokyo Bay, "indicates," says Chard, "that at least some coastal groups in Japan must have had adequate watercraft over 9000 years ago, and a late Initial Jomon site on one of the Izu Islands," he adds, "is even more convincing evidence of maritime capabilities, probably at least as early as 7500 years before the present. By around 6500 B.P. [that is, about 4500 B.C.] there is clear evidence of occasional trade between Kyushu and the Pusan area of Korea."[74]

Chard's tentative chronology for the more than 10,000 years of Jomon ceramic manufacture and (let us add) Jomon seafaring is as follows:[75]

Incipient Jomon	c. 11000–7500 B.C.
Initial Jomon	c. 7500–5300 B.C.
Early Jomon	c. 5300–3600 B.C.
Middle Jomon	c. 3600–2500 B.C.
Late Jomon	c. 2500–1000 B.C.
Final Jomon	c. 1000– 400 B.C.

Very cautiously and noncommitally, Chard makes reference to the announcement of Jomon pottery in Ecuador, neither affirming nor denying his belief in its possibility, though recognizing that in the vast region of the Pacific world, of which Jomon Japan was a part, "seafaring," as he writes, "must have reached a fairly high development thousands of years ago in order to account for the evidence of human occupation throughout the western Pacific from the Kyukyus, Taiwan, and the Philippines on out to Micronesia."[76]

a

b

493. (**a**) Japanese earthenware vessel, 11⅝" tall with a 35½" girth, Middle Jomon period, c. 3000 B.C.; (**b**) Ecuadorian pottery jar, c. 2¾" high, Valdivia phase 6, c. 1850–1700 B.C.

To the unstudied eye, these two pots might appear extremely dissimilar, but to Emilio Estrada (and, subsequently, to various ceramic specialists) key fragments of such Jomon and Valdivian vessels as these exhibited sufficient similarities of form, decorative motif, and technique of manufacture to suggest strongly that they were of common origin.

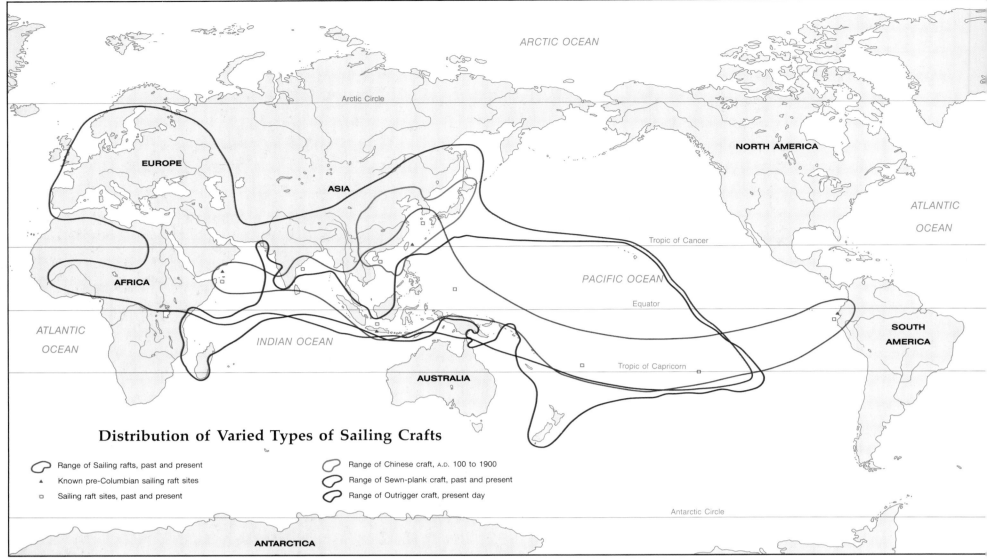

Distribution of Varied Types of Sailing Crafts

- Range of Sailing rafts, past and present
- ▲ Known pre-Columbian sailing raft sites
- □ Sailing raft sites, past and present
- Range of Chinese craft, A.D. 100 to 1900
- Range of Sewn-plank craft, past and present
- Range of Outrigger craft, present day

Map 40.

In Map 40 the occurrences and distributions of seaworthy rafts, sailing rafts, and outrigger canoes throughout the world can be seen to match in large part the areas outlined in Baumann's map (I.2:**Map 33**) showing the world-distribution of the mythologies of bisexual gods. Intriguing questions are also raised by a comparison of various sailing rafts from diverse locations—especially from the Coromandel Indian Coast (Figure 494), Java (Figure 495), Annam (Figure 496), Formosa (Figure 499), and Brazil (Figure 497)—with a similar craft from pre-Columbian Ecuador (Figure 498), recorded from exactly the site of Estrada's discovery of Early Middle Jomon pottery

sherds. The Brazilian example is, in Doran's view, post-Columbian. However, its local name, *jangada,* is Tamil, derived from Sanskrit, and the support for its mast is of a kind found otherwise only in India and Annam.[77] Its position (it is worth noting) is at the mouth of the river Amazon, several of the numerous headwaters of which originate in the Andean highlands, just across the mountains from coastal Ecuador and proximate to the sources of rivers that flow toward the Pacific. These rivers, cutting through the prodigious Andes mountain range, provide possible connective routes between the Ecuadorian coast and the Upper Amazonian rain forest, where the

494. From the Coromandel coast (India), a sailing raft with two leeway boards and a steering paddle.

495. This panel on the stupa of Borobudur (Java) depicts, in bas-relief, a sailing raft caught in a fierce storm. Assisting in the rescue of a mate being threatened by a sea monster, sailors fore and aft manipulate the craft's daggerboards.

496. From the Vietnamese state of Annam, this bamboo raft makes use of multiple daggerboards.

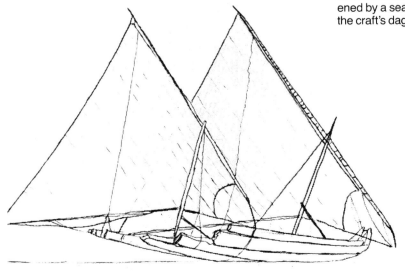

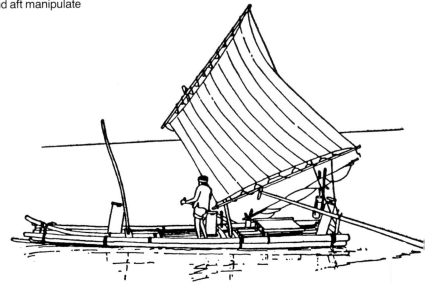

great latticework of river- and canoe-ways are thoroughfares for the Arawakan, Cariban, and Tupi-Guarani tribes.

Many observers have noted what appear to be more than coincidental likenesses between the cultures and racial features of the riverine tribes of the Amazonian Basin and those of the waterways of Southeast Asia: specifically, Malaysia, Borneo, the Celebes and Moluccas. Stephen C. Jett points out that physical anthropological data on the tribes of interior Borneo and on the Caribs and Arawaks of equatorial South America demonstrate between these two groups greater similarity than between either group and its neighbors. By way of explanation, some physical anthropologists have suggested convergence (following established biological "rules") under similar conditions of heat and humidity. But Jett concludes: "This greater similarity suggests actual migrations."[78]

"It is possible," he states further, "that the entire system of vegetative-reproduction-shifting cultivation in the New World owes its origin to Malaysian or other Southeast Asian immigrants. If so, local plants—such as sweet potato, yantia, and manioc—were largely substituted for similar Asian ones, such as yams and taro. However, there is evidence (of variable quality) that certain Southeast Asian food plants, such as the plantain, were brought to pre-Columbian tropical America…

"The old cultural pattern of Indonesia," he continues, "and that of equatorial America are strikingly similar. Points in common range from longhouses to head-hunting, and include a host of specific traits. Of these the blowgun complex has been studied in detail and was found to share a very large number of common points in the two areas concerned.[79] It may also be relevant that the Tucano of southern Colombia, though an inland tribe, have a tradition of having come from across the Pacific.[80]

497. The jangada, the post-Columbian sailing raft of Brazil, has a single daggerboard and a steering paddle, as well as multiple steps for the mast, a feature also found only in India and Annam, where the most complex of all sailing rafts are located.

"The aforementioned similarities," he then notes, "have been attributed by some to similar physical environments. Many of the shared traits, however, have no specific adaptive value in such environments. Further, the distribution pattern of the relevant traits—decreasing in frequency as one moves away from northwesternmost South America—is suggestive of transpacific introduction over a long period and sequential diffusion into the Amazon Basin, the Guianas, and Central America. As to those traits which clearly *are* adaptive, Malaysians' earlier adaptation to equatorial environments in Asia is exactly what would have enabled them to occupy such environments successfully in the New World while at the same time excluding them from other environments."[81] For the dating of these movements, Jett suggests "a probable time range from 3600 to 300 B.C. and a possible principal Malaysian source area on the shores of the Celebes Sea."[82]

Concerning the feasibility of transoceanic voyages by raft or dugout canoe, there is today no longer question. Thor Heyerdahl's drift voyage from Peru to the Tuamotus on the unguided raft, *Kon-Tiki,* and the passage from Hawaii to Tahiti and back of the large, double-hull, Polynesian type sailing canoe, *Hokuleia,* have put a term to that argument. However, as Jett points out, our academic colleagues need not have waited for those two demonstrations for the cure of their thalassophobia. The sea, for boatmen, is not a barrier but a highway; indeed, a challenge and invitation. J. Merrien, he reminds us, published a catalogue, following the *Kon-Tiki* adven-

498. A drawing made in 1619 showing an early Ecuadorian sailing raft with multiple daggerboards.

ture, of no less than 120 modern intentional solo and two-man ocean voyages,[83] which included: a solo ninety-three-day crossing from Japan to San Francisco in a nineteen-foot sloop; a sixty-eight-day raft drift from California to Hawaii; a solo voyage in a converted Indian dugout canoe (bottom length, thirty feet) from Vancouver to the Cook Islands (5500 miles in fifty-six days), followed by an ultimate landing in England; a solo journey in a nineteen-and-a-half-foot schooner from San Francisco to Australian waters without a single port of call (6500 miles in 162 days). Also included in Merrien's formidable catalogue were three solo round-the-world tours: one, a solo by Joshua Slocum in the *Spray* (thirty-six feet nine inches) of 46,000 miles in three years; another, by Vito Dumas in a thirty-two-foot ketch, which included a 7200-mile run from the Cape of Good Hope to New Zealand and a continuation to Valparaiso, Chile (5400 miles in seventy-two days), followed by a trip around the Horn; the third, sixty-two-year-old Francis Chichester's one-stop circumnavigation of the globe (28,500 miles with only one stop) in a fifty-four-foot ketch. Notable, also, were the voyages of Eric de Bisschop: first, in a double canoe with one companion, from Hawaii to Cannes in 264 days; next, some 5000 miles by bamboo sailing raft from Tahiti into the southeastern Pacific; and finally, 5500 miles by raft from Peru to Rakahanga. Among the 110 other examples cited and described was the pontoon raft journey of seventy-year-old William Willis in 1965, from Peru, 7450 miles to Samoa, and an additional 3000 miles, then, to Australia, though suffering (following various accidents and a wind that had ripped his mainsail apart) from an abdominal hernia, fractured sacrum, and paralysis from the waist down.[84]

Could a Jomon Japanese dugout canoe or sailing raft have landed in Ecuador, safely and intentionally, c. 3000 B.C.?

499. This sailing raft of bamboo, from Formosa, features multiple leeway boards that, when thrust down into the water, prevent the raft from being blown sideways, thus enabling it to make headway in any direction for unlimited periods of time.

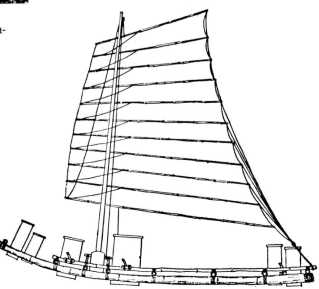

That America was already known to the seafaring people of East Asia is almost certain. For, as Robert von Heine-Geldern pointed out over thirty years ago, after reviewing an article published in 1875 in the Proceedings of the California Academy of Sciences,[85] *in the course of a single year,* no fewer than twenty Japanese junks, having lost in storms their masts or rudders, were carried by currents toward the North American coast, which they reached at various points from the Aleutian Islands to Mexico. And this sort of thing, Heine-Geldern infers, must have happened (if one thinks back to that period of Early Jomon maritime activities recognized by Chester Chard as occurring no less than 9000 years ago) to many many times twenty shipwrecked Japanese craft — not to mention similar craft from other East Asian shores. Accordingly, Heine-Geldern has reasoned, if the occupants of a single one of those many hundreds of shipwrecked craft had contrived to return home, that would have sufficed to reveal the existence of a continent on the other side of the ocean.[86]

Moreover, evidence that this continent must indeed have been known to Asia at an early date has been lately dependably reported from two sites near the southern Chinese coast (in Kiangsu and Chekiang provinces), where the peanut, a South American domesticate, now appears to have been cultivated c. 3300–2800 B.C.[87] — which is exactly the period of Estrada's and Meggers' Valdivia. Furthermore, the fashioning of bark cloth (Polynesian, *tapa*) in southern China no later than c. 2400 B.C. is made known by the appearance in Taiwan at that date of stone bark-beaters almost identical in form to those of Central and Western Mexico, Costa Rica, and El Salvador.[88] And still further: the presence throughout South America of chickens of Asian—not European—breeds at the time of the Spanish and Portuguese first arrivals indicates, as George F. Carter has observed, that at least some of the transoceanic voyages were made, not only intentionally, but with "such speed that they allowed the carriage of animals who had to be fed and watered and would surely not have survived a long drift voyage."[89]

On November 30, 1980, six Japanese scientists brought their forty-three-foot catamaran to land at Arica, Chile, terminating a six-and-a-half-month voyage. Their craft, the *Yasei-Gō,* "Wild Adventure," had set sail from Shimoda on May 8, following the Japanese Current (*Kuroshio,* the "Black Current"), which, they reasoned, might have carried the Jomon fishermen to America. And indeed, it brought them to San Francisco on July 5, and then carried them south to Ecuador, Peru, and Chile.

"We have proved," said the happy, though weary, Captain Kazunobu Fumimoto, "that such a voyage can be made in a boat like those used by Japanese fishermen 5000 years before Christ."[90]

Map 41.

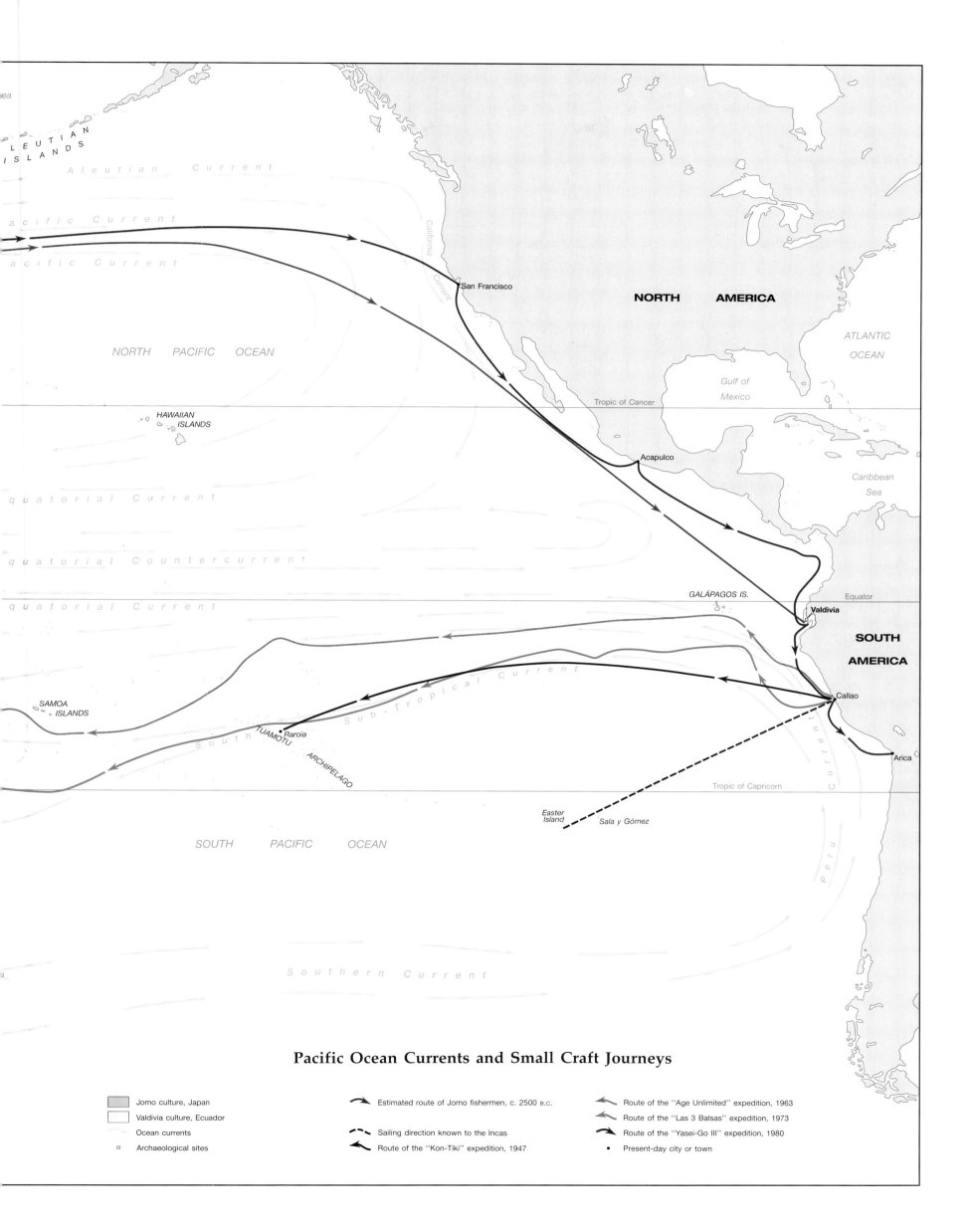

Pacific Ocean Currents and Small Craft Journeys

Jomo culture, Japan	Estimated route of Jomo fishermen, c. 2500 B.C.
Valdivia culture, Ecuador	
Ocean currents	Sailing direction known to the Incas
Archaeological sites	Route of the "Kon-Tiki" expedition, 1947

Route of the "Age Unlimited" expedition, 1963
Route of the "Las 3 Balsas" expedition, 1973
Route of the "Yasei-Go III" expedition, 1980
Present-day city or town

359

Ecuador As the American Formative Matrix

Comparisons between Jomon pottery from Japan (fragments, left column) and Valdivian shards from Ecuador (right) evidence numerous similarities in design and manufacturing techniques (see below). Consideration of these similarities, some experts argue, as well as the apparent absence of any clearly antecedent indigenous ceramic tradition, suggests that the art of pottery-making might have been introduced into the Americas by some prehistoric, trans-Pacific voyagers. The question has not been resolved.

The work of Meggers, Evans, and Estrada[91] suggests that, together with the primary idea and technique of pottery manufacture, there had crossed the sea, c. 3000 B.C., a distinctive cluster of secondary ideas and techniques for the non-functional embellishment of the ceramic vessels produced. Meggers has compiled a list of twenty-eight Valdivia traits that are shared, on the one hand, by the Jomon wares of Japan and, on the other, by potteries of the very same early period from Panama and the Colombian Caribbean coast.[92] Further evidence of Ecuador's seminal position in Early Formative America is provided by Valdivia figurines (Figures 505 and 506)—the earlier in stone, the later in clay—that are (by many centuries) *the earliest known female statuettes in the Americas*.

In 1969 the Smithsonian Institution published James A. Ford's *A Comparison of Formative Cultures in the Americas*,[93] which contained twenty-two charts that displayed essentially similar patterns of distribution throughout the Americas for bent-knee figurines, ceremonial centers and planned villages, grinding stones, bark-beaters, particular forms of bowls and pots, red-slip and zoned-relief decorations, and so forth. The distribution patterns pictured in these charts (which served as a principal source for portions of "From Nomadism to Seed Gardening" in this volume; see II.2:122–127) tend only to confirm the very strong impression already given by the distribution of the figurines, namely that coastal Ecuador was a matrix—possibly even *the* matrix—of Early Formative culture impulses in the Americas. The bark-beaters represent, almost certainly, a transoceanic influence; the grinding stones, for the preparation of vegetable food, suggest an agricultural background; while the ceremonial centers (notwithstanding earlier similar findings on the coast of Peru)[94] testify to an astonishingly early unfoldment toward the Classic temple forms of the South and Middle American civilizations.

A veritable gold rush of scientific teams to the Ecuadorian region shortly followed the appearance of the Meggers, Evans, and Estrada publication, and it was then not very long before claims were staked to evidences of potteries purportedly of an earlier date than certain of Estrada's sherds, although controversy continues over the accuracy of various so-called calibrated and uncalibrated datings.[95] Nothing, however, has yet been found of earlier figurines. Nor have possible sources for any of the antecedent techniques and wares been adduced, though many have been postulated. Some have piously hoped, of course, that an indisputably American origin for these earliest potteries might be uncovered, an antecedent in demonstrable independence of transoceanic inspiration.

500. Broad-line incisions with square-ended tool.

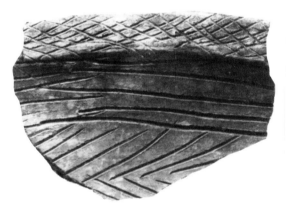

501. Row of punctuations at lower margin of an incised zone.

502. Combination of crosshatch at rim, horizontal incised lines on neck, and zigzag lines on body.

503. Zoned punctuation and incised lines.

Should that prove to be the case, however, a new and far more mysterious conundrum will have emerged, a mystery more perplexing than that of prehistoric transoceanic travel. As Clinton Edwards has remarked in comment on the papers

504. An array of early-Valdivian stone figurines.

collected in *Man across the Sea*: "We do have the problem of explaining how and why, after tens of thousands of years of very slow technological change and lack of any attributes of civilization anywhere in the world, both of the world's great land masses should rather suddenly and in many similar ways experience almost contemporaneously the phenomenon of change from the precivilized to the civilized state." He continues: "Students of Old World prehistory and history seem fairly well in accord that the major generator of change is the dispersal and interchange of ideas within a single, uncompartmented *oikumene*. On the other hand, many scholars in the United States assume that the forces and processes engendering change stem predominantly from the individual group itself, not from outsiders. The result of this latter theoretical persuasion was the compartmentalization of cultures as distinct entities in the Americas."[96]

To date, some of the more extensive of the reported researches in coastal Ecuador have been those of the expeditions organized by the University of Illinois at Urbana, directed by Donald W. Lathrap of the Field Museum of Chicago, and supported by both the United States National Science Foundation and the Banco Central of Ecuador. Among the sites excavated, two have been of outstanding consequence: Loma Alta, situated on a hill fifteen kilometers up the Valdivia River; and Real Alta, a coastal site southeast of Punta Concepción (see II.2: Map 16). From the materials accumulated, classified, and interpreted, Lathrap and his colleagues—recognizing three distinctive stages of development—have attempted to formulate a chronological reconstruction of one of the initiating culture-complexes of the American Formative era.[97]

505. These early-Valdivian ceramic figurines are distinguished by their elaborate hair treatments.

The first period they distinguish was of a *preceramic culture, dating from possibly 4000—certainly 3000—to c. 2450* B.C.,[98] when the Valdivians dwelt in small, beehivelike oval houses and practiced an intensive agriculture, which included cultivation of the bottle gourd. A finding of what appears to be spindle whorls at the bottom of one of the excavated trenches suggests that the Valdivians may already have been growing and spinning cotton, although they could equally well have been working with another wild fiber such as kapok. Their figurines were of the crudest kind, and of stone (see Figure 504).

What is generally known to American archaeology as the Formative stage of civilization (or Civilization) generally corresponds to what in Europe is known as the Neolithic (see II.2:122). Lathrap has described it as "the stage in cultural evolution…defined by the appearance of large permanent communities that derived the greater part of their food from farming."[99] Ford's charts—especially those showing

506. Detail of an enigmatic, dual-headed, early-Valdivian stone figurine, one of the earliest representations of the distinctive, universal, bifocal, mythological perspective that would later inform such aboriginal, American graphic metaphors as the Tlatilcan "pretty ladies" (see **342**), the Huichol sky goddess Our Mother Young Eagle Girl (see **404**), and certain early-Antillean zemis (see **430**).

507. The presence of the bottle gourd already in the garden plots of earliest Ecuador (Valdivia 1, c. 4000/3000–2450 B.C.) is suggested by the discovery there of bowls, with incised faces and rims carved in imitation of a carved gourd, similar to the examples pictured above: the top bowl has a diameter of c. 7¼", while the bottom is c. 3⁵⁄₁₆" high.

For the bottle gourd, or calabash, is native not to America, where it is known only as a cultigen, but to tropical Africa.[59] Its dissemination has been attributed by some to waves and currents, but as Carl Sauer pointed out some thirty years ago: "It is a cultigen as we know it in America and depends on the care of man for its preservation. It is in no sense a strand or marsh plant. The theory of its accidental dissemination involves, in addition to the undamaged transit of an ocean, a waiting agriculturalist who carried it from the seashore to a suitable spot of cultivation. It is at any rate an anciently grown plant in the New World, as many gourds in archaeological sites attest."[60] Two more recent authorities, Thomas W. Whitaker and Herbert G. Baker, have suggested in reply to this point that a gourd washed up by waves might have been picked up simply by a beach-comber and carried to the finder's village to be opened out of curiosity, with the contents finally thrown onto a trash pile, where the seeds took root.[61] So that, in Whitaker's considered view, "The gourd could have been introduced into the Americas by drift from Africa or Polynesia, but introduction by human transportation remains a distinct possibility."[62]

Lathrap's date of 4000/3000 B.C. eliminates Polynesia, however, which at that time was uninhabited. "On the northern border of Mesoamerica," Whitaker reports, "*L. siceraria* [the bottle gourd] is reported from strata radiocarbon dated at 7000–5000 B.C. This is the earliest date for this species in the Americas."[63] But here again, as in Ecuador, we are on the Pacific side of the continent; so that, one way or the other, either by ocean current or by sailing raft on the same current, the odds are for a trans-Pacific voyage of the bottle gourd from that part of the world around the Celebes Sea from which Stephen Jett has presumed the long-house, blowgun, bark-cloth beater, panpipe, and dugout canoe to have come to South America, together with the idea itself of vegetative-reproduction-shifting cultivation. Consideration, with Map 41 in view, of the distance that a bottle gourd would have had to have floated undamaged from the Celebes Sea to the American coast, to be picked up there by a beachcomber, opened out of curiosity, and thrown onto a trash pile, where its seeds (still alive and well) took root, will, one should think, suffice to settle the case for deliberate transportation by an agriculturalist who knew what he had.

the distribution of grinding stones, figurines, and ceremonial constructions—strongly suggest that in Formative Ecuador the passage from an economy of nomadic hunting and gathering to a sedentary life and to agriculture (a cultural transition that has elsewhere been viewed as being a prerequisite to the development of an archaic high civilization: literate and monumental, aristocratic and city-based) had already occurred in Ecuador by c. 3000 B.C., a date arguably earlier than any recorded elsewhere in the Americas. Lathrap's excavations both suggested and enlarged upon this demonstration: "One should consider," he declares, "even earliest Valdivia fully Formative."[100]

The origin of this agriculture is itself, of course, a question. Lathrap holds that both the agriculture and the life-style of the earliest Valdivians represented "an extension of Tropical Forest culture, which itself expanded out of the Amazon Basin, first to the Guayas Basin, and then on west to the coast. It was a Tropical Forest economy further enriched by the presence of developed races of corn."[101] Others counter, however, that "all evidence indicates settlement was earlier on the coast. Preceramic complexes—for example, the Vega—extend to 7000 B.C."[102]

If we accept Lathrap's reading of the evidence, it only presses back the origin of this agricultural development to the Amazonian Basin and the (undated) appearance there of what Stephen Jett suggested was a type of vegetative-reproduction-shifting cultivation possibly exported from insular Southeast Asia and applied in tropical South America to plants of the local forest: manioc, peanuts, and potatoes, in place of taro and yams.

The second stage of culture defined in Lathrap's reconstruction of the prehistory of coastal Ecuador was of a *pottery-fashioning population, during a period extending from c. 2450–1850 B.C.* (Valdivia 2 through 5, according to his reckoning), when large, elliptical houses appear (Figure 508), which by 2300 B.C. (Valdivia 3), at the coastal site of Real Alto, stood arranged along a central

509. Jar fragment with an incised and mottled design representing corn ears, c. 6⁵⁄₁₆" tall, from San Pablo, Valdivia phase 6, c. 1850–1700 B.C.

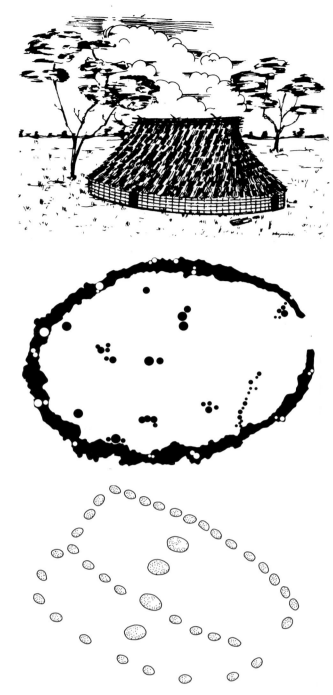

508. Hypothetical drawing (top) of a large early-Valdivian house, the frame of which was built of hardwood posts, up to c. 8" in diameter, deeply embedded in a trench serving as the foundation for an outer wall that encircled an oval area, 33'9" × 26'2½"; reconstruction based on one complete floor plan (middle), as well as traces of several others, from the site of Real Alto (bottom), a village, according to Donald W. Lathrap, of numerous similar dwellings "oriented around a central open plaza containing the remains of what appears to be a somewhat larger structure."[64]

plaza by way of a well-planned village (length, north-south, about 330 yards; breadth about 220). Two matching mounds, projecting from the house rows, divided the plaza into north and south. Potsherds decorated with what could plausibly be corn-kernel impressions (Figure 509) suggest that maize may have been in cultivation at the time. Other sherds have been interpreted as being in imitation of bottle gourds.[103] The figurines—no longer of stone, but of clay—appear to be of a totally different tradition from the earlier, beehivehut period; they are exactly those which Estrada found associated with nearly 40,000 pottery sherds suggesting some connection with the Early Middle Jomon ware of contemporary Japan.

Another reading of the archaeological record in Ecuador at this time points to increasing evidence of an enduring, landward, Tropical Forest connection that suggests a remarkably full and convincing reconstruction by analogy of the social manners of the period.

At the Real Alto site, for example, the complete floor plan of one of the dwellings was uncovered. It had been a large building, with walls enclosing an oval area some forty feet long and thirty feet wide. Massive hardwood posts, eight inches in diameter, forming the frame of the structure, were deeply embedded in a trench that served as the foundation for the outer wall. "The size of the house," states Lathrap, "is not compatible with the interpretation that it sheltered a single nuclear family. Rather, the structure is comparable to the *malocas* of the Upper Amazon which house large groups, several families related through the male line. A population of thirty people for the house does not seem excessive."[104]

Lathrap estimates a community of fifty to one hundred of such longhouses, all oriented according to an overall plan that has its closest parallels (in his view) "in modern Indian communities occurring in a broad belt from the highlands of northeastern Brazil to the south and west on up to the eastern foothills of the Andes in Bolivia....It is legitimate," he concludes, "to look to the village plans of Ge and Bororo communities and the social order they exemplify for clues to the interpretation of Valdivia society."[105]

And not only the social order, the religious practices, too, can be postulated to have been of the Upper Amazonian Tropical Forest type; for instance, in the ritualized use of hallucinogenic drugs, and in the prominence of the role and figure of the shaman. As discussed by Lathrap:

"Tropical Forest cultures of South America are remarkable in that they use far more hallucinogenic drugs and integrate the use of such drugs into their religion in a more complex way than any other peoples on earth. More species of plants containing chemicals which can alter the physiological or psychological state of the human organism have been identified and used by Indian groups of the Amazon than by any other people. Both species of domesticated tobacco were clearly brought under cultivation in the Amazon drainage. Coca, the source of the modern drug cocaine, was domesticated on the eastern slope of the Andes. The tropical vine, *Banisteriopsis,* frequently referred to as *ayahuasca,* and the seeds of the mimosa-like tree, *Anadenanthera,* are two of the most powerful vision-producing agents known, resulting in particularly intense and complex colored hallucinations. These are only a few of the most widespread and powerful mind-expanding drugs in the arsenal of the Tropical Forest religious practitioners. The visions and experiences achieved through the use of these drugs are of great religious importance, both in ceremonials binding the living group to the collective body of dead relatives, and in curing rituals. The most common religious practitioner in the Amazon Basin is the shaman, who gets his power through repeated sacramental use of *ayahuasca* and/or the snuff ground from seeds of the *Anadenanthera.* It is believed that while under the influence of these elements, the shaman is possessed by or turns into a ferocious animal, most typically a cayman [a kind of South American alligator] or a jaguar. While possessed by or transformed into his supernatural helper, or alter-ego, he is believed to be capable of traveling at incredible speed through both time and space and in this state can retrieve the soul of his patient or determine what other conditions must be met to insure the recovery of his patient.

"Over most of tropical South America east of the Andes the symbol of this kind of shaman is a wooden stool that is carved in the form of the ferocious creature who is the alter-ego of the individual shaman. Most typically the stool is in the form of a jaguar, although the cayman is also frequent and there are even examples implying a double load of power, with one end carved as a cayman and the other as a jaguar.

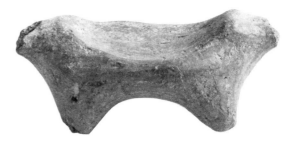

510. Two shaman's stools: top, a Valdivian ceramic miniature, c. 2⅜" long, featureless now, probably once represented a jaguar; below, from Cerrojupa, Manabi province, Ecuador, a full-sized stone seat with a jaguar in relief on the base.

511. A striking ceramic, c. 18¼" high, that is an outstanding representation of the anthropomorphic jaguar god, who, as has been demonstrated over and over again, is a dominant figure in the mythologies of most South American peoples; from coastal Ecuador, the La Tolita-Tuymaco culture, c. A.D. 1000.

"The uniformity of this complex of beliefs and practices throughout South America indicates that it is a very old system of thought and can be projected back to the earliest variants of the Tropical Forest culture. It is thus of tremendous interest that along with the solid human figurines of Valdivia, which may have served in curing rituals, we find exact miniature replicas of the zoomorphic wooden shaman's stools which are the prerogative of the Tropical Forest curer. One of the Valdivia examples is even clearly a jaguar, and is identical except in scale to a recently carved wooden stool from the upper Xingu Basin in Brazil...The presence of this kind of shaman's stool implies the use of either *ayahuasca* or the snuff from the *Anadenanthera* tree."[106]

"The Buena Vista series," he reported, "associated with a pottery-making culture, represents a very homogeneous brachycranic [broad-headed] type that probably corresponds to a family group…The Buena Vista physical type is totally different from the earlier preceramic Peruvian coastal population of Cabezas Largas, leading to the inference that the introduction of pottery also brought a new physical type. This new group may be to a large degree the source of the brachycrany observed in populations associated with the later pottery-making periods of the Peruvian coast."[109]

Another body of evidence to be taken into account is of the shell fishhooks found among Valdivia remains already from the earliest period (see Figure 513). As noticed by Meggers, Evans, and Estrada, "All are of pearl oyster (*Pinctada mazatlanica*) and similar in general size, proportions, and construction."[110] And as Lathrap has observed of the same: "It has been noted

512. An anthropomorphic grotesque jaguar head with deeply hooded eyes, a wry smile, prominent incisors, and a distinctive, cowl-like headdress; made of brownware pottery, c. 5¼" high × 7" wide, this suggestive specimen was recovered from an area located in the state of Manabi (Ecuador) near the confluence of the Peripa and Daule rivers; it is of the Jama-Coaque Culture.

All of this we recognize from what we have already learned of the Amazonian tribes. It is necessary to note, however, that the cultures of those tribes are not generally classified by anthropologists as being representative of the Formative stage of civilization. Furthermore, other scholars have difficulty accepting the certainty with which Lathrap pursues his Tropical Forest connection; they argue that equally plausible antecedent cultures can be found elsewhere.

During the period of occupation of the excavated longhouse at the coastal site of Real Alto, there gradually built up on the dirt floor some eight inches of trash and, as Lathrap reports: "This cultural deposit contains the remains of hundreds of pots and dozens of figurines made, used, and discarded by the inhabitants."[107]

Ceramic figurines are not characteristic features of Tropical Forest religious usage, but belong, on the contrary, to the complex represented in the ceramic wares of Jomon affiliation discovered by Estrada. If their association here is also with the Tropical Forest folkways, as Lathrap suggested, then early Ecuador may have been an arena for just such a coming together of two distinct traditions as can usually be found wherever significant formative cultural transformations have come to pass. As Heine-Geldern points out in his article on the origin of ancient civilizations: "How-

ever original and unique each of the ancient civilizations may appear to be, not one of them came into being independently. Fecundation by another civilization was always necessary…. Even the oldest of the higher civilizations, that of Babylonia, ancestor of all others, did not come into being through 'mutation'…but emerged as the result of mutual contacts of a whole series of cultures which had preceded it."[108]

From the now numerous sites of coastal and inland Ecuador, the reported evidence suggests very strongly a conjunction of two distinct traditions, one of the land, the other of the sea. The Guayas area is especially well suited for meetings of this kind, with its riverways affording passage to the trans-Andean interior and the trans-Pacific *Kuroshio*, "Black Current" (see Map 41), coming to land precisely at the well-named promontory of Punta Concepción. Its geographical location, then, is surely a major reason why coastal Ecuador might well have been a, if not the, Formative matrix of the New World civilizations; and why, during its initial centuries (from c. 3000 B.C. or earlier, to c. 1000 B.C.), with new influences arriving not once simply, but repeatedly, from Asia, it appears to have stood far in advance of any of its neighbors.

This judgment is reinforced by the skeletal remains unearthed by Meggers, Evans, and Estrada at their coastal Valdivia sites. Juan R. Munizaga, of the Universidad de Chile, Santiago, to whom these remains were entrusted for analysis, arrived at the conclusion that the Valdivia skulls taken from the site of Buena Vista were of a totally different physical type from skulls one thousand years older, unearthed at the *preceramic* Cabezas Largas site on the south coast of Peru.

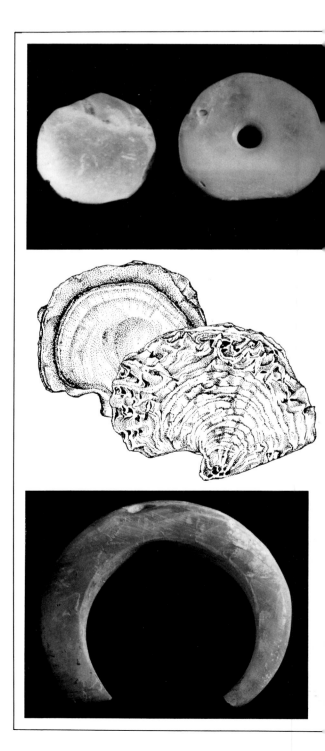

frequently that the hook of mother-of-pearl shell which functions both to engage the fish's mouth and to serve as lure, is remarkably similar over the whole Pacific. In the New World," he continues, "such hooks of an early date are known from the pre-ceramic occupation of the north coast of Chile [about where, by the way, the Japanese drift expedition of 1980 came to land]. The fishing equipment of the late prehistoric and historic Chumash Indians of Southern California is also remarkably similar. Comparable hooks were also in use on most of the Polynesian and Micronesian islands."[111] Such a distribution of evidence through immense reaches of both time and space speaks certainly of a long continued oceanic (Old Pacific) order of life in which a good part of the American Pacific Coast participated. And that this oceanic culture made its contribution to the Formative transformations of the Punta Concepción domain is surely evident as well. A little

ceramic bowl in the form of a dugout canoe (Figure 514), which Lathrap assigns to Valdivia 4, c. 2150–2000 B.C.,[112] and which might have represented either a vessel for coastal fishing or one for travel on the riverways that penetrate the Andes and lead to the Amazon, may be taken as a reminder, at this point, of the adaptability of artifacts to new purposes.

514. Restored ceramic bowl fragment with red slip, suggestive of a dugout canoe, c. 2″ high, Valdivia phase 4, c. 2250–2000 B.C.

Generally sociologists recognize that, complementary to the influences (no matter how strong) of what is known as *diffusion,* are the responses of *acculturation,* the processes of change that occur in any native culture following an alien infusion. These changes are of two orders: (1) "directed change," where the influence is of one people establishing, with its institutions, dominance over another through military conquest or political control, as, for example, in the instance of the Christian conquest of America and, centuries earlier, of Europe; and (2) "voluntary incorporation," where, through cultural interchange, borrowings occur without the exercise of military or political domination, as, for example, in the receptions by China and Japan of the Buddhism of India. In developments of this second kind the diffused complex or idea serves largely as a catalyst, releasing reactions which finally are of the society affected. And indeed, even in cases of a massively "directed change," the native character is what is definitive, finally, of the consequence. The Christianity of the Indians of Peru or Brazil today, for example, is hardly that of Ignatius Loyola in sixteenth-century Spain or of Oliver Cromwell in seventeenth-century England; not to mention Saint Paul. Indeed, even in Matthew, Mark, Luke, and John, there are differences enough to give one thought.

The term *diffusion,* that is to say, is misconstrued when taken to imply the annulment, rather than activation, of native creativity. As one distracted theoretician has complained: "If all the world can be linked in a single one-way claim of diffusion, comparison is unnecessary. Why compare the rise of civilization in Mesopotamia, China, Mexico, and Peru if China

received all its significant ideas from Mesopotamia, Mexico from China, and Peru from Mexico (or Peru from Ecuador from Japan)?"[113] To which the elementary answer is, of course, that the virtue of a scientist lies, in contrast to that of a theologian, in recognizing a fact, not in defending an idea. Moreover, no one has ever claimed that *all* of the significant ideas of China and Japan, Mexico and Peru, must have come from the Near East; or even that all those ideas which clearly *are* from that earliest source of what is known as "archaic high civilization" (literate and monumental, aristocratic and city-based) remained in sense and form unchanged in Egypt, India, China, Japan, Mexico, and Peru. There is such a thing, moreover, as "stimulus diffusion," where a dispersed idea becomes variously embodied, as in the instance recognized by Stephen Jett, of the idea of vegetative-reproduction-shifting cultivation carried from tropical Southeast Asia to tropical America, to be applied there to plants of the local scene.

For a date some time within the period of Valdivia 6 (c. 1850–1700 B.C.), the "impressions of two textiles of different weave," states Lathrap, "have been noted on a lump of partially fired clay from Real Alto.... It is conceivable," he adds, "that a plant other than the New World cultivated cotton was the source of the fiber that went into the yarn of the textile, but the very fine and even character of this yarn makes such an alternative unlikely...given the firmness of the yarn and the high warp count per centimeter, it is most likely that a heddle loom was used."[114]

Now, as reported by S. G. Stephens, "Of more than twenty species of *Gossipium* that have been recognized, only four include cultivated forms....Two of the species, *G. arboreum* L. and *G. herbaceum* L., have thirteen pairs of chromosomes and are confined to the Old World continents and neighboring islands. So far there is no convincing evidence that these species, or any nearly related wild species, have existed in the New World except in recent experimental culture....The other two species, *G. hirsutum* L. and *G. barbadense* L., have twenty-six pairs of chromosomes. They are commonly known as the New World cottons, because their centers of variability and archaeological prehistory lie in Mesoamerica and northern South America, respectively. Cultivated forms of both [American] species, however, are widely distributed in the subtropics of both Eastern and Western hemispheres and in Polynesia....There are two puzzling cases of cotton distribution that might be related to early transoceanic contacts, though alternative interpretations cannot be excluded. They are of particular interest because one case (cotton in the Cape Verde Islands) requires some form of transatlantic distribution; the other (cotton in the Marquesas Islands) may involve a transpacific contact."[115]

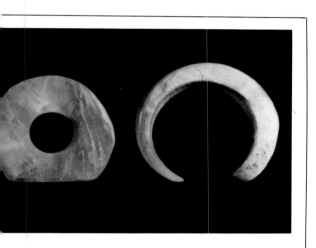

513. The sequence above depicts shell fishhooks in several stages of fabrication; beginning as a circular shell fragment, the hook is formed using stone reamers to make a central perforation that is gradually enlarged and shaped — a method of manufacture that is remarkably similar throughout the entire Pacific. That the early Ecuadorians were involved with marine fishing is evidenced by the recovery from Valdivia Phase excavations of seventeen such fishhooks or fishhook fragments (two exemplary, intact specimens are pictured below). These deeply recurved fishhooks — fabricated from the disklike, glistening shells of the pearl oyster (left, *Pinctada mazatlanica*), which is found in coastal waters from the Gulf of California to Peru — served a dual function, being both tantalizing lures that attracted fish and effective tools for ensnaring them.

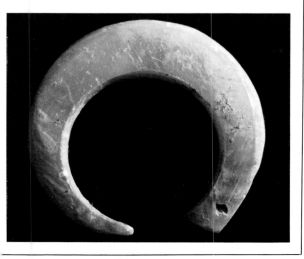

How these contacts might have been effected, Stephens does not pretend to know, though he does have a couple of quaint suggestions. One is of "transport by birds";[116] so that those who tremble to think of pre-Columbian passages by human navigation may now entertain the more likely idea of some bird of powerful wing consuming a cargo of durable seeds and then taking off in all haste, with neck outstretched, to attain some unseen distant land before nature would have worked the cycle of its usual course and discharged the burden into the ocean. The other suggestion was of European seamen of the sixteenth century or later throwing overboard their old worn-out mattresses, which, being stuffed with seed-bearing New World cotton, might then have floated to hospitable shores.[117]

The valuable observation here is of a New World cultigen distributed to coastal Africa and to Polynesia. The datings seem not to be known, but there is the obvious implication of pre-Columbian two-way voyaging, at least across the Pacific, where the evidence is in accord with that of Heyerdahl's drift-voyage from the Peruvian coast to the Tuamotus on the raft *Kon-Tiki*.

Cultivated cotton is one thing, however; a cotton fabric finely woven is another. Fragments of a cotton textile, dyed red and sticking to the side of a silver vase, were recovered from excavations at Mohenjo-daro in Sind: of the period, that is to say, of India's pre-Vedic, Indus Valley Civilization, c. 2300–1750 B.C. The yarn was of *Gossypium arboreum*. Textiles in Egypt, finely woven of flax, and in Mesopotamia, of wool, are of dates a millennium earlier. But the earliest known cotton has been, up to now, from Mohenjo-daro. Remarkably, half the world away, the Valdivia date, c. 1850–1700 B.C., is a close match.

Striking changes in the forms and ornamentation of Valdivian ceramic wares, from c. 2000 B.C., occurred at about the same time as, but seemingly were not influenced by, a substantial influx of potteries from a newly arrived ceramic tradition which was named by Meggers, Evans, and Estrada—after a type site north of Valdivia village—the Machalilla Phase. "The area occupied by these sites extends along the coast," they reported, "from South Manabi Province into northern Guayas Province."[118] And among the human skeletal remains associated with these sites there appeared a feature formerly unknown to the American Pacific Coast, namely, *artificial deformation of the human skull* (see II.2:312). Again quoting Munizaga, who analyzed these remains:

"Cranial deformation appears for the first time on the Pacific coast of South America in Ecuador at about 4000 years ago, as part of the Machalilla Phase. The type of deformation is fronto-vertico-occipital or tabular erecta, of the variety known as 'cuneiform' or 'Chavín.'

515. Machalilla solid ceramic figurines from the Barcelona site, c. 1500–1000 B.C.; both feature red-on-tan painting, coffee-bean eyes, and salient noses: left figure, c. 5″ tall; right fragment, c. 4¼″ high.

516. Two Chacras-style (Terminal Valdivia) ceramics: left, red-slip figurine of seated woman, c. 5½″ tall, from Valdivia Heights; right, fragment, 2½″ high, from Miguelillo, Manabi.

"Tabular erecta deformation appears along most of coastal Peru in the late Pre-ceramic, at a date subsequent to its occurrence in Ecuador, permitting the inference that it was diffused from north to south.

"The North-South diffusion current is most clearly demonstrated by the Formative Period complexes (Machalilla, Cupisnique, Early Ancon-Supe, Paracas Cavernas), in which identity in the variety of deformation implies diffusion of the same deforming apparatus, a rather complicated system that seems to be correlated with this time period and zone."[119]

"The different shapes that a normal skull can acquire by deformation have been classified into types and varieties according to the manner in which pressures were applied. This permits us to infer from the characteristics of a skull the kind of apparatus by which it was molded. The tabular erecta deformation shown by the Machalilla Phase skulls is the result of strong compression of the back of the head against a hard surface, to which it is fastened by appropriate binding. The 'cuneiform' variety of this type indicated that the head was held so that the face invariably looked forward; the pronounced occipital flattening shows that the bindings were tightly applied; the concavity of the occipital permits the inference that a pillow-like object was placed between the skull and the board."[120]

By 1700 B.C. (Valdivia 7, according to Lathrap's reckoning) the village at Real Alto had become, as he described it, "an administrative and religious center controlling several farmsteads scattered along the Rio Verde and other lesser rivers such as El Rio Real, thus managing some six hundred acres of riverine agricultural bottom lands. This system of a control center with satellite settlements," he adds, "implies a stratified society."[121]

517. This hollow figurine of a naked man, c. 11½″ tall, is noteworthy for its face and body painting (including incised designs that have been filled with white pigment), its distinctive hair (or headdress) treatment, and its prominent circular ear-spools, an ornamentation most often associated with Indians living in the Amazon Basin and eastern Brazil; Chorrera, c. 1000–200 B.C., from Cerro Verde, state of Manabi, Ecuador.

It appears thus probable, from the look of things, that a governing priestly caste (or perhaps race) was now in charge, such as in the classic periods of both the South and Middle American hieratic civilizations of the first millennium A.D. maintained in great ceremonial centers a formal ceremonial order of social festivals and observances, while a rural agricultural population, residing in villages round about, provided both the economic support and the required manual labor for the maintenance of a manner of life established equally in the energies of nature and the forms of a society oriented to cosmological coordinations. Two completely different types of figurine now appear: one quite crude and markedly stylized (Figure 515), with coffee-bean eyes and a salient nose; the other, of hollow forms (Figure 516)— as were the later, so-called Chorrera figurines of c. 1000–300 B.C. (named for an inland site in the Guayas Basin)— represents what Lathrap declares to be "the artistic climax of the Ecuadorian Formative."[122]

Across the Pacific the civilization of China had by now attained maturity. The dates of the Shang dynasty are from c. 1523–1027 B.C. Lathrap dates the Machalilla phase in Ecuador from c. 1500–1000 B.C. and the culminating Chorrera phase from c. 1000–300 B.C., which is the period in China of the Chou dynasty (c. 1057–250 B.C.). Among the hollow ceramic Chorrera figures Lathrap remarks a beautifully rendered dog forming the body of a whistling bottle (Figure 519). "This particular dog representation," he declares, "...is the ancestor of the whole range of delightful dog effigies from the state of Colima in western Mexico. Similar figures of dogs are particularly common in the late prehistoric Chimu empire on the North Coast of Peru where they are executed in a burnished black ware. All of these dog representations seem to form a single artistic tradition of which this Chorrera vessel is the oldest known example. It also appears to depict the particular breed of dog so faithfully portrayed by Colima and Chimu potters. This is the breed usually referred to as the Mexican hairless.

"The Mexican hairless was bred as a source of meat, its low massive body having the same relationship to the contours of a normal dog as our own Angus steer has to the basic configuration of wild cattle. The presence of this highly specialized breed of dog in Chorrera before 500 B.C. suggests a long prior history of attention to the food potential of this oldest of domesticated animals and argues that the breed first appeared in Ecuador and from there spread to Northern Peru and West Mexico. A dog is known from China where it was bred for eating before 2000 B.C. Some people have suggested that the presence of this particular breed in the New World is the result of contact eastward across the Pacific

518. Late Preclassic ceramic representations of Colima dogs that were interred with the dead for food and for companionship.

519. Chorrera whistling bottle in the form of a dog, c. 10¾" high, Manabi, Ecuador. "Similar figures of dogs," notes Donald W. Lathrap, "are particularly common in the late prehistoric Chimu empire on the North Coast of Peru where they are executed in a burnished black ware. All of these dog representations seem to form a single artistic tradition of which this Chorrera vessel is the oldest known example....This is the breed usually referred to as the Mexican hairless."[65]

around 1000 B.C. Such transpacific diffusion might account not only for the dog but also for the peculiar ceramic pillows to be discussed later, and for certain kinds of human figurines and house effigies that are peculiarly East Asian in appearance."[123]

It might account also, one might add, for a number of other novelties that appeared in the New World at just this time. For the date, c. 1000 B.C., is of the greatest moment as marking the almost simultaneous appearances in Middle and South America of *two monumental cultures,* one, the Olmec, in Mexico, on the torrid Gulf coast of Tabasco and Veracruz; the other, the Chavín, in the northern highlands and neighboring Pacific coast of Peru. The manifestation in Mexico was suddenly of a sculptural art, already of the highest standard, rendering colossi in basalt and miniatures in jade, associated (at La Venta) with a ceremonial compound containing a fluted pyramid. That in Peru was of a massive temple complex built of dressed rectangular stone blocks, honeycombed with galleries at different levels, ventilated by shafts and decorated with mythological figures carved in low relief on its stone pillars and lintels. Prominent in both art contexts is the figure of a jaguar-mask or -man, suggesting shamanic associations, but also, as Garry J. Tee has shown,[124] there is evidence

in the aesthetic handling of these forms of an influence from China.

Schematically, the dating of these two new cultures may be registered as from c. 1000 B.C. to c. 200 B.C., with the Olmec as perhaps the earlier. They are regarded as representing the initial phases of the monumental high civilizations of Mexico and Peru. In Ecuador the contemporary development, c. 1000–400 B.C., was of the Chorrera phase already mentioned, where, in addition to the superb unfoldment in ceramic wares, a number of signs appear of a cluster of ideas that can only have arrived from elsewhere: not only dogs bred for eating, ceramic pillows, and house effigies, but also, roller stamps of a kind long known in southeast Asia, large ear spools, and the flute.

The cultural lead at this time passes from Ecuador to Mexico and Peru, in both of which later centers the timeless, village-based, Neolithic order of life is irrevocably surpassed—through a time-factored acceleration of developments which, like an organic process working through its inevitable course, is to unfold, mature, and come to its period of full ripening, when, like a thunderbolt, the fire of the Spanish Inquisition arrives and by a handful of incredibly courageous, gold-maddened thugs, two civilizations are laid waste.

The Civilization and Despoliation of Peru

Reconstruction of the mythologies of the Pre-Incan peoples of present-day Peru is rendered difficult, first, by the fact that there are no written documents, either from their time, or from the period of the Incas; second, by the fact that the Incas, though their reign was short (hardly 150 years, c. A.D. 1380–1532), imposed their own mythology on the whole area, either eliminating or assimilating local cults and traditions; and finally by the fact that what late reports we do possess are from the pens of Spanish chroniclers, who were neither well informed nor particularly interested—with, however, two exceptions:

Garcilasso Inca de la Vega was the son of a young Spanish nobleman who had served under Alvarado as a captain of infantry and in 1538, in Peru, six years after the conquest, married a baptized granddaughter of Tupac Yupanqui, the eleventh Inca (fl. c. 1439). Garcilasso was born in 1540, in Cuzco, of which city his father was then governor. His mother died when he was twelve; his father, when he was twenty. Sailing to Spain, he served in the army, from which he retired when thirty or thirty-five, to settle in Cordova and devote himself there to writing, until his death, 1616, the year of the deaths, also, of Shakespeare and Cervantes. Garcilasso's principal opus, *The Royal Commentaries of the Incas,* reviews in Part 1 the history of Peru before the Conquest, and, in Part 2, the history of the Conquest and of the wars, thereafter, among the Conquistadores themselves for monopoly of the spoils.[125]

The second valuable chronicler, Pedro de Cieza de León, who was born in Seville about 1519, came to the New World at the age of thirteen and remained until 1550, during which season of seventeen years, while serving in various armies, he began in 1541 to keep diligently a journal, with intention of publication in four parts.[126]

"The attempt savors of temerity in so unlearned a man," he wrote, "but others of more learning are too much occupied in the wars to write. Oftentimes when the other soldiers were reposing, I was tiring myself by writing. Neither fatigue nor the ruggedness of the country, nor the mountains and rivers, nor intolerable hunger and suffering have ever been sufficient to obstruct my two duties, namely, writing and following my flag and my captain without fault....Much that I have written I saw with my own eyes, and I traveled over many countries in order to learn more concerning them. Of those things which I did not see, I took great pains to inform myself, from persons of good repute, both Christians and Indians."[127]

Of the people of those times before the founding of the Empire, however, not even this good man could learn. "From what I gathered from the accounts of the Indians around Cuzco," he recorded, "it would seem that in olden times there was great disorder in this kingdom we call Peru, and that the natives were stupid and brutish beyond belief. They say they were like animals, and that many ate human flesh, and others took their daughters and mothers to wife, and committed even greater sins, and had great traffic with the devil, whom they served and held in great esteem. Aside from this they had strongholds and fortresses in the mountains and hills, and on the least pretext, they sallied forth from them to make war on one another, and killed and took prisoner as many as they could. In spite of the fact that they were given over to these sins and worked these evils, they also say that some of them were religiously inclined, and for that reason in many parts of this kingdom they built great temples, where they prayed, performing their rites and superstitions before big idols, and the devil appeared to them and was worshipped. And while the people of this kingdom were living in this way, great tyrants arose in the provinces of Colla and in the valleys of the Yungas and elsewhere, who carried on war against one another, and committed many killings and thefts, and they all suffered great calamities. Many fortresses and castles were destroyed, but the struggle between them went on, at which the devil, the enemy of mankind, rejoiced to see so many souls lost."[128]

Cieza's own Roman Catholic mythology shows through here. For him, the devil was an actual personage who wandered through the world for the ruin of souls, as God too was a living, albeit invisible, personage. Invisible both, they are the ultimate antagonists in the great theater of world history, in competition for the capture of souls with which to populate their kingdoms: the one, of dark and total torment; the other, radiant of God's presence. Many peoples have ideas about God, but only Roman Catholics have true knowledge, namely, of God as three divine Persons: Father, Son, and Holy Spirit.

The first, the Father, created not only heaven and earth, but also hell, to receive that once luminous prince of the host of his angels, Lucifer, who in pride had set his own will above that of his Creator and so incurred the terrible wrath of God, who flung at him that awful sentence of rejection [undoubtedly in Latin]: "Depart from me, thou cursed, into everlasting fire!" And together with him went those of the heavenly host who had joined him in rebellion.

But God the Father created, also, Adam and Eve, male and female, in his own image, to live in timeless happiness in a timeless Earthly Paradise, out of which four rivers ran in the four directions. And Lucifer, now Satan, to avenge himself on his Creator's indignation, took the form of a serpent—wisest and therefore least trustworthy of God's creatures—wherewith to seduce the "weaker vessel," Eve (who had been fashioned from one of her husband's ribs), into tasting the fruit of a certain tree of the knowledge of good and evil, which by God's command, was the one tree in the garden the fruit of which had been expressly forbidden to the couple. Whereupon, having eaten, their eyes were opened to the knowledge, not only of good and evil, but also of male and female, and with leaves they clothed their nakedness. So that when the Father, whose pleasure it was to walk in the garden in the cool of the day, discovered them thus attired, he realized what they had done. And [as we read in the Book] lest they should eat of the fruit of a second tree, which also grew in that garden, the Tree of Eternal Life [compare the Bo-Tree of the Buddha; folklore motif: World Tree *axis mundi,* Tree of Life] and so become immortal and omniscient as himself, he withdrew from their sight and expelled them from the garden, setting to guard its gate two angels with a flaming sword between, to block the way to the Tree of Life.

Thus Satan, the devil, had mankind in his keep, and the Father, offended in wrath withdrawn, had abandoned the whole of creation to the malice and deceptions of that Antagonist and his ubiquitous host. It was he and his imps who inhabited all the idols of heathenness; he and they who appeared to shamanic seers in visions; and again, he and they, who, having thus deluded the progeny of fallen Adam and Eve, were harvesting souls unnumbered to the torments of their hell-pit of dark fire.

In heaven, however, a program of redemption had been conceived—at once to recover mankind from the devil's keep, and to atone mankind with the inaccessible Father—and the Son, Second Person of the Trinity, became the agent of this feat of rescue. Begotten of the Holy Spirit, Third Person of the Trinity, in the blessed womb of an immaculate daughter of the chosen race of Israel [a holy, priestly race, which had

520. Pope Alexander VI, Rodrigo Borgia, father of a dozen or more illegitimate offspring—some in Spain, others in Italy—of whom Juan, Cesare, Jofre, and Lucrezia Borgia are the best known. *Inter Cetera,* his 1493 Bull (see pp. 308–309), divided New World lands between Portugal and Spain (the last remaining great Catholic powers of Europe).

been set apart by God to become the vessel of the Incarnation; but which, alas!, on accomplishment of the Event, had shut its eyes and ears to the Word become Flesh, and so, having become accursed to God, was now, in this sixteenth century of the Years of Our Lord, to be scoured out of Catholic Spain, together with the devil's heretic brood of Mohamet], the Son had become Man, and, as at once True God and True Man, had been crucified, taken down from the Cross, and buried: by which Sacrifice the Father had been atoned in his wrath and mankind redeemed from the devil's keep. Not all of mankind was redeemed, however [and here, of course, was the crucial historical point], only those baptized into the One True Church, which the Son had founded in his lifetime and committed to the infallible charge of his disciples under Peter: wherein, by virtue of the sacraments, participation in the reconciliation of mankind with the Father was attained, and salvation thereby from the devil. *Extra ecclesia nulla salus.* Only under the sign of the Cross are the devices of the devil and his host undone.

Therefore, for the healing of mankind, frustration of the devil, and accomplishment of God's purpose in the world, the work of history was to enlarge the bourn of Peter's Church, which task, since the devil's recent calamitous triumphs in accomplishing the heresies of Luther and Henry VIII, had fallen upon the only two remaining great Catholic powers in God's Europe, namely Portugal and Spain. The Bull of Pope Alexander VI, Rodrigo Borgia (see Figure 520) had conferred God's charge upon these most Catholic nations, that (as therein written) "the health of souls should be procured and the barbarous nations subdued and brought to the faith."[129]

It is little likely that a sincere participant in such a world-restructuring enterprise should be able to understand anything of mythologies not his own. Moreover, in the matter of mythologies earlier than the Inca, Cieza's informants (as may be judged from the passage above quoted, page 368) were quite as ignorant as himself. An idea can be gained of the sense the Incas entertained of the superiority of themselves and their civilization to the tribal cultures, not only in former times, but also still around them, from an account recorded by Cieza of the subjugation of an aboriginal Colombian tribe by the Lord-Inca Huayna Capac (fl. c. A.D. 1475).

Having subdued in Ecuador "certain nations [to use Cieza's words] who had never wished to accept his friendship," he proceeded northward and "went exploring as far as the Angasmayo River, which was the boundary of his empire. And he learned from the natives that farther on there were many peoples, and that they all went naked without the least shame, and that all, all of them, ate human flesh, and he built several strongholds in the region of the Pastos. [See Map 39.] He sent word to their headmen that they were to pay him tribute, and they replied that they had

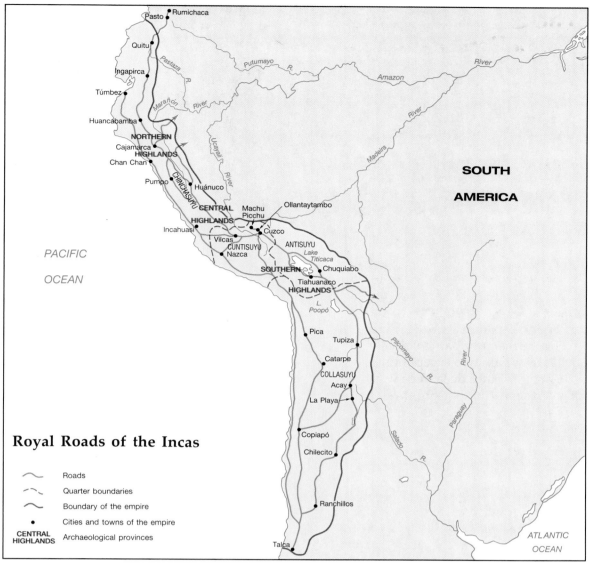

Royal Roads of the Incas

~ Roads
~ Quarter boundaries
~ Boundary of the empire
• Cities and towns of the empire
CENTRAL HIGHLANDS Archaeological provinces

Map 42.

nothing to give him. Whereupon, to bring them to reason, he ordered that every house in the land, every so many moons, must give him in tribute a large quill of lice. At first they laughed at his order; but afterwards, however lousy they were, they found they could not fill so many quills. So they tended the flocks the Inca had ordered left with them, and paid with those that were born of the foods and tubers grown in their lands."[130]

*   *   *

It was not until about 1940 that the archaeological investigation of Pre-Inca Peru began to be seriously pursued by university-supported expeditions, and although much remains to be learned, the chronology that has already emerged of earlier kingdoms and empires belies the reports that were given to Cieza of barbarism and chaos. The period under investigation is roughly dated from c. 1000 B.C. to A.D. 1380, when the Lord-Inca Viracocha consolidated the empire, and the geographical view extends from the Angasmayo River in Colombia, where the Inca Huayna-Capac discovered the above-noticed louse-bearing tribe, to Talca (below Santiago, Chile) in the south. The Royal Road to the Incas covered the greater part of this distance in two branches: one, the Highland Road, from Quito (Ecuador), through Cuzco (seat of the Inca Empire), to Talca, a distance of

3250 miles;[131] the other, the Coastal Road, from the Port of Tumbes (in northern Peru) again to Talca, 2250 miles.

At the time of the Spanish Conquest, the three outstanding peoples of the South American west coast were the Chebcha in Colombia, the Inca in Peru, and in Chile the Araucanians, nomadic, fiercely fighting hunting-and-gathering tribes who remained unsubdued by the Incas, or even by the Spaniards, until defeated in the Araucanian War (1880–82), after which they were settled on reservations.

At the first coming of the Spaniards, Araucanian-speaking peoples occupied the area west of the Andean highlands from the Rio Choapa, south, to the southern tip of the island of Chiloé (see Map 39). About the beginning of the eighteenth century, they began to spill over into Argentina, along the Andean foothills and into the western Pampa. As recognized today they are in five divisions: (1) the Picunche (*picun* "north," *che* "people"), (2) the Mapuche (*mapu* "land"), and (3) the Huilliche (*huilli* "south"), (4) the Pehuenche (*pehuen* "pine") in the Andean highlands; and finally, east of the Andes, (5) the Argentine Araucanians, who have been called by a number of names: Araucanos de Pampas, Patagon, Pampa, Mapuche, Puelche (*puel* "east"), Ranguelche (*rangh* "reed"), Hombres del Manzanar (*manzano* "apple tree"), Moluche, Pinunche, Huilliche, and Piche ("small") Huilliche.[132]

Archaeologically the Incan Highlands are now reckoned to consist of three geographical divisions: (1) the Northern Highlands, from the southern border of Ecuador to Huanuco, the most important site of this region being at Chavín de Huántar; (2) the Central Highlands, from Huánuco to Cuzco, seat of the Inca Empire; and (3) the Southern Highlands, from Cuzco into Bolivia along an extensive high plateau (the *altiplano*), which includes the vast Lake Titicaca, out of which, according to Inca legend, the first light came, when the sun rose from its waters. In the southern part of that lake are a number of isles, of which the largest was regarded by the Inca (according to Garcilasso) as their place of origin. For it was there, according to this legend, that Manco Capac, the first Inca, received from the Sun-God his cultural commission. On that island therefore, in memory of that moment, a great temple was constructed, the ruins of which are said to be in the Late Inca style (A.D. 1400–1500) and still in a fair state of preservation.[133] Cieza wrote:

The name of this great lake of the Colla [the Southern Highland] is Titicaca, from the temple that was built in the center of the lake. About this the natives had an idea that was pure superstition, and this is that they say their forebears asserted for a fact, like the other nonsense they tell, that for many days they were without light, and when they were all in darkness and gloom, there arose from this island of Titicaca the sun in all its splendor, for which reason they hold the island to be a hallowed spot, and the Incas built there a temple…which was one of the most venerated, in honor of their sun, bringing to it vestals and priests and great treasure. Although the Spaniards on different occasions have removed much of this, it is believed that most of it has not been discovered. And if these Indians were without light, as they say, it might have been caused by an eclipse of the sun.[134]

The vestals here mentioned, who were known as Chosen Women, or *mamaconas*, Virgins of the Sun, had been selected from the age of about ten for the promise of their beauty and intelligence. As described by G. H. S. Bushnell in his classic introduction to the cultures of pre-Pizarro Peru:

521. Portrait of Manco Capac, the first Inca, who received his commission from Inti, the Sun God.

522. Peruvians panicking during a solar eclipse, in Picart's *The Religious Ceremonies and Customs of the Several Nations of the Known World* (1731–37).

"An Inca official visited the villages at regular intervals to inspect any girls who had reached the age of about ten. He divided them into two classes; those of special beauty or promise were sent away to be educated in special institutions by the State, or reserved for sacrifice on special occasions or in emergencies, such as the accession or serious illness of an Emperor, and the remainder were left behind, to be married in due course to the boys of the village by the curaca [local supervisor], who picked their mates for them. Those who were taken away were placed in convents called Accla Huasi, the Houses of the Chosen Women in the provincial capitals or in Cuzco, and here they learnt such things as spinning, weaving, and cooking. Those destined for sacrifice were regarded as fortunate, since they were assured of a life of ease and comfort in the world to come. The others were divided into those who would be given as wives to nobles or successful warriors by grace of the Emperor, and the Mamaconas, some of whom would be secondary wives or servants to the Emperor, and some dedicated in perpetual chastity to the service of temples and shrines. Those who served the Emperor included specially skilled weavers, who made fine clothing for him. It is difficult to exaggerate the importance of cloth in the Inca polity, and examples like the textiles found in Paracas mummies [527–528] suggest strongly that this was nothing new, in fact the general excellence of Peruvian weaving would make it surprising if it were otherwise. In Inca times the weavers had to make cloth for the ruler and the goods from materials provided by the State, and in return the State gave them the materials from which to weave their own clothes. The finest fabrics were reserved for the ruler, and gifts of them from him were highly appreciated. Cloth was used in all sorts of gift exchanges, in the crises of life and for sacrifice. It was second only to food in the army's rations, and enormous quantities were found by the Spaniards in the storehouses, in addition to those which were burnt to keep them out of their hands."[135]

At Tomebamba, in the Northern Highlands, there was a temple of the Sun, the splendor of which so impressed Cieza, as he passed through, along the Highland Road, that he paused to write of it at length.

The lodgings of Tomebamba are situated at the joining of two small rivers in a plain having a circumference of over twelve leagues. It is a chilly land, abounding in game such as deer, rabbits, and partridges, turtle doves, and other birds. The temple of the sun was of stones put together with the subtlest skill, some of them large, black, and rough, and others that seemed of jasper. Some of the Indians claimed that most of the stones used in the construction of these lodgings and the temple of the sun had been brought all the way from the city of Cuzco by order of the Lord-Inca Huayna Capac and his father, the great Topa Inca, pulled with great

cables. If this is true, it is a remarkable thing, considering the size and number of the stones, and the distance. The fronts of many of the buildings are beautiful and highly decorative, some of them set with precious stones and emeralds, and, inside, the walls of the temple of the sun and the palaces of the Lord-Incas were covered with sheets of the finest gold and incrusted with many statues, all of this metal. The roof of these buildings was of thatch, so well laid that barring a fire, it would last for ages. Inside the dwelling there were sheaves of golden straw, and on the walls carved figures of the same rich metal, and birds, and many other things. In addition to this, it was said that there was a great sum of treasure in jugs and pots and other receptacles, and many rich blankets covered with silver and beadwork. Whatever I say I cannot give an idea of the wealth the Incas possessed in these royal palaces, in which they took great pride, where many silversmiths were kept busy making the things I have described and many others. The woolen clothing in the storehouses was so numerous and so fine that if it had been kept and not lost, it would be worth a fortune. The virgins dedicated to the service of the temple were numbered more than two hundred, and were very beautiful, chosen from among the Cañari [the people of this province] and the region of the district governed by the high steward of the Incas, who lived in these dwellings. They and the priests were well supplied by those in charge of the maintenance of the temple, at whose gate there were gate keepers (some of whom were said to be eunuchs), whose duty it was to watch over the *manaconas,* as the virgins living in the temple were called. Besides the temple and the palaces of the Lord-Incas there were a great number of dwellings where the soldiers were garrisoned, and still greater storehouses filled with the provisions I have described, howevermuch was used. For the stewards kept careful account after their fashion of all that entered and all that was given out, and the will of the Lord-Inca was observed in all things. The natives of this province, known as the Cañari, are well built and of goodly countenance. They wear their hair very long and coil it around their head, so by it and the round crown of wood, as fine as sieve wire, they can be recognized as Cañari wherever they go, and this is their identification.[136]

From Tomebamba there was a turn, a spur, from the Royal Highway west to the port of Guayaquil, on the coast of Ecuador, in the Guayas province of Estrada's Valdivia finds from c. 3000 B.C. And again, a little south of Tomebamba, there was another turn, southwestward, to Tumbes, at the head of the Coastal Road.

This valley of Tumbes was once thickly settled and cultivated, covered with fine, cool irrigation canals, channeled from the river, with which they watered their crops abundantly and harvested much corn and the other things needed for human consumption, and many delicious fruits. The ancient rulers, before they were subdued by the Incas, were more feared and obeyed by their subjects than any of those described, as they all state and recall, and they were served with great ceremony. Their clothing consisted of a shirt and blanket, and they wore a headdress which was a round affair made of wool, and sometimes of gold or silver

523. Picart's fanciful interpretations of Inca sun worship: above, inside the sun temple, an offering is made of a sacred vessel; below, the Peruvians celebrate their annual Grand Festival of the Sun.

or of small beads, which were known as *chaquira.* These Indians were much given to their religion, and performed great sacrifices...they are more self-indulgent and comfort-loving than the mountain-dwelling Indians. They are very industrious in the cultivation of their fields, and carry heavy loads. The fields are excellently cultivated, with much forethought, and they are very orderly in their watering of them. They raise many varieties of fruit and well-flavored roots. Corn is harvested twice a year, it and beans, and broad beans yield abundantly when planted. Their clothing is made of cotton, of which they gather as much as they need in the valley. In addition, these Indians of Tumbes are great fishermen...for by this and the other products they sell to the highland dwellers they have always been rich.

From this valley of Tumbes it is a two days' journey to the valley of Solana, which in ancient times was thickly settled, and had lodgings and storehouses. The highway of the Incas runs... between groves and cool, pleasant glades. through their valleys between groves and cool, pleasant glades.

From Solana one comes to Poechos, though some called it the Maicabilca, because beyond this valley there was a chieftain or lord by that name. This valley was very thickly populated, and beyond doubt many were the people who dwelt there, to judge by the numerous large buildings. These, though now in ruins, bear out what was told of them, and the esteem in which the Incas held them, for in this valley they had their royal palaces and other lodgings and storehouses. Time and wars have so wasted all that the only thing to be seen in proof of what is told are the many and very large burial places, and how the many fields that lie in the valley were cultivated by them that were alive.[137]

Like the highland sites, those of this coastal strip traversed by the Royal Coastal Road are distinguished archaeologically as of three zones, north to south. At the mouth of each of the valleys of the numerous short rivers that come down from the highlands to the sea, there had been before the Incan conquest a relatively independent local agricultural community. The three zones archaeologically distinguished are: (1) *The North Coast,* from Piura to Casma, which included the Moche, where, from c. 250 B.C. to c. A.D. 750, there had flourished one of the finest ceramic-sculpture traditions in the whole history of pottery, and where, from perhaps the twelfth to the late fourteenth century (when the city was entered and sacked by the Inca Capac Yupanqui) the opulent capital, Chauchan, of the empire of Chimu or Chimor, held dominion over a coastal range that extended from Tumbes south to the river Rimac; (2) *The Central Coast,* from Huarmay to Lurín, which included, just south of the river Rimac (near Lima), a very great pilgrimage center and temple dedicated to a deity, Pachacamac, whose age is unknown, but whose cult was of such antiquity and importance that the Incas accepted and assimilated its deity as an aspect of their own Virecocha.

This valley [of Pachacamac] is pleasant and fertile [Cieza wrote], and there stood there one of the most sumptuous temples to be found in these regions. They say of it that, despite the fact that the Inca lords built many temples, aside from those of Cuzco, and glorified and embellished them with riches, there was none to compare with this of Pachacamac, which was built upon a small, man-made hill of adobes and earth, and on its summit stood the temple which began at the foot and had many gates, which, like the walls, were adorned with figures of wild animals. Inside, where the idol stood, were the priests who feigned great sanctimoniousness. And when they performed their sacrifices before the people, they kept their faces toward the door of the temple and their backs to the figure of the idol, with their eyes on the ground and all trembling and overcome, according to certain Indians still alive today, so that it could almost be compared to what one reads of the priests of Apollo when the Gentiles [i.e. the Greeks] sought their vain oracles. And they say more: that before the figure of this devil they sacrificed many animals, and human blood of persons they killed; and that on the occasion of their most solemn feasts they made utterances which were believed and held to be true. In the terraces and foundations of this temple great sums of gold and silver were buried. The priests were greatly venerated, and the lords and caciques obeyed them in many things that they ordered. And it is told that beside the temple there were many and spacious lodgings for those who came there in pilgrimage, and no one was deemed worthy nor allowed to be buried in its vicinity except the lords or priests or pilgrims who came bearing gifts to the temple.

When the great yearly feasts were celebrated, many people assembled, carrying on their diversions to the sound of the musical instru-

ments they possessed. And as the Incas, powerful lords that they were, made themselves the masters of the kingdom and came to this valley of Pachacamac, and, as was their custom in all the lands they conquered, they ordered temples and shrines built to the sun. And when they saw the splendor of this temple, and how old it was, and the sway it held over all the people of the surrounding lands, and the devotion they paid it, holding that it would be difficult to do away with this, they agreed with the native lords and the ministers of their god or devil that this temple of Pachacamac should remain with the authority and cult it possessed, provided they built another temple to the sun which should take precedence. And when the temple of the sun had been built, as the Incas ordered, they filled it with riches and put many virgins in it. The devil Pachacamac, highly pleased with this arrangement, they say revealed his satisfaction in his replies, for the one and the other served his ends, and the souls of the misguided remained fast in his power....

The name of this devil meant "maker of the world," for *camac* means "maker," and *pacha,* "world." And when the Governor Don Francisco Pizarro (because God so willed it) took Atahualpa prisoner in the province of Cajamarca, as he had heard about this temple and the riches it contained, he sent Captain Hernando Pizarro, his brother, with a force of Spaniards to this valley to remove all the gold from that cursed temple, and return to Cajamarca. And although Captain Hernando Pizarro made his way to Pachacamac with all possible speed, it is common knowledge among the Indians that the headmen and priests of the temple carried away more than four hundred loads of gold which was never seen again, nor do the Indians alive today know where it is.

Notwithstanding, Hernando Pizarro (who, as I have said, was the first Spanish captain to enter the temple) found considerable gold and silver. Later on, Captain Rodrigo Orgoñez and Francisco de Godoy and others found a great quantity of gold and silver in the burial sites, and it is believed and held certain that there is much more. But as no one knows where it is buried, unless it is stumbled on by chance it will be lost. From the moment Hernando Pizarro and the other Spaniards entered this temple the devil was defeated and his power destroyed, and the idols in it cast down, and the buildings and the temple to the sun were lost, and most of the Indians have disappeared, so that there are very few left.

This valley is as lush and full of vegetation as those which border upon it, and in the fields much cattle and other livestock and mares are raised, which breed a number of good horses.[138]

Over 400 drawings such as these were included by the Cholo (part Inca, part Spanish) chronicler Felipe Guaman Poma de Ayalia (born 1534) in his *Nueva Cronica y buen gobierno,* a 1200-page letter addressed to the King of Spain, which was forgotten until 1908, when it was discovered in the Royal Library at Copenhagen. Pomo de Ayalia's illustrations are a primary source of information about Inca festivals, daily life, and ethnic groups. Top to bottom: (**524**) In the western part of the empire, an Indian brings offerings to a local *huaca* (anything imbued with spiritual force) honored along with Inca deities. (**525**) "Tupa Inca Speaks with All the *Huacas*," in order to learn of the past and divine the future. (**526**) "The Great Sorcerer" of the Inca ceremoniously burns a devil clearly drawn from the European imagination (see **428**).

The Paracas culture is arguably best known for wrapping its mummies in burial cloths that are considered preeminent examples of the art of textile making. Above left (**527**), a painted cotton shroud, Paracas-Cavernas culture, c. 1000–400 B.C.; above right (**528**), an embroidered sample, Paracas Necropolis culture, c. A.D. 1–400.

529. No satisfactory explanation of purpose has yet been given for the profusion of mysterious lines that covers the arid, otherwise empty pampas near Nazca. Clearly visible only from the air, some are straight, while others form trapezoids, spirals, and giant figures of such animals as spiders, monkeys, fish, and the hummingbird pictured below.

The last of the coastal valleys, namely (3) *The South Coast,* from the river Mala to the river Lomas, includes, besides the important archaeological site of Paracas, with its rich burials dating from c. 500 B.C. to about the second and third centuries A.D., the no less important center of the classic Nazca Culture, which flourished from c. A.D. 250–750 and differs from the contemporary Mochica of the north, as Bushnell has remarked, "in not providing any evidence for expansion or aggressive tendencies."[139] "The pottery," he states further, "does not provide the same sort of evidence about the structure of society as that of the Mochica, but, such as it is, it indicates an interest rather in the supernatural than in the rank and occupations of men."[140]

"When the traveller by air looks down on the desolate pampas round Nazca," observes Bushnell, "he sees a multitude of long straight lines, geometrical figures and other markings on the ground, a phenomenon which has also been observed, but on a small scale, in the Virú valley and in North Chile. They were formed by removing the dark brown pebbles which cover the yellow sandy surface in this neighborhood, and piling them up round the exposed areas. The lines may radiate from a point in almost any direction, form parallel groups, or be distributed irregularly, and they vary from half a kilometre to more than eight kilometres in length. They are associated with elongated, solid areas of more or less rectangular, trapezoidal or triangular form, one of the largest being 1700 metres long with a mean width of 50 metres. Spirals and zigzag lines are frequent, and there are irregular forms besides occasional birds and fish. Lines frequently intersect and figures may be superimposed on one another, but examples of the various types are associated in a way which suggests that no great time-difference is involved. An indication of their age is given by radiocarbon date of c. A.D. 500 for a post at the intersection of two lines, and some animal forms have appendages which recall in a vague way those of some Nazca monsters. Their object has not been satisfactorily explained....Whatever the explanation, the setting out and execution of these perfectly straight lines and other figures must have required a great deal of skill and not a little disciplined labor."[141]

* * *

The general history of the cultures of this Inca zone of six archaeological provinces (three highland and three coastal) unfolds from c. 3000 B.C. to the year of the Spanish Conquest through a sequence of four periods (variously named by various authorities) that date about as follows: *Formative* (c. 3000–300 B.C.), *Pre-Classic* (c. 300–1 B.C.), *Classic* (c. A.D. 1–900), and *Post-Classic* (c. A.D. 900–1532).

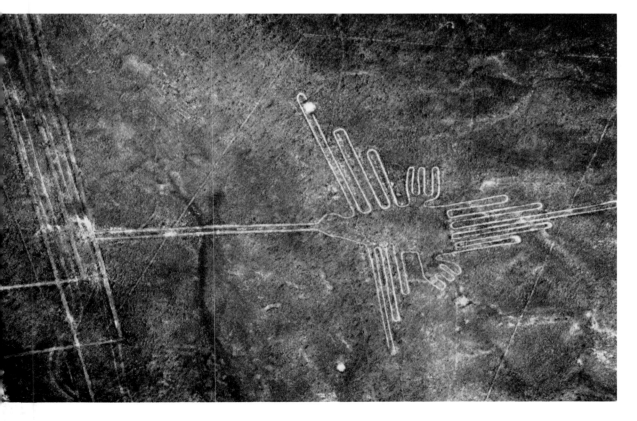

Following an indefinite, almost timeless era, first, of nomadic Paleolithic hunting, gathering, and fishing tribes, such as survived into the early twentieth century in the "marginal areas" of southeastern Brazil, Argentina, and Tierra del Fuego; then, during an as yet undefined period of what do appear to have been influences from Southeast and East Asia (the pearl-oyster shell fishhook, dugout canoe, longhouse, blowgun, panpipe, tapa cloth, bottle gourd, and so forth, in association with vegetative-reproduction-shifting cultivation) and the emergence of that tropical-rain-forest type of village life that still prevails throughout the Amazon Basin, there occurred in coastal Ecuador, c. 3000 B.C. (or perhaps earlier), a transformation of the local extension of the Amazonian style of village life (with deep-sea fishing as an added feature) which is now taken to mark the beginning of what is known in American archaeological circles as the Formative Period of New World high cultures. Donald Lathrap describes the criterion by which this culture-stage or -period is recognized and defined. "It is necessary," he declares, "to distinguish clearly between man's first manipulation of the plants naturally available to him as a source of food and his later achievement of a system of agricultural production that yielded a dependable supply of food."[142] "Man," he continues, "was transplanting and protecting particular species of plants long before he really achieved productive agriculture."[143]

With the achievement of such a dependable system of food production there followed an increase in both the size and the complexity of the village settlements and, with that, a specialization of the inhabitants' social functions. Among nomadic and tropical-village tribes, where every competent adult is in possession, or at least has some knowledge, of the whole cultural heritage, there is no more than a natural distinction of social roles according to sex, age, and individual talents—with the only radical separation being of the shaman, linked to a subliminal psychological, instead of immediately practical social-economic, ground of values and concern. With the improved economy and consequent enrichment and expansion of the agriculturally supported community, however, there followed such a differentiation of socially required specializations that the community was one, no longer of generally equivalent adults, but of distinct classes of specialists; and from that there followed a sociological mutation, from the condition, so to say, of an association of amateurs, to that of an enterprise of professionals: a quantum leap, immediately evident archaeologically in the appearance of a distinctive, monumental art informed by an advanced order of both cosmological and psychological insights, and characterized by a distinctive style which thereafter endures, develops, and degenerates

530. Before being fired, this stirrup-spouted funerary vessel portraying a Mochica flautist was burnished, covered with cream slip, and painted with an iron-oxide pigment. Of particular note is the striking verisimilitude with which the texture of the skin had been rendered.

During the Early Intermediate Period (c. 200 B.C.–A.D. 900, approximately synchronous with Bennett and Bird's "Mastercraftsman Period"), on the North Coast, the Mochica civilization, with a sharply divided class system given to warfare and expansion, flourished A.D. 200–700, developed a tradition of realistically modeled and painted pottery that spread into all the other coastal valleys, and was typified archaeologically by the remains of immense public buildings, "which," as Bennett and Bird remark, "display only limited architectural skill, but certainly suggest well organized mass labor."[66] On the South Coast, the contemporaneous Nazca culture was devoted, apparently, less to warcraft and expansion than to religious interests and the arts, the chief remains of the culture being not large buildings, but beautiful pottery and those enigmatic Nazca lines (see **529**).

531. Double-spouted Nazca stirrup vessel in the shape of a decorated trophy head, c. 8⅝" high.

through the relevant lifetime of the culture.

So defined, the Formative Period comprises those centuries during the course of which such an elite, time-factored culture acquired its form, from the moment of its inception to the first monumental manifestations of its achieved style.

In the New World this Formative Period (particulars of which we have already reviewed) extended, as now construed, from c. 3000 to 300 B.C., and was comprised of three phases: an *Early Formative* (Valdivia), c. 3000–1500 B.C.; *Middle Formative* (Machalilla), c. 1500–1000 B.C.; and a *Late* or *Culminating Formative* (Chorrera-Chavín) phase, c. 1000–300 B.C.

During the Early and Middle Formative periods, influences from Southeast and East Asia seem to have mixed with indigenous traditions and to have contributed substantially to the stimulation of the native imagination. From the period, on the other hand, of the Late or Culminating Formative phase, with the almost simultaneous appearance (at Chavín de Huántar in the Northern Highlands of Peru and at various sites in the swamplands of the Mexican states of Veracruz and Tabasco) of the earliest monumental ceremonial centers of two distinct yet related civilizations, the epochal transition was made from the timeless idyll of village horticulture, hunting, and fishing to the time-factored unfolding, maturing, and aging of distinct historical cultures. It was as though a spiritual threshold had been crossed and a self-consistent development initiated, with such a will and destination of its own that no influence whatsoever could now significantly alter its course.

In Peru, the first great phase of this culminating development was of a cultural unfoldment and maturation in two stages: (1) a *Pre-Classic* stage (c. 300–1 B.C.), termed by Wendell Bennett and Junius Bird in their exposition of Andean history, the "Experimenter Period," and described as characterized by "experimentation in new techniques and new controls...in the crafts, in building, and in the agricultural methods";[144] and then, (2) a *Classic* stage (c. A.D. 1–900), the "Mastercraftsman Period," described as characterized by "the mastery of agricultural techniques, by ambitious monumental architecture, by skilled craftsmanship in ceramics, weaving, and metallurgy, and by a florescence of art styles."[145] The period is represented by hundreds of sites and a number of major cultures, each covering an extensive area; notably, the Mochica culture in the North Coast Valley and the Nazca culture of the South Coast, alongside the closely related necropolis culture at Paracas; in the Southern Highlands, the Pucara and Early Tiahuanaco cultures, and in the Northern Highlands, the Recuay. It was a period of achieved civilization, accomplishment in the arts, abundance in the necessities of life, and stable, orderly states.

Toward the close of the ninth century and beginning of the tenth there occurred what Bennett and Bird have described as a shift from "technological advancement to manipulation of man-hour units and political organization," and with this change in emphasis, "expansion in the form of conquests in new regions became profitable." Moreover, "this general tendency for expansion and aggression was not limited to one region, but, except for the Nazca culture, seems to have been general throughout the Central Andes."[146]

With this we pass from the early to the late stages of the cultures of the area, from their centuries of maturation to age and disintegration—from cultivation to violence—through a sequence of three increasingly brutal phases:

(1) An *Early Post-Classic* phase (c. A.D. 900–1200), the "Expansionist Period," when from a center in the Southern Highlands around Tiahuanaco and Lake Titicaca some sort of "culture wave" somehow issued forth and along the whole coast left its mark in monuments of a distinctive "Tiahuanaco" stamp; whether this wave was military and political or purely aesthetic and religious is unknown, but its look and timing suggests a sort of Napoleonic or Alexandrian shaping of a sudden but ephemeral empire.

(2) A *Middle Post-Classic* phase (c. A.D. 1200–1450), the "City Builder Period," when "the disintegration of whatever type of unity the Expansionists had imposed was succeeded by new struggles for power....There is now evidence for large, well organized populations living in planned building units in a pattern which can be designated as urban, even though large cities are not found everywhere.

...Since all cultures now possess adequate technology and all are concentrating on political controls, the balance of power depends largely on the extent of territory. Consequently, it is not surprising that the North Coast cultures became stronger than those of the Central and South Coasts, since the northern valleys are larger and have a more permanent water supply."[147] In this "period of contending states," the empire of Chimu with its capital Chanchan, expanded from the valleys formerly of the Mochica to dominate an area extending some six hundred miles, from Tumbes south to the Chillón. To the south of that, a small but powerful state occupied the Rimac and Lurin valleys. Farther south the people in the Mula, Cañete and Chincha valleys also were united. Still farther south—in the Ica, Nazca, and Acari valleys—a fourth center was established. And it was over this whole arena, not of chaos (as Cieza told of it: see page 368), but of contending city- and state-building powers, that the armies of the Incas, proceeding from the Central Highlands, rapidly imposed through a few ferocious campaigns, the order of a Roman state.

Thus was initiated (3) the *Final Post-Classic* phase of the civilization (c. A.D. 1450–1532), the "Imperialist Period," the political genius and practical efficiency of which are demonstrated in those two Royal Roads, the length of the Empire, 3150 miles, from Quito in the north to Talca in the south, over which relays of runners could bear messages and orders at a constant speed of some ten miles an hour. As Cieza wrote of this marvel:

In the memory of people I doubt there is record of another highway comparable to this,

running through deep valleys and over high mountains, through piles of snow, quagmires, living rock, along turbulent rivers; in some places it ran smooth and paved, carefully laid out; in others over sierras, cut through the rock, with walls skirting the rivers, and steps and rests through the snow; everywhere it was clean-swept and kept free of rubbish, with lodgings, storehouses, temples to the sun, and posts along the way. Oh, can anything comparable be said of Alexander, or of any of the mighty kings who ruled the world, that they built such a road, or provided the supplies to be found on this one! The road built by the Romans that runs through Spain and the others we read of were as nothing in comparison to this. And it was built in the shortest space of time imaginable, for the Incas took longer to order it than their people in carrying it out.[148]

The kingdom of Peru was so vast that, if the Lord-Inca happened to be at one end of his territory, he had to be informed of what was going on at the other by a messenger, who, if he had to make the trip alone, however much he traveled each day, by the time he had covered the thousand leagues it would be too late to do what needed to be done or to make the necessary decisions. For this reason, and the better to rule the provinces, the Incas devised a system of posts which was the best that could be thought of or imagined, and this was the invention of Pachacuti, the son of Viracocha Inca, father of Topa Inca, according to the songs of the Indians, which the *orejones* confirm [the aristocrats, called by the Spaniards "long eared," because of lobes stretched to receive the large earspools of their rank]. Not only did Pachacuti invent these posts, but he did other great things, as we shall relate. Thus, from the time of his reign along all the highways every half league, more or less, there were little houses well built of wood and straw, and in the mountains they were built along the hillsides and cliffs, so the roads were full of these little houses every so often, as has been said above. And in

532. A section of the eroded, cast adobe or adobe brick walls (right), some up to 50 feet high, as well as a detail of one of the many varied designs in molded clay plaster (below) with which they were adorned, that were used in the construction of Chan Chan, the capital city of the Chimú empire. Founded c. A.D. 800 at the northern end of the Moche valley, Chan Chan was comprised of a civic center covering some 3.5 square miles and an 11 additional square miles of outlying buildings.[67] The Chimú seemingly mass-produced pottery, textiles, and metalworks at Chan Chan. They began to seize control of other coastal valleys c. A.D. 1200, and the empire continued to expand its territorial holdings and to consolidate its power until conquered by the Incas in A.D. 1465.

each of them two Indians were to be stationed, with supplies, and these Indians were to be drawn from the neighboring settlements, and were not to be there permanently, but replaced from time to time by others. This was so carefully observed that all that was necessary was to order it, and it never failed during all the time the Incas reigned.

Each province took care to supply the posts which came within its confines, whether in the wastelands and snow-covered highlands or near the highway. And when word had to be sent to the Lord-Inca in Cuzco or anywhere else of something that had happened or was required for his service, a runner set out from Quito or Tomebamba, or Chile, or Caranqui, or any other part of the kingdom, whether plains or mountains, and at full speed ran that half-league without stopping, for the Indians selected for these posts must have been the swiftest and most agile of all. And when he came near the other post he began to call to the one in it, saying to him, "Set out at once, and go to such and such a place, and tell that this and that has happened, or that this governor begs to inform the Inca...." And as soon as the one who was there heard this, he set out at full speed, and the one who had come went into the little house to rest and eat and drink of what was always kept there, and the other did the same when he reached the next post.

Thus in a short time the news had been carried three hundred leagues and five hundred, and eight hundred, of what had happened or was needed and should be ordered. And those who carried these messages observed such secrecy on their mission that neither plea nor threat could make them reveal the news they were bearing, even though the message had already been passed on to the next messenger. It is a known fact that over such roads, through rough sierras and perilous mountains, snow-covered peaks, and rocky wastes overgrown with every kind of briar and thorn, neither swift horses nor mules could carry the news with more speed than these messengers on foot. For they are very swift, and one of them could cover more ground in a day than a messenger on horse or mule in three; I do not mean to say a single Indian, but by the system they used, which was for each to travel half a league. And never, because of a storm or anything else that might happen, was any post deserted, but the Indians I have mentioned were always there, and never left until others had come to take their place.

In this manner the rulers were notified of all that happened in their kingdom and realm, and took the measures the situation called for. Nowhere in the world does one read that such an invention existed, although I do know that when Xerxes the Great was defeated, the news was carried in this way, by runners, in a short time. There is no doubt that this organization of the posts was very important in Peru, and it can be seen from this how good was the government of its rulers. Even today in many parts of the uplands, alongside the highways, certain of these post houses can be seen, and they bear out the truth of what is said. I have seen certain *topos*, which are like boundary markers, except that these here are large and better made, and by them they counted the leagues, and the distance between each was a league and a half by the measure of Castile.[149]

*   *   *

533. Artifacts crafted of gold, in the pursuit of which the conquistadors would come to ravage the continent and decimate its native inhabitants, first appear during the Early Horizon phase (c. 900–250 B.C.), when the distinctive style of the Chavín culture crystallized at the type-site of Chavín de Huántar in the Mosne valley and then began to spread rapidly throughout the northern highlands and along the northern and central parts of the coast, and, apparently, even into southern coastal regions, where it affected the ceramics there being made.[68]

Herewith, several outstanding early examples of craftsmanship in gold: (**a**) Chavín crown with a grimacing, jaguar-fanged, claw-footed deity (and many snakes) wearing a breast plate suggestive of the Chinese *t'ao-t'ieh* (see p. 383 and **549**); (**b**) Chavín disk, c. 4¾" in diameter, in the center of which is a similar feline face with snakes; (**c**) Chavín spoon, c. 4⁵⁄₁₆" long, the handle of which was made by soldering together two sheets of metal to form a hollow man (also a rattle), either blowing into or drinking from a silver conch shell; (**d**) Mochica plaque showing two masked warriors—each with an animal headdress and a belt terminating in an animal head, one with a conch shell hanging from his elbow—dancing around a pole surmounted by a grinning head.

a

b

c

d

As clues to the mythology or mythologies of the Pre-Inca eras of this great domain, we have, first, the evidence brought forth by Lathrap (see above, page 363) of shamanic practices supported by hallucinogenic drugs and visions, featuring werejaguar and -cayman associations of the shaman, such as are carried on today among the Amazonian forest tribes. The prominence of ceramic female figurines, however, among the Early and Middle Formative artifacts of this culture zone cannot but represent an accent of some kind upon what in the Orient is known as the "female energy or power" (Sanskrit, *śakti*), however interpreted in local mythology or cult practice. In the myths and rites of every one of the Old World Neolithic cultures personifications of this energy are not only prominent but dominant. They are not reflections of shamanic thought and experience, but arrive from another quarter. Indeed, among the Paleolithic remains already reviewed of the Dordogne (see I.1:66–79), a separation of the female and male energy fields and cultic associations is already evident, with the figurines (Paleolithic Venuses) assigned to dwelling sites and the representations of shamans (as semi-animal presences) confined to the temple-caves of the male initiation rites. Thereafter, in the later, Neolithic periods, when intensive agriculture had become the main support of society and the analogy was not only recognized, but stressed, of the power of Nature to bring forth and nourish life with the power of the female body to do exactly the same, representations of the shaman disappear from the iconography and there is a multiplication of female figurines beyond measure. In the accumulated rubbish in the dirt floor of the Valdivia *maloca* that Lathrap excavated he found "hundreds of pots and dozens of figurines made, used, and discarded by the inhabitants."[150] An interesting detail to know would be the relative density of fragment distribution in the rear and front of the *maloca*, since we know (pages 351–353) that during the house ceremonials of the Amazonian Barasana the women sit apart, screened away in the rear of the *maloca*, while the men and the youths being initiated partake of their hallucinogens and sound their various bark trumpets. Further, one of the outstanding characteristics of the cultures of both North and South America (as also, by the way, of both China and Japan) is a persistence even into the late high-culture stages of a robust shamanic strain, even along with the inevitable *śakti* observances of their agriculturally grounded seasonal ceremonials. I am inclined to see a prefigurement of this disposition in the observed conjunction, already in earliest Formative Ecuador, of the shamanic jaguar cult with its kit of hallucinogens and the multitude of little ceramic personifications of the *śakti*.

Around 1200–1000 B.C., however, at the opening of the Late or Culminating phase of the New World Formative development, something decisive occurred which has not been explained. Not only was there (as has already been remarked) the almost simultaneous, sudden appearance of two monumental ceremonial centers showing an immediate mastery of the arts of architecture and sculpture in stone, but there was also evident in the monuments of all of these Late Formative ceremonial centers an order of symbolic thinking, translated into symbolic art forms, that is altogether beyond the range of what, in contrast, can only be called "primitive art."

The astonishing Raimondi stela (now in the National Museum at Pueblo Libre near Lima), which is far and away the most *mysterious* iconographic image yet discovered anywhere, either in the New World or the Old, marks decisively the quantum leap that had been accomplished in the inward life and experience of the priestly élite of this Native American civilization in the period of its initial manifestation.

* * *

534. The mystery of the Raimondi Stela lies not only in the sophistication of its symbolic form, for which we have not a word of explanation (since during the whole history of this Andean civilization there was never developed a system of writing), but also in its early date (c. 1000 B.C.), which centuries earlier than any known work of comparable sophistication either in Europe or in Asia—though not, be it noted, in Egypt. The god that it shows (known to archaeology as the Staff God) is almost certainly the same as that represented, centuries later, on the great Monolithic Gateway at Tiahuanaco, where the deity appears to be weeping. A vase painting from Peru (Figure 539) exhibits the same interesting feature, and related, certainly, is the weeping Argentinian god shown in the copper plaque of the Frontispiece to Volume I. We have also seen weeping visages from the Antilles (see page 314).

All of these are popular representations, apparently, of the same dominant divinity, in various aspects, adapted to the folklore and conditions of the various local cultures, whereas in the remarkable stela at Chavín de Huántar, the initial ceremonial center of the widely spread civilization, the inward reality and transcendent import of the personification are disclosed.

As described by G. H. S. Bushnell, the revelation is of "a standing figure with feline face, holding an elaborate staff in each claw-like hand, while from the head projects a monstrous appendage facing upwards and consisting of a series of fantastic snouts with feline fangs and snakes projecting on either side."[69]

Observe the picture upside down (Figure 535) and the "fantastic snouts with feline fangs" will appear. There are three—each proceeding, as it were, from the tongue of the one above—all of which emanate from a tongue or snout that descends from the rectangle which, when right side up, is the head of what appears then as the god. Regarded upside down again, this rectangle shows two faces, one above the other, that below, of a bird, from which the trinity of faces proceeds, the other, of a jaguar. And we notice now that in each of the two elaborate staves there is a jaguar-face just above the bend of the god's elbows.

Now there is certainly a hidden doctrine here, as in the universe there is hidden divinity. Right side up, all that the icon shows is an image of the popular Staff God wearing an extraordinary headdress; whereas, upside down (and no one could possibly have turned this great stone stela upside down), an esoteric revelation appears of the one god's three aspects or faces proceeding from the composition's only readily visible image of a bird, its beak precisely at the top of the axial vertical (at the bottom of which are the twined serpents of a caduceus), while above the bird-face is again our old friend the jaguar, whose fangs, at either side of his jaw, are not centered like the bird's beak, and who, when we again turn the icon right side up, stands before us holding, right and left, the two staves of the one world-governing god's contrary powers: Justice and Mercy, in the vocabulary of the Christian cult. What they were called at Chavín, c. 1000 B.C., we do not know. But that the Jaguar aspect here confronting us holds with his two staves sway over this temporal world where all things are experienced as pairs of opposites—male and female, light and dark, future and past, good and evil, and so on—is clear; and further, that at that centering point in mid-forehead, where the inner eye of vision opens to the way of spiritual flight, transcending all dualities in axial ascent, there occurs an overturning of insights and values, and where only enigmatic shapes had been seen, now the forms are beheld of three divine faces.

Serpents, meanwhile, are everywhere: two hanging from either side of the god's belt, eight along either side of the quadrangle of his head, eight more along each side of the tower of his headdress, and then two at the summit, interlaced as a caduceus, bringing thus the two ranges of opposites together as aspects of one entity. At the top of each of the staves, furthermore, there are again two serpents, and a caduceus is an element at the base of each staff. Finally, along the snout of the first of the three faces are two runs of three serpents each, bringing the total number of serpents (if I have caught them all) to fifty two, which just happens to be the number of years in what was to be known as

Across the Pacific, in Southeast Asia and Indonesia, this same theme of the sun-bird (*garuḍa*) with a serpent (*nāga*) in its talons is paramount in the arts, both of the classical Hindu-Buddhist centuries (A.D. 800–1200) and of today. And do we not find in the *Iliad* the legendary account of an eagle soaring above the fleet of the Greek heroes approaching Troy, bearing in its talons a bleeding snake which was interpreted by Kalchas, the soothsaying priest of the expedition, as an augury of the victory of the patriarchal Greeks over luxurious Aphrodite's Troy?

One of the earliest known symbolic juxtapositions of the serpent and the winged solar bird is from ancient Mesopotamia, c. 2000 B.C., in an engraving on the libation vase of a certain King Gudea of Lagash. Two serpents interlaced across an axial staff, in the way of a caduceus, are flanked by a pair of lion-birds or cherubim, who are either opening the portals of a shrine to reveal its symbol of the mystery of life, or closing the same to contain the symbol's force. In the biblical version, according to Genesis 3, the gates are closed, the serpent with its life-wisdom is cursed, and two cherubim are stationed at the gate to guard the way to the tree of the knowledge of eternal life. In the Hindu and Buddhist traditions, on the other hand, the serpent power is to be fostered and increased.

The ability of the serpent to shed its skin and thus to renew itself, as the moon is renewed by sloughing its shadow, has recommended it, throughout the world, as an obvious image of the mystery of the will in nature, which is ever self-renewing in its generation of living beings. But also, in its threatening character, as a traveling aesophagus, the serpent is equally an image of the consuming power of the same will, foreboding death to all that lives. In its flowing form, the serpent suggests water. The forked flashing of its tongue, however, is flamelike. But in water, too, there is fire, a generative fire which carries life to deserts parched by the unmitigated fire of the sun.

For the solar fire is like a raptorial bird, a killer. The sun desiccates, evaporates, and draws to itself the waters of life, and can be thus appropriately pictured metaphorically as a raptorial bird bearing off and consuming the serpent of the earth-fertilizing waters.

The image is given in nature (see I.1:**68**). Anyone, anywhere in the world where there are serpents and raptorial birds, might be struck by this dramatic manifestation in the spectacle of nature, of its two extremes in conflict: the earthbound serpent and the bird of celestial flight. Anyone, anywhere in the world, might be struck, furthermore, by the analogy of the sun absorbing the waters of the earth and this bird dispatching a serpent. And still further, since there is more to a myth—or even to a poem—than the observation of similitudes in the spectacle of nature, we must add that anyone, anywhere in the world, might experience in himself an empathetic participation in the fascinating conflict, and go on to render in a work of art an image of the opposition of earthly and celestial energies as something to be experienced equally within oneself and in the constitution of the universe. And then finally, of course, anywhere in the world, once this image has been rendered by a creative poet or artist, others might experience its force and assimilate it to the local mythological vocabulary as a pictorial metaphor appropriate for representation in religious monuments.

Hypothetically, from the point of view of an abstract system of psychological suppositions, such imagined occasions might be thought to account for the unrelated appearances, here and there in the world, of identical mythological motifs. But in fact, then, why do we not find in the Paleolithic temple caves any painting of a raptorial bird killing a serpent? Might there be required some sort of psychological readiness for the insight? And would this readiness, then, be somehow a function of local social conditions?

The association of the image of the bird with shamanic flight is already evident in the art of the caves, specifically in that painting, for example, in the crypt of Lascaux, of a shaman in trance wearing a bird mask and with the figure of a bird on the shaman's staff by his side (see I.1:**105**). In the paintings of the Bushman trance-dancers, too, the imagery of flight is present in

their figures of flying bucks (see I.1:**176–177**). The earliest serpents, on the other hand, appear to be those three engraved cobras on the buckle of mammoth ivory discovered at Ma'lta (Siberia) in the grave of an elaborately ornamented boy (see I.1:**127**). Significantly, there were a number of ivory female figurines in that grave as well, besides ivory images of wild geese in full flight.

536. From Manabi, a Chorrera effigy jar, c. 10¾" tall, showing a laughing falcon (*Herpetotheres cachinnians*) holding in its beak and claws a snake, probably a fer-de-lance (*Bothrops*).

I know of no earlier raptorial bird and serpent image than that, already mentioned, of the *Iliad*, except one, engraved on a cylinder seal from Mesopotamia, showing an eagle clutching *two* serpents. The date of this seal is of King Gudea of Lagash, c. 2000 B.C., on whose libation vase we have already noted the earliest caduceus. The eagle is the sun-bird of Lagash, Im-gig, who is shown frequently with a lion's head, since the lion, like the eagle, was in antiquity metaphoric of the sun, which, in turn, is metaphoric of spiritual light. The teaching of the Buddha is known as his Lion Roar; for as the great sound of a lion's voice scatters the grazing herds, or as the light of a rising sun dispels the herd of stars of a moonlit night, so the word of the Buddha annihilates the lustful delusions of the unilluminated will. Waxing and waning, the light of the moon is of the sun, but tempered to the cycles of time: for the fire of the sun, full blast, annihilates. The moon is lord of the tides of life, but the sun, lord of an enduring light, is disengaged from the waxing and waning of time's ruins. Sloughing its skin, the serpent is an earthly counterpart of the moon shedding its shadow, and so, as illustrated in the Buddhist image of the World Enlightener and Teacher protected by the five- or seven-headed cobra, Muchalinda, there is a balance to be achieved in life between the blast of absolute illumination and the covering, tempering, life-sustaining and -loving wisdom of the serpent. The internal fire of the serpent that is evident in the flashing of its tongue is to be increased through reflection of the solar blaze, but not to such a degree as to incinerate the serpent. And so it was that Nietzsche, who understood such mysteries, in his *Thus Spake Zarathustra* gave as boon companions to his nineteenth-century prophet of a new wisdom for mankind an eagle and a serpent, "the proudest and the shrewdest among the beasts."

Thus the apparent polarity of spirit and will, celestial light and the values of earthly nature, is what in the earliest historic periods the bird and serpent duo symbolized. And the inward, psychological application and realization of the import of this mythologized symbolization is what is intended in the Indian practice of yoga—the earliest evidences of which appear on seals from the Indus Valley, of the period, exactly, of the libation vase of King Gudea of Lagash. The relationship of the symbolism of this piece to that of the Muchalinda Buddha (three thousand years later) is obvious. A little less obvious, but nevertheless discoverable through an exercise of the comparative imagination, is a relationship of the symbolism of the Indus seal, as well, to that of the great American stela (c. 1000 B.C.) at Chavín de Huántar, where the awakened (Buddha) eye at the center of the god's forehead is

535. Inverted drawing of Raimondi Stela.

a Knot or Bundle of Years in the much later Mayan calendar; and if this is not merely a coincidence, then the deity of this mystical early-Andean stela is a counterpart symbolically of the Platonic *Aion* and Zoroastrian *Zervan Akarana* ("Endless Time"), as a personification of the ever-returning, self-renewing round of the passing years.

The relevance of the serpent symbol to the pictorial exposition of this mythological "archetype" or "elementary idea" (see II.1:28) can be substantiated through a consideration of the serpent in other mythological associations.

The motif of a raptorial bird killing a snake is depicted in one of the powerful stone statues that have been found in the neighborhood of San Agustín (Colombia), in the highland Huila district, at the headwaters of the Magdalena river. These monuments are of the date, approximately, of the mystic Staff God of Chavín de Huántar, the Olmec ceremonial centers in southern Mexico, and the Chorrera ceramics of contemporary Ecuador. Figure 536 is of a Chorrera jar, where again we see a raptorial bird killing a snake. The motif appears today on the Mexican national flag, in memory of the Aztec legend of their settlement, after long wandering, at the site of Tenochtitlan (now Mexico City). They had halted there, by the waters of Lake Tezcuco, when they beheld an eagle perched on a tall cactus that was growing from a wave-washed rock; and while they watched, the bird rose to the rising sun bearing a serpent in its talons. This being taken as an augury, it was there that they founded their city of the Sun, Tenochtitlan.

represented as the visage of a bird and, instead of two serpents rising, one at either hand, we have fifty-two. Turn the monument upside down and, just above the triad of benign faces is the visage of the bird with its beak indicating the axial meridian, while at the base of this axial line is the caduceus. The symbolism is of the universal World Tree, as represented, for example, in the Icelandic Eddic Yggdrasil, with the eagle, perched on its peak, the dragon, Midhogg, gnawing at its root, and the busy squirrel, Ratatosk, running up and down the trunk between, bearing to each the words and messages of abuse from the other.

What can be said of all these likenesses? Too close to be disregarded, they have to be explained, if not by evidences of diffusion, then by a psychology of archetypes. The pictorial vocabulary of the Indian system of yoga by which they are most cogently interpreted is late, of the Tantric period, fourth century A.D., or later; so that diffusion is ruled out, unless (which is not impossible) there was a controlled verbal communication of some kind that was carried without fault across a vast ocean, not only of space, but of time. Alternately, one may conjecture that the extravagant use of hallucinogens in American shamanic practice must have produced transformations of consciousness, very like, if not identical with, those of the experiences of Indian yogis. The parallels, in any case, are much too numerous, too close and exquisite, to be attributable to chance or to undirected convergence.

Briefly resumed: The controlling image of what is known as Kundalini Yoga is of an awakening and unfolding of the "Serpent Power" (śakti, the will in nature), through breath control and other intentional exercises, rousing it from its animal lethargy in the lower, pelvic centers of the cerebro-spinal nervous system, to ascend through nodes of psychological transformation toward a realization, finally, of a full spiritual awakening, symbolized as the dissolution of the fully uncoiled serpent into the light by which it was waked.

The word yoga is from the Sanskrit root yuj, "to yoke, to join, to link"; specifically, to yoke one's waking consciousness to the ultimate source of consciousness, or, mythologically expressed, to unite the will of the individual with that of the Lord of the universe, whether known as Shiva, Aion, Zervan Akarana, or the Staff God of Chavín de Huántar.

The feminine noun kuṇḍalinī means, "that which is coiled"; for in this yoga the cosmic energy (śakti), which is of each of us the life, is symbolized as a coiled serpent lodged at the base of the spinal column, asleep until awakened, when it will uncoil and ascend along an inward spinal nerve to the ceiling of the brain, passing on the way five centers, nodes, or chakras ("circles"), at each of which the mode of consciousness of the yogi is transformed.

The total number of centers is thus seven. Three are of the pelvic region, three are of the head, and one, between, as the node of transformation, is of the great area between the diaphragm and shoulder yoke of the heart and the lungs:

1. Near the base of the spinal column, between the rectum and the genitals, where the kuṇḍalinī sleeps;

2. At the level of the genitals, where the will becomes of an erotic cast; and

3. At the level of the navel, where the wakened serpent's aim is to eat (consume), to master, and to control.

4. At the next center of the heart, a radical transformation occurs with an awakening to the prospects of a life given, not to torpor, physical lust, or conquest, but to further spiritual unfoldment and realizations. At this center of the heart, that is to say, there occurs what has been in many cultures recognized and mythologically symbolized as a "virgin birth," that is, the inception of an eminently human lifetime, addressed to ends unknown to the lower animal (pelvic motivated) orders of consciousness. Whereupon a tension is generated between two now contrary natures, one addressed to the popular world, the other to the inner life.

In the Raimondi stela of Chavín de Huántar these are represented by the two faces in the quadrangle of the deity's heads: that below, of the jaguar god, addressing the world with his two symbolic staves, and that above, at the point in the forehead of the opening of the Buddha eye, of a bird, turned upward to the towering revelation of an inward dimension of three successive transformations.

In the imagery of India the heart center of this transformation is symbolized as a lotus of twelve vermilion petals, each inscribed with a letter of the Sanskrit alphabet, and with the sign of the syllable yam at the center, enclosing a lingam-yoni symbol in gold, symbolic of the "virgin birth," as representing the male and female organs (lingam and yoni) in conjunction. At this level, at this station of indrawn consciousness, the sound OM is heard of the world-creating radiance of the immanent-transcendent ground (brahman). Once heard, this sound is recognized in all things. The six-pointed star enclosing the golden central symbol is of the color of smoke from the solar fire of this resounding sound. Its two triangles, upward and downward pointing, are significant of the tension and the relevant decision now to be marked between effort and inertia, ascent along the way of increasing consciousness and rapture against the impeding down-draft of the unregenerate senses. The two deities, upper right, are the gods patron of this center (Shiva and his śakti), personifications of the powers symbolized in the golden triangle at the center. And the animal is the black antelope on which (unseen) the wind god of the breath (prāna, spiritus) rides with his hands extended in the gestures known as "fear not" and "granting boons."[70]

Finally, the channel shown rising from the golden triangle is to be the passageway of the unfolding Serpent Power to the transforming raptures of further ascent. Leading to, and passing through, the three remaining centers of transformation, all of which are of the head, it matches in the Raimondi stela the towering "appendage facing upwards" in which are to be seen three faces. No practiced Freudian will have difficulty in recognizing in the inverted bird-face at the root of the towering gloriole a counterpart of the lingam and yoni in the Indian symbol. The bird is the golden sun-bird. Its position on the forehead of the rectangular head of the Andean Staff God is exactly at that point above the eyes where, in Hindu and Buddhist images, the eye of awakening uncloses. The second, the lower and principal face in this large, rectangular head is of the powerful were-jaguar, who, with his two symbolic shaman staves, is governing this temporal world of dualities. The downward-pointing triangle and the upward-pointing of the Indian heart chakra correspond in sense to the sense of these two faces. "Two souls," wrote Goethe, "dwell within my breast." And here they are.

Thus the interesting head of the Andean Staff God matches in its symbolic details the glorious lotus of the resounding syllable OM of the Indian symbolic system. The panel on the god's chest shows three pairs of volutes (Chakras 1, 2, and 3). The gloriole above his head is about to reveal three faces (Chakras 5, 6, and 7). The eight serpents on either side of the head are sideways reaching and small. Those above, upward reaching, are magnified (as in rapture) and are, also, the volutes. And if we now, once again, turn the icon upside down, to consider, stage by stage, the transformations represented in the faces, their messages from the silences of our own most inward space come loud and clear, in three transformations:

5. "This region," states an Indian text, "is the gateway of the great Liberation."[71] Its station is at the level of the larynx (the Voice, the Word, the Lion Roar). There is a purgation to be accomplished here: to put down, to quell, and to be quit of all the temporal lusts and fears of the lower centers, and so to become cleared for untrammeled spiritual flight. Accordingly, the snout is overcast of the first of the Raimondi stela's three faces, and it is crossed by threatening, tusk-like spikes and marked by the heads of six serpents.

6. Whereas here, at that point above and between the eyes where full awakening is achieved and the rapture experienced of what is known in the Christian vocabulary as the Beatific Vision of God, what are shown on the forehead of the second Raimondi face are the heads of a pair of eagles. Chakra 6, that is to say, corresponds to the experience that the angels know of the vision of God in heaven; as Chakra 5 was of purgatory. And since what is here beheld is a personification of the infinite, the Sanskrit term for the good is saguṇa brahman, "the infinite qualified," while the rapture known is of savikalpa samādhi, "qualified union with the infinite."

7. "The most difficult leave-taking," said the mystic Meister Eckhart, "is the leaving of God for G O D ":[72] overcoming the name and form of the historical "Ethnic Idea," that is to say, for an experience of transcendence. At Chakra 7, at the crown of the head, the mind-annihilating rapture is experienced of nirvikalpa samādhi, "unqualified identity" with nirguṇa brahman, "unqualified transcendence"; and accordingly, in the Raimondi stone, whereas the first revealed face showed six serpent forms and the second two eagle's heads, the last carries only an abstract design. For we have here gone beyond all names and forms—the names and form even of what had been earlier feared and revered as "God."

Turn the image right side up again!

537. Drawing of the Raimondi stela right side up.

All that we now see is a popular anthropomorphic god, represented as the avatāra, "descent into temporality," of a supreme power whose horned visage appears mysteriously near the summit of the radiant crown.

And one more detail: the menacing mouth of the were-jaguar turns into the cat-like grin of an amusing face with smiling eyes, when the panel is reversed and the beatifying revelation exposed of the mystic tower.

Mythology in the domain of any of the high civilizations will be of three orders, which, though they may appear to be of the same constitution, are not; nor can they ever be. They are, namely, mythology, (1) as experienced by the mystics; (2) as applied by governing authorities; and (3) as idolized by the folk. The aim of the first is rapture; of the second, power; and of the last, health, progeny, and wealth: or, in terms of the chakra system just reviewed, these aims are those proper, respectively, to Chakras 4, 3, and 2 (see pages 378–379). Mystics and the folk have in common the ability to turn to their use any mythology whatsoever. Politicians, on the other hand, not only are committed to one system, but also have the necessity to impose their system on others; for it is by engaging the folk mind in the idolization of the deities they propose that they engage the worshippers to themselves. Mystics can become an inconvenience, since their ability and need to read past the "ethnic idea" to the "elementary idea" disempowers the image politically intended to be idolized. And yet, paradoxically, as I believe we have found in the evidence of this *Atlas*, it has been out of mystic states that mythologies are derived.

Among the most primitive hunting and gathering tribes, of course, there is no place for the political factor. With the enlargement of settled communities, however, during Neolithic (Formative) eras, class distinctions originate, and ruling élites then emerge and take charge.

From the evidence, c. 1000 B.C., at Chavín de Huántar it appears that in Highland Peru this Formative élitism was not only of a social order, but also intellectual, vocational, of craftsmanship in the arts, and of inward spiritual insights. There has been discussion as to whether the distinctive style of Chavín art and thought, with its characteristic symbols, was in any way linked to a context of political domination. The influence became spread over broad areas, both in the Northern Highlands and along the North, Central, and South Coasts, but whether by political force or by some other manner of influence is unknown. As Bushnell has remarked of the archaeology of this culture:

"It is united by the presence of similar pottery types, and by evidence of a religion of animal worship, in which the cult of a feline god held the foremost place. There are a number of ceremonial centers which show a considerable variety in detail, and each seems to have been the nucleus of a group of scattered settlements, but there is no indication that the centers were united by any sort of political organization. Weapons are not common; flanged and spiked stone mace-heads and polished stone mace-heads occur in the graves of the Chicama region, the spear-thrower was in use, and a single long palm-wood bow was found at Ancón, but some of these must have been used for hunting. Fortifications

538. Mochica effigy vessel depicting an anthropomorphic creature that some suggest was a "bat god," holding a human head in its left hand and a knife in its right.

539. Ceremonial urn of the Tiahuanaco-Epigonal period, decorated with a figure — probably the Inca deity Viracocha — who wears a snake headdress, carries two staffs, and is seen to be weeping.

are unknown, as fighting can hardly have amounted to more than small-scale local raiding, and the carvings at Sechín indicate that head-hunting may have played some part in this. With a small population in a few scattered settlements, there cannot have been any of the competition for land which so often provokes wars.

"An important question which remains," Bushnell adds, "is, where did the bearers of the religious cult, ceremonial pottery and other new features come from?"[151]

Now "animal worship" is not at all the proper term for anything of which we have learned in the course of our review of the "primitive" cultures of mankind, let alone for such a figure as the Staff God of the Chavín de Huántar stela. As told by the Pawnee Letokots Lasa: "Tirawa, the One Above, did not speak directly to man. He sent certain animals to tell man that he showed himself through the beasts, and that from them, and from the stars and the sun and the moon should man learn. Tirawa spoke to man through his works, and the Pawnee understands the heavens, the beasts, and the plants. For all things tell of Tirawa" (see I.1: 8, 10, 25, 48–49).

Too many of our best scholars, themselves indoctrinated from infancy in a religion of one kind or another based upon the Bible, are so locked into the idea of their own god as a supernatural fact—something final, not symbolic of transcendence, but a personage with a character and will of *his* own—that they are unable to grasp the idea of a worship that is not of the symbol but of its reference, which is of a mystery of much greater age and of more immediate inward reality than the name-and-form of any historical ethnic idea of a deity, whatsoever. The feline god of the Andean Chavín Culture, accordingly, is not in any way evidence of "animal worship," but is of a sophistication that makes the sentimentalism of our popular Bible-story theology seem undeveloped. Where did the bearers of this truly mystical, profoundly poetic mythology then come from?

A rubbing from Chavín de Huántar (Figure 541) shows the symbolical were-jaguar holding two marine shells in his hands, a *Malea* in the right and a *Spondylus* in the left. Shells, as Lathrap has recognized, are important elements in Chavín religious art and are almost always presented as a pair: the conical univalve, *Malea*, being an obvious male symbol, and the bivalve, *Spondylus*, female.[152] Right, male; left, female: a worldwide archetypal association! The god in whose image the male and female aspects of the will in nature are comprised is also of an enormous domain (see I.2: Map 33). Another rubbing of a relief at Chavín de Huántar (Figure 542) shows an eagle, the claws of whose feet are exactly those of the feet of the jaguar god. Donald Lathrap has suggested that the birds represented in the symbolic arts of northwest-

540. Mochica ceramic effigy vessel, c. 4⅝" tall, depicting an anthropomorphic being about to consume a supine figure with a feline helmet (see 551–555).

ern South America at this date are the monkey-eating harpy eagle (*Harpia larpyga*), which is native to the Amazonian Basin and "by far the most impressive and powerful raptorial bird in South America....Many of the Tropical Forest tribes," he states further, "held the harpy eagle in great veneration, raising the young for their feathers and for purposes of ceremonial exchange and trade."[153] The serpent represented, he posits, is the prodigious Amazonian anaconda, whose mythological role as the Water Mistress, sister of the Moon, we have learned from the Makiritare of the Orinoco (see page 331); the Barasana of the Upper Orinoco Vaupés region tell tales of the same great snake in the character of the Manioc-stick Anaconda: of his birth as child of the Primal Sun (precursor of the visible sun and moon of today), of his marriage to Jaguar Woman, and of his death when he broke into flame and burned himself to ashes. From his bones were made the original trumpets of the men's rites, and from the ashes of his other remains grew manioc, edible fungi, and various other plants.[154] "It would appear appropriate," states Lathrap in comment

541. Rubbing from Chavín de Huántar of the principal Chavín deity, who holds a strombus shell in his right hand and a spondylus in his left.

on the imagery of Chavín, "...that the attributes of the most powerful known carnivore, the jaguar, were combined with the attributes of the most powerful raptorial bird, the harpy eagle, and the most powerful constrictor, the anaconda."[155]

These were all creatures of the neighboring Amazonian forest. The two seashells, *Malea* and *Spondylus*, on the other hand, were not only from a remote coast, but also difficult to obtain. Neither occurs along the coast south of Ecuador, and, as Lathrap points out, "large specimens of *Spondylus*, in particular, can be obtained only by diving to reefs at depths of fifty feet or more.

"Chavín art demonstrates," he continues, "that as early as 800 B.C. *Malea* and *Spondylus* were accepted as essential parts of the sacramental system. Indeed, there are representations of the *Spondylus* from a slightly earlier context at the site of Kotosh in the Huánuco Basin. The people of Chavín and Kotosh had to obtain these shells by long-distance trade from coastal Ecuador.... The Formative people of Ecuador used the bright red rims of the *Spondylus* shell for their own jewelry. They also traded this material to their southern neighbors as a most profoundly sacred and necessary commodity." And further: "In economic rituals of the modern highland Peruvian communities these marine shells still play an important part in ensuring proper rainfall and crop fertility."[156]

Uniting in his one person, thus, not only the powers of the male and female, as well as those of the celestial eagle and aqueous anaconda, but also the influences of two distinct mythological traditions, one of the neighboring rain forests to the east, the other of the sea to the west, the jaguar god of Chavín de Huántar appears and stands before us as a mystery god indeed, compounding in his one commanding presence practically all the enigmas and pairs-of-opposites of our subject. He is in no way the grotesque idol, merely, of some primitive local cult. Neither is he, finally, local—despite the appearances in the make-up of his person of the three most powerful animals of the nearby Rain Forest myths.

542. Rubbing of one of a row of harpy eagles on a stone slab that once may have rested over the entrance to the main temple at Chavín de Huántar.

543. Of note, but inexplicable, is the similarity of the headgear on such widely dispersed figures as these three: (**a**) stone figure, c. 18″ high, from Tiahuanaco, once on the shore of Lake Titicaca in Bolivia; (**b**) Tres Zapotes Monument A (see **350**); (**c**) stone sculpture from San Agustín, Colombia.

a

b

c

544. A tusked deity and his tiny companion, atop a ceremonial digging stick in a Mochica warrior-priest's grave at Huaca de la Cruz, the Virú valley.

545. Stela 2 from La Venta, Tabasco, Mexico.

The three figures shown in Figure 543 are wearing similar headgear. The first is from Bolivia, the second from Tres Zapotes, Mexico, and the third from San Agustín, Colombia. The posture of the Colombian figure is matched in a miniature, six inches high, from the Virú Valley (Figure 544). It is matched again at La Venta in a large stela, eleven feet five inches high (Figure 545), which is evidently the image of a god surrounded by a cloud company of attendants. Above the head of this figure is an immense headdress. Above the heads of the Colombia and Virú Valley figures are the apparitions of their feline "alter-egos." The shape of the headpiece of the Colombian apparition is exactly that of the jaguar-boy and jaguar-god heads and faces in Olmec art (Figure 356), where the boys are represented as sacrifices to the god. The earliest example of the mask in America, apparently, is from Ecuador, c. 2150–2000 B.C., on a piece of Valdivia pottery (Figure 546). It appears again, about a thousand years later, engraved and painted on two small bottle gourds (Figure 548) unearthed by Junius Bird in the late 1940s at Huaca Prieta, a site on the Peruvian North Coast, in the Chicama Valley. The radiocarbon date here was 1016 ± 300 B.C., and associated were some bits of bark cloth, cotton string, twined cotton fabric, looped and knotted pouches, fishing nets, and even true weavings: a context definitely of the sea.[157] And finally, of course, on the North American Northwest Coast, in the arts of the Haida, Kwakiutl and Tlingit wood carvers, the same unmistakable face appears on totem poles, carved boxes, and Chilcat blankets (Figure 547).

546. Valdivian bowl fragment with a diameter of c. 7¼″, an undulating rim, and incised mask-like facial treatments (see **507**).

547. Chilcat blanket of the Tlingit featuring an iconographic representation (arguably of a bear) that is suggestive of a *t'ao-t'ieh* mask.

Across the Pacific, on bronze ceremonial vessels of the Shang Dynasty (c. 1523–1027 B.C.) and Early (Western) Chou (c. 1027–772 B.C.), something very like this South and Middle American jaguar mask was an essential ornamental feature. Known as *t'ao-t'ieh,* the "Glutton," its earliest form is shown on the bronze *ting* (tripod with two ears: sacrificial cauldron regarded as a type of imperial power)[158] reproduced in Figure 549. It is here composed of two confronting dragons of the one-legged kind known as *k'uei.* "There is a difference of opinion," William Willetts states in discussion of this image, "as to how it originated; whether the confrontation of two animals or animal heads seen in profile first suggested the idea of a frontal mask, that is, or whether an original mask acquired, by a fanciful proliferation of its form, a *double entendre* in the shape of two confronting animals seen in side view....Chinese accounts as to the meaning of *t'ao-t'ieh,*" he goes on to report, "are conflicting. A passage in *Tso chuan* [a fourth-century B.C. history] speaks of noxious spirits at large in the hills and wastes,

549. Schematic drawing (above) explicating the iconography of one of the three *t'ao-t'ieh* masks (each formed from a pair of confronting *k'uei* dragons), all on a ground of squared spirals, on the Shang Dynasty bronze *ting,* c. 9¼" high, pictured in full at the right.

548. Carved gourd vessel with cover, from the Huaca Prieta site on the north coast of Peru.

and tells how these were depicted on the Nine Cauldrons of the legendary Yü the Great, to give people a fair idea of what they look like. By the third century A.D. the commentator Ku P'o is identifying the *t'ao-t'ieh* with one of these. But a passage in *Lü shih ch'un ch'in,* attributed to the third-century B.C. writer Lü Pe-wei, runs: 'On Chou vessels there was put a *t'ao-t'ieh* with a head, but no body. He is eating a man and thinks he is going to swallow him; but already the *t'ao-t'ieh's* body is destroyed.'"[159]

There is in Indian art and myth a comparable symbolic glutton called *Kīrttimukha,* "Face of Glory," also represented as a mask (Figure 550), of which the legend tells:

As a manifestation of Shiva's invincible majesty, Glutton was born of a lightning flash of wrath from the deity's third eye, whence he appeared as a ravenous monster avid to consume whatever was before him. And when nothing was seen available, Shiva ordered him to consume himself, which he promptly did. Commencing at his feet, he came chopping up the line until nothing was left but a face without a lower jaw, whereupon Shiva, delighted by this epitome of the nature of life, which lives on life, namely on itself, declared: "I name you 'Face of Glory,' *Kīrttimukha,* and shall place you above the entrances to my shrine. No one who cannot bow in obeisance to you is worthy to come to me."[160]

There is thus represented in this image a fierce philosophy of unqualified affirmation of the nature of life; a *yea!* that breaks past the barrier of fear to a recognition of sublimity. The mask appears over shrines, not only of Shiva, but also of his goddess, and in later Buddhist art, over images even of the Buddha with right hand lifted in the "fear not" posture.

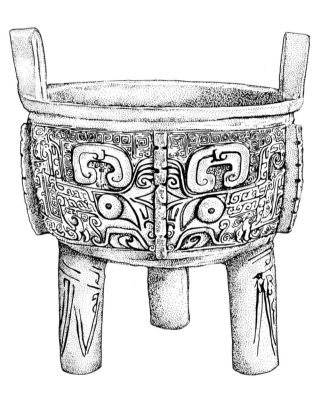

550. *Kīrttimukha,* as pictured in a detail of a larger work entitled *Durga Slayer of the Titan Buffalo,* Bhuvanesvara Vaital Deul, c. 1000 A.D.

551. Chinese bronze Yu vessel, Shang Dynasty, 1523–1027 B.C. On the back of this piece is an exceptionally fine *t'ao-t'ieh* design. Interpreters have differed as to whether the animal is meant to be eating or protecting the human being, who appears, indeed, to be rather more pleased than discomposed by what is happening. However, the tiger in China, like the jaguar in the Americas, is a beast symbolic of earth, and as such representative of the female, receptive, *yin* principle in nature; the *yang*, the male, being represented by the dragon—as by the Feathered Serpent. And we perceive that in this wonderful piece, symbolic of the sacrifice it was designed to serve, there are serpents of many kinds curling everywhere over the two bodies, together with auspicious spiral, thunder, and labyrinth motifs.

553. Ceramic Classical Recuay jar, found in a stone-lined grave in the Callejón de Huaylas Valley in the north highlands of Peru. Dating from the Early Intermediate Period (c. 200 B.C.–A.D. 600, contemporaneous with the Mochica), this vessel, painted with black negative designs over white and red, is typical of most extant Recuay pottery, both in its style of modeling and in its distinctive decoration.

Enlarged to a world-mythological perspective, the imagery of these alter-ego pieces can be compared to that in Mesopotamian and Indian art where gods are shown riding or standing on their animal vehicles. The animal in such an image is the alter-ego—the operative aspect in time—of the immortal, whose higher aspect is of eternity, disengaged from this field of birth, suffering, and death. Accordingly, where a god is slain by a beast, as was Adonis by a boar, the animal is in fact the alter-ego of the personification slain; representing the active, timebound and thus death-bound aspect of an immortal that has condescended to assume a form and play a mythic or historic role. The animal is thus an agent of the active aspect of the power that appears to be slain.

And so, too, in relation to a human being: the mythic alter-ego, where it appears, is symbolic of the person's active will and effective power in the field of space and time, the endowed person himself (like the Buddha seated beneath *Kīrtti-mukha*) being at once at one with and transcendent of the temporal manifestations.

This is an idea that was implicit in all of the archaic high mythologies where ceremonials of human sacrifice played an important role. It is what was implied in the Early Christian understanding of the Crucifixion, as stated in what has been called "the great Christological passage" of Paul's epistle to the Philippians 2:6–9, where the sacrificed God-Man is celebrated as one.

> *Who, being in the form of God, thought it not robbery to be equal with God:*
>
> *But made himself of no reputation, and took upon him the form of a servant, and was made in the likeness of men:*
>
> *And being found in fashion as a man, he humbled himself, and became obedient unto death, even the death of the cross.*
>
> *Wherefore God also hath highly exalted him, and given him a name which is above every name.*

Augustine states somewhere that Jesus "went to the Cross as a bridegroom to his bride," and so, too, we must suppose, those many who in Antiquity were sacrificed voluntarily must have greeted the grim threshold of their return from time to eternity. There is a famous Shang sacrificial bronze vessel, shown in Figure 551, in which this idea appears to be rendered. It will be noted that on the back of the symbolic beast there is an unmistakable *t'ao-t'ieh*. Figure 552 is a Mochica stirrup-spout jar from the Peruvian North Coast; Figure 553, a representation of the same theme from the Classical Recuay Culture of the Highlands; Figure 554 is a bone club from a Salishan tribe of Washington State; and Figure 555 a Chimú bronze.

552. Polished clay stirrup-jar, showing a man in the consumptive embrace of an anthropomorphic, cay-man-like creature, having special mythological significance to its Mochica creators (see **541**).

554. Detail of the head of a bone club, Salish tribe, Washington State.

Whatever the explanation may be, it seems to me to be evident beyond question that, in the monuments of the great werejaguar god of the Formative Cultures of South and Middle America, features appear that are of a kind with those of the equivalent high gods in Asia. How this came to be, we can only surmise; for the evidence that we have (and we have a lot) has been consistently interpreted in contrary senses by those qualified to judge. However, there can be, in fact, only three possibilities: (1) massive, politically directed influence; (2) completely independent, parallel development; and (3) creative native incorporation of unenforced influences from Asia.

For number (1), it seems to me, there is no evidence whatsoever; against (2), it seems to me, there is too much evidence of analogies to make any judgment of complete independence possible only as an article of blind faith (which for some, I understand, is a requirement of their school). And so, that leaves number (3)—which has been evident, of course, for over a century to most European scholars of this subject. The only remaining questions, then, must be of the period or periods, and of the kinds and extent of the Asian influences—to which the answers separate into two clusters. The first has to do with the period preceding c. 3000 B.C., and the second, with the Formative Period thereafter.

With respect to the first, there is the whole longhouse (maloca) complex to consider, along with the dugout canoe, pearl-oyster shell fishhook, blowgun, panpipe, headhunt, vegetative-reproduction-shifting cultivation, men's secret societies, and the rest. The key myth is of a deity killed and buried, from whose remains the food plants arose; and in the South American rain forests, the myths and rites of this horticultural tradition coalesced with a powerful, shamanic, hunting-and-gathering heritage, to which a lavish exploitation of the abundant hallucinogenic plants of the region had given a special accent.

And with respect, then, to the questions touching the Formative innovations fol-

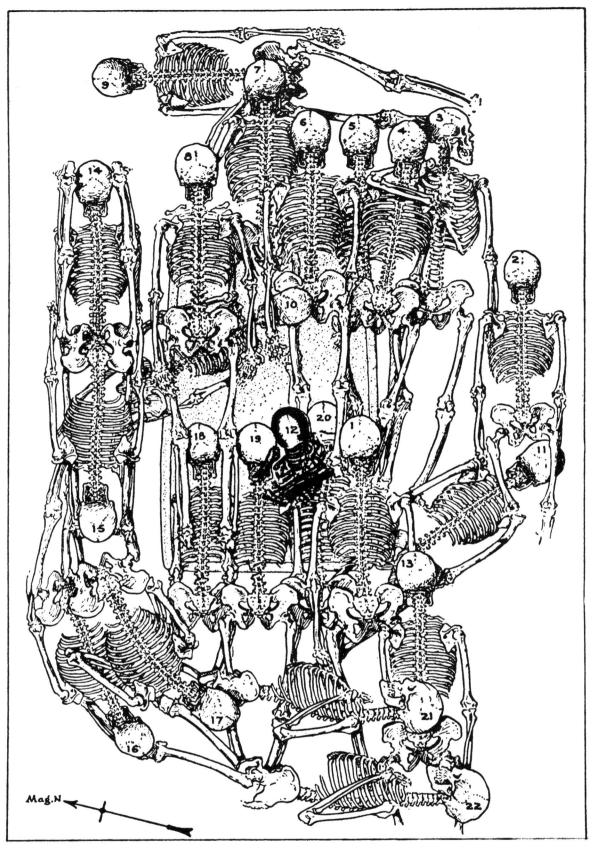

556. Plan of grave from Sitio Conté; Skeleton 12, the Cacique, has fallen from his seated position.

555. Chimú bronze figurine from North Peru.

lowing c. 3000 B.C, first to be noticed are the Valdivia-Jomon affiliations of the earliest ceramic female figurines in the New World; next the appearance in Ecuador, c. 1500 B.C., of the custom of artificial skull deformation. With the appearance of stone monuments in the Late Formative phase, from c. 1000 B.C., the signs of Asia greatly multiply, with ceramic pillows, ceramic roller stamps and flat stamps, dogs for eating, and, at Chavín de Huántar, an elegant esoteric art, comprising *double-entendre* motifs. At Paracas, on the South Coast, in the barren sandy wastes around the hill called Cerro Colorado, Julio C. Tello, in 1925, excavated a wall-enclosed necropolis, where the tombs were subterranean houses from which he extracted 429 mummy bundles, in an amazingly good state of preservation,

many of the skulls of which had been trephined.[161] The represented culture, contemporary with the Chavín, seems to have been culturally related to the Nazca. And finally, over three thousand miles to the north, on the western coast of Panama, by the Rio Grande de Coclé, in the tombs of a now famous burial ground known as Sitio Conte, from which over two hundred pottery vessels have been recovered, the graves of the Caciques contained, besides the dignitary himself (buried in a sitting posture, as though still in authority), the skeletons of over twenty retainers who had been sent along with him to eternal life (Figure 556).[162]

557. From Sitió Conte, Coclé, Panama, a beaten gold plaque, 6¼" x 6⅝", showing an anthropomorphic deity, depicted as an almost-prototypical "hocker" (German, "squatter"), with cayman-like claws, a spine rendered visible in "x-ray" style, and a headdress comprised of a pair of confronting mouths, with attached eyes and extended fish-like bodies, that some suggest are representations of hammerhead sharks. Miguel Covarrubias notes that the hocker motif "is a circum-Pacific element and is [found in] early China, Malaysia, Melanesia, and Polynesia [see I.2:**324–326**]. It appears with dots or disks between knees and elbows; in series, often losing the head and becoming a decorative pattern; or as hockers with claws, horns, death's head, and visible spinal columns, suggesting that it represents a spirit of the dead.... In some cases (Northwest Coast, Mexico, Peru, Borneo) hockers are flanked by two animals, which [another scholar] identifies with the guardians of the sun god in Mexico and Peru."[73]

Robert von Heine-Geldern (1885–1968), who for some five decades waged an almost solitary battle against the American Anthropological establishment, to demonstrate what, as an Orientalist, he had recognized of Asia in the Americas, identified the South Chinese coastal states of Wu and Yüeh as the probable seats of the influences evident in Chavín. In 333 B.C., however, when Yüeh, which had subdued Wu, was itself subdued, the Chinese transpacific voyaging ceased, and the adventure passed to their southern neighbors in northeastern Indo-China, the Dong-son, ancestors of the present day Vietnamese. "Traces of Dong-son influence are far more numerous in South America," Heine-Geldern claimed, "than those of Chinese influence. One finds them throughout the Andean region from Panama to northern Chile and northwestern Argentina....The trans-Pacific voyages of the Dong-son people may have come to an end as the result of the final conquest of Tonkin and North Annam by China toward the middle of the first century A.D."[163] Later Chinese evidences in Mexico and Guatemala suggest, however, to quote Heine-Geldern again, that the relations of China with Mesoamerica either continued after the fall of Yüeh or, as seems more likely, were resumed under the Han. They may have terminated as a result of the political troubles which, in the third century A.D., culminated in the fall of the Han dynasty."[164]

In working out the links between Asia and Mesoamerica, Heine-Geldern collaborated in research with Gordon F. Eckholm of the American Museum of Natural History, and, as he tells: "we experienced one surprise after another. The architecture and the art, the religious symbols, the cosmological ideas, the institutions of the states and the royal courts, the insignia of kings and dignitaries, even the games—all this to an unsuspected and overwhelming extent—reminded us of the civilizations of Southeast Asia and India."[165]

Although the high-civilization Mayan-Toltec-Aztec development cannot be dealt with properly in this context until we review the origins of writing and of solar and lunar calendric calculations in the Old World, the unfoldment of Peruvian civilizations—developed without writing and without any calendar, so far as we know—has been considered as a special curiosity, not matched anywhere in the histories of the higher civilizations: namely, as a relatively isolated development out of an initial Formative impulse of a preliterate civilization that can be compared to Egypt in the wonder of its monuments and with Rome in the organization of its culminating empire. Only toward the end, in the shaping of the Inca empire, do we find unmistakable evidence of a deliberate *political* emphasis in the shaping and enforcement of a mythology. There must have been something of the kind involved, also, in the structuring of the empire of Chimú. From what has been learned, on the other hand, of the period of Chavín de Huántar, there were evidently no fortifications, there was little weaponry, and of the possible social applications of the symbolized mythology, we have no evidence. The influence of the culture was nevertheless extensive and, in the full sense of the term, Formative. Bushnell describes it as "a religious cult which required imposing buildings...together with an elaborate form of pottery for ceremonial use...."[166]

"All the known sites of this period," he points out, "belong to some form of the Chavín Culture, of which the north coastal aspect is sometimes called Cupisnique. There is reason to believe that the new features were introduced by an immigrant people. The older inhabitants continued to live on and near some of their original sites, where their presence is shown by the persistence of the old types of utilitarian pottery, but the newcomers imposed their religious system on them."[167]

By what means imposed, no one can say; neither, indeed, whether it was imposed or, rather, caught on. Regardless, and notwithstanding all the historical obscurities surrounding its sudden appearance, the main impression is of a new level of metaphysical insight, which crystallized (c. 1000 B.C.) over a large part of the culture field of Peru, not only as an art form and local manner of life, but as the founding inspiration of a civilization. The precise whence and wherefore of it all remain to be learned.

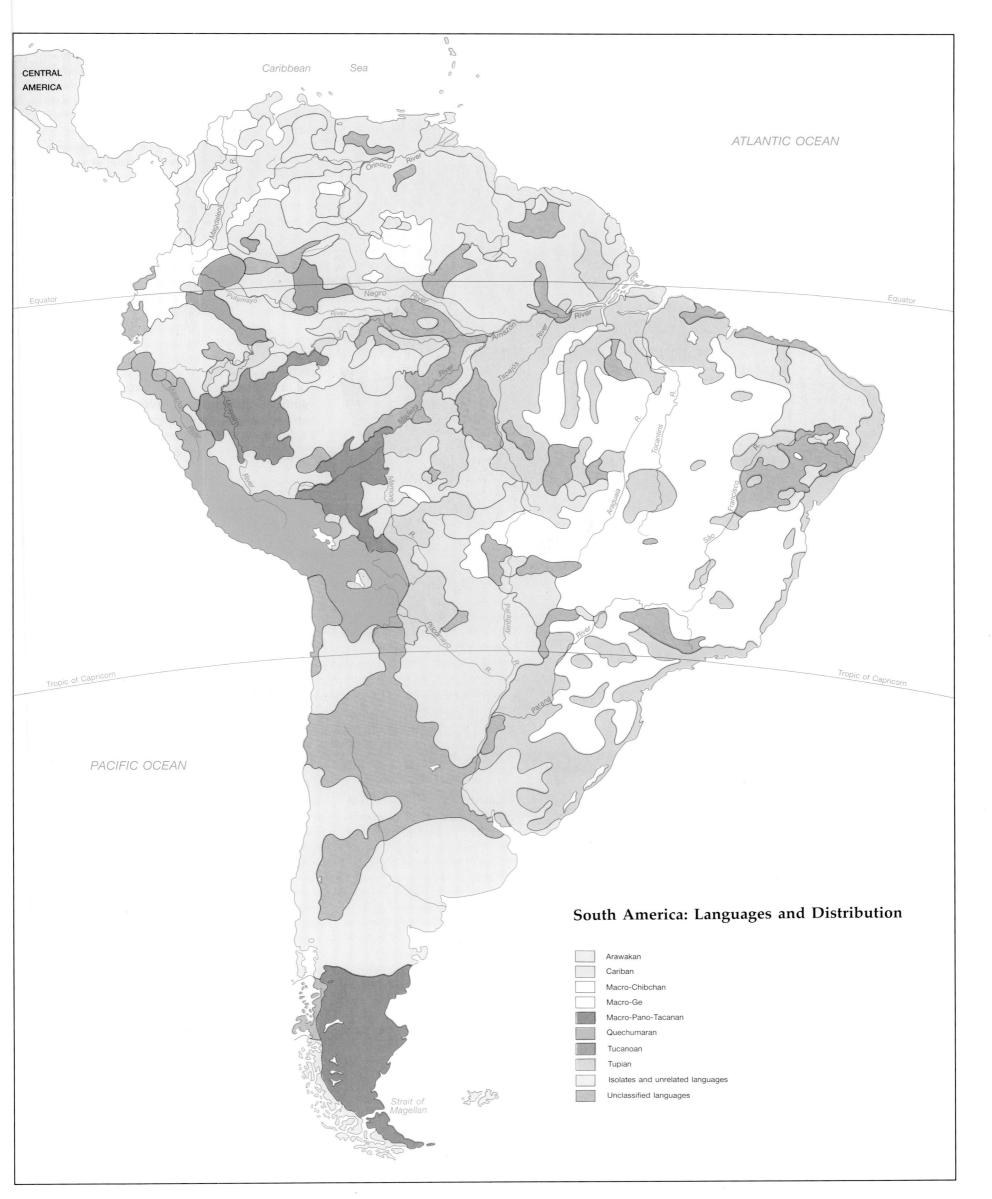

CENTRAL
AMERICA

Caribbean Sea

ATLANTIC OCEAN

Orinoco River

Magdalena R.

Equator

Putumayo River

Negro River

Amazon River

Tapajos R.

Madeira River

Marañón River

Ucayali

Mamoré

R.

Araguaia R.

Tocantins R.

São Francisco R.

PACIFIC OCEAN

Pilcomayo R.

Paraguay R.

Paraná River

Tropic of Capricorn

Equator

Tropic of Capricorn

South America: Languages and Distribution

	Arawakan
	Cariban
	Macro-Chibchan
	Macro-Ge
	Macro-Pano-Tacanan
	Quechumaran
	Tucanoan
	Tupian
	Isolates and unrelated languages
	Unclassified languages

Strait of Magellan

Map 43.

387

APPENDIX

ENDNOTES

AGRICULTURAL DEVELOPMENTS IN THE MESOAMERICAN MATRIX

[1]Susan Eger and Peter R. Collings, "Huichol Women's Art," in Kathleen Berrin, ed., *Art of the Huichol Indians*, Fine Arts Museums of San Francisco (New York: Harry N. Abrams, 1978), p. 35.

[2]Charles C. Di Peso, "Macaws...Crotals...and Trumpet Shells," *Early Man*, vol. 2, no. 3 (Autumn 1980), p. 5.

[3]Ibid., pp. 5 and 8.

[4]Ibid., p. 8.

[5]Ibid.

[6]Ibid., p. 11.

[7]Richard B. Woodbury, "Artifacts in the Guatemalan Highlands," in Robert Wauchope, ed., *Handbook of Middle American Indians*, 13 vols. (Austin: University of Texas Press, 1964–73), vol. 2, p. 169. The whole question of the hallucinogen in relation to religious visionary cults was introduced to modern anthropology largely through the researches of R. Gordon Wasson. See, for instance, V. P. Wasson and R. G. Wasson, *Mushrooms Russia & History*, 2 vols. (New York: Pantheon Books, 1957).

[8]Di Peso, op. cit., p. 11.

[9]Ibid., pp. 21–22.

[10]Ibid., p. 8.

[11]Richard I. Ford, "'Artifacts' That Grew: Their Roots in Mexico," *Early Man*, vol. 2, no. 3 (Autumn 1980), pp. 22–23. For detailed analyses of the matters here briefly reviewed, see J. Charles Kelley, "Mesoamerica and the Southwestern United States," and James B. Griffin, "Mesoamerica and the Eastern United States in Prehistoric Times," both in Wauchope, op. cit., vol. 4, pp. 95–110 and 111–131.

[12]Victor Wolfgang von Hagen, ed., *The Incas of Pedro de Cieza de Leon* (Norman: University of Oklahoma Press, 1959), opening maps.

[13]Oswald Spengler, *Der Untergang des Abendlandes*, 2 vols. (Munich: C. H. Beck'sche Verlagsbuchhandlung, vol. 1 in 1918, vol. 2 in 1922), vol. 2, pp. 51–52. Translation (slightly modified) by Charles Francis Atkinson, *Decline of the West* (New York: Alfred A. Knopf, 1926–1928), vol. 2, pp. 43–44.

[14]Jacques Soustelle, *The Olmecs: The Oldest Civilization in Mexico*, trans. Helen B. Lane (Garden City, N.Y.: Doubleday and Company, Inc., 1984), p. 1.

[15]Ibid., p. 25.

[16]Philip Drucker, Robert F. Heizer, and Robert Squier, *Excavations at La Venta, Tabasco, 1955*, Smithsonian Institution Bureau of American Ethnology Bulletin 170 (Washington, D.C., 1959), pp. 152–159 and plates 30–36.

[17]Ibid., pp. 93–95 and plates 14–17.

[18]Matthew W. Stirling, "Stone Monuments of the Rio Chiquito, Veracruz, Mexico," in *Anthropological Papers*, nos. 43–48, Smithsonian Institution Bureau of American Ethnology Bulletin 157 (Washington, D.C., 1955), pp. 8 and 19–20; also plates 2, 25, and 26.

[19]Ignacio Bernal, *The Olmec World*, trans. Doris Heyden and Fernando Horcasitas (Berkeley: University of California Press, 1969), p. 58.

[20]Michael D. Coe, "Olmec Jaguars and Olmec Kings," in Elizabeth P. Benson, ed., *The Cult of the Feline*, Dumbarton Oaks Research Library and Collections (Washington, D.C.: Trustees for Harvard University, 1972), pp. 10–11.

[21]Peter T. Furst, "The Olmec Were-Jaguar Motif in the Light of Ethnological Reality," in Elizabeth P. Benson, ed., *Dumbarton Oaks Conference on the Olmec, October 28th and 29th, 1967*, Dumbarton Oaks Research Library and Collection (Washington, D.C.: Trustees for Harvard University, 1968), p. 148.

[22]Soustelle, op. cit., p. 145.

[23]Bernal, op. cit., pp. 107–110.

[24]See, for example, Kent V. Flannery, "The Olmec and the Valley of Oaxaca: A Model for Inter-regional Interaction in Formative Times," in Benson, ed., *Dumbarton Oaks Conference on the Olmec*, pp. 79–177; also, David C. Grove, *The Olmec Paintings of Oxtotitlan Cave, Guerrero, Mexico*, Studies in Pre-Columbian Art and Archaeology Number 6 (Washington, D.C.: Dumbarton Oaks, Trustees for Harvard University, 1970), p. 32.

[25]Miguel Covarrubias, *Indian Art of Mexico and Central America* (New York: Alfred A. Knopf, 1957), p. 18.

[26]Paul Tolstoy, "Utilitarian Artifacts of Central Mexico," in Wauchope, op. cit., vol. 10, p. 271.

[27]Soustelle, op. cit., pp. 122–134.

[28]Ibid., p. 134.

[29]Ignacio Bernal, "Views of Olmec Culture," in Benson, ed., *Dumbarton Oaks Conference on the Olmec*, p. 137.

[30]Flannery, op. cit., pp. 98–102.

[31]From William H. Sears, "Seaborne Contacts between Early Cultures in the Lower Southeastern United States and Middle through South America," in Elizabeth P. Benson, ed., *The Sea in the Pre-Columbian World*, Dumbarton Oaks Research Library and Collections (Washington, D.C.: Trustees for Harvard University, 1977), p. 8.

[32]Gordon R. Willey, in discussion of Robert F. Heizer, "New Observations on La Venta," in Benson, ed., *Dumbarton Oaks Conference on the Olmec*, p. 40.

[33]Sears, "Seaborne Contacts," p. 9.

[34]Soustelle, op. cit., pp. 79–80.

[35]Ibid., p. 150.

AGRICULTURAL RITES AND MYTHS OF MIDDLE AMERICA

[1]Paul C. Mangelsdorf, Richard S. MacNeish, and Gordon R. Willey, "Origins of Agriculture in Middle America," in Robert Wauchope, ed., *Handbook of Middle American Indians*, 13 vols. (Austin: University of Texas Press, 1964–73), vol. 1, pp. 431–432.

[2]Carl O. Sauer, *Agricultural Origins and Dispersals* (New York: American Geographical Society, 1952), reedited and published with additional chapters as *Seeds, Spades, Hearths & Herds: The Domestication of Animals and Foodstuffs* (Cambridge, Mass.: M.I.T. Press, 1969), 2nd ed., p. 64.

[3]Gordon Vivian and Paul Reiter, *The Great Kivas of Chaco Canyon and Their Relationships*, The School of American Research Monograph 22 (Albuquerque: University of New Mexico Press, 1965), p.97, citing J. D. Jennings and E. K. Reed, eds., "Seminars in Archaeology, The American Southwest: A Problem in Cultural Isolation," in *American Antiquity*, vol. 22, no. 2, part 2, p. 86.

[4]Natalie Curtis, *The Indians' Book: An Offering by the American Indians of Indian Lore, Musical and Narrative, to Form a Record of the Songs and Legends of Their Race* (New York: Harper & Bros., 1907), p. 314.

[5]Vivian and Reiter, op. cit., pp. 97–99.

[6]Vivian and Reiter, op. cit., citing Gordon C. Baldwin, "A Basket Maker III Sandal Tablet," *Southwestern Lore*, vol. V, p. 49.

[7]Vivian and Reiter, op. cit., citing Paul S. Martin and John B. Rinaldo, *Modified Basket Maker Sites in the Ackman-Lowry Area, Southwestern Colorado*, Field Museum of Natural History Anthropological Series, vol. 23, no. 3 (1939), pp. 350–359.

[8]Vivian and Reiter, op. cit., p. 63.

[9]Stephen C. McCluskey, "The Astronomy of the Hopi Indians," *Journal for the History of Astronomy*, vol. 8 (October 1977), pp. 177–178.

[10]Anna Sofaer, Volker Zinser, and Rolf M. Sinclair, "A Unique Solar Marking Construct," *Science*, vol. 206, no. 4416 (October 19, 1979), pp. 283–291.

[11]Anna Sofaer, Rolf M. Sinclair, and L. E. Doggett, "Lunar Markings on Fajada Butte," in A. F. Aveni, ed., *Archaeoastronomy in the New World* (Cambridge: Cambridge University Press, 1982), pp. 169–186.

[12]Rolf M. Sinclair, Anna Sofaer, J. J. McCann, and J. J. McCann Jr., "Marking of Major Lunar Standstill at the Three-Slab Site on Fajada Butte," *Bulletin of the American Astronomical Society*, vol. 19, no. 4 (1987), p. 1043.

[13]Sofaer, Zinser, and Sinclair, op. cit., pp. 283–291; also Kendrick Frazier, "The Anasazi Sun Dagger," *Science 80*, vol. 1, no. 1 (November and December 1979), pp. 56–67.

[14]Anna Sofaer, M. P. Marshall, and R. Sinclair. "The Great North Road: A Cosmographic Expression of the Chaco Culture of New Mexico," in A. F. Aveni, ed., *World Archaeoastronomy* (Cambridge: Cambridge University Press, 1989).

[15]Anna Sofaer and Rolf Sinclair, "Astronomic and Related Patterning in the Architecture of the Chaco Culture of New Mexico," *Bulletin of the American Astronomical Society*, vol. 18, no. 4 (1986), pp. 1044–1045.

[16]Recent findings by Anna Sofaer and her colleagues have shown that eighteen major Chaco buildings located across two thousand square miles were symmetrically and possibly astronomically organized about the ceremonial center of Chaco Canyon. See Anna Sofaer, Rolf Sinclair, and K. Williams, "A Regional Pattern in the Architecture of Chaco Culture of New Mexico and Its Astronomical Implications," *Bulletin of the American Astronomical Society*, vol. 19, no. 4 (1987), p. 1044.

[17]Frank Waters, *Book of the Hopi* (New York: Ballantine Books, 1969), pp. 188–254. Also, McCluskey, op. cit., pp. 176–191.

[18]Florence M. Hawley, "Pueblo Social Organization As a Lead to Pueblo History," *American Anthropologist*, vol. 39 (1937), pp. 504–522.

[19]Waters, op. cit., p. 168.

[20]Ibid., p. 183.

[21]Ibid., p. 170.

[22]Ibid., pp. 169–173.

[23]Ibid., pp. 168–179 and 422.

[24]See Alexander M. Stephen, *Hopi Journal*, Elsie Clew Parsons, ed., 2 vols., Columbia University Contributions to Anthropology, vol. 23, in two parts (New York: Columbia University Press, 1936), vol. 2, pp. 981–982. Stephen, whose great two-volume journal is a classic source for Hopi lore, lived among the Navaho and Hopi from about 1881 to the year of his death in 1894. His account of Wúwuchim, as observed at Walpi in 1891 (vol. 2, pp. 957–993) differs greatly in detail from Frank Waters' observations at Oraibi, over half a century later. Unfortunately, he missed the kiva ceremony of the Night of the Washing of the Hair altogether. As he laments: "I have missed the whole of the novice initiation" (p. 978).

[25]Waters, op. cit., pp. 185–187.

[26]Waters, op. cit., pp. 185 and 188–191. Elsie Clew Parsons, who watched the arrival of Soyál Kachina at Oraibi in 1920 was told, not that the kachina was tottering like a child, but that "He acts like an old man and wears old clothes because he is an old kachina" (in Stephen, op. cit., vol. 1, pp. 3–4, note 5). Waters' interpreters, on the other hand, declared that such an interpretation "negates the meaning of the whole Soyál ceremony" (p. 189, note 3). At Walpi, where Stephen observed the festival in 1982, the first kachina to appear was not Soyál, but Au'halani Kachina with his two sisters, Blue Corn Girl and Yellow Corn Girl (the female roles enacted by men); and here, too, the interpretation given was that the costume was "very old." Stephen comments, "and it surely looks it" (Stephen, op. cit., vol. 1, pp. 34–35).

[27]Waters, op. cit., p. 188.

[28]Ibid., pp. 188–201.

[29]Ibid., pp. 213–230.

[30]Ibid., p. 247.

[31]Ibid., p. 250.

[32]Ibid.

[33]Ibid., p. 255.

[34]James G. Frazer, *The Golden Bough*, one-volume edition (New York: The Macmillan Company, 1922), pp. 11–37.

[35]Waters, op. cit., pp. 272–273 and 448.

[36]Ibid., p. 277.

[37]Ibid., pp. 271–276.

[38]Ibid., pp. 257–265.

[39]Ibid., pp. 283–287.

[40]Ibid., pp. 283–291.

[41]Betty Bell, "Archaeology of Nayarit, Jalisco, and Colima," in Wauchope, op. cit., vol. 2, p. 695.

[42]Carl O. Sauer and D. D. Brand, "Aztatlan: Prehistoric Frontier on the Pacific Coast," *Ibero-Americana*, no. 1 (Berkeley: University of California Press, 1932), p. 41.

[43]Bell, op. cit., pp. 695–696.

[44]Peter T. Furst, "The Art of 'Being Huichol'," in Kathleen Berrin, ed., *Art of the Huichol Indians* (New York: Harry N. Abrams, Inc., 1978), a catalogue published in conjunction with an exhibition organized by the Fine Arts Museums of San Francisco, p. 22.

[45]Barbara G. Myerhoff, *Peyote Hunt: The Sacred Journey of the Huichol Indians* (Ithaca: Cornell University Press, 1974), pp. 125–126.

[46]See ibid., pp. 84–88 and 199–204, for a discussion of these mercurial figures.

[47]Ibid., pp. 130–132.

[48]Ibid., p. 133.

[49]Ibid., pp. 147–148.

[50]Barbara G. Myerhoff, "Peyote and the Mystic Vision," in Berrin, op. cit., p. 57.

[51]Myerhoff, *Peyote Hunt*, pp. 123–124.

[52]Ibid., p. 166.

[53]The account is greatly reduced from Myerhoff, *Peyote Hunt*, pp. 118–172.

[54]Myerhoff, *Peyote Hunt*, pp. 172–173.

[55]Ibid., p. 174.

[56]Ibid., p. 175, note 20.

[57]Susan Eger and Peter R. Collings, "Huichol Women's Art," in Berrin, op. cit., p. 44.

[58]Ibid.

[59]Ibid., p. 37.

[60]Ibid.; also Furst, op. cit., p. 22.

[61]Eger and Collings, op. cit., pp. 47 and 49.

[62]Ibid., p. 46.

[63]Ibid.

[64]Prem Das, "Initiation by a Huichol Shaman," in Berrin, op. cit., p. 138.

[65]Joseph Campbell, *The Hero with a Thousand Faces*, Bollingen Series XVII (Princeton: Princeton University Press, 1962).

[66]Furst, op. cit., p. 33.

[67]Ibid.

[68]Ibid., pp. 33–34.

[69]Ibid., p. 33.

[70]The phrase, "transparent to transcendence," I have borrowed from Karlfried Graf Durckheim, *Erlebnis und Wandlung* (Munich: Otto Wilhelm Barth Verlag, 1978).

[71]Myerhoff, *Peyote Hunt*, p. 210.

[72]Myerhoff, *Peyote Hunt*, pp. 210–213, adapted.

[73]"Journal of the First Voyage of Columbus," translated and edited, with an introduction and notes, by Cecil Jane, *The Voyages of Christopher Columbus* (London: The Argonaut Press, 1930), pp. 148–149. This so-called "Journal" is actually a redaction by Bartolomé de Las Casas of an already-edited version of the original account sent by Columbus to the king and queen, which original has been lost.

[74]The Bull "Inter Cetera" was issued by the newly elected Pope Alexander VI (Rodrigo Borgia) on May 4, 1493, on terms highly favorable to the Castillian crown. Several years later at the Treaty of Tordesillas, the line dividing Spanish and Portuguese hegemony in the New World was moved westward and Portugal gained possession of what is now Brazil. The translation is from Richard Eden, *The History of Trauayle in the West and East Indies, and Other Countreys Lying Eyther Way, towardes the Fruitfull and Ryche Mollaccaes* (London, 1577), pp. 455–457, abridged.

[75]Bartolomé de Las Casas, *Historia de las Indias*, ed. Agustín Millares Carlo, 3 vols. (Mexico: Fondo de Cultura Económica, 1951). The original manuscript was completed by Las Casas in Madrid in 1561, but was not printed until 1875–1876.

[76]Bartolomé de Las Casas, *Brevíssima Relación de la Destrucción de las Indias* (Mexico: Libros Luciernaga, 1957). Finished by Las Casas in 1542, and first printed in Seville in 1552.

[77]Andrés Bernáldez, *Historia de los reyes católicos, Don Fernando y Doña Isobel* (Seville: Sociedad Bibliófilos Andeluces, 1st Series, 1978), chapter 118; translation from Jane, op. cit., p. 314.

[78]Ramón Pane, *Relación acerca de las antigüedades de los indios*, ed. José Juan Arrom (Mexico: Siglo Veintiuno, 1977). Pane's account can be found in Hernando Colon [Ferdinand Columbus], *Historie...della vita e de' fatti dell' Ammariglio D. Christoforo Colombo* (Venice, 1571). A good English translation is by Benjamin Keen, *The Life of...Columbus by His Son Ferdinand* (New Brunswick, N. J.: Rutgers University Press, 1959).

[79]Bartolomé de Las Casas, *Apologética historia sumaria cuanto a las cualidades, disposición, descripción, cielo y suelo destas tierras, y condiciones naturales, policías, repúblicas, manera de vivir e costumbres de las gentes destas Indias occidentales y meridionales cuyo imperio soberano pertenece a los Reyes de Castilla*, ed. Edmundo O'Gorman, 2 vols. (Mexico: Universidad Nacional Autónoma de México, Instituto de Investigaciones Históricas, 1967). Completed by Las Casas in 1560 and first printed in full in Madrid in 1909.

[80]José Juan Arrom, *Mitología y Artes Prehispánicas de las Antillas* (Mexico: Siglo Veintiuno Editores, 1975), p. 16.

[81]Ibid., p. 19, citing Pane, chapter 1.

[82]Arrom, op. cit., pp. 19–22.

[83]Ibid., p. 22, citing Pane, chapter 19.

[84]See, for example, Jesse Walter Fewkes, "The Aborigines of Porto Rico and Neighboring Islands," *Twenty-fifth Annual Report of the Bureau of American Ethnology* (Washington, D.C., 1907), pp. 3–220, especially pp. 111–132, and plates xxxi–liii; and Frederick J. Dockstader, *Indian Art in Middle America* (Greenwich, Conn.: New York Graphic Society, 1964), caption to figure 199.

[85]Arrom, op. cit., pp. 22–30.

[86]Ibid., p. 26.

[87]Ibid., p. 44, citing Pane, parraio preliminar.

[88]Arrom, op. cit., p. 44, note 3, citing Las Casas, *Apologética historia*, chapter 120.

[89]Arrom, op. cit., pp. 44 47, citing Daniel G. Brinton, "The Arawak Language of Guiana in Its Linguistic and Ethnological Relations," *Transactions of the American Philosophical Society*, vol. XIV (1871), p. 444.

[90]Arrom, op. cit., p. 47.

[91]Arrom, op. cit., pp. 47–48, citing *Vida de almirante don Cristobal Colon por su hijo Fernando*, chapter 62.

[92]Arrom, op. cit., p. 55, citing Pane, chapter 11.

[93]Arrom, op. cit., pp. 55–56.

[94]Ibid., pp. 55–57.

[95]Ibid., p. 60.

[96]Frazer, op. cit., p. 436.

[97]Arrom, op. cit., pp. 128–129.

[98]Matthew 14:17 ff., Mark 6:38 ff., Luke 9:13 ff., John 6:9 ff.

[99]Arrom, op. cit., p. 129.

[100]Ibid., p. 137.

[101]Ibid., pp. 126–128, citing Pane, chapters 9–11.

[102]Arrom, op. cit., p. 142, citing Niels Fock, *Waiwai, Religion and Society of an Amazonian Tribe* (Copenhagen: National Museum, 1963), p. 47.

[103]Arrom, op. cit., p. 143.

[104]Julian H. Steward, ed., *Handbook of South American Indians*, 7 vols., Smithsonian Institution, Bureau of American Ethnology Bulletin 143 (Washington, D.C., 1944–1950); reissued in New York by Cooper Square Publishers, 1963.

[105]Ibid., vol. 4, p. 2.

[106]Ibid., p. 23.

[107]Ibid., p. 41; also, Irving Rouse, "The Ciboney," in ibid., pp. 497–503; and Pedro Garcia Valdes, "The Ethnogeography of the Ciboney," in ibid., pp. 503–505. The lengths of these last two articles are due to the number of culture traits enumerated and described which the Ciboney did *not* possess.

[108]Steward, op. cit., pp. 6–7.

[109]Rouse, "The Ciboney," pp. 533–534.

[110]Hartley Burr Alexander, *Latin-American Mythology*, in Louis Herbert Gray, ed., *The Mythology of All Races*, 13 vols. (Boston: Marshall Jones Co., 1920), vol. XI, p. 32.

[111]Girolamo Benzoni, *Historia del Mondo Nuovo* (Venice, 1565), translated and edited by W. H. Smyth as *History of the New World by Girolamo of Milan: Shewing his Travels in America from A.D. 1541 to 1556; with Some Particulars of the Island of Canary* (London, 1857).

[112]Alexander, op. cit., pp. 33–34, translating from Francisco López de Gómara, "Historia de las Indias," in A. Gonzales de Barcia, ed., *Historiadores primitivas de las Indias Occidentales* (Madrid, 1749).

[113]Alexander, op. cit., pp. 33–34, translating from Francisco López de Gómara, "Hispania Victrix. Primera y segunda parte de la historia general de las Indias," in Gonzales de Barcia, op. cit.

[114]Alexander, op. cit., p. 33.

[115]Irving Rouse, "The Carib," in Steward, op. cit., vol. 4, p. 558.

[116]Ibid., p. 560.

[117]Ibid., p. 558.

[118]Ibid., pp. 558–559.

[119]Alexander, op. cit., p. 39.

[120]Rouse, "The Carib," p. 548.

[121]See ibid., p. 549, and Alexander, op. cit., p. 352, for the catalogues of their sources.

[122]Diodorus Siculus, 5.14.1–3. See C. H. Oldfather, ed. and trans., *Diodorus of Sicily*, 12 vols. (Cambridge, Mass.: Harvard University Press, 1939), vol. 3, p. 135.

[123]Strabo 3.4.17. See Horace Leonard Jones, ed. and trans., *The Geography of Strabo*, 8 vols. (Cambridge, Mass.: Harvard University Press, 1917), vol. 2, p. 113.

[124]E. Sidney Hartland, "Birth," in James Hastings, ed., *Encyclopedia of Religion and Ethics* (New York: Charles Scribner's Sons, 1928), vol. 2, pp. 635–636.

[123]Strabo 3.4.17. See Horace Leonard Jones, ed. and trans., *The Geography of Strabo*, 8 vols. (Cambridge: Harvard University Press, 1917), vol. 2, p. 113.

[124]E. Sidney Hartland, "Birth," in James Hastings, ed., *Encyclopedia of Religion and Ethics* (New York: Charles Scribner's Sons, 1928), vol. 2 pp. 635–636.

[125]Ibid., p. 636.

[126]Rouse, "The Carib," p. 557. Rouse comments: "The accounts of the couvade vary considerably from source to source. The above version is taken largely from [John] Davies [*The History of the Caribby*, London, 1666], pp. 336–338, with supplemental data from [Père de] La Borde [*Voyage qui contient un relation exact de l'origine, moeurs, coûtumes, réligion, guerres et voyages des Caraibes, sauvages des isles Antilles de l'Amérique, faite par le Sieur de la Borde, employé à la conversion des Caraibes, et tirée du cabinet de Monsieur Blondel*. A. Leide, Chez P. van de Aa, 1704. In Louis Hennepin, *Voyage ou Nouvelle découverte*, pp. 517–604. Amsterdam], 1886, pp. 249–250."

[127]Rouse, "The Carib," pp. 553–554.

SOUTH AMERICAN AGRICULTURAL RITES AND MYTHS

[1]Hartley Burr Alexander, *Latin-American Mythology*, in Louis Herbert Gray, ed., *The Mythology of All Races*, 13 vols. (Boston: Marshall Jones Co., 1920), vol. XI, pp. 38–39.

[2]"Satanam aliosque spiritus malignos, qui ad perditionem animarum pervagantus in mundo," from prayers at the foot of the altar at the conclusion of holy mass. Dom Gaspar Lefebure, *Daily Missal* (Abbey of St. Andre, Hophem-near-Bruges, Imprimatur, 1934), p. 78.

[3]The following is a radical abridgement of a few selected episodes from Marc de Civrieux, *Watunna: Mitología Makiritare* (Caracas: Monte Avila Editores, C.A., 1970), translated, with an introduction and glossary, by David M. Güss as *Watunna: An Orinoco Creation Cycle* (San Francisco: North Point Press, 1980).

[4]Guss, *Watunna*, pp. 21–22.

[5]Ibid., p. 28.

[6]Ibid.

[7]Ibid., pp. 28–36.

[8]Ibid., pp. 128–135.

[9]Ibid., pp. 47–50.

[10]Ibid., pp. 51–53.

[11]Ibid., pp. 55–61.

[12]Ibid., pp. 66–68.

[13]Ibid., pp. 80–82.

[14]Ibid., pp. 143–146.

[15]Ibid., pp. 147–153.

[16]Ibid., p. 161.

[17]Selections, greatly abridged and recast, from Gerardo Reichel-Dolmatoff, *Amazonian Cosmos* (Chicago: University of Chicago Press, 1971).

[18]Ibid., pp. 25–27 and 55–57.

[19]Ibid., pp. 28–29.

[20]Ibid., p. 26.

[21]Ibid., pp. 27–28.

[22]Ibid., p. 72.

[23]Ibid., pp. 29–30.

[24]Ibid., pp. 30–32.

[25]Ibid., p. 34.

[26]Ibid., p. 75.

[27]Ibid., pp. 36–37.

[28]Ibid., p. 172.

[29]Ibid.

[30]Ibid., pp. 172–174, 24–25.

[31]Ibid., p. 106.

[32]Ibid.

[33]Ibid., p. 135.

[34]Ibid., pp. 136–138.

[35]Ibid., p. 106.

[36]Ibid., pp. 138–139.

[37]Ibid., p. 139, note 6.

[38]Ibid., p. 127.

[39]Ibid., pp. 129–130.

[40]Ibid., pp. 64 and 130.

[41]Ibid., p. 81.

[42]Ibid., pp. 83–84.

[43]Ibid., p. 82.

[44]Ibid., pp. 82–83.

[45]Theodor Koch-Grünberg, *Zwei Jahren unter den Indianern: Reisen in Nordwest Brazilien, 1903–1905*, 2 vols. (Berlin: Ernst Wasmuth A.-G., 1909, 1910), vol. 2, pp. 292–293.

[46]Ibid., p. 293.

[47]Ibid., p. 293, note 317.

[48]Robert H. Lowie, "The Tropical Forests: An Introduction," in Julian H. Steward, ed., *Handbook of South American Indians*, 7 vols., Bureau of American Ethnology Bulletin 143 (Washington, D.C., 1944–48), vol. 3, "The Tropical Forest Tribes," pp. 1–56. 56.

[49]Ibid., p. 1.

[50]Stephen Hugh-Jones, *The Palm and the Pleiades: Initiation and Cosmology in Northwest Amazonia*, Cambridge Studies in Social Anthropology No. 24 (Cambridge: Cambridge University Press, 1979).

[51]Christine Hugh-Jones, *From the Milk River: Spatial and Temporal Processes in Northwest Amazonia*, Cambridge Studies in Social Anthropology No. 26 (Cambridge: Cambridge University Press, 1979).

[52]Christine Hugh-Jones, op. cit., pp. 6–9.

[53]Stephen Hugh-Jones, op. cit., p. 25.

[54]Ibid., pp. xiii–xiv.

[55]Ibid., p. 9.

[56]Ibid.

[57]Ibid., pp. 9–10.

[58]Ibid.

[59]Ibid., pp. 37–38.

[60]Ibid., p. 131.

[61]Ibid., p. 132.

[62]Ibid.

[63]Ibid.

[64]Ibid., p. 84. The whole above account is a radical abridgement of S. Hugh-Jones, op. cit., pp. 46–84.

[65]Emilio Estrada, *Las Culturas pre-clásicas, formativas o arcaicas de Ecuador* (Guayaquil: Publicación de Museo Victor Emilio Estrada, no. 5, 1958).

[66]Betty J. Meggers, "Did Japanese Fishermen Really Reach Ecuador 5,000 Years Ago?" *Early Man*, vol. 2, no. 4 (Winter 1980), p. 16.

[67]Ibid.

[68]Emilio Estrada, Betty J. Meggers, and Clifford Evans, "Possible transpacific contact on the coast of Ecuador," *Science*, no. 135 (1962), pp. 371–372.

[69]Meggers, op. cit., p. 17.

[70]Betty J. Meggers, Clifford Evans, and Emilio Estrada, *Early Formative Period of Coastal Ecuador: The Valdivia and Machalilla Phases* (Washington, D.C.: Smithsonian Institution Press, 1965).

[71]Ibid., p. 167.

[72]Chester S. Chard, *Northeast Asia in Prehistory* (Madison: University of Wisconsin Press, 1974), p. 111.

[73]Ibid.

[74]Ibid., p. 118.

[75]Ibid., p. 116.

[76]Ibid., p. 119.

[77]Edwin Doran, "The Sailing Raft as a Great Tradition," in Carroll L. Riley, J. Charles Kelly, Campbell W. Pennington, and Robert L. Rands, eds., *Man across the Sea: Problems of Pre-Columbian Contacts* (Austin: University of Texas Press, 1971), p. 131, citing R. H. Lane-Poole, "Primitive Craft and Medieval Rigs in South America," *Mariner's Mirror*, vol. 26 (1940), pp. 333–338; and p. 133, note 2, citing J. Hornell, *Water Transport: Origins and Early Evolution* (Cambridge, U.K., 1946).

[78]Stephen C. Jett, "Pre-Columbian Transoceanic Contacts," in Jesse D. Jennings, ed., *Ancient Native Americans* (San Francisco: W. H. Freeman, 1978), chapter 13, p. 606, citing his own paper, "Malaysia and Tropical America: Some Racial, Cultural, and Ethnobotanical Comparisons," *Congreso Internacional de Americanistas, Actas y Memorias*, vol. 37, no. 4 (1968), pp. 133–137.

[79]Jett, "Pre-Columbian Transoceanic Contacts," p. 606, citing his own paper, "The Development and Distribution of the Blowgun," *Annals of the Association of American Geographers*, vol. 60, no. 4 (1971), pp. 662–668.

[80]Jett, "Pre-Columbian Transoceanic Contacts," p. 606, citing Marcos Fulop, "Aspectos de la Cultura Tukana: Cosmología," *Revista Colombiana de Antropología*, vol. 3 (1954), pp. 97–137.

[81]Jett, "Pre-Columbian Transoceanic Contacts," p. 606.

[82]Ibid.

[83]J. Merrien, trans. J. H. Watkins, *Lonely Voyages* (New York: Putnam, 1954).

[84]Stephen C. Jett, "Diffusion versus Independent Development," in Riley et al., op. cit., pp. 17–18, abridged.

[85]Charles Wolcott Brooks, "Reports of Japanese Vessels Wrecked in the North Pacific, from the Earliest Records to the Present Time," *Proceedings of the California Academy of Sciences*, vol. 6 (1875), pp. 50–66.

[86]Robert von Heine-Geldern, "The Origin of Ancient Civilizations," *Diogenes*, vol. 13 (1956), p. 95.

[87]Jett, "Pre-Columbian Transoceanic Contacts," p. 603, citing Kuang-chih Chang, "Radiocarbon Dates from China: Some Initial Interpretations," *Current Anthropology*, pp. 525–528.

[88]Jett, "Pre-Columbian Transoceanic Contacts," p. 604, citing Paul Tolstoy, "Cultural Parallels between Southeast Asia and Mesoamerica in the Manufacture of Bark Cloth," *Transactions of the New York Academy of Sciences*, Series 2, vol. 25, no. 6 (1963), pp. 646–662.

[89]George F. Carter, "Pre-Columbian Chickens in America," in Riley et al., op. cit., p. 215.

[90]As reported in the *San Francisco Chronicle* (United Press International), Monday, December 1, 1980, p. 8.

[91]Meggers, op. cit., p. 16.

[92]Ibid.

[93]James A. Ford, *A Comparison of Formative Cultures in the Americas* (Washington, D.C.: Smithsonian Institution Press, 1969), charts 10, 3, 5, and 2.

[94]Betty J. Meggers, personal correspondence, 1982. She notes that "Ford refers especially to the ring plan. There are earlier ceremonial constructions on the coast of Peru."

[95]For a discussion of the value of calibrated versus uncalibrated dates see David H. Thomas, *Archaeology* (New York: Holt, Rinehart and Winston, 1979), s.v. "Calibration"; for a general discussion of dating techniques, see Ian Tattersall, Eric Delson, and John Van Couvering, eds., *Encyclopedia of Human Evolution and Prehistory* (New York: Garland Publishing, 1988), s.v. "Geochronometry."

[96]Clinton R. Edwards, "Commentary" in Riley et al., op. cit., Section II, p. 298.

[97]Jorge G. Marcos, Donald Lathrap, and James A. Zeidler, "Ancient Ecuador Revisited," *Field Museum Bulletin* (June 1976), pp. 3–8.

[98]The earlier start is suggested by Lathrap in his article on Formative Ecuador in *Ancient Ecuador: Culture, Clay and Creativity 3000–300 B.C.*, catalogue of an exhibit organized by the Field Museum of Natural History, April 18 to August 5, 1975.

[99]Lathrap, *Ancient Ecuador*, p. 13.

[100]Ibid., p. 19.

[101]Ibid., p. 43.

[102]Meggers, personal correspondence, 1982.

[103]Lathrap, *Ancient Ecuador*, p. 21.

[104]Ibid., p. 43.

[105]Ibid., p. 45.

[106]Ibid., pp. 45 and 47.

[107]Ibid., p. 43.

[108]von Heine-Geldern, op. cit., p. 96.

[109]Juan R. Munizaga, "Skeletal Remains from Sites of Valdivia and Machalilla Phases," in Meggers, Evans, and Estrada, *Early Formative Period of Ecuador*, appendix 2, p. 228.

[110]Meggers, Evans, and Estrada, *Early Formative Period of Ecuador*, p. 39.

[111]Lathrap, *Ancient Ecuador*, pp. 22–23.

[112]Ibid., p. 73.

[113]John H. Rowe, "Diffusion and Archaeology," *American Antiquity*, vol. 31 (1966), p. 339.

[114]Lathrap, *Ancient Ecuador*, p. 27.

[115]S. G. Stephens, "Some Problems of Interpreting Transoceanic Dispersal of the New World Cottons," in Riley et al., op. cit., pp. 401 and 413, abridged.

[116]Ibid., p. 406.

[117]Ibid., p. 407.

[118]Meggars, Evans, and Estrada, *Early Formative Period of Ecuador*, p. 110.

[119]Munizaga, op. cit., pp. 232–233.

[120]Ibid., p. 229.

[121]Marcos, Lathrap, and Zeidler, "Ancient Ecuador Revisited," p. 4.

[122]Lathrap, *Ancient Ecuador*, p. 34.

[123]Ibid., pp. 23–25. Others suggest a later date: see Emilio Estrada and Betty J. Meggers, "A Complex of Traits of Probable Transpacific Origin on the Coast of Ecuador," *American Anthropologist*, vol. 63, no. 5 (October 1961), pp. 914–920.

[124]Garry J. Tee, "Evidence for the Chinese Origin of the Jaguar Motif in Chavín Art," *Asian Perspectives*, vol. XXI, no. 1 (1980), pp. 27–29.

[125]Garcilasso Inca de la Vega, *Royal Commentaries of the Incas,* Part I (Lisbon, 1609) and Part 2 (Cordova, 1616).

[126]The journals of Pedro de Cieza de León were published according to the following schedule (the titles are here given in English): Part I, *The Divisions and Description of the Province of Peru* (published in Seville, 1553); Part II, *The Government, Great Deeds, Origin, Policy, Buildings and Roads of the Incas* (in manuscript until published in London, 1873); Part III, *Discovery and Conquest of Peru by Pizarro, and the Rebellion of the Indians* (published in part [15 chapters] in Lima, 1946); Part IV, Book i: *The War between Pizarro and Almagro* (London, 1923), Book ii: *The War of the Young Almagro* (Madrid, 1881; London, 1918), Book iii: *The Civil War of Quito* (Madrid, 1909; London, 1913), Book iv: *The War of Huarina* (lost), and Book v: *The War of Xaquixaguana* (lost); Commentary I, *Events from the Founding of the Audience to the Departure of the President* (possibly never written); Commentary II, *Events to the Arrival of the Viceroy Mendoza* (possibly never written).

[127]As quoted by John Fiske, *Discovery of America* (Boston: Houghton Mifflin Company, 1892), vol. 2, p. 304, note 1, translation of Cieza by Clements Markham.

[128]Victor Wolfgang von Hagen, ed., *The Incas of Pedro de Cieza de León,* trans. Harriet de Onis (Norman: University of Oklahoma Press, 1959), pp. 25–26, from Cieza's *Chronicle,* Part I, chapter 38.

[129]From the May 3, 1493, Bull "Inter Cetera" of Pope Alexander VI.

[130]von Hagen, op. cit., p. 50; Cieza, Part II, chapter 67.

[131]According to von Hagen, op. cit., map.

[132]John M. Cooper, "The Araucanians," in Steward, op. cit., vol. 2, pp. 687–760.

[133]von Hagen, op. cit., p. 280, note 3.

[134]Ibid., pp. 280–281; Cieza, Part I, chapter 95.

[135]G. H. S. Bushnell, *Peru* (New York: Frederick A. Praeger, revised edition, 1963), pp. 133–134.

[136]von Hagen, op. cit., pp. 70–71; Cieza, Part I, chapter 19.

[137]Ibid., pp. 300–302; Cieza, Part I, chapter 101.

[138]Ibid., pp. 334–337; Cieza, Part I, chapter 116.

[139]Bushnell, op. cit., p. 89.

[140]Ibid., p. 89.

[141]Ibid., p. 91.

[142]Lathrap, *Ancient Ecuador,* p. 13.

[143]Ibid., p. 13.

[144]Wendell C. Bennett and Junius B. Bird, *Andean Culture History,* 2nd edition (New York: American Museum of Natural History, 1960), p. 105.

[145]Ibid., p. 114.

[146]Ibid., p. 135.

[147]Ibid., pp. 149–150.

[148]von Hagen, op. cit., p. 138; Cieza, Part II, chapter 15.

[149]Ibid., pp. 139–140; Cieza, Part II, chapter 21.

[150]Lathrap, *Ancient Ecuador,* p. 43.

[151]Bushnell, op. cit., p. 54.

[152]Lathrap, *Ancient Ecuador,* pp. 57 and 59.

[153]Donald W. Lathrap, "The Tropical Forest and the Cultural Context of Chavín," in Elizabeth P. Benson, ed., *Dumbarton Oaks Conference on Chavín, October 26th and 27th, 1968* (Washington, D.C.: Trustees for Harvard University, 1971), pp. 76–77.

[154]Stephen Hugh-Jones, op. cit., pp. 287–294.

[155]Lathrap, "The Tropical Forest and the Cultural Context of Chavín," p. 77.

[156]Ibid.

[157]See Miguel Covarrubias, *The Eagle, the Jaguar, and the Serpent* (New York: Alfred A. Knopf, 1954), p. 16. For the date, 1016 ± 300 B.C., see Frederick Johnson, "Radiocarbon Dating," *Memoirs of the Society for American Archaeology,* no. 8 (Salt Lake City, 1951), pp. 10–18, sample no. 321. Others have placed the date much earlier, c. 2000 B.C. (Peter Kvietok, personal communication, February 1989).

[158]*Mathews' Chinese-English Dictionary,* revised American edition (Cambridge, Mass.: Harvard University Press, 1960), p. 927, character 6392.

[159]William Willetts, *Foundations of Chinese Art* (New York: McGraw-Hill Book Company, 1965), pp. 96–97.

[160]*Skanda Purāṇa* II. Visnukānda, Kārtvkamasa, 17; as in Heinrich Zimmer, *Myths and Symbols in Indian Art and Civilization,* Joseph Campbell, ed., Bollingen Series VI (Princeton: Princeton University Press, 1972), pp. 175–184.

[161]Wendell C. Bennett, "The Archaeology of the Central Andes," in Steward, op. cit., vol. 2, p. 96.

[162]Wauchope, op. cit., vol. 4, p. 148.

[163]von Heine-Geldern, op. cit., p. 93.

[164]Ibid., p. 94.

[165]Ibid.

[166]Bushnell, op. cit., p. 43.

[167]Ibid., pp. 43–44.

CAPTIONS

[1]Maya Deren, *Divine Horsemen: The Living Gods of Haiti* (London: Thames and Hudson, 1953), pp. 37–38 and 107–108.

[2]Roman Pina Chan, "Preclassic or Formative Pottery and Minor Arts of the Valley of Mexico," in Robert Wauchope, ed., *Handbook of Middle American Indians,* 13 vols. (Austin: University of Texas Press, 1964–73), vol. 10, p. 177, chart 1.

[3]Miguel Covarrubias, *Indian Art of Mexico and Central America* (New York: Alfred A. Knopf, 1957), pp. 18–19.

[4]Ibid., pp. 24–27.

[5]Michael D. Coe, "San Lorenzo and the Olmec Civilization," in Elizabeth P. Benson, ed., *Dumbarton Oaks Conference on the Olmec, October 28th and 29th, 1967,* Dumbarton Oaks Research Library and Collection (Washington, D.C.: Trustees for Harvard University, 1968), p. 60.

[6]Ibid., p. 63.

[7]David C. Grove, "Olmec Monuments: Mutilation As a Clue to Meaning," in Elizabeth P. Benson, ed., *The Olmec and Their Neighbors,* Dumbarton Oaks Research Library and Collection (Washington, D.C.: Trustees for Harvard University, 1981), pp. 49–68.

[8]Ignacio Bernal, *The Olmec World,* trans. Doris Heyden and Fernando Horcasitas (Berkeley: University of California Press, 1969), pp. 56–57.

[9]Bernal, op. cit., citing Philip Drucker, Robert Heizer, and Robert Squier, *Excavations at La Venta, Tabasco, 1955,* Smithsonian Institution Bureau of American Ethnology Bulletin 170 (Washington, D.C., 1959), p. 170.

[10]Drucker, Heizer, and Squier, op. cit., p. 156.

[11]Ibid., p. 155.

[12]Ibid., p. 156.

[13]Ibid., p. 158.

[14]Jonas E. Gullberg, "Technical Notes on Concave Mirrors," in Drucker, Heizer, and Squier, op. cit., appendix 3, p. 280.

[15]Bernal, op. cit., p. 78, note 106.

[16]Gullberg, op. cit., p. 283.

[17]Drucker, Heizer, and Squier, op. cit., p. 196.

[18]Bernal, op. cit., p. 94.

[19]Jacques Soustelle, *The Olmecs: The Oldest Civilization in Mexico,* trans. Helen B. Lane (Garden City, N.Y.: Doubleday and Company, Inc., 1984), p. 137.

[20]Both the iconography and the nature of this object are a matter of contention: while some scholars are of the opinion that it is certainly a jaguar mask, others insist, according to personal correspondence of March 1985 from Jerald T. Milanich, Curator of Anthropology at the Florida State Museum, that "the tablet, one of more than 50 metal ones known (there are wooden ones as well), depicts a stylized spider (see Allerton, et al., 'Ceremonial Tablets and Related Objects from Florida,' *Florida Anthropologist* 37:5–54). The spider motif is very similar to spiders depicted on Southeastern Ceremonial Complex shell gorgets (see *Sun Circles and Human Hands,* by Fundaburk and Foreman; also, John Griffin, 'Historical Artifacts and the Buzzard Cult in Florida,' *Florida Historical Quarterly* 14:295–301). Recent documentary information and analysis of the Fort Center tablets suggests that the metal tablets were copies of earlier wooden plaques. The metal tablets were apparently being made in the early seventeenth century in Cuba for trade to the South Florida Indians. The date is consistent with other European items found with the tablets. I suspect that the spider is a cosmogonic symbol associated with high status individuals. Its origin may lie in the Southeast Indian myth regarding the role of the water spider in bringing fire to humans (e.g. James Mooney, 'Myths of the Cherokee,' *19th Annual Report, Bureau of American Ethnology,* pp. 240–242)."

[21]Campbell Grant, *The Rock Paintings of the Chumash* (Berkeley: University of California Press, 1965), plate 27, note.

[22]Barbara L. Moulard, *Within the Underworld Sky, Mimbres Ceramic Art in Context* (Pasadena, Calif.: Twelvetrees Press, 1984), pp. xi–xiii, abridged.

[23]Gordon Vivian and Paul Reiter, *The Great Kivas of Chaco Canyon and Their Relationships,* The School of American Research Monograph 22 (Albuquerque: University of New Mexico Press, 1965), pp. 62–65.

[24]T. Y. Canby, "The Anasazi," *National Geographic,* vol. 162, no. 5, pp. 554–592.

[25]Stuart J. Feidel, *Prehistory of the Americas* (Cambridge: Cambridge University Press, 1987), pp. 211–221.

[26]Barton Wright, essay in *Year of the Hopi,* catalogue accompanying a traveling exhibition, "Paintings and Photographs by Joseph Mora, 1904–1906," organized and circulated, 1979–1981, by the Smithsonian Institution Traveling Exhibition Service, p. 17.

[27]Ibid., p. 30.

[28]Following ibid., pp. 47 and 54, abridged.

[29]Ibid., p. 60.

[30]Frank Waters, *Book of the Hopi* (New York: Penguin Books, 1977), p. 208.

[31]Ibid., p. 210.

[32]Peter T. Furst, "The Art of 'Being Huichol'," in Kathleen Berrin, ed., *Art of the Huichol Indians* (New York: Harry N. Abrams, Inc., 1978) a catalogue published in conjunction with an exhibition organized by the Fine Arts Museums of San Francisco.

[33]Prem Das, "Initiation by a Huichol Shaman," in Berrin, op. cit., pp. 140–141, abridged.

[34]Following an interpretation furnished by the artist, Eligio Carrillos Vincente, obtained and translated courtesy of Prem Das.

[35]Barbara G. Meyerhoff, "Peyote and the Mystic Vision," in Berrin, op. cit., pp. 57–59.

[36]Ibid., p. 56.

[37]Ibid., p. 59.

[38]Furst, op. cit., p. 18, quoting Carl Lumholtz, *Symbolism of the Huichol Indians,* Memoirs of the American Museum of Natural History 1 (New York: American Museum of Natural History, 1900).

[39]Joseph Judge and James L. Stanfield, "Where Columbus Found the New World," *National Geographic,* vol. 170, no. 5 (November 1976), pp. 568–569.

[40]Frederick J. Dockstader, *Indian Art in Middle America* (Greenwich, Conn.: New York Graphic Society, 1964), pp. 128–132.

[41]Hartley Burr Alexander, *Latin-American Mythology,* in Louis Herbert Gray, ed., *The Mythology of All Races,* 13 vols. (Boston: Marshall Jones Co., 1920), vol. XI, pp. 33–34, translating from Francisco López de Gómara, "Historia de las Indias" (Anvers, 1554).

[42]Girolamo Benzoni, *Historia del Mondo Nuovo* (Venice, 1565), translated and edited by W. H. Smyth as *History of the New World by Girolamo of Milan: Shewing his travels in America from A.D. 1541 to 1556; with some particulars of the island of Canary* (London, 1857).

[43]Dockstader, op. cit., plate 193.

[44]José Juan Arrom, *Mitología y Artes Prehispánicas de las Antillas* (Mexico: Siglo Veintiuno Editores, 1975), p. 99, citing Ramón Pane, *Relación acerca de las antigüedades de los indios,* chapter 22 (here abridged).

[45]Arrom, op. cit., p. 106.

[46]David M. Guss, *To Weave and To Sing* (Berkeley: University of California Press, 1989), p. 1.

[47]Marc de Civrieux, *Watunna: Mitología Makiritare* (Caracas: Monte Avila Editores, C.A., 1970), translated, with an introduction and glossary, by David M. Guss as *Watunna: An Orinoco Creation Cycle* (San Francisco: North Point Press, 1980).

[48]Guss, *Watunna,* p. 12.

[49]Ibid.

[50]Guss, *To Weave and To Sing,* p. 21.

[51]Ibid., p. 27.

[52]Ibid., pp. 29–30.

[53]Ibid., p. 30.

[54]Ibid., p. 65.

[55]Gerardo Reichel-Dolmatoff, *Amazonian Cosmos* (Chicago: University of Chicago Press, 1971), pp. 80–81.

[56]Ibid., p. 11.

[57]Ibid., p. 81.

[58]Ermanno Stradelli, "Inscrizioni Indigene della regione dell'Uaupes," *Bolletino della Societe Geografica Italiana,* series 4, no. 1, p. 476.

[59]Thomas W. Whitaker, "Endemism and Pre-Columbian Migration of the Bottle Gourd, *Lagenaria siceraria* (Mol.) Stanal.," in Carroll L. Riley, J. Charles Kelly, Campbell W. Pennington, and Robert L. Rands, eds., *Man across the Sea: Problems of Pre-Columbian Contacts* (Austin: University of Texas Press, 1971), p. 232.

[60]Carl O. Sauer, "Cultivated Plants in South and Central America," in Julian H. Steward, ed., *Handbook of South American Indians,* 7 vols., Bureau of American Ethnology Bulletin 143 (Washington, D.C., 1944–48), vol. 6, p. 506.

[61]Herbert G. Baker, "Commentary" in Riley et al., op. cit., Section II, citing Whitaker in note 1, pp. 431–432.

[62]Whitaker, op. cit., p. 327.

[63]Ibid.

[64]Donald W. Lathrap, *Ancient Ecuador: Culture, Clay and Creativity 3000–300 B.C.,* catalogue of an exhibit organized by the Field Museum of Natural History, April 18 to August 5, 1975, p. 43.

[65]Ibid., p. 23.

[66]Wendell C. Bennett and Junius B. Bird, *Andean Culture History,* 2nd edition (New York: American Museum of Natural History, 1960), p. 132.

[67]Feidel, op. cit., p. 333, citing M. E. Mosley and C. Mackey, "Chan Chan: Peru's Ancient City of Kings," *National Geographic,* vol. 152 (March 1973), pp. 319–345.

[68]Following Feidel, op. cit., pp. 319–320; also G. H. S. Bushnell, *Ancient Arts of the Americas* (New York: Frederick A. Praeger, 1965), pp. 152–154.

[69]G. H. S. Bushnell, *Peru,* revised edition (New York: Frederick A. Praeger, 1963), p. 48.

[70]Following Sat-cakra-nirūpana, verses 22–27, as translated and interpreted in Arthur Avalon (Sir John Woodroffe), *The Serpent Power* (Madras: Ganesh & Co.; London: Luzar and Co., 1931), pp. 369–381.

[71]Ibid., verse 30, p. 386.

[72]Meister Eckhart, "Sermons and Collations," no. 96, "Riddance," in Franz Pfeiffer, ed., D. de B. Evans, trans., *Meister Eckhart,* 2 vols., (London: John M. Watkins, 1947), vol. 1, p. 289.

[73]Miguel Covarrubias, *The Eagle, the Serpent, and the Jaguar* (New York: Alfred A. Knopf, 1954), p. 34, citing Carl Shuster, "Joint-marks, a Possible Index of Cultural Contact between America, Oceania, and the Far East," Med. XCLV, *Adfeling Culturele en Physische Antropologie,* no. 39, Koninklijl Instituut voor de Trpen, Amsterdam, 1951; also H. J. Spinden, "Ancient Civilizations of Mexico and Central America," American Museum of Natural History Handbook Series no. 3.

A NOTE ON THE INDEXES

References to pages, captions, maps, and map captions.

In the Place Name Index and the Subject Index, references to pages are page numbers, e.g.,

couvade, 320

which means that a reference to the practice of the couvade is to be found on page 320. In both indexes, commas, rather than dashes, are used to indicate separate mentions of a topic on adjacent pages, e.g.,

358, 359

References to captions consist of a boldface caption number (or range of caption numbers), followed by a hyphen and a page number, e.g.,

444-328

338–390-286

References to maps consist of a boldface capital "M" and a map number followed by a hyphen and a page number, e.g.,

M42-369

Map captions are referred to similarly, but with an additional letter "C," e.g.,

MC31-277

INDEX OF PLACE NAMES

CREDITS AND ACKNOWLEDGEMENTS

PICTURES

Key:
AMNH = American Museum of Natural History, New York; **BB** = Barbara Brandli, Caracas; **BM** = British Museum, London; **BJM** = Betty J. Meggers, Smithsonian Institution, Washington, D.C.; **CUL** = Columbia University Libraries, New York, N.Y.; **DG** = David Guss, Piermont, NY; **DO** = Dumbarton Oaks Research Libraries and Collections, Washington, D.C.; **FAMSF** = Fine Arts Museums of San Francisco; **FGA** = Fundacion García Arévalo, Santo Domingo; **FMNH** = Field Museum of Natural History, Chicago; **GG** = courtesy of Gilett G. Griffin, Princeton, NJ; **JBT** = John Bigelow Taylor, New York; **JM/JRW** = Jacinto Mora/John R. Wilson, Tulsa; **LB** = Lee Boltin, Croton-on-Hudson, NY; **MAI** = Museum of the American Indian, New York; **ML** = Mennonite Library, North Newton, KS; **MMA** = Metropolitan Museum of Art, New York; **MNA** = Museo Nacional de Antropologia, Mexico City; **MNM** = Museum of New Mexico, Santa Fe; **NGA** = National Gallery of Art, Washington, D.C.; **NYPL** = New York Public Library; **PC** = Peter Collings, Moorpart, CA; **PF** = Peter Furst, Santa Fe; **PMA** = Philadelphia Museum of Art; **RD** = Gerardo Reichel-Dolmatoff, Bogotá; **SI** = Smithsonian Institution, Washington, D.C.

COVER: JBT, from the collection of Gilett G. Griffin

AGRICULTURAL DEVELOPMENTS IN THE MESOAMERICAN MATRIX

339 MNA; **340a–b** CUL; **341** GG; **342** JBT; **343** Muriel Porter Weaver, New York; **344** top, left to right: JBT, MNA, LB, MNA, JBT; bottom, left to right: JBT, MNA, JBT, JBT, MNA, JBT; **345–347** PF; **348** FAMSF; **349** Bibliothèque Nationale, Paris; **350–352** GG; **353** LB; **354** MNA; **355–356** GG; **357** Brooklyn Museum, New York; **358** AMNH; **359a** MNA; **359b** BM; **359c** SI; **359d** AMNH; **360** GG; **361** JBT, MNA; **362a–b** GG; **363** Florida State Museum, Gainesville

AGRICULTURAL RITES AND MYTHS OF MIDDLE AMERICA

364 NYPL; **365** PMA; **366a** MNM; **366b–c** Karl Kernberger, Santa Fe; **366d** Campbell Grant, Santa Barbara; **367–368** JBT; **369–370** MNM; **371** David and Barbara Anderson, Cochiti Lake, N.Y.; **372** Edward S. Curtis; **373** Anna Sofaer, Washington, D.C.; **374a–b** Mary Challinor, "Science 80"; **374c** Karl Kernberger, Santa Fe; **375** Barbara Bohrer, American Academy for the Advancement of Science, Washington, D.C.; **376** Peter Dechert, Santa Fe; **377** Cynthia Petrowski, Stamford, Conn.; **378** Arizona State Museum, Tucson; **379** JM/JRW; **380–381** ML; **382** Barton Wright, Phoenix; **383** California Academy of Sciences, San Francisco; **384–386** JM/JRW; **387** SI; **388** JM/JRW; **389** SI; **390** JM/JRW; **391** ML; **392** JM/JRW; **393** Southwest Museum, Los Angeles; **394** ML; **395** PMA; **396–397** Natural History Museum of Los Angeles County; **398** JM/JRW; **399** ML; **400–402** JM/JRW; **403** PF; **404** Museum of Cultural History, UCLA; **405** FAMSF; **406** PF; **407** Joseph Campbell; **408–410** PF; **411** Susan Eger-Valdez, Oakland; **412** PC; **413** Prem Das, Covelo, Calif.; **414** PC; **415–417** PF; **418** MNM; **419** FAMSF; **420–423** NYPL; **424** LB; **425a** MAI; **425b–c** SI; **425d** MAI; **426** FGA; **427–428** NYPL; **429** Museum of Anthropology, History, and Art, University of Puerto Rico; **430** FGA; **431** Museum für Völkerkunde, Munich; **432** MAI; **433–434** NGA; **435–436** NYPL; **437** NGA; **438** NYPL; **439** SI; **440** NGA; **441** DG

SOUTH AMERICAN AGRICULTURAL RITES AND MYTHS

442 Phillip Galgiani; **443–451** DG; **452** BB; **453–454** DG; **455** BB; **456** DG; **457** BB; **458** Phillip Galgiani; **459–468** DG; **469** BB; **470** DG; **471** NYPL; **472** Jacques Jangoux/Peter Arnold, New York; **473–477** RD; **478** Albert E. Stevens, "The Amazon, Father of Waters," *National Geographic*, vol. 64, no. 4 (April 1926); **479–483** RD; **484** FMNH; **485** RD; **486** Loren McIntyre/ Woodfin Camp, New York; **487a** DG; **487b** RD; **487c–e** Steven Hugh-Jones, Cambridge, U.K.; **488** Theodor Koch-Grünberg, *Zwei Jahren unter den Indianern: Reisen in Nordwest Brazilien, 1903–1905*, 2 vols. (Berlin: Ernst Wasmuth A.-G., 1909, 1910); **489** Brian Moser, London; **490** Steven Hugh-Jones, Cambridge, U.K.; **491** RD; **492** Brian Moser, London; **493** FMNH, NMA; **494–499** NYPL; **500–503** BJM; **504** BJM, FMNH; **505** FMNH; **506–509** FMNH; **510** FMNH, MAI; **511** George J. Fery, Miami; **512** MAI; **513** Sally Black, Charlottesville, Virg.; **514** FMNH; **515** BJM; **516–517** FMNH; **518** JBT, AMNH; **519** FMNH; **520** Art Resources, New York; **521** Thomas Gilcrease Institute of American History and Art, Tulsa; **522–526** NYPL; **527** DO; **528** Hamlyn Picture Library, London; **529** Evan Hadingham, Cambridge, Mass.; **530–531** Michael Holford, London; **532** Victor Englebert, Cali, Colombia; **533** DO, MAI; **534–535** GG; **536** FMNH; **537** GG; **538** Cambridge Museum of Archaeology and Ethnology, Cambridge, U.K.; **539** AMNH; **540** MMA; **541–542** AMNH; **543** MMA, GG, RD; **544** G. H. S. Bushnell, *Peru* (New York: Praeger, 1963); **545** GG; **546** FMNH; **547** MMA; **548** AMNH; **549** William Y. Willets, *Foundations of Chinese Art from Neolithic Pottery to Modern Man* (New York: McGraw-Hill, 1965), as redrawn by Sally Black, Charlottesville, Virg.; **550** ACSAA Project, Ann Arbor, MI; **551** Musée Cernuschi, Paris; **552** Fernand Anton, Munich; **553** Musée de l'Homme, Paris; **554** FMNH; **555** Miguel Covarrubias, *The Eagle, the Jaguar, and the Serpent* (New York: Alfred A. Knopf, 1954); **556** AMNH; **557** DO

EXTRACTS

From Jacques Soustelle, *The Olmecs: The Oldest Civilization in Mexico*, Helen B. Lane, trans. (Garden City, N.Y.: Doubleday & Co., 1984).

From Prem Das, "Initiation by a Huichol Shaman," in Kathleen Berrin, ed. *The Art of the Huichol Indians* (New York: Harry N. Abrams, Inc., 1978) a catalogue published in conjunction with an exhibition organized by the Fine Arts Museums of San Francisco.

From Peter Furst, "The Art of 'Being Huichol'," in Kathleen Berrin, ed. *The Art of the Huichol Indians* (New York: Harry N. Abrams, Inc., 1978) a catalogue published in conjunction with an exhibition organized by the Fine Arts Museums of San Francisco.

From Barbara G. Myerhoff, *Peyote Hunt: The Sacred Journey of the Huichol Indians* (Ithaca: Cornell University Press, 1974).

From Marc de Civrieux, *Watunna: Mitología Makiritare* (Caracas: Monte Avila Editores, C.A., 1970), translated,with an introduction and glossary, by David M. Guss as *Watunna: An Orinoco Creation Cycle* (San Francisco: North Point Press, 1980).

From Gerardo Reichel-Dolmatoff, *Amazonian Cosmos* (Chicago: University of Chicago Press, 1971).

From Stephen Hugh-Jones, *The Palm and the Pleiades: Initiation and Cosmology in Northwest Amazonia*, Cambridge Studies in Social Anthropology No. 24 (Cambridge: Cambridge University Press, 1979).

From Donald Lathrap, *Ancient Ecuador: Culture, Clay and Creativity, 3000–300 B.C.*, catalogue of an exhibit organized by the Field Museum of Natural History, April 18 to August 5, 1975.

From Victor Wolfgang von Hagen, ed., *The Incas of Pedro de Cieza de León*, Harriet de Onis, trans. (Norman: University of Oklahoma Press, 1959).

MAPS

Map 26. Based in part on information adapted from Michael Coe et al., eds., *Atlas of Ancient America* (New York: Facts on File Publications, 1986).

Map 27. Based in part on information adapted from Michael Coe et al., eds., *Atlas of Ancient America* (New York: Facts on File Publications, 1986); Robert Wauchope, ed., *Handbook of Middle American Indians*, 13 vols. (Austin: University of Texas Press, 1964-73), vol. 3; Jacques Soustelle, *The Olmecs: The Oldest Civilization in Mexico*, trans. Helen B. Lane (Garden City, N.Y.: Doubleday and Company, Inc., 1984); *Past Worlds: The Times Atlas of Archaeology* (London: Times Books Ltd., 1988); and Michael Wood, ed., *The World Atlas of Archaeology* (Boston: G. K. Hall and Company, 1985).

Map 28. Based in part on information adapted from Jacques Soustelle, *The Olmecs: The Oldest Civilization in Mexico*, trans. Helen B. Lane (Garden City, N. Y.: Doubleday and Company, Inc., 1984); and Michael Coe et al. eds., *Atlas of Ancient America* (New York: Facts on File Publications, 1986).

Map 29. Based in part on information adapted from Michael Coe et al. eds., *Atlas of Ancient America* (New York: Facts on File Publications, 1986); H. P. Walker and D. Bufkin, *Historical Atlas of Oklahoma* (Norman: University of Oklahoma Press, 1979); W. A. Beck and Y. D. Haase, *Historical Atlas of New Mexico* (Norman: University of Oklahoma Press, 1969); James M. Goodman, *The Navajo Atlas* (Norman: University of Oklahoma Press, 1982); *Historical Atlas of the United States* (Washington, D.C.: National Geographic Society, 1988); and Gordon R. Willey, *An Introduction to American Archaeology*, 2 vols. (Englewood Cliffs, N.J.: Prentice-Hall Inc., 1966), vol. 1, "North America."

Map 30. Based in part on information adapted from R. H. Lister and F. G. Lister, *Chaco Canyon: Archaeology and Archaeologists* (Albuquerque: University of New Mexico Press, 1981).

Map 31. Based in part on information adapted from Douglas Anderson and Barbara Anderson, *Chaco Canyon: Center of a Culture* (Globe, N.M.: Southwest Parks and Monuments Association, 1984); and "Complex Culture in a Harsh Land" (map), *National Geographic*, vol. 162, no. 5 (November 1982).

Map 32. Based in part on information adapted from M. Benzi, *Les Derniers Adorateurs du Peyotl* (Paris: Gallimard, 1972).

Map 33. Based in part on information adapted from R. H. Fuson, trans., *The Log of Christopher Columbus* (Camden, Me.: International Marine Publishing Co., 1987); G. Roberts, *Atlas of Discovery* (New York: Crown Publishers, 1973); J. Engel, *Grosser Historischer Weltatlas* (Munich: Bayerischer Schulbuch Verlag, 1967); F. W. Putzger, *Historischer Weltatlas* (Berlin: Velhagen und Klassing Verlag, 1968); C. L. Lombardi and J. V. Lombardi, *Latin American History: A Teaching Atlas* (Madison: University of Wisconsin Press, 1983); Joseph Judge, "Where Columbus Found the New World," *National Geographic*, vol. 170, no. 5 (November 1986); and "Where Did Columbus Discover America?" (map), *National Geographic*, vol. 170, no. 5 (November 1986).

Map 35. Based in part on information adapted from *Academic American Encyclopaedia* (Princeton, N.J.; Arete Publishing Co., 1980); and National Geographic Society, *Indians of South America*, map (Washington, D.C.: National Geographic Society, 1982).

Map 38. Based in part on information adapted from Gerardo Reichel-Dolmatoff, *Amazonian Cosmos* (Chicago: University of Chicago Press, 1971); Stephen Hugh-Jones, *The Palm and the Pleiades: Initiation and Cosmology in Northwest Amazonia*, Cambridge Studies in Social Anthropology No. 24 (Cambridge: Cambridge University Press, 1979); and Christine Hugh-Jones, *From the Milk River: Spatial and Temporal Processes in Northwest Amazonia*, Cambridge Studies in Social Anthropology No. 26 (Cambridge: Cambridge University Press, 1979).

Map 39. Based in part on information adapted from Michael Coe et al. eds., *Atlas of Ancient America* (New York: Facts on File Publications, 1986); and *Past Worlds; The Times Atlas of Archaeology* (London: Times Books Ltd., 1988).

Map 40. Based in part on information adapted from Edwin Doran Jr., "The Sailing Raft As a Great Tradition," chapter 7 in C. L. Riley et al., eds., *Man across the Sea; Problems of Pre-Columbian Contacts* (Austin: University of Texas Press, 1971).

Map 41. Based in part on information adapted from Society cf Ancient Pacific Cultures, *Yasei-Gō III: An Experimental Voyage and Archaeological Research by the Double Canoe in the Pacific Ocean* (Tokyo: Kadokawa Publishing Co., 1982); and Thor Heyerdahl, *Early Man and the Ocean* (Garden City, N.Y.: Doubleday and Co., 1979).

Map 42. Based in part on information adapted from Michael Coe et al. eds., *Atlas of Ancient America* (New York: Facts on File Publications, 1986).

Map 43. Based in part on information adapted from Michael Coe et al. eds., *Atlas of Ancient America* (New York: Facts on File Publications, 1986).

HISTORICAL ATLAS OF
WORLD MYTHOLOGY

Developed and first published in part by
Van der Marck Editions, New York

Editorial Director: *Robert Walter*

Designer: *Jos. Trautwein/Bentwood Studio*

Art Editor: *Rosemary O'Connell*

Associate Editor: *Antony Van Couvering*

Indexer: *Maro Riofrancos*

Maps and Charts: *Cartographic Services Center of R. R. Donnelley & Sons Company*

Map Design: *Sidney P. Marland III*

Map Research, Compilation, and Project Coordination: *Luis Freile*

Map Drafting and Production: *Robert Hoover*

Type Composition: *Typographic Art, Inc.*

Printing and Binding: *Royal Smeets Offset, B.V., The Netherlands*

Grateful acknowledgement is made to the following for their noted contributions to this volume: John Bigelow Taylor; Spencer Throckmorton; John R. Wilson; Dr. Peter T. Furst; Cathleen Baxter, Smithsonian Institution, Washington, D.C.; Barbara Mathé, American Museum of Natural History, New York; Nina Cummings, Field Museum, Chicago; James Foerster, Field Museum, Chicago; Peter Kvietok, American Museum of Natural History, New York; and Drew Dutcher.

DALLAS

DALLAS

THE COMPLETE EWING FAMILY SAGA,
INCLUDING SOUTHFORK RANCH, EWING OIL,
AND THE BARNES-EWING FEUD
1860-1985

LAURA VAN WORMER

Introduction by Leonard Katzman

A Dolphin Book
DOUBLEDAY & COMPANY, INC. · GARDEN CITY, NEW YORK · 1985

Music available on Warner Brothers records and cassettes.

Library of Congress Cataloging in Publication Data:

Van Wormer, Laura, 1955–
    Dallas, the complete Ewing family saga.

    "A Dolphin book."
    1. Dallas (Television program)   I. Dallas (Television
program)   II. Title.
PN1992.77.D3V36   1985   791.45′72   84-28693
ISBN 0-385-23058-3 (pbk.)

Designed by Judith Neuman

Manufactured in the United States of America

First Edition

In Loving Memory of
Jock Ewing
1909–1981

CONTENTS

INTRODUCTION

Whenever I think about "Dallas," my mind flashes back to the first time I flew down there in search of Southfork Ranch, which at that point existed only on paper. I was coming from sunny Los Angeles, where we had received the go-ahead to film our miniseries about a wealthy Texas family on location instead of locally. Arriving that day, I found Dallas buried under four feet of snow. My only thought was, "Oh, Lord, what have we gotten into?" Well, what we had gotten into was destined to become the most-watched, most-successful hour dramatic show in the history of television.

In the beginning, "Dallas" was not a continuing drama (i.e., "soap opera"). Until halfway through its first year, each episode was complete unto itself, having no bearing on anything that happened before. And then when Sue Ellen found out she was pregnant and didn't know whether Cliff or J.R. was the father, we had to continue that story line in the following episodes. That story line necessitated parallel story lines, and as we grew more and more into a serialized show, our audience grew as well. By the end of the second season, "Dallas" had become a global phenomena with the cliff-hanging question, "Who shot J.R.?"

The other primary elements in making "Dallas" so compelling are the way the characters created by David Jacobs have evolved, and the fine actors who portray them. Over an eight-season period, the core characters we started out with—at the time so unknown to all of us—developed into distinctive human beings with complete life stories, individual family trees and roots. We came to know how they think, how they feel, the aspirations they have for the future, the lessons they have learned from the past. It has been an astonishing transformation to witness. From characters sketched out on paper, the Ewings have become people who are invited into one hundred million homes each week as intimate friends.

And then there is our wonderful cast. When we first started filming in that terrible, cold, dreadful winter of 1977 in Dallas, none of us knew each other very well. In fact, it was rather like being in the Army. We were all huddled together, looking at one another, and finally we said, "Well, we're all in this together, so let's do it." And we did. From the very beginning, it has been a very tight-knit family group working on "Dallas." The actors work as an ensemble group, where each respects one another and is generous with each other as performers. Behind the scenes, we really do have a family whose members love each other, who really care about each other, and I think that quality—which comes through on the screen—is a great part of "Dallas"'s appeal.

This is an American program, designed for Americans and presented in a thoroughly American perspective of what entertainment should be, and yet

ix

these special qualities of "Dallas" have allowed the show to cross every cultural boundary. While the dialogue is translated in any non-English-speaking country, the woes and troubles and fun and joy of the Ewing family remain the same. In short, the Ewings, as a family, have been accepted by every economic group and every social structure, including millions of people worldwide who have never seen or done any of the things they see on the show. This universal appeal is but one of the firsts we have been extremely proud to be a part of.

Finally, closer to home, one must cite the loyalty of our American audience as the mainstay of the "Dallas" phenomenon. In the beginning, "Dallas" was kind of a network stepchild. We premiered on CBS on Sunday nights, then were moved to Saturday, then back to Sunday, and then to Friday night, which was known in the industry as television's "graveyard." Historically it was the lowest night of viewership in the week. But our audience followed us and "Dallas" went on to change the television viewing habits of the entire nation. At the peak of its popularity, "Dallas" had more people watching television on Friday night than on any other night.

We—the cast and crew of "Dallas"—have nothing but the greatest affection for the show and the loyal audiences who have supported its ongoing success. What better way, then, to celebrate our mutual old friends—Jock, Miss Ellie, J.R., Sue Ellen, Lucy, Ray, Donna, Bobby, Pam, Cliff, and many others—than to immortalize their life stories in the annals of literature.

Here then, with the fondest regards, are the Ewings of "Dallas."

Leonard Katzman
Producer
Culver City, California

1 · THE LEGACY

Southfork Ranch

The Ewing Rodeo is open to all amateurs, offering a $500 prize for each event and a purse of $5,000 for best all-round cowboy.

"There's just no way to build another Southfork, not in six lifetimes."

—Jock Ewing, 1980

To the construction barons who are bulldozing the ranges, pouring concrete, and hoisting thick steel beams in the name of progress for the Metroplex, the area around Dallas–Fort Worth, Southfork Ranch stands as a defiant dinosaur, daring any would-be attacker. To die-hard Texans, however, Southfork is the symbol of a proud people fiercely protecting their rich cultural history.

Located in the town of Braddock, Southfork has largely preserved the ranching way of life for over a hundred and twenty years, despite its proximity to "The Big D," razzle-dazzle Dallas. It stretches over a hundred thousand acres. Mile after mile, the gentle rises, bluffs, and grassy plains, dotted with cattle and horses, never fail to produce a burning excitement deep within the visitor's heart. For this is the land of Texas. This is the unscathed horizon that reawakes man's inherent yearning to be one with the land.

The ranch is the home of the illustrious Ewing family, but, more important—certainly to Dallas County—it is a testament to the alliance between two often bitter adversaries: Great Ranches and Big Oil. For while ranch after ranch across the state was violated by the maniacal search for raw crude, Southfork too was almost lost, and it was in an ironic twist of fate that Big Oil proved to be its savior.

In 1841, Tennessee lawyer John Neely Bryan built a pole hut on the east bank of the Trinity River and named it Dallas. Pioneers started straggling in in the 1840s, sharing Bryan's vision of a great port for steamboats coming up the river from the Gulf of Mexico. By the 1850s, a new group of settlers had arrived—largely French, Belgian, German, Swiss, and Polish—whose skilled artisans and unusually high number of intellectuals promoted the cultural development of the envisioned city. But a man with a different dream, Enoch Southworth, steered clear of Dallas and bought up thousands of acres roughly thirty-five miles to the north.

Southworth was a man in love with the earth, its textures, its gifts of sustenance to the grasses, the animals, himself. He had carefully chosen this site for his ranch. He had grown up hearing of Bryan's boasts of Dallas as a major boat terminal, and in 1858 he shook his head in bafflement as he studied the shallowness and unpredictable nature of the Trinity River, knowing full well that it could never handle boats. No, Southworth thought, that water was not meant for shipping, it was meant for the regeneration of life.

He garnered one hundred thousand acres—all of which is still intact today—the choice Sections bountiful with water from a stream which divides at one point—hence the name Southfork—small ponds, and several underground springs. Other Sections, each equivalent to 642 acres, like Two Stick Pasture and Little Horn Country, were plentiful in the grasses and low-to-the-ground vegetation needed to support cattle and horses. And then there was an area that bore little of anything, except rattlers, which the deed called Section 40. But it was *land,* and Southworth bought it along with the rest. The soil on Section 40 was heavy with salt, rather than the limestone that permeated the rest of the area, but he thought that perhaps one day he could somehow channel water there and bring the land back to life.

3

Ray Krebbs, foreman of Southfork Ranch, supervising the segregation of infected cattle in Little Horn Country during the outbreak of screwworm in the fall of 1979. They caught the epidemic in time and lost only fifty calves, cows, and steers, while nearby ranchers were not so lucky.

Jock Ewing and Ray enjoying themselves at a cattle auction at the Fort Worth Stockyards Exchange. Southfork has been represented at the auctions for well over eighty years.

Bobby Ewing and Ray Krebbs. Bobby, the youngest of the Ewing sons, manages the finances of the ranch and at roundup or branding time is a regular out with the hands.

On the whole, Southworth's dream was realized in Southfork as the most splendid place in which to start his cattle empire. There was indeed a heavenly quality to this land: the mild temperatures, the brilliant blue skies and gentle breezes, the rolling magnificence of the prairie grasses, wildflowers of all kinds, and the clusters of mesquite, pecan, hickory, cottonwood, and live oak trees. Enoch himself felled some of the trees and began work on the main house, where he planned to bring a new bride and begin work on a family of his own.

By the fall of 1860, Southfork Ranch was well on its way as the leader of the territory. The first thousand head of Southworth Texas longhorns were driven north to market on the new Chisholm Trail and several hundred head of horses were rounded up by Southworth's small army of cowboys. But then on February 1, 1861, Texas joined the Confederacy and Southworth had no choice but to send himself and his "army" off to war.

When he returned to Southfork in 1865, he was faced with rebuilding almost everything. In his absence, fences had fallen, his cattle were roaming only the good Lord knew where, and his horses had been appropriated by the Army. But he set to his work with a vengeance, and by 1870 the ranch was resurrected in even greater glory. He then married, and his wife bore him a son, Aaron. In celebration, Enoch moved his family into the finally completed white clapboard house and began the tradition that is honored to this day: the Annual Barbecue.

Aaron, Enoch's sole child and heir, was every bit the man his father was, and more. His respect for the land was without condition, his way with animals extraordinary, and even as a young man his leadership abilities and fairness with the hands were the talk of cowboys throughout the territory. He was bright, strong, charismatic, and vital, and also gentle and kind, though on occasion he tried to hide those qualities.

Southfork was prospering along with Dallas, the growth of the latter not particularly delighting Enoch, since it was apparent that Dallas's future was attracting a level of sophistication that wasn't necessarily in the best interests of the ranching way of life. Dallas was now the intersection of the northbound Houston & Texas Central Railroad with the westbound Texas

Ray and Bobby confer on the heating system for the stables, 1978.

Square dancing at the annual Ewing Barbecue. Hundreds of guests attend each year, greeting friends and neighbors whose ties have extended for generations. The barbecue offers tons of ribs and Miss Ellie's famous chili. And, too, the prettiest gals in Texas.

Ray, J. R. Ewing, and Bobby with four of the Southfork hands. J.R. is an expert rider but has left Southfork to the care of Ray and Bobby in favor of concentrating on Ewing Oil.

and Pacific, which was good for the local economy, but the new wave of eager settlers chugging into the area were not of Enoch's liking. That was when he purchased miles of barbed wire from Betcha-a-million Gates (John W., the barbed-wire king who had been pestering Enoch for years) and ordered high fences to be erected. "Not to keep the cattle in, Son, to keep those crazy Eastern folks out."

Young Aaron's acceptance of new ranching ideas, integrating them compatibly with the old ways, brought even greater prosperity to Southfork. In the late 1880s, when the cattle trails to markets were more easily traveled, when the trains were more efficiently shipping beef to the north and east, he was responsible for Southfork's being one of the first ranches to raise less-tough, fatter cattle and slowly diminish their number of longhorns. "Daddy," he explained, "for every one of 'em with those eight-feet horns, I can git three Herefords on the boxcar." More revenues poured into the Southfork chest.

With their expanding funds, Aaron supervised the building of the best bunkhouses in the county for the loyal Southfork hands. New pens, barns, and corrals were also built, and more cattle and horses moved across the land.

Aaron began experimenting with open irrigation, with moderate success. Perhaps his most important contribution, however, at least in terms of the ranching community, was his cooperative effort with other ranchers to finance, launch, and support the Fort Worth Stockyards Exchange in the late 1890s—a move that put "Cowtown" on the map as the third largest exchange and meat-packing center in the United States.

Like his father, Aaron kept a wary eye on the ever-expanding Dallas. He didn't quite understand that city, what the people were doing there. Of the new arrivals he said, "Hellfire if I kin figure out why they come all this way just to live like they did back East." He felt the future lay in Fort Worth, where ranchers and cowboys could meet and talk and share ideas—feel like neighbors, like a community, like men who were born to be a part of the range and part of each other through their common bond. And, better yet, it was a place to hoot and holler and wheel and deal and parade their best livestock, to boast of their successes and advise one another in times of trouble.

On January 11, 1901, a very tired, elderly Enoch Southworth rode back to Southfork from Dallas. He tied up his horse, trudged up the stairs of the house, and summoned his son. Slowly, with a seriousness Aaron had never seen, he told his son the news. The day before, in Beaumont, Patillo Higgins and Anthony Lucas's well, the Lucas #1, had hit a gusher and raw crude was spewing up from the ground by the thousands of barrels. "I know that land," he said glumly, "and if there's oil there, then, God almighty, the entire state's swimmin' in it." He paused. "They're carryin' on in Dallas about Black Gold. Huh. What it is, is poison. It kills every living thing that it covers."

And right then and there, Enoch made his son pledge that he would never, *ever* let anyone drill for oil on Southfork Ranch. His son took the oath and Enoch nodded, satisfied. A few days later, he passed away.

Aaron married and had two children, the eldest a boy, Garrison, and then a little girl, Eleanor. Aaron was one of the most respected and powerful men in Texas and the children grew up in awe of him. Garrison, however, came to fear his daddy because, as he hit his teenage years, it was apparent that, by some freak accident of nature, Garrison was not cut out for the ranching way of life. But Aaron was not unkind to him, he just basically ignored him

Eleanor Southworth Ewing Farlow, "Miss Ellie," can be seen daily riding her bicycle along the same roads where she rode bareback in her younger days.

The second eldest son, Gary Ewing, gives away his daughter, Lucy, to Mitch Cooper at their wedding in 1981. Southfork has been a glorious backdrop to many weddings over the years, including Jock and Ellie's, J.R. and Sue Ellen's (twice), and Miss Ellie's to Clayton Farlow in 1984.

after—to his utter joy—he found out that it was his daughter, Ellie, who had inherited every bit of the Southworth spirit.

For Ellie it was a magical place to grow up in, a peaceful place that also held many moments of exquisite excitement: calving time, the round-ups, the rodeos, the auctions in Fort Worth. Southfork cattle were commanding some of the highest prices in the state, bulls and new breeds won prizes every year at the State Fair in Dallas, and money, well, it was just *there,* lots of it.

But then it all started to change. Oil—Big Oil—began its encroachment on all of Texas, bringing a wave of grimly determined men in search of it, the wildcatters. The state was reeling, drunk with new dollars from the new industry. Ellie watched her father speak out in Dallas, and then in Austin, bellowing, pleading with his fellow Texans to protect the ranchlands from this insane invasion. But who listened, who cared? Oil meant big money, much bigger than the ranching community could ever dream of.

And then, for Aaron, everything his father and he had worked for started coming apart. In 1929, following the stock market crash, the country slumped into depression and the money that was once so plentiful at Southfork began to dry up. Cattle prices plummeted to next to nothing and Garrison and Eleanor watched their father's face grow lean and more tense.

Oil. Oil. *Oil*—the only word that meant survival in the listless, dangling economy. Ranch hands, shrugging helplessly to Aaron, deserted Southfork to earn wages in the oil fields. Derricks were bursting onto the horizon, moving closer and closer to the region, as Southfork continued its sickening slide into decay. The year 1930 brought one of the most devastating droughts in Texas history, and it was plain to all that Southfork was dying. The stream was barely a trickle, the ponds just gaping holes in the ground. The fields and ranges were burned out, cattle carcasses rotting in the sun. Day after day Aaron rode back from Forth Worth with hardly any money as he sold what was left of his bulls and horses. As Garrison remembered years later, "He'd

bark orders in that tough, leathery voice of his like Southfork was the most prosperous ranch on earth, but his voice had an edge of fear."

It was a gut-wrenching day when the Sheriff of Dallas County drove up and knocked on the once beautiful main house, now in sad disrepair. Southfork was bankrupt, finished. The Sheriff was there to foreclose and evict the Southworths from the land. Garrison was too horrified by the scene to endure it, and he ran away. Aaron barely noticed or cared in his anguish.

And then, bursting through the door, came young Ellie, pulling in behind her a very tall, ruggedly handsome man. Glancing at the Sheriff, Ellie told her daddy that the man's name was Jock Ewing and that she was marrying him. Jock spoke up, telling Aaron that he would save the ranch. Aaron was thunderstruck. His eyes first lit up with hope, then narrowed in suspicion.

Yep. Jock Ewing was a wildcatter. Big Oil in the making.

Ellie smoothed things over, talking sense to her daddy and gratitude to her fiancé. The ranch was saved and Ellie was married to the maverick oilman. Things went along smoothly as Jock poured thousands of dollars into the revitalization of Southfork. Smoothly, that is, until he thought he should get something back on his investment and did some testing on the salty Section 40 and, to his delight, located the only oil reserve in all of Dallas County. Right there on Southfork. Without Aaron's knowledge, Jock moved in drilling equipment. When he made a strike, Jock proudly showed Aaron how Southfork was going to finance itself.

Local lore has it that the ensuing fight between Aaron and Jock over those wells caused the clapboard house to collapse from the sheer volume of it. (Jock built the new main house that presides over Southfork today.) In the end, Jock decided he needed Miss Ellie—who was as appalled as her father—more than he needed that oil, and he capped the wells.

When Aaron Southworth died, he bequeathed Southfork to Eleanor Southworth Ewing and to the Ewing family, on the provision that they maintain it as a working ranch and, as his father had instructed, that no one ever drill for oil. The family has respected that provision to this day.

Ray, his wife Donna Culver Krebbs, J.R., and Miss Ellie enjoying breakfast by the pool. Miss Ellie is a fanatic for the outdoors and orders that breakfast and luncheon be served outside on the patio or on the terrace (pictured here) whenever the weather permits.

Southfork is a mighty ranch out of the past, though it is slightly different with the times. Its traditions continue: the riding, roping, branding of cattle (some of the state's finest Charolais, Angus, and Santa Gertrudis), the buying of supplies from MacGregor's in Braddock, representation at the Monday and Thursday auctions at the Fort Worth Stockyards, and the holding of the (Ewing) Barbecue every year. However, there is daily evidence of the modern world: helicopters and jeeps used in roundups and chasing strays; an intricate network of underground irrigation pipes that feed water to all acres; an electronic intercom system that hooks up all points of the ranch to the main house; and a flood of paperwork necessitated by government regulation and price support system of the beef industry.

The ranch's foreman is Jock's son Ray Krebbs, and it is managed by the youngest of Ellie and Jock's sons, Bobby Ewing. There are fifty full-time hands, a loyal group still reminiscent of the personal army that stood with Enoch Southworth in the 1860s.

The Ewing family is by no means stuck in a bygone era. This is a family of immense wealth, power, and culture, but maintained through all the ups and downs that the family has endured in recent years has been their sacred duty to preserve every square inch of the land that Enoch staked out so many years before. The Ewings hold this land in trust. They're caretakers of a way of life, honor-bound to their roots in the Lone Star State.

While the city of Dallas may appear to be pushing its history away in favor of a world-class, sophisticated image, Southfork Ranch carries on as an awesome reminder of the past—the regeneration of life in all of its God-given glory.

In 1983, a raging fire broke out in the main house at Southfork. Pictured here is Bobby as he threw himself in the pool before braving the flames that engulfed the front foyer. His quick thinking and bravery saved the life of his brother, J.R., and his sister-in-law, Sue Ellen, while Ray rescued the first Ewing grandson, John Ross Ewing III. The house had to be completely renovated and today bears no scars from the near tragedy.

The front gate to Southfork, here being guarded by Braddock police. Because the Ewings are multimillionaires, they have often been the target for kidnappers.

2 · THE FAMILY

The Ewings of Southfork

John Ross Ewing, Sr.

"JOCK"

"He was tough, but he was fair. All he ever needed was a handshake to make a deal. I guess he was kind of a symbol of what the oil business was all about."
—Punk Anderson, 1982

He was the man who single-handedly made Ewing Oil the largest independent oil company in Dallas. He was the six-foot-three, blue-eyed powerhouse who fell madly in love with Eleanor Southworth. He was the aggressive wildcatter who saved Southfork Ranch from doom, only to be seduced by ranching itself. He was the man who sired four enormously talented, hearty young men to carry on the Ewing name. He was Jock Ewing, a legend in Texas, and a passionate believer in the superiority of the Lone Star State.

Jock was born just before World War I, one of two sons in a family of very modest means, their only distinction being that a distant relative, James L. Ewing, had given his life bravely at the Alamo. From the time Jock could walk, he was off to the burgeoning oil fields, learning all that he could. It was an exhilarating time. Since the oil strike at Spindletop, Texas, in 1901, the fortunes to be made in oil had been moving away from the Rockefellers' fields in Pennsylvania to the Lone Star State, where *any* smart, able-bodied man had a shot at instant wealth. The only trouble, Jock found, was that many of these men were also desperate cutthroats, men who would calmly shoot you in the back to steal your claim. A certain combination of toughness and cunning was required to survive, and Jock Ewing had it.

Jock was an extremely bright young man and he concentrated on his natural gifts, developing expertise in the methods of extracting oil from the ground, once it was located. Then nothing could stop him; no geological barriers could outfox him. A particular specialty of his in those days was the highly dangerous practice of breaking through limestone deposits by shooting the well with nitroglycerin. He was paid well for his work, and on one of his jobs he struck up a friendship with Willard "Digger" Barnes, who could literally smell oil, pinpoint exactly where to drill. A plan took shape in Jock's mind. In a matter of days, the two men had pooled their resources and struck out on their own as wildcatters.

At this same time, in 1927, Jock married a frail young girl named Amanda Lewis. There was trouble in the marriage from the start, stemming from Amanda's rather nervous nature. As Digger smelled out oil, as the two men started busting their guts to get equipment and start drilling, Amanda was left alone for long periods in the makeshift town around the fields. It was a rough, dirty "community," and Jock would carry enormous guilt for many years afterward for having put poor Amanda into the middle of it. For every new

13

Jock saved the day in the fall of 1978, when two strangers from Waco held the Ewings hostage. It turned out they had come to revenge J.R.

Ellie and Jock in the living room on Jock's birthday, 1978. "Miss Ellie, the older I get the less I understand these kids."

Above: Riding the range on his favorite horse, Blazer, with Ray Krebbs. After years of being a die-hard oilman, Southfork ultimately seduced Jock into ranching. He adored the wide open spaces and working the ranch with his bare hands, and once sighed to Ray, "Sometimes I think I was born a hundred years too late."

millionaire, there were hundreds of broken and angry men milling about, up to no good. Drunkenness and shoot-outs were rampant, fist-to-face violence a normal part of each waking hour. The temporary Ewing home was under attack nearly every night by men in search of food, of money. Amanda became terrified of leaving the house and barricaded herself in when Jock wasn't there. She did not complain. Instead, she grew thinner, paler, more drawn, and distant. Worried, Jock urged her to return to her family until he could find a proper home, but she persisted, saying that her place was with him. Finally, after another gunfight outside in the street, poor Amanda had a complete mental breakdown, from which, the doctors said, she would never recover.

Jock placed Amanda in the care of a hospital in Dallas and himself lived right out on the fields. He became a man obsessed. The fields were all he had, and he *had* to strike oil, he *had* to have money to send Amanda to a private hospital in Colorado where, in the doctors' opinion, lay the only remote chance of her recovery.

He pushed Digger perhaps harder than he should have. Yes, Digger could locate oil, but—darn it—he got drunk the minute he did, never pulling himself together long enough to put in a decent day's work on the rig. Jock was impatient and stern with him, not understanding his friend's compulsion, and more than once he ended up trying to knock some sense into Digger's drunken head. Jock brought in his brother, Jason, hoping he would help stabilize the venture.

Ewing #1 came in. That day, hat in hand, looking up to the Lord and thanking Him, Jock experienced a happiness he had never known before. He immediately moved Amanda to the Colorado hospital and channeled the rest of the income from Ewing #1 into new sites. But trouble was still in hand with Digger—and with Jason as well! Jock was at first furious and then disgusted when his partners kept losing their shares of the money in drunken poker games. As wells 2, 3, 4, and 5 came in, Jock soon found himself with new partners, each with a paper that showed he had won Digger's and Jason's interests in the well. Each time, Jock would search all over town and then finally find Digger and Jason holed up somewhere, nursing a bottle. When Jock could get them sobered up, they would stagger back to work.

This time, on #6, Jock was determined that his partners would keep their shares. He took the leases on the new site in his name only, so Digger and Jason couldn't lose their shares if they tried. When Ewing #6 came

An exhausted Ellie and Jock leave Dallas Memorial Hospital after their vigil following the shooting of their eldest son, J.R., in 1980. Jock had quit cigarette smoking many years before at Ellie's urging—and had been sneaking them for just as long—but during this crisis he resumed for a few days. Jock was adamant that the habit was not one he wanted his family to pick up; none of the Ewings smoke.

Miss Ellie lovingly comforts Jock in the intensive care unit after his massive coronary in 1978.

Jock listens closely to his sons while sitting at his desk in the Southfork library. Years before him, Ellie's father, Aaron Southworth, sat in the same seat.

Jock with his son Gary at Southfork in 1980. Jock loved him but couldn't for the life of him figure out what was wrong with Gary. He lacked all the Ewing traits: competitiveness, a head for business, and a taste for power. Gary was also an alcoholic, which Jock did not know how to help him with.

in—the biggest strike yet—Jock returned from town to the site to find two drunk, violent men with a menacing look in their eyes. Digger screamed at him, railed, shrieking that he had found out what a crook Jock was—that he had put his own name on the lease as sole owner. Jock tried to explain his reasons for doing so, about a separate agreement, but Digger was out of his head and tried to kill him. Jock finally had had it with both of them. If Digger and Jason wanted to drink themselves into oblivion, then fine, but not as his partners. Digger stayed on a murderous bender for a number of days, during which he firmly planted in his head and his heart that Jock Ewing had cheated him and that one day he would settle the score. Jason left for parts unknown.

Without Digger, the strikes in new fields were less precise, but Jock worked even harder and rapidly parlayed money from the working wells into the purchase of whatever raw acreage he could get, hoping to find more oil one day. The Ewing name was rising to prominence. His land was in thousand-acre parcels all over the state, and years later his investments paid off handsomely. For a few dollars an acre back then, Jock came to own not only new oil fields, but also natural gas fields, rich mineral deposits, and acreage to lease for cotton.

When the Colorado doctors told Jock that Amanda's condition was permanent, with no hope of any mental recovery, Jock sadly got a divorce in Dallas in 1930. Shortly thereafter, he happened to see a young woman named Eleanor Southworth. The second that Jock saw her—those dazzling blue eyes, that flashing smile, the laughter of her hair as she galloped on her horse (in the most unladylike fashion)—Jock felt his heart give way. She was wildly beautiful and Jock eagerly asked around about her. The news was not good. She was the daughter of the most distinguished rancher in the territory, Aaron Southworth, who made no secret whatsoever of his opinion of oilmen:

16

Jock telling Ray that he would publicly acknowledge that he was Ray's father, 1980. It was a dream come true for Ray, who said: "How I looked up to him when I was a kid. I idolized him. But, when I goofed something, he'd chew me up one side and down the other . . . and I thought, how could somebody I idolize be like that? Now I know—he was concerned about me, he was teaching me. He knew when to be firm, when to be affectionate . . . and he was all those things. And mostly, I just thought he was almost perfect."

he hated them. The second piece of news, which made Jock grimace, was that Digger Barnes claimed "Miss Ellie," as everyone called her, was his girl.

Jock wrestled with his conscience—and also his good sense, which told him not to tangle with Barnes one more time—but when he saw Ellie again, he was filled with an elation and passion that he could not contain. Not even when Ewing #1 came in had he felt this way. So, after one long deep breath, Jock went after her, hell-bent on marriage. Incredulously, Miss Ellie was just as overwhelmed by him, and she agreed to marry Jock. It was the happiest moment of his life.

The consequences of Jock and Ellie's love in those early years was decidedly mixed. Yes, the Southfork Ranch was saved by Jock's money, but Jock secretly was forced to find a way to make up the enormous financial drain fast, before he lost hold of his assets.

When he had agreed to get Southfork out of debt, he had no idea how much money it would take, and then, on top of that, how many thousands and thousands that Aaron needed to get it back to a proper working condition. But Jock knew that Southfork was Ellie's lifeblood and so, for her sake, he said nothing and continued to pour money into it. It was worth it to see her so happy. It was even worth it to take old man Southworth's constant haranguing about the ruination of Texas by oilmen.

But where was Jock to find the cash he desperately needed? Between the ranch, his payments due on equipment and mortgages, and the huge bills for Amanda's care, he was strapped. Then a good buddy from way back, a smart lawyer whom Jock trusted, Sam Culver, offered him a partnership on some fields that Sam's elderly uncle, Jonas Culver, owned. The only problem was that Jonas refused to sell. He was like Southworth, bitterly opposed to the oil industry. But Sam had an idea . . . When Jock first heard it, he refused to

17

go in on the deal. He told Sam he couldn't do it, couldn't put Jonas in a sanatorium, what with his former wife's condition . . . Sam said for him to think about it—it wouldn't be but for a month or so—and afterward they'd set Jonas up to live like a king for the rest of his life. When Jock got back to Southfork that night, Aaron handed him the estimates of how much it was going to cost to replenish the cattle. Looking at the man's lowered head, seeing Ellie's pained expression at her father's pride lying so vulnerably on the table, Jock just smiled and slapped Aaron on the back, assuring him that it was no problem. The next day, against his better judgment, Jock went to Sam and agreed to the partnership. Years later, in 1982, Sam's second wife, Donna Culver, discovered Sam's journals that told what happened:

"March 1st—Today I got a court order to have Jonas committed to Signal Mountain Sanatorium and had myself appointed custodian of his estate."

"March 27th—Today, as custodian of Jonas's estate, I sold to Ewing/Culver all but 40 acres of Jonas's land. The money is in an account in his name and he'll get a 25% royalty from all producing wells. Next week I'll release him from the sanatorium. Neither Jock nor I wanted to do things this way, but the old codger left us no option. Anyway, now he'll be a rich man despite himself."

"April 12th—Lord, oh, Lord, what have we done? Jonas killed himself today."

Jock was to carry this secret heavy on his heart for the rest of his life.

On the domestic front, things were progressing nicely until Jock started drilling on Section 40 and hit oil. Aaron was unspeakably angry and, for a moment, Jock saw that same mad gleam in his eyes that Digger Barnes had had so many years before. Jock explained that the land was obviously barren, useless, worthless, hell, they were building practically a highway along it from Braddock, and after all the money he had spent . . . Southworth raged, reducing Miss Ellie to tears and then to anger, directed at Jock. Unable to stand Ellie's distress for long, Jock reluctantly gave in and ordered the wells capped.

As if rewarding Jock, Miss Ellie gave him the most precious gift imaginable: a healthy, robust son named John Ross Ewing, Jr. Jock was on cloud nine over this child, as was Aaron. The two of them, walking together around the ranch one evening, discussed whether this boy, nicknamed J.R., would be an oilman or a rancher. Jock was certain the kid was oil but good-naturedly went along with Aaron's fantasy that he was going to be a rancher. Something then bonded the two men; it was more than respect, more than friendship. It was more a silent pact of trust of one generation with the next. Jock was to preserve both options for his son; he understood that. That evening Aaron gave Jock one of his most prized possessions, an 1892 six-shot Colt, double-action service revolver. It was his way of welcoming Jock to the Southworth family.

Two years later Miss Ellie presented Jock with a second son, Garrison, and Jock smiled even more broadly, envisioning the expanding executive offices of Ewing Oil.

After the bombing of Pearl Harbor in 1941, Jock enlisted in the Army Air Corps and, as a colonel, was stationed overseas. After two agonizingly long years in London, Jock had an affair with a young nurse from Texas, Margaret Hunter, that was abruptly ended when Jock was shipped off to France.

Jock at the Oil Baron's Club with Ray (left) and Punk Anderson (right), discussing the Takapa development project, 1981. The project nearly destroyed his marriage to Miss Ellie.

When Jock returned to the States in 1945, he couldn't live with his conscience and he told Miss Ellie about the affair, frightened that she would leave him, or, rather, throw him off of Southfork. He was forgiven by her and was amazed, not for the last time, by this extraordinary woman's depth of compassion and ability to understand. What neither of them knew at the time was that Margaret Hunter had returned to Texas carrying Jock's child.

The late 1940s brought another gift to the family, son Bobby, and the Ewing family line was ensured. Aaron passed away, but he had lived to see all of his grandsons.

By necessity, Jock had to struggle with managing the ranch and its finances, which drove him to distraction, since he absolutely abhorred bookwork and didn't know beans about ranching. It wasn't until 1950 that he found a foreman, Hutch McKinney, whom he felt he could trust with the running of Southfork. Now he could concentrate on Ewing Oil's expansion with a plethora of new wells in Kilgore, Midland, and Odessa and also, once again in his life, have some free time for himself.

Not since he was a child had Jock been able to pursue the interests that he adored: hunting and fishing. He had made two good friends in the oil industry who had tastes similar to his own, Marvin "Punk" Anderson and Lucas Wade. And when the boys were old enough, he took them along to Landowne Reserve, near Caddo Lake on the Louisiana side, where he taught them all about tracking and wilderness survival.

In 1952, on Election Day, as the rest of the Ewing family sat around the new Southfork television set watching the returns as Eisenhower beat Stevenson, Jock slammed the ranch books shut, took off his glasses, muttered something to Miss Ellie, and stormed his way into town. He found foreman Hutch McKinney drinking in the Wild Bronc Saloon and he fired him on the spot for padding the feed and supply bills. A fight ensued. After Jock beat the living daylights out of McKinney, he told him that no one could steal from Southfork Ranch and get away with it and if he so much as tried to steal one more thing, he'd kill him. Later that night, Jock found McKinney back at the

19

bunkhouse and threw him out of it. That was that; Jock Ewing was back running the ranch as well as Ewing Oil. It wouldn't be until the late 1960s, when Ray Krebbs was old enough, that Jock would have a foreman whom he trusted.

As the years went by, the differences between Jock's sons became apparent. The eldest, J.R., pleased Jock since he clearly had the makings of an oil baron—in fact, since he was five years old. And the youngest, Bobby —whom Jock unabashedly spoiled—was taken with both ranching and Ewing Oil. But it was the middle son, Gary, who proved to be such a disappointment to Jock. Although Gary had an affinity for ranching, Jock thought he had too much ranch air in his head. His whole attitude frustrated Jock. It was as if the boy were in another world—he loved to *paint,* for land's sake—so Jock left Gary's upbringing largely to Miss Ellie.

In later years, as Jock grew enamored with ranching and left more and more of the responsibility for running Ewing Oil to J.R. and Bobby, he drew very close to Ray Krebbs, who seemed to be just the kind of son Gary should have been. It was a shock—but somehow not nearly the kind of shock one would have thought—when, in 1980, Jock learned that Ray *was* his son, by Margaret Hunter Krebbs.

By 1978 Jock had largely retired from Ewing Oil, although he remained Chairman of the Board. For the next three years he would periodically step in when the going got tough for J.R. and Bobby, between whom the leadership fluctuated, but for the most part he concentrated on ranching.

In the fall of 1978 Jock suffered a massive coronary that landed him in the intensive care unit at Dallas Memorial Hospital and necessitated a heart bypass operation in order to save his life. It was a warning signal to him and his family of his advancing years. Before, no one, not even Jock himself, had even contemplated the notion that one day he might not be able to do everything he had always done. He had to slow down, and the family took this too much to heart. They patronized him, coddled him—particularly Miss Ellie —and if ever there was a man whose pride wouldn't allow such a thing, it was Jock.

It was only natural, then, that when the lovely former Ewing Oil employee, Julie Grey, returned to Dallas and was seeking companionship that Jock would be attracted to her, and she to him. To his family, he was an invalid. To Julie, he was the tall, powerful, handsome man he always was. But the two were careful to keep the relationship within the bounds of friendship, though passion was lurking dangerously close. But whether or not it would have progressed to anything more, neither had a chance to find out, as Julie was murdered by two of J.R.'s business associates.

As Jock more fully recovered, he and Ellie grew close once again, only to be threatened later by his confession of having been married previously. Amanda had been a secret all of these years. His timing was unfortunate. Ellie was undergoing severe medical problems—unbeknown to him—and it frightened her that Jock was apparently capable of divorcing someone who was ill. Her reaction—one of enormous anger—stemmed from fear, and she lashed out at him rather unfairly. But once she traveled with Jock to Colorado and saw Amanda for herself—what a state she was in—she forgave Jock completely, and the two of them vowed to care for Amanda for the rest of her life.

The past rose once again to threaten Jock in 1980. Jock had given Ray Krebbs a Section of Southfork upon which to build his own home, and when the ranch hands broke ground, they discovered a skeleton. It turned out to be the remains of Hutch McKinney, the foreman Jock had fired in 1952. In a nightmarish chain of events, Assistant District Attorney Cliff Barnes—Digger's son—built a case against Jock, accusing him of murder. The evidence at the trial was overwhelmingly against Jock. McKinney had been shot with Jock's gun (the one Ellie's father had given him), he had been killed the night that witnesses heard Jock threaten him, and evidence was presented that testified to Jock's sometimes volatile temper. But, in the end, Jock was cleared. On his deathbed, Jock's old friend and enemy, Digger Barnes, confessed to killing McKinney himself.

After that ordeal, Jock wanted to get back the rhythm of his life: riding, roping, jogging, talking with his family at the big breakfasts and dinners, spending time with the little grandson whom J.R. had presented him with, playing games of backgammon with Ellie at night, but it was not to be. And the cause this time, like so many times before, was Gary.

Ellie had blamed Jock for driving Gary away from the ranch, away from her, in the past. This time, in the fall of 1980, it was worse (though it was actually J.R., not Jock, who did any forcing). She was infuriated by Jock's deep affection for and camaraderie with his newfound son Ray and by the fact that, once again, J.R. and Bobby were at odds. Ellie felt that Jock had abdicated his role as father and was simply ignoring the other boys, *their* boys, in favor of Ray.

Matters between the couple took another turn for the worse when Jock entered into a partnership with Punk Anderson and Lucas Wade for the Takapa development project, a plan to convert swampland on the East Texas/Louisiana border into a resort. Miss Ellie, not knowing that Jock was one of its developers, was fighting the project with the Daughters of the Alamo on behalf of the state's environmental groups. When she found out that Jock was involved, she exploded. Their misunderstanding was so bad that Jock moved off Southfork, and Ellie began divorce proceedings in 1981. Only the personal and political savvy of Bobby resolved the Takapa issue amicably, and Jock and Ellie were reunited in an even stronger way than before. They celebrated with a lengthy second honeymoon in Europe.

The banner Miss Ellie had put up over the driveway on the day of the Ewing Barbecue, 1981, when Jock was supposed to have arrived home.

Upon their return, Jock was summoned by the State Department to Washington, D.C., where he was asked to lead a drilling venture in South America. Jock accepted the assignment, working down there for several weeks in some of the thickest, most deadly jungle territory in the world. If the terrain didn't worry him, the political unrest did. However, he successfully completed his assignment, and a jubilant Ewing family expected him to return to Dallas in time for the 1981 Ewing Barbecue. Then came the shocking news: the helicopter that was to have taken Jock to the South American airport had been caught in a storm and was reported lost. J.R., Bobby, and Ray flew down immediately to search for Jock, and on the bottom of a jungle lake in the middle of nowhere they found Jock's medallion—proof that he had gone down in the crash. The boys returned home with the confirmation. Their daddy, Ellie's husband, was dead.

Jock Ewing's death affected not only his family, but also hundreds of Ewing Oil employees, and the oil market itself. It was unthinkable that Jock was no longer there to control those Ewing boys, J.R. and Bobby. For control he did. He once said to Bobby, "I'm not trying to influence you, I'm tellin' you what I want you to do." Jock Ewing was a man who knew what was right, knew how to handle people, and tried to pass his wisdom on to his sons. The extent to which he succeeded is debatable.

Jock left many things behind him as remembrances. His Lincoln Continental with the license plate "EWING 1" is still parked at Southfork; and his corner table at the Cattleman's Club, his seat at the Jaycees, and his personal box at the Dallas Cowboys can only be filled by one of his sons. He also left a legend with a group of men at the Colverton oil field. They still remember their millionaire boss, with his bare hands, fighting the devastating fire there in 1960. And perhaps, in a way Jock would not have liked, he will also be remembered by the terms of the will he left, the cause of feud after feud within the family over the control and activities of Ewing Oil.

But the end of Jock Ewing's story was best summed up by Miss Ellie at the 1982 Oil Baron's Ball. The Texas Independents had set up the Jock Ewing Memorial Scholarships—which each year are awarded to four young oilmen in the making—at Southern Methodist University. That special night, Miss Ellie said of her husband:

"Jock Ewing was a great man, measured in the only true value of a man—not in money or power, but in friends. As I look around, I see so many of you that called Jock friend. And he was my husband, but more than that he was my best friend. I know how much you all miss him, but in a way he'll always be alive in your memories, and in his family. And now, through the scholarships at SMU, I know how proud he'd be if he knew what you had done for him, and perhaps he does. For him, and for me, I thank you.

"My life will never be the same without him, but Jock, of all men, believed that, whatever happened, you have to be ready to face tomorrow. And so we will. But I'll always know that my sons had the finest father and I was married to the finest man that God ever put on this earth.

"I love you, Jock."

With her sons Bobby and J.R. at her side, Miss Ellie tearfully thanks the Texas Independents for setting up the Jock Ewing Memorial Scholarships to Southern Methodist University. Her speech, at the 1981 Oil Baron's Ball, brought a thundering standing ovation from the guests.

Eleanor Ewing Farlow

"MISS ELLIE"

"Ellie, you haven't changed since you were a girl. You were always fighting other people's battles."

—Matt Devlin, 1980

She has been called the Empress Dowager of the Lone Star State. With her regal carriage, inherent grace, irradiating warmth, and compassionate heart, Miss Ellie is known as an awesome presence in the social and civic circles of Dallas County and beyond. With her keen mind and surprisingly adept business instincts, she is discreetly recognized as the safety net behind her boys, who are running Ewing Oil. But it is Miss Ellie's fierce pride in her heritage, her deep-seated courageousness, and her indefatigable belief in the strength of family that keep the Ewings a family rather than a splintered kingdom of personal fiefdoms.

Miss Ellie was born on Southfork Ranch and, with the exception of some of her school days, has never lived anywhere else in her seventy years. Her father, Aaron Southworth, taught her to ride before she could walk, and it is said in Dallas County that, until her mother made her attend Miss Hockaday's, the exclusive finishing school in Dallas, Miss Ellie had never walked on her own two feet. Indeed, she was a wild one, born with all the fiery spirit of the Southworth generations.

In contrast, Ellie's older brother, Garrison, seemed to be born in the wrong family. Though he liked the animals all right, the ranching way of life—Southworth style—was not for him. He preferred a quieter, more serene way of life and, much to his father's utter dismay, had a passionate attachment to, of all things, water and boats. So his father chose to ignore him, for the most part, and take Ellie as "his" child, bringing her to cattle auctions in Fort Worth when she was four years old, yahooing as she charged alongside him on her pony across the ranges, and winking his approval as she kept scores at rodeos. But Ellie had another side, one that she shared with Garrison. She thrived on music—country, classical, opera—as much as she did on the songs of nature. She was mesmerized by art of all kinds and, unlike any of the Southworths before her, had a gift for painting. Her subjects? Why, Southfork and its animals, of course.

She and Garrison were quite close, which Aaron thought all right, but . . . when he couldn't find Ellie, Aaron knew Garrison had her off somewhere, doing some kind of sissy stuff. And he hoped Ellie wouldn't go too far awry at that fancy schmancy school she was attending. Though Aaron knew he would have to leave Southfork to Garrison—it was unheard of to do anything else—he also knew that Ellie would have to run it behind the scenes, until she married a suitable rancher to take over.

25

Jock and Ellie playing an afterdinner game of backgammon in the living room. It was a ritual for them, and so was the outcome—Ellie nearly always won. The family was puzzled by Jock's willingness to play, but Ellie knew it was a sign of the trust between them. She was the only person on earth he could lose to in anything.

Ellie trying to have a peaceful breakfast with her sons J.R. and Bobby in the dining room, which is nearly always impossible. The boys inherited many of Jock's characteristics, including aggressiveness, stubbornness, and a taste for power. Trying to manage them is like trying to manage two Jocks, both competing for the control of Ewing Oil.

Miss Ellie was popular in school, but more because of the social standing of her family than anything else. She was a Southworth—which counted for an awful lot, no matter what you were like—and was quite beautiful with her billowing mane of hair, blazing blue eyes, and simply dazzling smile. She was certainly not like the other girls. Where they took their lessons seriously—in etiquette, cooking, French, etc.—Ellie would burst into laughter over her own helplessness and disinterest, and where they groaned and yawned—at mathematics and natural science—her face glowed with anticipation. And she was restless, constantly, yearningly, looking out the window as if she were about to expire if she didn't get outside soon. And her way with boys! The other girls shook their heads in astonishment and then jealousy—you could hardly call her a lady, carrying on and hootin' and hollerin', as pretty as she was in a stunning silk dress, but really! The boys were mad about her.

When Ellie was sixteen, an older man, a wildcatter, caught her eye. He was the son of a Southfork ranch hand, but his connection to oil was enough to break the blood connection. Since her father claimed that "They (oilmen) ruined the ranges and stank up the air," she was forced to see him on the sly. Eventually, all of Dallas murmured at seeing Miss Southworth together with Willard "Digger" Barnes, one of the craziest wildcatters around.

Digger was fascinating to Ellie—gentle one minute, raucous and humorous the next. And his occasional wild bursts of forbidden drunkenness captivated her. At those times he told her stories of the oil fields, of his daring feats, of the danger, and he always, always wound up telling her how desperately he loved her. He never ever, not even at his worst, behaved as anything but a gentleman with her.

How he adored her spirit! Many years later Digger described Miss Ellie in those days: "She was a wee little thing, Ellie was, with a great big laugh and a way about her. Sweet as sugar one minute, come at you with a shotgun the next. Oh, that temper. Fierce. But *fast,* like a firecracker. Flare up real big and loud—*boom!*—and then go right out."

Digger liked to think that they would one day manage to get married, but what little chance he had was blown away when Jock Ewing appeared. Jock simply swept Miss Ellie off her feet—or so they say. More than one Dallas resident has remarked on the coincidence that Ellie agreed to marry Jock on the day the Sheriff was foreclosing on Southfork, and that Jock was the only eligible man in Dallas who had the money to save it. But Miss Ellie said she loved him, and it was evident over the years that that was indeed the truth.

Her father didn't give the two of them five years together—said they were both too stubborn—but he was wrong. This is not to say that their marriage was smooth. They both had strong, independent wills, which often clashed mightily, but even stronger were their unrelenting respect, love, and passion for one another.

Miss Ellie and Jock's wedding was one of the largest in Dallas's history. Although everyone knew that Aaron was bankrupt, he refused to let Jock pay for the wedding and somehow came up with enough money (Ellie noticed the precious objects that disappeared from the house) to insist on the finest. He not only ordered that Ellie's wedding gown be made of imported French fabric but also paid for a seamstress to come along with it, all the way from Paris, to fit her. Hundreds of guests arrived, and out came the food, tons of barbecue and drink, and a band to beat the day.

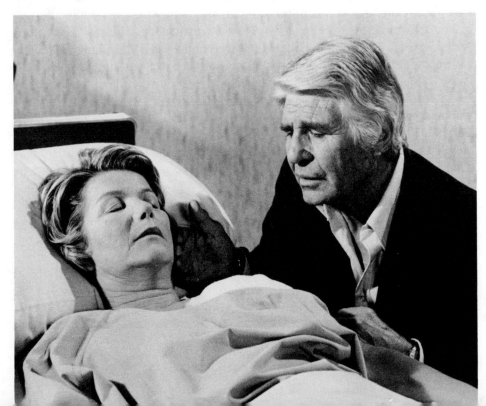

Jock lovingly at Ellie's side following her mastectomy operation in 1979.

Miss Ellie sips hot chocolate in the Southfork kitchen late at night with Bobby and, as she has done for years and years, listens thoughtfully to his problems, 1979. She said to him, "You're still a little boy to me . . . and as hard as you may find to believe it—so's J.R."

The event was slightly marred for Ellie by her brother's absence. He had written to wish her well and tell her that he had joined the Merchant Marines and would be at sea on the day of her wedding. A short time later, the family was notified that Garrison had been lost at sea. Ellie was deeply grieved.

After she bore their first son, J.R., Ellie began to settle down some. She participated in Aaron and Jock's discussions regarding the finances of the ranch in the library, and in the bedroom she listened to Jock's dreams that were being realized at Ewing Oil, but she began to see that her role in life could not be only a wife and mother at Southfork, but that it must involve the outside community. There were enormous changes taking place in Dallas, and she began to take an active interest in the city, particularly in the cultivation of its arts. She joined the Daughters of the Alamo, a woman's volunteer group centered in Dallas. Under Ellie's leadership—for almost forty years—the DOA went from being a social club for elite ladies to one of the most effective and influential civic groups in the state. They involved themselves in land reform issues, in protests against what they felt were dangerous precedents in housing developments, and established and supported many charitable agencies dealing with food, clothing, housing, and medical care for the disadvantaged.

Just prior to the outbreak of World War II, Ellie gave birth to another son and named him after her brother, Garrison. She had her third and last son, Bobby, six years later. Ellie adored her children. Nothing made her happier than to see the boys roughhousing in one of their infamous football games on the Southfork lawn. She'd give anything to encourage their love for Southfork, to keep them there all day—and, hopefully, for the rest of their lives. Up went the basketball hoop, stables with ponies inside were labeled "J.R.," "Gary," and "Bobby," and Ellie supervised the building of a swimming pool.

The boys were the center of her and Jock's life, but Ellie had one special son, and her favoritism was hard to hide. Gary, always Gary. Reminiscent of the scenes between her parents over her brother, Jock and Ellie's fights always seemed to be over Gary. J.R. was an oilman, just like his daddy. And no

28

wonder, Ellie thought; Jock stole the child away from her when he was five and plunked him behind a desk at Ewing Oil. Bobby was a rancher, just like Jock was now becoming, but Bobby was versatile enough, quick enough to be a Ewing Oil executive one day as well. Gary, poor Gary, was not quite fitting in anywhere. Oh, he loved ranching well enough, but he simply did not get along with Jock's rough-and-ready temperament. Gary was more like Ellie, in that he was artistically inclined, but he lacked her will on an everyday level. When he was a teenager, Ellie winced at what she saw. Gary started drinking to gain courage to stand up to Jock, and to J.R., who had been bullying him since the day he was born. When Gary ran away from Southfork after his brief attempt at marriage with Valene Clements, it nearly broke Ellie's heart, and deep down inside she harbored a resentment against Jock that would surface years later.

As her sons grew up into men of their own minds, Ellie missed having a child around. Though she was distressed that Gary and Valene's marriage had broken up, she was elated to bring up their tiny baby, Lucy, as the daughter she had never had.

The years rolled along, and in 1979 Ellie was handed a shock. Her brother, Garrison—after almost forty years of being thought dead—reappeared at Southfork. Since Ellie had inherited Southfork from her father only because of Garrison's alleged death, she felt honor-bound to offer him the ranch. The entire Ewing family recoiled in horror, but Ellie was persistent; she believed in the tradition of family land following blood lineage. To everyone's relief but Ellie's, Garrison was not interested in Southfork, since he was dying of cancer and only wanted to spend his final days on the land where he was born, near the sister he cherished. It was a sad day—yet somehow happy—when Ellie put her brother to rest on Southfork.

In 1979, Ellie had the scare of her life. She discovered a lump in her breast and was forced to have a lifesaving mastectomy, during which the malignant tumor and twelve lymph nodes were removed. It was so terribly frightening, because it was one of the few sets of circumstances where Ellie had absolutely no control over the outcome, no way to fight it herself. Her disfigurement and shaken self-image were something she had to wrestle with for years, but the brush with death also reaffirmed her zest and passion for life, for, indeed, it was more precious than ever.

The year 1980 proved to be even more painful for Ellie. Another fight erupted over Gary, and after Ray Krebbs was revealed to be Jock's son, all of Miss Ellie's anger over Gary's departure from Southfork came roaring to the surface. She accused Jock of abandoning, as a father, not only Gary but also J.R. and Bobby, in favor of Ray. And then, when Ellie and the DOA joined forces with Donna Culver Krebbs to stop the Takapa development project from destroying a wilderness area in East Texas and she found out that Jock, of all people, was one of the developers, her rage was complete. She felt betrayed on all levels. Worse yet, she thought that perhaps she had been married all of these years to a man she had never really known. Ellie's anger was further fueled by Jock's self-righteous response, and she went so far as to go to a lawyer and begin divorce proceedings. After their youngest son, Bobby, fortunately got involved, and settled the Takapa project problem to everyone's satisfaction, Miss Ellie and Jock rose above their mutual anger and stubbornness and were lovingly reconciled.

In 1981, while Jock was working down in South America, Miss Ellie had to step into the business of Ewing Oil to pull the company back on track from J.R.'s disastrous course. In an effort to force Clayton Farlow to kick

Ellie with her favorite son, Gary, on his visit home after the shooting of J.R. in 1980.

Ellie in court with Donna Culver Krebbs, fighting for an injunction to stop the Takapa development in 1981. Since the 1950s, Ellie has been actively trying to preserve the vanishing wilderness and wildlife areas in Texas.

Sue Ellen off the Southern Cross Ranch in San Angelo, J.R. had bought all the oil that normally fed Farlow's refineries. It was a great plan, except that J.R. used all the resources of Ewing Oil to do it, and the bottom fell out of the oil market. Ewing Oil was holding five million barrels of crude without a buyer in sight—a loss that endangered the solvency of the company. With her shoulders thrown back and her head held high, Miss Ellie flew to the Southern Cross in the Southfork helicopter and struck a deal with Clayton that saved the day. In addition, she won a new friend in Clayton. She was pleasantly taken by this robust man and thought how much like Jock he was, and how much Jock himself would like him.

The night of the Ewing Barbecue in 1981 was the worst night of Ellie's life. She was notified that Jock's helicopter had crashed in a storm in South America and that he was presumed dead. Her boys flew there and found evidence to confirm that Ellie's beloved Jock was truly dead. She was devastated. Her shock and her grief pushed her into a semicatatonic emotional state where she simply refused to believe that her husband was gone. The family agonized over her behavior, her denial, but it wasn't until 1982 that she came to terms with the truth. At a quiet family dinner one night, Miss Ellie rose from the table and rushed into the kitchen and there, venting all of her grief and anguish over Jock's death, smashed every piece of crockery within her reach. Following

Ellie getting acquainted with Rebecca Barnes Wentworth, 1981. Ellie hoped Rebecca could do her part to stop the Barnes-Ewing feud by controlling her son, Cliff, while she promised to do her best with J.R. The two women were not successful in their attempts. However, they did develop a warm friendship with one another.

the night of the Oil Baron's Ball, when the Jock Ewing Memorial Scholarships were announced, Miss Ellie told her family that it was time to declare Jock legally dead and to read his will.

The will was, in many ways, the last straw for Ellie. Its instructions—J.R. and Bobby each running half of Ewing Oil, and battling each other for a year—resulted in a nightmare for everyone in the family. No one took it harder than Miss Ellie. Power, and the struggle for it, may have suited Jock, but it had never brought out the best in her sons. For the next few months, Ellie was torn this way and that, trying to protect her sons from each other and keep some semblance of a family. Finally, in desperation at how ugly the competition had become, Ellie was pushed to move in and try to break Jock's will, under the pretense that he was not in his right mind when he wrote it.

It was the last thing on earth she wanted to do—to publicly denounce her husband's state of mind—but she was frantic to keep the family together. Despite her efforts, the court upheld the will and Ellie, exhausted, was forced to the sidelines while her sons battled it out. Had it not been for the counsel she received from Clayton Farlow and the support from her daughter-in-law Pamela, no one knew what would have happened to her.

By 1983 the family's problems had worn Ellie down, and her health started to fail. Alarmed, Clayton wisely took her away from all of the chaos at Southfork and brought her to Takapa Resort. There, while under a doctor's supervision, Ellie received badly needed rest and, perhaps the best cure of all, love from Clayton. She recovered fully, which was a good thing, since in her absence the family unity had been blown to kingdom come. Ellie became engaged to Clayton soon after and, with her strength supported by his, started to replenish Southfork with love.

Ellie had no pretensions about replacing Jock with Clayton, but certainly Clayton was the kind of man of whom Jock would have approved. The couple had their differences to work out—that he had to move to Southfork, for example—and their personal trials to overcome—Ellie's fear

31

One of Miss Ellie's most prized photographs—five minutes of peace for the sake of the camera: Donna, Ellie, Lucy, Pamela, Sue Ellen (center), Ray, Cliff Barnes, J.R., and Bobby.

Sue Ellen checking in with an exercising Miss Ellie before driving into town. The two women are extraordinarily close. Ellie has always admired Sue Ellen for something no one else is capable of—loving J.R. They have worked side by side in volunteer efforts, and when Miss Ellie is away, Sue Ellen assumes her role as mistress of Southfork.

Following the death of Jock in 1981, while Miss Ellie's first grandson, John Ross, was living with Sue Ellen in Dallas, Pam and Bobby's adopted son, Christopher, proved to be a godsend. Understanding Miss Ellie's need, Pamela generously included her in all aspects of her baby's life.

that Clayton would be turned off by her mastectomy—but they got through all of it, strengthening their bond, becoming solid and real.

Their path to marriage seemed clear. Then, in a ghastly incident just before their wedding in 1984, Ellie was nearly killed by Clayton's sister, Lady Jessica Montford. It was quite a shock that such a gentle man could have a psychotic killer for a sister. The quick reflexes of Clayton, along with J.R. and Bobby, saved Ellie, and it was Ellie and Clayton's love that saved their wedding the very next day at Southfork.

The wedding was a beautiful affair, a dignified ceremony marking the beginning of a new chapter for both. Miss Ellie was given away by her sons J.R. and Bobby; and Sue Ellen Ewing, her daughter-in-law, of whom she is extremely fond, served as matron of honor. Ellie and Clayton took a long, romantic honeymoon cruise among the Greek Isles.

To the outside observer, Southfork Ranch is a tranquil place. That is how Enoch Southworth foresaw it in the 1860s, and that is how Aaron tried to maintain it. But the union of Southworth and Ewing blood has created a family of inordinate will, power, and high passion, and no one but the possessor of the most fierce clan loyalty and unflagging love of family and tradition could possibly manage it. And Miss Ellie not only manages it, but also commands it. For more than their love for her, the family has an overriding, non-negotiable respect for this woman. When Rosalyn Carter was nicknamed the "Iron Magnolia," the family shared discreet looks and chuckles at the dinner table in Miss Ellie's direction. She was mildly amused, but really rather disinterested, for she knows better than anyone else that the name Miss Ellie needs no further amplification.

33

Miss Ellie with Sue Ellen,
J.R., Bobby, and Pam at the
Oil Baron's Ball, 1982. It
was her first public
appearance since Jock's
death in 1981.

Miss Ellie rereading War and Peace—*a suitable book, considering the emotional climate at Southfork. Though she was an avid reader before her marriage, it wasn't until after Jock was gone that she really had much time for it again.*

Clayton Farlow, Miss Ellie, and Rebecca Wentworth at the Ewing Barbecue, 1982. Clayton was dating Rebecca at this time and Ellie, though she liked Clayton enormously, was a little nervous about his friendly behavior toward her. She needn't have worried; Clayton was in love with Sue Ellen. It would be at Sue Ellen and J.R.'s remarriage in November of this year that Ellie and Clayton would look at each other with mutual attraction.

Clayton Farlow

"The Farlows have a lot of power down there. Nobody wants to go up against them. And they run San Remo, just like the Ewings do Braddock."

—Harry McSween, 1981

I t's haunting at times, watching Clayton's figure riding across a stretch of Southfork land, how like Jock Ewing he is. He's well over six feet, has a full head of silver hair, and has the same kind of manly good looks and purposeful stride as Jock. And, too, he made a fortune in oil and ended up as a full-time rancher. But Clayton Farlow is different from Jock in one major way. He never overtly made a quest for money and power. He simply attracted it and then handled the responsibilities that went along with it. Clayton is a man of deep, underlying faith, a man who is quick to realize what he can control and what he cannot. He has an attitude of acceptance of whatever comes his way, good and bad, and a sense that whatever will be will be, without his getting all fired up about it. This sixth sense has been his saving grace in the Ewing household and, in many ways, the key to his survival all his life.

Clayton Farlow was the heir to the magnificent ten-thousand-acre (small, only by Southfork standards) Southern Cross Ranch in San Remo, on the outskirts of San Angelo in central Texas. The community there is known to this day as the wool center for the Southwest, and, in addition to sheep, the region boasts of fine cattle and goats. Clayton grew up adoring ranching. His younger sister, Jessica, grew up adoring him.

As a young man, Clayton took his responsibilities seriously, took ranching seriously, and, after his father passed away, was forced to take Jessica, now his charge, seriously as well. She was more than a handful, all right, just screaming for attention from any man who'd look her way—and there was plenty, as Jessica was quite pretty. When Clayton wasn't out roping a stray calf, he was searching the countryside to find Jessica and pull her out of some scandalous affair.

When he fell in love and married his first wife, Amy, in 1939, Jessica flew into a jealous rage. She had been vastly unstable all of her life and now threw all caution to the winds for the benefit of the newlyweds. A short time later, Clayton and Amy were not surprised when Jessica told them that she was pregnant and wasn't sure who the father was. Amy—who had recently learned that she could not bear children of her own—suggested that they take Jessica away from scandal to England for her confinement, and then come up with a plausible story to bring Jessica and the baby honorably back home to the Southern Cross. Jessica and Clayton agreed to the plan, and Jessica bore a son during an air raid in World War II London.

37

SOUTHERN CROSS RANCH

The beautiful ten-thousand-acre Southern Cross Ranch, located outside of San Angelo. Although Clayton loved it, he made a clean break with the past by selling it in 1983 and moving to Dallas.

Immediately following the birth, young Jessica lapsed into a severe depression and the doctors, fearing a suicide attempt, advised Clayton and Amy that she needed extensive, round-the-clock supervision and therapy. On their recommendation, the worried couple placed Jessica in a rest home out in the English countryside and took the small baby boy back home to the Southern Cross. When they were told that Jessica's mental health had further deteriorated and that she was incapable of caring for herself, much less a baby, Clayton and Amy told the world that the boy was their son. Steven— later nicknamed Dusty when he learned to ride—was brought up as their own flesh-and-blood son and was never told his true parentage.

Things went along fairly smoothly for the Farlows until the early 1950s, when Amy's health started to fail, and so did the Southern Cross. Amy was soon confined to bed as an invalid. As a result of Clayton's worry being focused on Amy and a series of problems with the livestock and the weather, the Southern Cross started drifting toward bankruptcy. In the recent past Clayton had used money from mortgaging the ranch to invest in the opening of oil refineries—Texas was in desperate need of them—but the return on the venture was still a few years away.

In early 1954, Jessica was well enough to be released from the home in England, and she returned to the Southern Cross to help her brother look after Amy, who was growing weaker every day. Clayton was nervous about Jessica's reappearance, though her being with Amy while he tried to get his refineries on their feet made him gratefully accept her presence.

While Clayton was out of town on business that year, a monstrous fire broke out in the main house at the ranch. Jessica managed to save Dusty, but Amy perished in the fire. Clayton was nearly strangled with grief and unable even to look at the ruins of the once magnificent house. He ordered the lot to be completely bulldozed and planted over, and built the new house at another site. Jessica returned to England, where she met Lord Henry Montford, and married. Clayton, while he cared about his sister, was relieved that she had made no move to take Dusty away from him.

Amy had left Clayton a fortune—money that he wouldn't touch when she was alive. Now, horribly depressed, he used it to get the Southern Cross out of hock and bail out his refineries. What energy he had, what love he had left, he gave to his son Dusty. And so, while the refineries grew to an

empire and Dusty into a rodeo star, Clayton grew older alone. He had loved Amy completely, and he would not be interested in any other romantic relationship for twenty-seven years.

In 1981, Sue Ellen Ewing left her husband, J.R., and brought John Ross Ewing III with her to be with Dusty at the Southern Cross. She and Dusty were in love. It was to be a chaotic period, fraught with emotional turmoil for everyone concerned. Dusty was slowly recovering from his waist-down paralysis—caused by a plane crash in 1980—and was struggling with his inability to have sex with Sue Ellen. Meanwhile, J.R. was doing his best to get through the Southern Cross fortress and get his son. Clayton stood firmly in the middle of all this, protecting Sue Ellen on Dusty's behalf. The more J.R. tried to battle his way in, the more Clayton calmly flexed the Farlow muscles and fended him off.

At that time, Clayton's refineries were making millions, refining crude for Aroco, Bell, Carson, Davis, and Fowler oil companies. Suddenly, all shipments stopped and, tracking down the reason, Clayton came face to face with J.R., who had used every cent of money behind Ewing Oil to stockpile the five million barrels in question. J.R. would release the oil on one condition: Clayton must throw Sue Ellen off the Southern Cross. Although Clayton's business position was critical—without oil to refine, he couldn't keep his employees much longer, not even at one third their former wages—Clayton knew J.R. couldn't sit on that much oil for long, not in the middle of a glut that was pushing the price of crude down, down, down every day. So Clayton told him, flatly, no. Sue Ellen could stay at the Southern Cross as long as she wanted.

In the end, Sue Ellen left on her own volition when she and Dusty separated, and Ellie Ewing herself stepped in on behalf of Ewing Oil and sold the oil they were holding back to Clayton. So, everything was fine. Or so it

Clayton accompanies Bobby Ewing up to the main house at the Southern Cross, 1981. Bobby was the first Ewing to fly in on the Southfork helicopter; he was a nice man and Clayton liked him a great deal. But later, when J.R. arrived—well, that's another story.

Clayton, Sue Ellen Ewing, and John Ross Ewing III having a good time in the living room of the Southern Cross main house, 1981. Sue Ellen was living there to be with Clayton's son Dusty, but Clayton found himself falling in love with her. She was the first woman in his life since his wife's tragic death over twenty-seven years before.

Clayton with Ellie Ewing on the back terrace of the Southern Cross, 1981. They had just closed the deal for Ewing Oil to resell five million barrels of crude oil back to the Farlow refineries. Clayton was quite taken by Ellie's grace, beauty, and charm, but quickly reminded himself that she was a married woman. It wouldn't be until November of 1982 that they would be drawn together.

seemed. For while all of this was happening, not even completely aware of it himself, Clayton had fallen in love with young Sue Ellen Ewing.

Clayton started making frequent trips to Dallas on his plane. He advised Sue Ellen on how to handle her financial affairs after her divorce settlement—wisely, for she became a wealthy woman in her own right—and was there for her on any problem. But, Lord, it was painful at times. Over the course of the next year he had to stand by and watch as Sue Ellen got involved with Cliff Barnes, and then, of all people in the world, with her ex-husband, J.R. Clayton was seeing someone "suitable" at this time—Rebecca Wentworth— but he pined for Sue Ellen. At one point, in 1982, Clayton went away to think things over. When he returned, he was prepared to ask her to marry him. He took Sue Ellen to lunch at the famous Chez Martine restaurant, and then Sue Ellen told him that she was seeing J.R. again.

Though Clayton was crushed, he kept silent, just telling Sue Ellen that if she ever needed him, he'd be close by. Later on, his heart nearly broke when she asked him to give her away at her remarriage to J.R., but Clayton stoically accepted the honor. And it was fortuitous that he did, for at the wedding someone else caught his eye in a big way, someone he had been taken by earlier but who had been married at the time—the lovely widow Ewing.

When Ellie sought legal help to break Jock's will, Clayton came to her and, in the course of the ensuing battle within the family, saw a side of Sue Ellen he didn't like, much less love. That man, J.R., did something to Sue Ellen to bring out the very worst in her, and Clayton was repulsed by it. On the other hand, the fight showed him something he certainly did like—the beauty, gentle laughter, and vitality of Miss Ellie.

Clayton fell out of love with Sue Ellen, and when she tried to use her friendship with Clayton to force him to help J.R. in business, that clinched

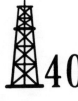

A jubilant Clayton and a distressed Sue Ellen watch Dusty ride in a rodeo, 1981. Dusty was still impotent after his physical recovery from his paralysis and he left Sue Ellen for the rodeo life. She moved back to Dallas, where Clayton often flew in to take care of her. By 1982 he was hopelessly in love with her and was prepared to propose marriage; he never got the chance.

Rebecca Wentworth dancing with Clayton at the Ewing Barbecue, 1982. Although in love with Sue Ellen, Clayton took to squiring Rebecca; she was, after all, more suitable. While he was quite fond of Rebecca, he had no interest in her beyond friendship—a fact that she did not particularly relish.

it. So when Clayton was on business in Galveston and he ran into Miss Ellie there, he spent time with her as a free man. Their friendship blossomed, edging toward intimacy, but Clayton didn't press Ellie, just went along at the pace she was comfortable with.

In the ensuing weeks, he spent more and more time in Dallas with Ellie and found himself increasingly involved with the Ewing boys—particularly J.R.—in an attempt to keep them from upsetting Ellie with all their shenanigans at Ewing Oil. In 1983, since Dusty was not in the least interested in having the Southern Cross, Clayton decided to put the past to rest by selling the ranch and moving to Dallas. Miss Ellie was surprised and delighted. She helped him look for a place, and the ensuing days around town together were enough to start their love in earnest.

Their courtship was not without problems. When Sue Ellen went on a drinking binge in 1983, Miss Ellie showed up at Clayton's hotel while Sue Ellen, half-dressed and in a blackout, was trying to seduce Clayton, reminding him how much he loved her. Clayton explained to Ellie that while, yes, he once had been in love with Sue Ellen, he now loved only Ellie. She believed him—finally.

And then when an internal conflict in the family was getting Miss Ellie down, dangerously down and shaky, Clayton whisked her away to Takapa Resort. The doctor who examined Ellie was worried about her nerves and her emotional health, and so what was supposed to be a short visit turned into a several-month vigil of Clayton shielding Miss Ellie from news of the family—Southfork nearly burned to the ground, Pam divorcing Bobby, Ray arrested for manslaughter—and nursing her back to health. J.R. was livid at the intervention and hassled Clayton endlessly. Shortly after Clayton and Ellie returned to Dallas, they announced their engagement.

The engagement brought on new problems. The first was the issue of Southfork. To Miss Ellie, it was simple. If Clayton wanted to marry her, then he'd have to live there; if he didn't, then they wouldn't get married. Clayton had a long talk about it with Ray Krebbs, whom he is extremely fond of, and Ray told him that if Jock Ewing could live on her ranch, then why couldn't Clayton? And, after all, it would be an enormous help to the family to have Clayton there to help run the ranch. This was all fine with Clayton, though he could do with a little less family—namely, J.R.

The couple worked through the result of Miss Ellie's mastectomy, which was difficult for her to talk about. She was terrified that he would be turned off by her physically, and Clayton at first wondered if that wasn't so. But that proved not to be a problem at all, for Ellie was the first woman since Amy that Clayton loved heart and soul. Moreover, regardless of the operation, he found her to be the most sensually enticing woman he had ever known. No, passion was no problem for this couple.

Then the nightmare. His sister, Jessica. It was a horrifying chain of events, but it did turn out all right, although Clayton still carries the emotional scars. The day before the wedding, in 1984, Jessica tried to kill Ellie out of jealousy and anger. And, to Clayton's utter grief, he found out that Jessica had deliberately set the fire at the Southern Cross in 1954 in order to kill Amy. She said she had been jealous and angry that Amy had Jessica's son, and now she couldn't bear to see Ellie take Amy's place with Clayton and Dusty. Jessica was sick, all right, but not nearly as sick at heart as Clayton at this revelation. The past had been bad enough to live with as it was. Instead of retreating into shock, though, Clayton turned to Miss Ellie and she to him, and they went ahead with the wedding.

It was a moving ceremony for Clayton, reflecting his feelings of true union after all those years alone. And the family wasn't *that* bad—there was Ray, who served as best man for Clayton—though he was eager enough to leave them behind in order to romance his beautiful bride on a long, quiet cruise among the Greek Isles.

Clayton's life has come full circle, back to the place where he always wanted to be: married to the woman he loves, riding across the ranges doing the ranch work he adores, running a mighty empire of oil refineries, and, for all of its ups and downs and explosiveness, having a family to come home to at night.

Clayton Farlow used to be one of the loneliest men in Texas. Now he is certainly one of the luckiest.

J.R. grins at a concerned Clayton at the reception following J.R.'s remarriage to Sue Ellen in November 1982. It was not just because of Sue Ellen that Clayton neither liked nor trusted J.R., it was because J.R. was unscrupulous in just about every area of his life. As Miss Ellie would say to Clayton the following year, when they were engaged, "J.R. has always been difficult. There were times when his own father couldn't control him. Clayton, when you marry me you get the whole Ewing family too. They're not always easy to live with. If you want to back out, I'll understand."

Clayton's sister, Lady Jessica Montford. When she was a young girl, Jessica was an accomplished pianist and Clayton an excellent singer and so they often performed together for family and friends. That was the only untroubled memory Clayton ever had of his sister.

"J.R."

"J.R. needs his secrets. That's his power. That's what he's all about."

—Pamela Barnes Ewing, 1978

As Roy Ralston of "Talktime" said, "Some call him saint, some call him sinner," but they call him. They call from Wall Street in New York, they call from the Petroleum Club in Houston, they call from Associated Press headquarters, and they call from frontline fighting in military coups in Asia. Everyone who's anyone in the oil business calls J. R. Ewing at least once in their life, for he is a man of ineffable power. To be with him is to be a winner, to be against him is exciting—to say the very least—but to be without him completely can mean certain kinds of financial death. He is the eldest Ewing son, and while most of Dallas is continually slack-jawed that he could be the offspring of Ellie and Jock, J.R. just bares his brilliant smile, tips his ten-gallon hat, and strides on toward more oil, more money and, of course, more power.

J.R. was born in 1939 on Southfork Ranch. In the beginning, he was just like any other little baby boy, except that he needed more love and affection from his parents than he ever got. Miss Ellie remembers: "J.R. was so shy, when I took him shopping I never had to look to see where he was. He had hold of my skirt so tight. I think Jock scared him at first. But when Gary came along, Jock just took over raising him. 'Make him a man's man,' Jock said. I guess then I fussed over Gary too much, because Jock had J.R. . . . and Bobby. We all spoiled him. Bobby was given everything J.R. had to fight for and Gary didn't bother with."

J.R.'s "man's man" training included, at the age of five, going to his daddy's office at Ewing Oil and learning the business. He liked that fine. He'd watch his daddy, hang on his every word and emulate his every move, and do everything he could in order to please him, for to him, Jock was perfect —a great big god whose boots were firmly stained with oil. J.R. had no interest in the ranch or the Southfork way of life. He thrived on the exchanges in the business, the deals, the way his father's eyes lit up in delight when he got his way, when he closed a deal, when the well came in, when the oil commanded the best price of the day. And it wasn't just the figures, the finances, although J.R. proved to be an absolute wizard at them. There was also the thrill of pursuing the unspoken goal: if bigger was better, then *biggest was best.* Jock encouraged that attitude in J.R. but did nothing in the way of teaching J.R. when to stop, and so when young J.R. went overboard with enthusiastic purpose—which he often did—then Jock would come down hard on him, seemingly from out of the blue. That was the way it was. Jock expected J.R. to

45

Luther Frick holds a gun to J.R. during the great storm in the fall of 1978. J.R. had a fling with Luther's wife, Wanda, in Waco one weekend and Frick came to Southfork to get revenge.

succeed and gave him little attention until he did. And if J.R. made a mistake, then, Lord help him, Jock'd nail him.

From this relationship, J.R. learned the one word that would guide him for the rest of his life—*win.* To do this, J.R. took a shortcut in his early years. He relied on his lightning-fast reflexes, keen intellect, and beguiling charm to wheel and deal and bedazzle, and it worked. In later years, when he had gained all the practical knowledge concerning oil, he was, quite literally, unbeatable in most situations.

It was clear early on that J.R. also had a great flair for wheeling and dealing in another area—women. Since he was thirteen years old, J.R. had this almost spooky way with women of all ages. He charmed, flattered, and seduced women in no time, and if for some extraordinary reason he failed, then he just bought them in intricate ways that on the surface appeared to be something else. The ladies offered a great deal more attention than J.R. ever received at home.

As the eldest son, J.R. was expected to be a good big brother, but it wasn't easy. J.R. thought Gary was a wimp and bullied him in private every chance he got, not so much because he hated him, but because his mama gave Gary *everything.* She was always fussing over him, tending him, hugging him, taking him for rides and walks—none of which she did with J.R. And Gary did nothing to deserve it! When he wasn't having a tantrum, he was off moping somewhere. He was athletic but didn't like to play with anyone—he'd always quit and run to Mama. J.R. did take his role with little Bobby seriously, though, and honestly loved the kid. Everyone did. J.R.'s parents lavished attention on Bobby, but J.R. didn't mind so much, he was so little—ten years younger—and he was cute. And cute was no threat to J.R., because he wasn't competing in that category. However, it didn't pass his notice that *both* parents acted differently with Bobby. They were freer with him; for one, they always touched him. No one ever touched J.R. except to spank him. How was it that no one wanted to hug and kiss him like they did Bobby, and his mama did Gary? Why? He excelled at everything his daddy and mama wanted him to, but how was it that they didn't seem to care half as much about his accomplishments as they did about some diddly-squat thing that Bobby did?

From the moment J.R. had brothers, he had a lifelong fight on his hands. Not for money, not for power, but for the love and affection and ap-

46

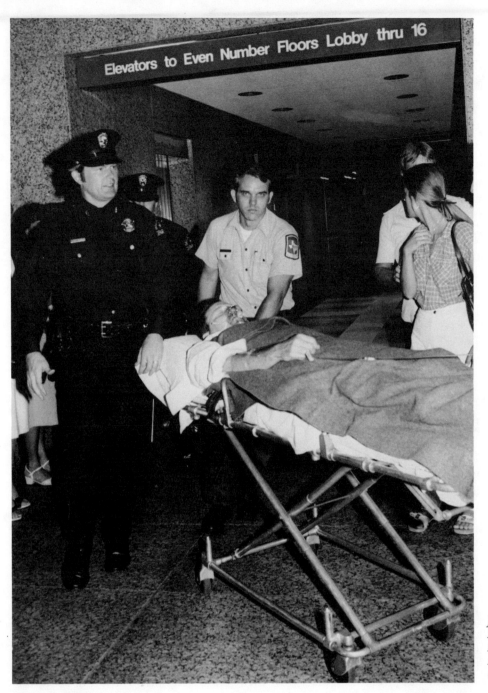

J.R. is rushed to Dallas Memorial Hospital after his near-fatal shooting in his Ewing Oil office in May of 1980.

proval of his parents. It certainly wasn't too much to expect from one's parents, yet it was the very thing J.R. couldn't bring himself to ask for outright. He thought his daddy would think him a sissy. And he thought he would probably be right.

     In 1956, J.R. enrolled at the University of Texas and went off to Austin for four years. He was an excellent student, extremely popular fraternity brother, and a party goer and thrower extraordinaire. He had an enormous capacity for women, of course, and food and drink, Texas style. His drink of choice, bourbon and branch, became the illicit rage on campus.

     After he graduated, Jock pushed him to do a stint in the Army—part of his "man's man" training—and was shipped off to South Vietnam in

Ray visits a paralyzed J.R. and exhausted Sue Ellen at Dallas Memorial. Sue Ellen, thinking she had shot her husband in a blackout, never left his side—until, that is, she was arrested for attempted murder.

1960. Although he was a good soldier and won several medals in the field, he grew sick at heart at what he saw and was told to do, so he put his wheeling and dealing to use and got himself transferred to Japan, where he finished out the rest of his hitch.

J.R. returned home, and to Ewing Oil as a Vice President. Gary was gone—and would never ever have a head for business anyway—and Bobby, at that time, was more interested in chasing skirts and cattle than being bothered with Ewing Oil, so J.R. had the field all to himself. He plunged right in with his father's blessing. Business boomed, along with the family's personal fortune, because of his efforts.

Still, there was a void in his life. He saw scads of women, and his parents wondered out loud if he had thought about marrying, settling down, producing some heirs. J.R. assured them that he was looking, and indeed he was, but like everything else, J. R. Ewing was determined to bring home the best, and, more important, and most difficult, he wanted to love and be loved. Of the hundreds of women he dated, wooed, bedded, none fit the bill. Then, in July 1963, serving as a judge at the Miss Texas Pageant in Fort Worth, out came young Miss Dallas. As J.R. later said to Sue Ellen, "When it came to the bathing suit contest all the rest of the girls were strutting and trying to look sexy. You didn't try, but you sure looked sexy and . . . something else . . . you looked like a lady." Sue Ellen Shepard won the pageant and J. R. Ewing's heart.

It was quite a lengthy romance. Sue Ellen loved J.R. and he her, but he was hesitant about marriage. After all, every girl in the state was after him. How could he be sure Sue Ellen was the one? Unlike every other girl in the state, Sue Ellen flatly refused to go to bed with J.R. unless they were married. It made her all the more desirable, and the more he desired her, the more aloof she became. Then, finally, crazy in love with her, convinced that she had to be

J.R. during his recuperation from the shooting, in the Southfork pool, 1980. During J.R.'s long road back to full health, Jock put Bobby in as head of Ewing Oil, and J.R. was beside himself at what he saw as reckless mismanagement of the company. Here, he smiles at the headline about the tanker that sank while carrying needed oil to Bobby's new refinery. J.R. was sure that this disaster would be enough to reinstate him.

the one, he asked her to marry him. They had a huge wedding at Southfork in 1971.

The marriage was a great disappointment to J.R. Oh, he loved Sue Ellen, but he had trouble in the one place he had never had before—bed. It wasn't that Sue Ellen was exactly cold, it was just that she was so restrained, so ladylike, that J.R. was practically afraid to touch her. J.R. honestly believed that Sue Ellen was a lady, a great lady, and, based on their first time in bed together, he came to believe that true ladies weren't interested in such things and shouldn't have to be sullied that way. So he left Sue Ellen pretty much alone after the honeymoon. It wasn't that he wanted to, but it seemed to be what she wanted, although they never talked about it. So rather than debase his beautiful wife, J.R. discreetly took his desires elsewhere. (He found solace with his secretary, Julie Grey, who not only met his appetite in bed, but who also was a confidante, one who generously gave him affection. She would be more a wife to J.R. than Sue Ellen would be for several years.) The other disappointment that was related to this was that Sue Ellen didn't conceive, and J.R. very much wanted to have children.

When his daddy retired in 1977, J.R. was made President of Ewing Oil. It was a wise choice, for J.R. was a man of the times and his new ideas and ventures were highly successful—so long as he had absolute power. Though J.R. had wonderful business schemes, they were so intricate, often so cloak-and-dagger, that they required a great deal of secrecy and shooting from the hip. Their success depended on J.R.'s masterminding them, without any outside interference. One naïve step could result in the undoing of months of ground-work and cost the company millions. Until 1978, J.R. had no such interference and the company was in blazing good health.

In late 1978, J.R.'s previously discreet sexual liaisons came home

49

J.R. and Sue Ellen put on smiles for the press at Bobby's victory party when he won the election for Texas State Senator, 1980. The Ewings, no matter what their problems at home, have always maintained a near-perfect image together in the public eye.

J.R. relaxing at the bar at the Ewing Barbecue, 1981. He is one of Texas's most congenial hosts and, as any red-blooded female will attest, one of the most attractive men in the world. His good looks, aura of power, and charming ways are among his most effective assets.

to Southfork to haunt him, and nearly kill him. J.R. and Ray Krebbs had gone on a weekend fling with a certain Wanda Frick and Mary Lou Allen in the Tropicana Motel in Waco. It wasn't anything special, just a jaunt to blow off a little steam after a hard week's work. But Wanda's husband and Mary Lou's brother followed the men back to Southfork and held the family hostage during the great storm that fall. The incident, on the whole, turned out all right, though J.R. was shot in the arm and the entire family became wise to some of his activities on his "business" trips. Sue Ellen reacted bitterly, and their marriage started to rock.

That year also presented problems at Ewing Oil. After Bobby married Pamela Barnes (that was enough to test J.R.'s patience—Digger's daughter!), Bobby demanded a bigger executive role in the home office. J.R. was sorely tried by Bobby's interference, and this would mark the beginning of J.R.'s efforts to get him out of Ewing Oil altogether. It wasn't that he didn't think him bright—in fact, he thought Bobby was better suited to running Southfork, which was no easy job—but that he lacked qualities needed to do business in the oil industry: a sense of divine duplicity, for example. Bobby was just too naïve, soft.

In 1979, after eight years of marriage, Sue Ellen announced that she was pregnant. J.R. was elated. His happiness was only momentary, however, for they were having horrendous problems in their marriage. Then J.R. found out that Sue Ellen was having an affair. And leave it to her to have it with the man whom J.R. hated most in all the world—Cliff Barnes. To top everything, Sue Ellen began drinking heavily, despite J.R.'s efforts to prevent her. Fearing that Sue Ellen was doing permanent damage to the unborn child with her round-the-clock drinking, J.R. was forced to place her in a sanatorium. Then, the final blow: Julie Grey was murdered. J.R. paid all of her funeral expenses and tried to put her to rest in his heart.

John Ross Ewing III was born with apparently no bad effects from Sue Ellen's drinking. That was the good news. The bad was that J.R. was informed that the baby was Cliff Barnes's. J.R. reeled—it just couldn't be. Sophisticated paternity tests were taken and J.R., to his utter joy, found out that John Ross was truly his flesh and blood. J.R. could not be with his son enough after that. He loved him, held him, talked with him, and touched him with tenderness. No matter how bad things got, J.R. would have this son to love.

On a dove-hunting trip with Jock, Bobby, and Ray Krebbs, J.R. was accidentally shot in the leg. He recovered quickly, and it was fortuitous, since the biggest deal of his life—the purchase of offshore drilling leases in Asia (see chapter III)—was occurring, and so was the collapse of his marriage. Following John Ross's birth, Sue Ellen was seriously depressed, and it worried J.R. that she was virtually ignoring the baby. Then Sue Ellen started disappearing, staying out afternoons and nights, giving no explanation but sly smiles. J.R. was beside himself. He loved Sue Ellen, but she wouldn't come near him. Tired, lonely, under enormous pressure at work, he resigned himself to the fact that Sue Ellen must be having an affair. J.R. turned to Sue Ellen's sister, Kristin, for comfort.

Then J.R. got in a whole mess of trouble with his parents, which upset him more than the actual problem. He had been forced to mortgage Southfork to finance the Asian wells, and Jock and Ellie, outraged, lashed out at J.R., with Jock stepping back in to run Ewing Oil. The fact that the wells came in, as J.R. knew they would, that the venture for a period made Ewing Oil the richest independent oil company in the world, didn't seem to count for much. J.R. was not to be trusted by his parents for quite some time. Now, everyone seemed to be out to hurt him, and Sue Ellen, who had begun drinking again, openly declared her hatred of him and her desire for a divorce.

Late one night in the spring of 1980, while working in his office at Ewing Oil, J.R. was shot twice. He nearly died. The bullets bruised a kidney and nicked his spleen and left him in the most horrible condition J.R. could imagine—paralyzed from the waist down. The situation brought one aspect of happiness however: Sue Ellen came lovingly to his side. He underwent a very dangerous operation to regain the use of his legs. As he began the long road to recovery, he was hurt to learn that his daddy had put Bobby in as President of Ewing Oil. And then came the ultimate betrayal: Sue Ellen was arrested as the prime suspect in the shooting. She hadn't come to him because she loved him; she only came because she thought she had shot him in a blackout and was feeling guilty. It turned out, though, that Sue Ellen was innocent—it was her sister who had done it—but their marriage was still in ruins. J.R. chose not to prosecute Kristin because she told him she was pregnant with his child. J.R. could not bear the thought of a child of his, or any child for that matter, being

51

born in prison. He let her go and supported her financially throughout her pregnancy in California.

After intensive therapy and sheer persistence, J.R. regained the use of his legs. He has, to this day, worked hard at exercising and is in better physical condition than ever before. Back on his feet, he was back in full action, with one major problem to take care of: Bobby refused to step down from Ewing Oil. J.R. was alarmed by what he saw as Bobby's reckless leadership, and so he persisted in striking some kind of deal to get back into the power seat before the company was run into the ground. Bobby finally resigned in 1980, after J.R. agreed to set him up in a business of his own.

The year 1981 was the worst of J.R.'s life. Sue Ellen walked out on him and J.R. managed to wrestle John Ross from her, but Pam—that Barnes girl! —stole John Ross from Southfork and took him to Sue Ellen. Then Kristin showed up in Dallas, alone. She had gotten into trouble after the birth of her baby—she was on drugs—and, after ingesting too much PCP, she fell from the second-floor landing of the main house and died. J.R. was accused of murder by Cliff Barnes, but he was cleared of any wrongdoing.

J.R. hardly cared, in comparison with the other loss he was feeling. Sue Ellen was shacking up with some cowboy in San Angelo—committing *adultery*—and she had *his* son with her. Sitting in John Ross's empty room at Southfork one night, J.R. broke down and wept. So what if Sue Ellen had fallen in love and run away with another man, so what if all was not well at Ewing Oil or with his family, what mattered to J.R., what he loved more dearly than any other thing in the world, was his little son. That child was a part of him, and to have him taken away was to tear out a piece of his heart.

J.R. watches grimly as Sue Ellen displays more than casual interest in seeing Clint Ogden, her college flame, at Lucy's wedding reception in 1980. In the ensuing weeks, J.R. was nearly mad with jealousy, suspecting—with good reason—that she was having an affair with Ogden.

The cool, beautiful, devilishly bright Leslie Stewart, with whom J.R. thought he had fallen in love, 1981. Leslie was a public relations expert, but her real work at Ewing Oil was to play hard to get to J.R. Lucky for J.R., he found out her true nature.

J.R. became obsessed with getting him back. When he and Sue Ellen went to court, he was prepared to bring up her past—the drinking, the affairs—not giving a damn about the publicity, only wanting to get his son, but Miss Ellie restrained him. He tried to take John Ross off the Southern Cross Ranch by helicopter, and Miss Ellie stopped him again. J.R. tried to reason with the Farlows, get them to kick Sue Ellen off of the ranch—all to no avail. So finally, desperate, he embarked on the most risky and dangerous business venture of his life. Using Ewing Oil Company as collateral on a loan, he bought up all the oil that was being fed into Clayton Farlow's refineries. By glory, he'd *make* them give him back his son.

The plan failed, and put Ewing Oil on the brink of disaster. Miss Ellie stepped in. Backing off from her wrath, J.R. had to sit helplessly by as she sold the oil, at a loss, to Clayton Farlow. Then she lectured J.R. that she would be watching his every move and that, when the time was right, when she found someone else to run Ewing Oil, she was going to get the family to vote him right out of the company.

Sue Ellen left her cowboy at the Southern Cross and moved into a Dallas town house. Thanks to Miss Ellie, the court had awarded her custody of John Ross, a huge settlement over and above alimony and child-support payments, and gave J.R. visitation rights only on alternate weekends. The money didn't bother J.R., that's not what he wanted; he just wanted to be with his son.

When his daddy died in South America in 1981, J.R. couldn't handle the loss and went into a deadly depression. He didn't have his son living with him, he had lost his wife, and Jock . . . His daddy, the man he passionately revered, the reason why he had done everything all his life—to make him

J.R. confronting Afton Cooper at the Stardrift Lounge, 1981. She was launched into a singing career by J.R. but became disloyal to him when she fell in love with Cliff Barnes.

proud of him—was gone forever. J.R. slumped into day-long drinking and listlessly let Ewing Oil run itself. He just didn't care anymore—it was all over, finished, a journey with no destination. He cried at times and wondered what to do, where to go. He went to a prostitute, Serena, for comfort, but found that he had lost all desire for sex. J.R.'s world had come to a stop, and he felt like it was time to jump off.

J.R. protectively clutches John Ross in the front hall of Southfork, 1981. Sue Ellen tried to take him with her on her sordid affair with rodeo star Dusty Farlow and, initially, J.R. succeeded in keeping his son at Southfork. But then his sister-in-law kidnapped John Ross and took him to Sue Ellen. J.R. was put through excruciating pain over the whole ordeal. As Bobby said, "When you're inside the family you'll understand that J.R.'s a very complex character. Family is very important to him. He always put Mama and Daddy first, then it was little John Ross. They're more important than anything else in his life."

J.R. meets Dusty Farlow face to face at the Cotton Bowl, 1981. He had tried several methods to make Farlow return his son and wife, and finally resorted to common sense—he asked Farlow what Sue Ellen's chances at happiness were with an impotent man.

A deliriously happy J.R. with his new—second time round—bride just after their wedding at Southfork on November 24, 1982.

J.R. has his brother Bobby to thank for bringing him out of it. Bobby forcefully reminded him that Jock had built an empire for *them,* and it was his and J.R.'s responsibility to preserve that empire for *their* sons. J.R. realized that Bobby was right, and his heart lifted at the thought of John Ross Ewing III. If J.R. couldn't go on living for himself, then he'd do it for John Ross. He went to Jock's office at Ewing Oil late one night and, talking aloud, said:

"I let you down for a while, Daddy, I know I did. I lost my backbone down at that lake when I saw you'd never be back. I'm coming back, though, and I'm coming back strong. You built Ewing Oil from the ground for your sons. I know that, and, Daddy, I'm gonna build it stronger for mine. You're gonna be proud of me again, Daddy. I'm gonna put such a lock on the company that nobody, nobody will ever take it away, not from you and me, and not from your grandson."

J.R. wanted his son back at Southfork, that was no secret, but it was a secret that he desperately wanted Sue Ellen back, too. There had been something about their separation—something had been restored in Sue Ellen that had been lost for many years—that stirred his heart. He had forgiven her, and his original feelings for her resurfaced. After all, they had been married for ten years, and Sue Ellen was still one of the most beautiful, and desirable women in all of Texas. And her affairs and the birth of their son had brought

55

J.R. and Holly Harwood toast J.R.'s acceptance of the position of silent Chief Executive Officer at Harwood Oil, 1982.

J.R. calmly watches the proceedings at the 1982 hearing of the Texas Energy Commission, where Donna Culver Krebbs tried to get J.R.'s special drilling variance rescinded. She was not successful that day.

out a side of her that had long been hidden. Instead of being detached, cold, Sue Ellen was actually a loving, affectionate, and passionate woman.

It caused J.R. untold pain to find out that Sue Ellen was seeing Cliff Barnes again, and while everyone else said that J.R. was upset only because it was Cliff, that J.R. wanted John Ross back at Southfork because of his voting shares in Ewing Oil, the truth of the matter was that J.R. only wanted his family back, and that included Sue Ellen.

In 1982, J.R. learned that Christopher, the dear little boy whom Bobby and Pam were adopting, was his child by Kristin. J.R. had loved the baby the moment he saw him, before he had even known. But then he was crestfallen. It turned out that Kristin had miscarried *his* baby and that this child was someone else's. J.R. would have loved to have had another child and, although he was happy for Bobby, he would always play with Christopher a bit wistfully.

J.R. slowly made progress with Sue Ellen. No matter what they had done to each other and themselves, there was still an undeniable bond between them. If nothing else, they were survivors, they were the parents of John Ross, and Sue Ellen was, by this time, a Ewing at heart. The spark of the years before came back and their love rekindled. J.R.'s dream of having her back as his wife seemed to be realized when she agreed to marry him again. Meanwhile, though, J.R. had quietly aided Cliff Barnes's greediness and watched as Barnes destroyed his own company career. But to J.R.'s shock, Barnes then tried to kill himself. Sue Ellen and Miss Ellie held J.R. responsible —which J.R. didn't understand, since it was obvious that Barnes's own greed and stupidity had been his undoing, with little help from him—and Sue Ellen put off their pending marriage while an angry Miss Ellie led the family in voting J.R. out of Ewing Oil.

Not to be left out in the cold for long, J.R. became the silent Chief Executive Officer of Harwood Oil, for a 25 percent interest in the company. The position had been offered by Holly Harwood, the beautiful young thing who had just inherited the company from her father, Al, and didn't know how to run it. So, J.R. had something to do until his father's will was read and he was reinstated at Ewing Oil to run half of the company in the yearlong contest with Bobby. Despite that workload, J.R. continued to run Harwood Oil until well into 1983.

On November 24, 1982, J. R. Ewing's dream came true and he and Sue Ellen were remarried at Southfork. This time, he pledged not only his love and devotion to her, but monogamy as well. And he meant it. He resisted the advances of Marilee Stone, whom he had tangled with before, and the pesky Holly Harwood, who was hell-bent on seducing him. But J.R. was completely in love with Sue Ellen, and how Sue Ellen loved him back! It was a wonderful period for J.R., being reunited with Sue Ellen and his son, and not having to fight his brother in the Ewing Oil contest alone. Sue Ellen was right there by his side every step of the way, and right there beside him in bed every breath of the night. He was deliriously happy.

Later that year, when J.R. went into the cheap gasoline business and received 1,431 letters from people who had seen him on "Talktime," the local television talk show, saying they'd vote for him if he ran for a political office, it gave J.R. food for thought. Politics had always caught his fancy. However, being an oilman through and through, J.R. declined when a grass-roots organization tried to talk him into running for Dave Culver's U.S. Senate seat.

As the contest with Bobby grew more complicated, one side and then the other vying for the lead in profits, J.R. remained confident. But Miss

57

An icy Sue Ellen with John Ross and J.R. in the lobby of the Quorum Hotel following the near-fatal fire at Southfork, 1983. After she finally stopped drinking, Sue Ellen refused to be anything but an appearances-only wife to J.R. It caused him enormous heartache.

Ellie could not stand to see the personal repercussions of what was happening between her two sons. She took Jock's will to court to contest it, break it, and the scene in the courtroom did not bring out the best in anyone, including J.R., who was outraged at Pamela's interference in the matter.

J.R.: That make you feel good, Bobby? Your wife over there, comforting the opposition?

SUE ELLEN: Opposition? J.R., that's your mother.

In 1983, while on a fact-finding trip to Cuba, J.R. was thrown into prison, but he soon emerged, unscathed, and with a consummated deal for an enormous oil sale. He made piles of money for Ewing Oil and pulled ahead in the contest. In the process, he alienated Holly Harwood, who began gunning for revenge. Holly set J.R. up, not realizing the tragic consequences of her actions. It took weeks to plan, but she finally succeeded in getting J.R. drunk and in bed. She timed it perfectly so that Sue Ellen would arrive and see them.

The incident was to cause a rift in their marriage that has yet to be fully repaired. J.R. tried to explain. He told Sue Ellen how much he loved her and pleaded with her to forgive him. Instead, Sue Ellen elected to start drinking. J.R. helplessly watched her self-destruction, so horribly reminiscent of her alcoholic rampage of years before, and it broke his heart to see little John Ross not understand what was the matter with his mother. J.R. did his best to shield John Ross and stop Sue Ellen, but to no avail.

J.R.'s half brother, Ray Krebbs, accidentally set fire to Southfork. J.R. was knocked unconscious and almost died, but he came to in time to grab John Ross and leap off the second-floor landing to safety in the pool, while Bobby pulled an unconscious Sue Ellen to safety. It was a narrow escape for J.R.'s little family, and it made J.R. redouble his efforts to patch things up with Sue Ellen. But she would have no part of it and demanded a separate bedroom.

J.R. and Sue Ellen bringing John Ross to Windsor Meadows Camp, 1983.

At that time, after the fire, J.R. noticed that little John Ross was quiet, withdrawn. J.R. and Sue Ellen sent him to a camp where he could get special counseling. J.R. felt terrible; he knew his relationship with Sue Ellen had been partially responsible for John Ross's condition. There was just so much damage in general in the family of late; J.R. had had his fill of all the unhappiness and got Bobby to agree to call off the contest and split the control of Ewing Oil between them. They did, and at least that front quieted down.

John Ross was enthralled by a young counselor, Peter Richards. J.R. grew jealous of the young college man's close relationship with his son, but he refrained from interfering, hoping that John Ross would come back to him in the same loving, admiring way as before. Then J.R. noticed something else. At first he thought he imagined it, but then he really thought he saw it: Sue Ellen was attracted to this counselor, this *boy.* He grew more suspicious when Sue Ellen refused to let J.R. so much as touch her.

Things were not going well at Southfork. In fact, the whole family seemed to be coming apart. When Bobby brought up the subject of the 1983 Oil Baron's Ball, J.R. threw up his hands at the dinner table, saying, "Wonderful, the Oil Baron's Ball. Ray's gonna be in prison, Mama's off somewhere with Clayton Farlow, you and Pam divorced . . ." And, too, he was thinking what a mess his own marriage was.

The night of the ball, however, Sue Ellen surprised and then elated J.R. by inviting him to bed. Afterward, though, when J.R. tried to hold her in his arms, happy that she had forgiven him, Sue Ellen haughtily said no, she had just felt like using him. J.R. was hurt, and his hurt turned to anger.

Later, in 1984, after Sue Ellen was hit by a car, J.R. found out that she had miscarried. He was terribly upset. First of all, he hadn't known that she was pregnant—it had to have been from the night of the ball—but to lose

59

J.R. is indeed a man of the world, but even he was shocked when he found out that Sue Ellen was carrying on an affair with the young Richards boy, John Ross's counselor.

the child . . . He wanted another so much. He also loved Sue Ellen still, but when he tried to comfort her, she was still cold to him, distant.

One afternoon, J.R. happened to overhear Sue Ellen and Peter Richards talking at Southfork. He felt as though someone had plunged a knife in his heart. They were talking about their affair and that Peter could have been the father of the lost child. It hurt J.R. in every vulnerable place. The betrayal was complete. Sue Ellen had rejected J.R. and his love to tramp around with a *boy*. It was a cruel return on the love and trust he had invested in her. And it was, in his mind, unforgivable. If Sue Ellen was going to act like a prostitute, then, hell, he figured she might as well be treated like one.

J.R. framed Peter for possession of drugs and then told Sue Ellen if she didn't move back into his bedroom, he would see that Peter went to prison. Sue Ellen chose to comply, which hurt J.R. even more. Peter left the area, and although J.R. was relieved about that, he was miserable about his relationship with Sue Ellen. He didn't want to take advantage of her, he didn't want to use her, he wanted her to love him like he loved her.

What J.R. didn't know was that Sue Ellen did love him. It only took family misfortune to bring it out. After Bobby was shot at Ewing Oil and J.R. was nearly overwrought with concern for Bobby and finding the killer, Sue Ellen's coldness slowly began to melt. Hoping against hope that the occasional look in her eyes was a glimmer of love and concern, J.R. tentatively tried sharing his worries with her. Slowly, with time, Sue Ellen started to grow closer. And then, at last, there she was, holding her arms out to him.

Their reconciliation was joyous, but short-lived. The minute Jamie Ewing—the daughter of Jock's dead brother, Jason—appeared in late 1984, J.R.

Sue Ellen and J.R. sharing a quiet, tender good morning at Southfork. Truth is, despite their rather turbulent marriages, theirs is one of the greatest love stories ever told.

smelled trouble. He was right. In no time Jamie had manipulated Sue Ellen into friendship and turned her against J.R., and, on top of that, slapped a lawsuit against the Ewings for a third of Ewing Oil. Although J.R. was deeply distressed by Sue Ellen's rejection and outraged by his cousin's actions, he remained calm, reminding himself, "As Daddy used to say, the opera ain't over till the fat lady sings."

The name J. R. Ewing can be heard in any given circle of Dallas at any given moment. Often the discussion is bitter, laced with accusations of ruthlessness in his quest for power, but let it be said that Dallas has been warned. The fact is, J.R. never attacks unless provoked. You can call him any name in the book, and he won't bat an eye, but if you make the slightest move that threatens the well-being of the things closest to his heart—his son, his parents, Ewing Oil, or his wife—then he will quickly take care of you in a way you'll never forget. It is best to let J.R. be that for which he was destined: the most powerful independent oilman in Texas and the indisputable patriarch of the Ewing clan.

61

Sue Ellen Shepard Ewing

"Fight? Sue Ellen doesn't fight. She takes it all inside. That's why she's the one who always gets hurt."

—Bobby Ewing, 1983

She is the most poised of the great Texas beauties. She's Sue Ellen Ewing, J.R.'s wife, John Ross's mother, the President of Daughters of the Alamo, the chairperson of the fund-raising committee for the underprivileged, and a founder of the Dallas Home for Wayward Boys. But she's also an alcoholic and an adulteress, and an excellent actress because of it. It's hard to imagine her any other way than what she projects at a luncheon at Gardens Restaurant or at an exclusive showing at Madam Claude's—a lady, a gracious Southern belle, a savvy, sophisticated woman of extraordinary hospitality— but when Sue Ellen falls off her stage, she falls hard. Whether the real woman is the one in public or the one in private, no one can be sure, but there is one sure thing: all the world can love Sue Ellen, except Sue Ellen herself.

Sue Ellen Shepard was born and raised in Dallas. Her father was an alcoholic, and soon after Sue Ellen's sister, Kristin, was born, he deserted the family. A short time later, he died. Her mother, Patricia, with a modest income of her own, never remarried but chose, instead, to concentrate on her lovely daughters. As Sue Ellen recalls, "Mama wanted her girls to have everything she wanted and couldn't get by herself. We were like dolls, created just to fulfill Mama's wishes. Mama wanted wealth, position. She decided to get it through us. It wasn't in Mama's plan to fail." Sue Ellen was reared to be the best, to marry the best, and, growing up as a born people-pleaser, she did exactly as she was told.

She was a straight A student in high school, with particular talents in French and cooking—a combination which her mother readily approved of. She developed an awesome set of social graces, which, though gratifying to her mother, made Sue Ellen a little scared inside. Oh, yes, she enjoyed being well liked—and perhaps worshiped a little—but the Sue Ellen she was projecting was not necessarily the Sue Ellen she felt inside. People thought her extraverted, when, in fact, she was quite shy. She felt uncomfortable meeting new people but found herself mechanically offering a radiant smile and what she hoped was an agreeable persona. It was an act, and she knew it, but that was the way life was. Everyone pretended that way, right? Her job was to please her mother and others, and, in exchange, she would grow up and be happy. And so, as insurance for the future, Sue Ellen banked on being perfect.

When she entered the University of Texas at Austin, she was quickly launched as the reigning queen of the campus—unheard of for a freshman. She was undeniably the most gracious, beautiful creature to appear on the social scene for some time. She was invited to join _all_ of the sororities and she moved into one her freshman year, where she had two roommates—which

63

she liked, since she had never been away from her mother and sister before. Sue Ellen made varsity cheerleading and had her choice of virtually any man on campus, but it was Clint Ogden with whom she fell in love, and he didn't fit into any of her carefully laid plans.

Clint was a poor student—their dates usually consisted of picnics with peanut butter and jelly sandwiches—and Sue Ellen did the unthinkable: she found herself wanting to physically consummate their love. Clint cut basketball practice and Sue Ellen cut cheerleading and the two checked into a four-dollar-a-night motel with a bright neon sign, and the deed was done. Sue Ellen was elated with this side of life and felt no guilt, as she loved Clint and wondered how to manage to marry him (her mother would have a stroke!). But it was not meant to be . . .

At her mother's urging, Sue Ellen went for the highest honor for a young woman in Texas: to be Miss Texas and represent the Lone Star State at the Miss America Pageant. She won the local competition in Dallas hands down and went on to grace the stage in Fort Worth at the Miss Texas Pageant in July 1963. The lights were bright on stage, but Sue Ellen could see that there at the judge's table sat the infamous J. R. Ewing, heir to the throne of Ewing Oil. She was attracted to him instantly, as he was to her. They formally met after the pageant, after Sue Ellen was crowned Miss Texas.

Sue Ellen had many suitors other than Clint, men with a lot of money, so that wasn't what overwhelmed her about this man. It was his eyes. "They always seemed to be hiding secrets," she said later. And when he spoke, his powerful voice and hearty self-assurance sent splendid shivers down her spine. Their first date was to dinner at Donahue's (Sue Ellen politely ordered a spinach salad but couldn't eat, she was so nervous), followed by the best seats at the Dallas Symphony. J.R. was bored by classical music—he stared at Sue Ellen the entire performance—but Sue Ellen was enthralled by the music and

Below, left:
Luther Frick holding a gun to Sue Ellen's head at Southfork, 1978. The hostage incident brought J.R.'s infidelities to the attention of the entire family. It was a horrible ordeal for Sue Ellen, as Frick forced her at gunpoint to parade in her Miss Texas swimsuit and threatened to rape her.

Below, right:
Sue Ellen packing her bag as J.R. looks on, 1979. Sue Ellen tried to leave him, and J.R.'s view of her took a nasty turn: "Don't flatter yourself. You're just another Ewing possession. Like an oil lease in the Midlands, easily disposable."

by this man beside her. With her stunning beauty and his dashing good looks, they made an incredible couple, turning heads everywhere they went in Dallas.

Poor Clint got lost in the shuffle. Sue Ellen had met her man. She loved J.R., and, he was rich, powerful, and distinguished. He would satisfy both her *and* her mother's needs. Only, how to catch him? Sue Ellen played it exactly the way her mother had always told her—hard to get, and under no circumstances should she go to bed with him until they were married. It was not easy to maintain her ladylike reserve with J.R.—his animal magnetism made her dizzy with desire at times—but he respected her wishes. Eventually the strategy worked and J.R. asked her to marry him. Sue Ellen gleefully accepted, but was terrified when J.R. brought her to Southfork to meet his parents, the legendary Jock and Ellie Ewing. She knew how devoted J.R. was to them and was sure they'd never like her. To her nervous surprise, Ellie liked her right off, and J.R.'s daddy soon did too. Oddly enough, it was Sue Ellen's mother who was not so keen on the marriage. She wanted Sue Ellen to marry Billy Frampton, heir to an empire in oil *and* coal *and* diamonds *and* uranium. But Sue Ellen, exasperated, had it out with her, and Mrs. Shepard finally settled for J.R. as a son-in-law.

65

In a blackout, following the 1979 Barbecue, Sue Ellen rides around the stables without bothering to change her clothes. Her alcoholism baffled the Ewings. As Miss Ellie once said, "It's just such a shock. Sue Ellen was always so poised, so proper, she's the last person I thought this kind of thing would happen to."

The Southfork wedding was one of the biggest and most expensive in Dallas to date. White orchids, flown in from Hawaii, cascaded over the ranch, and hundreds of guests attended. Sue Ellen was positively glowing, and J.R. was at his most handsome—such a happy, prosperous couple, with their whole lives ahead of them.

The couple went off on their honeymoon, and Sue Ellen was in for a baffling disappointment. Sex with J.R. was nothing like it had been with Clint. There just wasn't anything romantic or passionate about it. She blamed herself, thinking that she didn't turn J.R. on, for he never lingered, never ventured beyond just doing the act and getting it over with. She loved her husband and felt ashamed for expecting anything more. So she said nothing, and wondered if it would change in time. It was clear, however, that it would not be up to her to change anything. J.R. took on a pained expression if Sue Ellen made even the slightest sexual overture.

The following seven years at Southfork were ones of slow letdown for Sue Ellen. She was increasingly sad, year after year, when she didn't conceive. She had herself checked out and the doctors said, no, there was nothing wrong with her, but she dismissed the obvious conclusion, as she could never, even broach the subject to J.R. Instead, she channeled her energies into volunteer work. Sue Ellen adored Miss Ellie, and together they made an awesome team, civicly and socially. After Jock retired and Ellie wished to spend a little more time at Southfork, Sue Ellen began to emerge as the new social matriarch of Dallas. As she once said, "There was a time I used to live for those meetings. They were all that gave meaning to my life."

Despite her efforts to keep active, Sue Ellen became increasingly afraid—afraid that this was all there was ever going to be for her. Oh, yes, it was nice to be Mrs. J. R. Ewing and have millions of dollars and dominating social clout. Yes, it was nice to be beautiful and smart and active. And, yes, it was nice to live at Southfork. But then, so what? What did it all add up to? It was agonizingly apparent to her that J.R. did not love her anymore, although

Sue Ellen was in love with Cliff Barnes and desperate to leave J.R. for him. Her drinking was excuse enough for J.R. to have her committed to the Fletcher Sanatorium in Fort Worth in 1979. She was seven months pregnant.

Lucy greets Sue Ellen on her arrival home from the hospital, 1979. Sue Ellen had produced a son, but she was so chronically depressed, so terribly unhappy to be trapped with J.R., that she was barely conscious of anything around her.

she was still very much in love with him, that J.R. would never be sexually interested in her, and that she was destined not to have a child. And the family gatherings, where Sue Ellen and J.R. did their best acting, trying to maintain the façade of total happiness, were becoming some kind of hideous joke that the family was all in on. If Ellie and Jock asked one more time when they were going to have a child . . . And then it was worse—they stopped asking.

How desperately she wanted a child! That longing, that pain, that inadequacy, combined with this feeling of being trapped, pushed Sue Ellen toward drinking a little more at these family gatherings. There was simply no

Rodeo star Dusty Farlow, with whom Sue Ellen fell deeply in love. They started their affair in January 1980 in Suite 1701 of the Regent Hotel in Fort Worth. It ended five weeks later when Dusty allegedly died in an airplane crash midway between San Angelo and Dallas.

other way to get through the masquerade; she just didn't have her old energy. It was infinitely easier to drink a lot of wine and be physically present, smiling no less but mentally miles away, fantasizing about how life could have been . . .

Sue Ellen reluctantly accepted J.R.'s infidelities. She *had* to after they were exposed to the whole family during the Wanda Frick from Waco incident in 1978 at Southfork. But still she didn't give up hope for a child. Finally, when her sister-in-law, Pam, announced that she was pregnant in 1978, Sue Ellen considered adopting a child, but she found that it could take years. Desperate, she located an unwed mother, Rita Briggs, and paid her expenses at 6245 West Street in Dallas, planning to pay Miss Briggs a lot of money to take the baby when it was born. J.R. found out about it and, outraged, put an end to the arrangement. Crushed, Sue Ellen emotionally withdrew from the family, solemnly watching them over the rim of a glass.

And then Sue Ellen met Pam's brother, Cliff Barnes, and fell in love with his earnest, gentle ways. Or so she said. Cliff once asked her, "Well,

68

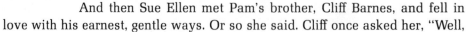

Sue Ellen during her drinking relapse following the news of Dusty's death in 1980.
J.R.: You've lost your class, Sue Ellen. Maybe that is the worst thing that's happened to you.
SUE ELLEN: No, J.R. The worst thing that's happened to me is you.

if it's not money"—he didn't have any—"what is my fatal charm?" Sue Ellen thoughtlessly replied, "Maybe it's that J.R. dislikes you so much."

Shortly after ending the affair, Sue Ellen discovered that she was pregnant. She was ecstatic, and so were the Ewings. That is, until Sue Ellen, fed up with more of J.R.'s unfaithfulness and roguery, resumed her affair with Cliff and J.R. found out about it. In the following explosion between the two, Sue Ellen told J.R. that the baby was probably Cliff's, and that she was in love with him. The couple's estrangement was complete. J.R. retaliated by destroying Cliff's career and keeping Sue Ellen virtually a prisoner at Southfork. Angry, depressed, Sue Ellen's latent alcoholism came roaring to the surface.

She drank and drank and drank and didn't care. She hated J.R., she hated that she couldn't be with Cliff, and she hated herself. The Yellow Rose of Texas was bent on killing herself, drink by drink. J.R. had her locked up

69

Sue Ellen and Kristin arrive at Dallas Memorial Hospital after J.R. was shot in May 1980. Kristin led Sue Ellen to believe that Sue Ellen had shot him during a blackout—which to her seemed more than likely. Their marriage had been absolutely a mess, with J.R. involved in a number of affairs, including one with Kristin herself. Their fights had become extraordinarily vicious, one of the latest no exception:

SUE ELLEN: Tell me, J.R., which slut are you staying with tonight?

J.R.: Does it matter? Whoever it is, she'll be more interesting than the slut I'm looking at right now.

An attentive Sue Ellen caring for J.R. during his recuperation after his shooting, poolside at Southfork, fall of 1980. He was more concerned with his getting back to Ewing Oil than he was in keeping her. As Sue Ellen said to her psychiatrist that fall:

"Dr. Ellby, maybe I'm not as crazy or maladjusted as I thought I was. Maybe what I have is the 'Ewing disease.' You only catch it if you fall in love with one of them. First they lavish you with attention, affection, and all the material possessions you could ever hope for. Then, suddenly, for no reason, they turn away from you. And you compete with the only thing they do love . . . power, and more power."

in Fletcher Sanatorium in Fort Worth for the duration of her confinement, and the experience nearly drove Sue Ellen crazy. She managed to bribe an assistant to bring her alcohol, and on a binge, following a visit from J.R., she escaped from the hospital and was in a horrible car accident that sent her into early labor. She was seven months pregnant. The crash caused bleeding in her uterus and the placenta started separating. The doctors had to perform an emergency cesarean to save both Sue Ellen and the child.

John Ross Ewing III's life hung in the balance for a few days, but with little notice from Sue Ellen. She had slumped into a massive depression and could barely even feign interest in her son, or in anything, for that matter. Zombie-like, she returned to Southfork and was kept under careful guard by J.R. The subsequent kidnapping and safe return of John Ross scarcely registered with her—she was just too depressed, despondent. Her life was a shambles and there was nothing she could do about it. J.R. tried to patch things up between them for the sake of appearances, but Sue Ellen openly hated him. When he bought her a terribly expensive maternity ring, she merely said, "I'm no longer for sale, J.R." And when he reminded her that she was *married* to him, she glared at him:

SUE ELLEN: I am not your wife, J.R. A wife is someone who shares her husband's life, who cares for him and is cared for in return. That hardly describes our relationship.

J.R.: How would you describe it, Sue Ellen?

SUE ELLEN: I would say it was sick—very sick, J.R.

Near emotional collapse, Sue Ellen started seeing a psychiatrist, Dr. Ellby, four times a week. J.R., of course, tried to blackmail him into telling him everything Sue Ellen said in her sessions, but Ellby resisted him and con-

Above, left:
Sue Ellen finds her beloved Dusty at the Southern Cross Ranch, early 1981. Dusty refused to start up their relationship again because he was crippled. Sadly, Sue Ellen went back to Dallas, but she would return.

Above, right:
Sue Ellen offers a radiant smile at the Ewing Barbecue, 1981, while holding an equally gleeful John Ross. No matter how tough life gets for Sue Ellen, John Ross never fails to lift her heart and spirit.

Sue Ellen is dragged away by a security guard as J.R. clutches John Ross in the front hall at Southfork, 1981. Sue Ellen had tried to take her son with her to the Farlows at the Southern Cross, but J.R. cut her off at the pass. However, Sue Ellen's friend and sister-in-law, Pamela, took John Ross out for "a ride" that delivered him safely into her arms.

tinued to treat her. Over the next months, he was crucial in her sorting out her feelings about her son and breaking through her depression. She came to love her son with an intensity that surprised even J.R.—particularly after they found out it was J.R.'s baby, not Cliff's.

At the Ewing Rodeo in 1979, Sue Ellen met rodeo star Dusty Farlow and, in the ensuing weeks, had a wonderfully passionate love affair with him. He fulfilled her every desire, emotionally as well as physically, and she began to plan her escape from J.R., taking John Ross with her to Dusty. She hadn't been able to leave J.R. for Cliff because Cliff was too vulnerable to J.R.'s power, but Dusty was the son of the immensely wealthy and powerful Clayton Farlow, who had enough resources to protect her. The problem was that if she divorced J.R., in light of her drinking history and this "desertion," the court would surely give custody of John Ross to J.R. And so Sue Ellen started working on building her image as the perfect mother and devoted wife, while having a private investigator compile a file on J.R.'s constant infidelities. (He was having an affair with Sue Ellen's own sister, for starters.) J.R. caught on to what was happening and mounted his counterattack. He framed Sue Ellen, making it appear that she had started drinking again, and destroyed the investigator's file on him. It appeared to all the Ewings that Sue Ellen had relapsed again, and they all clucked their sympathies to J.R. Not being able to withstand the pressure J.R. was putting on her, Sue Ellen decided that she had to leave Southfork immediately—divorce hearing or no divorce hearing. When she went to meet Dusty to confirm her plan, she was met with the news that his plane had

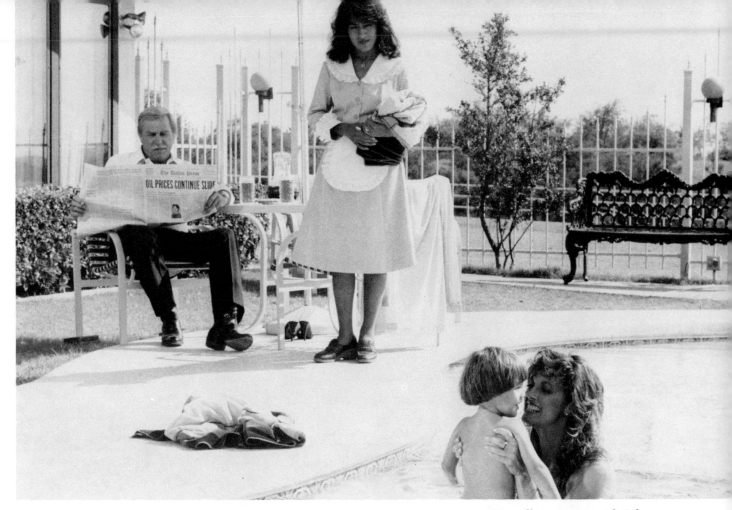

crashed en route to Dallas and he was dead. Sue Ellen was stunned. Her rising grief and despair said that her life had ended right along with Dusty's, so she picked up a drink for real and didn't stop.

One day in 1980, Sue Ellen was told by her sister, Kristin, that she had shot J.R. during a blackout. Plagued with guilt, Sue Ellen never left his side at the hospital. When the gun used in the shooting was discovered in Sue Ellen's closet at Southfork, she was accused of attempted murder and taken to jail. The Ewings refused to bail her out. Someone else did. Who, Sue Ellen didn't know.

It turned out that Kristin had shot J.R. and framed Sue Ellen, who was so beaten by the experience that she wanted only to return quietly to Southfork and be with her son. She and J.R. tried a tentative truce for a while, but when J.R. started playing around with Lucy's fiancé's sister, Afton Cooper, Sue Ellen angrily gave up on the marriage and told her husband that she would follow his style and seek her own romantic life.

At Lucy's wedding reception, Sue Ellen ran into Clint Ogden, who was still as much in love with her as ever. Sue Ellen and he resumed the passion of their college years, until she was confronted by Clint's wife, who was so much in love with Clint that she offered to share him with Sue Ellen. Sue Ellen knew the kind of pain the woman was feeling and immediately put an end to the affair.

After being followed for a number of weeks, Sue Ellen was shocked to find that her mysterious tail was Dusty. He had not died but had been crippled by the plane crash and, because he couldn't walk, didn't think he

Sue Ellen romps with John Ross in the Southern Cross pool while Clayton reads about plummeting oil prices, 1981.

73

Sue Ellen passionately kisses Dusty in the Southern Cross pool, 1981. It was a cruel blow to the lovers that Dusty was only impotent with Sue Ellen; it eventually caused their breakup.

could be a full man for Sue Ellen. He had wanted her to go on with her life, thinking him dead. He was the one who had posted her bail. Sue Ellen didn't care whether he was in a wheelchair or not—she was joyous that he was alive —and it restored her desire to be alive as well. Alive and happy! She left J.R., and dear Pam brought John Ross to her, and the two Ewings moved onto the Southern Cross Ranch with the Farlows.

In the spring of 1981, Sue Ellen's sister, Kristin, died in an accident at Southfork. It was tragic in that Kristin, addictive like Sue Ellen, had gotten herself in serious trouble with drugs. Despite Kristin's indiscretion with J.R., Sue Ellen had loved her sister very much, and she mourned such a senseless, wasteful way for the young woman to die.

There were problems with Dusty. Though he gradually learned to walk again, even ride, he was impotent, which made him feel hopelessly inadequate. Actually, all this turned out to be fortuitous. When these facts came out at the temporary custody hearing, they made Sue Ellen look like a saint and she was able to get custody of John Ross. (J.R.'s case had been built on grounds of adultery.) Sue Ellen was loving, patient, and willing to forego sex, but Dusty couldn't handle it, particularly after J.R. had hammered home the point to him that "My wife—she is still my wife—is a lady of tempestuous moods. Mostly sexual." The couple could not overcome Dusty's frustration, and they lovingly ended the relationship.

Sue Ellen moved off the Southern Cross and into her own condominium in Dallas at 56 Fayette Road. When her divorce from J.R. came through, the Honorable Jade William Parker awarded her a very generous settlement,

74

Sue Ellen nervously awaits the outcome of the custody hearing over John Ross, 1981. She won custody when J.R. tried to portray her as an adulteress and Dusty testified that he was impotent.

plus $5,000 a month in alimony and $1,000 a month in child support. She was able to live in the style she had gotten used to at Southfork, though she was pretty miserable at first. Little John Ross was a comfort, heaven knew, but it was the first time in her life that she had lived alone. She tried to fend off the interminable loneliness by reading, crocheting, and watching television at night, but she was starved for companionship. She went on one blind date and the man came back to the condo and literally attacked her. Her friends' husbands made passes at her.

Clayton Farlow was a godsend in this period. He helped Sue Ellen with her finances and occasionally acted as her escort. He was enormously kind, attentive, amusing, and warm. "Clayton is very special to me," she said. "He's the father I never knew. And, right now, he's probably the best friend I have." And she was right, though she did not realize that Clayton—Dusty's father—had fallen in love with her.

J.R. was surprisingly nice to Sue Ellen when she moved back to Dallas. It frightened her that even then, so soon after their divorce, she still felt attracted to him. She began to see him on occasion. He was sincere, courteous, extremely gentle, and positively loving, though at first she thought she must be imagining it. And there was something else, something undeniable: a sexual electricity flowing between them. Though she kept her distance, the air was fraught with it. Sue Ellen found herself, in spite of herself, falling in love all over again. But when Bobby came to see her, asking for her help in completing his and Pam's adoption of Kristin's son Christopher, all of her old wounds

75

about J.R.'s past affairs opened up. Full of anger over the past, she held herself in check against him, and started seeing Cliff Barnes.

She cared mightily about Cliff, but the old love she had once felt for him was gone—he had changed, somehow. He was in love with her and, for a while, enough so that it seemed to make up for her own feelings. Cliff kept talking about the fortune he was going to make on a deal and kept dreaming of their future together. He asked her to marry him in the spring of 1982. Sue Ellen almost accepted, but decided to think it over. Days later, Cliff was back at her house, using their relationship to get Sue Ellen to bail him out of a mess of trouble when his alleged deal fell apart. She was shocked, then livid, and then threw him out.

What to do? She loved Dusty, but he now belonged to someone else (he had married a rodeo cowgirl). She was no longer in love with Cliff, and she did not love Clayton. She was in love with J.R., but he was such a scoundrel. How long could it last? She gambled that he had changed.

Sue Ellen and J.R. were married again on November 24, 1982, at a lavish wedding at Southfork. They only had a two-day honeymoon, since J.R. was called back to business to try and buy a refinery for his half of Ewing Oil. Sue Ellen asked, and J.R. grinned his approval, that she share his work problems with him. She wanted to be a real part of J.R.'s life, which meant his life at Ewing Oil as well. She joined him in his quest to win the contest.

Every aspect of the Ewings' love—emotional, physical, even almost spiritual—was being realized for the first time. However, Sue Ellen's relationship with the rest of the family was not very good. She felt that they simply did not understand J.R. and his motives the way she did. Her friendship with Clayton was severely strained—almost finished—when she asked his help on J.R.'s behalf. She had to oppose Ellie on the attempt to break Jock's will. And her friendship with Pam and Bobby was on shaky ground because of the contest. It was very difficult for Sue Ellen. She loved all of them dearly, but her complete loyalty was to her husband.

Until Holly Harwood. When this bombshell of an oil tycoon told Sue Ellen that she was having an affair with J.R., Sue Ellen refused to believe it, dismissing it as Holly's vengeance against her husband for business reasons. But then Holly told her to look for her lipstick on J.R.'s collar one night, and it was there, and Sue Ellen began to panic. But again, she believed in her husband, and confronted Holly, telling her that the ploy had not worked. One night, knowing that J.R. was at Holly's house, Sue Ellen went over there and saw, right before her very eyes, J.R. making love to the woman. It nearly destroyed her. Not *again,* not like *this,* not when she and J.R. had been so happy. She drove directly to a bar and, after only a moment's hesitation, started pouring alcohol into her system. She wanted to die but was too afraid to. This was the only way out of her pain.

She crashed at Clayton Farlow's hotel until Miss Ellie came and took her back to Southfork. She did not stop drinking. When J.R. tried to explain about Holly, Sue Ellen threw a drink in his face, grabbed his car keys and ran out of the house. She jumped into Ewing 3 and tore out of the driveway, with the family running after her. Mickey Trotter jumped into the front seat and, as they turned out of the front gate, a car hit them head on.

Mickey went into a coma, while Sue Ellen was unhurt. With her marriage in ruins, her guilt over the car crash, Sheriff Washburn's threats to arrest her for manslaughter, Sue Ellen tearfully continued to drink. At one point, she tried to apologize to Lucy for what happened, but the young woman

76

rebuffed her, increasing her guilt. J.R. ordered all the liquor on Southfork locked up, but Sue Ellen still found cooking wine to drink. When J.R. confronted her, they had a horrendous fight, and Sue Ellen hurled the bottle at him, splashing wine all over the front staircase wall. The decorators came to redo the wallpaper the next day, and Dr. Danvers came to sedate Sue Ellen in the hope that she would sleep it off. That night, the wallpaperer's materials caught fire and Southfork was soon in blazes, with an unconscious Sue Ellen upstairs. Only the quick thinking and enormous strength of her brother-in-law Bobby saved her.

The Ewings moved into the Quorum Hotel while Southfork was being repaired. Still agonized with guilt over Mickey, Sue Ellen persisted in drinking. But when she overheard J.R. and Pam discussing Walter Driscoll, a former business associate and now mortal enemy of J.R.'s, and the fact that he had confessed to purposely running into the Mercedes at Southfork because he thought it was J.R. driving the car, Sue Ellen's drinking binge was over. She hadn't caused the accident after all. She was nearly wild with outrage that J.R. had not told her about Driscoll's confession, that he had let her go on thinking she was responsible for the accident.

Sue Ellen made three key decisions at this point. One, that she would not ever drink again, and if that were to be possible, then at all costs she

A blissfully happy Sue Ellen and J.R. on their second honeymoon, in November 1982.

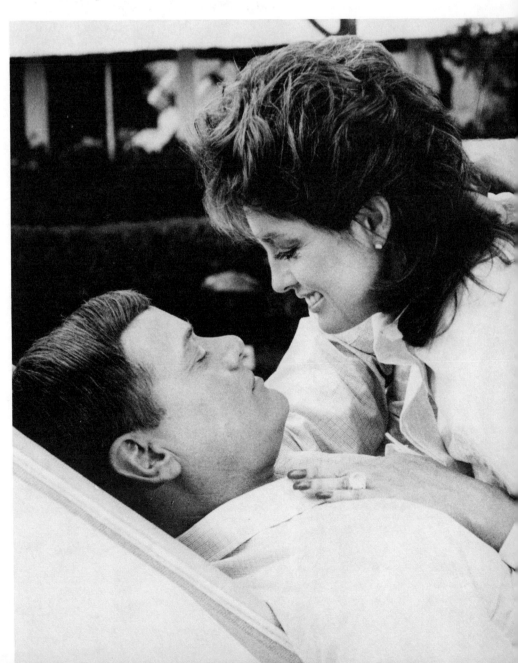

had to keep an emotional distance from J.R. Two, she would have separate bedrooms, and they would be man and wife in name only. And third, and most important, she was going to devote herself to nurturing John Ross back to the healthy, happy boy he was supposed to be. Her little boy, she realized, after all of the recent drama—the fire, the fighting, her drinking—had been left with scars. He was withdrawn, shy, slipping away from them.

Over J.R.'s protests, she took John Ross to a child psychologist. Then she talked J.R. into joining her at the next session. J.R. went along with the psychologist's recommendation that John Ross attend a special camp with counselors having strong backgrounds in psychology.

Little John Ross fell in love with his counselor at camp, Peter Richards, a twenty-year-old SMU student. And Peter Richards, a softly handsome, sweet young man, fell in love with Sue Ellen. Given her loneliness, Sue Ellen cast more than a casual eye at him, but she reprimanded herself, reminding herself of his age, his future, of the fact that she was married, and that it simply wouldn't work. With Cliff, Clint, and Dusty, there had always been the possibility of something working out. They were men. But this boy . . .

Sue Ellen is a highly sensual, passionate woman. After weeks of being sexually attracted to Peter, but not going near him, she was beside herself. One night, before the Oil Baron's Ball in 1983, she seduced J.R. and, afterward, had no desire to go near him again.

Peter was lovesick. He'd follow Sue Ellen. He'd show up at Southfork. He even played on his relationship with John Ross and Lucy Ewing

Firemen carry an unconscious Sue Ellen out of the burning Southfork, 1983. She had been heavily sedated by the family doctor, and if it hadn't been for Bobby Ewing, she would surely have died.

Sue Ellen joins John Ross's fun at Windsor Meadows Camp, 1983.

to get to see Sue Ellen. Sue Ellen was torn. She did not want to get involved with this young man, but she did not want Peter to stop working with John Ross, either. After a rejection by Sue Ellen, Peter didn't show up at camp, and little John Ross had gotten hysterical. Peter disappeared again, later, dropping out of school, and Sue Ellen frantically tracked him down. She promised to see him platonically if he promised to go back to school and continue working with John Ross. However, she didn't bargain on her own passion and feeling for him and, against her better judgment, ended up in bed with him.

It was the first and last time. She couldn't bring herself to do it again. It was just wrong, there was no future. She still had strong feelings for him, but she didn't want him to get hurt, nor did she want herself to be hurt, which would be inevitable.

In early 1984, as Sue Ellen was leaving Jenna Wade's boutique, she was hit by a car and rushed to Dallas Memorial Hospital. When she came to, the doctors informed her that she had lost her baby. *Baby?* Sue Ellen hadn't known she was pregnant, and even if she had, she still wouldn't have known who the father was—J.R. from that one night, or Peter from that one afternoon.

J.R. thought it was his. Peter thought it was his. Sue Ellen, painfully, tearfully, had to tell Peter that it could have been J.R.'s. Sadly, Peter said how much he wanted to have that baby, how he dreamed of being with Sue Ellen and bringing up their child . . . Sue Ellen was dumbstruck. Did this boy really think that it would have worked, with nearly twenty years' difference in their ages? She decided it had to end right there, right on that note. It was over, done, finished. Peter had to understand that.

To her bewilderment, J.R. then hired Peter to work privately with John Ross at Southfork. J.R. befriended the lad, encouraged him to join the

79

family in their activities, and seemed to push him on Sue Ellen. But Sue Ellen was firm in her resolve and warily watched all of this, warning Peter to be careful of J.R. and under no circumstances let him think that they had been anything other than what they now were: a counselor and the counselee's mother.

Lucy got smashed at a Ewing party and accused Sue Ellen and Peter of having something going. To Sue Ellen's amazement, J.R. defended her and reprimanded Lucy for thinking such a thing. Peter, feeling guilty, came close to telling J.R. about the affair, but Sue Ellen stopped him. It didn't matter, because it turned out that J.R. knew anyhow. And that's why J.R. proceeded to have the Braddock police sergeant, Harry McSween, plant drugs in Peter's jeep, have him arrested and thrown in jail, and then bailed him out. He told Peter that if he didn't go away, stay away from his wife, then J.R. would see to it that he would go to prison. And, he added, if Sue Ellen didn't move back into his bed, be a wife to him again, the same thing went: Peter would go to prison.

She had been beaten again. Angry, sullen, Sue Ellen resigned herself to J.R.'s demands. However, as the weeks went by and crisis hit Southfork (Bobby's shooting and subsequent blindness), the qualities she loved in J.R. resurfaced: his loyalty, his gentleness, his fierce determination to protect his family. And, most important, his emotional need of Sue Ellen in times of trouble. Once again they had a loving reconciliation—a respite for her weary heart —and once again it all went to pieces.

Jamie Ewing arrived at Southfork in the fall of 1984 and when J.R. immediately started bullying her, Sue Ellen stepped in to protect her. Jamie was so young, so lost, so vulnerable. She had no family but this one, and Sue Ellen could not help but take care of her. At first she was like a kid sister. Sue Ellen taught her how to dress, how to carry herself, and how to laugh again. In return, Jamie offered Sue Ellen her complete loyalty and love. The relationship was a sorely needed breeze in the balmy emotional air of Southfork.

When Sue Ellen overheard Jamie confronting J.R. over his infidelity in 1985, she tried to believe J.R.'s lies, but ultimately she believed Jamie because she believed so much *in* Jamie. Lord, it had been years, if ever, since Sue Ellen could believe in anyone, and in Jamie she found an integrity, an emotional purity and bond of mutual trust that made it possible. When her relationship with J.R. exploded with its usual agonizing pain, Sue Ellen didn't drink. He had expected her to, and she herself thought she would too, but she didn't, for Sue Ellen, through Jamie's support, had begun to believe in herself.

In April, however, with J.R. flaunting an affair with Mandy Winger and a medical emergency with John Ross for which J.R. cruelly blamed Sue Ellen, she broke down and drank.

Sue Ellen Ewing is a woman possessing an enormous capacity for love. By the same virtue, she is cursed with a dire need of it from others, something she has not readily received in the past. Her love and need for J.R. is only surpassed by that for her son, but whereas John Ross is so young, so dependent, his love so unconditional, J.R. is constantly fluctuating. When J.R. is down, frightened, he depends on Sue Ellen's love to survive, but when he's up, on top of the heap, he reverts to the "man's man" persona Jock taught him too well, a persona that drops a sheet of glass between him and Sue Ellen. When J.R. needs her, Sue Ellen flourishes; his love is the magic ingredient she has needed to love herself. When he detaches from her, cheats on her, she despairs, feeling all is lost. More than alcohol, J.R. may well be Sue Ellen's most dangerous addiction.

80

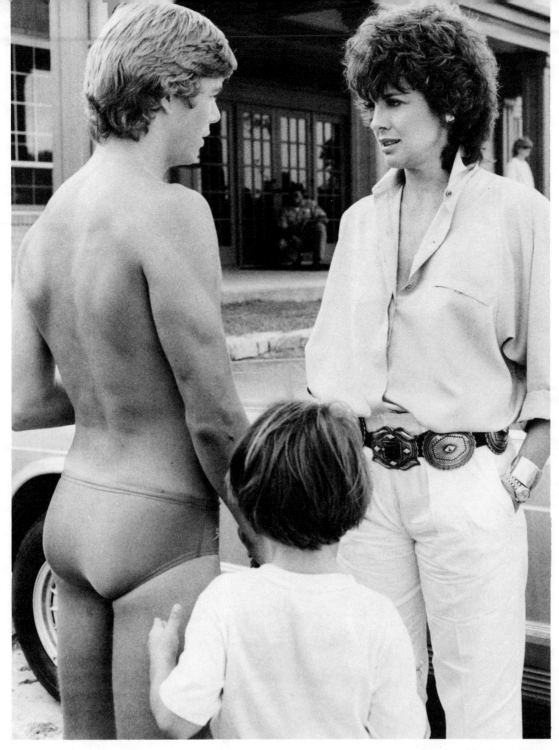

Sue Ellen checks herself against the attraction she feels for John Ross's counselor, Peter Richards, at Windsor Meadows. It was to no avail.

John Ross Ewing III

"In John Ross's few short years, he has experienced not only the burning of his home, but the breakup and divorce of his parents, a total change of life when he lived with his mother on another ranch with another family, the remarriage of his parents . . . and now a second breakup of his parents."
—Dr. Suzanne Lacey, 1983

There is nothing sedate about the short life of John Ross Ewing III, but this is by nature a loving, smart, energetic little boy with amazing emotional recuperative powers.

He is the only son of Sue Ellen and J. R. Ewing. He was born eight weeks prematurely, in the fall of 1979, his birth having been induced by a car accident that his mama was in. When he was barely three weeks old, he was kidnapped from Dallas Memorial Hospital by Priscilla Duncan, a distraught woman who had lost her own child. His Aunt Pamela found him, and John Ross was finally able to go home with his parents to Southfork Ranch. As a baby, he slept in the very same crib that his cousin Lucy had slept in.

John Ross has J.R.'s eyes and healthy appetite, but otherwise favors Sue Ellen. His family and friends call him John Ross, though his mama often calls him "sweetheart," and his daddy, "little John." His first word to the world was "Mama."

John Ross has always had people, in addition to his mother, taking care of him. When he was a baby at Southfork, he had a nurse, Mrs. Reeves, and his devoted Aunt Pamela. During the time he lived at the Southern Cross Ranch with his mama and the Farlows, he had a nanny named Maria, and when he and his mother lived in the Dallas town house on Fayette Road, he was often looked after by Mrs. Chambers, whom he loved very much. But no one, outside of the family, did John Ross love more than his counselor at Windsor Meadows Camp, Peter Richards. Peter was John Ross's idol, and he missed him dearly when he left Dallas in 1984.

In April of 1985, John Ross suffered a chronic appendicitis and underwent emergency surgery at Braddock Medical Center, from which he fully recovered.

John Ross worships his daddy and adores his mama. Both parents are extremely affectionate and playful with him. J.R. taught him how to swim, invites him each day to work out with him in the exercise room, and often takes him along to his office at Ewing Oil. Sue Ellen, who otherwise is quite proper, never hesitates to change her clothes and romp with John Ross outside at the ranch, at the pool, or with his friends. She is currently teaching him how to ride. Both parents enjoy reading with him nightly.

John Ross's future is bright with promise. In his granddaddy's will he was left a trust fund and voting shares in Ewing Oil. And one day little John Ross won't be little anymore and will take his rightful place in the Ewing empire.

83

John Ross's parents, J.R. and Sue Ellen Ewing, the most famous couple in all of Texas.

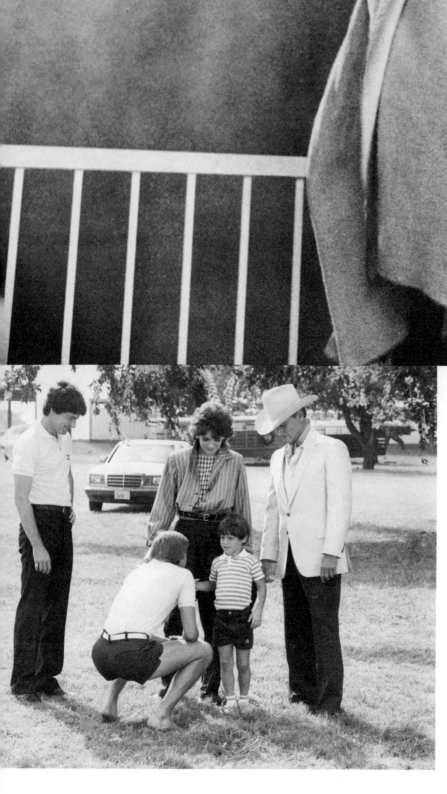

John Ross's half uncle, Ray Krebbs, saved his life in the horrible fire at Southfork, 1983.

John Ross meets his counselor, Peter Richards, at Windsor Meadows in 1983, with his parents and the camp director looking on. John Ross was heartbroken when Peter left Dallas in 1984.

Garrison Arthur Ewing

Valene Clements Ewing

"GARY" and "VAL"

"I hurt sometimes, but I can handle it. What I can't handle is you comin' back again . . . And then one day finding out you're gone again."

—Lucy Ewing Cooper, 1979

(Editor's Note: Since Gary and Val have spent barely a few months' time at Southfork in over twenty years, theirs is but an introductory note. For their complete, detailed biographies, you can look forward to *Knots Landing*.)

Gary Ewing is the second son of Jock and Ellie, and was named after Ellie's brother, Garrison Southworth. He was clearly Miss Ellie's child from the very beginning. Not only did he inherit her talent in painting and her love of the land, but he also possesses all of the gentle, nurturing qualities that have served Miss Ellie so well over the years. She adores him, and it has been an ill-kept secret that he is Miss Ellie's favorite, while also being the son whom Jock Ewing tried to write off.

Gary was born with an addictive temperament. His attitude from birth was "all or nothing," either striving to be a perfectionist or not trying at all and giving up completely. His father's rough and gruff ways and booming voice left him a little afraid. And so did his older brother, J.R., who seemed to be able to do everything brilliantly. Gary's greatest dream in life was for these two to leave him alone. Everything he did seemed to irritate his father and invite torture from J.R. If only, Miss Ellie thinks now, Jock had fallen in love with ranching earlier, he would have had a respect for Gary's talents in that area.

Gary was devoted to his mother, but that was not enough. He always felt like an outsider in the family, the one Ewing who couldn't compete. On top of that, he felt—and rightly so—that no one understood him at all. When he was a teenager, he fell in love with a young girl named Valene Clements. She sparked the self-confidence he so desperately sought but was unable to provide for himself. She *believed* in him, in his talents, even if his father and brother scorned them. Their love resulted in an unplanned pregnancy and Gary, defying the wrath of his father, insisted on marrying the fifteen-year-old.

Valene bore him the most beautiful little blond girl Dallas had ever seen. He cherished the newborn, at night dancing her gently around the room to a hushed "Rock-a-Bye, Baby." But constant harassment and pressure from Jock and J.R. pushed Gary into heavy drinking. Gary couldn't metabolize alcohol and became a blackout drinker, not remembering what he did. The otherwise gentle man turned violent when drunk, horrible, and the terror he saw in Val's eyes the morning after plagued him with guilt.

87

Unable to stop drinking, unable to face his responsibilities and his family, Gary ran away in 1962. Val, fearing the Ewings, left Southfork with her precious daughter and went to Virginia. At this writing, the details remain sketchy, but it is known that J.R. went to Virginia and took Lucy back from Val, leaving her with dire threats of what would happen if she ever set foot in Texas again.

Gary drifted around the country for several years. During that time he made two quick visits to Southfork. Though he had stopped drinking, being at Southfork always managed to start him on another bender.

Valene secretly moved back to Dallas County and worked as a waitress. She was frightened of J.R. and made no effort to see Lucy. She just wanted to be near her daughter as she grew up. Her heart was wrenched each time that Lucy was mentioned in the newspapers.

Lucy located her mother in late 1978, at a time when Gary happened to be visiting, and she set up a surprise reunion. After seventeen years of separation, in the fall of 1979, Gary and Val remarried in Dallas—although technically they had never been divorced. The ceremony was conducted by Judge Jensen and Val wore the same wedding dress as she had when she was fifteen. Lucy, Bobby, Pam, Ellie, and even Jock attended. For a wedding present, Miss Ellie gave them a house in Knots Landing, California, where the couple was going to make a fresh start.

Val and Gary were divorced in 1982. Val is a bestselling novelist and still lives in the house that Ellie gave them, while Gary is remarried and lives on a California ranch. In December of 1984, Val was delivered of twins, the result of a single night's reconciliation with Gary.

Proud papa, Gary, poses with the lovely bride, Lucy, after her marriage to Mitch Cooper in 1980.

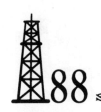

Lucy Ann Ewing Cooper

PAMELA EWING: *They all treat her like a china doll, but she's not. She's got the Ewing temper* and *the stubbornness,* and *the spitefulness.*
BOBBY EWING: *And the spirit.*

Jock Ewing used to swear that those genes had to be from the Clements, because no Ewing or Southworth ever came *that* small. Five feet. Five feet of sheer energy, electricity, high-flying temperament, sparkling laughter, and sizzling sexuality. Lucy Ewing Cooper is never not noticed, never not known, and never ever forgotten.

All of Dallas County has watched this girl grow up, and there have been many whispered comparisons to the poor little rich girl. Though she was spoiled beyond belief by her grandparents, Jock and Ellie Ewing, and virtually had everything she wanted at her fingertips, there was one painful exception—her parents. Love in general has not been a successful area for this young woman. It has always seemed to be that the more she has sought it, needed it, the more cruelly she has been deprived.

Lucy was delivered by Dr. Harlan Danvers in Dallas Memorial Hospital in 1961 to the recently married Gary and Valene Ewing. Gary was having terrible problems living at Southfork with his family, and, shortly after Lucy was born, he began drinking heavily. When Lucy was approaching her first birthday, her father ran off and her mother, frightened, unsure of what to do, but knowing that she did not want to be near the family that had driven her husband away, took Lucy to Virginia. She didn't get very far. Lucy's Uncle J.R. brought the baby back to Southfork to live.

Jock and Ellie raised Lucy the best way they knew how. Jock's child-rearing theory was simple: give her everything she wants that makes her happy. Ellie tried to be a little more disciplined, but this fussy, stubborn, beautiful youngster had her wrapped around her finger. It took hours to feed her, hours to catch her once she got outdoors. All of the old-timers in Dallas compared Lucy to young Ellie Southworth, in that the girl was virtually born on a horse. It was common to see her streaking across a field faster than almost any man, hair streaming wildly in the wind, and then—after a brief, silent, suspended moment as she took a fence and soared through the air—her figure growing smaller as she galloped off toward the horizon.

Lucy attended the public schools in Braddock and exhibited many talents—as a singer, pianist, guitar player, and dancer—but showed almost no interest at all in academics. She was a voracious reader of romance novels but little else. She was not sure of what she wanted to do in life—besides having parents—but, after all, thanks to her grandparents, she would be one of the wealthiest women in Dallas one day, and so she really didn't have to plan on doing anything. But, as she grew older, she moved from one dream to another. At fifteen, she wanted to join a circus—seriously—and dance on a horse's back. (She actually did this quite well and probably wouldn't have had much trouble getting hired, but Miss Ellie put her foot down.) At sixteen she wanted to be a photographer, and while she was indeed extremely talented in this field, she abandoned it at seventeen in favor of being a singer.

Lucy with her new Aunt Pam, 1978. Lucy resented Pam's intrusion in her life and did her best to get her out of it. However, by 1979 the two had become fast friends.

Lucy doing some fancy retailoring of a blouse that Pam bought her, 1978. She wore it to school the next day under her sweater, and when her guidance counselor took her behind closed doors to reprimand her about her absences, she took off the sweater and ran out into the hall, the blouse hanging in shreds, shrieking that he had attacked her. Pam was wise to her game and made her behave from there on in.

Lucy's greatest interest, however, was usually about six feet tall, with a deep voice. Attracting men was second nature to Lucy, and controlling them gave her a kind of emotional compensation for not having any control over her parents. She openly relished men's attentions and offers of love, but out of the dozens drawn to her, it would be Lucy's curse that she would invariably fall in love with those she could not have or control.

By the time Lucy was seventeen, she was a handful. Though she was affectionate and loving to her grandparents and to her Uncle Bobby, she was, at best, a rascal with everyone else. She rarely attended school, preferring to spend her days hiding out on the ranch, trying to seduce the foreman, Ray Krebbs. At school, Lucy was a kind of legend, in that she was remembered but almost never seen, though somehow she always managed to pass her courses.

When Pamela Barnes married Uncle Bobby, Lucy's world began to change. Pam quickly caught on that Lucy had given up school as a hobby; she was also onto the evolving affair with Ray. Both secrets were enough to get Lucy in a lot of trouble with her grandparents—and get Ray fired for sure—but

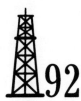

Pam did not reveal them. Instead, provoking Lucy's fury, Pam stepped in as a self-appointed disciplinarian and literally blackmailed her into behaving. In the course of Pam's catching on to Lucy's rather devious method of operation, Lucy's view of Pam changed. She realized that Pam was not namby-pamby, but was, in fact, pretty savvy and could be as crafty as Lucy. In spite of herself, Lucy not only liked Pam, but grudgingly respected her. It was to be the beginning of a lifelong friendship that Lucy would need desperately in later years.

Lucy out-and-out hated her Uncle J.R. Just the fact that he had been the one to steal her back from her mama so many years ago was enough. And so was the way he slammed her father, Gary. No-good loser-drunk was all Lucy ever heard from J.R. about her father. And her Aunt Sue Ellen, well, Lucy didn't hate her, but, in her opinion, anyone who was married to J.R. couldn't possibly be right in the head, and certainly was not to be trusted.

In 1978, Lucy located her mother, working as a waitress in Fort Worth. Their reunion was wonderful. Lucy began visiting her in secret as often as she could. Then Bobby and Pam ran into Gary in Las Vegas and talked him into coming home for a visit. Now not drinking for some time, Gary surprised

Lucy, Sue Ellen, and J.R. at a family celebration of Jock and Ellie's anniversary in the Southfork living room, 1978. Theoretically J.R. and Sue Ellen were supposed to be parental figures for Lucy, but the arrangement really never worked well, with Lucy hating J.R., J.R. despising her, and J.R. and Sue Ellen hating and despising each other. Their parental chats ran much like this one in 1979:
J.R.: I knew that tramp mother of hers would start filling her up with false hope if she came back to Dallas.
SUE ELLEN: Somehow, J.R., the role of social worker doesn't fit you.
J.R.: She's my niece, Sue Ellen. I don't want to see her hurt.
SUE ELLEN: How touching, your concern for children. I'm almost sorry you didn't adopt me instead of marrying me.

Lucy with her mother, Valene, 1978. Lucy would do anything to be near her mother and father, but given the disparity in their lives, it appears this will never happen.

the family by declaring he was ready to try living at Southfork, make a shot at being a businessman, and, the most important thing, be a good father to Lucy. Thrilled, Lucy orchestrated a meeting between her parents, who hadn't seen each other for years. It was clear, at least to Lucy, that her parents were still in love. Her happiness was short-lived, however, as J.R. piled on Gary an overwhelming amount of work and pressure, purposely giving him a dying company to run, and Gary's old insecurities started to rise and nearly drove him to drink. Knowing that everything would be lost if he went back to drinking, Gary chose to leave Southfork again. Lucy was heartbroken.

Lucy's granddaddy refused to let Lucy invite her mother to her birthday party and, furious, Lucy took J.R.'s car to go to her mother. But she was kidnapped by Willie Gust, a psychotic thief, who believed Lucy was his dream partner in crime. It was a terrifying experience. He wielded a gun, and Lucy was in fear for her life. Thankfully, Bobby—and the police—located her and she was safely returned to the Ewing household.

And then—crushing Lucy completely—her mother disappeared. J.R. told her that he had paid Val to leave, that all she had come for was money. Lucy emphatically refused to believe it, but J.R. seemed to have proof. Lucy was bitter and angry.

In 1979, Lucy met a young man who took her breath away: the smart, gentle, handsome Christopher Mainwaring III, heir to the Mainwaring Oil empire. Lucy fell deeply in love with Kit. Despite the fact that Lucy was so young, the Ewings were by and large ecstatic when the young couple got engaged. The Dallas *Press* ran the announcement with a large portrait of Lucy on the cover of the social section, describing the impending marriage as "the social event of the season, uniting as it does two of the Southwest's most prominent oil and ranching families." And then Lucy's dream shattered in a heartbreaking way. Kit told Lucy that he was a homosexual—despite having slept with her once—and he could not bring himself to put her through the mockery of a marriage. Lucy argued valiantly, declaring that she didn't care, she loved him so, and would do, or put up with, whatever he wanted. But in her heart, she knew that, with her jealous nature, she wouldn't be able to bear the situation, and she agreed to call off the wedding. Lucy was indeed in love with Kit. Instead of revenge—which had been such a part of her emotional makeup in the past—she never revealed to anyone why they had ended their engagement. She merely took a deep breath and lied, saying that she and Kit had found out that they did not truly love each other.

The loss of Kit from her life dropped Lucy into despondency. Her school friends rallied round, trying to push her into partygoing, which she had no interest in. In fact, she had little interest in anything—no energy, no motivation. A friend pressed some diet pills on Lucy to pick her up, and that first experience led her into a month-long stint of drug abuse with speed and Quaaludes. Sue Ellen, at the time, was on a horrific bender, and Lucy, drugged out of her head one day, barely registered the scene as Sue Ellen plunged headlong down the Southfork front staircase, nearly killing herself. Lucy just stood there, blankly watching. Afterward, the incident really frightened her and, with her Uncle Bobby's loving help and support, she stopped drugs altogether, without her grandparents ever knowing that she had been taking them.

With Pam's help, Lucy graduated from Braddock High School and enrolled at Southern Methodist University in Dallas. She was unsure of what she wanted to major in, and the family raised an eyebrow at some of her course selections—Interpretive Dancing was one of them—but they encour-

A drunken Lucy is barely cognizant of having just met the man of her dreams, Mitch Cooper. Lucy, upset over the end of her affair with Professor Forrester in 1980, went out to drown her sorrows, and Mitch, the parking lot attendant, refused to let her drive and sent her safely off in a cab.

A beaming Lucy throws a barbecue in the fall of 1980 so her friends can meet Mitch. The day was a disaster. Mitch was appalled by her friends' arrogant wealth and life-style, and Lucy's friends were unimpressed with the struggling medical student.

aged her willingness to attend. She tried out for cheerleading and made the team, much to the family's delight.

That fall, her mother reappeared, trying to reestablish an understanding with Lucy. Still enraged over her previous abandonment, Lucy lashed out at her mother, accusing her of being bought off by J.R. Valene enlisted Bobby's help in getting Lucy to listen to her, to hear that J.R. had threatened her. In the end, the two did get the past sorted out, and they renewed their mother-daughter bonds of love. Lucy's parents were back together again, and when they decided to leave the area, Lucy understood. So long as J.R. was in Dallas, there could be no safety for them.

At the annual Ewing Barbecue, Lucy thought she had found the new man of her dreams in Alan Beam. He was a young lawyer who had stood up against J.R. in public—which was enough of a character reference for Lucy. The relationship took off immediately, and within weeks Alan had proposed to Lucy and she had accepted. Fortunately, Lucy soon came to see that she didn't love Alan after all and that she shouldn't marry him. It was more fortunate than she knew at the time. Later she found out the rest of Alan Beam's story.

Lucy and Mitch enjoying each other's company on the lawn at Southern Methodist University. Despite the differences in their life-styles, the two fell madly in love.

The face-off with J.R. at the barbecue had been planned to convince Cliff Barnes of Alan's hatred for J.R., while Alan was actually on J.R.'s payroll to set Barnes up. And then there was the little matter of Alan's being in love with another woman. It was at J.R.'s urging that he had pressed Lucy to marry him. J.R. had wanted him to take Lucy out of his hair to Chicago. The experience rocked Lucy—what if she *had* married him?—and made her hate J.R. all the more.

The end of that relationship pushed Lucy straight into another. Her attractive English professor, Greg Forrester, caught her eye. She won Forrester easily, and they fell into a passionate affair at 11044 Dunbar Street, supposedly his apartment (it wasn't). When Lucy learned that Greg was not only married, but also the father of a new baby, she immediately put an end to their relationship. She has never been interested in stealing another woman's man, for she knows how she would feel in their place—a trait that all the Ewing women share.

One night, upset, depressed over her bad luck with men, Lucy went out drinking with friends. She got plastered, and when she went to the bar's parking lot to retrieve her Porsche, the attendant refused to let her drive and put her in a cab instead. Even as loaded as she was, Lucy was completely enthralled by this handsome man, and after she sobered up, she went about finding out who he was and where he lived. His name was Mitch Cooper, and she dropped in at his Platt Street apartment to thank him in person. In her winning way, which normally never fails, she invited him to pursue her. He said he was sorry but he simply did not have the time. He was a second-year medical student and had more important things to do. Lucy smiled—though disappointed—and hoped that he had been smitten anyhow. He was, and soon they were seeing each other.

Mitch takes Lucy up to the minister at their Southfork wedding, 1980. Gary and Val (seen behind the couple) flew in from Knots Landing, California, making it an extra-special day for their daughter. Lucy's best friend, Muriel Gillis, was maid of honor (seen at right).

Mitch simply did not come from Lucy's world. She found him alien, altruistic, and wonderful. He was born and raised in Biloxi, Mississippi, and his father, a farm laborer, had died at age thirty. His mother, Arliss, had brought up Mitch and his older sister, Afton, single-handed. Mitch always wanted to be a doctor and, after going to college on a full scholarship, he spent two years working full-time to earn enough money for medical school. He was accepted at SMU and had the funds to cover the tuition, but he had to sandwich in between his studies any lab jobs he could find to finance his books, food, and clothing. That was the priority order, Lucy learned, and there was no room for play. He didn't have the money *or* the time, but, despite his circumstances, he fell hard for Lucy and tried to make time.

From the beginning, the relationship was fraught with problems around money. The most painful part was that, as Lucy and Mitch realized how very much they loved each other, they began tiptoeing around each other, trying to change their natures. Mitch tried to be more tolerant of Lucy's upbringing, her money, extravagance, and style, and Lucy tried to adapt to Mitch's sparse, monk-like existence, which, incidentally, she found ghastly oppressive.

She brought him to Southfork to meet her friends at a barbecue, and Mitch was horrified by what he saw as the arrogance and ostentatious wealth of her friends. But the two kept working at their relationship and then, to the nervous surprise of the Ewing clan, Lucy announced their engagement. She couldn't have been happier; Mitch couldn't have been happier.

The wedding was a joyous event. Gary and Valene flew in from California. Gary gave his daughter away. Lucy wore her grandma's wedding dress (which was something old), an exquisite strand of pearls that her parents

97

bought her (which was something new), carried the lace handkerchief that Pam had held when she had married Bobby (which was something borrowed), and slipped on the garter Sue Ellen had worn at her wedding (which was something blue—and should have been an omen, Lucy thought later).

The opulence of wealth, the staggering resources of the Ewings and their guests were all a bit much for Mitch, but he tried to remain calm and confident. He accepted that Lucy had bought dresses for his mother and sister to wear at the wedding, that she had them "made over" (all to their delight), he accepted the honeymoon trip to Padre Island from Jock and Ellie, and also he accepted the Ewing Oil condominium in which to live (it had been vacant since the departure of Kristin Shepard).

The honeymoon was wonderful, and when they returned to Dallas, Mitch was touched by how earnestly Lucy tried to be a good homebody. However, she was an absolutely horrendous cook, and an even worse housekeeper. But she was trying, and he loved her and she loved him, and on they went—Mitch off to school and lab jobs, Lucy sitting at home. And then, suddenly, home became model perfect. The dinners were sumptuous, the condo spick-and-span, and Mitch was all smiles. Lucy was so happy—until Mitch came home unexpectedly and encountered the daily cleaning lady whom Lucy had hired. Mitch was furious. Lucy knew he would be, but she tried to make him understand how very much she wanted to please him and, anyhow, if she had the money, why shouldn't she use it to make them happy?

It was their old battle all over again. Lucy wanted to use her Ewing money in their life, and Mitch wanted no part of it. *He* wanted to make their way, earn their income. So Lucy said fine, she wouldn't use the money

J.R., Sue Ellen, Arliss Cooper (Mitch's mother), Jock (caught at an awkward moment), and Ellie watch the ceremony.

*Lucy in one of her poses for
Young Miss Dallas, 1981.*

given her, she'd go out and earn a living too. Mitch allowed as that might be all
right.

Lucy sought help from Pam, who arranged an interview with Alex
Ward, the magazine tycoon, about the possibility of doing some modeling. Not
only did he hire Lucy, but he hired her as *the* official Miss Young Dallas, the
woman who for a year would represent the new *Young Dallas* and other Alex
Ward publications in all public relations work.

For Lucy, it was a paradise; for Mitch, it was a nightmare. Lucy
was virtually making a fortune, while Mitch was still slaving over lab jobs for
fifty dollars, if he was lucky. Lucy was supporting him, and he couldn't stand it.
And he couldn't stand her hours, either. Her work often demanded a 5:30 A.M.
call, with the workday lasting until 10:30 at night. She modeled for layouts in
the magazines, did interviews on radio and television, and starred at special
events at the Ward Publications headquarters in Houston.

After argument after argument, Lucy—exasperated with Mitch for
what she saw as unreasonable behavior (after all, she worked darn hard for
this money)—moved back to Southfork in 1981 to think things over.

With her stint as Miss Young Dallas drawing to a close in the fall
of 1981, Lucy began working with Roger Larson, one of the country's most
talented fashion photographers. She liked him, adored the way he made her
look, and took Larson up on his offer to work exclusively with him for national
clients. She also took his suggestion and signed with the exclusive Blair Sullivan Modeling Agency.

As Lucy worked with Roger, she sensed that he wanted their
relationship to take a romantic turn, but she restrained herself, still hoping for

99

Lucy and Mitch dancing at the 1981 Ewing Barbecue. The couple tried several times to save their marriage, but it finally collapsed under the strain of their life-style differences.

Lucy listening to Miss Ellie's marital advice, 1981. Lucy is extremely close to her grandmother and the two share many traits—stubbornness, a love of the outdoors, and a sensitive nature among them. Lucy, like Miss Ellie when she first married Jock, can't cook worth a darn, but perhaps, like her grandmother, she'll learn.

a reconciliation with Mitch. Then Lucy dropped in on Mitch at the condo one day in an attempt to patch things up and found him on his way out with an attractive former patient—and older woman—Evelyn Michaelson. Lucy was beside herself. And then the woman took her out to lunch and told her that she and Mitch were sleeping together (they weren't), and Lucy angrily fell into the arms of Roger Larson that very afternoon. Afterward, Lucy felt she had made a mistake with Roger and was in the process of easing it to a stop when Mitch came storming in to the photography studio to demand a divorce. Again, out of anger, Lucy went to bed with Larson. Little did she realize how obsessed the photographer was becoming with her.

Lucy started to get frightened of Roger's excessive, intense behavior toward her. He was practically violent in his declaration of love and adoration. She confided her worry to Pam and also talked to her agent about getting another photographer to work with. In the middle of this, Mitch asked Lucy over to the condo and Lucy, thinking he wanted to work things out, was devastated when he said he still wanted a divorce. Lucy tearfully made her way to a bar and drank too much, and, as she was making her woozy way out, Larson kidnapped her.

When Mitch went to Southfork looking for Lucy, the Ewings knew something bad must have happened. Ultimately, it was Pam and Bobby who found her at Larson's studio at 960 Bowie Street, and they were shocked at what they found. Lucy had been severely beaten, raped, and was near a complete nervous breakdown. They rushed her to the hospital. Though Lucy soon made a complete physical recovery, her mental anguish was to go on for a long, long time.

Mitch landed a position at the Atlanta Burn Center and said his final good-byes to her. After all that had happened, even though Lucy still dearly loved him, she agreed it was best to let him go. They filed for divorce.

The fall of 1982 would test every ounce of emotional endurance Lucy had left. She found out she was pregnant—the result of Larson's violent assault. She was sick at heart, agonized, unable to confide in anyone except her friend Muriel. Finally, near collapse, she turned to Pam. After a lot of careful discussion, thought, and soul-searching, Lucy decided that she would have an abortion. Pam went with her, and afterward, during the aftermath of depression, she gave Lucy a tremendous amount of love and support. No one else but Bobby knew what had occurred.

Pam pushed Lucy back to work, and Blair Sullivan arranged for Lucy's photographer to be a woman, the dynamic photographer known simply as Annie. Work went along fairly well, and it was a blessing to have as Lucy went through the painful final stages of her divorce. One of the clients, a nice guy named Bill Johnson, tried to romance Lucy, but, after the divorce was final, she found that she couldn't respond. To let a man so much as touch her brought on a hysterical wave of panic. So the relationship ended before it started.

Then Lucy met young Mickey Trotter, Ray's young cousin, whom he had brought to Southfork from Kansas to "straighten out." Lucy hated the pip-squeak on sight, but, as she got to know him, she felt oddly attracted to him. They were both very traumatized young people, and yet both of them were loving by nature. Although Mickey was usually a loud, brassy, wiseass kid, with Lucy he treaded very softly, gently. Eventually, in the spring of 1983, they fell in love, and Lucy confided to him her secret about Roger, the rape, the

Mickey Trotter, 1982. Lucy hated him when she first met him, but it was Mickey who eventually helped her overcome the scars from her rape. The young couple had dreams of marriage until the tragic car accident at Southfork.

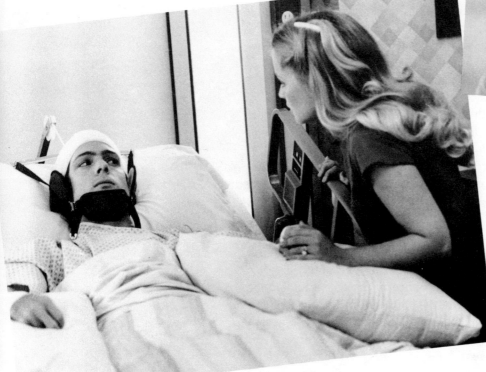

Lucy tries to cheer up Mickey as he lay paralyzed in Dallas Memorial Hospital, 1983. She stood vigil over his bed every day and insisted that his physical condition was no obstacle to her everlasting love for him.

abortion, the whole nightmare. Slowly, gently, Lucy was soon able to make love with Mickey. And happily so.

The two of them, in private, talked of getting married. And then the night that drunken Sue Ellen went tearing out of the Southfork driveway, Mickey jumped into the car to stop her and they were hit head on at the front gate by another car. Mickey was critically injured and lapsed into a coma. When he came to in the hospital, Lucy was by his side. She was still there when it was announced that he was paralyzed, probably for life. Lucy kept vigil, attempting to raise Mickey's spirits, to reassure him of her love and devotion. In the fall, he suffered a cardiac arrest and slipped back into a coma.

And then Mickey was dead. Ray, at the tearful urging of Mickey's mother, had pulled the plug to the life-support system to put him out of his misery. Lucy was ravaged with grief. She eventually forgave Ray, because she knew it had had to be done. It had been unbearable to see Mickey lying there day after day, brain-dead, his body wasting away to nothing.

A hysterical, grief-stricken Lucy lashes out at Ray, after learning that he had unplugged Mickey's life-support system and let him die.

At the urging of her family, Lucy reluctantly attended the 1983 Oil Baron's Ball to award the first four Jock Ewing Memorial Scholarships to SMU. Sue Ellen arranged for John Ross's counselor, Peter Richards, to serve as her escort. The evening was okay, and Lucy thought Peter was nice.

As the fall progressed, Lucy started to feel better, and she impulsively asked Peter to take her to the movies. He was such a sweet guy—he had all the good qualities of Mitch and Mickey—but Lucy was baffled by his aloofness with her. He liked her, she knew that, but something was holding him back. Though they dated a few times, nothing changed. Was he shy? No, not really. And then she worked with him on a modeling job at Southfork, and he pulled away again. Thinking back to her experience with Kit, she wondered, is he gay? The answer was no. Was he so wrapped up in his work with John Ross that he didn't have time? Not a good-enough excuse.

Finally, after drinking too much at the party welcoming Clayton Farlow's sister to Dallas in the spring of 1984, she had it all figured out. It was because he was seeing someone else. And that someone, she bet her bottom dollar, was none other than her Aunt Sue Ellen. She made the accusation and J.R. reprimanded her, telling her that it was nonsense. Lucy felt badly about her outburst, but, on the other hand, something told her that she was not completely off. Peter told her that he wasn't interested in her because he had a number of personal problems—and, indeed, it appeared that way when he was arrested for possession of drugs. But deep down inside, all of her wily instincts told her that it had to be Sue Ellen.

In an attempt to find out who she really is, in the fall of 1984 Lucy took a waitressing job at a diner. No one there knew her as anything but a working girl named Lucy Cooper. She was elated to find that people liked her

103

for herself, and it did much to boost her self-esteem. (The family at Southfork, however, couldn't imagine what was making Lucy so darn tired every day.)

Lucy's true identity as a Ewing was found out by the man she was seeing, a young construction worker named Luke Cronin. His affection for her seemed sincere, though, and they got increasingly involved. Lucy offered to go into partnership with him on a small housing project. She'd underwrite everything, and Luke would build the houses. In early 1985, Lucy found out Luke was two-timing her and she ended their relationship and partnership.

All of her life Lucy Ewing Cooper has been told who she is—a Ewing, a beautiful, wealthy, smart young woman who has the world at her disposal—but few have ventured beyond that. *Who,* past the birthright, is *she?* Had she been born in less advantageous circumstances, had she had parents, had she had brothers and sisters, would she be different? Happier? Would she know if it was true when someone said they loved her? Would she have reason to trust anyone? *Would people stop abandoning her?*

It is Lucy's saving grace that she has refused to give in to the sense of loss that has permeated all her life. And, she has finally stopped looking at others and has focused on herself—who *she* is inside. It is a difficult journey, one full of unanswered questions, but she senses that her key to happiness lies in her own heart.

In 1985, Lucy moved off Southfork and away from Dallas. Like her parents, she needs a life of her own, a life separate from the Ewing dynasty. Happily, Lucy's new life includes her former husband and love of her life, Mitch. The couple remarried in May.

Punk Anderson looks on as Lucy announces the first recipients of the Jock Ewing Memorial Scholarships to SMU, at the Oil Baron's Ball in 1983. It was Lucy's first public appearance since Mickey's death.

The Ewing table listens as Peter Richards tells a story at the Oil Baron's Ball, 1983. Sue Ellen had arranged for Peter to escort Lucy. Lucy liked him, but when she pursued him, he was strangely disinterested in her. Lucy suspected Sue Ellen had something to do with it. She sure did.

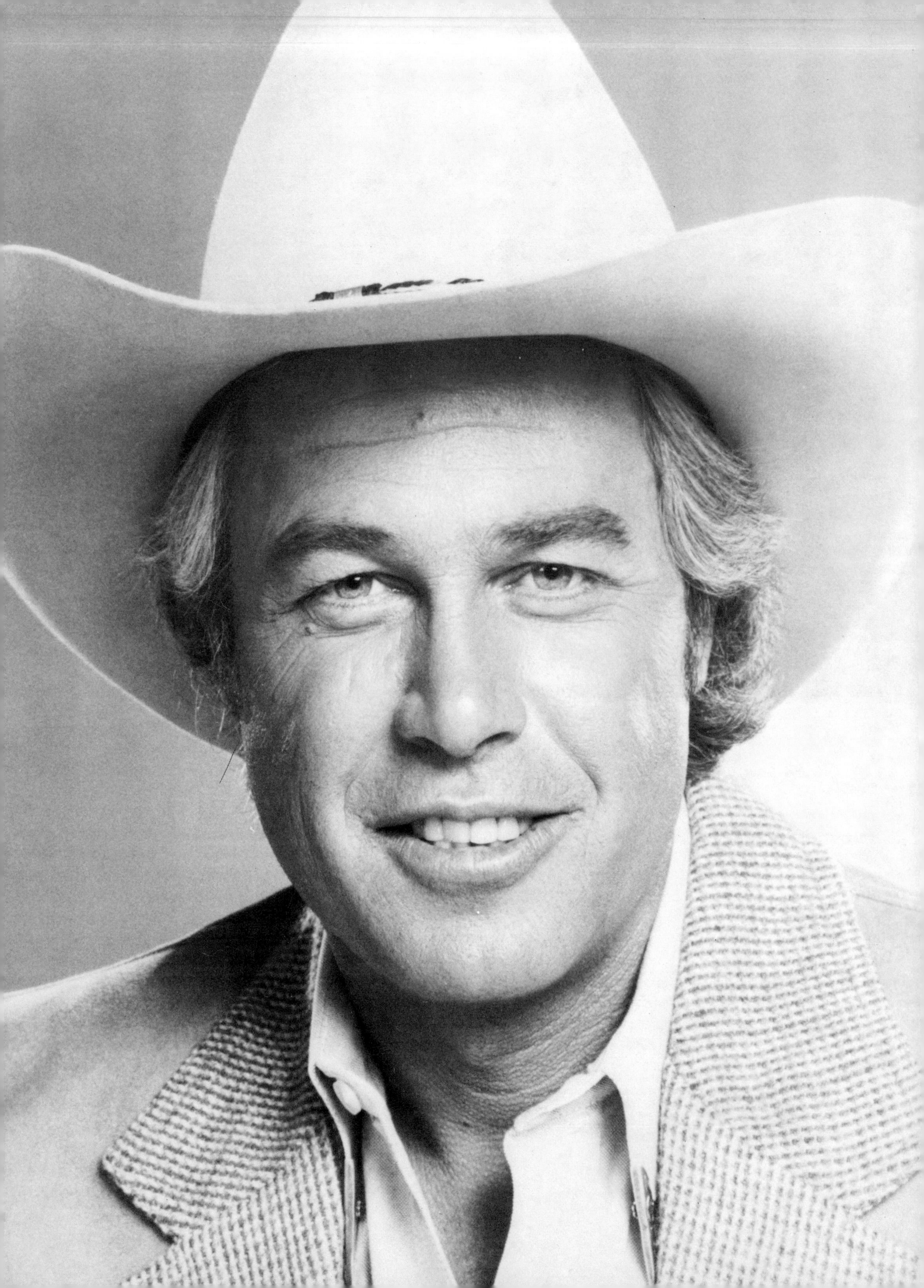

Raymond Krebbs

"Ray, you can sit where Gary used to. The two of you have a lot in common."

—J. R. Ewing, 1983

It's rather startling that no one ever commented on the resemblance between Ray Krebbs and Jock Ewing. At six feet one, Ray is two inches shorter than Jock was, but those vivid blue eyes, cut of the jaw, and head of brown hair turning to gray are unmistakable. So is the stubbornness, the infrequent but fiery temper, and the yearning to work hard with his hands. And, too, there is the love of the land, its animals, the wide open spaces, and an occasional hoot and holler over a couple of beers.

If people had missed the resemblance as the two men walked, rode, and talked together, then they would have seen it if Gary Ewing had joined them, standing side by side with Ray. It couldn't be mere happenstance, this resemblance, and indeed it wasn't. Ray was a Ewing, unbeknown to all for years.

Ray and Jock might unconsciously have recognized their true blood relationship, as there was an unmistakable tug between the two men, some unspoken bond that felt like father and son, although neither openly acknowledged it. If Ray could have had a father of his choice, it certainly would have been Jock, and had Jock been able to exchange Gary for another son, then it certainly would have been for Ray.

As he had known his story, Ray Krebbs had been born in Emporia, Kansas, toward the end of World War II. He was the only child of a free-floating handyman and town drunk, Amos Krebbs, and a recently discharged Army Air Corps nurse, Margaret Hunter Krebbs. When Ray was three years old, his father abandoned the family, leaving no money and never writing. His mother, accepting the situation, went about raising Ray as best she could.

He was a lot to handle. He always felt different from the other kids—mostly because of the absence of a father—and was a troublemaker at school, constantly disrupting the class. From the moment he opened his mouth, it was clear that he had no use for being kept indoors or even in town, but wanted to be on a horse and out on the plains. He wanted to be a cowboy—and, to be left alone. His mother promised him he could do as he wished when he was older and explained how much she needed him at home. He loved her and tried to obey. Outside of the house, he was constantly getting into some kind of trouble. He always played the tough guy, which was ironic, since he was physically immature for his age. So, in essence, Ray was just a little, skinny juvenile delinquent who fancied himself a big shot.

In 1962, his mother fell very ill and, unable to take care of Ray, she sent him to Braddock, Texas, with twenty dollars in his pocket and a letter addressed to Jock Ewing. Jock, who had known Margaret during his World War II London assignment, took Ray under his wing and made him a hand on the ranch. Margaret shortly thereafter died, leaving Ray essentially an orphan.

107

Ray and Pamela Barnes
Ewing at one of the large
ponds that are prevalent on
Southfork land. They had
seriously dated until Bobby
Ewing stole her away, and
it was difficult for them
both when she moved to
the ranch in the fall of
1978. Ray gave her a tour of
the ranch by helicopter and
tried only this one time to
see if she still cared for
him. She didn't—not in
that way.

Ray riding the range with Jock, before either of them
knew that Ray was his son by Margaret Hunter Krebbs. It
is astonishing that no one noticed the physical
resemblance between the two men, or if they did, no one
commented on it.

Ray was a wiseass kid and Jock was strict with him. In fact, some
said he was downright hard on the sixteen-year-old, but he broke Ray's bad
habits, lifted his spirits in a constructive way, and soon Ray was right in there
with the rest of the cowboys, working his heart out. Over the years he became
invaluable to Jock, in that he knew more about the ranch than Jock did himself.
He was completely loyal, and he was *good,* boy, was he good at what he did.
The skinny little kid grew into a robust man who could outride, outrope, out-
brand any other hand. He won prizes in all of the county rodeos and proved to
be a solid, responsible leader. Jock made him foreman of the ranch while Ray
was in his twenties.

There was still a wild side to Ray—his social side. He loved hanging out at the Longhorn Bar, tossing back a few drinks, indulging in a good
fistfight on occasion, always flirting and romancing the pretty girls and finishing out the night by roaring all over town in his pickup truck.

Ray attracted loads of women but couldn't seem to find one he
was interested in settling down with. Then he met Pamela Barnes, a beautiful
young woman who possessed a quiet demeanor along with a high-running,
vivacious spirit. Their courtship was full of fun and good times. She was a
terrific dancer, loved to laugh, was smart, alive, interested, and quickly learned
about Ray's work so she could discuss it with him (she was reared in the city).
Although Ray was aware of Pam's feelings about the legendary Barnes-Ewing
feud, he talked her into attending the Ewing Barbecue with him in 1977. He was

having strong feelings for this girl and was anxious to get Jock's opinion of her —without telling him that she was Digger's daughter.

The barbecue started out well enough. Pam was gorgeous—as usual—and it was with more than a little pride that Ray arrived with her on his arm. He introduced her around. They danced, and then suddenly Bobby Ewing was cutting in on him. Oh, he liked Bobby well enough—in fact, Ray thought him a good man through and through—but he didn't cotton to what he saw happening on the dance floor. It was not polite interest passing between Pam and Bobby, it was downright electricity. Ray managed to cut in and pull Pam away and keep her away from Bobby for the rest of the evening, but things were never the same again between them. The light in Pam's eyes was no longer directed toward Ray. Much to Ray's agonized frustration, Pam soon eased out of the relationship.

Still hurting from Pam's rejection, Ray found himself tempted by Jock's teenage granddaughter, Lucy. She was a lovely girl and—whoa!—promised a good time, but Ray knew Jock would kill him if he knew of the fooling around that was going on. Besides, Ray had no interest in using anyone—it just wasn't part of his nature—and he kept the brakes on their involvement as best he could.

In September of 1978, Ray was first astonished and then crushed when Bobby Ewing arrived home at Southfork with Pamela Barnes. It was worse than he suspected. The two of them had run into each other in New Orleans and whisk-bang-boom, Pamela was now Mrs. Bobby Ewing. It was extremely awkward the first couple of weeks—and painful for Ray—but then the two settled into a peaceful friendship that would last a lifetime.

Ray had always been a part-time buddy of J. R. Ewing's. It wasn't that Ray admired him in any way, or even liked him, for that matter, but when he felt like kicking loose and raising a little hell, J.R. always knew how and where to do it best. They would go on jaunts together—usually centered on a lot of women and a lot of bourbon—but their arrangement, even their tolerance of one another, would come apart completely in early 1979. Ray had fallen hard for the pretty country and western singing sensation in the Southwest, Garnet McGee. He thought he had found the woman of his dreams and asked her to marry him. Then he found out he had competition, from none other than J.R.

A happy Ray indeed escorts country western singing sensation Garnet McGee to the Ewing Barbecue, 1979. Ray planned to marry her, but J.R. lured her away from him with a recording contract.

Ray was torn apart by the whole affair. The object of his love and devotion was an exceedingly ambitious woman, and Ray found that she was willing to sell out to J.R. for a recording contract. It caused him a great deal of anguish that she could be so unfeeling and that he was unable to do anything to change things. But that was the way it was, and Ray had to let go of Garnet and his dreams for the future. However, he did hold on to his anger toward J.R.

One uplifting thing did happen to Ray during this period. For his years of service at Southfork, Jock gave him a prime Section—642 acres—of Southfork to call his own. It solidified Ray's commitment to stay, at a time when, given the Garnet situation and J.R., he was sorely tempted to get the heck out.

To take his mind off his troubles, Ray began clearing away part of the land and mapping out a blueprint for a house. While hanging out in the Longhorn Bar one night, Ray struck up a conversation with a beautiful, fair-haired woman named Donna. She liked him instantly, he knew—he felt it in himself, immediately, the attraction—though the lady was slightly aloof—which kind of added to the attraction. He kept going back to the Longhorn to "run into her" and he played along with her mysterious game, which included not telling him what her last name was.

Their unusual courtship came to a halt when Ray found out that his lady was none other than Donna Culver, the wife of the former Governor of Texas, Sam Culver. Donna hastened to explain to him that she and Sam were separated, but in the end she went back to Sam, and Ray was heartbroken. He didn't know her that well, this brilliant, classy lady—and that was what she was, a *lady*—but somehow she had reached in and taken a piece of his heart.

He threw himself into his work and, in his free time, built every bit of his house with his own two hands. When he had finally bounced back from the Donna affair, when it looked like life would go on, Sam Culver passed away. Gunshy, Ray cautiously saw Donna, and she explained that Sam had found out that he had terminal cancer and that was why she had gone back to him—to be with him in those final days.

The two resumed their relationship, though there were plenty of problems. First of all, Donna was extremely wealthy now, a millionairess. Second, she was intellectually inclined, politically a tigress and a powerful figure in Texas and Washington, D.C. He, on the other hand, was a basically uneducated cowboy with a modest ranch house and a little land. In his mind, he was woefully inadequate for her and, besides, they had virtually nothing in common—not in movies, books, work, or friends—including the fact that Donna was a night person, and Ray was always up at first light. In the face of these differences, Ray backed down on his marriage proposal and they split up.

In the fall of 1980, Amos Krebbs, Ray's alleged father, whom he hadn't seen in years, turned up at Southfork to show Margaret's diary to Ray. It was proof of his claim that Margaret had been carrying Jock's child—Ray—when Amos married her. Ray threw him off his property when he tried to blackmail him; Jock, however, paid him ten thousand dollars to get him on his way. Jock didn't doubt Amos's story at all and had a talk with Ray about it. To Ray's quiet joy, Jock was delighted by the news—he had always thought of Ray as a son, and now, indeed, he was.

Jock generously wrote Ray in for 25 percent of the Ewing boys' trust fund, over Ray's protests. He really didn't want any of Jock's money, particularly after Jock had given him something that was priceless—public recognition as his son. It did something for Ray's self-esteem. Now he knew the

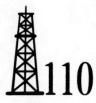

whole story—where he had come from, *who he was*. With new self-assurance, in 1981 he asked Donna to marry him. The happy couple were married in Braddock City Hall, with Bobby and Pam serving as best man and matron of honor.

Jock started including Ray in many of his business meetings, most notably with Punk Anderson on the Takapa project, a land development deal. Ray was in over his depth—he has virtually no head for figures—but he stubbornly pushed himself to prove himself to Jock and, in his mind, to Donna. He wanted to show that he could make money too, support Donna in the style she was accustomed to on *his* money. The Takapa deal went well, and Ray was lucky it did. While Donna was inaccessible on a trip to Washington, he withdrew $1,000,000 from their joint account, which was actually Donna's money. Out of a $3,000,000 investment, Ray made a profit of $1,000,000, with which he set up a development account so he would not have to ask Donna for money again. "The point is," he explained, "it's not right for a man to have to ask that. Now I don't have to."

Ray gently tries to push Sue Ellen Ewing away, 1979. When she and J.R. were having horrible marital problems, Sue Ellen took to drinking and to just about any handsome man at hand.

111

Ray pushed on with another deal—an upper-middle-class housing project—with Punk Anderson while Jock was away in South America, but he was a bit nervous, feeling that he might be overextending himself, given his lack of experience. Donna expressed caution, which only pushed him onward; he was determined to prove himself by doing this deal without Jock. At the last minute, Punk Anderson was forced to drop out, having been asked to join Jock in South America. Punk suggested that Ray do the project alone. He debated— he didn't have all the money he would need and he was skitterish about that— and then Donna agreed to put up the rest of the money as a silent partner.

Then the project—Krebbs Park Villas in San Antonio—started to teeter toward disaster. Before plunging those millions into it, Ray had neglected to thoroughly check out the water table under the land. The soil was soft and the water table high, and so the site had to be compensated for in the construction of the buildings, escalating the costs twofold. He desperately needed another three million dollars. When he went to the bank for a loan, they turned him down because of his lack of experience. Then, feeling low, he gave in and told Miss Ellie about it, and she said she would gladly give him the

Ray married Donna McCullum Culver in 1981. Bobby served as best man and his former flame, Pam, served as matron of honor.

The cowboy and the lady alone at last, 1981. Ray said to her, "Only thing I wish is my mama was still alive so she could meet you. Make her real proud of me, marryin' someone like you."

money. But when they went to the bank, they found out that Miss Ellie—indeed, all of Ewing Oil—didn't HAVE three million. J.R. had tied up everything in the gas he had stockpiled from Clayton Farlow's refineries. Ray was forced to sell out of the project at a huge loss.

He felt like he was a loser. More than a loser, a born loser. His depression deepened when Donna's book was bought by a major publisher for a lot of money. Donna seemed to be able to do anything and everything well, while Ray, he thought, was just destined for failure. And he had no one to talk to about it; he always confided in Jock, but he was thousands of miles away.

When Jock died in the helicopter crash, Ray gave in to his depression and started drinking heavily. Until Jock's will was read in 1982, Ray had control of 10 percent of the voting shares in Ewing Oil. J.R. doggedly tried to wrestle them from him, but Ray continued to resist him in memory of Jock's wishes. But everything else started to slide, fast. Miss Ellie, for the first time ever, was forced to confront Ray about his responsibilities at the ranch. He simply was not functioning like himself. As all around him began to worry, his drinking stretched to around the clock. He had furious fights with Donna, who made him feel even more a failure. Finally, so low a dog could have kicked him, Ray started fooling around with Bonnie Robertson, his girl of long ago.

J.R. stepped in to do two things to Ray. He had him thrown in jail during one of his binges and, while he was still groggy with booze, made him

113

sign over his Ewing Oil voting shares. Then he arranged it so that Donna would walk in on Ray and Bonnie in bed in a motel. The Krebbses had a raging fight, with Donna doing most of the raging. But when her shouting turned to a vow, her main message began to penetrate Ray's still-hazy mind: Donna loved him heart and soul, and if he wanted to divorce her, then he'd have to do it all by himself, because she wasn't letting go of him, no matter what. She was prepared to take Ray any way she found him.

What began to crystallize in his mind was that if Donna was so wonderful—which he knew she was—and *she* loved him so much, then maybe there was something worthy in himself. He slowly began to feel better, and he stopped drinking, resuming his responsibilities at full steam.

Ray adored Donna and now loved her even more. Their marriage was cemented with a stronger bond. Ray started regaining his confidence and ventured to learn about Donna's world, and invite her into his. And the romantic side of their marriage, well, suffice it to say that "the cowboy and the lady" let no dust settle.

In the fall of 1982, Ray received a letter from his Aunt Lil (Lillian Trotter)—who knew nothing about Ray's being Jock's son—informing him that Amos Krebbs had fallen ill and needed financial assistance. Ray sent some money to her, and just as he and Donna were leaving for a trip to New York, Lil

Ray splitting wood in back of his ranch house, an activity he often engages in to unwind. He built the house himself, and it is situated on the Section of Southfork land that Jock gave to him.

Donna interrupts Ray's meeting with Punk Anderson at the Oil Baron's Club, 1981. Ray assured her that he was not in over his head in the San Antonio building project, but when Punk had to drop out, that's exactly where he ended up.

called to say that Amos had died. Ray and Donna went back to Emporia for the funeral service.

While staying with Lil at her old house at 17 Briar Lane, Ray was distressed that Lil's son, Mickey, was not making life easy for her. He was a cocky, smart-alecky, self-interested juvenile delinquent. The similarity between Mickey and himself when young did not go unnoticed, and when it was readily apparent that Lil had given up on Mickey, Ray suggested that he go with him to Southfork, where Ray could do for Mickey what Jock had done for him.

It was not easy. When Mickey wasn't mouthing off, he was lollygagging, and when he wasn't doing that, he was running a crap game in one of the bunkhouses, and if he couldn't be found, then he was probably getting drunk in Braddock. But Ray was determined to get this kid back on track and, miraculously, it seemed to start happening in 1983—all because of, of all people, Lucy Ewing Cooper. Mickey fell in love with her. Ray beamed as Mickey started shouldering his load, learning about and being truly interested in the facets of the ranch. The kid was starting to have plans of his own. Ray was elated with the change.

115

Ray reads to Donna the letter he received from his Aunt Lil about his "father," Amos Krebbs, being ill, fall 1982. It was a blessing that the Krebbs marriage had grown stronger, for Ray was heading into the most heartbreaking period of his life.

When Sue Ellen and Mickey were in the car accident at the Southfork gate, it was as if Ray himself had been told he was paralyzed. Ray was beside himself with grief and rage that Mickey had been robbed of his chance at a normal life, and when he found out that the accident had been caused because Walt Driscoll had been trying to kill J.R., Ray crossed the line and tried to do it himself. He did not succeed, but his vicious fistfight with J.R. accidentally started the fire that nearly destroyed Southfork.

As Mickey layed helpless in the hospital, Ray grew thin, sad, exhausted. When Mickey fell into his second coma, Ray could not bear to watch the boy's body, once so young and strong, decay, shrivel so he looked like an old man. Mickey's mother, Aunt Lil, begged that he be put out of his misery and Ray, anguished, near emotional collapse, pulled the plug on the life-support system and barricaded the hospital room door until he was sure that Mickey was gone.

It was over. Ray was arrested, and he resigned himself to the fact he was guilty. He would do the same thing again, if he had to. Donna charged to his side, trying to compensate for his fatalistic attitude, and found a good legal defense. Case number 8046, the State of Texas versus Raymond Krebbs, made headlines around the country. The Honorable Judge Emmett Burke of the Third District Court found him guilty. Ray's sentence was five years in the state penitentiary—suspended—with eighteen months of probation.

To lift Ray's spirits, Donna took him away to New York on a vacation. A kind of second honeymoon, it helped him put the past behind.

Ray continued to run Southfork smoothly and, in addition, began taking a more active role in Donna's political causes. He was heavily involved, for example, in the investigation of the 1984 government auction of offshore drilling leases in the Gulf.

Ray was delighted when Clayton Farlow became a familiar figure at Southfork. Farlow loved ranching dearly and Ray found his easy, yet tough manner reminiscent of Jock. The two became very close. As Clayton's sister, Jessica, remarked, "I noticed the resemblance the first time I met you. You're both strong, silent men. Men of the fields . . . men of the soil."

In 1985, however, after years of watching the Ewing clan seemingly bypass him with entrepreneurial success, Ray has begun to yearn to try a new career of his own. His disaster with the San Antonio project has left him cautious, so until the time comes for him to move on, the once-skinny wiseass kid from Emporia remains a widely respected ranch foreman, an impressive landowner, a loving husband, and an heir to the Ewing empire. And, as always, the cowboy extraordinaire.

Ray plays the good guy to his cousin Mickey Trotter at Southfork. He couldn't be yelling at Mickey all *the time, although he might as well have in the beginning. Ray patiently waited for him to come round and act responsible, and leave his boozing and gambling ways behind.*

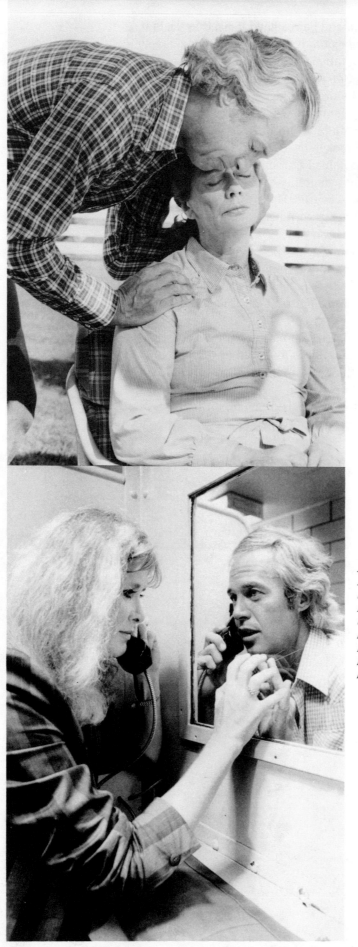

An agonized Ray tries to comfort his Aunt Lil at home, 1983. Mickey had suffered a cardiac arrest, had lapsed back into a coma, and was being kept alive by machines.

A terrified Donna visits Ray in jail, 1983. Ray had been arrested for manslaughter and was held until bail was posted. He had unplugged Mickey's life-support system in his room at the hospital, letting him die a merciful death.

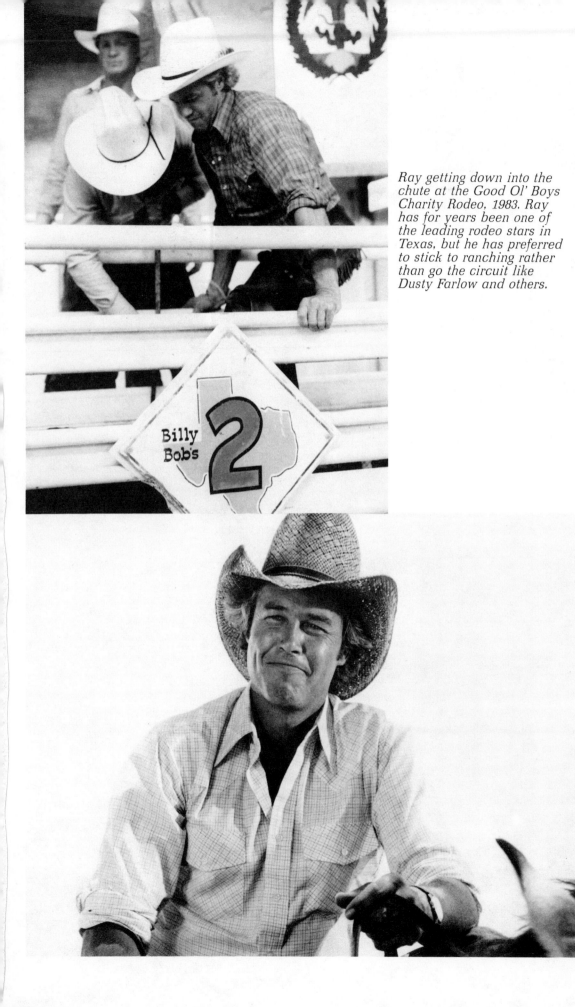

Ray getting down into the chute at the Good Ol' Boys Charity Rodeo, 1983. Ray has for years been one of the leading rodeo stars in Texas, but he has preferred to stick to ranching rather than go the circuit like Dusty Farlow and others.

Donna Culver Krebbs

"The girl who's got everything. You've got looks, you've got money, you've got brains, you've got political savvy. You sit down to write a book and—like that—boom! I guarantee it'll be a bestseller."

—Ray Krebbs, 1981

Looks and brains she was born with, but the rest only came with years of hard work and perseverance. "Fiercely dedicated" is an apt description of this woman, and in combination with her extraordinary sensitivity to the needs of others, everything she has touched has ultimately blossomed into something wondrous and good. As some folks in Dallas cast an envious eye toward her—watching this beautiful woman so confidently address the public through mass media, taking note of her extremely handsome husband, having heard about the interest her millions are accruing in local banks—they should keep in mind that *nothing,* neither her life nor her causes, came easily.

Donna McCullum was born in Marshall, Texas, the only child of a hardworking couple of modest means. She excelled in schoolwork of all kinds and, despite the fact that she was very heavy as a child, was quite popular with her classmates. She worked part-time through high school and won a full scholarship to the University of Texas at Austin. There she did brilliantly, majoring in political science, with a special concentration in environmental resource management. It was in the latter classes that she became friendly with Bobby Ewing. They shared similar political convictions, and the respect they developed for one another would endure to this day.

In her junior year, Donna's parents were killed in a car crash, leaving little else but a few debts behind them. Donna had no choice but to drop out of school and go to work full-time. About a year later, at a political fund-raiser, she met the former Governor of Texas, Sam Culver. Donna was drawn to this liberal hero, and Sam was drawn to this young, vulnerable beauty.

It was, at best, a winter/spring relationship; Culver was over thirty years older than Donna. They decided to make a go of it, however, and they married in 1973. Donna did her best to ignore the whispers around the Capitol in Austin and in Washington, D.C., but once she and Sam demonstrated their happiness and effectiveness over a period of months, people stopped noticing the age difference—or, at least, they stopped commenting on it.

Donna's obvious affinity to politics, her blazing strength and energy, and her brilliant, tactically shrewd mind were an enormous boon to Culver, and, in return, he gave her the benefit of some forty years of political experience.

In Texas, being married to Sam Culver was being married to God. He was by far the most popular governor in the last hundred years, and, until his death, the most powerful member of his political party. She learned to be a perfect hostess, not batting an eye at receptions for over two hundred, a visit from the President or from dignitaries from the Middle East.

Donna presides over the fund-raiser to elect her former husband's son, Dave Culver, to the U.S. Senate, 1980. Cliff Barnes, at left, was Dave's legal counsel and Donna's love interest at the time.

Donna and Ray. Their reconciliation led them to be married in 1981.

Despite the work of both Donna and Sam, their marriage began to sway and strain because of their age difference. Donna was just coming—bursting—into her own, as Sam was leaving his. They had never been in love; their relationship from day one had been more like teacher/student. Amicably, they agreed to a trial separation, and in March of 1979 Donna moved to 2701 Jessmine Street in Dallas.

One night, when Donna couldn't bear to be alone, she went into the Longhorn Bar by herself and met a cowboy named Ray. Donna was startled by how instantly attracted she was to him. She cautioned herself and kept her distance but found herself wanting to get to know him. She ran into him several times there, and though constantly reminding herself that she was still married, still Sam Culver's wife, she could not bring herself to reveal it to Ray.

The dilemma was taken out of her hands. Ray found out. She had felt badly for her deception (well, she never lied, she just didn't tell him), but now she felt relieved. Although distressed, Ray seemed to be still interested in trying to work things out, and Donna was prepared to make the final break with Sam. When she started to tell Sam, he gave her some news of his own: he

Donna arrives at a downtown Dallas bookstore to autograph copies of her book, Sam Culver: The Political Years, *with a proud Lucy and Miss Ellie looking on. The book was published in early 1982 by Chapman & Whitnow and rose to number five on the national bestseller lists.*

A beautiful but pensive Donna in 1982 as she decided to fight to save her marriage to Ray.

was dying of cancer and had only months to live. Donna moved back into the Preston Hollow mansion and stayed at Sam's side until he died, shortly after the new year of 1980.

Donna started seeing Ray Krebbs again, and it got serious, but then they split up over Ray's feeling that they had absolutely nothing in common. The money Donna had inherited from Sam's estate—some $10,000,000 *after* taxes—did nothing to win the esteem of the Southfork foreman.

Donna threw herself back into politics. She helped Sam's son, Dave Culver, move from his State Senate seat into the U.S. Senate. She was also a major force in obtaining ratification of the Health Care Reform Bill of 1980. On the personal front, she was still yearning for Ray, but when the rather dashing, difficult Cliff Barnes started pursuing her, Donna started seeing him.

Since Cliff was also Dave's legal counsel, they mixed politics and pleasure. Cliff didn't appeal to Donna in the way Ray did, but he was the first man of her own age group that Donna had had in her life since college. So it worked for about seven weeks, until the fall of 1980, when Ray and Donna were reunited in love and quickly married. Donna moved into Ray's newly completed house on Southfork, and all seemed well for the newlyweds.

That same fall, Donna joined forces with Ellie Ewing and the Daughters of the Alamo to stop the Takapa development in East Texas. Eventually a suitable compromise was worked out, thanks to Bobby Ewing. In the middle of that lengthy proceeding, Donna was approached to run for the State Senate seat that Dave Culver had vacated, but she declined, stating that she had no interest in public office. She did, however, join the party committee with Phil McKenna, Charlie Rowe, and Mike Whittaker to convince her old classmate Bobby Ewing to run. He did and won.

Donna started editing Sam's memoirs and then decided to turn it into a definitive biography, focusing on his later years. She worked at home on this while Ray was immersing himself in real estate deals, an activity that worried her. Although she knew her husband was smart, she felt he was simply in over his head with the wheeling and dealing and horrendously complicated financing. She had never known him to so much as balance his checkbook before this.

Donna finished the manuscript at the end of the summer and sent it off to New York. In the fall of 1981, she was astonished and then pleased beyond words when Edward Chapman of Chapman & Whitnow offered $50,000 as an advance for *Sam Culver: The Man and the Legend.* Donna was elated, but her success came at a time when Ray was feeling like a failure. He was depressed, drinking too much, and openly resentful of her newfound career and success. It wasn't fair at all to Donna. The good Lord knew how she had slaved over that book, and now here was Ray robbing her of the gratification and pride she should have about her efforts. But Donna loved him so, worried about him so, that she tried to overlook his hostility.

And fight she did! Donna seen here after delivering a neat right hook to the jaw of Miss Bonnie Robertson, the cowgirl who had been wrangling with Ray.

Donna joins Bobby and Ray at the weekly cattle auction at the Fort Worth Stockyards. Her reconciliation with Ray brought her closer to his world, and he to hers. However, it was not without incident. A chronic gesturer as she talks, this day Donna mistakenly bought herself a bum steer.

When the book was published in early 1982, it met with a deluge of wonderful reviews across the country. Despite, or maybe because of, the nightmare going on at home—Ray was drinking around the clock—Donna went out and promoted the book. Soon it soared up to number five on the national bestseller lists. Chapman & Whitnow quickly offered her another contract, this for *Sam Culver: The Early Years,* and Donna tried to concentrate on this new book while her husband seemed bent on destroying himself. It wasn't as if she hadn't tried to talk with Ray; he just wasn't in his right mind.

When Donna was set up by J.R. to find Ray in bed at a motel with his old girlfriend Bonnie, Donna was heartsick, but, like the best of her ancestors in the Old West, she decided to take matters in her own hands. She confronted Bonnie and offered her money to leave the state of Texas. As a reply, Bonnie threw a drink in her face, so Donna just flattened her out on the bar floor with one punch. Then she marched home and told Ray that she still loved him, no matter what, and that was the way things were. No matter what he did, that's how she felt, and she would take him any way she found him. Miraculously, the message apparently penetrated Ray's fog—and not so surprisingly, Donna's message to Bonnie got through as well, for she steered clear of Ray thereafter.

Donna went away to do some research on Sam Culver, giving Ray a few days to think things over. On the trip, she discovered the whole story about Sam and Jock Ewing having committed poor old Jonas Culver to a sanatorium back in 1930. She was horrified by the revelations in Sam's diary and called Ray to tell him the news. To her surprise, Ray offered to help, and even told her that he loved her. Well, that was one problem solved, but it was replaced by another. What should Donna do with this information? Tell the world that Sam Culver and Jock Ewing made their fortunes by pushing an old man to kill himself? She decided that she better talk to Miss Ellie.

Donna was nervous about her talk with Ellie, and her fears were realized. Still unable to accept Jock's death, Ellie lashed out at her, accusing her of printing lies about her husband. And then, snap, like that, Ellie refused to acknowledge Donna's existence. It was overboard behavior, but those days around Southfork were fraught with deceit and ill will and it was all taking its toll on Ellie. Donna was so upset by Ellie's response that she was prepared to call off the whole book. In late spring, Ellie came to terms with Jock's death,

125

and she apologized to Donna for the rift she had caused. She told her to proceed with the book, saying that Jock was a good man, but mortal too, and that he had made a mistake, one that shouldn't be concealed.

In September 1982, Donna finished *The Early Years* and wanted to deliver the "box full of my blood, sweat, and tears"—containing a manuscript of over six hundred pages—directly into the hands of her editor in New York, but the Krebbses were called away to Emporia for Amos Krebbs's funeral, and they had to cancel their trip.

After they returned from Kansas, Donna was terribly restless. She had no book to work on, nor a job. Dave Culver, as a U.S. Senator, asked her to get involved with a political group that was looking into the effectiveness of the state's Office of Land Management. Donna was swept right into the middle of things, as the group claimed there was corruption in the Office. In particular, it was evident that the head of the Office, Walter Driscoll—who had recently disappeared on an extended vacation—had been illegally catering to the needs of J. R. Ewing, granting him a special variance that permitted him to pump hundreds of thousands of barrels of oil over what state regulation allowed. The committee felt it would be in the best interests of the public if they simply disbanded the Office and started afresh with a new agency, complete with new people. The committee drew up a set of proposed guidelines for the agency—the Texas Energy Commission—whose function would be to watchdog the oil industry on behalf of the state of Texas and its people, and Donna helped Dave Culver push the agency bill through the State Senate. However, the Senate approved it on the condition that Donna Culver Krebbs herself would be on the commission in its early stages. Donna checked with Miss Ellie—since it meant for sure that she would have to meet J.R. head-on—and Ellie gave her full approval. And so the Texas Energy Commission was born, with Donna, Elmer Lawrence, George Hicks, Henry Figueroa, and Doug Reed as its members.

Their first job, in Donna's opinion, was to revoke J.R.'s outrageous variance. The committee, however, feeling politically vulnerable, turned on Donna and protested the revocation because the public was so swayed by J.R.'s P.R. work and enamored of the low prices at Ewing Gas. Donna was

A determined Donna in a crucial Texas Energy Commission meeting, 1982. The Texas State Senate approved the formation of the commission to replace the corrupt Office of Land Management, on the condition that Donna herself be a part of it. She did an exceptional job till she stepped down in the fall of 1984.

furious. Not only was Ewing Oil overpumping, draining capacities of wells needlessly in the middle of an oil glut, but J.R., with his temporary string of gas stations, was putting hundreds of independent gas station owners out of business, not to mention deescalating the price of crude—an act that was endangering the economic stability of all of the members of the Texas Independents. Donna suspected foul play in the committee, particularly from George Hicks, who seemed to be an ardent supporter of J.R.'s, but in early 1983 Hicks reversed his position and joined Donna in leading the commission into finally retracting J.R.'s variance. Donna was baffled, but pleased. (No one but Bobby Ewing knew the truth—that he had blackmailed Hicks about his rampant cocaine abuse, thus terminating his under-the-table employment by J.R.) J.R., of course, went gunning for her, but that was life. J.R. was always gunning for someone.

A frustrated Donna and Bobby outside of the Texas Energy Commission hearing, 1982. Although it was clear to everyone that J. R. Ewing had somehow bought his dangerous (to the oil community) drilling variance from the former head of the OLM, Walter Driscoll, the new commission failed to revoke it.

Donna's face was well known in the state from appearing frequently on television and in the newspapers, but there was no preparation for her next splash in the press—as the supporting wife of Ray Krebbs, the man on trial for manslaughter for pulling the life-support plug on the comatose body of Mickey Trotter.

Donna understood why Ray had done it, and was terrified by Ray's indifference to his own fate. His own will to live had died inside him along with Mickey, and he was morbidly resigned to accept whatever sentence the courts handed him. At that time, the very best to hope for was a ten-year prison term. Donna sprang into action, frantically searching for a lawyer. No one would take the case since Ray was sure to be found guilty. Donna pleaded with an old friend, Paul Morgan, who had been Sam Culver's assistant legal counsel, and he agreed, for Donna's sake, to take the case. After the trial was

Donna's relationship with her half brother-in-law, J. R. Ewing, can best be summed up in one word—war. J.R. was particularly obnoxious at breakfast one morning at Southfork in 1982, and Donna lost her temper and gave him a shove by the pool.

over and Ray was on probation, Paul confessed to Donna that he was in love with her. Donna gently explained to him that she was already married to the man she loved. Paul reluctantly and graciously backed off, but asked that Donna remember him, should she ever change her mind about Ray.

That night, Donna packed their bags for their long-awaited trip to New York. It proved to be just the ticket to bring Ray back to life. He threw himself into the fast pace of Manhattan, which surprised and delighted Donna. She had no idea he could cotton to any city, much less New York. Ray squired Donna all over town, to shows and restaurants, and, as a surprise gift, bought her a gorgeous fur coat. Relieved, wildly happy, Donna could see that her husband, the man she had married, was back.

After Bobby Ewing was shot in 1984, Donna resigned from the Texas Energy Commission and stepped in as co-Chief Executive Officer at Ewing Oil, where she had to steel herself against the wrath of her old friend and new co-worker, Mr. J. R. Ewing.

When Bobby returned, Donna surprised everyone by announcing that she had bought her own oil company. Smiling at the Ewings' astonishment, she was delighted to show them little Krebbs #1, a single well on acres and acres of land. But to say it will never be a threat to Ewing Oil is to dismiss the wily instincts of this woman, for if she believes that the land holds rich oil deposits beneath it, well, then, consider her track record: she has never been wrong, and she has never failed.

At this writing, Donna is expecting the couple's first child.

Nothing stops this lady, and little fazes her, and Donna's enormous fortitude, strength, and courage on behalf of those whom she loves is legendary. And she's wicked smart, and, on occasion, wicked good. If ever there will be a person one day to put J. R. Ewing in his place, then surely Donna is a leading candidate.

129

Donna being told by reporters that Ray had been arrested for the murder of Mickey Trotter, 1983.

Donna trying to comfort Ray's Aunt Lil during the trial.

Donna trying to calm Lucy after she learned of Mickey's death. Donna's role in the Ewing clan has been as an emotional rock of support to all (well, except J.R.).

Donna rides the mechanical bull at Billy Bob's Charity Rodeo in 1983. Although she hadn't been near cattle and horses for years, her marriage to Ray led her back to them and, surprise, surprise, she's a natural-born cowgirl.

Donna and Ray at the Oil Baron's Ball, 1983. Although Donna is a political activist at heart, 1984 was the year that she made the transition to the oil business.

Bobby James Ewing

"Oh, you're still handsome, but I think the sweetness is gone—the naïveté. Your edges are all sharp and hard and there is a kind of sadness about you now."

—Sue Ellen Ewing, 1983

Many have said that Jock and Ellie Ewing saved their best genes for last, almost as an afterthought. There was a ten-year stretch between their eldest son, J.R., and Bobby, and the span seemed only to more highly focus the family's love, adoration, and generosity on this youngest heir.

And why not? He was completely winning, possessing the best traits of both the Ewing and Southworth bloodlines. He was born with a ready smile, a keen intelligence, athletic prowess, and a competitive nature that was overshadowed only by his compassion for others. Indeed, he was a child born to be spoiled, and, heaven knows, the Ewing family did just that, but it is a credit to Bobby that he escaped being a baby for the rest of his life. In fact, he grew up to be every inch of the man Jock Ewing was, and, for many years, he was as widely loved and trusted as Ellie.

Everything in his life was special; to start with, a hundred-thousand-acre ranch to call home. His parents did, however, insist on Bobby's attending the public schools in Braddock, and he mixed well with the other children. He was enormously popular—something he would be all of his life—and was considered just one of the gang . . . that is, until the gang went to his home. Not every kid in the class had a Shetland pony, a buzzy bike, and an honest-to-god merry-go-round with handcarved horses.

Jock often took Bobby along to the office, which Bobby loved, and also the oil fields, which Bobby loved even more. And Bobby also took to the ranch in a way that made Miss Ellie beam with pleasure. He learned to ride before he was four years old, and by the time he was six, he was off on his pony on his own adventures, visiting other ranches.

To be more specific, he rode over to Lucas Wade's ranch. Lucas was one of his Daddy's best friends, but it wasn't Lucas that Bobby went to see. It was his daughter, Jenna. If it is possible to be seriously in love at six, then Bobby was. This spitfire of a girl had won his heart.

At eight, they were riding together. At ten, Bobby pulled Jenna off her horse. They fell on the ground, and he kissed her. At twelve, Jenna pushed Dotty Maypack into the Southfork pool because she had asked Bobby to a movie. At fourteen, they had picnics at Missing River. At sixteen, Bobby took Jenna to the Country Club dance, and when she danced with Butch McKeon, Bobby cut in and Butch took a swing, and a fight was on. At eighteen, Bobby went to the University of Texas at Austin, and Jenna was shipped off to Bennington College in Vermont. Their weekend reunions were written up in gossip columns across the country. For two young people, it was indeed a glamorous whirlwind that their peers were not accustomed to: champagne, caviar, and colored lights . . . private planes to Paris and golden yachts to Rio. And Jock didn't bat an eye, he just paid the bills.

133

Bobby and Pam, a few days after their wedding in September 1978. As Bobby explained to the family: "So I said, 'I love you,' and Pam said, 'I love you.' And I said, 'Are you sure?' and Pam said, 'Of course I'm sure,' and I said, 'Let's get married right here in this beautiful old city of New Orleans.' 'Why, Bobby,' Pam said, 'that's just the craziest idea I ever did hear.' But twenty minutes later we were standing in front of that Baptist minister, saying, 'I will, I will,' and that was that."

Bobby and Jenna were going to announce their engagement at the Oil Baron's Ball (it was no big secret; no one ever considered that these two wouldn't marry), but Jenna, at the last moment, balked and ran away to Europe. Bobby heard that she married an Italian practically the minute she stepped off the plane. When Lucas told him that Jenna had given birth to a child, a baby girl, Bobby knew he had to give up any idea of their ever being together. He had lost his beloved Jenna and didn't really know why.

The aftermath of his loss pushed Bobby into a rather cavalier, freewheeling kind of life-style. He became a tad wild, but in the most stylish sense of the word. He made a great friend at school in Taylor "Guzzler" Bennett, a loud, boisterous senior. Bobby found Guzzler's rambunctious ways diverting from his heartache and the two did a lot of heavy-duty partying and hell-raising.

It was Guzzler who inspired Bobby in football. Jock was a fanatic about the game, and Bobby loved it too. He had played for years at Southfork in his older brother's games, although he was so much younger. Sometimes his best defense had been biting his opponent on the leg, since he couldn't bring him down. It was Guzzler who gave Bobby the confidence and discipline to go out for the team. Every morning Guzzler made him work out (which is not to say that they hadn't partied the night before) and when this rich kid showed up for "hell week," the team (largely made up of scholarship students who sneered at Bobby's fashionable clothes) was downright hostile. Until they saw him play. The kid was a gifted athlete. Bobby not only made first string, he was made quarterback.

When the Ewing clan gathered to watch the Texas-Colorado game and saw their "baby" run eighty yards for the winning touchdown, they nearly burst with pride. He was indeed a star and perhaps the best quarterback the University of Texas ever had, but upon graduation, Bobby turned down the pro offers in favor of a career at Ewing Oil.

And what a career *that* was. Bobby was the best roadman of any oil company. And what does a roadman do? Another name for it is "goodwill ambassador," specializing in the three Bs: broads, booze, and booty. Bobby's job was to slick down the way for Ewing Oil with politicians and businessmen of all kinds, smooth ruffled feathers, and just give the good ol' boys a good ol' time they'd never forget—a woman, a trip, and various freebie junkets in the state. He *was* a good ol' boy, the youngest of them all, and the guys loved him. He was a Ewing, but he got along just like anybody else. And he had charisma and—the most important, impressive thing, nearest and dearest to every Texan heart—he was a football star. "Bobby Ewing?" they'd ask. "The UT captain, the one who made All-Southwest Conference? That Bobby Ewing?"

He learned virtually nothing about running Ewing Oil or Southfork, for that matter, preferring to leave it all to J.R. and his daddy. He was having fun, darn it, with or without Jenna Wade. He was known as the Ewing playboy: the expert horseman, swimmer, tennis player, skeet shooter, scuba diver, and dancer. He adored children, and on weekends he coached the Dallas Little League and, in the fall, Pop Warner's football. He had everything he wanted—except in love.

Bobby's romantic conquests in those years are legendary. There was virtually no eligible woman (he was never interested in married women) in Texas who hadn't set her cap for him, but as hard as he tried, he couldn't get over Jenna Wade, and he drifted aimlessly through scores of women.

Above, left:
Bobby taking a break from skeet shooting. He is an athlete extraordinaire. He was a football star in college and turned down offers to play pro ball; he is an Olympic-caliber swimmer, an excellent tennis player, a superb squash, racquetball, and basketball player, an adept rodeo rider, and a crack shot with a pistol or rifle.

Above, right:
Father and son glare at each other in anger at the Oil Baron's Club, 1980. Bobby was furious that Jock had withdrawn millions from the Ewing Oil cash reserves for his Takapa project without telling him, leaving Bobby in a very tight business spot, and Jock was outraged that his son would demand that he check with anyone about any amount of money he wished to use.

135

Bobby and Pam relaxing around the Southfork pool on a Saturday afternoon. Pamela was everything Bobby had dreamed of for a partner in life, but pressures from the family and Ewing Oil took their toll on the couple.

And then came beautiful, soft-spoken, bright, voluptuous Pamela Barnes. Bobby Ewing fell head over heels the instant he laid eyes on her. What he didn't know at the time was that underneath that gentle exterior was a woman every bit as strong, vital, and passionate as himself, but he must have sensed it, otherwise no Ewing would have dared go near the daughter of Digger Barnes.

They first met at the 1977 Ewing Barbecue, when Pam was dating Ray Krebbs. They wouldn't see each other again until the fall of 1978, when they ran into each other in New Orleans. Their mutual declarations of love came almost immediately and then Bobby just said, "Let's get married right here," and they did. And so, that September day, in a justice of the peace's office, Bobby Ewing became a married man.

He brought his new bride back to Southfork, where the reception was chilly, to say the least. There was no graceful way to say, "I just married Digger Barnes's daughter yesterday and here she is," and so Bobby just tried to barnstorm the family with his happiness. He also announced that he was ready to take his place alongside J.R. at Ewing Oil. His playboy days were over; Bobby was ready to settle down and make Pam proud of him.

It was a strange year. To start with, Bobby found that J.R. was not only protective of his power in Ewing Oil, but was just plain dishonest and crafty about getting Bobby out. Bobby learned quickly about the oil business, and the more he learned, the more he realized just how shady his brother's business dealings were. Right from the beginning he sensed that there would be no ball-playing with J.R.; that he'd have to prove himself to his father and his colleagues, while keeping a step ahead of J.R.'s poised knife. No short order.

With Pam at his side, Bobby prepares to give his victory speech when he won the election for State Senator, 33rd District, in the fall of 1980.

To his joy, Bobby was told that Pam was pregnant. Eager, excited, the couple made plans, but then Pam had a miscarriage. It was a deeply sad moment in their marriage, and Bobby reluctantly stepped aside to let Pam resume her career to take her mind off of it. In the meantime, Bobby's own career was accelerating rapidly—which meant that he was meeting J.R. head-on at almost every turn. But Bobby was learning, and growing stronger and more confident every day.

One morning, shortly after the plane crash that he and J.R. survived, Bobby borrowed J.R.'s Mercedes. A trio of kidnappers, thinking he was J.R., forced the car to the side of the road and spirited Bobby away. They held him for one and a half million dollars in ransom money. The Ewings were prepared to pay it, but J.R. managed to throw the kidnappers off balance at the drop-off point and Bobby returned unharmed to Southfork.

When Julie Grey was murdered in 1979, Pam found out that J.R. had framed her brother, Cliff, for the murder. Although Cliff was cleared, Pam

137

was outraged and moved off Southfork to get away from J.R. Bobby, confused, upset, stayed on at Southfork, as his whole family was having problems and were depending on him for emotional support. During this period, Bobby—who was as sick to death of J.R. and his dealings as Pam was—spun off a separate company from Ewing Oil and went into construction. It was a highly successful enterprise, and it also afforded him time to help run the ranch.

Pam returned to Southfork to be with Bobby, and soon she conceived again, and Bobby was ecstatic. But the joy was short-lived. Pam lost the child.

Bobby desperately wanted a baby. Seeing Pam's despondency, he delicately suggested adoption, but Pam just didn't have the emotional strength to contemplate it. However, it was apparent that her need to be in contact with a child was great. She began tending John Ross as if he were her own child, much to J.R. and Sue Ellen's consternation. And Bobby, in this period, found himself acting like a father to Luke Middens, the son of one of Southfork's ranch hands. They would make such wonderful parents—that was the tragedy. They had so much love to offer.

In 1980, after the Asian wells J.R. had gambled on were nationalized and the incident wiped out the fortunes of the Ewings' friends and caused Seth Stone to kill himself, Bobby and Pam, united in disgust and contempt for J.R., left Southfork to start over in California. There Bobby could at least be

Below, left:
A heartsick Bobby listens to Pam's psychiatrist, Dr. Dagmara Conrad, after Pam's suicide attempt in 1981. She explained to Bobby that it was Pam's inability to carry a child that drove her to it.

Below, right:
Bobby meets Jeff Farraday during his frantic quest to adopt Christopher in 1981.

near Gary, his other brother, and he and Pam would have a chance to get their lives back on track without interference from J.R. As Bobby and Pam were speeding along the highway, a police helicopter swooped down to give them the news: J.R. had been shot and was critically wounded. Reluctantly, dutifully, the Ewings returned to Dallas, where Jock asked Bobby to take over as President of Ewing Oil for the duration of his brother's recovery.

In J.R.'s absence, Bobby proved to be an extraordinarily adept businessman, but Pam was not very keen on the life-style his job demanded. Bobby had little time outside of Ewing Oil, and he asked her to be patient. When Bobby succeeded in buying a refinery—something Jock had always wanted and J.R. was unable to swing—J.R. flew into a rage and, from his wheelchair, got on the phone and moved quickly to screw up all of Bobby's pending deals. Under enormous pressure, Bobby spent even less time at Southfork, and his marriage started to crack over the issue of how the job was affecting him. It was clear to all that Bobby was personally thriving on the power of the presidency. Pam also maintained that his priorities had shifted. Now it was the job first, his family second. Bobby didn't feel that way. Yes, of course, he did enjoy the power and prestige, but the only reason he was running Ewing Oil was for the benefit of his family—including Pam and their future. When J.R. came back in—after undermining every one of Bobby's big deals—Bobby made his choice: to get out. To hell with J.R.—he'd run his own company.

Above, left:
Bobby listens to oil heiress Holly Harwood as she tells him what J.R. is up to, 1982. Holly made a big play for Bobby, but Bobby, despite his marital troubles, gently rejected her and instead helped her eventually to get J.R. out of her company.

Above, right:
Bobby and Pam share a laugh while dancing at the 1982 Oil Baron's Ball. In a few short weeks their marriage would collapse under the strain of interference from Ewing Oil, J.R., and Pam's sister, Katherine Wentworth.

139

Bobby's alternative energy company gave him his own territory, free from interference by J.R., but it necessitated a lot of groundwork and a bit of traveling, which Pam complained about. Bobby understood her complaint, but he felt it was a two-way street. Her career at The Store was taking off, and she made little effort to support Bobby in his work, or even at home. He hoped things would eventually straighten out.

In 1980, Bobby's career took a surprise turn. Donna Culver approached Bobby about running for the Texas State Senate. The political committee wanted to replace Dave Culver with someone who was experienced in the oil industry, had a background in geology and resource management and conservation, and held political beliefs sympathetic to their own. Donna and Bobby had been friends since their days at the University of Texas. She introduced him to the election committee as "a man who's proved, more than once, that he cares about people, about the quality of life, rather than just the success of the Ewing enterprises. Bobby, many of us hold beliefs like your own: equality, an improved life for others, supporting the greatest good for the greatest number. You and I have talked about that since we were in school."

He accepted the nomination and won the election. Bobby Ewing was now the State Senator for the 33rd District, Dallas County. His new job landed him smack in the middle of Jock and Miss Ellie's family feud over the Takapa development. Bobby's first act in office was to settle the vicious battle to everyone's satisfaction. He bought—at the cost of a few million of his own personal funds—an alternate site to the original and offered to trade it for the land Jock and his partners currently held. The exchange was agreed upon, and then Bobby donated the original site to the State of Texas as a wildlife preserve forever.

His problems at home were not so easily solved. He and Pam became more distant from each other. At first, it was because of their separate

Below, left:
Proud daddys Bobby and J.R. show off their sons, Christopher and John Ross, in the Southfork nursery, 1982. Sue Ellen remarked once of the two men, "They may look different, they may talk different, but they're both Ewings."

Below, right:
Bobby despondently looks to his bourbon and branch for the answer to his marital problems, 1983. He loved Pamela with all his heart and yet was helpless to stop the divorce he thought she wanted.

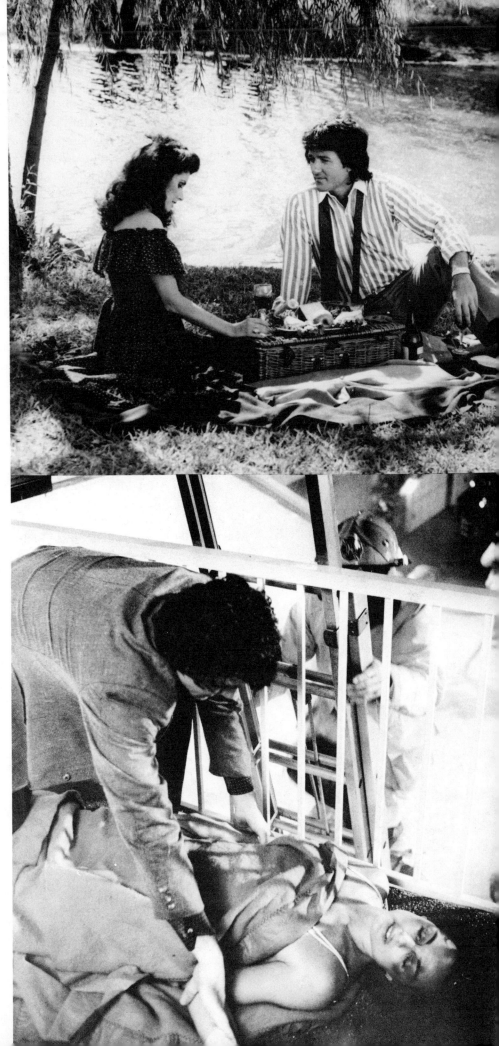

Bobby picnicking with the beautiful, deadly Katherine Wentworth, 1983. Her entry into Bobby's life caused him endless pain—from helping to break up his marriage to Pam, to trying to murder him, twice, in 1984. All because she loved him!

Bobby gets ready to hand an unconscious Sue Ellen to the firemen at the tragic Southfork fire in 1983. Had Bobby not arrived when he did, Sue Ellen, J.R., and John Ross would all have died.

careers, or so he thought—Pam was doing extremely well and was as busy as he. After Bobby's needless jealousy over the time Pam was spending with Alex Ward, they were able to draw a bit closer. But, still, something was wrong. Bobby couldn't put his finger on it. He noticed that Pam was beginning to behave oddly, being there physically but mentally far, far away, and she was becoming increasingly distant to everyone, not just himself. Then he realized that she was increasingly slipping away into a private world centered around her inability to have a child. Worried sick about her, Bobby looked into adoption and was distressed to learn that it could take years to get a baby. After Pam's suicide attempt, he placed her in the care of Dr. Conrad and wondered what to do next.

Then Bobby was contacted by Jeff Farraday from California, who said that Kristin Shepard—Sue Ellen's sister—had borne a child before she died. He would give Bobby more information for two thousand dollars. Bobby paid him and, through investigative work, found out that the baby had been fathered by J.R. Bobby took the little boy, Christopher, from Farraday and brought him back to Southfork to confront J.R., but just as he entered the house, he ran into Pam, who was on a surprise visit from the sanatorium. She looked at Bobby—frozen in his tracks—then scooped up the baby, beaming, assuming that Bobby had found him for them to adopt.

This was an agonizing moment for Bobby. The child was J.R.'s, and now Pamela, already having taken possession of him, was happier than he had seen her in months and months. He just didn't have the heart to take the baby from her, and, after conferring with Dr. Conrad, who said the child was the best possible therapy for Pam, he decided to try to keep him, and not reveal the natural parents to anyone.

After Jock's death, Bobby was running half of Ewing Oil in the contest with J.R. and he was under enormous pressure to win. The entire family wanted J.R. out of the company, and Bobby also wanted to prove that he was a better businessman. So the fact that Pamela was so joyously happy with this baby, was an enormous relief to him.

Ray watches as Bobby gets down into the chute for the Good Ol' Boys Charity Rodeo, sponsored by Billy Bob's, 1983.

Billy

When Bobby's lawyers started adoption proceedings, on the basis that the baby had been abandoned, and the court ordered that Bobby place ads about Christopher and the intention to adopt, J.R. picked up the trail. He soon traced the child to Kristin and discovered that Christopher was his. In the meantime, knowing that Bobby wanted to adopt Christopher, Farraday decided to blackmail Bobby over the baby's identity. Bobby was up a creek, but he knew one thing for sure: he would do anything to keep this child, because he loved him, and because the loss of Christopher would surely mean another emotional breakdown for Pam.

J.R. approached Bobby. He said, sure, Bobby could have his son, but in exchange Bobby would have to vote his twenty shares in Ewing Oil in whatever way J.R. dictated. Bobby agreed to his terms—and was horrified that even J.R. would stoop so low as to so callously use his own son to this end. Then Farraday gave Bobby an ultimatum. He said, to keep him quiet, he wanted fifty thousand dollars in cash and a one-way ticket to Rio. Bobby agreed, got the money, purchased the ticket, and went to Farraday to pay him off and pick up some medical documents about the child that Farraday said would be of interest to him. When Bobby arrived, he found that Farraday had been murdered. Worse yet, the police hauled Bobby in for questioning.

Farraday, it turned out, was a drug dealer and had been murdered by one of his business associates. Bobby cooperated with the police, who were holding the documents he wanted, and made contact with the drug dealers, which led to their arrest and conviction. The police handed over the documents, which raised some new questions about Christopher's parentage. Bobby finally told Pam the whole story and together they flew to Los Angeles, where they found out the truth: Christopher was *not* J.R.'s baby after all. He had been Farraday's. And now Christopher was theirs.

Above, left:
Bobby arrives with his long-lost love, Jenna Wade, at the Oil Baron's Ball in 1983.

Above, right:
Bobby more than helps Jenna off the mechanical bull at the charity rodeo at Billy Bob's in 1983.

143

Bobby vowed to flatten J.R. for this whole mess. The idea that he would blackmail him with what he thought was his own flesh-and-blood son was simply too much. His determination to win the Ewing Oil contest doubled; he wanted to bounce his brother out and far away.

Things went well for Bobby for a while, but then Miss Ellie tried to break Jock's will and end the contest. Pam supported Miss Ellie, while Bobby was forced to side with J.R. It was a difficult time. Bobby couldn't understand why Pam wasn't supporting him. She insisted that she was sick and tired of the feud between the brothers and just wanted the whole thing over. J.R. and Bobby won the case and the contest continued, but Bobby and Pam's marriage was never to be the same.

After Rebecca Wentworth's death, Bobby and Pam separated for what he hoped would be a short time, while Pam got things sorted out. She blamed her mother's death on J.R. and wanted to be away from the Ewings altogether for a while. Bobby desperately wanted her to come home with their son, but Pam's half sister, Katherine Wentworth, continually interfered. Unbeknown to Bobby, Katherine had fallen in love with him. She consistently lied and misrepresented things so that he thought Pam was not interested in a reconciliation. It was a long, painful mess.

Bobby would call the hotel and Katherine would say that Pam was asleep (she wasn't). He was encouraged to believe that Pam was having an affair with Mark Graison (she wasn't). Once, when he and Pam were left to their own business (without Katherine or J.R. meddling), they spent a loving night together, and Bobby assumed that Pam would come back to Southfork. She flatly refused, saying that she wouldn't unless he stopped the Ewing Oil contest. He refused, saying that it was the only way he could stop J.R. And then Mark Graison showed up at the door, and Bobby exploded with jealousy and stormed off, hurt, feeling helpless and misunderstood.

Bobby's daughter and wife-to-be, Charlie and Jenna Wade. Bobby and Jenna became formally engaged in 1984. She missed the wedding.

When Pam went off on a trip to France with Graison, Bobby was despondent, sure he had lost her. But once she returned, and they met alone, they discussed the possibility of a reconciliation. Pam said she couldn't go

back with him as long as he was living at Southfork. Bobby was caught in a bind. He couldn't leave at that time. His daddy was dead, his mama was recovering from an emotional breakdown, Sue Ellen was on a bender, Mickey Trotter was in a coma, and there was no one else to tend the ranch and no one to keep an eye on J.R. He said he had to stay. Pam said that since he had made his choice, then, so had she—she wanted a divorce.

But still they tried to work out their differences. Then, one night, when Bobby was supposed to have met Pam, Katherine was at the hotel instead. She insisted on reading him a letter that Pam allegedly had written to her lawyer. It said that she no longer loved Bobby and, should she return to him, it would only be to make him happy, even though it would no longer make *her* happy. Bobby was devastated. Thinking that she really was no longer in love with him, he acted as if he was no longer in love with her, either, in order to let her go, let her be happy with whomever she wanted.

In the fall of 1983, the Ewings were divorced. Pam had custody of Christopher, and Bobby had visitation rights on weekends. Bobby won the contest for Ewing Oil—he and J.R. agreed to split the company—but he had lost his marriage. It was a hard reality for him to accept.

Women descended upon him. To the oil heiress Holly Harwood, he gently said he wanted to remain friends; he also confessed that he could not be interested in anyone who had slept with J.R. And he didn't see Katherine, for a while, as anything but Pam's well-meaning sister; she was around a lot, and he welcomed her comforting ways. For Bobby was *lonely,* something he had never been before in his life, and it was awful.

One night, he saw Jenna Wade again. His heart leaped with hope and, after some touch-and-go romantic negotiations, they began to see each other regularly. Bobby had always loved Jenna, though not as intensely as he did Pam. But he thought Pam was not available to him. He thought she was permanently ensconced with Graison.

Bobby's courtship of Jenna was still clouded by an old question: Was Charlie—Jenna's daughter—Bobby's child? Jenna neither confirmed or denied it. Bobby adored the girl and treated her as if she were his own, and had the notion in the back of his mind that indeed she might be. He waited for what he thought would be a proper time to ask Jenna outright about it.

Bobby reached out to Pam one last time, asking her if she loved him still. She said that a part of her always would. Encouraged, he pressed to find out if she was still not sleeping with Mark, as she had told him before. She merely reminded Bobby that they were no longer married. Bobby took this to mean that she was sleeping with Mark, and he stopped pressing her.

He pushed into his relationship with Jenna completely. He took the children, Christopher and Charlie, with them on outings, the foursome acting like a family. He set Jenna up in business with her own boutique and bought Charlie a horse to keep at Southfork. He was working his way back to happiness. Jenna declared that she was in love with him again, and they began sleeping together, having fantasies about the future.

When Jenna's ex-husband, Renaldo Merchetta showed up in Dallas, Bobby found out the truth about Charlie: she was not his daughter. He was deeply disappointed, more so in Jenna than in the news about Charlie. Why had she led him on, implying that Charlie was his daughter? Her reasons were weak, and he sadly broke off their relationship.

His spirits lifted a little when Sue Ellen told him that Pam had decided to turn down Mark Graison's proposal of marriage, but then, just as

145

quickly, his hopes were dashed. Pam came out to Southfork to tell him that she had changed her mind and was marrying Mark after all. Bobby threw himself in his work and the ranch for a while, then gravitated back toward Jenna. They decided to try and start over, as if they had just met, with no past history bearing down on them. It worked, and the two became inseparable. This delighted all of the Ewings—even J.R.!—since they had all known Jenna for years and loved her. And, as Lucas Wade's daughter, Jenna was one of their own kind.

Meanwhile, Katherine Wentworth came bursting out with a confession to Bobby, that she and J.R. had slept together. She apparently thought that J.R. had already told him, and she said she had been forced to sleep with him in her effort to win Bobby. She pleaded her case of how much she loved Bobby, of all she had done for him, and why he should turn to her and not Jenna. Bobby was shocked. First of all, this was the first he had heard about J.R. and Katherine—J.R. hadn't told him anything. Second, he thought he had made it clear that he had never felt anything but friendship for her. Finally, Bobby asked her if being Pam's sister meant anything to her. Katherine said that she had waited until they were divorced to make her move. Bobby shook his head at all the deception she had spun over the months and, disgusted, ordered her to stay out of his life.

After wrestling with his emotions about Pam, Bobby finally went ahead and asked Jenna to marry him. He did love her and he adored Charlie— and he *had* lost Pam—and didn't think he would ever do better. It would be a family anyone would be blessed to have.

Just as Bobby and Jenna were announcing their engagement to the family, the news that Mark Graison had been killed reached Southfork. Bobby quickly assured a nervous Jenna that this would not affect their wedding plans, but when he went to see Pam to express his condolences, he was not so sure. He had little time to wonder, since Katherine made another desperate play for him, waving her Wentworth properties at him as a bribe. Bobby told her firmly that she could not buy him, and that, in any event, he was marrying Jenna. Katherine flew into a rage and blamed J.R. for poisoning Bobby's mind against her—as if J.R. needed to do anything to reveal this woman's true nature. On her way out of the Ewing Oil offices, Katherine threatened J.R.

Katherine came back to Ewing Oil one night and shot Bobby in the back. Afton Cooper discovered him lying on the floor and he was rushed to Dallas Memorial Hospital. He was temporarily blinded for several weeks and, as if that weren't bad enough, Katherine stole into the hospital and tried to kill him again, with a lethal injection. J.R. arrived in the nick of time.

In December of 1984, Bobby and Jenna went on with their wedding plans. The big day arrived, the guests gathered at Southfork and . . . nothing. Jenna never showed up. Renaldo Merchetta had taken Charlie hostage and forced Jenna to remarry him. Renaldo was then murdered and Jenna was arrested.

The year 1985 brought more chaos. After Bobby found Charlie, after he put up millions to get Jenna out of jail during her trial, he happened to run into Pam. She told him why she had agreed to marry Mark Graison; she told him how she still fantasized that she and Bobby could get back together; and she reminded him how much Jenna needed him, so that would not be possible. Bobby was stunned. So Pam did love him after all. Somehow, he always knew it, because he has always loved her too.

Bobby always maintained great personal ambitions. He throve on working hard, building something of his own, and enjoying the power and exhilaration it brought. But he also had a great collective ambition. He genuinely wished everyone to be happy, content, with enough in their life to call their own. Although enormously wealthy in his own right, he was something of a Robin Hood and made it his business to discreetly offer support to anyone who needed help—from Lucy to Ray, from Sue Ellen to Cliff Barnes, from J.R. to Jenna Wade. People never needed to ask; Bobby's greatest love in life was to help those in need, whether it was his family or the entire state of Texas. In return, Bobby Ewing's name will go down as one of the best-loved men in Lone Star history.

Bobby teaches Christopher how to ride, 1983. After he and Pam were divorced, Bobby would take him to Southfork every weekend.

Pamela Jean Barnes Ewing

"When I see you, Pam, I know that something wonderful came out of that awful time."

—Rebecca Barnes Wentworth, 1981

She is one of the savviest newcomers in big business today. She is known for her gorgeous appearance, elegant good taste, stunning smile, cool head, and warm heart. She is the former wife of Bobby Ewing, a dedicated mother, an heir to the great fortune of Wentworth Industries, and the woman who landed playboy millionaire Mark Graison's heart. But, unknown to the public, the circumstances behind any one of the above would have completely destroyed any lesser human being.

Pamela Ewing is a *survivor.* Everything about her past and present has been fraught with deception created by those she loves most. It is indeed a miracle that she has survived her own family and her family by marriage, and that somehow, *somehow,* she has managed to escape annihilation at the hands of injustice. But an even greater miracle is that this is a loving, forgiving woman, gentle by nature and strong by necessity.

The story of her early life, as she was told, was that she was born in Corpus Christi, Texas, to Willard "Digger" Barnes and Rebecca Blake Barnes, and that she had an older brother, Cliff. Her mother died when she was a baby. The *real* story, as Pam was to learn years later, was that, yes, she was born in Corpus, but, no, Digger was not her father. Her father had been the foreman of Southfork Ranch, Hutch McKinney, who had had an affair with her mother, Rebecca. Digger murdered her father, and, no, her mother didn't die, she had run away from Digger, in fear of her life.

However, this little girl was a happy baby. Pamela giggled and laughed almost from the day she was born. She never howled; she was well-behaved, even as an infant. She started walking at ten months; with no premeditation, she just stood up one day and walked across the living room to Digger. She could barely remember her mother. She and Cliff were left in the care of Digger's sister, Aunt Maggie, and were brought up in a small, well-kept house in a rundown neighborhood of Dallas. Her aunt, though something of a religious fanatic, was warm and loving, and Pam adored her. All in all, as Pam would say in later years, "When you get right down to it, Cliff and I were just two poor kids who grew up on the wrong side of the tracks."

They had infrequent visits from their nomadic father. When he did show up, it was usually during one of his sober periods—which got shorter and shorter as Pam grew older—and if there was one thing he liked to talk about, it was his hatred for Jock Ewing. Pam grew up believing that Jock Ewing had cheated her father out of his oil fortune, and that was the reason why her father drank so much, and that was why she and Cliff had to live with Aunt

149

Bobby and Pam shortly after their marriage, 1978.

Above, right:
Pamela's fall from the loft at Southfork, which caused her miscarriage in 1978. She had interrupted a romantic interlude of J.R.'s (hence the lipstick on his face) and, in the heat of an argument with him, lost her footing and fell.

Maggie. Digger filled Pam's head with visions of how Barnes money built the Ewing empire. In adolescence, a period when her lack of parents and money seemed to be an insurmountable social liability, Pam was, as Cliff later said, "worse than I was. You used to break windows in the old Ewing building downtown. You used to plot revenge."

But as Pam grew older, she began to wonder about her father. He was, after all, a drunk. She loved him dearly, Lord knew, but there was something pathetic about how he railed all the time and never did anything. Why didn't he fight for what was his? Why did he just let Jock Ewing take it all and then not fight back? Could it be that Digger just *let* it all happen?

Pam's revenge fantasies began to fade in her teenage years, as she realized that hating the Ewings would do little to improve her lot in life. *She* would improve her life, her future, turn it around, make her own way. *She* could be happy. She, Pamela Barnes, could be somebody.

She tried out for cheerleading in high school and made the team. The squad was an excellent one, winning local competitions, and they were asked to perform at the Sun Bowl in El Paso. It was Pam's first big trip, and she went off terribly excited at her first look of "the world." She found it in a young man, Edison "Ed" Haynes, a dashing soldier who was being shipped off to Vietnam the next day. It all happened so quickly. Pam was barely fifteen years old, she had never been away from home, from Aunt Maggie, and so when this handsome man declared that he loved her and promised her a happy marriage, her head filled with fantasies. Swooning, she agreed to marry him, envisioning a husband, a house, and children of her own—her own normal, loving family.

Ed whisked her across the border into Juárez to get married. Digger found them just in time. They were married, but, thank heaven, the mar-

150

An ecstatic Pamela hugs Bobby for his surprise present of a black Corvette, 1978. Cars are not inconsequential items at Southfork; they are personalized statements to advertise the Ewings' presence on the road. The license plates are as follows:

EWING 1 belonged to Jock's long Lincoln Continental, which is still kept in the garage at Southfork.

EWING 2 belongs to the ranch Ford station wagon that Sue Ellen usually drove. Now she has a Mercedes station wagon.

EWING 3 belongs to J.R.'s conservative four-door Mercedes.

EWING 4 belongs to Bobby's two-door Mercedes sports coupé.

EWING 5 was reserved for Lucy's first car, a Porsche, given to her by Bobby and Pam in 1979.

EWING 6 belonged to Pamela's Corvette, which she gave up when she divorced Bobby in 1983.

Bobby and Pamela are pulled over to the side of the highway by the police and told that J.R. has been shot, 1980. It would be the couple's last opportunity to leave Southfork and save their marriage.

Pamela being led away from the doctor's office by her mother, Rebecca, 1981. Pam was told that she could never carry a child to full term.

Jock beams as the new Texas State Senator Ewing kisses Pamela, 1980. If only, Pamela wistfully thought later, she and Bobby had spent more time kissing and less time listening to other people, they might have saved their marriage.

riage had not been consummated. Ed was shipped off to Vietnam the next day and Digger dragged a crying Pamela back to Dallas, where Digger had the marriage annulled. It was fortunate, because Pamela soon forgot all about Haynes in the months ahead.

When she graduated from high school, Pam started working in The Store, a clothing store in Dallas. It was not a terrific job, but she had a flare for fashion, a classic taste in clothes, and she earned enough to maintain a place of her own, a modest one-bedroom apartment. She took enormous pride in that apartment, and also pride in herself. She took great care with her appearance, in the way she talked, the way she greeted people, and in her manners. An avid reader, she kept up with current events and issues, and was well read in the classics as well as the bestsellers. She was a beautiful, hardworking, charming young lady whom people admired and liked enormously.

She dated frequently. For quite some time, she dated Jack Eastlin, who was one of the wealthiest bachelors in Dallas, and even a State Senator, but then she met a cowboy with rugged good looks and a winsome way—Ray Krebbs, the foreman of Southfork Ranch. She and Ray made a happy couple. They both loved fun and a good time, and yet both were earnest, sincere, with no illusions about themselves. She cared for him a great deal and had idle notions in the back of her mind of perhaps marrying him one day, but then, in 1977, Ray brought her to Southfork for the annual Ewing Barbecue. At first, Pam balked—the *Ewings?* How on earth could she go there after all that had happened between her father and Jock? In the end, she decided to go, if for no other reason than just plain curiosity.

She was dancing with Ray when she first noticed Bobby Ewing. At six feet two, with warm hazel eyes and jet-black hair, Bobby was hard not to notice. He was standing there, on the sidelines, watching her. And then he came over and cut in. Pam forgot Ray, the barbecue, Southfork, *everything,* the moment this man held her. She looked into those eyes, and it was all over. It didn't matter that this man was a Ewing; he was Bobby, and one day he was going to be Pam's.

Pam's vision of her wedding had not been of a ten-minute service in a New Orleans justice of the peace's office with a Southern Baptist minister presiding, but it was a wedding. In 1978 she became Mrs. Bobby Ewing and was suddenly a member of one of the most powerful families in Texas. The transition was not easy.

When she arrived at Southfork, the family was clearly mortified at what Bobby had done, at *what* he had married. Jock was contemptuous, Miss Ellie cool, J.R. hostile, Sue Ellen as if she didn't exist, and Lucy! Pam was astounded at the behavior that little brat got away with. And then, of course, there was Ray to contend with. Silent, sad Ray, standing outside, forever hovering around the house.

But Pamela had Bobby. She had him to wake up with in the morning, she had him in her arms at night, and she had him to make a life with, to make a future. That made everything worth it.

Oh, Lord, was there ever trouble, though, in that house. First off, J.R. accused her of being a spy for her brother, Cliff, who was building a case against Ewing Oil. Bobby vigorously defended her, and the family eventually found out that Pam was innocent. Score 1 for Pam.

When Pam announced that she was expecting, all the Ewings except J.R. and Sue Ellen forgave her for being a Barnes. The family's joy was terminated, however, when she lost the child, due to a fall from the loft in the barn. To get her mind off her misfortune, Pam took back her old job with Liz Craig at The Store, and she did extremely well, eventually earning a promotion as a buyer.

As Pam was beginning to recover from the trauma, Ed Haynes turned up in Dallas to claim that they were still married and that during the

Below, left:
Pam, dazed, suffering from an emotional breakdown, ready to jump off the top of Reunion Tower in downtown Dallas, 1981.

Below, right:
Bobby, crying with relief that he got there in time, holds Pam in his arms after her suicide attempt.

Dr. Dagmara Conrad stands by as Bobby says good-bye to Pamela, who went into Brooktree Psychiatric Hospital for round-the-clock supervision and therapy, 1981.

Rebecca brings Pam's half sister, Katherine Wentworth, to meet her in the hospital, 1981. It lifted Pam's heart to know she had more family, and for that, Pam would always be grateful. However, everything else about Katherine would only bring destruction.

years he was in a POW camp, only Pam's memory had kept him alive. Pam was shocked beyond words and couldn't imagine how this could be happening. J.R. gleefully brought the news—that Pamela was a bigamist—to the family dinner table, and though Pam hastened to explain to the Ewings that the marriage had been annulled, the papers testifying to that fact had mysteriously disappeared. Eventually Pam was cleared, and Haynes was found to be a blackmailer. Pam kept a wary eye on J.R. after that. His desire to get her out of the family was all too apparent.

Trouble was forever being generated by J.R. He openly despised Pam. Pam thought that was mild compared to the feelings she was developing for him. When her brother was framed by J.R. for the murder of Julie Grey, Pam threw in the towel and moved off Southfork. She moved in temporarily with Leanne Rees, one of The Store's models. What was supposed to be a chance to get her head together turned out to be the most embarrassing incident of her life. One night in her room she woke to find Leanne lying across the bed with a drunken man, both of them in stages of undress. Pam bolted upright and yelled at the two of them, while a photographer snapped away from outside the window, the record of the event courtesy of J.R. The next morning at the Ewing breakfast table, the Dallas *Press* displayed the not-so-discreet headline: FINAN-

CIER IN LOVE NEST and there, splashed across the front page, was a photograph of Pam in bed with Leanne and Ben Maxwell. Fortunately for Pam, Bobby always believed in her innocence, and this time was no exception. But boy oh boy, it really cinched the saddle on Pam's hatred for J.R.

In 1979, Pamela was told by Digger's doctor that Digger was a carrier of neurofibromatosis, and that she and Cliff, as his children, were carriers. It was a disease that could be fatal to infants, and the doctor strongly advised them never to have children. Shortly thereafter, Pam discovered she was pregnant. She was in agony; she couldn't bring herself to tell Bobby. But before she could go ahead with the abortion the doctor recommended, Bobby found out about her pregnancy, and he was so happy, she didn't have the heart to tell him the rest. Then tragedy struck. A rattlesnake scared Pam's horse while she was riding and she was thrown, causing a miscarriage. Later she found out that she was not Digger's daughter and thus was not a carrier of the disease. Then she was told that, after those two miscarriages, she could not bear children. Deeply grieved, Pam tried to push on in life as best as she could.

Her career was moving along at The Store—she was handling the spring catalog alone for the first time—but she started losing interest in her work when Sue Ellen and J.R. brought little John Ross home to Southfork. Sue Ellen, who was in a chronic state of depression, barely acknowledged the child's existence, and J.R. rarely went within two feet of the child. Pamela stepped in as if she were his mother—feeding, changing, and playing with him, getting up before the nurse did in the middle of the night when he cried. She soon became obsessed with the child, as a kind of mourning for what she could not have herself.

Pam's boss was suddenly transferred to the Houston store and Pam was promoted to head buyer, which kept her extremely busy. But she still was obsessing over John Ross. Bobby was drifting away from her with the demands of his work.

To top off 1980, Pam watched Digger painfully and slowly die as a result of his years of alcoholism. She was overwhelmed by a sense of loss and her great loneliness pushed her to find out about her mother. She developed a notion—a dream born out of grief—that perhaps her mother wasn't dead after all. Then a private investigator turned up evidence that her mother had *not* died as Digger had said.

Meanwhile, Bobby had taken over Ewing Oil while J.R. was convalescing after being shot, and it made Pamela nervous. She watched her husband get deeper and deeper into the heart of the business in an effort to prove himself, and she took note of Bobby's instinctive attraction to power, which she realized might be dangerous to their marriage. Pam knew that their chance of leaving Dallas and J.R. was over. Now that Bobby had tasted power, he wouldn't be anxious to let go of it.

Pam's private investigator, after following seemingly endless leads, located a woman he believed to be Pam's mother. But instead of the waitress or maid whom Pam had envisioned, the woman was the matron of a fabulously opulent mansion in Houston. Pam approached her, and Rebecca Wentworth flatly denied that she was her mother. She was, she said emphatically, Rebecca *Wentworth,* and she had never heard of anyone named Digger Barnes.

Depressed, Pamela pushed on with her work, trying to shut out the pain, the loneliness penetrating her very heart. She met Alex Ward, the millionaire publisher of Dallas *World,* who fell head over heels in love with her

Pamela holds her new son, Christopher. His entry into her life made her psychological recovery complete.

Pam happily plays with Christopher as Bobby looks on with worry. He finally confided to Pam in 1982 that Christopher could be J.R.'s son.

the first time they met. Alex was ardent, persistent, and he was tempting. Bobby, at this point, had resigned as President of Ewing Oil but had begun an alternative energy company that still took all of his time. He consistently missed lunch and dinner dates with Pam, and by the time he got home at night, he was too tired or too wrapped up in business problems to pay much attention to her. Alex, by contrast, was charming, attentive, and totally available. It was difficult to keep pushing him away, particularly since he had business ties with The Store, but Pam couldn't bring herself to betray Bobby, and she curtailed any involvement with Alex.

Pam is stunned when Bobby says that perhaps it's best that they go their separate ways, 1983. Unbeknown to them both, Katherine engineered the misunderstanding that made each think the other wanted a divorce.

Mark Graison sits beside Pam outside her house, 1983. He fell very deeply in love with her, but Pam held out for many weeks, still in love with Bobby.

Then something wonderful happened. Rebecca Wentworth called Pam and asked for a meeting. Rebecca broke down and confessed that, yes, indeed, she was Pammy's mother. To Pam, it meant a confirmation of her identity, which she badly needed. Rebecca arrived at a time when Pam needed family most, when she was trying to come to terms with her past, with her inability to have a child, with her problems fitting into the Ewing family. Rebecca came to cherish her daughter, and soon the past was behind them. They became extraordinarily close in a very short period of time.

The baby issue continued to haunt Pam, after the doctors had told her that she could not carry a child past the third month of pregnancy. Despite Bobby's and Rebecca's support, she floundered in depression, without quite being aware of what was happening. She started to drift off at work, her concentration gone, lapsing into short periods of remorse, of some kind of grieving. The depression culminated in near-fatal tragedy: Pam tried to kill herself by jumping off the top of Reunion Tower in downtown Dallas. Bobby got there in time to stop her, but it was clear that Pam would try again and was in dire need of psychiatric help.

Bobby took her to Brooktree Psychiatric Hospital, where Dr. Dagmara Conrad began intensive therapy with Pam as an inpatient. Pam explained to her that being unable to bear a child made her feel "like nothing matters. Like I'm worthless, empty. Like I'm dying . . . or already dead." She diagnosed Pam's depression as stemming largely from suppressed anger and self-hatred. The therapy continued, and little by little Pam came to terms with her problem. As Dr. Danvers explained to Bobby, "Her desperate desire for a child is rooted in her own unhappy childhood. She wants to give a baby the love and attention she feels she missed. That way she thinks she can make things right for baby Pam."

While still in Brooktree, Rebecca brought in Pamela's half sister, Katherine Wentworth, whom she had never met. She was a lovely girl and Pam took to her immediately. Katherine made Pam feel better, more secure; it was a

157

nice feeling, having more family, and even nicer to have a sister, which she had always wanted.

On a surprise visit home to Southfork, Pam walked through the front door and saw Bobby standing there with the most precious little baby boy in his arms. Her heart skipped a beat. She assumed it was a child they could adopt. As she took the little fellow into her arms and looked into his eyes, she felt all the heaviness fall away from her heart. With this son to love and nurture, Pam's remotional recovery was complete within weeks.

In soaring spirits, Pam quickly settled into her life as Christopher's mother, while Bobby continued with the adoption proceedings. She was never happier than in those days, sharing the child with Rebecca, Ellie, Cliff— all those who wanted to participate in her joy. When Liz Craig asked her about returning to The Store, Pam said no, explaining that she didn't want to leave her son. Bobby expressed a little concern about what he saw as obsessiveness with her mother role; he reminded her that she herself had always maintained how important working was to her. Pam sidestepped the issue. Then her husband surprised her with a gift of a business, Pam's Aerobics Unlimited, an exercise salon, complete with a day-care room where Christopher could happily be taken care of, right near his mama. Pam thrived, as did the salon. She had always been extraordinarily fit, and she proved to be a terrific instructor and example.

She and Bobby grew closer during this period. Though terribly overworked, and often exhausted, Bobby fought for time to spend with Pam and their son. Pam noticed that he seemed to be under some kind of emotional strain, which he consistently shrugged off when she asked him about it. In May of 1982 Bobby finally told her about Farraday, Kristin Shepard, and the fact that J.R. could be Christopher's father. Pam was shocked that Bobby had kept this news from her all this time, but she didn't hesitate to jump right in and fly to California with him to find out the truth, prepared to fight whoever she had to to keep her son.

The Ewings formally adopted Christopher in the fall of 1982, and the little Ewing family seemed on good ground. But, alas, the calm was not to last. Pam's brother, Cliff, made a suicide attempt and it revived the Barnes-Ewing feud. Now Rebecca was brought into it; she was hell-bent on revenge against J.R. in particular. And the contest between Bobby and J.R. for Ewing Oil compounded the stress. Pam saw that the corporate battle was changing her husband—he was becoming more like J.R. in his tactics—and she didn't

Pam forlornly listens to the court proceedings during her divorce from Bobby, 1983.

like it one bit. As she said, "Power, money, and control mean nothing to me. I want a nice, ordinary life with my husband." She wanted them to leave Southfork, to leave Texas if they had to, and start life over elsewhere. Bobby refused.

Tension escalated to unbearable proportions when Miss Ellie, in her attempt to break Jock's will and stop the contest that was tearing the family apart, sought support from Pam, who gave it. Bobby was angry with Pam, since he sided with J.R. on the issue. As emotions rose at Southfork, Pam leaned more and more on her mother for support.

And then Rebecca was no longer there. As she was leaving for Houston on business concerning the feud, the Wentworth jet was involved in a midair collision, forcing it to crash-land at Love Field. Critically injured, Rebecca died in Dallas Memorial Hospital. She spent her last minutes alive with Pam at her side, and her last words to her were:

"Cliff's a sweet boy. But—he's not—so strong. Look after him, Pammy, please. He needs someone strong. Like you . . . Keep him safe. Protect him. Promise me you'll protect him . . . You always were the stronger one. Don't tell him I said so. It'll be our secret."

Pamela made her promise to her mother and, quietly, Rebecca passed away. Pam was devastated—and angry—if it hadn't been for that infernal contest between Bobby and J.R. . . .

She went to her mother's house, where she finally broke down and cried her heart out. When she had calmed down somewhat, she knew she could not go back to Southfork. She decided to take Christopher and move into the Fairview Hotel with her sister, Katherine, and try to get her head straight.

Katherine and Cliff's girlfriend, Afton Cooper, join Pam and Christopher for a little poolside brunch, 1983. Divorced from Bobby, missing her mother and father too, Pamela reached out to whatever family she had left.

159

Rebecca's death left Pamela a millionairess in her own right. Her mother left her 50 percent of all income and voting shares in Wentworth Industries (the other 50 percent went to Katherine), and 33.3 percent in Wentworth Tool & Die (the other two thirds to Katherine and Cliff). It would be a while before she paid interest in her new status and responsibilities.

Thanks to Katherine, and later J.R., Pam and Bobby were led into deception after deception about each other, making a reconciliation impossible. Meanwhile, the wonderful man Pam had met recently, millionaire Mark Graison, persistently appeared on the scene, offering help, love, and encouragement. Pam found herself drawn into a friendship with him, although he clearly wanted more. After an emotionally exhausting confrontation with Bobby at the hotel, Pam expressed a need to get away from all the chaos in Dallas, and Mark offered to fly her to the Riviera on his private jet. At first she was hesitant and said no, but then she thought, why not?

There, enjoying the sun and the quiet, Pam realized that she was enormously attracted to Mark, but, no matter what, while she was still married to Bobby, she would never sleep with anyone else. That is just her nature. Then, when she was leaning toward violating her own moral code, Pam received an urgent transatlantic call from Afton Cooper, her brother's girlfriend, who warned her that Katherine was moving in on Bobby. Confused, not sure what it was all supposed to mean, Pam left immediately for Dallas.

She confronted Bobby first, then Katherine, and believed them when they said they were merely close friends and that Katherine was working on helping him get a Wentworth Tool & Die drill he desperately needed for his Canadian fields, despite Cliff's veto.

Pam was put in an awkward position. Bobby wanted the Tundra Torque for Ewing Oil, and Cliff did not want him to have it (he wanted to force Bobby to sell the fields to him instead). If Pam sided with Katherine and voted to let him have it, then Bobby would probably win control over Ewing Oil. And that would mean Bobby would go on as he had been recently—tense, a bit ruthless, and never having time for anything but work—leaving few of the qualities that made Pam love him. But if Pam voted with Cliff not to give Bobby the drill, it would mean the end of their marriage for sure. Pam voted with Katherine and hoped for the best.

The best was no alternative, she realized then. Bobby had changed greatly, and there was a no-win label on this marriage. She met with him and said she thought they should be divorced so that she could try to build a new life, since the old one was in such a shambles. Then the fire at Southfork occurred and Pam backed off the divorce issue to let Bobby have some time to sort out the mess at the house. Before Pam spoke to him again, J.R. stepped in to say that as long as Pam stayed away from Bobby, J.R. would leave Bobby alone, but if Pam came back into Bobby's life, then J.R. would do everything in his power to destroy not only Bobby, but also her brother, Cliff. J.R. had never made an idle threat in his life, and Pam knew it.

Katherine tricked Pam into signing a paper that made it appear that Pam had written a letter to her lawyer saying she was no longer in love with Bobby. Katherine read Bobby this made-up letter. So when Pam met with Bobby, having decided to ignore J.R. and reconcile with him, she was speechless with pain when Bobby told her to her face that he was ready to let go, and that it was time for both of them to realize that their marriage was over. Unable to say anything, Pam left.

Pam waiting to ride the mechanical bull in Billy Bob's Charity Rodeo, 1983. When she saw how Jenna Wade kissed Bobby that night, she finally gave in and went to bed with Mark.

Pam and Bobby met with their lawyers, and the proceedings began. Pam went to court—Bobby didn't need to appear—and the divorce was granted to the Ewings in the fall of 1983.

Cliff had been pestering Pam to join forces with him and Mark Graison to create a new company. Pam had been slow to agree to the arrangement—her brother was clearly overwhelmed by Mark's money, good breeding, generosity, and kind heart—because she didn't want Cliff taking advantage of him, using the fact that Mark was in love with her as leverage. Mark's love was something she had yet to act on. Oh, she cared for Mark, but Bobby . . .

It hurt Pam deeply when she saw Bobby with, of all people, Jenna Wade. It pushed her closer to Mark, and her jealousy and anger the night of Billy Bob's Charity Rodeo pushed her over the edge and into Mark's bed. As the possibility of any reconciliation with Bobby grew more and more remote, Pam began to be more seriously involved with Mark.

Mark asked Pam to marry him. She was caught off guard and said she needed to think about it. Katherine and Cliff jumped all over her, urging her to say yes. Pam told Bobby, who remained silent on the subject. Mark, impatiently waiting for her answer, went on a trip and said he wanted an answer when he returned. After thinking long and hard about it, after searching her heart, Pam confided to Sue Ellen that she was going to turn Mark down. Sue Ellen asked her if it was because of Bobby, and Pam admitted it was.

And then the world turned upside down. Pam accidentally met Mark's doctor and good friend, Jerry Kenderson, who had been searching frantically for Mark. When Pam pressured him, the doctor reluctantly revealed that he had to tell Mark he had leukemia, that it was hopeless, and that he would have, at best, a year to live. Pam pleaded with the doctor to postpone telling

161

Mark, which he agreed to. And so, when Mark arrived home to Dallas, Pam told him, yes, she would marry him.

The ensuing weeks were sheer agony for Pam. Mark's love for her, his bright banter about their future together, all the things they would do, the home they would create, made her ache inside, as she knew he would never live to see any of it. Pam wanted to be married right away and have a small wedding, but Mark kept insisting on a big wedding, which would take more time to organize. Pam succeeded in keeping the doctor at bay for a little longer. Pam also had to tell Bobby that she would be marrying Mark, with no mention of why.

One night Mark was called to the Oil Baron's Club to pick up a completely smashed Katherine, who in her stupor told Mark the only reason he was getting married was because of Dr. Kenderson. She passed out then and, when she came to, Mark pressed her for an explanation. She tried to cover, but Mark was suspicious and went to Kenderson for an explanation. He got it.

Pam, not knowing that Mark now knew, spent one last loving, beautiful night with him. The next day she received the horrible news—Mark had flown his plane out over the Gulf and had blown it up. He was gone forever, unable to face being an invalid, a burden to those he loved. The letter he left behind said, in part:

"Pam, I realize now why, after so long, you suddenly wanted such a quick wedding. You wanted to make sure I wouldn't be alone at the end. Knowing that means more than I can tell you. You're a wonderful and beautiful woman, Pam. This past year has been the best in my life, and I'm deeply grateful for the happiness you gave me. I only regret I had so little time to

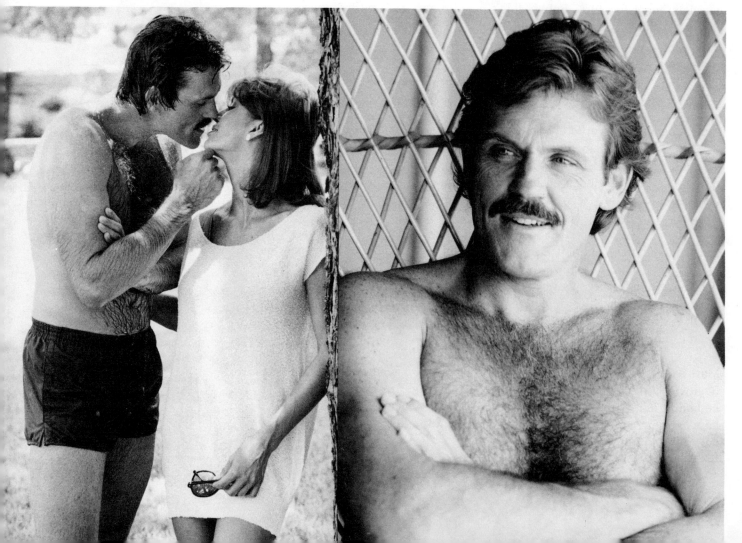

Cliff tries to cheer up Pam, 1984. He might be a braggart, headstrong and weak, but he is all the family besides Christopher that Pam has left.

return it. But you'll find happiness again. Maybe it'll be with Bobby. I think you two still care for each other."

But that would not be possible, for Bobby was marrying Jenna Wade.

In 1984, Pam was led to believe that Mark had not died, but that he had only appeared to die and, in fact, was secretly going from clinic to clinic worldwide in search of a cure for his disease. Pam's desperate search for him was fueled by a pilot who said he had flown Graison to the Caribbean. Later, after exhaustive inquiries and expense and a trail that was going to take Pamela to Hong Kong, the pilot broke down and confessed that J.R. had paid him to make her believe that Graison was still alive. He wanted to keep her away from Bobby.

For years Pamela has been willing to forgive and forget, as one loved one after another has hurt her, but the day has arrived where she is crossing the line from fatalist to catalyst. With her father and mother gone, with her lover Mark Graison gone, with her sister's betrayal complete and her ex-husband's estrangement almost total, Pamela has chosen to stand her ground against the Ewing family. She has joined the infamous feud and, if she has her way, J. R. Ewing will live to regret it.

163

Christopher Shepard Ewing

"Notice of Intention to Adopt. To all interested parties. Male child, age seven months. Abandoned at Dallas, Texas, on December 11, of last year."

—Daily Commercial Record, 1982

This gentle-natured, charming young boy will grow up with a rather extended and confusing family, but, no matter what, he will grow up with the Ewing name. He was born on August 18, 1981, to Kristin Shepard and Jeff Farraday in Los Angeles, California. Both his parents passed away, and so his Aunt Sue Ellen's sister- and brother-in-law, Pam and Bobby Ewing, who were unable to have children, adopted Christopher as their own son.

His adoptive parents were divorced in 1983 and Christopher lives with his mother at her house in Dallas. He spends his weekends with his daddy at Southfork Ranch, where his grandma and his cousin John Ross are.

When Christopher grows up, he will be a millionaire several times over. His granddaddy Jock Ewing left him an enormous trust fund, as did his grandmother Rebecca Wentworth. He will also—as his parents' and Uncle Cliff's wills provide—one day have substantial voting shares in Ewing Oil, Wentworth Industries, Wentworth Tool & Die, and Barnes-Wentworth Oil.

Christopher is always called by his full name. His favorite toys to sleep with are his pet teddy bear and giraffe.

Little Christopher was sound asleep at the most important moment of his life—when Bobby and Pamela Ewing legally became his parents in 1982.

165

3 · THE EMPIRE

Ewing Oil and the Texas Independents

The official portrait of John Ross Ewing, Sr., "Jock," the founder of Ewing Oil. The painting hangs in the company's headquarters in Dallas.

"We may be right, we may be wrong, but we're Ewings. We stick together. That's why we're unbeatable."

—Eleanor Ewing, 1981

Soaring upward from the Dallas skyline, the Ewing Oil building is right up there, at fifty stories, with the Republic Bank and Reunion Towers. It is the home of Ewing Oil, the family owned and operated corporation. The executive offices are on the top floor, where for decades the Ewings, literally, had Dallas at their feet.

Jock Ewing founded Ewing Oil in 1930 and ran it until 1977, when he retired as Chief Executive Officer. He retained his seat as Chairman of the Board. His years of leadership were ones of solid expansion in what Jock knew best—bringing up oil out of the ground. The company's substantial natural gas leases were almost incidental in the beginning; they were a kind of well-why-let-that-land-go-to-waste-we-might-as-well-get-something-if-not-oil venture. His company was a strong example of the Independents who survived over the years (for many didn't): prudent sense, a game plan of research/acquisition/development, a no-nonsense approach based on the Puritan work ethic, a word that was good on a handshake, and a virtual army of loyal employees who faithfully carried out orders.

Today there are several family owned and operated oil companies like Ewing Oil, though certainly not the number that Texas had in previous years. These companies—although multimillion- and sometimes billion-dollar operations—are nowhere near the size and resources of the international, publicly owned conglomerates like Exxon or Mobil. In order to maintain a strong voice in the oil industry, these companies are bonded by the IOA, the Independent Oilman's Association. They vote on various issues internally and then present a united front in political and economic arenas.

Within the IOA, there are cartels—groups of companies who invest in major ventures together. The cartels limit the competition within the Independents, provide an opportunity to go up against such awesome conglomerates as Westar Oil, and share the risk of any venture between companies. The other usefulness of a cartel is that it brings together the diverse brilliance and expertise of the companies. As Independents have changed hands over the generations, cartels have apprenticed and cared for many a new heir and their legacy.

Jock Ewing was a founding member of one of the first and most powerful cartels in the industry, to which many of the original companies still belong. The original charter of the Dallas-based cartel had the following members:

Jebson Ames, Sr. (deceased), Ames Oil
(Expelled from the cartel in 1980, due to illegal activities by Jebson's son, Jeb Ames, who is Chief Executive Officer.)

Punk Anderson, Anderson Oil
(Still belongs; Punk is still CEO.)

169

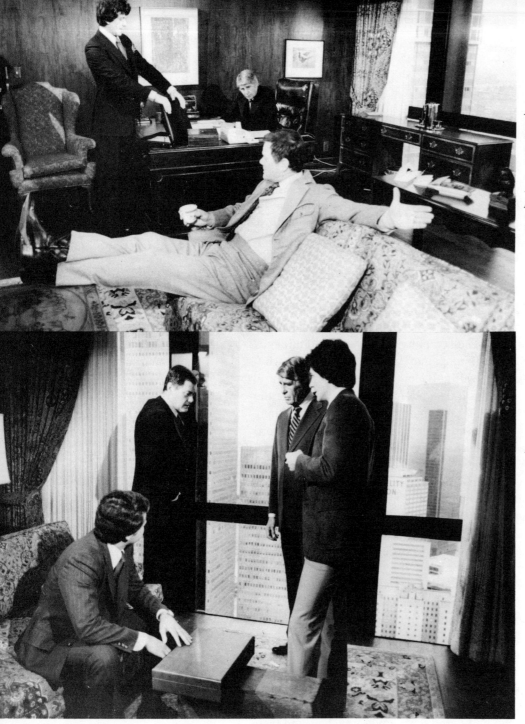

J.R. and Bobby discuss business with Jock in Jock's office, 1978. All of the executive offices at Ewing Oil are amply furnished, but more out of a sense of necessity rather than prosperity—the executives often live in their offices during times of trouble.

Ewing Oil is one of the tallest buildings in Dallas.

Andy Bradley, Bradley Oil
(Still belongs; Andy is still CEO.)

John Ross Ewing, Sr. (deceased), Ewing Oil
(Still belongs; sons John Ross Ewing, Jr., and Bobby Ewing are joint CEOs.)

William Joseph Garr, Sr. (deceased), Garr Oil
(Expelled from the cartel in 1980, due to illegal activity by William's son, Billie Joe, Jr., who is CEO.)

Martin Hurst (deceased), Hurst Oil
(Still belongs as Stonehurst Oil—name changed when Martin died and his daughter named her husband, Seth Stone, CEO. Upon Stone's death in 1980, Martin's daughter, Marilee Hurst Stone, became CEO.)

Marilee Stone, President and Chief Executive Officer of Stonehurst Oil. Marilee's father made her husband, Seth, President and CEO of the company, and when Seth killed himself in 1980 after nearly bankrupting the company, Marilee took control of the company herself. She has proved to be a mighty tough lady in the boardroom and has developed a reputation similar to J.R.'s in the bedroom.

Jordan Lee, Lee Oil

(Still belongs; Jordan still CEO.)

Wade Luce, Luce Oil

(Still belongs as Barnes/Wentworth Oil; Luce sold the company to Rebecca Wentworth and it kept its place in the cartel; upon Wentworth's death in 1983, her son, Clifford Barnes, became sole owner and CEO.)

Lucas Wade (deceased), Wade Oil

(The company went bankrupt after Lucas's death and its assets were auctioned off by the banks.)

When Jock stepped down from an active role at Ewing Oil, leaving the reins to his son, J. R. Ewing, as President, the company began to change. Some say it changed for the better, many said for the worst, but one thing is certain: since 1977, Ewing Oil has had to weather some of the most chaotic and explosive corporate management in the history of the oil industry.

In the fall of 1978, the youngest of the Ewing sons, Bobby, joined the executive management team, and rumors began to fly in Dallas and Houston. J.R. was indeed the President of the company—everyone knew that—but rumor had it that J.R. was not happy with his little brother nosing around certain files and wanted him out of his domain. Those in the industry who had been pushed around by Ewing Oil in years past began to smile at the thought of internal problems within the family, but no one smiled when the news came that the Ewing company jet, carrying both J.R. and Bobby to New Orleans, had crashed in a thunderstorm and the two men were presumed dead. With Jock Ewing recovering from a cardiac arrest and the two boys gone, the fate of Ewing Oil and its hundreds of Texan employees hung in the balance. (Anyone who knew anything about anything knew that Gary Ewing could run Ewing Oil about as well as a cow could run Southfork.) It was with a great cheer that Dallas and Houston received word that J.R. had pulled his brother and the pilot safely out of the wreck, got them to shelter, and set out signals for the search team. At the tail end of 1978, Bobby Ewing resigned from Ewing Oil management to start a subsidiary, Ewing Construction.

*Doing business where the
business is. J.R. confers
with Holly Harwood,
President of Harwood Oil,
aboard
her yacht.*

The year 1979 did not begin well. J.R. was closing one of Ewing
Oil's most profitable domestic deals in decades, securing all the land that made
up the recently discovered Palo Seco Field. All the land, that is, except a strip
owned by rancher Wally Kessel. It was the key, in that all the surrounding land
tied into this strip, and it was a major factor in the profitability of the entire
venture. The land was swiped right from under Ewing Oil's nose by none other
than Cliff and Digger Barnes, Jock's former partner and enemy since 1930. The
Palo Seco fields still came in profitably, but the millions Ewing Oil lost out on
that strip in pumping revenue and economical transportation of equipment and
crude was a major disappointment to the company, and its President, and its
Chairman of the Board.

In the spring of 1979, they ran into more bad luck. Cliff Barnes,
Digger's son, was appointed Commissioner of the Office of Land Management,
and he unabashedly declared war on Ewing Oil and unduly harassed them—or
so said Ewing Oil. Barnes said it was in the public interest that he was tying
most their deals in knots by consistently turning down new drilling variances.
Cartel members nervously watched as the Barnes-Ewing private feud became
a major issue in the oil marketplace.

In October 1979, Barnes halted all the new drilling sites of Ewing
Oil in Texas and began shutting down their working fields. J.R. was forced
quickly to find new sources of oil outside of the state—outside Barnes's jurisdiction—and he located some promising offshore leases in Asia. They promised a king's ransom in oil, but the cost and overhead of the operation was
staggering. J.R. examined the geological reports, ran the figures again and
again, saw that Barnes was going to be in the OLM for a while, and so, quietly,
he began to put his plan into operation. It was expensive.

Ewing Oil needed $200,000,000 in cash for the deal, of which it
had $100,000,000 on hand. J.R. debated and then, holding his breath, mortgaged
Southfork for $100,000,000 to complete the deal. A typhoon hit the sites in Asia,

172

causing a postponement of drilling. When the first bank loan became due, Ewing Oil had no money free and J.R. was forced to report this to his father, who, in turn, was ashen with shock. In a few short months, J.R. had taken Ewing Oil from a mighty million-dollar corporation and teetered it onto the verge of bankruptcy, taking all of Southfork and its hundred thousand acres with it.

J.R. waiting to speak with his brother in Bobby's office, 1979. The hard hat hanging on the coatrack is more than decoration; Bobby often travels out to the fields to get a firsthand look at any problems that arise.

Just before the loan note was due, much to J.R.'s relief and jubilation, the Asian wells came in. He found out about it himself from the Associated Press. It was one of the biggest oil strikes in the history of the world, flinging Ewing Oil to the top of the IOA and making the Ewing family *billionaires*. Jock Ewing wanted to step back in to run Ewing Oil, but J.R., in order to prevent that, elected to bring back Bobby.

Things went along smoothly for several weeks. Everyone was surprised when J.R. offered to sell shares of his Asian leases to some of their friends in the cartel. He'd sell 75 percent of the Asian holdings at $10,000,000 a point, plus a 25 percent royalty on every barrel of oil taken out of Asia. Any interested parties had twenty-four hours to make up their minds, and four did: Andy Bradley, Jordan Lee, Seth Stone, and banker Vaughan Leland. The deals were consummated, and Ewing Oil received $750,000,000.

The next day, there was a political revolt in Asia, and the wells were nationalized. The investors were ruined. Leland was run out of town (he had "borrowed" money from his bank), Bradley was close to bankruptcy and so was Lee, but Seth Stone, oh, Lord, how awful it was. Stone was faced with bankrupting his wife's company, and he just couldn't bear to tell her that he had lost everything, and he killed himself.

Jock Ewing, believing along with the public that perhaps J.R. had known that the wells were going to be nationalized, fired J.R. from Ewing Oil and named Bobby President. Bobby stepped into what was an awful mess. Bradley and Lee were friends of Jock's for years and years, and the cartel,

Bobby Ewing lands at La Mesa Air Field in the Ewing Oil helicopter to meet Gillis's extortion demands of money and a plane in exchange for not blowing up Ewing 23.

J.R. surprises Bobby and Gillis by striding out of the plane with security men, who open fire on Gillis.

Shot, Gillis falls to the ground, where he is about to detonate the explosives on Ewing 23.

Bobby runs out onto the field as the smoke from the remains of Ewing 23 can be seen drifting up from the horizon.

Bobby strong-arms his brother for interfering. This would be one of many, many disagreements the two brothers would have over how to handle Ewing Oil business.

seeing what Ewing Oil had done to them, refused to go into any deal with *any* Ewing anymore. Half of field Ewing 23, which Bobby had reopened for $6,000,000, was legally declared Digger Barnes's, so half of that revenue was lost. Marilee Stone was suing Ewing Oil for millions for the death of her husband. (Bobby managed to settle it out of court for $500,000.) The Asian wells had cost them a $250,000,000 loss, plus any earnings, and although they did have the $750,000,000 in cash from the cartel, the natural gas wells on the East Coast needed $650,000,000.

Bobby is a smart, savvy businessman. After settling various problems inherited from J.R., Bobby carried out his own dream for Ewing Oil. He bought a refinery in Galveston—something Jock had wanted for years but J.R. never managed to do—but he couldn't get anyone in the cartel to invest with Ewing Oil, so he had to swing it alone, using all available cash.

The financing was tricky. The key to it was the shipment of 600,000 barrels of crude oil to the refinery by way of the Venezuelan tanker *Antioch*. The tanker mysteriously sank in mid-voyage, and it was discovered that the owners had failed to supply Ewing Oil with anything near adequate insurance. It looked like Ewing Oil was going to lose its refinery altogether, due to cash flow problems. But then Bobby's people discovered that someone had pulled an oil heist on them. The oil had been lifted from the *Antioch* while it was still in Venezuela and transferred to the *Marsh Baron*. They tracked it from its departure from the harbor on October 2 to its docking in Corpus Christi, where they claimed it. The refinery was back in business.

As if this weren't enough to handle at the time, Bobby was contacted by a man named Gillis, who said if Ewing Oil didn't hand over $5,000,000, he was going to blow up Ewing 23. He wanted the money and a jet delivered to him at La Mesa Air Field. After Gillis demonstrated that he did indeed have all the wells wired to explode, Bobby followed Gillis's instruc-

Following his resignation from Ewing Oil in 1980, Bobby Ewing ran for Texas State Senator representing District 33. He won the election and was a valuable asset in Austin for the Ewings. His first order of business was to settle the Takapa dispute.

Sue Ellen, J.R., and Ellie Ewing chat with Cliff Barnes of Wentworth Tool & Die at the Oil Baron's Ball, 1982. The ball is held every fall and is one of the most illustrious social events in all of the Southwest.

Sue Ellen, J.R., Miss Ellie, Bobby, and Pamela Ewing listen as the Jock Ewing Memorial Scholarships to SMU are announced, 1982.

tions to the letter, but when the jet he had arranged for landed, the door burst open and J.R. stood there while two gun-wielding security men opened fire on Gillis. Gillis detonated the explosives by remote control and the ground shook. In the distance they could see Ewing 23 being blown to kingdom come.

Life was not easy for Bobby as President of Ewing Oil that year, and there were more problems ahead. Jock was used to going into deals of his own, withdrawing funds from Ewing Oil with which to invest. At this time, he went in with Punk Anderson on the Takapa project, which was to turn swampland on the Texas/Louisiana border into a hunting and fishing resort. Jock withdrew $12,000,000 from Ewing Oil, unbeknown to Bobby. Bobby, in the meantime, had committed Ewing Oil to an investment with the cartel. Now he didn't have the funds on hand to make good on his word. It was a crucial deal in several respects. First of all, Jordan Lee had put it together, and it was the first time the cartel had let Ewing Oil in on a deal since J.R.'s Asian well

177

Mark Graison of Graisco Industries, Pamela Ewing of Wentworth Industries, and Cliff Barnes of Barnes-Wentworth Oil went into a limited partnership in 1983 and lifted several deals out from under Ewing Oil. The arrangement dissolved when Graison killed himself in 1984.

disaster. It was Bobby's first test as a man of his word—a man who supposedly was different from his brother. And the deal itself was a very sound investment. There was enormous pressure on Bobby to come through. Eventually he did, with a staggered payment schedule.

The situation forced a severe argument with his father, since Jock had not notified Bobby of the withdrawal. (Jock said it was *his* company, darn it!) And J.R. was getting to him in subversive ways. Both soured Bobby's taste for the role of President.

Bobby resigned in the fall of 1980, and a gleeful J.R. moved back into the office as President, but his smile faded when he saw the terms of his brother's resignation:

· Control over Ewing 23 (which had been completely rebuilt)

· An alternative energy division, financed by Ewing 23 and 12½ percent of all profits from the Ewing refinery.

The alternative energy division would be in Bobby's sole control, researching and developing economical methods of producing power through solar, geothermal, and wind sources.

Following Bobby's resignation, J.R. hired one of the most effective corporate public relations experts in the country, Leslie Stewart, to shine up his and Ewing Oil's somewhat tarnished image. The initial slogan for the Ewing campaign was "People Before Profits" and, when it moved into high gear, the second stage of the campaign called for ads in the *Wall Street Journal,* the New York *Times, International Herald Tribune,* and the London *Financial Times,* blazing forth the line: EWING OIL—THE COMPANY FOR TOMORROW'S WORLD. Rumors began to fly in the financial world, and J.R.'s office was besieged with interested parties investigating the possibility that Ewing Oil would go public.

Most fortuitous for the Ewing image, however, was the toppling of the Asian government that had nationalized the wells. The new government returned the oil wells to their Texan owners, and Marilee Stone, Jordan Lee, Andy Bradley, and Vaughan Leland were made staggeringly rich. Ewing Oil, too, regained massive financial stability, and J. R. Ewing was riding high in the industry.

When Jock and Ellie Ewing separated in the spring of 1981, word had it that, should they divorce—which it looked like they would—Jock would sell Ewing Oil. The next underground scoop said that J.R. jumped the gun on

Sue Ellen and J. R. Ewing at the 1983 Oil Baron's Ball, representing the royal oil family of Dallas.

his father, moving ahead to sell the company to Westar, the eighth largest oil company in the world. It was alleged that Ewing Oil would remain a separate entity and still be run by J.R., who personally would garner a huge salary, preferred and common stock with annual options, profit sharing and a sweet provision for retirement. However, the sale did not come to pass.

In May, scandal for the company broke out, as the Dallas *Press* headlines screamed: ALLEGED COVER-UP IN ASIAN COUP BY SENATE COMMITTEE: J. R. EWING LINKED TO OVERTHROW OF SOUTHEAST ASIA GOVERNMENT. Bobby Ewing, now serving in the State Senate, was on that committee, which was moving on evidence produced by Cliff Barnes, Bobby's legal counsel. As Senator Horbin explained at the hearing:

"We are investigating charges brought against Ewing Oil Company, J. R. Ewing, President, that they have violated the Charter granted them by the State of Texas. The specific charge is conspiring to overthrow a foreign government. If we find evidence of wrongdoing, a recommendation will be made for the prosecution to the State Attorney General to deprive Ewing Oil of its State Charter and for an appropriate criminal charge against Mr. Ewing."

It was a grueling hearing, and things looked very bad indeed for Ewing Oil, but J.R. won his case when he proved that the $9,920,000 that was in question—the money allegedly used to overthrow the government that had nationalized the wells—was, in fact, donated for use in Asian schools and hospitals, as a gesture of goodwill from an American company who had interests there. The charges were dismissed on the strength of J.R.'s evidence for the defense.

The company was barely stabilized when it suffered another burden. Critics claim that a personal vendetta clouded J.R.'s judgment, but, whatever the case, the President ordered that the company buy up 5,000,000 barrels of crude that the company could not use, sell, or store. It was all of the crude that normally would be channeled into the Farlow refineries. This seemingly insane maneuver cost the company $200,000,000 in cash, the money for which came from a loan that was backed by Ewing Oil itself as a guarantee. Oil prices were dropping, and Ewing Oil immediately began losing money. On a single day in the fall of 1981, oil prices dropped $3 a barrel—a loss of $15,000,000—and that said nothing of the money spent on storage.

The Ewing table at the Oil Baron's Ball, 1983. From left, clockwise: Lucy Ewing Cooper, Peter Richards, Sue Ellen Ewing, J. R. Ewing, Jenna Wade, Bobby Ewing (hidden), Donna Culver Krebbs (of the Texas Energy Commission), and Ray Krebbs.

Members of the cartel were led by Cliff Barnes to buy J.R.'s loan notes, so that, should he default (they said, *when* he defaulted), the Ewing Oil assets would be divided up among their companies. The company barely escaped this disaster when Jock's wife, Ellie, intervened and sold the 5,000,000 barrels of crude to the Farlow refineries. There was a slight loss to the company, but the loan was repaid on time.

In this period, between Jock's fateful trip to South America (where he died) in 1981 and when his will was read in the fall of 1982, the voting stock in Ewing Oil was held by:

Ellie Ewing   30 shares

J. R. Ewing   20 shares

John Ross Ewing   10 shares (Ellie voted them if John Ross was living off of Southfork; J.R. voted them if his son was living on the ranch.)

Gary Ewing   10 shares (which he signed over to Lucy Ewing Cooper)

Bobby Ewing   20 shares

Ray Krebbs   10 shares (which he ultimately signed over to J.R.)

In September 1982, after the near collapse of the company over the stockpiling of Farlow oil, the family voted J.R. out and Bobby in as company President. There was an oil glut on, and Bobby's first and only action was to cut back production by 25 percent. His other plans were terminated by the reading of Jock's will.

In a special codicil, Jock instructed that Ewing Oil be equally divided between J.R. and Bobby, and that each run his half as a separate company for one year. At the end of that year, whoever had shown the greatest gain for their half of the corporation would inherit 51 percent of the voting stock and control of the company. The loser would receive 19 percent, and the additional 30 percent was to be equally divided between Ellie, Gary, and Ray Krebbs. The will was to start one of the fiercest internal battles in the history of corporate America.

Bobby's major maneuver in the contest was to invest with Thornton & MacLeish in northern Canada—a plan that was plagued by delay from frozen ground that missed its usual thaw. Drilling was postponed until very

Cliff Barnes accepts the Oil Man of the Year Award, 1983, on behalf of Wentworth Tool & Die, who developed the Tundra Torque. The irony is that the Torque would never have been used if Barnes's sisters, Pamela Ewing and Katherine Wentworth, hadn't overridden his veto to let Ewing Oil try it in Canada.

near the end of the year, when Wentworth Tool & Die lent Ewing Oil the experimental Tundra Torque, a drill bit that penetrated the frozen ground and made oil strikes possible.

J.R.'s route was to overpump oil with a special variance from the OLM, refine it, and open a string of cut-rate gasoline stations. By underpricing the competition severely, Ewing Gas was wildly successful with the public—and hated by the gas companies.

Bobby tried to move the cartel to open their collective Wellington wells, but the cartel refused on the grounds that that oil would further flood the market and bring prices crashing down, hurting them all. Then Bobby, incurring the wrath of the entire cartel, held them to their contract, which specified that, in the event they wouldn't open the wells when Ewing Oil wanted to, they had to buy it out as the buyers of the last resort—at five times the amount Ewing Oil had initially invested. The cartel was furious but was forced to comply. It wrote off Bobby as being as bad as J.R. himself.

When J.R.'s variance was rescinded by the new Texas Energy Commission in the spring of 1983, he had no choice but to shut down Ewing Gas. He then made a major oil sale of 1,000,000 barrels, supposedly to Puerto Rico, but word had it at the Oil Baron's Club that it was actually made to an embargoed nation. Bets were on Cuba, since J.R. had gone there recently on a fact-finding mission, but nothing was ever proved. The deal brought in $40,000,000 before expenses. J.R. also sold out interest he had in Harwood Oil, for which he received $20,000,000.

In the fall of 1983, the brothers agreed to split control over Ewing Oil fifty-fifty, no matter who technically won the contest. Both felt the contest had overtaxed the structure of the company and that it was time to pull the company back into one solid piece. Ironically, it was the relative novice, Bobby Ewing, who would have won—which came as a surprise to the industry. At the very last second, the Canadian wells came in, bringing in a check for $26,000,000 to add to his other earnings of $24,160,000 for the year, and making his total profits $50,160,000, compared to J.R.'s $40,220,000. All in all, despite all the feuding that had occurred over the year, Jock would have been proud of his

sons' $90,380,000 profit. Ownership of Ewing Oil to this day is: J.R. 35 percent, Bobby 35, Miss Ellie 10, Ray Krebbs 10, and Gary Ewing 10.

The brothers united their forces to run the company, requiring both men's signatures on all deals, but it was evident that fall that something was internally amiss. Deals were being stolen right from under Ewing Oil. First it was the Murphy Oil leases, which mysteriously ended up at Barnes-Wentworth Oil, and then it was Kesey's oil service company. Just swiped—poof!—like that—and there it was with Barnes/Wentworth/Graison. J.R. discovered an internal leak and let Barnes-Wentworth go ahead and outbid Ewing Oil on one more deal—Gold Canyon 340 Tract in the government auction.

The Ewings were busy in the spring of 1984. Bobby ordered a geological survey of all the Ewing wells, and the reports were not good. After all the full-out pumping they had done during the contest, many of the fields were drying up earlier than expected. Second recovery methods were ordered for the older fields and a search was launched for new domestic properties. Bobby bought Travis Boyd's company for $40,000,000. J.R. approached Katherine Wentworth about the properties she was holding. She eventually sold them to Bobby.

J.R. also moved in to make Ewing Oil the silent banker financing Barnes-Wentworth's acquisition and drilling of Gold Canyon 340, so that if Barnes couldn't meet the payments, Ewing Oil would take over Barnes-Wentworth. That didn't happen, but Ewing Oil did score big when Barnes, still caught short for cash while drilling, had to sell the Kesey and Murphy holdings to J.R., and at one heck of a bargain.

In the late spring of 1984, Bobby Ewing was shot at the Ewing Oil offices, and during his recovery—he was temporarily blinded—Donna Culver Krebbs stepped in on his behalf. Bobby regained his eyesight and returned to Ewing Oil. It was a fortuitous thing, since the Ewings in 1985 have been slapped with a lawsuit that threatens to wrest away two thirds of the company. Cliff Barnes and Jamie Ewing are claiming that their fathers, Digger Barnes and Jason Ewing, were legal partners of Ewing Oil, from its formation in 1930.

The fight is on. For J. R. Ewing it feels like it's for his very life.

Ewing Oil was built from below the ground up by the hands, brains, and determination of Jock Ewing. His sons J.R. and Bobby have brought a chaotic kind of new prosperity to the firm, and what their sons, John Ross and Christopher, will bring to the company only time will tell. But thousands of Texans—working the fields, the refinery, the offices—will attest to the ongoing tradition of Ewing Oil: to be in the forefront of the Texas Independents as a proud leader and prime provider for the magnificent Lone Star State.

The Barnes-Ewing feud flares up, 1983. Barnes denounced Jock Ewing and so J.R. paid a courtesy call on him. J.R. threw a platter at Barnes, Mark Graison punched J.R., and then all the oil barons started walloping each other.

4 · THE FEUD

That Barnes Family

Willard Barnes

"DIGGER"

"Oh, I liked Digger well enough but I wouldn't say I was his girl. And then when I met Jock, well, everything changed. Jock swept me off my feet. Digger never forgave him for it. And that, mixed with the oil, made for one long, awful feud."
—Ellie Ewing, 1983

Poor old Digger.

That's what all of Dallas always said about him. Not so much, perhaps, because of what had been done to him—his incredible run of bad luck with people he cared about most—but for what he did to himself. Digger was a notorious alcoholic for years, staggering along the city streets, talking to himself, only periodically trying to sober up—and even then, for someone he loved. And, of course, sobriety never lasted, since the people Digger loved, according to him, always let him down. His daughter, Pamela, to this day thinks that if Digger had tried to stop drinking for himself, to display any kindness to himself, things might have turned out different. But, sadly, as it were, Digger's life was just one bad nightmare after another until the day he died.

Willard Barnes was born and raised in Dallas County. His father worked for Aaron Southworth on Southfork Ranch as a hand. Willard was rebellious from the day he was born. As a youngster, he flatly refused to learn how to ride a horse; he much preferred to keep his own two feet on the ground, he said. He was a hell-raiser, hated ranching and despised school. But those who knew him well, knew that he possessed a deep, gentle nature that he chose to hide, electing instead to project his natural storytelling ability, often twisting the truth a mite to fit his need for dramatics.

What was peculiar to Willard, and which gave him his nickname, Digger, was his affinity with the ground—the earth, sands, clays, the geological compositions that lay beneath the surface. His parents raised their eyebrows at this strange passion of his and wondered what on earth good this weird fascination would produce, beyond finding water.

Digger was just a kid when Standard Oil of New Jersey lost its monopolistic hold on oil production from its Pennsylvania wells and Texas reared her head as the new, booming oil center of the country. As Digger grew older, his mother began to see where this sixth sense for geology might come in handy, and she encouraged Digger in his interest. Digger's father, like most of the folk at Southfork, abhored even the word oil.

Digger just *knew* what was under the ground. He tried to explain that he could just sort of smell what was down there. As a teenager in the 1920s, he began working in the oil fields, and on one of them he met Jock Ewing. The two became friends. When Jock discovered Digger's "nose," the two went into partnership as wildcatters. As Digger explained: "Jock Ewing

187

A beardless Digger glares at his old adversary Jock Ewing at the Ewing Barbecue, 1979. It killed him to see all that Jock possessed, particularly since Digger felt they were rightfully his—Miss Ellie and millions of dollars, for starters.

had the head. I had the nose. He was the smarter . . . but without my nose, he had nothing. I found the oil; he claimed it. I drilled; he sold what bubbled up."

Digger upheld his end of the partnership. He located and drilled five major strikes and made piles of money for Jock. Digger personally was having troubles on the money front. He was working so dang hard that he often wanted to blow off a little steam in town, an activity that invariably led him to the poker table and debts. So, Digger used his money from the first five wells to pay off his debts. They were all taken care of, and he was looking forward to the sixth well as the one that would provide him with enough money to marry.

Digger located and struck oil at the sixth well and was busily working away at the site when he learned from someone who had just returned from town that that low-down skunk Ewing had put the claim on the well in only *his* name. Digger didn't have claim to one cent of his own well! Furious, he confronted Ewing, who gave him some pile of horse manure about how he was going to give Digger his share, but . . . Digger took a shot at him and then Jock darn near killed him with his fists, and Digger left the partnership.

Digger made Dallas his home base, working with the various Independents in the area. He seriously started to woo Ellie Southworth, Aaron's wild, passionate young daughter, whom he had been smitten by since he was a boy. Digger was crazy in love with her and began to dream of asking for her hand in marriage.

And then Jock Ewing stole Miss Ellie away from him. Bought her, was more like it, Digger ranted. Took Digger's money and bought Southfork back from the bank for her daddy.

Digger's hatred for Ewing was complete, and he vowed one day to get Ewing and to get back what was rightfully his. His hurt over the loss of Ellie sent him reeling into a drinking binge. Later, in a somewhat dry period, he married a young girl, Rebecca Blake.

Rebecca bore him a son, Tyler, who took sick and died when he was six months old. The Barneses slowly overcame their grief and tried again. Rebecca gave birth to a second son, Clifford, who was as healthy as the day

was long. A year later, Rebecca had a daughter, Catherine, who died when she was approaching her first birthday. The death of the baby rocked the couple badly; they didn't understand what had happened, nor did the doctors, and Digger's drinking burst full-out in despair.

Digger tried to stop drinking, but he couldn't bear the look in Rebecca's lovely brown eyes. Somehow, he knew, she blamed the children's deaths on him. He could feel it. He couldn't stand the guilt she provoked in him, and he was forced back to the bottle, again and again, for solace.

When Cliff was five years old, Digger's heart broke when he found out that Rebecca was having an affair with the foreman of Southfork Ranch, Hutch McKinney. And then, to make matters worse, Rebecca confessed that she was pregnant, and they both knew it wasn't Digger's child. Nearly mad with the betrayal, Digger shot and killed McKinney and buried his body out on Section 40 of Southfork.

Digger immediately moved his family to Corpus Christi, where Rebecca spent the rest of her confinement. When she bore McKinney's child, a little girl, Digger was prepared to hate it. Instead, in spite of himself, he loved her on sight. She was so little, so helpless, and she was such a joyous child. It wasn't her fault what union she had come out of. There was not a moment after Digger first held her that he thought of Pamela as anything but his own daughter.

But Digger's bad days—drinking days—still plagued him. Although he remembered little, if anything, of those days, his rage at Rebecca had apparently surfaced, since afterward she always raged at him. When Pam was still a baby, and Cliff nearly six, Digger came to one morning and found that Rebecca had cleared out. Gone. No note, nothing.

To hell with her, he thought, and he started on plans for the only thing he knew to do, to put the children somewhere safe before he went drinking again. He told the children that their mother was sick in the hospital—that's where she had gone—and packed up their things and took them to his sister's house in Dallas. Maggie was a good person, though a bit too God-fearing for Digger's taste, and she agreed to care for the children. They decided it was best to tell the children that Rebecca had died. (What else could he say to little Cliff—your mama didn't want you anymore and ran away?)

The Barnes-Ewing feud continues on through the second generation of Cliff and J.R.

*Digger's daughter Pam—
who actually was Hutch
McKinney's daughter—
clings to Digger's long-lost
wife, Rebecca, whom Pam
searched for following
Digger's death. Digger
would not have been
pleased to see Rebecca
again; however, he might
have approved of her
contribution to the feud.*

Over the next twenty years, Digger would make periodic visits to Dallas in his "good" periods to see the children. But those times were less and less as his drinking took a monstrous hold on his life. Those years were one long blur—dead years, years of telling stories, in exchange for drinks from any interested listener, about how Jock Ewing had cheated him.

However, it was Digger's hatred for Jock Ewing that often kept him going. Running away from his failures, trying to shut out his inability to be a significant part of his children's lives, he was lost without his dreams of revenge. He passed his hatred for the Ewings to his son, Cliff, of whom Digger was enormously proud. Cliff was smart as a whip, a rising politician, and hell-bent on getting the Ewings, so when his career really began to take off in the late 1970s, Digger chuckled contentedly, delighted that his strong son had taken up his battle.

To say that Digger was shocked at Pamela's marriage to Bobby Ewing is to put it mildly. He was outraged, mad with another betrayal, and it took its toll in drinking. Pamela just didn't understand the consequences of what she had done. He could see in her eyes that she didn't understand the pain he was feeling. Those eyes . . . He winced—eyes just like Rebecca's. How could he make her understand that Jock Ewing had now taken her away from him, too?

Eventually, in time, Digger forgave Pamela, and in 1978 and 1979 he tried to take an active role in his children's lives, but a clash with the Ewings made his drinking get the better of him, and he left Dallas for a stint in California. There he sobered up, got some work, and then returned to Dallas in late 1979, at his son's urging.

Cliff told his father that he had a grandchild, a boy, whom Sue Ellen Ewing had borne after their affair. The child was at Southfork, being guarded by Sue Ellen's husband, J.R., who was pretending that the child was his. Digger was furious, but wary. He knew Jock would be lording it over the child, but it gave him deep satisfaction that it was *his* grandson, not Jock's. Cliff was smart and would get him back, Digger was sure.

Although not drinking, Digger felt ill and, after much arguing, Cliff managed to get him to see a doctor. It was the first time Digger had seen a doctor since he broke his leg on an oil rig in 1949, and the first thing the doctor ordered was a complete physical. Besides telling Digger that oil field work was far too strenuous for him, that he had a virus, and that his overabused liver would not tolerate any more drinking, the doctor also told him that he was a genetic carrier of neurofibromatosis, a disease that is often deadly to infants. The disease, which Digger did not himself have, could spring up in future generations, and those babies who got it would be afflicted with tumors along their

nervous system, usually resulting in death in their first year. The doctor said that since Digger had the genes, then Cliff and Pamela were carriers too, and he strongly advised them against having children.

The news deeply grieved Digger for, oh, so many reasons. First of all, after all these years, he knew what had killed his two little babies, Tyler and Catherine. Rebecca had been right; it had been his fault. And Cliff's anguished look went straight to Digger's heart—his little grandson could have the disease. And then Pamela . . . Oh, Lord, Digger couldn't look at her, couldn't tell her that she *didn't* have it because she was not his daughter. The past was so awful, so full of pain, he just couldn't face it.

Ellie Ewing invited Digger to the Ewing Barbecue that fall in an attempt to stop the feud, and Digger happily accepted. He would see his grandson! But the barbecue proved to be too much. He looked at the magnificence of Southfork and he looked at Jock. Jock had Ellie, he had Digger's money, he had Pamela and, now, his grandson. He started drinking at the barbecue, and it turned out to be one of his worst binges.

Later, it was revealed that John Ross was not Cliff's baby, not Digger's grandson, and Digger met this news with mixed emotion, deeply sad not to have a grandson, that Cliff couldn't have a son, but still somewhat relieved that the child's life was not in danger—even if it was a Ewing.

Digger's life-style finally caught up with him. As he lay dying in Dallas Memorial Hospital in 1980, his body simply worn out from years of abuse, he chose to disclose the great secrets he had carried for so long. He cleared Jock Ewing by confessing to the murder of Hutch McKinney, and he told Pamela that she was not his daughter by blood. He also told Ellie Ewing, who sat by his side as he passed away, that he still loved her as much as he had in 1930. That was no secret.

His passing was peaceful. His feud with the Ewings was over.

The feud did not die, though. It would be continued in the next generation through Cliff and, as Digger would be stunned to know, through his former wife, Rebecca, and his sweet little Pamela.

In commemoration of his father's contribution to the pioneering days of the Texas Independents, Cliff established the Willard Barnes Memorial Scholarships to Southern Methodist University in 1983.

Digger's son Cliff accepts the Oil Man of the Year Award at the Oil Baron's Ball in 1983. That night Cliff announced the establishment of the Willard Barnes Memorial Scholarships in memory of his father's contribution to the early days of the oil industry in Texas.

"If Jock's will puts J.R. back in the saddle, Rebecca'll blast the horse to get to the rider."

—Clayton Farlow, 1982

No one in Dallas even had a glimmer of recognition of her as anyone but who she appeared to be—Rebecca Wentworth, wife of industrial tycoon Herbert. When she and her husband attended a political fundraiser in Dallas in 1980, high society chatted with her the way they always had: How was Houston? How was lovely Katherine doing? Were plans in place for the annual ball for the Houston Heart Fund, of which Rebecca was chairperson? But there was one woman there who asked nothing, and whose eyes followed Rebecca around the room.

Rebecca had wanted to cry. She saw her own eyes in the young woman's face, the face of her long-lost daughter. And in them, she could see the same pain and loneliness that she had carried in her heart for so many, many years. And yet, she still just nodded to the young woman, as if but merely a social acquaintance.

Rebecca Blake was born and raised in the slums of Dallas. She was sweet, terribly shy, and pretty, but couldn't imagine what Digger Barnes saw in her. She was barely a teenager and Digger was so worldly! He had been all over the state, had made and lost a fortune already (although, he assured her, another one was only a moment away), and he had the most wonderful twinkling blue eyes and uplifting sense of humor. And what she loved best—he appeared so rugged and arrogant in public, but in private he was so gentle and affectionate.

It wasn't until after she married him that she ever saw him drunk. It terrified her. His eyes were bloodshot, his face screwed up in an angry sneer, and his voice turned vicious, constantly spewing venom about Jock and Ellie Ewing.

It only happened a couple of times in the first year, and Digger was always so apologetic, so loving afterward, that she didn't really say too much about it. She figured if he was happy, he wouldn't drink, and so she did her darnedest to make him happy.

Rebecca conceived her first child. She was elated, and when the boy, Tyler, was born, she was as thrilled as Digger over how much he looked like him. They adored the child and shamelessly spoiled him with the fruits of Digger's inspired labor in the oil fields, and it looked as if the large family they both wanted was off to a great start. And then when Tyler was only six months old, he started to get sick, rapidly. Something was wrong with his spine, his nervous system, the doctors said; his tiny body was causing him pain. And then he died.

They were both devastated by their loss. Rebecca wept quietly at home, while Digger went out on a bender. After months had passed, and Digger had settled down some, the sad couple nervously agreed to try again. Rebecca

A radiant Rebecca Blake Barnes Wentworth poses with her children Pamela Barnes Ewing, Katherine Wentworth, and Clifford Barnes, 1981.

tiptoed through this pregnancy, praying mightily every day. Her prayers were answered when she delivered a big, healthy boy—Clifford. Rebecca handled him like glass throughout his infancy and, to the couple's mutual relief and joy, he was every bit as healthy as he appeared to be. But still, Rebecca hovered over him constantly, to the point where Digger warned her about making him a mama's boy. Rebecca would only smile, drawing her son close to her breast in a hug.

Two years later, Rebecca gave birth to a daughter, Catherine. She too appeared to be healthy, but then, toward the end of her first year, Rebecca became sick with fear when she noticed the same symptoms in Catherine that Tyler had displayed. Her fears were confirmed, and Catherine died too.

It was more than either of the parents could bear. Digger disappeared for weeks, and Rebecca, clinging to her small son, cried and prayed to get through each day. She didn't have family to turn to, didn't have any money, and she didn't have her husband when she needed him most.

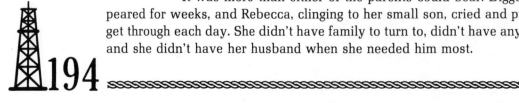

When Digger did arrive home, it was a nightmare. He was so ill from alcohol abuse that she could barely see any trace of the man she had fallen in love with. In fact, at his worst times, she wondered if she didn't hate him. But none of that mattered, as she had nowhere to go and was too scared to leave. He did, at least, bring home some money now and then—although, unless she hid it well, he was sure to take it to drink with.

Rebecca was thin and drawn but still very pretty. And lonely. She knew Hutch McKinney, the foreman of Southfork Ranch, who had openly paid her more than a kindly eye ever since she married Digger. She didn't want to—God knows, she really didn't—but she was so lonely, so anxious for some relief in that horror of a house, that she had an affair with McKinney. It really never occurred to her that Digger would find out, since he was so busy being drunk all the time, so it came as a shock when she realized she had to tell him herself.

Rebecca was pregnant. She knew that it had to be Hutch's baby—she hadn't slept with Digger in months. Finally, tearfully, she told him. He looked at her oddly at first—for a moment she thought she saw love in his eyes—but he said nothing and left the house. She assumed he went out on a bender. Then, to her surprise, Digger came home late that night only mildly drunk and instructed her to pack up their belongings because they were moving to Corpus Christi, which they did. Later, Rebecca heard that Hutch McKinney had disappeared from Dallas. Talk was that Jock Ewing had fired him, but to vanish completely was not Hutch's way.

The calm Digger had shown during the move ended, and he resumed drinking heavily, hurling vicious verbal abuse at Rebecca. It increased as her pregnancy progressed, and she began to fear for her safety. Thank heaven, Digger had never gone near Cliff while drunk, but with those blackouts . . .

Rebecca gave birth to the most enchanting little girl she had ever seen. She was simply a blessing in every way. Her big brown eyes looked at her mama and they told her that all was not lost in the world. And stunned, disbelieving, Rebecca watched as this beautiful, tiny baby took possession of Digger's heart. No matter what awful things he said to Rebecca, he only whispered to the little girl that she was his own precious daughter.

And that's the way it was, drunk or sober: Digger worshiped the children and despised Rebecca. Finally, she couldn't take it anymore. She had one huge, last confrontation with Digger, a blackout in which he nearly hurt her

Rebecca reveals to Pamela Ewing that she is indeed her mother, 1981. Pam had confronted Rebecca in 1980, but Rebecca, terrified of hurting her husband, Herbert, denied being the person the young woman so desperately wanted her to be.

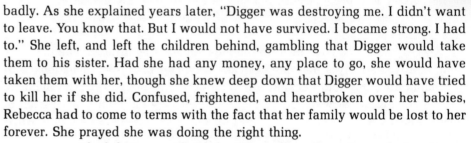

Rebecca listens to Cliff as he bemoans his inability to be hired in Dallas, 1981. Rebecca revealed to Cliff her true station in life when she surprised him with the job of Chief Executive Officer of Wentworth Tool & Die.

Right:
Rebecca frowns as Cliff makes an unfair comment to Pam's husband, Bobby Ewing. Rebecca initially tried to put an end to the feud, but J.R.'s attacks on her son fired up her revenging spirit. Her greatest wish was for Cliff to destroy J.R. professionally and rise to prominence, with lovely Afton Cooper at his side as his wife. As for Bobby Ewing, she was quite fond of him, but she wished he'd simmer down and be a better husband to Pam.

badly. As she explained years later, "Digger was destroying me. I didn't want to leave. You know that. But I would not have survived. I became strong. I had to." She left, and left the children behind, gambling that Digger would take them to his sister. Had she had any money, any place to go, she would have taken them with her, though she knew deep down that Digger would have tried to kill her if she did. Confused, frightened, and heartbroken over her babies, Rebecca had to come to terms with the fact that her family would be lost to her forever. She prayed she was doing the right thing.

She left Corpus Christi for Kingsville, where she worked under an alias as a waitress in Jerry's Coffee Shop. She met a nice man there, a salesman, and he talked her into traveling with him on the road. She didn't like what she was doing; she just didn't know what else to do. She changed her name almost twenty times after leaving Kingsville, always using the first letter of her maiden name, the last alias being Rebecca Burke. She left the salesman and settled in Houston to start her life over. She was still quite young. Rebecca put herself through secretarial school, learning typing and stenography, and she landed a job at Morrison & Pitz, a brokerage firm. After that successful experience, she was offered a job as executive secretary to Herbert Wentworth, the president of Wentworth Tool & Die. Their office relationship turned to romance, and Rebecca married him in 1960.

Rebecca loved Herbert very much. He was a smart, kind, gentle, handsome Texan, and could take or leave alcohol (she would never make that mistake again). Together they had one daughter, Katherine, a simply gorgeous —and willful—child. Rebecca tensely hovered over her the first year, remembering her poor Tyler and Catherine, but this child flourished and actually kept Rebecca running to keep up with her. The Wentworths had a happy family life, no one knowing that it was Rebecca's second time round.

In the 1960s, Herbert's company expanded into a conglomerate and went public. The Wentworths were millionaires, and the mansion they bought was the talk of Houston. Rebecca settled easily into the role of a grande dame of Texas social circles, but during all those years, not a day went by that she didn't think of her children Cliff and Pamela. By 1978, it was impossible not to—they were constantly in the newspapers. Her heart twinged when she read about Pamela's marriage to Bobby Ewing—and she immediately thought that if Digger was still alive, this news would surely kill him. And her boy, her son, appointed Commissioner of the Office of Land Management!

But she had to push down those thoughts, those memories, those intense feelings, and concentrate on her real life, her life as a Wentworth, as Herbert's wife and as Katherine's mother. And Katherine made that easier to do—though what a handful that girl was! She had brains and beauty, and Rebecca was hard put to tell her anything after the age of thirteen—the child seemed to know it all.

And then, in the fall of 1980, Rebecca was standing face to face with her other daughter, Pamela Barnes Ewing, who was saying that it had taken a long time to find her. Pamela didn't have to say who she was; Rebecca would have known those eyes from twenty yards off. But Rebecca panicked. The feelings were coming up too fast. There was so much at stake, so much for so many people. She couldn't, wouldn't respond to Pamela, and so she told her that she was mistaken, she was not her mother. After her daughter left, Rebecca cried her heart out—for Pamela, for Cliff, for herself, for the whole rotten nightmare. And, too, she even cried for Hutch McKinney, Pamela's father, because she had only recently learned that Digger had murdered him on that night so many years ago. Oh, it was all a door that was better left closed!

Katherine was attending college in New York City and she asked if her parents would come to visit her. Rebecca gratefully made the trip, desperately needing to be close to her little family, this family. At one point she wondered, just for a moment, if she could ever tell Herbert about her past, but she dismissed it. He was a wonderful man, and she didn't want to hurt him.

Their stay in New York began well. Katherine was vibrant and dynamic as always, and the three had fun making all of the obligatory social rounds in Manhattan. And then Herbert was stricken with a heart attack and died.

Rebecca beams at Clayton Farlow at the Oil Baron's Ball in 1982. Rebecca became progressively fond of Clayton and was distressed when he began casting an eye toward her friend Ellie Ewing.

Rebecca, Cliff, and Katherine arrive at the Ewing Barbecue, 1981. It was a day of mixed feelings for Rebecca. To begin with, she hadn't set foot on Southfork land since her affair with Hutch McKinney in 1952.

Rebecca mourned his death deeply and turned to Katherine for emotional support. But she needed more. She knew what she needed, what she wanted; she wanted *all* of her children, her babies, near her. In early 1981 she flew to Dallas and revealed herself to Pamela, who was forgiving (where did this child get so much goodness in her heart?) and eager to love her. With Cliff, it took more time, and Rebecca took seriously Pamela's caution against making too fast an entry into his life. Eventually Cliff came around and Rebecca took him under her wing.

Rebecca lived temporarily in a condo, and in the fall of 1982, when she had told all to Katherine and had decided to make her permanent home in Dallas, she bought a gorgeous mansion at 227 Antioch Drive.

Rebecca was a godsend to the Barnes children. Pamela was in a massive depression over her inability to have a baby and institutionalized after a suicide attempt. Cliff's political career was a shambles, and so was his relationship with the woman of his dreams, Sue Ellen Ewing. Rebecca gave both children all the love, attention, and support that she had been holding for all those years, and they gratefully received it, needing every bit of it.

Rebecca was pleased that Katherine took to Pamela immediately but was dismayed that she didn't like Cliff, whom she called a weakling. Rebecca paid her no heed and, over her protests, made Cliff President of Wentworth Tool & Die.

Over Cliff's protests, Rebecca made peace with Ellie Ewing, a wonderful woman and a compassionate friend. Both women wanted to put an end to the awful Barnes-Ewing feud which their sons had continued, and they did their best to stop it—unsuccessfully. Their friendship became strained over that issue, and then again over another—Clayton Farlow. Rebecca had begun dating Clayton, and although they had begun merely as friends, she had a notion or two about not minding very much if they got more serious. To her dismay, however, Clayton started showing more than a casual interest in Ellie.

Meanwhile, Cliff, riding high on his success as President of Wentworth Tool & Die, was swindled by J. R. Ewing, and Cliff, despondent over nearly losing the company and indeed over losing Sue Ellen altogether, to J.R., tried to kill himself. J.R., J.R.—that name kept coming up everywhere. He had a habit of cursing Pamela's life, too.

Cliff survived, but every ounce of wrath Rebecca possessed was focused on J.R., who had almost killed her son. In her mind, he might as well

198

have shoved the pills down Cliff's throat with his own hands. Her son's recovery was terribly slow. He was chronically depressed, but Rebecca pushed him and pushed him to fight back and fight back *hard*. She would help him destroy J.R. and, if need be, anyone who stood to protect him.

She bought the Luce Oil company from retiring Wade Luce and shot the company full of Wentworth money—enough so that the cartel *had* to let them keep Luce's seat. She then put Cliff at the helm of the new Barnes-Wentworth Oil. She actually didn't care whether the company made any money or not; she wanted Cliff to use it as the muscle needed to snap J.R.'s neck.

In early 1983, Cliff had J.R. in a corner, frantically searching for a refinery. The cartel was refusing to help Ewing out, and this one refinery in Houston was his last chance to save his Ewing Gas stations. Cliff was going to step in and buy it out from under him, except that Cliff got into a fight with his girlfriend, Afton Cooper, and went out on a drunk instead. Knowing how crucial it was to cut J.R. off at that moment, Rebecca took it on herself to fly to Houston.

As the Wentworth jet was taking off from Love Field, it was struck in midair by an incoming plane. Rebecca's plane crash-landed. She was just barely alive and was rushed to Dallas Memorial Hospital. Her daughter, Pammy, was there, and her loving eyes were the last thing Rebecca Wentworth saw.

Rebecca's will set forth that money from cash, stocks, and bonds of her estate was to be set up in a trust fund, with a provision for Christopher Shepard Ewing and any future grandchildren. Rebecca also left a generous amount of cash to Afton Cooper, whom she hoped Cliff would marry. In accordance with her husband's wishes, Wentworth Industries was to remain a public entity and be run by an elected Board of Directors. All income and voting shares of Rebecca's were divided equally between Katherine and Pamela. Cliff inherited all of her stock and continued as Chief Executive Officer and sole owner of Barnes-Wentworth Oil. Wentworth Tool & Die, Herbert's original company, was divided equally among Katherine, Pamela, and Cliff. On any given decision, two had to agree for approval.

Rebecca's children were now as rich and powerful as the Ewings.

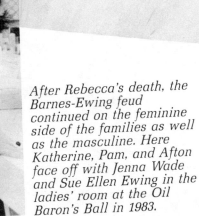

Katherine, Rebecca's daughter by Herbert Wentworth. An extremely bright, willful beauty, she took after her mother in every way but goodness. Little did Rebecca know how much damage her precious youngest would do to her other children—and the Ewings.

After Rebecca's death, the Barnes-Ewing feud continued on the feminine side of the families as well as the masculine. Here Katherine, Pam, and Afton face off with Jenna Wade and Sue Ellen Ewing in the ladies' room at the Oil Baron's Ball in 1983.

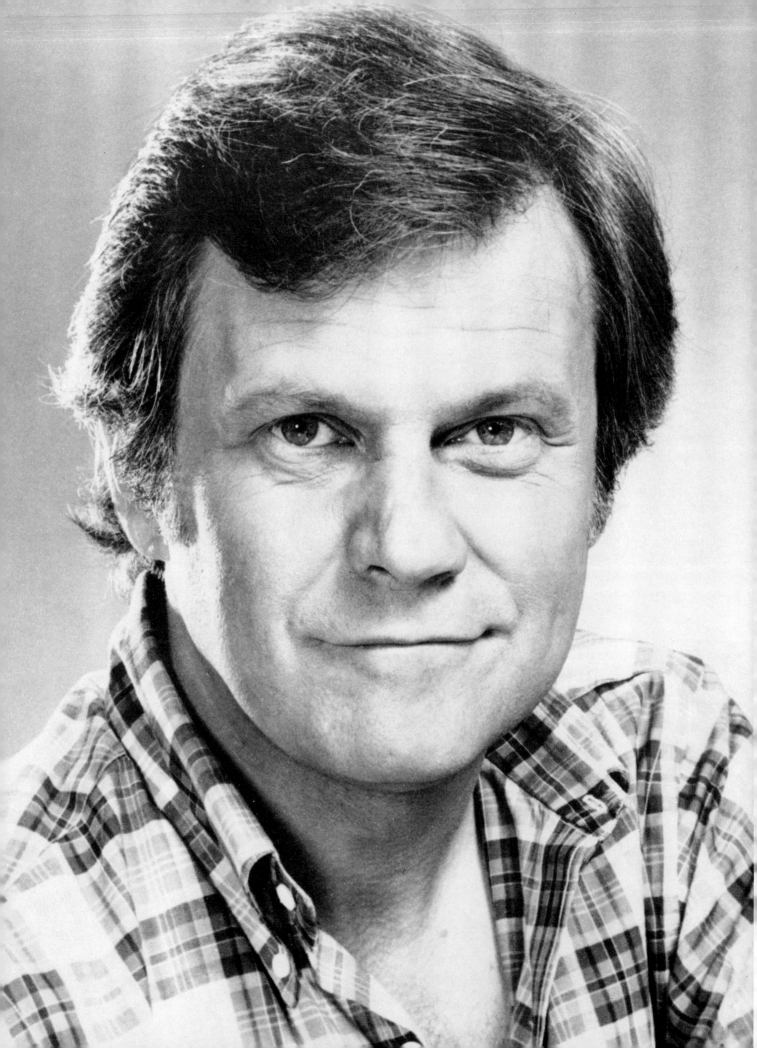

Clifford Barnes

*"Sometimes I think your hatred of the Ewings is like a cancer
eating up all of your good sense."*

—Bobby Ewing, 1978

As Cliff Barnes strides into the Oil Baron's Club, head held high, one
might presume that he was born to success. His charismatic charm,
bright intellect, and confident ambition are compelling qualities, ones
that have lifted him from the emotional and financial poverty that
grounded his early life. But there is another side to Cliff Barnes, a dark under-
side of insecurity, fear of inadequacy, and permeating loneliness that is constantly pulling, pulling him down to despair.

His professional and personal life has been as rock and roll as his
emotional makeup. From the day he graduated from law school he appeared to
be a man of great promise—as a lawyer, then a politician, and then a businessman—but something always seemed to happen to him. Every time he reached
prominency, he was catapulted out of his glory and into relative obscurity—
back and forth, up and down—while folks in Dallas murmured, "What happened to that Barnes fella?"

What has happened to him in the past has been J. R. Ewing, the
son of Jock Ewing, the man Digger Barnes, Cliff's father, had had a bitter feud
with for over fifty years. While many in Dallas—namely the Ewings and their
friends—have claimed that it is Cliff's instinct to bring misfortune upon himself, Cliff maintains that it has almost all been J.R.'s doing and that J.R., indeed,
has a second career as a silent assassin, bent on destroying Cliff or anyone
who stands to oppose his corrupt practices. It is Cliff's ultimate goal in life to
settle the score with J.R., and to make right the long list of wrongs the Ewings
in general have inflicted on the Barneses.

Cliff Barnes is the only surviving blood child of Willard "Digger"
Barnes and Rebecca Barnes Wentworth. He was born two weeks early, in
Dallas, and very nearly made his debut in a taxicab as Rebecca tried to get to
the hospital. This was not the last decision Cliff made that would catch people
off guard; it is his nature to make sweeping changes in his life plan at a moment's notice.

He was five years old when the Barneses moved to Corpus
Christi, where his sister Pamela was born and his mother disappeared. As he
explained years later, "I came home from school one day and she was gone.
Daddy said she was in the hospital, sick. A little while after that he brought us
to Aunt Maggie's. I remember I cried for her a lot at first." After that, Digger
told Cliff that his mother had died, and that was what Cliff believed until well
into his thirties.

Cliff learned to read early and easily, and would prefer to bury
himself in books, rather than athletics, for the rest of his life. He was a superior
student in school, always at the head of the honor roll. And, he was a day-
dreamer. He had fantasies of being rich, of being powerful, and, after the years
of Digger's bitter, drunken rages, he had fantasies of bringing down the Ewing
family to make his daddy happy. In fact, his greatest fantasy was to fulfill his

201

Above:
Cliff and his sister, Pamela, in 1978.

Above, right:
Cliff's Aunt Maggie, Margaret Barnes, who brought up Cliff and Pam after their mother allegedly died. Though Maggie bordered on being a religious fanatic, she was an enormously warm, loving guardian.

father's fantasy—revenge—and his second was how life would have been if Jock Ewing hadn't stolen Digger's fortune. Cliff was *entitled,* he knew, but to how much, would be for him to find out.

He won a scholarship to the University of Texas at Austin, where he majored in political science and worked as a busboy in the cafeteria. He had few friends—by choice—and dated little, preferring to concentrate on his studies. His predisposition as a lone wolf was occasionally haunted by an old, vague pain that came from watching classmate Bobby Ewing. Cliff knew he was every bit as smart and good-looking as Bobby, but Ewing had the entire campus as his own personal kingdom, had millions of dollars and one of the most powerful families in Texas to back him up, which kicked up a longing, as Cliff had virtually no one but himself. Cliff didn't hate Bobby, although he tried. There was nothing inherent in Bobby not to like, but his popularity, his jazzy clothes, his car, his girls, his athletic prowess all seemed to Cliff an embarrassment of riches—an overendowment not deserved. So, Cliff basically tried to ignore him, as he picked up Ewing's dirty dishes and piled them on his tray. There would be a time and place later on to settle the old score with the Ewings.

He graduated with honors and won a scholarship to the University of Texas Law School. After graduation, Cliff landed a job as a legal assistant in a prestigious law firm in Dallas and fell in love with a young woman, Jenny Ames, who was working there as a secretary, saving up for law school. They moved in together, and Cliff began thinking about marriage. Jenny made him so happy, made him feel so alive. His future seemed bright with possibility and void of the darkness of his childhood. The couple's happiness was interrupted when Jenny found out that she was pregnant. The couple debated what to do. Cliff wanted her to marry him, to have the baby, but Jenny insisted she was not ready for marriage, much less to have a child, and was determined to go to law school first. Finally, very reluctantly, Cliff gave her the money she needed to have an abortion, which was illegal in Texas at that time. Severe complications arose and Jenny went into massive hemorrhaging, and the inadequate medical care proved fatal. She died.

Cliff was nearly destroyed by the tragedy. It took him a long time to emotionally recover and he would forlornly back away from any relation-

202

Never lacking for female companionship, Cliff is awakened by a playful Julie Grey, 1979. Julie was for years J. R. Ewing's secretary and mistress, and she was in the process of helping Cliff build a case against Ewing Oil when she was murdered.

ships with women for almost ten years. He used his work as a ballast, throwing himself into it full-out. His job in the firm proved too staid, sedate for his temperament, and he yearned for participation in the "real" world, the community. He decided to leave the firm and move into the public and political arena. He worked for the state, building an impressive record and reputation as an investigator of corruption within the independent oil companies. It was no coincidence that his investigations often cited or targeted Ewing Oil.

In the fall of 1978, Cliff ran for the U.S. Senate on a platform heavy with ecological issues. His main campaign promise was to stop the wasteful drilling procedures that were destroying the future of the state's mineral and wildlife resources. It was a fierce race, but Cliff's campaign was eminently successful and, as the election drew near, he was far ahead of his Ewing-backed opponent, Martin Cole, in the polls. And then, disaster—courtesy of a certain Mr. J. R. Ewing. J.R. had found out about the whole tragedy concerning Jenny Ames and revealed it to the public in a less than sympathetic light: Cliff Barnes had murdered his girlfriend by making her go to a butcher for an illegal abortion. Cliff faced up to the newsbreak and explained the circumstances, though he had no choice but to withdraw from the race.

Cliff did get something out of the campaign. In the course of it, he met and conquered the devastatingly beautiful Sue Ellen Ewing—J.R.'s very own unhappy wife—and proceeded to fall in love with her. He otherwise wouldn't want to be involved with a married woman, but the fact that she was married to J.R. was like a red flag in his face, certainly adding fuel to their already passionate attraction. When Sue Ellen discovered she was pregnant, Cliff was elated and immediately began to plan his future with Sue Ellen and what he believed to be his child. When J.R. found out about the affair, he blackmailed Cliff into temporarily backing off.

Cliff resumed a state case against Ewing Oil corruption and enlisted the help of Julie Grey, J.R.'s former secretary. Julie was going to turn over a set of files to him, but when Cliff arrived at her apartment, she had been murdered. J.R. helped to frame Cliff for the crime, and he was arrested and thrown into jail. Bobby Ewing cleared Cliff of all wrongdoing and the real murderers, Jeb Ames and Billie Joe Garr, who were business associates of J.R.'s, were arrested.

Cliff's career took an upward swing when he was appointed Chief of the Office of Land Management, the enormously powerful state agency that coordinated and approved all ventures that affected the surface or geological texture of Texas land, including oil drilling permits. It was a tremendously

203

Above, left:
Handsome, charming, and
extremely well-spoken, Cliff
had a future bright with
promise in politics until
J. R. Ewing intervened.

Above, right:
Cliff being taken away by
Dallas policemen, accused
of trying to murder J. R.
Ewing in 1980. He was
proved innocent.

influental position, and Cliff was adept at handling it. He made his first and foremost project the harassment of Ewing Oil. The job also offered a salary that Cliff hoped was an acceptable financial future for Sue Ellen, and by undermining J.R. in business, Cliff hoped to batter his resistance to letting her go.

Some say Cliff went overboard with his authority. He denied permits for all new drilling sites for Ewing Oil and eventually even started shutting down their operating wells. But Cliff rightly pointed out that he had to be overboard to catch up with the host of illegal activities J.R. was up to: blackmail, politicians on the take, riding roughshod over ranchers; corruption of all kinds was the food that this shark lived on. If it meant destroying Ewing Oil to stop J.R.'s corruption, then so be it.

On the personal front, Cliff was deeply worried. Sue Ellen was being kept virtually a prisoner at Southfork, where she was drinking to alarming excess. And then J.R. had her committed to a sanatorium, which Cliff could do nothing to stop. When Sue Ellen's child was born—they had the nerve to name him John Ross Ewing III—Cliff was more determined than ever to destroy J.R. and get her back. And his son.

In the fall of 1979, Cliff was voted Man of the Year by the Dallas Civic Group. It was indicative of his popularity, and a young lawyer, Alan Beam, demonstrated the power of grass-roots support in the area for Cliff that would work politically. He was approached to run for Congress. After lengthy consideration, Cliff stepped down from the OLM to run in the election, and he made Alan Beam the head of his election committee. Shortly thereafter, Cliff's life ran smack into a wall, personally and professionally.

Digger, while on an angry drunk, announced to the press that Cliff was the real father of John Ross. This brought on a series of lawsuits between

the Barneses and the Ewings, which were resolved with a series of sophisticated blood tests that revealed that J.R., not Cliff, was the blood father of John Ross. Cliff was crushed, angry, but in a way relieved, too, for it meant that the little boy—no matter whose he was—had not inherited the dreaded disease, neurofibromatosis, the genes for which Cliff had recently learned he carried. It meant, however, that Cliff could never risk fathering a child in the future, a prospect that depressed him.

Cliff kept running at full steam for the congressional seat on a liberal platform, with what he believed to be his solid backing by minority groups. He was anti-oil and anti-nukes, and his speeches were received with resounding enthusiasm. And then, suddenly, he had no more money in his campaign chest. It was just gone. Cliff soon learned that Alan Beam worked for J.R. and that J.R. himself had financed Cliff's campaign to lure him out of his seat at the OLM. Once he was out, J.R. pulled the money out from under him and Cliff's following, mostly the poor, couldn't make up the loss. Cliff was forced to drop out of the race. Another one he owed J. R. Ewing.

Cliff felt like he was in no-man's-land. He was having a very hard time finding a job. In the spring of 1980, he found a spot as an Assistant District Attorney for Dallas County. It was by no means like the OLM job, but it was effective, and Cliff was quickly all over the Ewings again.

The case which Cliff thought would bring down Jock Ewing once and for all—the murder of Hutch McKinney in 1952—turned around to damage the Barneses. When the skeleton had been discovered at Southfork, Cliff led a brilliant investigation, recreating the circumstances of the night of the murder and even the face of McKinney when he died (in a forensic sculpture from the skull). Everything pointed to Ewing—his firing McKinney, their two fights, Jock's gun as the murder weapon—but on his deathbed, Cliff's very own father confessed to the murder.

Digger's death deeply saddened Cliff. Though Digger really hadn't been much other than a drunk for as long as Cliff could remember, he was the

The lovely Afton Cooper, singer in the Stardrift Lounge, 1981. She was working on the sly for J. R. Ewing—and sleeping with him.

Afton smiles at Cliff during their first meeting at the club. Initially it was Afton's connection to J.R. that attracted him, but it wasn't long before he started falling in love with her.

Above, left:
Cliff offers a gleeful grin to his long-lost mother, Rebecca, 1981. Her reentry into his life catapulted him into the big-time oil business. He also gained a few pounds. Although Cliff is a Chinese and Mexican food junkie, he adored his mother's gourmet cooking.

Above, right:
A heartsick Cliff dances with Sue Ellen at the reception following her remarriage to J.R. in 1982. He had come so close to winning her . . .

only parent he had ever had, and one that inspired Cliff in his career. Cliff had always wanted to make good in his father's stead, and he vowed to continue in his memory.

Cliff was hit with yet two more blows. He was arrested in the fall of 1980 for the attempted murder of J.R., and although he was cleared, the incident ruined his career in the D.A.'s office. And then Sue Ellen ran off to San Angelo with a rodeo star, Dusty Farlow, but at least, Cliff thought, it meant that J.R. couldn't have her either.

Then, on a brighter note, Cliff crossed paths with former governor Sam Culver's widow, the young and lovely Donna Culver. They had known of each other at the University of Texas, and politically they were sympathetic. Donna helped him get a job as Dave Culver's (Sam's son) legislative counsel during his campaign for the U.S. Senate. Meanwhile, Cliff and Donna had begun dating. When Culver won the election, it left his seat in the Texas State Senate open. Cliff thought the political committee would ask him to run—which he very badly wanted to do—but instead they asked Donna, who declined and endorsed Bobby Ewing. Cliff was upset, and more than a little hurt. When he confronted Donna, she said, "Remember when you said you'd be a great second man, Cliff? You were right. You are a great second man. We just don't think you'd be a great first man." That apparently meant personally as well, for Donna abruptly dumped Cliff for Ray Krebbs.

However, surprise of all surprises, after Bobby Ewing won the election, Cliff was appointed his legal counsel. In the course of the spring of 1981, while Cliff was compiling state's evidence against J. R. Ewing for engineering the overthrow of the foreign government that had nationalized his Asian wells, Cliff's mother, Rebecca Wentworth, made a dramatic reentry into his life. She was a lovely woman and, after much debating, Cliff gave into his love for her and forgave her for her desertion. It also, to be frank, delighted Cliff that one of his parents was so important a lady, so wealthy and powerful

206

in her own right. His newfound family provided some comfort, too, when J.R. managed to bribe and blackmail himself out of a guilty verdict in the state hearing. It was outrageous that anyone, even J.R., could get away with over-throwing a foreign government. The case caused a parting of the ways between Cliff and Bobby.

Another positive note during this difficult period was Cliff's involvement with stunning Afton Cooper, Lucy Ewing Cooper's sister-in-law and J.R.'s former mistress. She was a singer in Cliff's longtime watering hole, the Stardrift Lounge, and he was first lured to her because of her connection to J.R. After he stole Afton from J.R., he found himself becoming truly interested in her as a person, though he was hesitant about making any commitment. The first time they went to bed together, she said, "You're about the best lover I've ever had," and that was saying a lot, in light of her rather flamboyant past in Biloxi, Mississippi, and in Dallas. But what pleased Cliff most was her statement that he was a much more considerate, tender lover than J.R. had ever been.

One evening, in the late spring of 1981, Cliff was at Southfork and discovered the body of Kristin Shepard, Sue Ellen's sister, floating in the pool. He dived in and pulled her out, tried to revive her, but it was too late. J.R. accused Cliff of murdering her, and Cliff accused J.R., since he was the only one who had been with her before she died. Eventually the coroner declared the death accidental and the case was dismissed. It was decided that Kristin had fallen into the pool from the second landing of the house while under the influence of a great quantity of PCP.

After all the bad publicity in recent months, Cliff was unable to find a job in Dallas. As he confided to his mother, "My long fight with the Ewings left me with powerful enemies. Dallas may look like a big city, but in many ways it acts like a small town. The people who count all know each other . . . I'm now on their list." Rebecca enthusiastically offered him the presidency of Wentworth Tool & Die, a small subsidiary of Wentworth Industries which made parts for oil rigs. Cliff happily accepted and did extraordinarily well during the fall of 1981.

When J.R. stockpiled five million barrels of oil in his effort to shut down the Farlow refineries, Cliff approached and convinced members of the cartel to go in with him and buy up J.R.'s promissary notes to the bank, which held Ewing Oil as collateral. In a deft maneuver, Cliff was in the position of offering J.R. a desperately needed ten-day extension on the loan, for which J.R. had to pay him Ewing 6, the field that Jock Ewing had stolen from Digger so many years ago. Cliff received the transfer of ownership and christened the field Barnes-Wentworth #1.

After Sue Ellen Ewing obtained a divorce from J.R. and then broke up with Dusty Farlow, she moved back to Dallas. Cliff saw her again and found that he was still deeply in love with her. He had Afton Cooper in his life as a sure thing, and, though he didn't want to hurt her, he started seeing Sue Ellen again on any terms she granted. He finally told Afton the truth and Afton, very much in love with Cliff, opted to wait and see.

Despite the corporate structure that Rebecca's husband had set up at Wentworth Industries—with an overall, ruling President in the Houston headquarters—in early 1982 Cliff asked for, and got, complete autonomy at Wentworth Tool & Die. His relationship with Sue Ellen was going extremely well, and it was a very happy man who pounced on the deal that fellow cartel member Marilee Stone presented him with: a rich oil field in Lubbock that she and Cliff could buy out from under J.R. Cliff gleefully plunged into the deal,

207

putting in $3,500,000 of Wentworth Tool & Die cash (which the company comptroller warned Cliff against doing), plus his own savings of $500,000 (from the profits of Barnes-Wentworth #1), while Marilee's company, Stonehurst, put in $2,500,000. Once the acquisition was completed, Cliff drew out another $500,000 from Wentworth to cover the starting-up costs for drilling.

Betting that this well was going to make him a very rich man, Cliff asked Sue Ellen to marry him. Her loving request for a little time to think things over led him to believe that there was a very good chance that she'd accept.

Cliff was completely flabbergasted when J.R. walked into his office one day, grinning from ear to ear, and announced that he had tricked Cliff into buying a dry hole. An awfully expensive one. When Cliff cited the geological reports, J.R. said they were fake. Cliff, stunned, then redoubled drilling efforts for a short while, but he realized that, yes, indeed, he had been swindled out of $4,500,000.

He was frantic. The $4,000,000 could put Wentworth Tool & Die out of business and, not knowing who to turn to, he went to Sue Ellen to borrow money to pay back the company. She blew up and threw him out, along with his proposal of marriage. Then J.R. showed up again, offering to buy Barnes-Wentworth #1 back from Cliff for $4,000,000, which he could in turn pay back to Wentworth Tool & Die. Cliff had no choice but to do so, although the field was worth far, far more. He had lost all of his own money *and* his mother's respect. Regardless of the fact that he paid back the money he had borrowed from Wentworth Tool & Die, Rebecca fired him.

Cliff was, simply, blasted out of the water. He had lost Sue Ellen, his mother's trust, his job, and all of his money. He began to drink heavily, but he managed to pull himself together just long enough to make one last attempt with Sue Ellen. She broke his heart by telling him that she had decided to remarry J.R. For Cliff, that clinched it—there was nothing left. When Afton came to his apartment that night, she found him lying unconscious on the floor. He had tried to kill himself with an overdose of tranquilizers, washed down with alcohol.

Cliff pulled through, but he was on very shaky emotional ground. When Sue Ellen came to see him and said she wanted to be friends, he replied,

deeply depressed, that she should just go on without him. Though Afton was still lovingly at his side, he didn't feel that he deserved her. Rebecca and Pam were there to support him, but he was so troubled, so sick at heart, he could barely hear their words.

When he got out of the hospital, a remorseful Marilee Stone offered him a job at her company. Cliff was so demoralized, he wavered, leaning toward no, but when Rebecca offered him his old job at Wentworth Tool & Die, out of pride he turned it down and accepted Marilee's offer, becoming Senior Vice President of Operations for Stonehurst Oil.

Cliff left Stonehurst shortly thereafter, when Rebecca bought out Wade Oil and asked Cliff to run it for her. At first he turned her down, saying that he did not have the stomach to fight J.R. anymore, which he knew his mother wanted him to do. But Rebecca, with fiery revenge glistening in her eyes, persisted, literally pushing him into the President's chair of the new Barnes-Wentworth Oil Company. It was to Cliff's liking, and he stayed.

Cliff made his first big deal, leading the cartel behind him, by acquiring Al Thurman's very profitable oil refinery. It was not a coincidence that J.R. had been trying desperately to buy it, and Cliff wasn't exactly sure why Thurman had swung the deal his way and not J.R.'s, but he didn't care, so long as he got it. The cartel was very pleased at the acquisition.

Cliff won there, but not on the personal front. J.R. not so nicely offered him an invitation to his wedding to Sue Ellen. Despite Afton's protests —she was now living with Cliff—he insisted on attending. It was painful for Cliff to watch, and at one point in the ceremony he had to leave before he burst into tears.

With the cartel's blessing, Cliff continued to block J.R.'s search for a refinery to service his newly created Ewing Gas, but Cliff was sidetracked on the eve of his victory. He was supposed to leave for Houston to lock up the last available refinery when he found out why Al Thurman had sold his refinery to him. Afton had prostituted herself on his behalf. Cliff was horrified by the news and couldn't bear Afton's pleas for understanding. He left the apartment and ended up drifting from bar to bar, on a drinking binge. When Cliff couldn't be located, Rebecca decided to close the refinery deal herself. Shortly after take-off, the Wentworth plane crashed and Rebecca died soon after.

Cliff was close to suicide again, from the guilt, the grief. It barely registered that he had inherited Barnes-Wentworth Oil lock, stock, and barrel, and a third of Wentworth Tool & Die. He just didn't care. Eventually, with time.

Below, left:
Cliff pours champagne for Pam, Mark Graison, and Afton in celebration of a business acquisition, 1983, on the back terrace of Pam's house.

Below, right:
Cliff gazes at Afton at the Ewing Barbecue, 1982. Although he never really said it much, he loved Afton like no other woman.

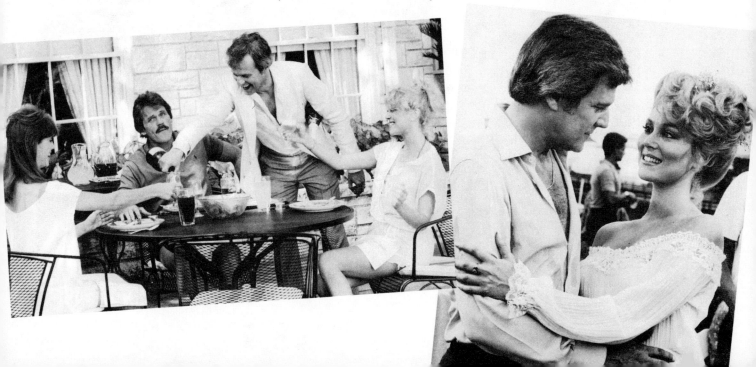

Pamela's retelling of Rebecca's deathbed declaration of forgiveness and of love for Cliff penetrated his guilt and he was able to forgive himself.

But those Ewings . . . still trouble, always trouble. After Pamela and Bobby had separated, Bobby Ewing tried to pry out of Cliff's half sister, Katherine Wentworth, the use of Wentworth Tool & Die's experimental Tundra Torque, which could penetrate icy, rock-hard ground. He wanted to use it on his frozen Thornton & MacLeish fields in northern Canada. Cliff was opposed to letting him have it. Cliff knew that Bobby would have to sell the fields if he didn't have the Tundra Torque—the Ewing Oil contest with J.R. was going on—and he mightily wanted to buy the fields himself. However, Pamela, still mooning over Bobby, voted with Katherine and let him have the drill bit.

Though Cliff was angered by Pamela's action, he was more worried about her well-being. Her separation from Bobby had taken a heavy toll on her, and he thought it best that she get involved in something to take her mind off it. He arranged for the creation of a new company with a division of Graison Industries, which was owned by Pam's new beau, Mark Graison. To his delight, his sister joined him as a senior executive of Barnes/Wentworth/Graison.

Cliff found a better way to counterplay the Ewings—by employing a spy there, a secretary named Sly. She fed him information on pending deals at Ewing Oil, and Cliff managed to pull several profitable ones out from under them.

At the Oil Baron's Ball in the fall of 1983, Cliff, as the head of Wentworth Tool & Die, was named Oil Man of the Year for the development of

Afton, Cliff, and Pam cheer Mark on at the Good Ol' Boys Rodeo, 1983. These were happy days for Cliff . . .

Holly Harwood of Harwood Oil once said, "As many oil deals are made in bedrooms as in boardrooms." Here, Cliff and Marilee Stone of Stonehurst Oil consummate the agreement to be partners in the offshore drilling lease auction, 1983. She was better in bed; she pulled out of her agreement at a crucial moment.

the Tundra Torque. Upon acceptance of the award, Cliff announced the establishment of the Willard Barnes Memorial Scholarships to SMU in memory of his father.

Still being fed information by Sly on Ewing Oil activities, Cliff thought he was getting the inside scoop J.R. had on government offshore drilling leases that were being auctioned. Cliff discussed the possibilities with Marilee Stone—which also resulted in a brief affair that caused a rift between Cliff and Afton. Marilee agreed to go in with Cliff as a silent partner on the bidding of one tract, the oil-rich Gold Canyon 340. Sly fed Cliff the bidding figures that J.R. had apparently blackmailed the auctioneer for, and so, in the allegedly blind bid auction, Cliff put in a bid that he believed to be just over that of Ewing Oil's bid—a bid that would win the tract. Ewing Oil did not bid the $155,000,000 they were supposed to. They actually bid quite low, almost as if they did not *want* to win. Though confused by this, Cliff was still pleased by the acquisition of Gold Canyon 340 for $157,000,000.

It was a staggering amount of money, but Cliff knew the tract was almost a sure bet. Then Marilee mysteriously pulled Stonehurst out of the deal on the angry declaration that Cliff had spread the word that she was his silent partner. It wasn't true—he hadn't; he smelled J.R. in this somewhere. Now Barnes-Wentworth had to shoulder the venture by itself, risking all assets.

Cliff got financing for the project from Vaughan Leland, and Cliff, in haste to start drilling, waived some of the fine print concerning the collateral against nonrepayment. The drilling began and . . . nothing. The overhead was staggering, frighteningly expensive. When Cliff continued to come up empty, he nervously persisted, sweating all the while. He had to pay back the first of the loan payments while still maintaining drilling, and he was forced to start selling off Barnes-Wentworth assets unrelated to Gold Canyon 340. Once these were gone, Cliff was going to approach Mark Graison for a loan, but Mark committed suicide. He couldn't talk to poor Pam in her present state, so he went to Katherine, offering his interest in Wentworth Tool & Die. It was worth at least $25,000,000, but he was so desperate for cash, he accepted the mere $18,000,000 she offered him. That money ran out quickly, and suddenly, with

211

only a few days left to drill in May of 1984, with his sister Pamela off somewhere in retreat, Cliff turned to Jordan Lee for advice. Lee said he should change crews on the site. In his opinion, if the present crew knew what it was doing, then they would have hit oil long before this. And so, with his last dollar, Cliff followed his advice and then, during the final remaining hours left to drill, he went out on the biggest bender of his life.

For you see, that night he learned that J.R. had engineered the whole thing, that J.R. had set him up on this oil tract, made him have to bid alone and too high, and counted on Cliff's inexperience not to figure out that the crew boss was working for J.R., and working darn hard to make sure they didn't hit oil. If Cliff didn't hit in the next hours, if Cliff defaulted on his loan, then both Barnes-Wentworth and Gold Canyon 340 would belong to Ewing Oil. For Vaughan Leland's alleged bank, in actuality, was Ewing Oil.

But, hooray! The tides of fate finally turned for Cliff Barnes. His new crew struck oil before the clock ran out and they didn't just hit some oil, they hit with the biggest oil strike in the history of the Gulf. Cliff was not only a millionaire, but a billionaire.

However, Afton Cooper left him, which saddened him more than he had imagined. And when Bobby Ewing was shot, Cliff was framed and arrested for the attempted murder. Courtesy of—yes, you guessed it—Mr. J. R. Ewing.

Cliff was cleared (his half sister, Katherine, had done it) and he was, at long last, free to enjoy his new prosperity. He immediately got involved with a gorgeous model, Mandy Winger, and life was on the up-and-up.

And it got better. Jamie Ewing came to town, with proof that Digger and her father, Jason Ewing, were legal partners in Ewing Oil, from its formation in 1930. Bound together by mutual hatred for J.R. in 1985, Cliff and Jamie were married in May have gone to court to break the Ewings and take over two thirds of the company. At this writing, the outcome is unknown. But, rest assured, this may be the most courageous thing Cliff will ever do—or, the most foolhardy.

No matter what you hear about Cliff Barnes around Dallas in the days ahead, just remember, the man is a fighter. And if J. R. Ewing persists in overshadowing Cliff's every move, Cliff will do more than shadowbox. He'll strike harder than Spindletop itself.

Cliff being arrested for the attempted murder of Bobby Ewing, 1984. He was cleared when Mandy Winger stepped forward to testify that Cliff was having a one-night stand with her at the time of the murder. Cliff has probably been arrested more times than any other lawyer in Dallas. J.R. framed him in the cases concerning Julie Grey, Kristin Shepard, and Bobby; the other arrest was when J.R. himself was shot.

*Cliff hears that he has won
the Oil Man of the Year
Award at the Oil Baron's
Ball, 1983.*